Trade and Diplomacy on the China Coast

Museum of Fine Arts, Boston

CH'I-YING

Portrait presented by the Imperial Commissioner to the Honorable Caleb Cushing of Massachusetts in 1844

Trade and Diplomacy on the China Coast

THE OPENING OF THE TREATY PORTS

1842–1854

By

JOHN KING FAIRBANK

Originally published in
the Harvard East Asian Series

STANFORD UNIVERSITY PRESS
Stanford, California

This book was originally published in two volumes in 1953 by Harvard University Press. The two volumes were bound together in a one-volume edition in 1964. The present Stanford University Press paperback edition is essentially the 1964 edition, with the addition of a new Preface by the author and minor changes in the presentation of the back matter to make it more accessible to the reader.

Stanford University Press
Stanford, California

First published in 1953 by Harvard University Press
Paperback edition first published in 1969 by Stanford University Press
by arrangement with Harvard University Press
Printed in the United States of America
L.C. 69–10365
Last figure below indicates year of this printing:
78 77 76 75 74 73 72 71 70 69

IN GRATEFUL MEMORY OF

HOSEA BALLOU MORSE

(1855–1934)

A.B., Harvard, 1874, LL.D., 1924.
Commissioner of Chinese Maritime Customs.
Historian of Chinese Foreign Relations.

DR. MORSE'S contribution to our understanding of modern China's relations with the West was based on his two careers, in the Customs, and in historical research. After graduation from the Boston Latin School and from Harvard in 1874, he entered the Chinese Imperial Maritime Customs Service with three of his classmates. In the next thirty-five years he served at Shanghai, Peking, Tientsin, Pakhoi, Tamsui, Lungchow, Hankow, and Canton, and on many special assignments, concluding with the post of Statistical Secretary in the Inspectorate General. On retirement in 1908 he settled in England, publishing his first large work, *The Trade and Administration of the Chinese Empire* that same year, the first volume of *The International Relations of the Chinese Empire* in 1910, and the second and third in 1918. In 1926 he completed *The Chronicles of the East India Company Trading to China* in four volumes, with a fifth in 1929. These books still constitute the starting point for study of China's foreign relations, particularly with Britain, between 1634 and 1911.

Dr. Morse's second career, as a scholar, was informed and guided by his earlier practical experience as a civil servant of China. Though he lived through the decades of foreign imperialism and the collapse of the Chinese Empire, his historical work avoids the obtrusive chauvinism of the Western treaty port community of that period. He was a scholar unusually devoted to the ideal of scrupulous, impartial, and accurate presentation of the facts. To me, as to other beginners, he offered generous encouragement and wise counsel, while his work gave us firm ground upon which to build our smaller contributions.

AUTHOR'S PREFACE TO THE STANFORD EDITION (1969)

How did this book come into being? The reprinting of it in paperback by the Stanford University Press gives the author an opportunity for biblio-biography, an account of how the book developed in the twenty-four years between its conception in the mind of a graduate student in 1929 and its birth in print in 1953. Even for the China field, this was a long gestation. A geneticist would be amazed at how the book changed in the process.

I think authors ought to look back and give us some record of how their works developed, not because their works are important (they may turn out to be unimportant) but because we need to know more of the process of history-writing. Historians today generally recognize, like social scientists, that their scholarship is an activity in which they are themselves participants. Writers of history are not just observers. They are themselves part of the act and need to observe themselves in action. Their view of what "really" happened is filtered first through the spotty and often hit-or-miss screens of available evidence, and second through the prisms of their own interest, selection, and interpretation of the evidence they see. The result can be only an imperfect approximation. Fortunately, no one has to regard it as the last word.

Once an author looks back at what he thought he was trying to do, many perspectives emerge. Foremost is that of ignorance, at least in my case. When I went to Oxford in 1929 I had never had any kind of instruction in Chinese history, or even seen anyone in the field, which, as a matter of fact, hardly existed. Moreover, Oxford University, although willing to indulge Americans by letting them work for higher degrees, had no preliminary examinations to test their knowledge of a field. One merely started research and writing. Consequently, unlike a thesis writer today who has just passed his Ph.D. general examination and is perhaps more knowledgeable over the whole scope of his field than he will ever be again, I was unencumbered by learning. Perhaps this helped, perhaps not. Suppose you had never heard of the gentry class, the White Lotus rebellion, salt merchants, compradors, *mu-yu,* cultural imperialism, Feng Kuei-fen, Wang T'ao, the anti-Christian movement, or the *kuan-tu shang-pan* system. Your situation would be at least simplified, and so was mine.

While crossing the Atlantic by steamship, as one did in those days, I read

H. B. Morse's *International Relations of the Chinese Empire*. Dr. Morse had hoped in Volumes II and III, on the period 1860–1911, to make use of Sir Robert Hart's diary, for the Inspector General of Chinese Maritime Customs had played a key role in the history of that period. After Hart died, his family had refused all access to his papers. Nevertheless it seemed to me that the Customs as a central institution in the treaty ports could be studied rewardingly, to begin with, through the British correspondence in the Public Record Office in London. And so, to get a running start, I picked as a research topic for the B.Litt. at Oxford "The Origin of the Foreign Inspectorate at Shanghai, 1850–1854." Completing this in 1931—its residue is in Chapters 19–23 in this volume—I then undertook a D.Phil. thesis on "The Origins of the Chinese Imperial Maritime Customs Service, 1850–1858." But by the time I completed this and received the degree in 1936, several things had happened.

First, I went to Peking (then Peiping) in 1932 and studied Chinese, initially at the missionary-oriented College of Chinese Studies and then with a succession of urbane and skillful teachers, old hands at the training of Westerners in the Legation Quarter. After a couple of years I found that the newly published Ch'ing documents on foreign relations could be read by foreign learners, especially if they were helped by Chinese (or ex-Manchu) gentlemen who knew what the documents meant. Thus the Ch'ing correspondence between Peking and the treaty-port provinces could be dovetailed with the British, American, and French correspondence to produce diplomatic history of the sort that was still so much in vogue in the 1930's. One could work from the foreign side, which was reasonably well known, to an understanding of the Chinese side, which was still obscure. But this raised many problems about the institutional processes of the Chinese state.

Second, after three years spent mainly in language work in Peking, I was able to take trips with my wife and her sister to the five earliest treaty ports. We sailed from Shanghai south to Ningpo by overnight steamer and then again from Shanghai down the coast to Foochow, Amoy, and Canton. In the last three ports in particular we found the British consular archives still intact and *in situ*. An introduction from Professor Charles Kingsley Webster of the University of Wales at Aberystwyth to the librarian of the Foreign Office had led to an introduction to the British minister in Peiping, with whose help we were installed in the consulates, usually in the consular courtroom where no one would disturb our perusal of the worm-eaten files. But these records led one straight back to the opening of the ports and the origin of the many problems of consular residence, communication with the Chinese authorities, control of British nationals, opium imports, coolie exports, and the like, which continued to provide the daily fare of Sino-British relations from the 1840's on into the 1850's. My research was

pulled backward in time rather than forward. (The use of these port archives is most evident in Chapters 10, 12–13, and 17–18 in the present volume.)

Thus the Chinese documents raised the question, what institutions had produced them? And the treaty-port consular files raised the question, how had the treaty system been created? I had two bears by the tail, and both were pulling me back to earlier times. In my observation this regression in time is typical of Ph.D. thesis research and has its innate, genetic-oriented logic. As a result, would-be modernists have wound up as medievalists. The rule seems to be, if you want to study the mid-period of a century, begin at the end of it and let problems lead you back. *Never* try to begin at the beginning. Historical research progresses backward, not forward.

After returning from Oxford and the P.R.O. in 1936 and starting to give a course at Harvard with the peculiarly British-oriented title "The Far East since 1793" (the date of the Macartney embassy to Peking), I had time to pursue the background in the 1840's out of which the Foreign Inspectorate principle had emerged in the treaty-port crisis of the early 1850's. Instead of writing a book on the period 1850–58 covered by my thesis, I found the logic of events led me toward a book on the period 1842–54. By accident I had begun at 1850, which turned out to be the critical midpoint in the era of the first treaties, 1842–58. Yet these studies of the rise of the first treaty system led into the whole question of the administration of the Ch'ing empire and its established mode of dealing with foreign affairs.

The fascination of historical research is that it lets your human craving for abstraction lead you to generalizations. Confronted with myriad bits and pieces, you seek a knowable formulation to cover them. The individual incident begins to stand forth as one of a kind. You look for its significance in a broader pattern of events. In this case the main thrust of this book comes from the broader context in which my original thesis research was subsequently placed.

I was led to this context by a post-doctoral research effort to understand how the Chinese government operated, especially in its foreign relations. Luckily I was able to collaborate with an able researcher who had come to Harvard from Yenching University, Teng Ssu-yü (now university professor of history at the University of Indiana). From 1938 to 1941 we produced three articles: on the postal system that transmitted Chinese documents, on the procedures by which they were handled at Peking, and on the tribute system that in the early nineteenth century still dealt with China's foreign relations (reprinted in 1960 as *Ch'ing Administration: Three Studies,* Harvard University Press). These beginnings were interrupted by World War II, but after five years in wartime service, I was

able to join in another project with Dr. Teng and others to select materials, translate them, and connect them in a volume to show the main outlines of *China's Response to the West.* In 1950 we got out a preliminary draft of that book and it was eventually published in 1954 (Harvard University Press), almost contemporary with this volume of 1953. Plainly it provides background for Chapter 1 of this volume, just as our studies of the tribute system contributed to Chapters 1, 2, and 24.

By this time I had found a name (though I hesitated to use it) for the institutional phenomenon studied in this book, namely "synarchy," meaning joint administration carried on in Chinese territory by Chinese and foreigners. This is of course a phenomenon that goes far back in Chinese history. It is most interestingly interpreted in the writings of Owen Lattimore (see his broad and stimulating work *Inner Asian Frontiers of China,* Oxford University Press, 1940). I had also by this time as a matter of self-training made a survey (working with Professor Masataka Banno) of *Japanese Studies of Modern China* (published for the Harvard-Yenching Institute in 1955). I found that this theme of foreign rule in China, or joint administration by foreign invaders and Chinese officials, had been extensively pursued by Japanese historians who saw a historic role that Japan might revive (and certainly tried to revive) in nationalist China.

A historical interpretation of this kind, even though it may cut athwart the presuppositions of a later time, has its own vitality and calls for further work. I tried to formulate my own conclusions in an article, "Synarchy under the Treaties" (published in *Chinese Thought and Institutions,* University of Chicago Press, 1957). The idea crops up in our textbook volumes (*History of East Asian Civilization*). In a current symposium, *The Chinese World Order* (Harvard University Press, 1968), I offer another article on the same theme: "The Early Treaty System in the Chinese World Order." In my case I came to this general theme partly from the institutional problem I had studied, how to tax and control Westerners in China when they had extraterritorial privileges.

Because this preface attempts only to observe the history-writing process, there is no point here in summarizing or arguing for the validity of the synarchy concept. Sino-"barbarian" relations and alien rule in China constitute a central historical theme in Chinese history, like that of the influence of the frontier in American history or of sea power in world history; but my generation are latecomers in dealing with it, at least a thousand years too late to play the seminal roles of a Frederick Jackson Turner or an Alfred Thayer Mahan. On the other hand, joint Sino-foreign administration in China, of which the treaty system was the last great example, will be explored in more and more detail as historians get down to the sophisticated analysis of how the vast Chinese populace has been governed in the past.

Certain cautions are in order. A central theme may be very central, but it can be overdone, if only because an author knows more about it and less about other themes. It is the nature of specialists to dig in, to deepen and ramify the shafts where they struck pay dirt. Some become identified with major themes like class struggle or water control. They may become possessive toward their brainchildren and get into great polemics defending them. But every concept has its limits, and synarchy obviously fades from the Chinese scene as modern nationalism arises. One may see the tradition of synarchy facilitating the establishment of the first treaty system of the 1840's, but thereafter modern nationalism begins to grow, partly in direct response to the aggression of the foreigners and partly no doubt simply from contact with and awareness of the world outside China.* The moral seems to be: as you find your unifying concepts, follow them out; but don't let them carry you off. They probably don't belong to you in any case.

How much of this book has been superseded since 1953? The late Hsin-pao Chang, a talented researcher, lived only long enough to complete his first volume, *Commissioner Lin and the Opium War* (Harvard University Press, 1964), which carried the story up to 1840. A brilliant Japanese researcher, Sasaki Masaya, has unearthed from the Public Record Office the Chinese-language drafts of the British communications sent in Chinese to the Ch'ing officials of the period 1834–59.† These, and not the Blue Book documents in Victorian English, were what the Chinese side responded to. This simple fact, apparently never recognized by the hundreds of commentators and historians before Sasaki, requires a new look at Ch'ing diplomacy in closer, textual terms. Masataka Banno, *China and the West, 1858–1861: The Origins of the Tsungli Yamen* (Harvard University

* Certain patriotic critics on Taiwan have taken umbrage at the whole idea of synarchy. Some historians want a decision "whether the unequal treaties were simply an extension of the relations between the Chinese . . . and the 'barbarian' tributaries . . . or whether they represented a complete reversal of relations between China and foreign countries, at China's expense." (Jean Chesneaux, *The Chinese Labor Movement, 1919–1927,* Stanford University Press, 1968, transl. from French edition of 1962, p. 438, note 36.) My own view is that events of this sort are multicausal, not either-or, and that the unequal treaties can really be understood only as an "extension" that indeed led to a "reversal."

† See his three volumes *Ahen sensōmae Chū-Ei kōshō monjo* for the period 1834–39 (Tokyo, 1967), *Ahen sensō no kenkyū* for 1840–43 (Tokyo, 1964), and *Ahen sensōgo no Chū-Ei kōshō* for 1844–59 (Tokyo, 1964), all published by or through the Toyo Bunko Seminar on Modern China. For other Chinese sources published since 1953, see J. K. Fairbank, *Ch'ing Documents, An Introductory Syllabus,* 3d ed. rev. (Harvard University Press, 1965), pp. 93–105. Note also Kuo T'ing-i, ed., *Ssu-kuo hsin-tang* (Taipei, 1966), four volumes of archival documents for 1850–63 published by the Institute of Modern History, Academia Sinica. Another collection of 708 documents for 1842–62, cited in the present book in manuscript as "IWSM Supp.," has now been published by the Institute of Modern History as *Tao-kuang Hsien-feng liang-ch'ao Ch'ou-pan i-wu shih-mo pu-i,* Kuo T'ing-i, ed. (Taipei, 1966).

Press, 1964), deals with another institutional development but in the subsequent period. Frederick Wakeman, *Strangers at the Gate: Social Disorder in South China, 1839–1861* (University of California Press, 1966), illumines the local Canton scene of the 1840's and 1850's.

Meanwhile this volume, *Trade and Diplomacy on the China Coast,* seems to have suffered the fate of "apparent overkill" that befalls some studies. A book that to its author is a mere antechamber to a whole unwritten library, bursting with problems awaiting exploration, may seem to his readers to have a solidity which shunts their research elsewhere. It is useless to assure them that the book is really full of holes. At the same time, its subject matter, in this case Sino-foreign relations, may seem unpromising in comparison with China's domestic scene, where landlordism, guilds, secret societies, peasant rebellion, social mobility, the New Text school, statecraft, and many newly perceived official personalities vie for attention, each with a wealth of sources.

If I had had an opportunity to guide the author of this book from the vantage point of today's sophistication, I would have urged him to look at the treaty ports in sociological terms, as a community where in the terms of economic history the expanding foreign firms nurtured their Chinese counterparts, and in the terms of social-cultural history the missionaries posed their threat to the Confucianist scholar-official class. I would urge him to tie together power politics, the transport revolution, international trade, commercialization, urbanization, local government, the growth of geographic knowledge, the press, scientific technology, chauvinism—all the institutions that brought foreigners and Chinese into contact, all the processes that were at work tearing down the old China and stirring up the Chinese revolution. Such a broad approach might have produced a book on the founding of modern Shanghai. The present volume, following a single institutional thread, is a simpler affair.

Prospective authors must realize that to produce a manuscript is to jump only halfway across the river. Book production, though undoubtedly aided by mechanical inventions, is still one of the few remaining handicrafts. In 1953 the technique of reproducing Chinese characters in American scholarly books was still in an experimental stage. The back matter for this book was set up in large type and characters were written by hand on large proof sheets, which were then reduced photographically and printed by photo offset, originally as a separate volume. The photoreduction ratio proved to be excessive and the notes came out in the mini-type you will see if you look carefully. This illustrates how a work can serve as a doormat on a steppingstone to the future. What more can one ask?

J.K.F.

September 1968

ACKNOWLEDGMENTS

In my senior year at Harvard, in 1929, (Sir) Charles Kingsley Webster suggested that the study of modern China, using the voluminous Chinese documentation which was then becoming available, could shed much light on the ominous problems of East Asia. Subsequently at Oxford I took up this suggestion, and in the Public Record Office in London began research on British relations with China. At this time I made the acquaintance of a fellow-alumnus of Harvard, the late Dr. H. B. Morse, to whom this volume is dedicated. After the Rhodes Trust had kindly let me transfer to Peiping in 1932, I studied Chinese there and began to use Chinese documents under the guidance of Dr. T. F. Tsiang, then head of the History Department at Tsing Hua University.

Twenty years ago I thus entered upon two approaches to the study of modern China — through Far Eastern languages and Sino-Western relations. Their confluence has at length produced this book, yet it seems a shallow product, compared with the problems and materials with which it deals and the mountainous load of obligation which I have accumulated. I am obliged to many scores of friends and strangers — teachers of Chinese in the old Peking Legation Quarter, consular and Customs officers and taipans in the treaty ports of a bygone era, students and colleagues in the Departments of History and of Far Eastern Languages and in the Regional Studies Program at Harvard. This list of persons, to whom I feel most indebted in large ways or small, is incomplete but may serve at least as a bare acknowledgment: the late Sir Stephen Gaselee, the Foreign Office, and British diplomatic personnel at Peiping, Tientsin, Shanghai, Ningpo, Foochow, Amoy and Canton (for access to the British consular archives in China); former Ambassador Nelson T. Johnson, the Department of State, and American consular officers (for access to American records); the late Dr. John C. Ferguson and authorities of the Palace Museum, Peiping, and Dr. T. F. Tsiang (for access to unpublished documents from the Ch'ing archives); Sir Frederick Maze, sometime Inspector General of Chinese Maritime Customs, Stanley F. Wright, L. K. Little, Everitt Groff-Smith and others of the Customs Service, and members of the pioneer British firm of Jardine, Matheson and Company.

This research has received generous support successively from the Rhodes Trust, the General Education Board, the Harvard-Radcliffe Bureau of International Research, and the Rockefeller Foundation. For scholarly aid and encouragement in diverse ways, I am particularly indebted to

Masataka Banno, Ida M. Cannon, Chang Te-ch'ang, W. C. Costin, Wilma C. Fairbank, the late Roger S. Greene, Kwang-ching Liu, the late William E. Soothill, the late B. Humphrey Sumner, Ssu-yü Teng, James R. Ware, Mary Wright, L. S. Yang, and Gerald Yorke; and for practical help of the most tangible sort to Rosamond Chapman, Marjorie Ellms, Wilma Fairbank, Norma Ford, Hope Kay, Marian Schlesinger, and especially E-tu Zen Sun, who read over most of my translations and contributed particularly to Chapter 14.

J.K.F.

CONTENTS

PART I

CHINA'S UNPREPAREDNESS FOR WESTERN CONTACT

PART II

THE FIRST BRITISH TREATY SETTLEMENT 1842–43

MAPS AND TABLES

MAPS

TABLES

PART I

CHINA'S UNPREPAREDNESS FOR WESTERN CONTACT

CHAPTER I

THE PROBLEM OF CHINA'S RESPONSE TO THE WEST

THE CENTURY OF THE TREATY PORTS IN CHINA, from 1842 to 1943, is now at an end, and historians may examine it for clues as to the future of Sino-Western relations. We can be sure that these three generations of steadily increasing contact have been more than a strange interlude in the long drama of China's ethnocentric history. For better or worse, the treaty ports remade Chinese life. Through them flowed Western goods, people, and ideas. The result was to give the West a privileged position in China not unlike that of earlier barbarian conquerors.

Should we view the present rejection of the West as an anti-foreign resurgence among the Chinese people? Is it, on the contrary, part of still another barbarian conquest? Or is it really an unstable mixture of the two? These are the imponderables of present day policy. They can be assessed only against the background of history.

The historical context of the period 1842–54. The modern invasion of China by the Western world really began in the middle of the nineteenth century, after the first Anglo-Chinese treaty was signed at Nanking in 1842. Until that time relations with the West had been based upon the ancient Chinese tribute system; after that time they were based upon the "unequal" foreign treaties. Under the tribute system foreign trade had been restricted to the picturesque "factories" of old Canton. But 1842 began a new era — the opening of China to Western commercial exploitation. This was characterized by the treaty ports and the opium traffic, extraterritoriality, the treaty tariff, and the most-favored-nation clause. By the end of the nineteenth century China had been placed in a semi-colonial status, the after-effects of which have not yet passed away. In this context the years from 1842 to 1854 have significance as the transition between two unilateral, Chinese and Western, schemes of things.

These middle years of the nineteenth century saw new developments in all the Far East. The first enunciation of American manifest destiny, the development of the clipper ship and the Shanghai trade in the 1840's, were followed by the opening of Japan and the establishment of Russia on the Pacific between 1853 and 1860. The center of all this international development, however, was the British activity in China, where the treaty port consuls labored to break down the Chinese system of foreign relations and set up the Western treaty system in its place. Their initial achievement was the first treaty settlement of 1842–44; further efforts led to the invention of the Foreign Inspectorate of Customs in 1854; their final success, after the second war of 1856–60, was marked by the treaties of 1858 and 1860 which opened the interior to trade and established the Western legations at Peking.

The treaty system which had thus been created to serve as a vehicle for British and other Western trade, diplomacy, and evangelism in China, was also set up in Japan, Siam, Korea, and other Far Eastern states. It may justly be taken as the symbol of the recent century of Western superiority in the East. It forms a striking contrast with the preceding millennia of the tribute system, when the great empire of China dominated the Far Eastern scene. It contrasts perhaps less sharply with the new international order of communism of which China has become a part.

We should not forget that the treaty system represented chiefly a state of affairs in the treaty ports, a mode of Sino-foreign intercourse which was an aspect or function of the larger situation within the Chinese body politic. It must be viewed in the context of the great revolutionary process of disintegration and rebirth which has convulsed the Chinese people since 1842.

The fall of the Chinese empire is an epic still to be written. Seen from the Chinese side, no political collapse in history has been more cataclysmic — a decline from an age-old recognized supremacy over the known world to an abject partitioning into spheres of foreign domination, all in the space of one lifetime between 1842 and 1898. The causes of this fall were many and various. The decay of the Manchu dynasty after two centuries of power within China and the rise of the great Taiping Rebellion in 1851 (an epic that would require another volume to tell) coincided with the invasion of Western arms. Western-inspired efforts at industrialization and the growth of nationalism followed hard upon this dynastic civil war. All these processes, native and foreign, have combined to produce the chaos and ferment of social change in modern China.

The resulting experience of the Chinese people in modern times has been overcast by a pall of frustration and uncertainty, owing to their inability to meet the West on equal terms. The inherited institutions of their society have played them false. More than any other mature non-Western state, China has seemed inadaptable to the conditions of modern life. Nationalism and industrialism, which triumphed so easily in Japan, were retarded in the Middle Kingdom. Neither the scientific method nor the rule of law, the inventor or the entrepreneur, have yet had their heyday in this strangely different society. Perhaps the very maturity and stability of Chinese social structure and political institutions have proved a handicap. Their dissimilarity to the West was so deep and ingrained that adjustment to the modern world has been possible only through the break-up of the old order. China's society has had to be thrown into the melting pot and her people have had to accept revolution as the law of modern existence; for the process of modernization has involved intense and rapid changes on all levels of social life and practice.

This process of modernization began only a bare three generations ago. In the days of Calhoun and Webster, Bentham and Mill, China's old ruling class was still firmly in the saddle, thinking in the accepted patterns of the Confucian system — universal monarchy, dynastic rather than national politics, tribute relations abroad and the Chinese way of life at home.

This ancient Confucian order and the expanding commercial empire of Britain had their first contact, on their lowest levels, through the Anglo-Indian opium traffic and the petty corruption of a demoralized Chinese bureaucracy, through piracy, brutality, and racketeering, without benefit of common speech or writing, and with little but uncomprehending contempt for each other's ideals and values. As we look back it seems amazing that so great a catastrophe as the invasion by the West could have been visited upon the Chinese people without producing more violent friction. No doubt this was due in part to the tolerance and passivity of a populace long inured to hardship, as well as to their relative inaccessibility to direct Western contact. It was due also to the effort of the British government to serve as the handmaiden of commerce, the civilizing benefit of which was deemed obtainable only through the establishment of the rule of Anglo-Saxon law. The energies of the British consuls were bent for a generation toward the creation of a framework of legal regulation within which foreign trade might prosper and Sino-foreign relations remain tranquil. Yet in the last analysis China's response to the West was determined most of all by the peculiar nature of her state and society.

Thus far the political collapse of the Chinese empire has been studied almost entirely from the alien view of the Western invaders, whose imperialist rivalry is recorded in numerous volumes. Nothing is more plain, however, than that the key to the story lies within. The startling contrasts between the responses of Japan and of China to the West since 1842 make it clear that imperialism was no juggernaut running roughshod over native peoples, but rather a stimulant capable of invigorating the strong or debilitating the weak, depending upon the internal condition of the recipient. Japan, for example, had a patriotic and adaptable ruling class. China did not. Japan had the medieval tradition of the samurai as a basis for modern chauvinism. The early bankers of Osaka and Tokyo were forerunners of the modern Zaibatsu. By the nineteenth century, Japan, indeed, was a nation somewhat like Western nations, while the Middle Kingdom was a state of a different political species altogether. Any study of China's modern adjustment to the West must therefore begin with those peculiarities of the Chinese state which made it uniquely inadaptable to the Western scheme of things.

The nature of Chinese society and its reponse to the West. The recognition of China as a society different in structure and character from our own suggests the need of defining and formulating this difference. All Western observers since Polo and the early Jesuits have tried to do this, either by description or by analysis. I have made my own brief attempt elsewhere.[1] Here let us note merely that fruitful socio-historical analyses are now being developed under the general headings of "Oriental Society," "the gentry state," or the like — bodies of theory which are not simple magic formulae but rather broad avenues of approach that afford new insights into Chinese social behavior. With these has come a fresh appreciation of the role of the barbarians of Inner Asia in Chinese history.[2]

All such theories assume, of course, that the record of events is still basic to our understanding. While conceptual schemes can inspire and guide research, they are not meant to substitute for it. The meagreness of our knowledge of modern China leaves us still in the stage of descriptive portraiture. Exactly how the men and events, the personalities and circumstances, the data and interpretations should be combined to form our picture of modern China's contact with the West is a problem of artistic composition more than of scientific measurement. Theories are not self-evident, any more than facts can speak for themselves. Our understanding of China must be accumulated painstakingly and in detail, through monographic research on one aspect of the record after another.

Not having a final formula for Chinese society, we can hardly invent one for China's response to the stimulus of Western contact,[3] yet certain points may be noted. First, in the expansion of the Western state system during recent centuries, the incorporation of China into this nascent world order has proved unusually difficult. China's political behavior has not easily been assimilated to that of the West, presumably because of the difference in her institutions. Second, the so-called Western "impact" on China has been a stimulus rather than a shattering blow. Personal contact in treaty ports and mission stations, material changes in economic life and social custom, have led to the eventual metamorphosis of Chinese institutions. But this modernization has been effected by the Chinese people through the adjustment of their own ways; it has not been simple westernization. Third, the response has worked both ways. In the hybrid society of the treaty ports, Western forms of law, finance, industry, and individualism have been subtly modified: the treaty ports have represented not the Western way of life transplanted to the China coast so much as China's accommodation to the Westerner and his ways. The handful of foreigners in the ports adjusted their lives to Chinese conditions. Your genuine Shanghailander was really a half-breed, typical of neither East nor West.

In the course of decades the new stimuli operating through the treaty ports led China into revolution. The response to the West upset traditional patterns of behavior which went far back into the past. Other great developments had indeed occurred throughout China's far from static history, but down to the nineteenth century they had all remained within a distinctive and persistent Chinese pattern. Thus repetitive phenomena like the political cycle of dynastic disintegration, warlordism, and re-unification had all taken place within the unshaken framework of the Confucian culture. Similarly the pattern of China's foreign relations with the barbarians of Inner Asia had been manifested inside the structure of the universal Confucian monarchy.

Although Western contact eventually destroyed this old political and cultural framework, the first phase in China's response to the West was neither inaction nor innovation, but merely repetition of the established pattern of behavior. In short, the first overt Chinese activity in the beginning of Sino-Western relations was to apply to the West those traditional attitudes which were already inbred within the Chinese way of life. This was to treat the West as though it were not the West at all, but merely a new form of Inner Asian barbarian.

This conditioned reflex made China's adjustment to the West much more difficult than it might otherwise have been. If the British barbarians had been an entirely unprecedented phenomenon in Chinese life, the Manchu rulers of the day might easily have formed a fresh and realistic view of them. Unfortunately, this was impossible because the British (*Ying-i*) were the unwitting inheritors of the status which had been reserved for barbarians (*I*) in Chinese society since time immemorial. Age-old stereotypes took the place of a creative response.

The first step in understanding the Western influence on China is, therefore, to understand the traditional role of the barbarian in Chinese society. The most cursory glance at this subject will indicate that the barbarians of Inner Asia had played a constant and, indeed, an integral part, in the long history of the Chinese people. Their experience had included not only recurrent phenomena like the dynastic cycle but also the recurrent phenomena of barbarian conquest. Doubtless these rhythms were not so regular and uniform as Chinese scribes have liked to assume. Yet the rise and fall of dynasties were expected, like the waxing and waning of the seasons, and have formed the main theme of the Chinese dynastic chronicles. Modern historians may be interested less in the obvious existence of these broad rhythms than in their multiplicity and interaction; China's history gives us today an oversupply rather than a lack of patterns. Nevertheless, since

Chinese historical thinking traditionally looked forward to repetitive cycles, the expectation that one dynasty would eventually be succeeded by another was an important factor in political life. Expectations or fears concerning barbarian conquest were similarly important in the conduct of foreign relations. In this way the British and other Westerners who moved into China in the nineteenth century became the heirs of the ages without knowing it.

As a first step in exploring this attitude toward the barbarians, let us note the curious alternation between Chinese and barbarian political domination of the empire in the four periods of T'ang-Sung, Liao-Chin-Yuan, Ming, and Ch'ing. Their sequence has been tabulated by Wittfogel and Feng as follows: [4]

TABLE 1. DYNASTIES OF IMPERIAL CHINA (221 B.C. — A.D. 1912)

I. *Typically Chinese Dynasties*	II. *Dynasties of Conquest (and "Infiltration")*
1. Ch'in and Han (221 B.C. — A.D. 220)	
2. The Chinese dynasties during the period of disruption (220–581)	
	3. Wei (T'o-pa) (386–556) and other northern barbarian dynasties directly before and after
4. Sui and T'ang (581–907)	
5. Sung (960–1279)	
	6. Liao (Ch'i-tan) (907–1125)
	7. Chin (Jurchen) (1115–1234)
	8. Yuan (Mongol) (1206–1368)
9. Ming (1368–1644)	
	10. Ch'ing (Manchu) (1616–1912)

During the last thousand years, in short, the Chinese people have been almost half the time under alien domination. Barbarian rule has been an integral part of their political life. We may assume that the aggression of the Western barbarians in the nineteenth century seemed to the Chinese of that day to be nothing new in principle, even though in the end it had the effect of shattering their traditional polity. This intellectual complacency about the barbarian world was an element of weakness in China's political heritage.

China's conception of the Western barbarians. The concept of Europe and America which became current in Chinese thought after the beginning of Western trade in the sixteenth century was certainly as significant as the trade itself, but has been little studied. Generally speaking, in the highly categorized and hierarchic Confucian world, the Western merchants who reached the east coast of China by sea in modern times were designated, literally, "eastern barbarians" (*I*).[a] Being of a different, and therefore inferior, culture, they could hardly qualify for any other appellation. Yet by this simple fact of terminology they were prejudged and stigmatized with the characteristics traditionally assigned to barbarians. In a society already stultified by its classical tradition, this ancient designation and the assumptions which went with it dulled the edge of curiosity and inhibited the Chinese scholar's intellectual response to Western contact.

That the tributary view of the West survived beyond its time in the minds of the Chinese literati is evident from any examination of their writings. Official publications of the court, private works, and the memorials of officials who were in contact with the British, American, and French invaders in the 1840's and 1850's all exhibit this stultification. The first type of material, chiefly official compilations of the eighteenth century when the Manchu power was at its height, gives one the impression that there was little interest in the study of the West. The traditional Chinese idea of the barbarians seems to have been applied to the West, lock, stock and barrel. It is plain from later documents that the traditional terminology was so applied. The British minister was called the "English barbarian chieftain" for twenty years after the first treaties. In Chinese documents the British continually seemed grateful for the emperor's compassion and stood in awe of his name. Like all barbarians, even the British had a sense of shame at their own uncouthness. Thus the bearers of Western civilization in the Orient were described to the court at Peking in the terms which were traditional for barbarous tribes like the Burut of Central Asia and the Miao-tzu and Lo-lo of China's southwest.[6]

In the latter days of the Ming, Matteo Ricci and his Jesuit colleagues had interested the Confucian literati in maps of the world which showed strange countries to the west. Many of the Jesuit transliterations of these place names have survived in modern Chinese usage. But this new knowledge presented to Chinese scholarly circles in the period after 1600 did not survive for long, or at least did not retain its significance, after the establishment of the Manchu dynasty. It was generally disregarded during the eighteenth century.[7] This is one of the puzzles of Chinese intellectual his-

[a] In the classical tradition this term had become one of the four generic terms for the barbarians on the four quarters of the compass: *I* (barbarians on the East), *Man* (barbarians on the South), *Jung* (barbarians on the West), and *Ti* (barbarians on the North).

Originally, however, the term *I* had not been so restricted to one point of the compass, for the oracle bones and ancient bronzes bear inscriptions indicating that there were many types of *I*, on the South, East, and West. Similarly, there were several types of *Man*, not merely on the South, but to be found in all the five quarters — East, South, West, North and Central, while the term *Jung* indicated backward tribes in any quarter of the compass, as did the term *Ti*. One scholar suggests that the differentiation by the four quarters appeared first in the book of Mo-tzu, after which it became well established in the Han period.[5]

tory, and without venturing upon an explanation, it may be strikingly illustrated.

The confusion regarding European countries. The countries of the Western Ocean were irretrievably confused with one another, even in the official publications of the imperial government.[8] For example, from medieval Europe via the Arabs had come the term *Fo-lang-chi*. This was a transliteration for "Franks," that is, the Europeans in the Near East at the time of the Crusades. When the Portuguese traveled to China by sea after 1500, they were identified as *Fo-lang-chi* because they came from the West. The same term was also applied to the Spanish after their arrival in the Philippines in the sixteenth century. Since Portugal was under Spanish rule from 1580 to 1640, this confusion was no doubt inescapable. The arrival of the French created a further terminological enigma because of the similarity of France and Franks. Time and again *Fa-lan-hsi*, *Fo-lang-hsi*, *Fu-lang-hsi* and similar transliterations for France were erroneously identified by Chinese scholars with *Fo-lang-chi*, which now meant the Portuguese-Spanish. Meanwhile, the term *Kan-ssu-la* for Castilla, the Spanish, had also been applied to the Portuguese; in addition, two tribute missions sent by the King of Portugal, in 1670 and 1727, had been recorded in official Chinese works as from two separate countries, *Po-erh-tu-chia-li-ya* and *Po-erh-tu-ka-erh*. But, in the meantime, the Jesuit missionaries in China had identified themselves as coming from Italy, *I-ta-li-ya*, and yet by their use of the Portuguese settlement of Macao, as a port of entry, had become associated with Portugal. Consequently, as late as 1844 the name *I-ta-li-ya* was being applied to the Portuguese at Macao, and when a genuine Italian turned up in 1848, his country had to be identified as *I-ta-li*, an entirely new and separate country from *I-ta-li-ya*.[9] There were also other ways of referring to Portugal, in addition to the five just mentioned. It would have taken a strong mind to identify *Fo-lang-chi*, *Kan-ssu-la*, *Po-erh-tu-chia-li-ya*, *Po-erh-tu-ka-erh*, and *I-ta-li-ya* as all referring to the same small Western country.

Confusion was, of course, not confined to the books. Just as Chinese, Japanese, and Koreans look much the same to the Western man in the street, so the Westerners in China, as in Japan, were indistinguishable in their common outlandishness. The colloquial term, *Hung-mao-fan*, "red-haired barbarians (or foreigners)," was applied to both the Dutch and the English, whose blue eyes, red complexions, beak noses, and tawny hair made them all indiscriminately exotic.[10]

Since the Jesuit map of the world had not gained much acceptance in China, the native habitat of these Europeans remained shadowy. They all arrived by sea from the southwest, and the *Collected Statutes* of 1818 therefore opined that their homelands were "in the southwestern sea," the same as Siam, Sungora, Ligor, Patani, Johore and way stations on the route to Singapore and the Straits of Malacca. One of the Portugals (*Kan-ssu-la*, or Castilla), however, was in the northwestern sea, as were also Sweden and Denmark. The exact location of the Western Ocean (*Hsi-yang*) was a bit hazy since the term had originally been applied to the waters west of Borneo leading into the Indian Ocean, on the ancient western trade route, the route which went down the Indo-Chinese-Malayan coast and was to be distinguished from the eastern route through the Philippines and Moluccas. When the early Europeans used the term Western Ocean to refer to the Atlantic it was not illogically objected that the Western Ocean, as known to the Chinese, had been sailed through, from end to end, by the great Ming expeditions under Cheng Ho, without anyone noting a trace of Europe. A compromise was finally worked out by referring to the Indian Ocean as the Little Western Ocean, *Hsiao-hsi-yang*, while the Atlantic became the Great Western Ocean, *Ta-hsi-yang*. *Ta-hsi-yang*, incidentally, was another of the names applied to Portugal.[11]

The relations between these minuscule kingdoms in the Great Western Ocean were naturally difficult to keep straight, particularly when they were not too permanent in actual fact and were differently described by the patriotic members of each nationality on their visits to Chinese ports.

This official knowledge of the West was reflected, for example, in a special compendium entitled "Illustrations of the Regular Tributaries of the Imperial Ch'ing" which was compiled by imperial decree during the 1750's.[12] The high officials of the border provinces supplied materials to indicate how "within and without the empire united under our dynasty, the barbarian tribes submit their allegiance and turn toward civilization." It is significant that among these ten elaborate volumes, the great bulk of which dealt with the tribes of Inner Asia and of Southwest China, the first volume was devoted to the overseas tributaries. They are listed in the regular order: Korea, Liu-ch'iu, Annam, Siam, Sulu, Laos, Burma, and Great Western Ocean. The last named, however, is described in twelve plates with text as opposed to twenty-six plates for all the preceding. This is followed by sections on Small Western Ocean, England, France, Sweden, Holland, Russia, and the Philippines. The European countries occupy twenty-eight out of seventy-four plates, and are thus considerably more prominent than in the antiquated Ch'ing dynasty lists based on Ming sources, in which the European countries are almost lost to view among the numerous small states of Southeast Asia and India.

Considering this prominence given the Europeans, it is surprising how little is recorded in this work concerning them. First of all, there is great confusion as to the European states. The Great Western Ocean country is identified both with Ricci and the Pope and with the Portuguese at Macao.

Modern France is again confused with *Fo-lang-chi* or the Portugal of the Ming period. England and Sweden are recorded as countries dependent upon Holland. In religious matters, the Portuguese-French are reported to have been Buddhist countries before they accepted Catholicism, and the Pope is said to have come from Italy to present tribute in 1725.

The characterization of the Western barbarians stresses superficialities: "their flesh is dazzling white, and their noses are lofty . . . their custom is to esteem women and think lightly of men. Marriages are left to mutual arrangement. The men are violent and tyrannical and skilled in the use of weapons. They wear short coats and tip their black felt hats as a sign of politeness. The Swedes and the Englishmen like to take snuff, which they carry in little containers made of golden thread."

In view of the trouble which the Manchu court had already had with the British at Canton, the scant attention given to England is particularly noteworthy: "This barbarian people's clothing and adornment resemble those of a country which is very wealthy. The males mostly wear wool and love to drink wine. The females, when they have not yet married, bind their waists, desiring that they be slender. They wear disheveled hair which hangs over their eyebrows, short clothing and layers of skirts. When they go out for a walk, then they add a big coat."[13]

Rather curiously, space is devoted to central European countries like Hungary and Poland, whose people are said to resemble Mongols. The Hungarians ride on horseback, educate their women, and are rich in natural resources of livestock and metals. Poland is very cold and the people wear furs. Presumably this sort of information was secured by the Chinese compilers from Russian rather than Cantonese sources. Russia is said correctly to have presented tribute in 1676 and to have made a boundary agreement in 1689.

The illustrations in this work are obviously copied by Chinese artists from foreign originals. The Europeans have Chinese eyes, but authentic Western costumes. One interesting sociological reference is to the "Black-devil slaves" (*hei-kuei-nu*) born in the islands beyond the seas, who serve the Dutch.[14] But the final effect, after the major states of Southeast Asia have been listed, is an utter and indiscriminate confusion among the barbarians of England, France, Sweden, Japan, Borneo, Johore, Holland, Russia, Sungora, Cambodia, Spain in the Philippines, Java, Malacca, and Sumatra.

How long this confusion persisted was strikingly shown by the imperial commissioner Ch'i-ying in November 1844, just after he had negotiated the treaties with Britain, the United States, and France which opened China to the West. No one in China should have been better informed than he about the barbarians. He explained to the emperor that France (*Fo-lan-hsi*) was the same as the *Fo-lang-chi* (Portugal) of the Ming period; that under the influence of Matteo Ricci, the great Jesuit, the French had been induced to give up Macao to the Portuguese, even though France was ten times as strong.[15] France, of course, had never held Macao. This whole cock-and-bull story probably illustrates the Paul Bunyan quality taken on by the legend of Matteo Ricci, who had already become the tutelary deity of clocks in China (known popularly as *Li-ma-tou p'u-sa*).

The lack of real intercourse. This vagueness of the Confucian mind regarding the West was no doubt a product of lack of interest and lack of contact, combined with genuine distaste. Outland merchants on the fringe of the empire were more often heard of than seen. Printed sources of information regarding them were few and out of date. As merchants they were beneath attention, and as barbarians with powerful arms they were no doubt easier to forget about entirely. The Westerners in China had never been numerous, and in the eighteenth century they were effectively quarantined. The decadent, part-half-caste community of Macao remained walled off on its peninsula; the Thirteen Factories at Canton were outside the city walls, from which foreigners were excluded. All contact with foreign merchants was mediated through a special class of compradores, linguists, shroffs and Chinese merchants, as well as through a special language.

Semanticists have paid too little attention to this early international language of eastern Asia, known as pidgin, that is, business, English. This medium of communication was the bastard offspring of Portuguese, Chinese, and English, with numerous local additions. It followed the Chinese word order, which fortunately agreed with that of English, and it included duplicatives like *chop-chop* (quick), in the Chinese fashion. From the Portuguese came words like *joss* (dios), which by the nineteenth century produced "joss-pidgin man" for missionary. From the Anglo-Indian culture were added words like *chit* and *tiffin.* In general this language amounted to a translation of Chinese into a restricted international vocabulary. Since all aspects of life, from table-talk to homicide and philosophy, were discussed during the East India Company period in this medium, it is small wonder that cultural understanding did not proceed more rapidly.[b]

[b] Pidgin English, being spoken and not written, changed rapidly with the passage of time. Carl Crow gives this example from the more recent past:

Taipan: "How fashion that chow-chow (miscellaneous) cargo he just now stop godown inside?"

Compradore: " 'Lat (that) cargo he no can walkee just now. 'Lat man Kong Tai (the purchaser) he no got ploper sclew (security)."

Taipan: "How come you talkee sclew no ploper? My have got sclew paper safe inside."

Compradore: "Aiyah! 'Lat sclew paper he no can do. 'Lat sclew man he have go Ningpo more far (i.e., absconded into the hinterland)."

Modern linguistic analysis shows the characteristic pidgin English use of suffixes like " — side" (top-side, bund-side), " — time" (plenty-time, what-time), " — fashion" ('merican-fashion, how-fashion), " — piecee" (three-piecee rickshaws) as well as the use of compounds like "chow-water" for drinking water, "look-see" for look at or watch over, "more-proper" for better, "have-talkee" for said or told, "makee-die" for die, etc., etc. Conversation in pidgin was usually a question-and-answer dialogue

The European tribute embassies which penetrated the veil of Chinese exclusiveness were relatively few and far between. After the first abortive Portuguese embassy of 1520–21 there were only about seventeen Western missions, so far as we now know, which got as far as an audience with the emperor (see Table 2). They all occurred in the years between 1655 and 1795, and six of them were from Russia, an Asiatic power in a somewhat different category from the maritime West. There were four from Portugal, after the first one; three (or perhaps four) from Holland; three from the Papacy; and one from Britain under Lord Macartney in 1793. All but the last appear to have performed the kotow. (The second British ambassador, Lord Amherst, in 1816 failed to obtain audience.) Of these various embassies only four occurred after 1727 and the last one, that of the Dutch in 1795, fitted perfectly into the traditional tributary system.[18] The established order was not challenged by this contact.

Russian relations with China had also fitted into the tributary pattern: the treaty of 1727 set up two trading posts on the Russo-Chinese frontier and allowed a caravan of two hundred merchants to visit Peking once in two years. A permanent mission was allowed to stay in Peking and did so, very quietly, for more than a century until after 1858. In it a handful of Russian Orthodox priests ministered to a secluded community of less than two hundred Russians (originally composed of prisoners of war) but made no effort to seek Chinese converts. The language students sent to study in the mission produced some results, like the dictionary of Archimandrite Palladius (1817–1878). But until the middle of the nineteenth century, Russian policy toward China remained quiescent and this rather mysterious little outpost in Peking continued inactive.[20]

The only other Western contact aside from trade was that of the Catholic missionaries. After 1725, however, the Jesuits' defeat in the famous rites controversy, and the Son of Heaven's denial of the Pope's oecumenical claims, had made them impotent at Peking, long before their dissolution in Europe in 1773. The Lazarists who succeeded the Jesuits at Peking in the late eighteenth century did not become influential. As of 1800 the Christian converts in China, all Catholic, numbered somewhere between one-fifth and one-quarter of a million. Their priests (about thirty Europeans and eighty Chinese) still suffered spasmodic persecution: in 1814 the Vicar Apostolic in West China was beheaded, in 1816 a French priest was executed at Changsha, and in 1819 a French Lazarist at Wuchang. The scientific mission at

---

between master and servant: "Boy, just-now missy have-got, no-have-got?" (Boy, is your mistress here now?). "Yes, no-have-got" (No, she is not.).[16]

On the other hand, until late in the nineteenth century, it was considered practically impossible for foreigners in the treaty ports (except perhaps missionaries with divine assistance) to master Chinese — the feat would require "a head of oak, lungs of brass, nerves of steel, a constitution of iron, the patience of Job, and the lifetime of Methuselah."[17] The result was a compromise on pidgin, which still persists in Hongkong.

TABLE 2. EARLY EUROPEAN EMBASSIES TO THE COURT OF PEKING[19]

	PORTUGAL		HOLLAND		RUSSIA		PAPACY/BRITAIN
1520–21	Thome Pires sent by Emmanuel	1656	Pieter van Goyer and Jacob van Keyser	1656	Feodor Isakovitch Baikov by Alexis I Mikhailovitch		
1670	Manoel de Saldanha by Alfonso VI	1665?	Pieter van Hoorn	1676	Nicolas G. Spathar Milescu by Alexis I		
1678	Bento Pereyra de Faria	1686		1689	Feodor Alexievitch Golovin by regent Sophia (to Nerchinsk, not to Peking)		
				1693–94	Isbrand Ides by Peter I	1705	Patr. T. Maillard de Tournon by Clement XI
1727	A. Metello de Souza y Menezas by John V			1720–21	Leon Vassilievitch Izmailov by Peter I	1720	Patriarch Mezzabarba by Clement XI
				(1721–25	Laurent Lange trading agent)	1725	PP. Gothard and Ildephonse by Benedict XIII
				1726–27	Sava Vladislavitch ("Raguzinski") by Catherine I		....
1753	F.-X Assis Pacheco Sampayo by Joseph I	1795	Isaac Tithsing	1767	Capt. I. Kropotov by Catherine II	1793	Lord Macartney by George III
				1805–6	Count Golovkin by Alexander I (turned back at Urga)		
				1808, 1820	(no audiences)	1816	Lord Amherst by George III

Peking was reduced to six timid Lazarists and an aged Jesuit. The revived activity of the Jesuits in the nineteenth century, which centered in the Lower Yangtze (based at Zikawei outside Shanghai) did not begin until the Opium War. Protestant missions in China were to be a vigorous new growth radiating from the treaty ports. But until that time the representatives of Christianity were in no position to influence the tone and trend of Chinese thought about the West.[21] All in all, the first decades of the nineteenth century seem to have been a low point in Sino-European relations at Peking, where the Catholic and Russian missions remained almost vestigial.

Examples of barbarian lore. In this situation a body of folklore grew up concerning the new overseas barbarians. A number of Chinese are known to have reached Europe in the seventeenth and eighteenth centuries, chiefly under Jesuit auspices, but none of them described Europe to their countrymen in any written record, so far as is known.[22] It remained for the more extensive contact of Sino-European commerce to produce such descriptions.[23] The type of information about the West available through the Chinese junk trade to Southeast Asia is recorded in an interesting work derived from a blind interpreter at Macao named Hsieh Ch'ing-kao. During his youth this man had traveled abroad for fourteen years (1782–95) and learned the languages and customs of the Southern Ocean (*Nan-yang*) region. In 1820 a Cantonese literatus named Yang Ping-nan used Hsieh as an informant and compiled the *Hai-lu* (A maritime record). This work systematically presents sailing directions and brief descriptions concerning more than sixty countries or trading ports on the routes around the Malay peninsula to India and through the Philippines to the East Indies, concluding with a third section on the countries of the Great Western Ocean. The authentic first-hand quality of the work is indicated by its description of the British at Singapore and Penang and their eclipse of the Dutch at Malacca, which had occurred in 1819.[24] In this first-hand account many romanizations are made de novo, representing both Portuguese influence and Hsieh's Cantonese accent. Except for Portugal, the sections on Europe seem obviously based on hearsay, but this work was later used by the famous Chinese geographers of the 1840's, Wei Yuan and Hsü Chi-yü (see Chapters 11 and 15 below), and its comments on the British represent one strand of early nineteenth-century barbarian lore.

Hsieh says that the British population is rather thin but extremely wealthy. Their houses are many-storied and they make their living by maritime trade and the establishment of overseas bases. The population give the king military service from the ages of fifteen to sixty, and they also train foreign armies, so that their nation, although small, has strong military forces of more than one hundred thousand men and other overseas countries fear it. Hsieh also describes London as a great emporium, with its three bridges and its city water pipes providing clear water to the inhabitants. England also has a great many prostitutes; but illegitimate children have to be reared and they do not dare to destroy them. Men and women both wear white clothes but black for mourning. Military officers wear red and women wear narrow-waisted dresses, tight above and full below. On festive occasions the young and pretty girls dress up and perform dances to the accompaniment of singing. The army is organized in squads of five and companies of twenty and relies chiefly on the technique of volley-firing (? *lien-huan-ch'iang*). When their trading junks go overseas to trade and meet a ship in distress they have to send boats to succor it, feed the survivors and return them to their countries under penalty of law, such is the excellence of their administration. Otherwise, their customs are similar to the rest of Europe. Their products include metals, woolen goods, and the like.[25]

Hsieh states that North America, about ten days to the west of England, is also an isolated island, rather small, with customs similar to the English, to whom it once belonged, and with similar products. The Americans are chiefly distinguished for their steamers, which have a fire box in the hold and (paddle) wheels turned by the fire, which makes the boat go without human effort. He also says that no American has two wives, whether king or commoner.[26]

Another work which reflects the learning of the time was the *Yueh hai-kuan chih* (Gazetteer of the maritime customs of Kwangtung), compiled by Liang T'ing-nan at the time of the first war with England. This is a systematic treatise on the history and administration of the Canton customs with sections on tributary trade and the overseas nations. This work seems to have been based partly on previous publications and partly on archival records and must have been regarded as a most authoritative source in its day. It discloses a few facts about the British, including the following: England was once a dependency of Holland but became rich and strong and eventually her enemy. In England there is a mountain which produces black lead (lit., graphite, or coal?); people mine it and pay duties to the officials. Liang's general description also mentions ports and fortresses and a series of recent rulers named *Ching-yeh-chih* ("George"). In summarizing certain highlights of Sino-British relations in the preceding hundred years, he emphasizes the British request to present tribute in 1792, the receipt of twenty-nine different items of tribute presents in 1793, and the gifts bestowed by the emperor in return. Ch'ien-lung's famous edicts to Britain are quoted at length. Liang then states that in 1796 England presented some "yellow colored broadcloth of a new sort" as tribute (presumably sent from Canton by the East India Company). Communications from the British in 1804 are quoted as "tributary memorials" and the dispute with the British government over forms of communication in that year appears to conclude with an apologetic statement from the British headman at Canton. The British tributary ambassador of 1816 is recorded as refusing to follow the usual ceremonies, but the failure of his mission is magnanimously excused on grounds of ignorance, while the edict to the English king reminds him that his ambassador of 1793 showed a proper respect for the ceremonies. To conclude this utterly consistent account of Britain's tributary status, Liang remarks that Britain formerly presented tribute through Canton, as is fully on record year by year.[27] As Professor Pritchard has shown, the idea that Macartney had actually kotowed in 1793 was widely spread throughout nineteenth-century Chinese documents and accounts.[28]

Much of this barbarian lore, being in the minds of officials, found its way into their documents. In June 1844 the Shansi censor Ts'ao Lü-t'ai, for example, denounced the wiles of the British, their insatiable cunning and deceit, and their friction with the Cantonese populace. He was particularly outraged over an incident in which a foreign woman had rushed into a government yamen at Chen-hai near Ningpo to pay her respects to the Chinese officials. "What kind of propriety is this? A clear proclamation should be issued to the barbarian chieftain to make him understand what is right." [29] The censor then without acknowledgment of any source quoted the following statements which had originally appeared in the sections on England and Singapore in the *Hai-lu*: The British live by their overseas trade, and by getting hold of profitable spots overseas like Bengal (*Ming-ya-la*), Madras (*Man-ta-la-sa*), and Bombay (*Meng-mai*). They have more than one hundred thousand troops and the overseas nations all fear them. In the Chia-ch'ing period (1796–1820) they occupied *Chiu-jou-fo* (Singapore, lit. Johore) which the people of Canton and Fukien call *Hsin-chou-fu*.[30] The censor then stated that he had recently heard of a book, the *Wan-kuo ti-li t'u* (Illustrated geography of all countries) in which the British author had marked the Chinese ports newly opened to trade as *Hsin-chou-fu* (lit. "new departments and prefectures"). This seemed to claim the ports as new British territory — "a most hateful thing to do." He requested that the provincial authorities ascertain whether barbarian presumption had gone so far; and an imperial edict of June 18, 1844, ordered the imperial commissioner Ch'i-ying to investigate.

Ch'i-ying reported in September that his assistant, through barbarian merchants, had got hold of this illustrated universal geography, the *Wan-kuo ti-li t'u*, in three volumes. On examination these volumes were found to contain the barbarian writing, which there was no way to comprehend. As to the year of its origin and author, and whether the ports where trade is now conducted were included, this was all very difficult to determine. So he had a translator extract in Chinese all references concerning China. It was found on minute examination that this work contained merely references to the geography, flora and productions of China and to the clothing, food and customs of the population along the coast, although among these data there were many gaps. But the trading ports listed were all in foreign countries and the *Hsin-chou-fu* mentioned was undoubtedly the same as Singapore (transliterated *Hsin-ch'i-p'o*), which the British had seized in the Ch'ien-lung period (1736–1795) (sic). The Cantonese commonly called it *Hsin-chou* (lit. "new island") and also *Hsin-fou* ("new port") and *Hsin-chou-fou* ("new island port"), which no doubt had caused the censor to mistake it for the similar-sounding *Hsin-chou-fu* which meant "new departments and prefectures." [31]

While this incident may seem like confusion confounded by a pun, it illustrates the actual vagueness of the official mind at the time of the first treaties. Perhaps if the censor had explicitly acknowledged the *Hai-lu* as his source instead of tacitly copying it (or some source that had previously copied it), he would have avoided the imperial commissioner's imputation of muddle-headedness. But Ch'i-ying's secretaries also evidently failed to spot the *Hai-lu* as the origin of the quoted passage.

As a keen contemporary student, the British interpreter, Thomas Taylor Meadows, testified in 1852: "The Chinese do habitually call and consider Europeans 'barbarians'; meaning by that term 'peoples in a rude, uncivilized state, morally and intellectually uncultivated'. . . . Those Chinese who have had direct opportunities of learning something of our customs and culture — they may amount, taking all Five Ports, to some five or six thousand out of three hundred and sixty millions — mostly consider us beneath their nation in moral and intellectual cultivation. As to those who have had no such opportunities, I do not recollect conversing with one, and I have conversed with many, whose previous notions of us were not analogous to those we entertain of savages. They are always surprised, not to say astonished, to learn that we have surnames, and understand the family distinctions of father, brother, wife, sister, etc.; in short, that we live otherwise than as a herd of cattle." [32]

In effect, during the 1840's the barbarians were a good deal more incomprehensible to Chinese observers than the "inscrutable Celestials" were to Western observers. As one modern historian has summarized it: "Ch'i-shan learned that the woman ruler of England had chosen a mate, and he memorialized, saying: 'This is naturally a country of barbarians, with the nature of dogs and sheep [i.e., fickle and greedy], fundamentally ignorant of rites and of modesty; how can they then know the distinction between ruler and subject, and upper and lower?' Regarding these people, Lin Tse-hsü said that their legs and feet stretched out and bent with difficulty;

Ch'i-ying stated that at night their vision was confused. Tao-kuang commented: 'Everyone says the same thing, it must be true.' Lo Ping-chang memorialized, saying: 'The said barbarians' troops and chieftains take elephant skin [*hsiang-p'i,* the modern term for rubber] and copper strips and wrap the upper part of their bodies for protection, so that the edge of a sword cannot wound them; the volunteers of Canton province take long cudgels and bend down to strike their feet, and immediately they fall down.' . . . All this unfounded talk, of which the origin is unknown, was actually believed by the officials and furthermore was memorialized to the court. They had no capacity to discriminate between true and false; hence it was difficult to weigh what was important and what was not, find out what was profitable and what was injurious, and make exact decisions." [33]

And hence, it may be added, they were the more readily subject to panic in the field and to a suspicious timidity in the council chamber. An edict of June 1842 commented: "The rebellious barbarians' cunning is manifested in a hundred ways; their ships separate, and some go north and some south . . . and their number changes constantly. Also, they take troops that have been captured on successive occasions [i.e., prisoners] and successively send them back. Although they take trade as their excuse, they do not wait for an answer but suddenly raise anchor and sail away — all sorts of craft and secrecy. One cannot get any clue to it." [34]

This intellectual unpreparedness for Western contact, so evident in the folklore and thought of China in 1840, was made the more grievous by the dry sterility which had overtaken the Chinese scholarly tradition. The wide-ranging intellectual vigor of seventeenth century scholars like Ku Yen-wu had become stultified, their search for new evidence had given way to empty combing of classical texts — the "textual research" (*k'ao-chü*) of literati divorced from the world around them. This fault was well demonstrated at Canton by the famous compiler Juan Yuan. He was governor-general of Kwangtung and Kwangsi for a decade (1817–26), during which he put together 366 volumes of classical commentary, compiled the provincial gazetteer, and printed 40 *chüan* of his collected writings, 5 *chüan* of bibliographical notes, and an anthology of Kiangsu poets. Although the highest authority in contact with the barbarian problem, he had little time to spare for it.[35]

These examples of Chinese folklore, ignorance, and confusion about the Western barbarians do not strike one as representing a distinct set of ideas and evaluation. On the contrary, the conception of the West in early nineteenth century China seems to have had that fuzzy-minded fairy-story quality which has characterized the Western approach to China in more recent times — quaintness taking the place of reality. Like us a century later, the Chinese of the 1840's were unprepared for what was to come.

The interaction of dynastic decline and Western invasion. The conclusion of the first set of treaties with Britain, France, and the United States in 1842–44 coincided with the end of exactly two centuries of Manchu rule in China. Judging by evidences of decay in the Ch'ing dynasty, it is not surprising that the great Taiping Rebellion began in 1851. Yet in this case the extremely complex processes of dynastic change within the country had already become further complicated by the Western pressure from without. Britain's defeat of the Manchus in the war of 1840–42 was an important, though as yet imponderable, political and psychological factor in the origin of the Rebellion. The opium trade which had precipitated the war of 1840 was only one aspect of the growth of China's foreign commerce. Like the rapidly growing exports of tea and silk, it heralded the spread of a commercial economy in South China which later had profound repercussions on the old agrarian society. The circumstance that the Taiping religion was a bastard offspring of Protestant evangelism was undoubtedly a factor in the rebels' failure to win the Chinese upper class to their cause. Western influences had already intruded upon the Chinese pattern.

But the long-term patterns of Western history as they impinged upon China contributed to the destruction more than to the creation of any observable rhythm in the Chinese social process. The seemingly irreversible trends of Western history, manifest in the growth of science and technology, trade and industry, nationalism and the modern state, destroyed the old China and created one of mankind's greatest problems — how to integrate into a world community one-fifth of the human race whose social heritage is essentially at variance with that of the West. The fact that this effort is currently being made under the banner of communism makes our study of its early history all the more urgent.

Unfortunately, an analysis of the old Chinese government must be a tour de force for the historian. Western political scientists, with very few exceptions, have so far succeeded in avoiding the study of the Chinese language and of the Confucian state. Apparently without loss of self-respect, they have neglected this greatest human achievement in the art of government, leaving its secrets unexplored, its amazing stability and persistence unexplained in professional terms. Until "comparative government" becomes less parochial, the historian must clutch at what straws he can.

The weakness of the Chinese state in contact with the West after 1842 sprang partly from its own essential nature and partly from its condition at the moment. These two types of weakness, inherent and circumstantial, may be usefully distinguished. The atrophy of dynastic leadership, the demoralization of the bureaucracy, evils of landlordism, over-population, and financial bankruptcy — these were mainly recurrent cyclical factors which by ill chance became acute as the nineteenth century wore on. They would not have been as pronounced a century earlier, for China was caught by the West at a moment of weakness, in the trough of the so-called dynastic cycle. But at the same time the old China suffered from inherent weaknesses in thought and in institutions which would have made her at any time a prey to the modern West.

Among these latter factors we may discern, first, a degree of intellectual blindness or inability to face the crisis presented by the West. This intellectual failure was due in part to China's ancient ethnocentricity, institutionalized in the tribute system for the conduct of foreign relations and evident also in the traditional idea of the barbarians. Second, there was a persistent lack of effective political leadership. This may be attributed partly to an administrative system which stultified initiative and was dominated by alien rulers, who sometimes may have put the defense of their dynasty before that of China. It came also from a social and economic system in which gentry and officials were traditionally in league and sometimes on the defensive against the peasantry. Finally, beneath these institutional weaknesses, lay the broad fact that the Confucian society was agrarian and bureaucratic, of a type not able to adapt itself to the commercial, industrial, and nationalist revolutions brought about by free-trade and free contact under the Western treaties.

The following chapters of Part I concern this theme of China's unpreparedness for Western contact — as seen in the tribute system and its application to the West before 1842. Later sections deal with the Sino-British contact which led to the working out of the first treaty system, its attempted application at the treaty ports, its gradual breakdown, and the beginning of its resuscitation through the creation of the Foreign Inspectorate of Customs at Shanghai in 1854.

CHAPTER II

TRIBUTE AND THE GROWTH OF TRADE

AS INDICATED ABOVE, the Manchu-Chinese response to the West in the nineteenth century was predetermined by an ideological structure of assumptions, expectations, and evaluations inherited from China's long history and institutionalized in the tribute system. Tribute was a Chinese-barbarian institution. It had been jointly created on the Sino-barbarian frontiers of China and jointly operated as the medium for Sino-foreign intercourse over the centuries. The ideology of tributary relations occupied a place in Chinese-Manchu thinking not unlike that which nationalism and international law had come to occupy in the Western mind. The idea of tribute was closely connected with that amazing characteristic of the Confucian monarchy — the fact that barbarian invaders could so often take it over and become the rulers of China. There is more to this problem than the myopia of Western political scientists has yet permitted them to see. The Confucian monarchy was a peculiarly non-national institution. It rested on a Confucian-Chinese social and cultural base but could be seized and manipulated by barbarian invaders quite as well as by Chinese rebels, sometimes indeed even more easily. It is hardly too much to say that by modern times the Confucian monarchy in China had itself become a joint Sino-barbarian institution.

The role of the barbarians in the Chinese state. The barbarian role had grown out of a great, continuing geographical fact, which limited the Chinese empire as a political body — namely, that the intensive agriculture which could be widely practiced in Eastern Asia, south of the soil-and-rainfall boundary marked by the Great Wall, could not be extended far beyond it to the north. The expansion of the most ancient Chinese state, which appears first in archeology as a culture-island around the Shang dynasty capital at Anyang north of the Yellow River in Honan, led to the gradual absorption and acculturation of areas and peoples to the south and east, all the way to the borders of Burma, Siam, and southern Indochina. In the course of three thousand years the Chinese way of life has incorporated a great variety of native tribes and Chinese colonists in central and south China, where an intensive rice culture permits a dense agrarian population. Yet in all these millennia the Chinese way has not expanded far onto the Mongol steppe, where cultivation must give way to an extensive pastoral economy and the tribal social institutions which accompany it.

Thus the descendants of the Anyang kings spread their civilization fifteen hundred miles across the hills and rice-fields to the south, to the seacoast of Annam, but have been unable to extend it more than a few hundred miles to the north.

This is merely another way of saying that the nomadic peoples of the Mongolian steppe have been a constant factor in the Chinese state. They have provided a permanent frontier beyond which the Chinese way of life could not extend. The Chinese state from its earliest inception had to adjust itself to this barbarian contact. China and the barbarians have co-existed throughout their history. From ancient times the civilization of China received stimuli and cultural ingredients through the medium of the barbarians of Central Asia. The use of iron and of the horse, methods of warfare, and cultural elements of the Near East all came by this route.

Thus the Chinese state and monarchy were from the earliest days up against this fact that the barbarians existed and could never be made Chinese. China's geographic isolation from Europe prevented her direct contact across the wastes of Central Asia with any settled power of equal size, and this, no doubt, conduced to the ethnocentricity which has roughly corresponded in China to the nationalism that grew up in Europe. Yet this isolation from the nationalistic competition of equal powers did not preclude the long struggle between China and the barbarians. The Chinese society seldom had equals within its sphere in eastern Asia, but it always had enemies. It was by no means left alone in solitary grandeur and to this degree it was by no means unprepared for contact with the West.

The nature of China's relationship to the barbarians was far different from any it could expect to work out with Western powers in modern times. In brief, this ancient relationship was based on supernationalist sanctions derived from the Confucian social order.

The superiority of the Chinese way of life was exhibited in China's culture as well as in her economic wealth. Yet this superiority in material goods as well as in intellectual and artistic life, and this greater complexity of social and political institutions, were both inadequate to save China from periodic barbarian domination. The key to the constant barbarian influence on China lay in the fact that the military force which could be based on the horsemen of the steppe, once it was concentrated, usually had superior striking power against any force which could be mobilized from the sedentary farming population of the North China plain. Farm boys were no match for trained hunters and horsemen. This simple fact remained a constant factor in favor of the nomad invaders. The barbarians' power in China was limited, however, by another constant factor — that they lacked the clerical personnel and local roots necessary to conduct the bureaucratic administration of populous Chinese territory once they had conquered it, and so had to rely upon Chinese assistance or partnership in government.

In short, the slowness of China's response to the Western impact in modern times, which forms the chief enigma of her modern history, can be understood only within the framework of China's traditional relations with the barbarians. The tragedy of the Chinese state has been that her adjustment to the barbarians of Inner Asia was such poor preparation for contact with the modern West. On the contrary, it was the most misleading possible precedent, for it left China to deal with the industrial West through institutions and preconceptions developed over three thousand years of contact with pastoral nomads. The tribute system could not be successfully applied to the modern West, yet it was China's only defense, for it was the established mode through which the Confucian monarchy dealt with foreign powers.

If we look for the ancient sources of this institution, we find first of all that the early Chinese states of the period before and after Confucius (up to 221 B.C.), in their relations with one another, had developed conceptions and procedures which may be compared in some ways with those of modern international law. The classics recorded relations among ancient rulers on an egalitarian basis — the tribute institution was not the only precedent in China's experience.

In this ancient legal system of the Warring States period, before China's unification as an empire, the concept of the state required that there be territory, people, sovereignty and organization or institutions. Because the barbarians moved about with a pastoral economy and no fixed territory, they were regarded as not being states at all. Among the Chinese states each had its capital as well as the above four attributes. There were sovereign states and subordinate states. New states received a form of recognition by a certain procedure, sometimes at a conference of other states. Recognition could also be implicit, as by concluding a treaty, permitting a state to attend a conference, sending representatives to it, or extraditing criminals. Whether explicit or implicit, recognition was permanent. States could also be destroyed or divided. They had their rights and duties, including rights of equal treatment and trade, and rights of reciprocity. Their duties included documentary and legal functions, while their moral duties were to preserve orthodoxy and save each other from danger. Procedures concerning the dispatch of envoys and other forms of inter-state relations were fully developed at this early time.[a] There was plainly no lack of diplomatic machinery in the Chinese heritage.

[a] Four types of personnel were recognized in these inter-state relations: sovereigns, envoys, military representatives, and officials in charge of foreign relations. Envoys were sent abroad to other countries to represent their rulers. Unlike modern diplomatic agents, however, they did not reside in the other country, but were sent back and forth on missions, usually concerning a single subject at a time. As

Theoretical basis of tribute. This early Chinese development of ritual procedure in inter-state relations formed part of the classical tradition after the imperial unification of 221 B.C. But it could not be fully applied outside the Chinese world, and hence arose the early distinction between Chinese and barbarian.

From their age-long contact with the barbarians roundabout, including both the nomads of the northern steppe and the aborigines of the south, the Chinese developed one major belief: that their superiority was not one of mere material power but of culture. Such things as the Chinese written language and the Confucian code of conduct were visible signs of this culture. So great was their virtue, so overwhelming the achievements of the Middle Kingdom in handicrafts and letters and the art of living, that no barbarian could long resist them. Gradually but invariably the barbarian in settled contact with China tended to become Chinese. By this most flattering act he reinforced the Chinese conviction of superiority. On their side the inhabitants of the Middle Kingdom, themselves in large part descendants of barbarians, stood always ready to judge a man by a cultural rather than by a racial or national standard. After centuries as the center of eastern Asia, the Chinese developed what may be called, by analogy to nationalism, a spirit of "culturalism." Those who did not follow the Chinese way were considered inferior and therefore dangerous when strong. This view was supported by (and emanated from) the entire Confucian cosmology.

Another ancient idea which supported this culturalism was the concept of the power of example. Confucianism held that *right conduct* for all persons consisted in the performance of the proper rites and ceremonies and the preservation of the proper social relationships according to status. Just as

---

to types, they included 1) envoys to conferences, 2) envoys sent to maintain alliances, 3) envoys sent to transmit inquiries — as on customary occasions, or when a ruler ascended the throne, or to maintain friendly relations or the like, 4) envoys sent to pay respects, by a ceremony either to return homage or to render thanks, 5) envoys sent to make announcements, including the announcement of disorder, disaster, mourning, natural calamity or defeat, 6) envoys sent to offer condolence for mourning, burial, natural calamity or defeat, and finally, 7) envoys to marriages. There were also customary procedures concerning guests or attachés and the followers of envoys such as bodyguards, interpreters, and servants.

The ceremonies for the reception of envoys were carefully detailed in the *I-li* and other works, while the actual practice was recorded in the *Ch'un-ch'iu* and *Tso-chuan*, in which references correspond to the regulations in the *I-li*. The ceremonial for the dispatch of envoys included the following procedures: 1) When the envoy arrived at the frontier of the other country, he announced his arrival and was then welcomed at the frontier and exchanged gifts and extensive civilities with the officials appointed to receive him, both there and at the capital. 2) The envoy went to his lodgings. 3) On the next day he had audience, being treated as the guest of honor. 4) He presented the valuable objects and gifts. 5) He might present an official letter. 6) He was entertained at a big official banquet, and there were various other ceremonies which might be used. Other rules governed the refusal of envoys, and their privileges, among which were immunity from attack, a sort of extra-territoriality freeing them from local law, and exemption from the customs duties. According to the ancient records there were also military representatives of various kinds, and officials in charge of the several aspects of foreign relations. Numerous regulations governed leagues and alliances; and customs duties, passports, settlement of disputes, and international law concerning war and neutrality, were all to be found in one form or another.[1]

it was the duty of the minister to be loyal, of the son to be filial, and of each person in society to preserve the social order by acting as demanded by etiquette, so it was particularly the duty of the ruler, as the one man who represented his people before Heaven, to set the model for the rest of mankind. There was felt to be a certain virtue or power (*te*) in right conduct such that it could move others. The virtuous ruler gained prestige and influence over his people merely by exhibiting his virtue. In this way Confucius and his followers had defined an ethical basis for the exercise of political authority over all mankind, including the barbarians.[2]

By a logical expansion of this theory the emperor's virtuous action was believed to attract irresistibly the barbarians who were outside the pale of Chinese civilization proper. "The kings of former times cultivated their own refinement and virtue in order to subdue persons at a distance, whereupon the barbarians (of the east and north) came to Court to have audience" — so reads an official statement of the Ming period about 1530.[3] A century and a half later the first Manchu edition of the *Collected Statutes* records that "When our Dynasty first arose, its awe-inspiring virtue (*te*) gradually spread and became established. Wherever its name and influence reached, there were none who did not come to Court." [4]

Thus the relationship between the emperor and the barbarians came to symbolize the actual historical relationship between China as the center of culture and the rude tribes roundabout. This relationship was clearly recognized and formed the theoretical basis for the tributary system. The first tenet of this theory was that the uncultivated alien, however crass and stupid, could not but appreciate the superiority of Chinese culture. Naturally he would seek to "come and be transformed" (*lai-hua*), so as to participate in its benefits. To do this it was chiefly essential that he should recognize the unique position of the Son of Heaven, the One Man who constituted the apex of the Chinese scheme of things. This conformed with the fundamental dogma that China was the center of the human scene and that the emperor exercised the mandate of Heaven to rule all mankind, Chinese and barbarian alike. It also accorded with the basic assumption of Confucian ethics that the organization of society is naturally hierarchic rather than egalitarian, that all superiors should be models for their inferiors, and that the family of nations is just what the name implies — an organized group dominated by the Chinese ruler as its patriarch.[5] In this family, barbarians were uncouth country cousins.

The relationship which thus inhered between the outer barbarian and the emperor was by no means unilateral and indeed could hardly exist except on a reciprocal basis. It was the function of the emperor to be compassionate and generous. His "tender cherishing of men from afar" (*huai-jou yuan-jen*) is one of the clichés in all documents on foreign relations. The humble submission of the foreigner came in direct response to the imperial benevolence, which was itself a sign of the potent imperial virtue.

Finally, it was unavoidable that these reciprocal relations of compassionate benevolence and humble submission should be carried out in ritual form, without which they could hardly be said to exist. Tribute became one of the rites of the court, a part of the ceremonial of government. In fact, the presentation of tribute was not a rite limited to barbarians. Under the Manchus tribute (*kung*) was also received by the court at Peking from the provinces of China proper. Its presentation by the barbarians was a sign of their admission to the civilization of the Middle Kingdom — a boon and a privilege, not an ignominious ordeal. In this way the formalities of the tributary system were a mechanism by which formerly barbarous regions outside the empire were given their place in the all-embracing Sino-centric cosmos.

Tribute as ritual. This will appear most plainly from an analysis of the rules and regulations of the tribute system as published in the various editions of the *Collected Statutes* of the Ch'ing.[6] First of all the tributary ruler who tendered his submission was incorporated into the charmed circle of the Chinese state by several forms. An imperial patent of appointment was bestowed upon him — a document which recognized his status as a tributary. A noble rank was also conferred upon him, sometimes, as with the Mongol princes, a relatively high rank in comparison with those of Chinese subjects. An imperial seal was also granted him, to be used in the signing of his tributary memorials. Such memorials and other communications were to be dated by the Chinese dynastic reign-title — that is, the Chinese calendar was extended over the tributary state. A tributary envoy who died within the Middle Kingdom received unusual Confucian honors: a funeral essay was recited and burned at his grave, where sacrificial offerings were made, and later a stone was placed above it with an imperial inscription. Even for the burial of an attendant of the mission, if he died at the capital, a wooden coffin and red satin were to be supplied.

The tribute missions themselves were carefully limited in size but, within the limit, were well provided for. The officers and servants of a mission were not to exceed one hundred men, of whom only twenty might go to the capital while the rest remained at the border under the care and on the provision of the local authorities. A mission coming by sea should not consist of more than three ships, of one hundred men each. On the way to the capital the mission received its keep and transportation, the latter being supplied by the men, horses, boats and carts of the imperial post (the service of transport and communication maintained in each province for imperial use). At the capital the mission was lodged at the official Residence for Tributary Envoys — a collection of hostelries where statutory daily amounts of silver, rice, or fodder were paid from the imperial treasury for the maintenance of men and animals. When an envoy returned to the frontier he was escorted by a ceremonial usher. Both going and coming he was accompanied by troops who combined protection with surveillance.

In the court ceremonies there was an exchange of courtesies. The tribute mission was entertained at banquets, not once but several times, and feasted also in the presence of the emperor, from whom they might receive tea or even delicacies of the table. On their part the tributary envoys performed the kotow. European participants were inclined to feel that this ceremony more than made up for the imperial benevolence which filtered down to them through the sticky hands of their official supervisors. The kotow in principle is a knocking of the head upon the ground, in itself an act of surrender, but the full kotow as performed at court was a good deal more. It consisted of three separate kneelings, each kneeling accompanied by three separate prostrations, and the whole performed at the strident command of an usher—"Kneel!", "Fall prostrate!", "Rise to your knees!", "Fall prostrate!", and so on. An envoy went through this calisthenic ceremony not once but many times, since it was the chief means by which he repaid the imperial board and lodging, and his official supervisors were charged to see that he did it before the emperor with accomplished ease. It was the rite of all others which left no doubt, least of all in the mind of the performer, as to who was the superior and who the inferior in status.

Yet it should not be forgotten by egalitarian Westerners (who invariably did forget) that the kotow was merely a part of the universal order of Confucian ceremony which symbolized all the relationships of life. The emperor performed the kotow to Heaven and to his parents, the highest officials of the empire performed it to the emperor, and friends or dignitaries might even perform it mutually to each other. From a tribute envoy it was, therefore, no more than good manners.

The tribute itself was no gain to the imperial court. It was supposed to consist of native produce, a symbolic offering of the fruits of the tributary country. "Things that are not locally produced are not to be presented."[7] Rare and strange items might be included, like the auspicious giraffes which were brought from Africa in the early Ming period as unicorns (*ch'i-lin*), omens of good fortune.[8] But there was little benefit to the imperial treasury in anything that a tribute mission might bring. The value of the tribute objects was certainly balanced, if not outweighed, by the imperial gifts to the various members of the mission and to the vassal ruler. The expense of entertaining a mission was not inconsiderable, but the court was repaid in kudos. Tribute was ordinarily presented at the time of a great audience at the New Year, when the bureaucracy of all the empire paid reverence to the Son of Heaven and when the dramatic submission of foreign lands could most effectively reinforce the imperial prestige within China proper.

Functions of the tribute system. This brings us to the interesting question, what made the tribute system work? Why did missions from neighboring states come to the Chinese court year after year, century after century? Something more tangible than the imperial virtue must have lain behind this impressive and persistent institution. The question is essentially one of motive. Without a constant incentive on both sides, the system could never have functioned as it did.

The motivation of the court is not difficult to see. The ruler of China claimed the mandate of Heaven to rule all mankind. If the rest of mankind did not acknowledge his rule, how long could he expect China to do so? Tribute had prestige value in the governing of China, where prestige was an all-important tool of government.

More than this, the tribute system was a diplomatic medium, the vehicle for Chinese foreign relations. Whenever a new ruler ascended the throne of a tributary state, he was required by the regulations to send an envoy to obtain an imperial mandate from the Chinese court. By imperial command he was then appointed ruler of his country, and the imperial patent of appointment was given to his envoy. After receiving this document, the new ruler sent a tribute mission to offer thanks for the imperial favor. In other words, his regime was recognized. In the Far Eastern scene, this recognition, or perhaps we might say "investiture," by the Middle Kingdom was perhaps at times comparable to recognition in Europe by the Pope or by the concert of powers. It might help to establish a claimant upon his throne. A recognized vassal might appeal in time of need for Chinese help, as did the king of Malacca after his ousting by the Portuguese in 1511.

Chinese influence abroad was also exerted through personal contact with tributary rulers, who sometimes came to court. In the ancient period this had been a chief form of submission. When the chieftain of the Hsiung-nu (Huns) visited the Han or when the king of the Uigurs or of Korea came to the Mongol court, they placed themselves literally under the imperial control. In later periods such activity grew rare, although several visits to Peking of kings from Malacca and such places are recorded in the Ming period; perhaps they came for the junket. Sometimes the heir-apparent of a tributary state might appear in a mission, an almost equally useful custom.

Even more important was the tradition of sending Chinese envoys abroad. Chang Ch'ien, who was sent to the Western Regions in the years 138–126 B.C. to gain for the Han an alliance against the Hsiung-nu, is only the most famous of these envoys. Even before the time of Chang Ch'ien, the first emperor of the Han had sent Lu Chia on an official mission to Nan-yueh, the region of Canton, and numerous envoys were later sent to deal with the Hsiung-nu of the northern steppe. Under the T'ang such an emissary was called "an envoy to foreign countries" (*ju-fan shih*); under the Sung, "an envoy with a state message" (*kuo-hsin shih*). The Mongols in the course of their expansion sent officers of this sort in all directions, to the Uigurs and Japan, and to Annam and various countries of southeastern Asia. This diplomatic activity was, of course, to be expected. It is unfortunate that it has not been studied systematically.

One function of these envoys was to confer the imperial seal and recognition upon vassal rulers. Plainly such a formality could be two-faced and of use to China as a mere cover for practical negotiations. Another function was to make condoling inquiries when the local ruler had suffered a bereavement or had himself died. In A.D. 55, after the death of the dangerous and troublesome chieftain of the Hsiung-nu, the Han sent a lieutenant-general "to go and offer condolences," and it is further recorded that he went "in command of an army." [9] Thus all types of international intercourse, if they occurred at all in the experience of China, were fitted into the tribute system. It permitted spying out the enemy, seeking allies, and all manner of negotiations, including the threat of force.

At different times tribute served different purposes, and the system could be used by China for defense quite as much as for aggression. Broadly speaking, it appears to have been used mainly for defense under the Sung. Under the Mongols it served for expansion; under the Ch'ing it promoted stability in foreign affairs. In the first of these periods, one of weakness, it has been suggested that the suzerain-vassal relationship was an isolationist device, a means of avoiding the dangers inherent in foreign relations on terms of equality.[10] In a sense this is the secret of the whole system. Outsiders could have contact with China only on China's terms, which were, in effect, that the outsider should acknowledge and enter into the Chinese scheme of things and to that extent become innocuous. So China tried to derive political security from her accepted cultural superiority. Tribute was a first step toward Sinicizing the barbarian and so neutralizing him. Apparently the dogma of superiority waxed when China grew weak. This interpretation, if supported by further research, may indicate the perennial value of the institution to the Son of Heaven.

If tribute had this obvious political value for the Chinese court, what was its value to the barbarian? Did the tributaries subscribe to the Chinese view of their position, or is the whole great tradition partly an official Chinese myth, foisted with great consistency upon the emperor's subjects and later historians? When we find that Lord Macartney, sent by George III in 1793 to demand trade concessions, refused to kotow but is faithfully enshrined in the Chinese records as a tributary envoy, what are we to think of the preceding millennia of so-called tribute missions? Why should an upstanding barbarian come and kotow? The answer is partly, of course, that he had little choice in the matter, being obliged either to accept the conditions of the gargantuan Middle Kingdom or stay away. But the unbroken continuity of tributary relations between China and surrounding states argues for a strong and consistent motivation on the foreigner's part as well as on that of the court. This motivation seems clearly to lie in trade, so much so that the whole institution, viewed from abroad, appears to have been an ingenious vehicle for commerce.

Tributary trade. That tribute was a cloak for trade has been axiomatic ever since merchants from the Roman orient reached Cattigara in southernmost China in A.D. 166 claiming to be envoys of Marcus Aurelius. Testimony on the subject abounds, particularly regarding the sham embassies of merchants on the Central Asian caravan routes. The Kansu governor in 1502 reported that there were more than one hundred and fifty self-styled rulers (*wang*) trading with China from the Western Regions. The Jesuit, Benedict de Goez, who crossed Central Asia a century later in 1604, described how the caravan merchants "forge public letters in the names of kings whom they profess to represent" and "under pretense of being ambassadors go and offer tribute to the Emperor." [11]

So fundamental was this commerce that the regulations for tribute devote a whole section to it.[12] Tribute missions arriving at the frontier normally included merchants, either as private individuals or as agents of the tributary ruler, who often monopolized the trade. They brought with them commercial goods which they were allowed to sell to the Chinese merchants at the frontier emporium or, alternatively, they might at their own expense bring these goods duty free in the train of the envoy to the capital and sell them there at a special market set up at the Residence for Tributary Envoys. This market lasted for three or five days, according to the regulations of 1690, and was carefully superintended by officers of the Board of Revenue. Trade outside of the official market and trade in certain types of goods were both strictly prohibited. The contraband list included works of history, implements of war, saltpetre, and copper and iron — things which might weaken the defense of the realm.

Meanwhile, for independent foreign merchants who did not come in the train of an embassy there were emporia on the frontier. For Korean merchants there was a market on the Manchurian frontier. For the Western border peoples there were one or two markets a year near Chengtu and Lanchow, each lasting twenty days. These appear to have been similar to the market set up in the eighteenth century at Mai-mai-chen for the caravan trade with Russia. For the maritime nations the chief market was at Canton. Foreign merchant vessels were forbidden to carry away contraband goods, or Chinese passengers, or rice and grain beyond the ship's own needs. Exports in a tribute vessel, however, were exempt from customs duty. In these terms the tribute system was made to cover foreign trade as well as diplomacy.

This sketch is, of course, only a faint reflection of the plethora of rules and regulations on the subject of tributary trade. Considering their extent, and the extent of the trade, it seems anomalous that foreign trade could be considered in Chinese theory to be subordinate to tribute, but so it was. It was officially regarded as a boon granted to the barbarian, the necessary means to his sharing in the bounty of China, and nothing more. No doubt, this quixotic doctrine reflected the anti-commercial nature of the Confucian state, where the merchant was low in the social scale and nominally beneath both the farmer and the bureaucrat, who lived off the produce of the land. It was strengthened perhaps by the self-sufficiency of the empire, which made supplies from abroad unnecessary. At all events, it was the tradition that foreign trade was an unworthy objective for high policy, and this dogma was steadily reiterated in official documents down into the nineteenth century. Meanwhile, foreign trade developed and grew ever larger within its ancient tributary framework.

This brings us to a paradox in the history of modern China and one of the fundamental reasons for the collapse of the Confucian state. Trade and tribute in the Confucian view were cognate aspects of a single system of foreign relations. The important thing to the rulers of China was the moral value of tribute. The important thing for the barbarians was the material value of trade. The rub came when the foreign trade expanded, and finally, in some cases, eclipsed tribute entirely, without changing the official myth. Tribute continued to dominate Chinese official thought after trade had begun to predominate in the practice of Chinese foreign relations. In the modern period the Confucian bureaucrats tried to treat the new trading nations of the West as mere tributaries. When this proved impossible, they were incapable of changing their immemorial theory to fit the new situation. The paradox in this tragedy lies in the fact that the new situation to which the Chinese government could not adjust itself had been created largely by the maritime trade of Chinese merchants. China had been for too long a continental empire, accustomed to foreign relations across a land frontier. Her new maritime relations not only caught her unprepared but destroyed her ancient defense, the tribute system itself.

The eclipse of tribute by trade. The high point of recorded tributary activity in China came early in the Ming period. Between the years 1403 and 1433 seven imperial expeditions were dispatched into the waters of southeastern Asia and the Indian Ocean.[13] They were under the general superintendence of the famous eunuch Cheng Ho, and are said to have included as many as sixty vessels and twenty-seven thousand men at a time.

Some forty states were included in their points of call and most of them sent back envoys with the Chinese fleets and became enrolled as tributaries. These included Pahang, Kelantan, and Malacca on the Malay peninsula; Palembang (ancient Srivijaya), Samudra, Lambri (mod. Achin), and Aru in Sumatra; Ceylon, Cochin, Chola, Calicut, and several other places on the southern coasts of India; Barawa and Mogadisho on the Somali coast of Africa; Aden and Djofar in Arabia, and the ancient port of Hormuz on the Persian Gulf. These distant places of Africa and Arabia were visited but a few times and by few vessels, yet the fact remains that representatives of the Chinese court touched there in the early fifteenth century, a generation before the Portuguese came into the Indian Ocean round the Cape. A party from one Chinese expedition even saw the sights of Mecca.

To call these Chinese voyages spectacular is an understatement, but it it not easy to comprehend their object or to understand the reason for their complete cessation after 1433. Professor Duyvendak,[14] the closest student of the problem, has pointed out that they were the work of the palace eunuchs, a group whose considerable power depended upon the imperial favor, and that the flow of vassal envoys and rare objects, unicorns and black men among them, was well calculated to please the imperial fancy. The cessation of the voyages was dictated, he suggests, partly by their expense, which plainly must have been considerable when one includes the largesse bestowed upon prospective tributary rulers to win them over. No scholar has as yet ventured a complete explanation. The Chinese historians' tradition that the expeditions went to seek out a vanished claimant to the Ming throne does not give us much satisfaction. The suggestion seems in order that these official voyages must have been connected with the private Chinese trade which we know had been expanding for some time into the waters of southeastern Asia. This commercial background deserves attention.

We know, first of all, that tribute from this area had begun long before the time of Cheng Ho. "Java" (perhaps then Sumatra) sent tribute as early as A.D. 132.[15] A regular and extensive maritime trade with China from the regions of the Indian Ocean had begun at least as early as the T'ang period (618–907) under the aegis of the Arabs. In the Sung period it had attained very considerable proportions. Mongol fleets had swept the seas of Java and Malaya in the time of Khublai,[16] and by the end of the fourteenth century a number of states in Southeast Asia had become regular tributaries of the Ming. They included Java, Brunei (in Borneo), Pahang on the Malay peninsula, Palembang and Samudra on the island of Sumatra, and even Chola from the Coromandel coast of India in 1372. It is patent that Cheng Ho after 1403 was following well-known commercial paths. He was exploring the established sources of trade and tribute rather than terra incognita.

It is most significant that tribute from Southeast Asia declined after the time of Cheng Ho, although trade did not. In the early fifteenth century the official Ming list of tributaries from which tribute missions were received included Japan, the Philippines (Lü-sung, i.e., Manila), Cambodia, Java, Pahang on the Malay peninsula, and Achin and Samudra on the island of Sumatra. Later, under the Ch'ing, none of these places was listed as tributary.[b] But in the 1818 edition of the Ch'ing *Statutes* these various places — Japan, the Philippines, and the others just mentioned — were listed in a special section as "trading countries" (*hu-shih chu-kuo*), that is, countries that traded with China but did not send tribute. Of course, this is understandable in the cases of Japan, the Philippines, and Java (Batavia), where the Tokugawa shōgun, the Spanish, and the Dutch respectively, could not easily be considered tributary (although the Dutch had actually sent tribute as recently as 1794). But this classification is less logical in the case of the small places of Malaya. The full list of "trading countries" printed in 1818 was as follows: Chiang-k'ou (i.e., Siam), Cambodia, Yin-tai-ma, Ligor, Jaya (Chaiya), Sungora, Patani, Trengganu, Tan-tan, Pahang, Johore, Achin (defined as the same as Samudra, by error), Lü-sung (the Philippines), Mindanao, and Java (Batavia). Most of these were small kingdoms under petty sultans, similar to the states of Pahang and Achin which Cheng Ho had enrolled as Ming tributaries. Why were they not now listed in the early nineteenth century as vassals of the Ch'ing?

The answer plainly lies in the fact that it was no longer they who came to China but the Chinese who went to them. Chinese trade with Southeast Asia had developed since the days of Cheng Ho to the point where the barbarians, or the Arab traders of the region, no longer came to Canton to obtain the products of the Middle Kingdom. Instead, the great junk fleets of Amoy and Canton now carried Chinese produce into all parts of the archipelago. The list of "trading countries" made out in 1818 really constitutes a catalogue of the ports of call on the two great sea routes of the Chinese junk trade, which went down the Malay peninsula and through the Philippines, respectively. Indeed, it shows an almost one-to-one correspondence with a list of the trading countries of the region made by Francis Light, the British founder of Penang, about 1788: he listed Siam, Chantebon, Chia, Sangora, Pattany, Ligore, Tringano, Pahang, Jahore, and others, including Acheen.[17]

That Chinese junks had long been the local carriers of Malaya hardly

[b] The official Ch'ing lists published in the five editions of the *Collected Statutes* between 1690 and 1899 included only Korea, Turfan, Liu-ch'iu, Holland, Annam, Siam, the countries of the Western Ocean, Burma, Laos, and Sulu, and not even all of these at one time; these tributaries of the Manchus were fewer in number, although it must be admitted that they were more substantial political entities than were some of the small islands and out-of-the-way principalities induced by Cheng Ho to become vassals of the Ming.

seems to require documentation, although it is a much neglected subject. The Portuguese at Malacca after 1511, the Spanish at Manila after 1571, and the Dutch at Batavia after 1619 had all found Chinese traders much in evidence. It is not too much to say that the early European trade in eastern Asia was actually grafted onto the junk trade which already flourished there, much of it in Chinese hands. The British and French East India Companies appear to have been well aware of the desirability of tapping this local commerce. Manila, indeed, lived upon it, the cargoes of the Acapulco galleons coming not so much from the Philippines as from the vast storehouse of China, whither the Spanish themselves were not allowed to go.[18] In short, it seems incontestable that the migration of the Chinese into southeastern Asia, which has been one of the significant phenomena of the nineteenth and twentieth centuries, is merely the later phase of a Chinese commercial expansion which had begun much earlier.

To this early Chinese maritime trade it would seem that the tribute system had been for some time successfully applied. The system had developed on the land for operation across easily controllable land frontiers, and every approach to China from the continental side had offered convenient points of control like the Jade Gate (Yü-men kuan) on the west or Shanhaikuan on the north. Under the Ch'ing the missions from Korea were required to enter via Feng-huang-ch'eng and Shanhaikuan, those from Annam via P'ing-yang or T'ai-p'ing-fu in Kwangsi, and those from Burma via Yung-ch'ang or T'eng-yueh in Yunnan.[19]

Over maritime tributaries a similar control had been established by requiring missions from Liu-ch'iu to enter only at Foochow, those from Sulu only at Amoy, and those from Siam only at Canton; the Dutch were reprimanded for coming to Fukien instead of Kwangtung. The greater volume of maritime trade had led to the growth of foreign communities in the seaports, like those of the Arabs at Zayton (Ch'üan-chou) and Canton, but these communities had been kept under control through their own headmen in their own restricted quarter, and trading operations had been supervised by Chinese officials. So long as the foreign traders came to the frontier of China, whether by land or by sea, tributary forms could be preserved and tribute missions could be sent to the capital, either on the initiative of acquisitive merchants and rulers or at the instigation of the face-seeking Chinese bureaucracy.

These observations offer some support for the hypothesis that the first blow at the Chinese tribute system was struck not by the Europeans who refused to accept tributary status after 1500 but by the expansion of Chinese trade even before that time. We know in a general way that the Arabs who had once dominated trade between China and Southeast Asia were supplanted by Chinese merchants, that traders from the southeast by degrees no longer came to China, that the Chinese went to them. As this foreign-carried trade dried up, tribute probably dried up with it.

If we look at the great fifteenth-century voyages of Cheng Ho in this light, perhaps we can regard them as an effort to bring the sources of Chinese maritime trade back into the formal structure of the tribute system, so as to make the facts of foreign trade square with the theory that all places in contact with China were tributary to her. Foreign places communicating by land, like Samarkand, Isfahan, Arabia, or the Kingdom of Rum in Asia Minor, were enrolled as tributaries of the Ming although contact must have been extremely tenuous (particularly when the Kingdom of Rum, for example, had long since ceased to exist). Was it not logical to enroll similarly the places communicating by sea? Mixed motives naturally must be assumed, but this desire to preserve the traditional system must have been one of them. In any case, the tribute system gradually ceased to operate by sea although it continued to do so by land.[20] From the first it had been a passive system, the Middle Kingdom waiting for the barbarians to approach, and it could not be maintained when the Chinese were themselves active. By the beginning of the nineteenth century its demise was officially acknowledged in the case of the "trading countries" of Southeast Asia which traded without sending tribute, as recorded in the *Collected Statutes* of 1818.

The increase of trade in the early nineteenth century may also be evident in the fact that the number of recorded tribute missions showed a decided increase.[21] From 1662 to 1761 the total of recorded embassies was about two hundred and sixteen. In the following century from 1762 to 1861 it was about two hundred and fifty-five. This increase must be examined as a possible index of greater commercial activity taking the form of tribute missions.

From the data available in the records the fact stands out that tribute missions coming by sea, from Liu-ch'iu and from Siam, increased remarkably in the half century beginning about 1800. They became decidedly more frequent than required by statute.[c] Since we must suppose that their

[c] The statutory frequency of tribute missions under the Ch'ing was as follows: from Korea annually, from Liu-ch'iu every two years, Annam every three, six, or four years (the regulations changed), Siam every three years, Sulu every five years, Laos and Burma every ten years, Holland every eight and later every five years, the Western Ocean (Portugal, etc.) indefinite. How did this square with practice?

With perhaps a couple of exceptions, Korea sent tribute every year steadily until 1874 and so need not be considered. Tribute from Liu-ch'iu was recorded in some seventy years out of the one hundred and forty-four years from 1662 through 1805, that is, on the average almost exactly as required by statute. But in the next fifty-four years from 1806 to 1859, tribute from Liu-ch'iu instead of being biennial was recorded forty-five times, on the average in five out of every six years: this is doubly significant when we remember that the Liu-ch'iu islands, in themselves unimportant, served as an entrepôt for trade between Japan and Korea on the one hand and China on the other, in this period before either Japan or Korea was open to foreign trade. Tribute from Annam was recorded forty-five times in the two hundred years from 1662 to 1861, somewhat less than an average of one in four years, which agrees fairly well with the shifting regulations for Annam. There was no significant increase.

motivation was commercial, this evidence lends strong support to the theory that tribute missions functioned chiefly as a vehicle for trade. Whether the commercial profits were gained by the tributary rulers and their merchants or mainly by Chinese merchants and officials remains to be investigated.

At least in the case of Siam the missions came over a route dominated by the Chinese junk trade. The arrival of this tribute at the Chinese court was therefore an ill omen, a sign of the rising tide of maritime trade conducted by Chinese merchants, with the help of which the merchants of the West were about to burst the dike of the tribute system and invade the Middle Kingdom. It is a fascinating question whether the court was not, on the contrary, lulled into a false sense of security by this apparent increase of barbarian submissiveness. This prostitution of the tribute system for commercial ends seems to have confirmed the Chinese idea of superiority just when it was most urgently necessary to get rid of it.

Siam was recorded as sending tribute only eleven times in the one hundred and fifteen years from 1662 to 1776, an average of about one year in ten instead of one in three as required by statute. But in the next seventy-seven years from 1777 through 1853, Siamese missions were recorded thirty-eight times, on the average every other year, and half again as frequently as the regulations prescribed! Significance is added by the fact that Siamese tribute came by sea along the main coastal trade route connecting Canton with Southeast Asia and the Straits. Tribute from Burma came only three times before 1788; from then until 1853 it came thirteen times, an average of once in five years instead of once in ten years as prescribed. Tribute from Laos came seventeen times between 1730 and 1853, averaging somewhat better than the statutory decade. Sulu is recorded only seven times, between 1726 and 1754, and may be left out of account.

CHAPTER III

CH'ING POLICY AND THE CANTON SYSTEM

ANOTHER SOURCE OF CHINA'S WEAKNESS in dealing with the problem of Western trade lay in the Manchu dynasty. By the same factors which gave them strength on the Inner Asian frontiers of China, these alien rulers were handicapped in facing the maritime West.

The Manchu position in China. As the last and most successful of the half dozen invaders of North China, the Manchus had profited by the trials and errors of many precursors, whose record is only beginning to be seriously examined. It is now plain that the early barbarian dynasties of conquest did not become "absorbed" or "assimilated." Beginning with the Ch'i-tan Mongols, who set up the Liao dynasty, these rulers "continued to maintain the center of their political and military power in their old tribal territory."[1] They did not abandon their tribal culture nor its political and military organization. They continued to be mainly pastoral people organized on a tribal basis. While ruling in North China, they also had a homeland beyond the Wall.

In similar fashion, the Chin, Yuan, and Ch'ing rulers all maintained centers of their native life outside of China proper. This gave rise to a profound dualism in their economy and society and also in their administration. The Chinese were agricultural while the Ch'i-tan and their successors relied upon stock-breeding, hunting, and some fishing. Different regulations and standards of treatment were applied to the Chinese and the barbarian populations. In the bureaucracy, key positions were normally reserved for the conquerors, and barbarian military domination was preserved. This duality applied to all aspects of both societies — food, clothing, religious observances, kinship relations, and many other cultural traits. The Jurchen who set up the Chin dynasty maintained their cultural and political independence of the Chinese. For example, they continued to use their own language and script, parallel to Chinese, in official documents. When one looks at the Yuan dynasty of the Mongols, the division between Chinese and barbarian is even more striking. Wittfogel and Feng call it a "brutally divided world," in which Marco Polo could become a bureaucrat under the Mongols and have only minimal acquaintance with the Chinese language and people. Like their predecessors, the Mongols of the Yuan dynasty exerted a military domination, used their own language parallel to Chinese in administration, and forbade Mongol intermarriage with Chinese. Indeed, the rigor with which the Mongols remained separate from Chinese society, constantly reinforced as they were through their contact with the Mongol homeland on the steppe, had much to do with their failure to retain control over China in the fourteenth century. Wittfogel suggests that this situation, in which the barbarian conquerors preserved themselves as a non-Chinese social group in China, may be termed *symbiosis*: cultural exchange did not result in the creation of a new homogeneous culture but merely in the coexistence of two mutually adapted cultures.

By the time of the Manchu conquest in 1644, it was possible for this symbiosis to be consciously institutionalized by a mixture of political, military, social and cultural arrangements. Perhaps under the Ch'ing it approached more closely a "synthesis" between the Chinese and their highly sinicized rulers. Nevertheless, something of the spirit of earlier conquerors persisted, and the Manchus sought vigorously to maintain their separate identity while minimizing their barbarian origin.

In politics the Manchus' first policy, as an alien dynasty on the defensive, was to champion the established order. They took over the Ming government almost as it stood, merely inserting themselves at the top. Their administrative innovations, like the Grand Council, were made gradually and unobtrusively. To the inherited political edifice they added certain safeguards of their power but these merely served to reinforce the traditional structure. Change thus became their enemy.

The fundamental Manchu political problem was how to succeed where the Mongols had failed. Like the Mongols they entered China as a small alien minority. But unlike the hordes of Monka and Khublai, they were from the beginning much closer to the Chinese in culture.[2] In their capital at Mukden they had imitated the Chinese court a generation before the incursion of 1644. There, in southern Manchuria, the settled arts had long superseded those of the steppe nomad and the forest hunter. Once at Peking the Manchu rulers became Confucian scholars and calligraphers, patrons of learning and of the arts in the Chinese tradition. They kept the examination system and used a majority of Chinese in the provincial governments. This system of joint Chinese and Manchu civil administration — a Manchu governor-general often being bracketed with two Chinese governors — amounted to a sort of dyarchy. The Manchus were loyal and the Chinese did the work.

To preserve this dyarchy — Chinese administration under Manchu supervision — the first essential was that the Manchu minority should maintain its social identity. Several measures were taken to this end. Outnumbered as they were, a few million Manchus might easily have been lost in the great body of China if they had not preserved their homeland as a base. They therefore closed Manchuria to immigration from China in

1668 — partly, it must be noted, to preserve the valuable monopoly of ginseng (a supposedly rejuvenative root) by the imperial household, and partly also, to keep Chinese settlers from the hunting lands.[3] For this purpose they built the famous willow palisade which stretched for several hundred miles in a great arc from the Wall at Shanhaikuan to the north of Kirin and southeastward to the Yalu river. This was not, of course, for defense but to mark a boundary as a means of checking Chinese migration beyond it. In spite of the inevitable overflow of Chinese migrants into the Three Eastern Provinces, Manchuria in effect remained a vacuum down to the late nineteenth century. Thus it is that Manchuria today is a new country with but a brief tradition of civil government from Peking.

The racial purity of the conquerors was also preserved by the ban on intermarriage with Chinese. Manchu separatism was emphasized by the ban on Manchus engaging in trade and other activities in competition with Chinese. Manchu women were customarily allowed much greater social freedom than Chinese women. In addition to these practices, the clan organization of the Manchus, supported by the religious system of shamanism, was preserved and used to prevent the assimilation of Manchus by the Chinese around them.[4]

No argument is necessary to prove that the Manchus adapted their own institutions to meet their major problem of holding power in China. Many specific procedures were developed so that the conquerors might rule over China in a Chinese way, but without becoming Chinese. For example, they early arranged to use Chinese troops as an important though subordinate part of their military organization. Military control of China was sustained by the banner organization of the Manchu nation-in-arms, from which were drawn garrisons stationed at strategic points in a military cordon around the symbol of imperial rule, Peking, and in big provincial centers such as Chengtu, Nanking, Hangchow, Soochow and Canton. Meanwhile the Chinese provincial army (*Lü-ying*, "Army of the Green Standard") was little more than a provincial constabulary for use against bandits and was never allowed to become a unified military power under central control.

In any situation of symbiosis, influences operate in both directions. Chinese institutions were themselves profoundly influenced by the successive barbarian conquerors, whose rule had a pervasive effect on many aspects of Chinese society. Barbarian influence is symbolized most vividly in the Chinese wearing of the queue under the Manchus. This was a compulsory sartorial custom which became part of everyday life among the masses and served as a constant reminder of Manchu domination.

Among their political innovations, the Manchu ruling house departed from the Chinese tradition of primogeniture.The emperor's eldest son was not made a crown prince and the heir to the throne was chosen among all the sons, with greater benefit to the dynastic interest. The Ch'ing further sought to avoid the fate of the Yuan by preserving effective rule within the imperial clan, whose members were kept out of power to avoid family squabbles over the succession. Until the late nineteenth century the imperial princes were not given important posts nor great wealth nor were they made territorial lords. Government by women and by eunuchs was also checked until after 1860. By such devices the Manchus succeeded in ruling for 267 years over a Chinese population one hundred times more numerous.

Behind all these safeguards lay a basic motive, the preservation of power. Manchu rule was from the first a contest to see how long an invading minority could rule the Chinese state; the welfare of China and its people was an essential but secondary consideration. To put it another way, there was no use in any measure which might benefit the country but destroy the dynasty. Any attempt at a purely Chinese "national" policy might conflict with dynastic policy. In the end, this division of counsels must be taken as one cause of the debacle which overtook both the country and its rulers.

This intricate Chinese-Manchu relationship awaits further analysis. Tentatively it may be useful to approach it through two channels, political and social. The political approach leads us to consider first the Manchu conduct of foreign relations.

Early Manchu foreign policy. This was by no means always the same as a Chinese foreign policy and was strongly colored by the fact that the Manchu empire embraced a good deal more than China proper. The Inner Mongols had become vassals of the Ch'ing before 1644. The vast areas of Outer Mongolia, Tibet, and Turkestan where the Manchu power was later established became subject not to China but to the dynasty — a fact which was to provide the logical basis for their defection from the Chinese Republic at the time of the revolution of 1911. Inner Asia until then was not under China but under the Manchus. Thus until the nineteenth century Inner Asia had been the focus of the dynasty's foreign policy, for there on the steppe was the great traditional source of danger. The legend of Chinghis Khan and his successors and the long struggle between the Mongols and the Ming dynasty in the early fifteenth century were still in the memory of Peking. The security of the Mongol border was, therefore, considered all important. Successful Ch'ing campaigns against the Outer Mongols in the seventeenth century were followed in the eighteenth by the conquest of Chinese Turkestan, which was eventually to be formed into the New Dominion (Sinkiang). This absorption of the Tarim basin, completed by 1759, followed the precedent of the Han and the T'ang. It placed Chinese and Manchu forces in the oases of Central Asia on the flank of the Mongol tribes to the north and served as strategic insurance against them. Meanwhile tribal boundaries were fixed and the law of succession among the

Mongols was arranged to split up inherited lands and so prevent the rise of a new Chinghis Khan or any feudal leader who might create a striking power upon the steppe through the organization of his personal following. Tribe was used against tribe. The Lamaist church was encouraged as a balance to the power of the temporal princes.

This importance of Lamaism as a political tool in Mongolia naturally reinforced the Ch'ing interest in Tibet. The Dalai Lama, temporal ruler at Lhasa, had received his title from a Mongol prince in the sixteenth century, and the Mongols had intervened at Lhasa and put the Dalai on the throne in 1641 just before the Manchu entrance into China.[5] It was not unnatural, therefore, that the Manchu rulers became patrons of Lamaism as a means of influence in both Tibet and Mongolia. The copy of the Dalai's palace at Lhasa, the Potala, which was built at the Ch'ing emperors' summer capital at Ch'eng-te in Jehol, is a symbol of this interest. To forestall Mongol control, the K'ang-hsi emperor intervened and established imperial residents (amban) at Lhasa in 1720. This was followed by extensions of Ch'ing control in 1751 and again after 1792.

Activity on the Inner Asian frontiers of China had constituted the great part of Ch'ing foreign relations. It is true that friction with Burma had led to hostilities in the 1760's and that there had also been friction with Annam in the late eighteenth century. There was also, of course, contact with Russia which led to the treaty of Nerchinsk in 1689, the Russian mission resident in Peking, and later intermittent relations in the northeast. The fact remains that Manchu foreign relations had been almost entirely continental and had been concentrated upon the problem of safeguarding the Manchu position in China. This meant that the arrival of the English by sea posed utterly novel problems, and at the same time inspired the court at Peking to act primarily with a view to preserving the political control over China which it had built up with such care.

Since the object of the alien conquerors was primarily to keep their political power, we might naturally expect their influence to be greatest on Chinese political institutions, especially on the monarchy. The hypothesis may be advanced that the Confucian monarchy in the last six or seven hundred years of its existence was profoundly molded and influenced by the barbarian rulers who controlled it during so much of that period. This influence applied both to policies and procedures, and to theories. It may be suggested that the general effect upon the monarchy was to keep it denationalized, inoculated against an ethnocentric Chinese nationalism. This result was achieved from both the barbarian and the Chinese sides.

The Chinese of the Sung period who reintegrated their philosophy in Neo-Confucianism had found themselves at the very same time subject to increasing pressure from northern barbarians. The alien Liao dynasty in

North China (907–1125) preceded the lifetime of Chu Hsi, and its successor, the Chin dynasty (1115–1234), outlasted him. These barbarian rulers of North China were but precursors of the Mongols who subjugated all China in the thirteenth century. It was therefore natural that Neo-Confucianism, which achieved its final formulation in a period of barbarian invasion, should tacitly or by implication take account of the barbarians. In fact the new world view of medieval China incorporated the barbarians in the Confucian system by stressing their position under the emperor's personal rule.

Equally on their part, alien invaders once in power found it expedient to emphasize the universal nature of the emperor's personal sway. The power structure which the emperor represented rested upon a complex foundation which included an elite military force, socio-cultural separatism between Chinese and barbarian, and the universal ethical sanction of Confucianism by which the economic and political processes of Chinese society were fostered and supervised within a traditional social order. The monarch's function was to maintain the order of society. But, since ancient times, he had been expected to do this both within the area of China and over the border regions of the steppe. The emperor's sway was not exclusively confined to the settled area of intensive Chinese agriculture. Under barbarian dynasties it had equally extended over the barbarian homeland beyond the Wall. This fact had the effect of emphasizing the monarchy's universality and playing down its peculiarly Chinese character.

This brings us to the second of the two channels of approach to Manchu-Chinese relations mentioned above — that by way of the social structure of the Confucian state, into which the Manchus had fitted themselves. Judging by the strongly bifurcated class structure of the Chinese state (the division between the literate ruling elite and the politically inert mass of the peasantry), the Manchus in China had their position already prepared for them before they took power, for the dynasty was the institutionalized leader and patron of the landlord gentry class. The latter dominated the local scene in the countryside, just as the court dominated the bureaucracy in the cities and major towns. Dynasty and gentry were necessarily allies, over against the Chinese peasant masses. Neither ally could normally dispense with the other, even though one were of alien race.

The result of all this was that the policy of the Manchu dynasty was never synonymous with a policy of the Chinese people as a nation. This in turn meant that the response of the Chinese imperial regime to the Western influx of the nineteenth century was not a purely Chinese response, but rather the response of a hybrid institution, the Manchu-Chinese Confucian monarchy. It would not be fair to say that the government at Peking during the early part of the century reacted to the West on the basis of a purely selfish concern for Manchu power and prestige. The Confucian monarchy of that day, by its nature as an institution, represented both the Manchu rulers and the Chinese landlord-scholar-official class at the same time. In this dyarchy it cannot be said that either racial group arbitrarily called the tune for the other. The regime as a whole, because of its dual nature, was inhibited from responding to the West in either a purely Manchu or a purely Chinese fashion.

Under this synthesized Sino-barbarian Confucian monarchy, there was no room for popular movements and, therefore, no room for nationalism in its modern mass form; the xenophobia of the Chinese scholar class was the response of a cultural and social elite. In the Confucian scheme of things the Chinese literati had been trained to treat as barbarians those who acted like barbarians, and to treat as Chinese those barbarians who behaved in a Chinese fashion. The Manchu dynasty at its height under Ch'ien-lung in the latter part of the eighteenth century had gone to great pains to proscribe and destroy literature which emphasized the non-Chinese character of barbarian conquerors. In the imperial literary inquisition of that period some two thousand works had been suppressed. At the same time some thirty-five hundred were brought together in the gigantic imperial collection known as the *Ssu-k'u ch'üan-shu*.[6] The *Gleichschaltung* thus effected, by which the content of Chinese scholarship was kept in line with the dynastic interest of the Manchus, appears to have been on the whole successful. In the first half of the nineteenth century there is little evidence of anti-Manchu thought or feeling among the Chinese officials who served the emperor.

The identity of interest between the Chinese and Manchu ruling classes who jointly participated in the government of China under the Confucian monarchy made them stand together both against the Western invaders from without and against rebellion from within. It was therefore impossible for them, as the joint rulers of China, to utilize the latent resources of popular anti-foreignism in any formal way. They could not rouse a spirit of mass resistance to the British without endangering the Confucian system of elitist government. This became evident when the imperial authorities at Canton, in their effort to use the local Cantonese anti-foreignism against the British in the 1840's, found that it was a two-edged sword which, if sharpened, might endanger the local authority of the imperial government itself.[7]

This integrated Manchu-Chinese response, both to the West and to domestic rebellion, was evident throughout the nineteenth century. It is noteworthy that after the early Manchu effort to suppress the Taipings had failed, the Confucian monarchy was eventually saved by its Chinese, instead of its Manchu, component. The strength of the common bond between the Manchu and Chinese ruling groups was attested by the fact that the Confucian monarchy, though headed by Manchus, survived for another fifty years on the loyalty of its Chinese supporters. While not pro-Manchu, these Chinese were pro-Confucian, as were the Manchus themselves. The Confucian order was the common bond which commanded their loyalty, not the Chinese "nation."

Imbedded as they were in the old social order of the agrarian-bureaucratic Chinese state and in the power relations of their Inner Asian empire, the Ch'ing rulers were in no position to respond creatively to the growth of maritime trade with Europe. From earlier dynasties they inherited certain administrative mechanisms for the regulation of commerce at Canton and other southern ports, but they had little to add themselves.

The background of Ch'ing policy at Canton. The record of official regulation of China's maritime trade is long and detailed,[8] even though the record of the trade itself is hard to find. The Arab trade at Canton was under government regulation at least as early as the T'ang. By the eighth century a Superintendency of Merchant Shipping (*Shih-po-ssu*) was set up there to keep a register of foreign vessels and captains, inspect their manifests, collect duties, and enforce laws against smuggling. In the ninth century it appears that the cargoes of Arab vessels arriving at Canton were held by the authorities until the arrival of all the season's fleet, whereupon three-tenths of each kind of merchandise was taken as import duty and the balance returned to the owners. Ch'üan-chou in Fukien (the Arab Zayton) became a second port as the trade expanded. Under the Sung by the year 1000 a state monopoly had been established which forbade private trading with foreigners and obliged all foreign goods of value to be deposited in government warehouses. Meanwhile a central office was set up at the capital to control the superintendencies at the ports. This system was preserved under the Yuan Dynasty, which had Superintendencies (*Shih-po-ssu*) in the time of Marco Polo at Canton, Zayton, Wenchow, Ningpo (then Ch'ing-yuan), Shanghai, Hangchow and nearby Kan-p'u (Polo's Canfu).

By the thirteenth century the main features of this system were well established: the supervision and taxation of trade by officials responsible directly to the capital, the confinement of trade to certain ports (chiefly Canton and Ch'üan-chou), the confinement of foreigners at these ports (chiefly the Arabs) to their own quarter, where they were under the authority of one of their own number. The rate of taxation varied in the statutes but was usually below 30 per cent ad valorem. In practice it was the object of the government to see that Sino-foreign trade was carried on under official surveillance so that the duties might be levied before trading began. All these arrangements were, of course, a recognized application of the tribute system which has already been described.

The Ming dynasty preserved these features,[9] setting up Superintendencies under inspectors (*T'i-chü*) at Canton, Ch'üan-chou, and Ningpo. Tributary envoys were entertained and sent to Peking, where they might also trade; foreign merchants at the ports were allowed to trade after their goods had been taxed.

Already the Chinese merchants had been brought into the system as official agents, one of their functions being to report to the authorities all arrivals of foreign ships as a first step in the process of taxation and trade. The object of the foreign trader, meanwhile, was to dispose of as much cargo as possible before reporting it for formal taxation. This he was able to do by exchanging part of it in illegal trade with the Chinese merchants, while at the same time presenting part of it to the Chinese officials as "squeeze" to gain their connivance. Apparently, the classic pattern was already fixed: the officials partly served the emperor and partly profited themselves, the Chinese merchants partly aided the officials and partly sought to evade them, and the foreign traders did the best they could. When the palace eunuchs, who usually monopolized the Superintendencies of Merchant Shipping, lost some of their power in the later Ming, the local and provincial authorities had their innings and began themselves to tax foreign merchant vessels. In 1522, however, the Superintendencies at Ch'üan-chou and Ningpo were closed because of the raids of Japanese pirates[10] who were then ravaging the coast, and only that at Canton remained. Meanwhile the Portuguese had arrived in China, shortly after their seizure of Malacca in 1511, and were gradually fitted into the system.[11]

The early Western commerce in China went through four chief periods.[12] (1) The first century, from the arrival of the Portuguese in 1514 to the demise of the Ming in 1644, saw little direct trade between China and Europe. Canton and Macao from the European point of view remained outposts of the main emporia at Malacca and Batavia.

From 1521 to 1554, while Sino-Portuguese trade was officially banned because of Portuguese violence, it continued in clandestine fashion, particularly along the coasts of Fukien, where the gentry, the officials and the fisher-folk all had an interest in it. After 1557, the first recorded date of its existence, the Portuguese settlement at Macao (*Ao-men*) rose rapidly. Chinese control over Macao and its commerce was never relinquished, even though the Portuguese set up their own local government. Chinese authority was exercised both by the local magistrate of the district of Heung-shan (*Hsiang-shan*), to whom a ground rent was paid annually, and by Chinese customs officers stationed in the port. By the high provincial authorities and the court above them, Macao was at first officially ignored and the customs duties, therefore, went to enrich the local officials and their superiors within the province. Duties were collected jointly: the procurator of Macao, a Portuguese official, announced the arrival of a vessel and sent the manifest to the Chinese customs authorities, who then in company with the procurator and captain measured the ship for anchorage dues (the measurement fee). After 1578 the Portuguese merchants at Macao were able, by a judicious use of presents, to establish the custom of going to Canton themselves to buy cargoes for export, so that export duties came to be collected by the local authorities of Canton. For the Portuguese alone the dues and duties were, reputedly, reduced two-thirds. In this way, by the end of the Ming, the manner of taxing foreign trade had been modified. Instead of the traditional control by officials from the court who both received tribute-bearing envoys and taxed the merchants in their train, foreign trade was for a time taxed by the local and provincial authorities for their own needs and advantage.

(2) In the first forty years of Manchu rule, from 1644 to 1684, foreign trade was inhibited by internal disorder and especially by the prohibition of sea intercourse after 1661, when the new dynasty combatted the rebel Koxinga (Cheng Ch'eng-kung) in Formosa by forbidding Chinese on the coast to sail abroad. In 1679 the Manchus used the same expedient which the Ming had used against Japanese pirates and ordered the coastal and island populations to move inland.[13] Merchant junks going abroad were severely restricted. Western contact was consequently limited and dependent upon the Western merchants' arrangements with the local officials at ports like Canton and Amoy. Direct Sino-European trade was at last made possible by the lifting of the imperial ban on sea intercourse in 1684 after the pacification of Formosa. Western traders had by then become interested in silk products, which they first found in Siam, as well as in tea, which was entering upon its vogue in Europe.

(3) The seventy-five years from 1685 to 1759 were a period of multiport trade, during which the English and other European companies tried out the market in a fitful manner at Canton, Amoy, Foochow, and Ningpo.

(4) The eventual confinement of this trade to Canton during the period of eighty-two years from 1760 to 1842, came as the final solution to the Chinese problem of control and administration. Since the growth of the Canton system was continuous during these last two periods, they may be considered together even though from the Western point of view they were successive phases.

Evolution of the Canton system. After 1685 the Ch'ing established a system of customs control partly by local officials and partly by an agent sent from the court.[14] The governors of Kiangsu and Chekiang and the Tartar-general of Fukien (the highest Manchu military authority in the province) were put in charge of the maritime customs in their respective areas, so that they became assimilated to the provincial administration. This relinquishment of central control perhaps recognized the growth of local customs authority as a fait accompli. At any rate, the court did not give up direct control in the case of Canton, where the bulk of foreign trade was already concentrated.

The first "Hoppo" or Superintendent of Maritime Customs for Kwangtung was appointed in 1685 as a representative of the Imperial Household Department (*Nei-wu-fu*) at Peking. His job was to collect the duties on the foreign trade of Canton and remit them to the Board of Revenue at the capital (the *Hu-pu*), from which some say he derived his famous Western name of Hoppo.[15] He controlled the central offices in Canton; the native customs (*ta-kuan*) and inspectors of foreign trade at Macao; and offices under deputies (*wei-yuan*) at five central ports in the Canton delta.

The innumerable streams and channels through which the waters of the West River and the Pearl River made their way between Canton city and the sea created, however, a most difficult administrative problem. The policing of such an area, inhabited by fishermen and pirates who could not be differentiated, and comprising several hundred square miles, required a strong preventive organization. The local officials must sincerely coöperate if the emperor were to receive even a part of his revenues. A long struggle seems to have resulted between dynastic and provincial interests, marked by periodic reforms of the administration. About 1724 the office of Hoppo was abolished and the management of the customs vested in the local authorities under the supervision of the provincial governor, who was to remit the duties according to the regulations. In 1729, the Hoppo's office was reëstablished but underwent various vicissitudes until 1750.[16]

One reason for these frequent administrative changes, aside from local rivalry, was given in an edict of 1734 which pointed out that an official sent directly from the court, though he could organize a reliable administration of his own, nevertheless had no official connection with the local authorities, who therefore offered his establishment no coöperation, and indeed often created friction which permitted smuggling and piracy. The Hoppo's functioning had therefore been impeded. To remedy the situation the emperor gave the Kwangtung governor-general and governor concurrent charge of all minor ports, so that they could impeach local officials who did not coöperate with the Hoppo and the customs. Meanwhile the Hoppo would handle the collection and remission of duties as before, independently of the governor-general and governor.[17] Soon thereafter, the Kwangtung maritime customs appear to have been under joint control. From 1750 on, the Hoppo collected the duties, but his report to the Board was made conjointly with the governor-general. Eventually, after 1792, the governor-general and governor reported secretly to the Board every month, and at the year's end their reports were compared with the collections reported by the Hoppo.

Thus all the high officials on the spot at Canton came to have a connection, official as well as private, with the foreign trade of the port. A fixed sum was expected by Peking, to which, in course of time, certain fixed "surpluses" were added. Amounts in excess of these fixed sums were to be reported if and as collected;[18] this left the Hoppo free to choose between pleasing his imperial master and profiting his own pocket. He was invariably a Manchu and held office usually for three years, during which, as Dr. Morse puts it, "it took the net profit of the first year of his tenure to obtain his office, of the second year to keep it, and of the third year to drop it and provide for himself."[19]

Meanwhile, the Hoppo and his official rivals at Canton had followed the tradition of using a group of Chinese merchants as their agents. This mercantile body, best known as the Cohong, was the product of a long evolution which, being unofficial, is not easy to document.[20] Evidences have been found that the Canton Superintendency of Merchant Shipping in the late Ming period had begun to employ a group of thirty-six brokerage firms (*ya-hang*) as agents in the supervision of foreign trade. These middlemen were comparable to the salt brokers who were licensed by the government to supervise the management of that official monopoly. They were also in the tradition of the Chinese merchant guilds organized in major lines of trade.

The famous Thirteen Hongs of Canton (*hang* or *hong* means business firm) dated as a recognized body from the seventeenth century, if not also from the Ming, and of course antedated the Cohong which was created by them in 1720. As agents of the government, the heads of these Thirteen Hongs now acquired a certain official status, such as the ninth official rank and the title of *kuan* (official) or at first *hsiu* (bachelor) — later known to foreigners as the suffixes *qua* and *shaw*, respectively, as in the name of their most famous member, Howqua (see further details in Ch. 14 below). Several of the early hong merchants were from Fukien, but at least three came from Kwangtung and one from Anhwei. Their activities in foreign trade early became concentrated in the suburb outside the southwest wall of the city of Canton where the "foreign quarter" (*fan-fang*) had flourished as early as the Sung period. With the growth of foreign trade in the eighteenth century their functions steadily increased and eventually became almost as much political as commercial.

Originally the Thirteen Hongs had supervised the trade of natives of the Southern Ocean (*Nan-yang*), that is, Malaya, the Straits, and the Indies. Only later did they begin to devote most of their attention to the European trade at Canton (they never concerned themselves with the Portuguese at Macao). This fits our picture of European trade as growing up from small beginnings within the framework of commercial relations already well established between China and Southeast Asia. For some time there were efforts at Canton on the part of one or another local official to set up his own monopolist of foreign trade in the person of a single hong, known to the Westerners as "the Emperor's merchant," "the Governor's merchant" or the like. In the formative period of the early eighteenth century, the governor-general, the Tartar-general, and others including the Kwangtung governor tried in this way to engross the profits of trade, each through his own agent. Finally in 1720, aided apparently by the sudden demise of one of the monopolists of the day, the Thirteen Hongs (their number varied from time to time) were able to form themselves into a monopolistic guild, the Cohong (*kung-hang*), thus providing a broader and more continuous base for monopoly regulation. The firms which took this action in 1720 subscribed by a blood oath to a code of thirteen articles which governed their commercial practices and enabled them to put up a common front against both the foreigners and the officials.

From then on, though not without much pulling and hauling, the Canton system took firm shape. In 1745 the security merchant system was instituted, some one hong being required to assume responsibility for each foreign ship, its conduct, and its duties. By 1760 European trade had been confined to Canton, and the tea and silk trades there to the Cohong. Its members were divided into three classes, one of which dealt with European merchants. The forms of taxation had proliferated. The famous restrictions on the freedom of Europeans in the Thirteen Factories were promulgated. In the period of the Canton trade's best days, 1760–1834, the hong merchants assumed more and more duties. They not only settled prices, sold goods, guaranteed duties, restrained the foreigners, negotiated with them, controlled smuggling, and leased the factories to them; they also had to manage all the aspects of a banking business, act as interpreting agencies, support the militia and educational institutions, and make all manner of presents and contributions to the authorities far and near.[21]

Official profit and imperial policy. Among the many ramifications of the Canton system which cannot here be touched upon, one fact stands out — that the Cohong was the agent and not the principal on the Chinese side. This is most evident in the long history of bankruptcy and failure among its members. One of the most persistent foreign complaints was that the hong merchants were perpetually insolvent and in need of capital — hence their foreign debts, which eventually became an international complication. The principal on the Chinese side of the Canton trade was the imperial bureaucracy which fed the imperial coffers and lined its pockets without satiety. The evidence abounds and need not be adduced at this point.[22] Year after year the profits of China's maritime trade (among which the formal revenue hardly held a candle to the informal presents and contributions made by both the Cohong and the Hoppo) flowed toward Peking or were used upon the Yellow River conservancy or in the suppression of banditry in the interior, or enriched the mandarins. This is not suprising and merely reflects the ancient domination of the mandarin over the merchant, a deeply imbedded characteristic of Chinese society which made it possible for a dynasty to affect indifference to trade and its taxation while its officials waxed fat upon it. In a sense, the imperial mandarinate had merely transferred its inveterate parasitism from the wealth of the land to the easy wealth of the maritime trade. Seen more sympathetically, the dynasty after 1800 was, no doubt, clutching at every straw to maintain itself. At all events, the result at Canton seems clear — a tradition of "squeeze" was developed such as had seldom been equalled in Chinese history, even allowing (as Sansom puts it) for the customary "difference between principle and practice."[23]

It is most significant that the fiscal importance of this growing foreign trade seems never to have been acknowledged in the official ideology of the Manchu dynasty. The formal policy of the government remained anti-commercial, in keeping with the traditional idea that foreign trade was, at best, a boon granted to barbarians and, at worst, a channel through which the latter could spy out the strength and weakness of Chinese power. This defensive policy is reminiscent of more recent times. It forbade the outflow of saltpetre, gunpowder and iron goods. It prohibited foreigners bearing arms on Chinese soil, and tried to prevent their studying the Chinese scene either by wintering at Canton, buying certain Chinese books, or learning the language. Toward the promotion of foreign trade the policy of the Ch'ing government at Peking was purely opportunist. It usually handicapped rather than aided the Chinese merchant. When the Dutch massacred Chinese merchants at Batavia in 1741, an angry proposal to stop the Dutch trade with China was overruled and the Hoppo expediently asked two Dutch ships to trade at Macao so as to avoid trouble at Canton. Rather than support Chinese merchants abroad, the court was inclined to forbid their going there and to call them home. Peking seems to have been fearful of overseas commercial expansion on the part of Chinese merchants. Thus the Ch'ing government opposed rather than assisted the extensive and increasing activity of Chinese merchants in conducting tributary trade with China on behalf of states like Siam and the small sultanates of the Malay peninsula. The sizable community of Chinese traders who already lived overseas and were in large part the actual operators of the tributary trade, were ignored in the formulation of imperial policy. When Siamese tribute vessels came to Canton in 1807 in the charge of Fukienese and Cantonese, the Canton authorities secured the issuance of an imperial edict which denounced Chinese merchants who conducted the tributary trade of foreign countries and declared that they should be treated as traitors.[24]

Yet, in spite of this policy, the Canton trade which had begun as a disesteemed boon to the barbarian turned out in fact to be a rich private booty for the court and for one group of officials after another. The ingrained rapacity thus produced among Chinese officialdom was to be one factor in the collapse of the Canton system and later a problem for the British treaty makers.

From the various types of evidence adduced above it should be obvious that China's unpreparedness for contact with the modern West was part and parcel of her old way of life. In modern times the economic and administrative patterns of the old society have been as much a handicap as the Confucian ideology or the theory of tribute relations, for no part of this well-knit and remarkably stable society could be remade without an eventual pulling apart and remaking of the whole structure. This has been a century-long continuous process, marked by successive phases, among which the creation of the treaty system was the starting point.

PART II

THE FIRST BRITISH TREATY SETTLEMENT
1842–43

CHAPTER IV

OPIUM AND THE COLLAPSE OF THE CANTON SYSTEM

The British treaties of 1842–43, so justly celebrated as the foundation of China's century-long "unequal" relations with the West, were charters which promised a new order in Chinese foreign affairs. But as with so many famous constitutional documents, the rights, duties, and procedures specified in the treaties were at first no more than words on paper (indeed, it was later found that some of the English and Chinese words differed). The fact that these legal documents of 1842–43 actually foreshadowed the new order of Sino-Western relations, instead of becoming waste paper like so many other solemn post-war compacts, is due to the way they were drawn up, through trial and error, by men on the spot, one side being backed by superior force. The treaties were not British-made blueprints but Anglo-Chinese compromises. They took account of Chinese values and institutions almost as much as Western. They were end-products of a century of Anglo-Chinese relations and must first be studied in the context of the old Canton system which they were meant to replace. The next several chapters recount the breakdown of this system, the war and negotiations which followed, and the process by which a rule of law was agreed upon for the legal foreign trade of China, while informal arrangements still remained the most that could be devised to regulate the opium trade. The chief defect of the first treaty settlement was the failure to bring fully within its scheme of things that expanding drug trade which had so largely contributed to the collapse of the old order at Canton.

The Hoppo and the Cohong have both been portrayed so vividly in Western records that their urbane relations with the British East India Company have taken on the color of a golden age. The old Canton trade, before 1834, was indeed a picturesque meeting ground for the hong merchants and the Honorable Company, who dominated their respective sides of the Sino-foreign commerce in teas and silks, and the Canton scene has been described by many writers.[1] Our interest here, however, is not the Canton trade in its halcyon days but rather the evils which beset it and the unsolved problems which it left behind. The pathology of the Canton system developed in three different areas — first among the Chinese officials, whose corruption has been mentioned above, second among the private traders, and third in the opium trade. The old Canton system finally broke down when venal Chinese officials and Western private traders joined hands in the drug traffic. The abolition of the East India Company's monopoly of British trade in 1834 was merely the coup de grace that killed the old order and precipitated the Anglo-Chinese struggle over the new.

Decline of the Company. The Company monopoly of all British trade in the Far East had been accompanied by the grant of wide powers such as were necessary for trade in the seventeenth century across perilous seas and in distant lands. Although the Company used these powers in India to grow into a government, at Canton it never lost its mercantile character. It was an organization run for profit, but not mainly for dividends.[2] On the books it was usually tending toward bankruptcy while at the same time profiting its servants through patronage, opportunities of private trade, and similar devices. Thus the governor-general in Bengal received a salary of $125,000 a year, and the president of the Select Committee at Canton sometimes earned $100,000 a year in commissions, while the dividends in England remained fixed at 8 to 10½ per cent. The Honorable Company had, so to speak, the body of a government with the brain of a merchant. In China it represented the British nation and yet it was recognized to be a trading concern, its policy being dictated by commercial considerations.

Until the latter part of the eighteenth century, the British Company in the Far East had met vigorous competition from other European nations. First the Portuguese and Dutch, and later the companies of the Austrian Netherlands ("Ostenders"), Sweden, Denmark, France, Prussia and other continental powers profited by smuggling Canton teas into the English market. This competition reached its height in 1783–84 when twenty-one continental ships at Canton exported nineteen million pounds of tea,[3] most of which would find its best market inside the British Isles. In 1784 the British government met the combined menace of smuggling and competition in the tea trade by passing the Commutation Act. It cut the tea duties in England from 119 per cent to 12½ per cent and made smuggling unprofitable. Within a few years the French Revolution further impeded competition from the continent and left England dominant in the China trade, where American participation had barely got under way after 1784.

By this time the Canton system had become firmly established, partly, in fact, with British help; for the Company had given up its early efforts to trade at Amoy or Chusan Island, preferring to do business in the well established and dependable market of Canton where native capital was sufficient for large dealings. No doubt this outcome was in part engineered by the jealous merchants of Canton, a point which has not yet been studied. At any rate, by the end of the eighteenth century, the Company found itself the dominant monopolist on the foreign side, dealing with a powerful Chinese merchant guild. The two could afford to be friends; and while the Company chafed and fretted at the restrictions, bad debts, and stoppages of the Canton trade, it eventually became conservative and inclined more and more, as the nineteenth century began, to let well enough alone and tone down its efforts at future reform lest they impede present profits.

The new day of the industrial revolution was heralded by the famous Macartney embassy which was dispatched by the Crown, paid for by the Company, and motivated partly by the desire to find an outlet for new British manufactures (*vide* the serious overproduction in the cotton industry in 1788).[4] Macartney was properly announced via Canton and arrived by sea at Taku (Tientsin) in the summer of 1793 on H.M.S. *Lion* with presents for the emperor worth fifteen thousand pounds sterling. These were labelled in Chinese "Tribute from the Kingdom of England," and Macartney was politely urged to get himself in trim for the appropriate tributary ceremonies. He refused to kotow, however, and felt sure that the Chinese saw "that superiority which Englishmen, wherever they go, cannot conceal."[5] The Ch'ien-lung Emperor, on his part, in his famous letter to George III, used the traditional phraseology of the tribute system, "I have already taken note of your respectful spirit of submission . . . I do not forget the lonely remoteness of your island, cut off from the world by intervening wastes of sea."[6] The British learned a good deal about China, but their requests concerning trade were not granted.

It is significant, however, that Macartney asked for trade at northern ports (Chusan, Ningpo, and Tientsin), for island depots near Chusan and Canton, and for a printed tariff. These requests of 1793, which can be traced back even further in the writings of Company officials at Canton,[7] formed a substantial part of what the British finally gained in 1842. Thus the needs of British trade were apparent for at least a generation before action was taken to obtain them. The delay must be attributed in part to the fact that the East India Company was more and more on the defensive. It lost its monopoly of British trade in India after 1813. Seeing the handwriting on the wall, the directors in England pursued a *carpe diem* policy. The Amherst embassy of 1816 was not strongly supported and got no results, and it remained for economic and military forces to succeed where diplomacy had failed in breaking down the barriers to trade.

The most powerful economic factor at Canton was the need for cargoes to sell to China. Something more than British woolens was required in the tropical climate of Canton to balance the mounting exports of tea and silk. The Company's tea shipments out of Canton rose from 2,626,000 lbs. (worth £831,000) in 1761 to 23,300,000 lbs. (worth £3,665,000) in 1800. Here the so-called "country" trade (the trade between India and China) entered the scene as the necessary link in a triangular commerce between India, China, and England.[8] This country trade was conducted by private individuals who were licensed by the East India Company in India and remained under its control in the Far East. It represented the final entrance of the British flag into the native carrying trade of Southeast Asia, the ancient coastal traffic which brought to China cotton piece-goods, opium, and elephants' teeth from India, and birds' nests, camphor, rattans, tin, and spices from the coasts and islands of Malaysia. The country trade increasingly and directly competed with the Chinese junk trade to the Straits and served a very useful purpose by importing products for which there was an established demand in China. Until 1823 raw cotton from India was the largest staple import. The funds realized by this trade in its sales at Canton were paid into the Company treasury there in return for bills of exchange on London. Between 1775 and 1795 the Company was already deriving more than a third of its funds from this source.[9]

Origins of the private trade. The private traders first appeared at Canton in the late 1760's. By the eighties bills of exchange were regularly being issued to partnerships such as Hunter, Vansittart and Law of London, and Fairlie, Ferguson and Company of Calcutta. More than two score of these firms were active in Canton at various times before 1800. Samuel Smith and Sons, Capt. William Mackintosh, Capt. James Farquaharson, David Scott and Company, Lance and Fitzhugh of London, Dady Nasserwanjee of Bombay — Scotsmen and Parsees (Indians of Persian extraction) were already a significant element.[10]

This growth of private trade is epitomized in that of Jardine, Matheson and Company, a firm which has played a dominant role in the China trade ever since the dissolution of the East India Company monopoly and which has held much of the British stake in Chinese coastal shipping, docks, railroads, mines, and cotton mills. While this firm was but one of many Western commercial enterprises in China, its preëminence among them and the happy fact that its voluminous records have been preserved, make it of major interest to the historian.

Jardine's did not take its present name until 1832. Before that date the style of the firm varied, as was the custom, with each change of partners. But its lineage can be traced back to 1782 [11] when a certain John Henry Cox was in Canton with the Company's permission to engage for three years in the selling of clocks and automata. These devices, such as "snuff boxes concealing a jewelled bird which sang when the lid was opened," [12] were known as "sing-songs" and had a great sale as curios for the imperial court (a collection of them may still be seen at the Palace Museum in Peking). Cox soon expanded his activities, entering the country trade, acting as Canton agent for British Indian firms, and experimenting with the importation of furs from the northwest coast of America. In 1787 he entered into partnership with Daniel Beale, formerly purser of a Company ship, who had obtained consular papers from the King of Prussia. As the agent of a foreign government, Beale was beyond Company jurisdiction and could not be expelled from China. By 1801 the firm had become Reid, Beale and Company, David Reid having arrived under the protection of a commission as captain of Danish infantry. The succession, including the indispensable Prussian consulship, by 1819 had passed to Charles Magniac and Company.

Dr. William Jardine (1784–1843) was taken into this partnership by 1825. He had been a Company ship surgeon at the age of eighteen but after fifteen years had left the service to enter the China trade on his own as an agent for firms in India. James Matheson (1796–1878), likewise a Scotsman, had received an education at the University of Edinburgh and then entered the counting house of Mackintosh and Company at Calcutta. By 1820 he had established himself at Canton as Danish consul and was soon in trade with Manila and Singapore. About 1827 he joined forces with Jardine, who was now in charge of Magniac and Company.[13]

It should be emphasized that the early British merchants (including "representatives" of Sardinia, Sweden, Sicily, and Hanover, as well as of Prussia and Denmark) survived and prospered in the China trade not only because they circumvented the Company monopoly by obtaining the commissions of foreign governments, but also because they performed a very necessary commercial function. As Michael Greenberg's illuminating study of the Jardine, Matheson archives makes clear, they were the Canton correspondents and agents of private firms in London and India who were rapidly building Britain's great nineteenth century nexus of trade, credit, shipping, insurance, and investment activity all over the world. These "agency houses" not only traded themselves but also "acted as banker, billbroker, shipowner, freighter, insurance agent [and] purveyor" all at once. The surplus production of Britain's new machine industry could be sent overseas on consignment to such agency houses, to be sold by them on a commission basis. This required a modicum of capital but a maximum of enterprise. Partners in an agency house might invest their personal funds in a "speculation" or purchase of goods, but the firm made its money chiefly from commissions, earned at rates varying from perhaps one-half per cent to five per cent on a great diversity of operations — sale or purchase of goods for others, remittance of returns in goods, bills, or treasure, guaranteeing of bills or bonds, insuring cargoes, chartering vessels, handling freight, recovering debts, and in short all manner of commercial transactions which could be performed for correspondents at a distance. Thus the agency houses became involved in various forms of banking, set up insurance companies, and acquired fleets of vessels long before the first treaties made it possible for them to develop their warehouses and establishments on Chinese soil in the new ports.

A curious tendency toward duopolistic competition runs through the history of these early firms in China — as though the circumstances of commercial enterprise called for rivalry between two organizations but no more. Dent and Company had its origin in W. S. Davidson, another Scotsman, who came to Canton as a naturalized Portuguese subject in 1811, thereby assisting his business by his legal immunity to Company control. Greenberg points out that the Jardine and Dent firms, while they dealt with all comers, developed especially close ties with their principal correspondents in Calcutta, Bombay and London, who were often mutual rivals already. Among the many firms (with constantly changing names) in Calcutta "the two leading ones were the 'Fairlie' and 'Palmer' houses. . . . The Canton firms were largely outgrowths of these India houses, frequently stemming directly from them in personnel and capital." The bitter rivalry of Jardine, Matheson and Company and Dent and Company, which enlivened two generations of life on the China coast, seems to have reflected a pattern already visible elsewhere in British commercial expansion.

Family connections played a great part in establishing these relations as well as in determining partnership within the firms in China. Jardine's dealt principally with Lyall, Matheson and Company (after 1832) in Calcutta, and in London successively with Magniac, Smith and Company, Magniac, Jardine and Company (from 1841), and Matheson and Company (from 1848). Intermarriage among the Scottish clans of the principal partners made the kinship tie even more pervasive than their names would indicate (see App. A, sec. 2, partners of Jardine, Matheson and Company, who included seven nephews of the founders). The firm's articles as redrawn in 1842 provided that management should be vested in the immediate Jardine and Matheson relatives. Nepotism, however, seldom if ever was allowed to triumph over business ability. One of Jardine, Matheson and Company's principal correspondents in Bombay was Jamsetjee Jeejeebhoy and Sons.

The most striking thing about these pioneers was their ingenuity and enterprise. Investing in furs from northwest America was only one example. They developed a direct trade with England through the device of buying from Company officers the private space to which each was entitled in the East Indiamen. In the late 1820's they invented a system of unloading China cargoes at the free port of Singapore, reloading them on the same vessels, and so shipping them to England without infringing (?) upon the Company monopoly of direct Canton-London trade. To profit from the dearth of capital at Canton, they regularly accepted fortunes from India on deposit, paying ten and twelve per cent interest on them year after year while making loans in turn to the Canton hong merchants at even higher rates. To avoid dependence on the British Company's rate for bills of exchange on London, the British private traders bought bills of exchange from American merchants. With these they could remit funds from Canton to London more advantageously than could be done from Bombay. These operations helped funnel the profits of India through Canton to England.

Imagination, assiduity, and an eagle eye for profit and loss characterized the successful Canton agent. James Matheson studied the Chinese taste and found that blue bandanas, for instance, "with weaving white lines sell for considerably more than if marked with round white spots." [14] His ships avoided British restrictions when necessary by sailing under Danish or Portuguese colors. For several years he worked in partnership with a Spanish firm at Manila which had outlets in the Americas, but most of his business was done in the country trade for British firms in India and Singapore. In all this he was indirectly aiding the Honorable Company to lay down funds for the tea trade, which at times had provided a tenth of the revenues of Great Britain. By 1834 "more than half the British trade with China was already in private hands."

Rise of the opium trade. As the next step in the disruption of the old Canton system, the ingenuity and energy of these newcomers on the Chinese scene became focussed upon the importing of opium. This grew into a tide which could not be checked.

The origin of the drug traffic lay first of all in the Chinese demand for opium — a social phenomenon which is the more perplexing because it is decidedly recent in Chinese history. Though the poppy was known early, smoking was not widely practiced in China before the late eighteenth century and the growth of the poppy there was not extensive until after 1850. Opium being a modern vice, it raised novel problems of regulation and had destructive social repercussions the limits of which could not be foreseen. The most obvious economic reason for its importation has been noted above, namely, the constant pressure to balance the Canton tea trade. Indian raw cotton had at first served this purpose equally well, but the Chinese demand for the drug increased so rapidly that it soon eclipsed all other commodities. Finally, by the time the traffic was well established, the production of opium in India had become a great vested interest on which the government had come to rely for revenue. This vicious spiral, demand and supply each stimulating the other, is worth examining in more detail.

When the Company first began to use opium for revenue in India it was in a position to take it or leave it alone, but not for long. There were two general types of opium, grown in the eastern and western areas of northern India, respectively.[15] The chief type grown in Bengal was called Patna, and its cultivation there was directly under the Company's control. The Indian peasant cultivator received an advance from the government and promised to sell his product only to the official agency and at a stated price. The raw opium so collected was refined and sold under Company auspices at auctions held periodically in Calcutta. The Company opium thus produced was of standard quality bearing the Company's stamp. It was purchased at auction by private individuals, chiefly British and Parsee, and taken by them to China. After a brief period of experimentation in the eighteenth century, the Company itself had refrained from carrying opium to the East. It is important to note, however, that the private traders who did the carrying were required to be licensed, and the Company granted the licenses.

Unfortunately, this profitable opium monopoly in Bengal was stimulated by the competition of opium from western India, partly shipped by the Portuguese from Damaun and partly from native states through Bombay. The latter opium was called Malwa, and at the beginning of the nineteenth century it was produced in territories which were not under the control of the East India Company. Since the Malwa product competed with that of Bengal, a long struggle ensued in which the Company tried to control both sources of supply in order to prevent competition and keep up prices. Their efforts were not successful until 1830. By that time the Company had obtained control of the Bombay area and the best ports for shipment of Malwa, so that opium produced in areas beyond their control still must come through their territory or follow a difficult, circuitous route. As the Malwa opium passed through Company territory, a transit tax was levied on it, high enough to produce revenue and yet not so high as to divert the trade. This control was perfected in 1843 by the conquest of Sind.

Partly because of this early competition and partly because of the pressure for funds, the production of opium steadily increased, as did also its importance in the Indian revenue. About 1800, for example, opium provided less than 3 per cent of the Company revenue in India. In 1826–27 this had risen to over 5 per cent and by the 1850's it was more than 12 per cent, a sum of almost four million pounds.[16] In this way the Company became dependent, in the short term at least, upon its opium revenue and therefore upon the sales in China. It is true that an expanding market was found in the Malay Peninsula and the adjacent islands, where Singapore served as the distributing center after 1819, but the numbers involved could never compare with the China market. On the other hand, the total number of smokers being supplied in China in the 1840's, judged by the quantity of opium available, can hardly have exceeded one million and was probably less.[17]

The process of preparing and smoking opium in China was rather simple. At the height of the opium trade in the 1880's, for example, Patna and Benares opium arrived in China in the form of round balls weighing about four pounds apiece and packed forty to a chest. Each ball contained some three pounds of opium inside an inch-thick cover of many layers of poppy leaf. Malwa opium came in irregular lumps, averaging four to six ounces in weight and loosely packed.

Preparation of opium for smoking proceeded through two stages. In the first stage the crude opium was boiled with water in copper pans for three to five hours over a slow fire. During this process it was constantly stirred until it attained the consistency of pill mass. It was then pressed into thin sheets an eighth of an inch thick, porous and friable. Water was then poured over the sheets and allowed to stand overnight. In the second stage, on the following day, the water in which the opium had been steeped was carefully filtered. This liquid filtrate, which now contained the opium, was boiled and stirred from four to seven hours until it had the consistency of treacle. It was then poured into jars, three pounds of crude opium having produced about two pounds of smoking extract. In the process a proportion of dross or seconds, collected from smokers' pipes, had been mixed in with the fresh opium.

The opium smoker, lying on his couch, took a bit of the opium extract on the point of a wire and warmed it over his lamp flame, dipping it again in his opium jar until he worked it into a soft solid by partial evaporation of the water in it. When the little bolus of opium had swelled into a light porous mass, the smoker dexterously deposited it in the bowl of his pipe. "The stem of the pipe being applied to his lips and the bowl held over the lamp, the heat of the flame is drawn in over the opium, converting into vapor all the volatizable material in the bolus." Thus the opium vapor which is inhaled into the lungs of a smoker is not a smoke produced by combustion but merely a water vapor containing the soluble alkaloids of the opium extract in a volatile form. The process is not like tobacco smoking but is an efficient mode of introducing morphine into the system.

Opium on the China coast. In the 1830's the competition in India led the East India Company to increase the supply of Bengal opium in order to maintain their revenue. They soon found that they were selling more chests at lower prices per chest to get the same return. In 1831–32 the Company production doubled, by 1836 it had tripled and the import of opium in China had risen to 30,000 chests. Quite fortuitously, this sudden boom in opium coincided with the end of the Company monopoly of trade with China in 1834, and both together precipitated the Canton crisis.

One fundamental cause of the crisis at Canton after 1834, and so of the first Anglo-Chinese war in 1840–42, was the expansion of trade beyond the limits of the ancient Canton system of regulation. In this expansion opium provided the profits which motivated both the Western and the Chinese merchants and the Chinese officials, who all coöperated with mutual benefit.

In his first year in the opium business Dr. William Jardine sold 649 chests of Malwa for a price of $818,000.[18] The drug had the small bulk, imperishability, steady demand, and wide market most to be desired in a product, and the expansion of its sale was very rapid. At times gross profits were as high as $1000 a chest. As early as 1806 Magniac had sought to avoid the trammels of the Canton system by delivering Bengal cotton "at an anchorage near the port of Amoy." [19] The occasional delivery of opium on the coast on orders arranged at Macao appears to have begun early in the century. In 1821 the exactions and fears of the Canton officials, concerned both for their profits and for their official positions, drove the opium receiving ships from the Whampoa anchorage below Canton to Lintin Island in the outer seas of Macao, and to the Cumsingmoon anchorage near Hongkong. Serious expansion up the coast began soon after. In 1823 James Matheson tried out the east coast (toward Fukien) with two opium cargoes that brought in $212,000. According to his testimony, this was the first attempt to effect sales on the coast without prearrangement.[20] Other firms like Dent and Company and Portuguese from Macao were soon competing, but the officials made trouble, and the new market appears to have been given up for a time, to be resumed in the following decade.

By 1834 sales on the coast of Kwangtung and Fukien were being undertaken by a fleet of fast, armed, running vessels which soon were supplying armed receiving ships stationed at definite points. The armament was necessary against pirates. The decade of the 1830's was the experimental period in the growth of this distribution system and it naturally saw a certain amount of friction between the foreign traders and their colleagues, the Chinese opium dealers, on the one hand, and the Chinese officials on the other. But the chief problem appears to have been not whether the trade was to go on but how much the parties involved were to gain from it.

Evidence of the early situation on the China coast can be gleaned from the report of Hugh Hamilton Lindsay, who in the year 1832 conducted a market survey on behalf of the East India Company in the ship *Lord Amherst*. He was accompanied by sailing men several of whom later had careers in the opium fleet and by a versatile German missionary, the Rev. Charles Gutzlaff, as interpreter. (Gutzlaff came from Pomerania. He married, altogether, three English ladies, meanwhile becoming frontier scout for Christian missions, visiting Siam in 1828, Tientsin and Korea in 1832, and Liu-ch'iu and Japan in 1837). Lindsay of course had no opium aboard. He held extensive intercourse with the Chinese authorities at Amoy, Foochow, Ningpo and Shanghai — the later treaty ports. His lengthy report became an important document, formulating opinions which influenced the course of British expansion in China.[21]

At this early date, a decade before the treaties, he found European woolen manufactures on sale in the Chinese shops of Foochow and Ningpo. At Shanghai he saw many shops with European goods. When Lindsay landed on the north bank of the Yangtze opposite Wusung, he found a village three miles inland with a shop "which announced in large characters that it sold Company's camlets and broad cloth; but on inquiry I was told that they had none of these precious commodities at present, but merely kept the characters on their sign to look respectable."[22] While woolens were known, opium at this date was already in great demand. At every place where the *Lord Amherst* stopped, both the officials and native merchants expected opium was aboard and could hardly be convinced of the contrary. Since the experimental voyages of foreign opium vessels were just beginning in 1832, we must assume that the demand for opium had been built up by Chinese rather than foreign distributors. This suggests that the Chinese opium trade along the coast had begun with Chinese merchants and officials distributing it from Macao in the 1820's, without waiting for the foreigners to inaugurate this service. But the foreigners soon took it over, organized and expanded it on the lines already laid down by Chinese initiative.

Chinese official connivance. The Chinese officials whom Lindsay encountered were all under the pressure of responsibility to see him gone. They assumed various attitudes, some bullying the barbarian until Lindsay and Gutzlaff took a high tone themselves (they broke in the doors of the taotai's yamen at Shanghai and were thereupon served tea), while other mandarins adopted a soothing manner from the beginning. In each case, some official was punished because of the barbarians' arrival in the city. Many pleas were made by the endangered officers to secure their departure. Some minor officials, for example, knelt and offered to perform the kotow, in private interviews with Lindsay, if only he would depart. At Ningpo they even offered to pay.[23] In most cases they readily promised trade outside the port.

The timidity which made these minor officials acquiesce in foreign trade, if only it were conducted outside their jurisdiction, was at times mixed with greed to participate in it. At Foochow an officer named Yang introduced Chinese merchants and arranged for the *Lord Amherst*'s sale of cloth to the value of $6,200, of which he received 3 per cent as commission. Yang came alongside in a small war-junk in broad daylight to effect payment. "Strange and almost incredible as it will appear to those practically unacquainted with the complicated machinery and habitual deception of the Chinese government, only three days subsequent to an admiral and several superior officers having been degraded from their rank for having permitted a foreign merchant ship to force the entrance of the port of one of the principal towns of the empire, and while edicts are placarded in every quarter, prohibiting all natives under the severest penalties of the law from holding the slightest intercourse with the barbarian ship, two war-junks hoisting the imperial flag come in the open face of day and trade with her in the presence of hundreds of spectators, while the civil mandarin of the district stays on board the whole time, examines the goods, and assists in the transaction." [24] This mandarin named Yang was disappointed that the *Lord Amherst* had no opium for trade. "He was our daily visitor and usually dined on board," [25] and appears to have typified the corrupt official whose venality was to provide such facilities for the growth of the drug traffic.

A similar sycophant appeared at Foochow in the person of Ch'en, whose ingratiating letter to Lindsay has been preserved in the original Chinese. He held the rank of *Tso-ying tu-ssu*, "Lieut. col. in the army," [26] but had been degraded because the *Lord Amherst* entered the river. He inveighed against his superiors and admired the Western products shown to him on the vessel.[27]

At Ningpo a mandarin named Ma played this role. A colonel on the staff of the *T'i-tu,* Ma was "a fine handsome-looking man of about fifty," who "indeed would make a finished courtier and possessed the talent of pleasing flattery in the highest possible perfection." [a] He took charge of the barbarians and began preparations for the clandestine trade of the *Lord Amherst* outside Ningpo, sending out merchants who inspected the cargo and especially asked after opium. Ma's plans were thwarted by the publicity of his proceedings, the ship being in full view of all the officials who had assembled on shore; but he tried to establish his position as future agent of the barbarian trader by offering a present of $600 plus provisions.[29]

From this and similar evidence it seems plain that the connivance of Chinese officials in the opium trade was a *sine qua non* without which the traffic could not have gone on.[b] On the coast of China, as everywhere else in the country, all things are known — a smuggling trade could be kept out of sight, but it could not be kept secret. Official protection was therefore essential to it. The merchants and the officials needed each other, if either of them was to profit, for alone the mandarin could do little and

[a] Colonel Ma was a realist, as well as a flatterer. He explained to Lindsay why the mandarins suspected England of wanting more than trade. "We are afraid of you; you are too clever for us. For instance, no sooner does a ship of yours arrive than out go your boats in all directions, you sound, you make charts, and in a week know the whole place as well as we do. Now, some Coreans were wrecked in this place last year; they were placed under restraint but were allowed to go everywhere, and were finally sent home through the provinces. We do not fear them; they are stupid, they look at all things, but observe nothing." [28]

[b] A leading Chinese scholar analyzes the reasons for the growth of the opium trade under two heads: 1) the officials charged with suppressing it were those who profited from it. For example, the rapid growth of imports at Canton occurred *after* the establishment of an official river police; this preventive service, by seeking profits through connivance or participation, acted as a stimulus to the growth of the traffic. 2) the profits to be got in legal trade between the foreigners and the hong merchants were not as great as those to be made from smuggling opium.[30]

without "protection" the Chinese merchant's dealings would be most precarious. In this way the tradition of venality which already flourished at Canton easily spread up the coast and set the style for a generation to come.

The pattern of paper denunciation of illegal trade was also established in this early period. As the *Lord Amherst* moved up the coast, her movements were reported to the throne.[31] By the time she reached Chekiang, the court had already instructed the provincial authorities all along the coast to forbid commercial intercourse. When she got to Kiangsu in June, Lin Tse-hsü, who was then governor, reported to the court his measures to drive the foreigners away. He said that they were afraid of force, and that Lindsay finally realized his errors and foreswore trade. The foreign account is different: Lindsay spent eighteen days at Shanghai, which he rated highly as a port. Having traded very extensively with Chinese vessels from all quarters, he proceeded to Shantung. Governor Lin meanwhile consciously or unconsciously gave the emperor a highly circumstantial and completely untruthful account of how the foreigners' trade was prevented and how they returned to Canton. The Shantung governor, after they got to Wei-hai-wei, gave an even more mendacious report. The emperor was entirely misled. Instead of returning southward, the *Lord Amherst* went to Korea, and then back to Liu-ch'iu, Formosa, and Macao.

From this voyage the British learned much of the coast and its lack of defenses in both guns and troops. They saw the ineffectiveness of official decrees. As Gutzlaff put it, "All of China's thousand war-junks cannot withstand one small frigate." They became convinced that to expand British trade through negotiation was impossible, as Palmerston later believed at the time of the war. Gutzlaff said that as a result of this voyage he became convinced that a firm demand on the part of the British government would gain access to the ports and that in each port certain local officials would coöperate if they could keep their superiors in the dark.[32]

The early coast trade as seen from the inside. Much light is thrown on this situation on the coast by the letters of opium captains preserved in the archives of Jardine, Matheson and Company. In 1832, for example, the *Jamesina* tested the Fukien coast[33] under the command of James Innes. He was the doughty individual who had settled a dispute with the Canton Hoppo by firing skyrockets into the latter's yamen and setting it ablaze.[34] Under date of November 29 his journal reads,[35] "Chinchew Bay [i.e., Ch'üan-chou, north of Amoy],[36] just before daylight I sent ashore two Chinese servants with a list of twenty-eight opium dealers to ask them to come off and do business, or if not prepared with dollars, to inform them that our station next month was off How-tou-san in Dansborg Bay. . . ."

"Dec. 2. Employed delivering briskly. No time to read my Bible or to keep my journal."

"Dec. 5. Still delivering briskly. Today several small mandarin junks sailed round us once or twice, when some smuggling boats were alongside, but whether they did not like our look, or remembered the reception they got in this Bay from the little *Kronberg*, I know not. They gave us no trouble and the opium boats came and went easily close to them."

In 1833 another of the firm's captains, W. McKay, was exploring the coast north of Amoy assisted by Dr. Gutzlaff as interpreter.[c] The latter distributed religious tracts from one side of the vessel while opium went over the other. Under date of June 8, Captain McKay reported: [38] "The mandarins are not troubling us much, but in the harbor and on shore they are very vigilant. Shortly after we arrived a fleet of six of them anchored near us. Dr. Gutzlaff (dressed in his best, which on such occasions is his custom) paid them a visit accompanied by two boats made to appear rather imposing. He demanded their instant departure and threatened them with destruction if they ever in future anchored in our neighborhood. They went away immediately, saying that they had anchored there in the dark by mistake and we have seen nothing more of them."

On the lower Fukien coast in the middle thirties the opium smugglers paid the local Chinese authorities a flat rate of ten dollars per chest,[39] but recalcitrant mandarins could of course be dealt with in other ways if necessary. In April 1835 when government junks anchored too close for the comfort of Jardine's vessel *Governor Findlay*, "A jolly boat with an officer and four armed lascars was immediately dispatched to insist on their moving further off. As they appeared disinclined to acquiesce the officer boarded the first boat and seized the whole of her arms both large and small; then boarded the second boat, tumbled all the great guns overboard, seized the small arms, and made them both quit the Bay." [40]

These letters show plainly the high degree of coöperation required among all those who participated or connived in the trade. At the end of August 1833, Captain McKay reported, "A merchant came off and purchased forty chests paying bargain money and engaging to clear the whole in fifteen days. . . . We assisted in landing twenty-two chests and guarded them up to the old gentleman's door, which was some distance from the landing-place and in the suburbs of the town. . . . At this place (Chinchew Bay) it will not do to lay constantly off the port. We are not sufficiently hid to enable the mandarins to connive at our presence. The nature of the coast will not permit our keeping out of view, but I hope an occasional cruise will

[c] Gutzlaff was a prolific translator of the Bible and writer of missionary tracts, and his piety never deserted him. On this opium voyage he wrote to Dr. Jardine: "At such a general prospect of increasing trade I heartily rejoice, but am equally grieved that the inhabitants of one village, with whom we have never had any [previous] communication, showed themselves very hostile when our boat went on shore [to water]. This . . . gave us no favorable impression of the populace. We have in fact to deal with ragamuffins, the scum of the nation, villains by nature and habit. . . May the Gracious God and Saviour protect you." Gutzlaff to Jardine, Jan. 2, 1834.[37]

relieve the merchants on shore and enable us to go quietly." [41] In May 1836 Jardine's Captain Rees reported, from near Chinchew (Ch'üan-chou), "We have not yet settled with the mandarin of this bay. He has been off to the ship and we made the proposal of 20,000 dollars per annum and not to allow strangers to trade. I have every reason to think he has taken the business into consideration. One of the head brokers told me yesterday that he had gone to consult the higher authority. He said that he . . . required a further sum for the expenses of the mandarin's boats . . . that are to anchor near the ship for the security of the trade when strange vessels are here, the cash to be paid every month." [42]

The competition of rival opium vessels appears to have been at least as great a problem as the activity of Chinese officials, but it was met successfully by price wars.[d] By the late thirties the leading rivals, Jardine's and Dent and Company, were already beginning to coöperate against third parties in order to maintain a joint duopoly on the coast. "Place one of your vessels alongside of . . . each of the strangers, and by taking the first of the sales, following prices down to the lowest rate that would pay the other craft, you might possibly sicken them of the trade." When such measures failed the resourceful Captain Rees arranged through the Rev. Gutzlaff with the local authorities to attack Chinese smuggling boats which patronized his rivals.[44]

In the end the corruption which facilitated the drug trade often infected the foreigners engaged in it. One of the British consuls later based his objection to the traffic mainly on the practical ground that it corrupted the personnel of the British merchant marine.[e]

[d] Opium captains of course lived in a strict moral universe. Capt. McKay wrote to W. Jardine in 1836: "The elder Rees [Capt. Thomas Rees of Dent and Co.'s *Lord Amherst*, a brother of Jardine's captain] is so entirely guided by his Chinamen, who are cheating him right and left, that we have difficulty in managing with him . . . To draw the boats to the *Lord Amherst* he has lately been practicing a piece of deceit which has compelled us to break off all terms with him. While under engagement to keep at fixed prices, he sold his opium at the proper prices on board and his Chinamen on shore refunded to the purchaser first four then six and lastly ten dollars (a chest) . . . ". Jardine replied to McKay: "Your account . . . did not surprise me . . . and I am not sorry for it, farther than feeling regret that such mean acts should be resorted to by men placed in a respectable situation in life . . . As you have more vessels than your opponents, how would it answer to place one of them alongside the *Amherst*, and run prices down as low as thev may think fit to go, while you keep prices up in the distant bays? Cured they must be of such evil practices, even at the sacrifice of reducing prices. . . ." [43]

[e] T. H. Layton to Lord Aberdeen, April 6, 1843: " . . . Our Mercantile Marine (which will be ever the great nursery of our Royal Navy) its Commanders, Mates, and Seamen, are engaged and paid not only to violate all laws or prohibitions of the Chinese Government, but the spirit which the Opium Service (as it is called) infuses into them is highly destructive of those eminent characteristics of the British Seamen — Courage — Humanity — and Obedience. . . .

"Almost every Mate and Petty Officer, in the Merchant Service in China has been allowed to take a share in retailing those petty quantities of opium which his superiors have granted him permission to deal in; and whilst they have themselves retained the wholesale traffic of the Chest — the Mate — the Apprentice, or the boatswain, with Scales in hand have sold retail by the pound. But whilst the dealings of these juniors are small in amount, it is to be regretted that they follow that example of self will, oppression, and self sufficiency, given to them by others — that same course of bullying, threatening, and cheating which may be too readily learnt in this unhappy system of smuggling, violence, and fraud.

The British spirit in the 1840's. This early expansion on the China coast was not motivated solely by the spirit of adventure or the lust for gain. Evangelism was also a powerful force. Thus the Reverend Walter H. Medhurst (Sr.), of the London Missionary Society, in 1835 explored the evangelical prospects on the coasts of Shantung, Kiangsu, and Chekiang in the American brig *Huron.* An outspoken foe of the opium trade, he distributed 6,000 portions of scripture, disappointing those who inquired for drug. His impression of the Chinese officials' contempt for barbarians indicates how wide was the gulf between Chinese and Western attitudes, quite aside from the opium question.[f]

The expansive vigor of Britain and America in this period was of course an offshoot of the great changes taking place at home. By the 1840's the industrial revolution had already given Britain her leadership in the developing international community, and industrialism had also begun to have its effect on British institutions. The two major political movements of the 1840's — Chartism and the Anti-Corn Law League — both took form around 1839, after the depression which began at the end of 1836. The abortive Chartist movement (1839–48) represented the attempt of the new industrial laboring class to secure full political democracy as a means to improve their condition. Meanwhile, the agitation against the corn laws which eventuated in their repeal in 1846 was part of the successful effort of the new middle class to secure the blessings of free trade. Thus Britain in the 1840's saw the more clear-cut emergence of those principles of liberalism which were to characterize later decades of the nineteenth century. Sir Robert Peel's second cabinet (1841–46), with Gladstone at the Board of Trade, administered a country which felt itself on a rising tide of economic and institutional development. The reforming principles of Benthamism had been applied to the law, the courts, and the prisons. Reform of local administration and the poor law, new developments in education, the growth

"Schooners, Cutters and Small Craft are also fitted out from these Ships, and are manned by the most desperate of their Crews for service upon the Canton River. I do not believe that there is a Gang of Burglars and Highway Robbers in England more relentless, more unfeeling and more cruel in their occupations, more thoroughly lost to all our common feelings of humanity, than these British semi-pirates upon the Canton River, and upon some portions of the China Coast.

"The Commanders of the Opium Ships upon the Coast do not tell their deeds of violence, and therefore they can be known comparatively but by few. I heard these words however from a young man who was a Mate on board one of these boats. The Truth of his word I can rely upon —

" 'We always make a practice of running over the Chinese fishing boats by night; for they will not get out of our way — call as you will.

" 'We are rather particular on board our Ships about firing into the Junks. I remember we once fired into a War Junk, and it was truly astonishing to see how high her splinters flew into the air.

" 'I have known Captain ——— of the ——— to fire into Junks frequently, and he once sent a Shot into a Junk which raked her fore and aft.

" 'Our boats frequently guard the Chinese Smugglers in taking the Opium on Shore. I have often gone in Command of armed boats to land the opium.' "[45]

[f] As Medhurst put it, "The Chinese assume to be . . . the *only* civilized and powerful nation in the world . . . If now we admit the justice of their pretensions, we must either confess ourselves vassals . . . liable to be bambooed at pleasure; or irreclaimable savages, incapable of reflection . . . upon a level with the filthy Coreans or naked Siamese."[46]

of social services, all were following upon the great changes which had already occurred in technology, production, and transportation. A new scientific view of mankind, expressed in utilitarianism and soon to be represented by Darwinism, had permeated the upper class and formed part of the new liberalism. Another component, humanitarianism, had been nourished by the non-conformist religious revival which had already sent Protestant missions overseas.

The result of all this rapid evolution at home was that the British who took the lead in the opening of China were a self-confident, righteous and energetic lot, uninterested in comparative cultural studies and impatient with Chinese ethnic differences. Sir John Bowring, author of the hymn "In the Cross of Christ I glory" and Her Majesty's envoy in the mid-1850's, whose energetic administration fostered the Customs Inspectorate at Shanghai and led up to the second British war with China, had a vigorous faith in laisser-faire which was only less comprehensible to his Chinese adversaries than it would be acceptable to his own compatriots today. He had written in 1821: "that which nations have most earnestly to entreat from governments is, that the latter would cease to honor them with any officious interference: 'their tender mercies,' however well intended, 'are cruel.' The best boon they can give is to let the stream of commerce flow as it will; its tide is strong enough to bear away all impediments; and governments are but too much the victims of self-deception, when they imagine that their Decrees of prohibition or of encouragement do really produce the effects they contemplate. Those Decrees are erected against and opposed to the natural tendency of things, and are in the end as absurd and ineffective as it would be to direct the winds by Order in Council, or to manage the tides by Act of Parliament." [47] No philosophy could have been more antithetic to the fundamental beliefs on which the Confucian monarchy and its foreign relations were founded, nor less conducive to Anglo-Chinese harmony.

CHAPTER V

THE OPIUM WAR, 1840–42

THE COMBINATION OF SCOTCH ENTERPRISE, opium, and Chinese official apathy or connivance which produced the pre-treaty expansion of Sino-British trade along the southeast coast of China naturally reached its height in the crowded waters of the Canton River and produced there a degree of disorder which was bound to attract the attention of both the Chinese and British governments. The main part of the import trade was no longer conducted at Canton. No longer were all the foreign merchants under the control of the Company and the Cohong in the Thirteen Factories. The hong merchants themselves were beginning to fail in their function of milking the foreign commerce of China. All the latent issues of diplomatic equality, commercial freedom, bad debts, legal jurisdiction, and Sino-foreign friction generally, combined in the late 1830's to poison the once genial atmosphere of Canton and create an explosive situation. Without going exhaustively into the ramified background of the first Anglo-Chinese war, certain elements in it may be noted in passing.

Historians generally agree that opium provided the occasion rather than the sole cause of war. One leading Chinese historian has concluded [1] that the Opium War was essentially a conflict between Eastern and Western cultures. Specifically it represented a clash between two conceptions of international order. The Western system of national states clashed with the traditional Chinese idea of a universal ethico-political order under the Son of Heaven. Second, the two sides had conflicting economic conceptions. China's self-sufficiency and disesteem of the merchant led her to regard foreign trade as unimportant, not as a national economic necessity. Western free traders could never understand why the Chinese government restricted its merchants' trade. Third, the Opium War had its immediate origin in a dispute over legal institutions. British ideas of the impersonality and supremacy of the established codes, their view of evidence and of legal responsibility, came into direct conflict with the Chinese view that the emperor's administration should operate on an ethical basis above the mere letter of the legal regulations. When the Chinese authorities in 1839 blockaded the British community in the Canton factories, they were merely applying their idea of collective responsibility.[2]

The Chinese anti-opium movement. This famous act of Commissioner Lin Tse-hsü in 1839 was inspired directly by the Chinese anti-opium movement, which was caused in turn by a moral dislike of narcotics as expressed, for example, in the imperial edicts on the subject. But the moral aspect was hardly the most important, for opium became an urgent fiscal problem to the Chinese government. If individual Chinese chose to poison themselves, the authorities were not bound to stop them. But when opium smoking threatened the economy of the state and particularly the imperial finances, the problem could no longer be avoided. This more practical concern was aroused over the question of the drain of silver, which in turn affected the bimetallic currency system used in the imperial accounts. Each of these factors deserves passing notice.

As the foreign trade increased at Canton and later in the treaty ports, the Ch'ing currency system broke down first of all on the side of the supply of silver. Growth of foreign and domestic trade increased the demand for silver more rapidly than the demand for copper cash, because large commercial transactions had to be settled in the more valuable currency. But the government by statute was supposed to receive tax payments and make its own expenditures using both currencies in the proportion of three parts of copper to seven parts of silver; and the populace, who used copper day by day, were obliged to convert it into silver very extensively when making tax payments. If silver became more valuable in terms of copper, they would suffer. The government would then be faced with the alternatives of popular discontent or decreased revenue. (The alternative of changing the statutory proportions in which silver and copper should be used seems to have been strangely neglected; possibly the rule was a dead letter.)

Unfortunately, silver was not extensively produced within China, and its use as a currency was constantly threatened with short supply. After the early use of silver had begun under the Sung, it became necessary to prohibit its export, a prohibition reiterated at various times later. The Ch'ing government decrees rigorously demanded the direct exchange of commodities in foreign trade without the use of silver to pay for imports. Thus the Canton hong merchants were required to exchange goods for goods. But as we know from the East India Company records, silver became a currency in the Canton trade, and the various types of Spanish (or Mexican) silver dollars imported by foreign traders were used not only to buy exports but also to pay for some foreign imports. One great impetus to the rise of the opium trade was the utility of opium imports as a substitute for silver imports. Yet the circumstances of opium smuggling required that the small bulk and high value represented in opium chests be exchanged for something equally precious and transportable, and so silver inevitably moved out as opium moved in. Eventually the expansion of the opium market illegally along the southeast coast began to make the silver dollar popular as a currency in that region. Since the supply of Spanish silver dollars was inadequate to the needs of the trade, cargoes of silver bullion actually began to leave China. This outflow was first denounced in 1822 and was quite evident by the end of the decade.

It is plain that the absorption of silver in the opium trade did not necessarily drain it from the country, since the opium receipts were largely used to purchase silk and tea. An apparent drain thus set in before the actual drain. The latter does not appear to have begun before 1830 when the balance of trade, judging by foreign figures, appears to have shifted slightly against China for almost the first time in history.[3] The prohibition of the export of silver was repeated in 1832 and a flood of memorials began to denounce the opium trade because of the drain of silver and its repercussions upon the populace.

In this period the rise in the price of silver in terms of copper cash produced a fiscal crisis in some respects comparable to that created in China by the rise in the price of gold in terms of silver during the early 1930's. By 1836 some officials estimated that China was losing Tls. 10,000,000 a year. Meanwhile, the increasing scarcity of silver within the country seemed to be indicated by the fact that one tael (the Chinese silver "ounce" or unit of account), which had traditionally exchanged for 1,000 copper cash, was now exchanging for 1,200 or 1,300. By 1838 the increasing demand for silver had raised this rate to 1,600 cash and had precipitated the great debate over opium.

The Chinese belief of the day that the silver crisis was due to the opium trade has only partially stood up under modern economic analysis. Among the many other factors involved were the increased demand for money, attendant upon the growing foreign trade and money economy, the contemporary debasement of the copper coinage, and possibly the hoarding of silver and rising prices. Complexity was increased by the growing substitution of the imported Mexican dollar for sycee silver (silver bullion) in foreign trade; the foreign dollar became more widely used as foreign merchants continued to pay it, in exchange for Chinese goods, while receiving Chinese silver in exchange for foreign goods.[4] In 1829 and 1831 memorialists drew attention to the silver problem and urged the prohibition of opium imports even before there had been much rise in the copper price of silver.

The thinking of some Chinese officials seems to have verged on hysteria. In 1837 a censor claimed that the annual drain of silver amounted to Tls. 30,000,000 from Kwangtung, Tls. 10,000,000 from the south China coast north of Kwangtung, and Tls. 20,000,000 from Tientsin — a total of Tls. 60,000,000. This sort of claim roused the emperor to order a general investigation. It appears that Chinese officialdom had been slow to associate the scarcity and assumed outflow of silver with its higher exchange rate in terms of copper. But when this idea gained general acceptance in 1836 it was thereafter stressed to the neglect of other factors. Gresham's law and the possible influence of silver hoarding were given little consideration. The Chinese fiscal experts assumed, first, that the increased value of silver was due entirely to its scarcity and, second, that its scarcity was due entirely to the import of opium.[5]

In actual fact, as has long been recognized, the steady debasement of China's copper coinage in the early nineteenth century was so great as to account for a large part of the appreciation in the copper price of silver. During the early reigns of the Ch'ing the statutory weight of minted cash had varied between ten- and fourteen-hundredths of a tael (*liang*, or ounce). Year by year the provincial and central governments minted cash according to local needs. Most of China's copper was mined in Yunnan and sent elsewhere for minting. The annual needs of the Boards of Revenue and of Public Works had been listed as 6,160,000 catties (*chin*), but it appears that the supply of copper from southwest China had become progressively less between the middle of the eighteenth and the middle of the nineteenth century. Production had averaged 6,000 tons a year from 1754 to 1772, between 6,000 and 7,800 tons from 1773 to 1822, but only 4,800 to 6,000 tons in the period 1823–58. In the early days of the dynasty, copper had been in sufficient commercial demand to induce "traitorous merchants" to melt cash and sell the copper. After this evil was denounced in the early years of Ch'ien-lung (after 1736), the minting of cash by the government and by forgers and the diminishing of their copper content apparently began to turn the scale: silver exchanged for increasing amounts of copper. By the early nineteenth century the average weight of cash had fallen to less than one-tenth of a tael, and in the Tao-kuang reign after 1821 the weight of a minted cash dropped to one-twelfth or even one-twentieth of a tael. This loss in intrinsic value of the copper currency "fully accounts for the loss of 20 to 30 per cent in its exchange value." [6] To this was added the effect of private coinage (forgery) of cash, a traditional evil which might arise whenever it became unprofitable to melt down copper cash for sale as commercial copper, and more profitable to turn commercial copper into minted cash. This increased the debasement of the copper coinage. Finally, hoarding of sycee silver increased in proportion as the public lost confidence in copper cash, which made silver all the scarcer and dearer. Copper production also seems to have increased in this period. But these varied and complex factors were largely beyond the grasp of the mandarin economists of the day,[7] who appear to have been unaware both of Sir Thomas Gresham and of his law that bad money drives out good because the latter is hoarded.

The great opium debate began in 1836 with the proposal of Hsü Nai-chi that opium should be admitted on a barter basis which would prevent the outflow of silver, that it should be taxed as a medicine for revenue purposes, and that its production within China should be viewed as relatively harmless. His fundamental argument was that silver would flow out as long as opium came in through a smuggling trade. A legalized barter trade would obviate this outflow. This general proposition received support from the Canton authorities but was denounced by other officials for its obvious errors and irresponsibility. By 1839 Chinese opinion was generally agreed that the opium trade must be stopped in order to stop the outflow of silver. Proposals to stop the foreign trade as a whole, or to prevent opium smuggling by a careful customs control, or to allow opium production in China, eventually gave ground to the idea that the only solution was to stop the demand by forbidding smoking under heavy penalties and to enforce the prohibition through the *pao-chia* system in every local community. Provincial governors doubted that so severe a prohibtion could be enforced, but it became the official policy. The Jardine-Matheson archives reveal that a very considerable and rather effective effort to suppress the opium trade was made in South China even before the arrival of Commissioner Lin at Canton.[8]

The British contribution to the crisis. Meanwhile British policy helped to precipitate the crisis at Canton. To the Chinese "crimes" and "nuisances" recorded in British blue-book history must be added certain errors or omissions on the part of the foreign minister, Lord Palmerston.[9]

When the Company's Select Committee lost its control over British trade at Canton in 1834, the Chinese authorities had asked for a headman to be sent to take its place. This preserved the custom of a thousand years according to which Arab headmen had been designated at Zayton in the tenth century. By sending a British *official*, and, of all things, a naval officer, Palmerston was shattering Chinese precedent. The representative of the British king had no place in the Chinese system, unless he chose to assume that of a tribute bearer (which he did not). Yet he was dispatched by Lord Palmerston in 1834 without credentials and merely told to announce his arrival "by letter to the Viceroy." Lord Napier, as an obedient officer of the king, took his instructions literally and asserted his equality with the governor-general of Kwangtung and Kwangsi. That the presumptuousness of this Palmerstonian gesture was unconscious is evidenced by the fact that Lord Napier was backed by no show of force. His attempt to alter the constitution of the empire was doomed from the beginning.

Lord Napier's position as chief superintendent of British trade in China was complicated by the fact that he was ordered to administer British law. For this the Chinese had given no permission. Moreover, the superintendent's authority outside the limits of the port of Canton remained for a decade uncertain and this handicapped his assumed control over British subjects. He arrived three months after the expiry of the Company's charter.

His arrival caused within three weeks a stoppage of the British trade which it was intended to promote, for his attempt to correspond with the authorities as instructed led to a Cohong embargo. In the uncomfortable humidity of August in Canton Lord Napier was not mollified to discover that the transliteration of his name, *Lü-lao-pi*, might be translated "laboriously vile." The governor he considered "a presumptuous savage"; the governor-general he felt had "committed an outrage on the British Crown which should be equally chastised." [10] He fell ill and died in October. His assistants who succeeded him, at a distance of eight months or more from London, were dependent upon the Foreign Office for new instructions. The whole venture betrays the inexperience of the British government in the Far East.

In effect, the abolition of the Company monopoly over British trade with China had finally upset the balance of responsibility and economic power which was already shaky enough within the Canton system.[a] In the restrictions maintained at Canton the free traders could see small chance for expansion. Abolition of the Cohong and the opening of more ports seemed to them the indicated remedy. Likewise the new situation was unsatisfactory to the Chinese. The free traders assumed with gusto the trading privileges bequeathed by the Company, and the Jardines and Dents soon revived the vanished splendor of the Select Committee, but they were individuals without official powers even of the sort previously delegated to the Company, each his brother's competitor rather than his keeper. It was thus left to the British government to assume that responsibility which the Chinese, according to their fashion, expected someone to assume. His Majesty's government, however, as a government, could do no less than assert equality of status. Chinese suzerainty, confinement of the trade to Canton, the Cohong monopoly, the Hoppo and security merchants, all formed one consistent scheme of things in which John Company had played a not inconsiderable part, though ever in a proper and subordinate station. Lord Napier in 1834 could not deny Chinese suzerainty without shattering the hereditary Chinese scheme of things entirely. Conflict was thereafter only a matter of time.

[a] Greenberg, *British Trade*, makes plain the degree to which the hong merchants, never accustomed to corporate business activity as a group, had become increasingly dependent on private foreign capital, especially to sustain their unprofitable import of British goods. After 1834 they were undercut by the foreigners' dealing directly with their erstwhile clients, the tea middlemen from upcountry (for more on these middlemen, see Ch. 16 below).

Mr. Greenberg's economic anatomy of the old Canton trade in its final phase indicates the imbalance which had overtaken it: "(a) Western products paid for about a quarter of the Company's tea investment; (b) the Company's total imports were equal to about half of its tea investments; (c) the private trade was practically all 'Country Trade'; (d) its India exports were now predominantly composed of opium, though raw cotton was still a substantial item, greater than the Company's quantity of the article; (e) the proceeds of opium sales alone were enough to pay for more than the whole tea investment of the Company; (f) but since only a portion of this was taken by the Company's Treasury for that purpose, a very large quantity of silver had to be shipped to India in return for Bills of Exchange on private account as remittance to the exporters of the opium." (p. 14).

For the next five years after Napier's death the situation at Canton remained uncertain. Napier's chief successor, Captain Elliot, was left almost without instructions and followed an ambiguous policy of alternately negotiating for a new dispensation and trying to keep the trade going by corresponding in the traditional manner under the character *ping*, "petition." This was just the period of the opium boom and the increasing friction which it induced. A policy of drift was followed also by the Chinese government. The proposal of Hsü Nai-chi in 1836 to legalize opium encouraged the trade. The official attempts to suppress the trade by acting against the Chinese dealers were sporadic and unconvincing. Many foreigners at Canton confidently expected legalization. The situation demanded decisive action by a strong man.

Lin Tse-hsü versus William Jardine. The famous "Commissioner Lin," governor-general of Hunan and Hupei, was 53 years of age in 1838 and one of the most vigorous Chinese in the imperial service. He presented three memorials in the summer of 1838 outlining the steps necessary for the eradication of the opium evil and reporting his own success in the territory under his control. The combination of elementary economics and moral denunciation in these memorials was impressive. Lin was called to the capital and had nineteen interviews with the emperor. On December 31, 1838, he was made imperial commissioner to settle the opium problem at Canton. On March 10, 1839, he arrived at Canton and a week later took decisive action against the foreign community, who were imprisoned in their factories. Captain Elliot, then at Macao, bravely hastened into the net and eventually promised to deliver some twenty thousand chests of opium. Through an error, this was five hundred chests more than the British community had in China; but fortunately new stocks arrived from India in time to make good his promise. The British opium merchants thus got rid of "half the annual crop of Indian opium at a fair price guaranteed by the British Government." [11] The opium was publicly destroyed and Commissioner Lin appears to have felt that he had solved his problem. Actually, this overt action was a *casus belli* which the British could not ignore. Had Commissioner Lin known more of the barbarian problem at the beginning, he might have acted with greater finesse. Handicapped as he was by the traditional Chinese idea of how to manage the barbarians, he was incapable of realizing that the Canton system was smashed beyond restoration and could only be reformed on British terms. Within a year a British expeditionary force was on its way from India to secure reparation or take reprisal. Lin's failure to solve the barbarian problem was spectacular and disastrous, and probably demoralized a whole generation.[b]

[b] Lin's role in history is criticized by Dr. T. F. Tsiang as that of a strategist who discovered China's military weakness but feared to announce it, and a champion whose removal from the fray provided a misleading excuse for China's defeat.[12]

The first Anglo-Chinese war which got under way in the summer of 1840 was a conflict between some ten thousand British troops of all sorts and the decadent forces of the Manchu dynasty. The local Chinese populace were largely neutral spectators, except when some of them might be hired to form a British coolie corps. It is uncertain how much the millions of the interior ever heard about the war.

Like more recent invaders, the British had technical superiority. Instead of airplanes or tanks their chief weapon was the armed steamer which could go anywhere, against the wind and in shallow water, to reconnoiter, carry dispatches, or effect troop landings. The famous *Nemesis*, for example, was an iron sidewheel steamer of 630 tons, 184 feet long. She was flat-bottomed, drew only 6 feet of water, carried 90 men and two 32-pounders on pivots fore and aft, and appeared invulnerable.[13]

Britain's superior firepower had its limits. For example, in May 1841 two thousand British troops established themselves on the walls of Canton but could find no solution to the problem of what to do with the million or so people inside. Illness and lack of supplies induced them to accept the so-called "ransom" of Canton and withdraw, whereupon the Cantonese believed themselves undefeated. Under the vacillating direction of Captain Elliot, the British expedition had advanced northeastward along the coast defeating the Chinese garrison at Tinghai on Chusan Island and blockading Amoy, Ningpo, and the mouth of the Yangtze. This British advance cast Lin Tse-hsü into disrepute. The court appointed a high Manchu, Ch'i-shan, then governor-general of Chihli, to try to neutralize by persuasion an invader who evidently could not be overcome by force. The facile Ch'i-shan met the British in August 1840 at Taku near Tientsin, persuaded them to return to Canton to negotiate there, and succeeded Lin Tse-hsü as imperial commissioner in charge of the barbarian problem. As a conciliator, however, Ch'i-shan soon found himself caught between the mounting demands of the British and the renewed pugnacity of the court. In January 1841 the British seized the forts at Chuenpi (Ch'uan-pi) below Canton and Ch'i-shan negotiated with Elliot the abortive convention of Chuenpi. By this deal the two emissaries both sought to effect a settlement, but the attempt undid them both. For ceding Hongkong to the British (who occupied it at once) and making other concessions like equality of diplomatic intercourse, an indemnity of $6,000,000, and a resumption of trade, Ch'i-shan was promptly cashiered, had all his wealth confiscated, and left Canton in chains. Elliot fared a little better. For having "completely disobeyed his instructions and *tried* to get the *lowest* terms he could" (as Queen Victoria put it), he was promptly recalled and the Chuenpi convention disavowed. Great Britain wanted much more fundamental concessions, while the Manchu dynasty was again determined to fight. Ch'i-shan's negotiations were denounced as double-dealing intimacy with the barbarians and his spectacular rise and fall served as another object lesson to barbarian-tamers for a generation thereafter.[14]

This failure of their first expedition necessitated a second British campaign which lasted from August 1841 to August 1842 under a new plenipotentiary, Sir Henry Pottinger, who followed the principle of putting diplomacy before trade and force before diplomacy. The objectives of British policy had meantime been laid down after consultation with the persons most concerned, the private British firms interested in the China trade. In the nine months from September 1839 to May 1840 half a dozen memorials were presented to Her Majesty's Government from organized groups of mercantile firms in London, Manchester, Leeds, Liverpool, Bristol, and Blackburn, all urging strong action. Dr. William Jardine had left Canton shortly before Lin's arrival and retired to England, where he became a member of Parliament in 1841.[15] As early as September 1839, when commercial opinion in England was starting to demand action in China, Jardine began to make his views available to Palmerston. He saw him in September, presented detailed suggestions in December, and saw him again in February 1840. His advice was to blockade the coast of China, send a force toward Peking, and get a commercial treaty allowing trade "with the northern ports . . . say Amoy, Foochow, Ningpo, Shanghai and also Kiaochow if we can get it." To enforce these demands "we must proceed to take possession of three or four islands, say Formosa, Quemoy and Amoy . . . also the great Chusan island." In his second interview he brought to Palmerston's notice the hong merchants' debts to foreign firms at Canton. His Lordship said "no one had brought these claims to his notice, inquired how they arose," and asked for a memorandum on the subject.[16] About the end of 1839 a committee of British merchants headed by Jardine's London agent, John Abel Smith,[17] and others had suggested similar treaty terms: admission to essentially the same list of ports, legal protection, an equitable tariff, diplomatic contact with Peking, and an island base.[18]

It is perhaps superfluous to remark that the ports eventually demanded were the first four named by Jardine and that British troops garrisoned Chusan and the island of Kulangsu in Amoy harbor (Quemoy is the adjoining island) until 1846 to ensure payment of the indemnity, of which three million dollars was for the hong debts. Before Sir Henry Pottinger came to China he had consulted the members of the firm in London in May 1841. Jardine wrote to James Matheson, "I have had two or three conferences with him of a very satisfactory nature, and he has spared no trouble to gain information. He had a conversation with Captain Rees[19] on Saturday last, and on Friday he dined with me, no one present but

Alexander Matheson until John Abel Smith joined us about ten p.m. We had the chart of the coast of China before us, and discussed many knotty points no doubt most ably. I intend to send him a few hints on paper through the foreign office tomorrow." [20] When Sir Henry reached Hongkong, Matheson's house was the first one he entered.[21] The Jardine, Matheson papers indicate that the firm's influence on British policy was as great as might be expected, considering that the government's chief aim in China was to open a path for that general commerce in which this firm already played one of the dominant parts, both in tea purchases at Canton and in drug sales on the coast. Palmerston wrote to Jardine's London agent: "To the assistance and information which you and Mr. Jardine so handsomely afforded to us, it was mainly owing that we were able to give our affairs, Naval, Military and Diplomatic, in China, those detailed instructions which have led to these satisfactory results. It is indeed remarkable that the information which we procured from yourself and various other persons whom we consulted in the Autumn of 1839, which was embodied in instructions which we gave in February, 1840, was so accurate and complete that it appears that our successors have not found reason to make any alterations in them, and it has turned out that the decisive operation has been that in the Yang tsi Kiang which we suggested to our Naval Commander as far back as our instruction of February, 1840, and that the Conditions of Peace imposed upon the Emperor are precisely those which we had instructed our Plenipotentiaries Elliot and Pottinger to obtain. There is no doubt that this event, which will form an epoch in the progress of the civilization of the human races, must be attended with most important advantages to the commercial interests of England." [22]

This survey of the famous Anglo-Chinese conflict of the period 1839–42 suggests that the Chinese officials were far removed, in their thinking, from the economic realities which they faced, whereas the representatives of Britain's economic expansion, particularly the pioneer opium merchants, knew clearly what they wanted and how to get it. It was soon to appear that the British officials on their part, as has been true more recently in the course of Sino-Western relations, were confident that they could win military victories in China, but were less certain how to capitalize upon them. Once the fighting stopped, they found themselves in a diplomatic contest which was more evenly balanced.

CHAPTER VI

MANCHU DIPLOMACY AND THE TREATY OF NANKING, 1842

WARFARE AND THE BRITISH VICTORY brought Chinese and Manchu high officials into direct and serious contact with Western barbarians as they had never been before. The Treaty of Nanking provides a case study (as well as the prototype) of this new situation[1] — the imperial negotiators caught midway between emperor and barbarian, the British knowing what they wanted but only half aware of what they were obtaining. In 1842, for the first time, the Ch'ing monarchy had to face up to the fact of Western military superiority.

Fears of the Manchu court in 1842. Ch'ing policy toward Britain in the preceding decade had vacillated between resistance and appeasement. During the debate over opium after 1836 the proponents of legalization and of prohibition had both been vociferous, but until Lin Tse-hsü arrived at Canton, the Chinese government cannot be said to have taken a strong stand. As noted in the preceding chapter, Lin's uncompromising vigor against the barbarians in 1839 had been followed by the soothing compromise policy of Ch'i-shan in 1840.[2] By 1842 the British menace was greater than ever and the alternative programs advocated by Lin and by Ch'i-shan still had their powerful advocates.[a]

Appeasement, on the whole, was advocated by Manchus, who were concerned for the dynasty, rather than by Chinese, who disliked the invaders perhaps more thoroughly. This has been widely noted and perhaps illustrates the unlucky conflict of interests which sometimes handicapped Ch'ing policy.[4] Mu-chang-a (1782–1856), for example, was the close and trusted friend of the Tao-kuang emperor, and in this period held power approaching that of a Western prime minister. His official biography indicates that he became a metropolitan graduate at the age of twenty-three and rose rapidly in office at the capital, but did not really come into power until the death of the Chia-ch'ing emperor in 1820. At that time, as a reward for his "reverent management of bridges and roads along the way" as the late emperor's coffin was brought back from Jehol, Mu-chang-a was suddenly raised one

[a] In the Grand Council the leaders of these two camps were Wang Ting, a Chinese who supported Lin's root-and-branch extermination policy, and Mu-chang-a, a Manchu who stood for making peace. These two were the senior of the six grand councillors then serving, Wang Ting having entered the Council in 1825 and Mu-chang-a in 1827. The others were P'an Shih-en, a Chinese scholar now seventy-two years of age who had entered the Council in 1833; Sai-shang-a, a Mongol, who had been a councillor in 1835–37 and again since 1841; Ho Ju-lin, a Chinese, who had entered in 1840; and Ch'i Chün-tsao, also Chinese, entered in 1841.[3]

degree in rank. Shortly afterward he was put in charge of the imperial household, given a peacock feather, and raised another three degrees in rank. Thereafter he rapidly became the leading official of the empire, holding commanding positions successively in nearly every important department of government. The wide range of his administrative offices, the special investigations on which he was sent, and the frequency with which he acted as examiner at the capital, all combined to give him by 1842 an exceptional knowledge of the empire's official personnel — knowledge which meant power.

During the years of the first treaty negotiations Mu-chang-a was at his height. When the high officers at the capital were duly asked to advise the emperor regarding the treaties and other documents presented by the negotiators, it was "Mu-chang-a and others" (he being the chief councillor) who consistently recommended approval. We are warranted in assuming that both Ch'i-shan and his successor Ch'i-ying conducted their negotiations in the provinces with the assurance that Mu-chang-a supported their policy at the capital. It is significant that the membership of the Grand Council remained the same throughout the period of Ch'i-ying's management of foreign relations (1842–47) and that the first act of the "anti-foreign" Hsien-feng emperor, after his accession in 1850, was to degrade both Ch'i-ying and Mu-chang-a.[5]

With the Grand Council dominated by the Manchu interest, it was inevitable that the Chinese government of 1842 should undertake negotiation as a necessary policy for the survival of the dynasty, fearing that if peace were not made the dynasty might be undone.

Judging the British by themselves, the Manchus could not help suspecting that they had designs of territorial conquest. The British conquests in India were well known, and it was customary for barbarians to invade China whenever they were strong enough — witness the Manchus themselves. There was no logical stopping point to be expected between British victories on the frontier, the invasion of the provinces, and the final seizure of the capital, which would symbolize the defeat of the reigning dynasty. British headmen at Canton had been notoriously interested in the profits of trade, but the British government obviously had higher pretensions than a trading company. Consequently they felt no assurance whatever that the British were interested only in trade. If the emperor and his court could have seen Palmerston's instructions to his new plenipotentiary, Sir Henry Pottinger, they would neither have understood nor believed them. The barbarians' chief characteristic reported by Manchu negotiators, the love of trade,[6] was considered worth reporting so frequently precisely because it was so unexpected in powerful fighters who could plainly seek more than trade if they wanted to.

Looking back at its own past, the court ordered preparations for the defense of the Manchurian homeland and of the passes leading to it through the Great Wall. Shanhaikuan, for example, had been of vital strategic importance at the time of earlier invasions, which had usually come from the north; and the British had explored the coast there in 1840. Therefore, when the emperor heard of the fall of Shanghai in June 1842, troops from beyond the Wall were called to the defense of Shanhaikuan. Others had been stationed at Hsi-feng-k'ou, a gateway to Jehol from the North China plain. On June 28 Sai-shang-a was ordered to Tientsin as imperial commissioner, to defend the approach to the capital. During the negotiations at Nanking in August the court energetically prepared to continue the resistance if necessary.[7] In short, in spite of British declarations, it was not convinced that the barbarian menace could be eliminated merely by paltry concessions of trade.

Once the bare possibility of British territorial designs had been admitted, there was every occasion for alarm over the inadequacy of the Manchu-Chinese defenses. Manchu military arrangements had been made for protecting the frontier of North China along the Wall and for controlling the Chinese populace in the provinces, not for resisting invasion along the southeastern coast. The Manchu and Chinese armies were both decentralized organizations, adequate at times against local pirates or bandits but not coördinated between one province and another. Worst of all, there was no naval tradition in Chinese history, and therefore nothing one could call a fleet — merely small garrisons of "water forces" for maintaining local order on the coasts and waterways. Their war-junks and fire-rafts were of no avail against iron steamers like the *Nemesis*. Corruption and inactivity had long since made these forces inefficient, and there was a complete lack of technical competence among the bureaucrats at Peking who were supposed to coördinate their operations. On July 28, 1842, for example, the court ordered Szechwan and Hu-kuang to build ships for the coastal provinces; and on August 23 it received the governor-general's reply explaining why junks of the Upper Yangtze type obviously could not sail in coastal waters, although they could be used in the Lower Yangtze. In his extremity the emperor considered every suggestion, even the proposal that several hundred or a thousand divers (*shui-mo*), of a type who "could lie hidden half a day on the river bottom," should be sent to terrify the British from the silt-laden depths of the river. The Hupei authorities reported having ordered divers from Ichang, and an edict of August 28 urged them to hurry. The emperor also ordered the secret carrying out of a proposal that good swimmers be enlisted to bore holes in the hulls of the British ships and ruin their rudders.[8]

Probably the consideration of greatest importance at Peking, although it was less openly discussed, was the state of popular opinion — that tacit consent which for every dynasty constituted the mandate of Heaven. In the summer of 1842 the court seems to have been as much afraid on this score as it was of the British invasion. Banditry, riots, aid to the enemy, and the activity of anti-dynastic secret societies were all indices of the dynasty's weakened hold upon the people. It is a truism that neither the expansion of the opium trade nor the British campaigns of 1840–42 could have been as successful as they were without the connivance of a certain type of Cantonese and the apathy of the populace north of Kwangtung. Consequently "traitorous Chinese" (*han-chien*) who collaborated with the barbarian were a fearful phenomenon to the dynasty, and memorialists refer to them repeatedly, usually on the basis of hearsay evidence.

When the British in 1842 blocked the southern entrance of the Grand Canal at Chinkiang, for instance, the "awe-inspiring general" (*yang-wei chiang-chün*) I-ching feared that the grain junkmen, if allowed to collect in numbers at one spot, might cause trouble and, with the salt bandits (*yen-fei*) of that region, might join forces with the British. "Rebellious barbarians without, and bandits within," and "barbarians enticing traitorous bandits" were a constant nightmare to this commander. He even feared the activity of traitors at the northern terminus of the Canal at Tungchow outside Peking.[9] When the British fleet sailed upstream from Chinkiang on July 29, imperial troops who saw it depart, entered the city to check the looting of local bandits.[10] But instead they found foreign "devils," both white and black, together with Chinese traitors, patrolling outside the walls and some two thousand more "devils" still within.[11] It was reported that in the battle of Chapu, on the coast of Hangchow bay, traitors had guided the British into position and had even wounded a Manchu officer. At Yangchow the authorities offered rewards for the seizure of traitors who were giving information to the enemy. According to their description, "the *bona fide* Chinese traitor has his hair and queue all cut off, his arm is branded with the figure of an insect or the figure of a butterfly, and on his body he carries a small belt-ticket with barbarian characters as a mark of identification." A censor warned that salt smugglers at Hwaiyang might be enticed by the barbarians to cut the dikes there. Orders were given to prevent it.[12] On August 17 another censor termed it an "urgent necessity" to capture the traitors who guided the British. He related rumors that the Manchu commander at Chinkiang had killed many innocent persons as traitors, and had thereby provoked a rising of the populace, upon whom he had fired with cannon. Aided by this riot within the city, the British had captured Chinkiang.[13] Still another censor reported the flight of officers defending Shanghai and the destruction of magistrates' yamens by the common people. Friction had reached the point where "the troops do not attack the (British) pirates but attack the people, and the people do not fear the pirates but fear the (imperial) troops. The rebellious barbarians declare they are enemies only of the troops and will not disturb the country people."[14] It was already known that the British at Shanghai had distributed imperial grain to the people and proclaimed their friendship for them — obvious moves toward seizing the mandate of Heaven.[15]

Statements of this sort indicate a situation which is also described by British observers: invariably the Chinese populace of captured areas suffered less from the British attack than from subsequent pillaging by native robbers. As an English officer recorded at Nanking, "Anarchy, discontent, and open revolt are daily increasing; nor can the lawless outrages committed in the interior, by gathering hordes of plunderers, be suppressed until the garrisons are left free to act, by a settlement with us."[16] To check the growing disorder, the Chinese authorities resorted to a traditional expedient. A proposal was made to "use bandits to attack bandits . . . make proclamations with great righteousness, entice them with large profit"; furthermore, "to subdue bandits, one must first subdue the bandit leaders." To this it was replied that of the militia already organized along the Yangtze, a half had previously been smugglers, but among the smugglers there were no outstanding leaders.[17] By the offering of sizable rewards, some three thousand such banditti had been enlisted as troops at Yangchow and elsewhere, which removed the possibility of their being led astray and used by the British. Nevertheless shops had been closed and the people terrorized, and the authorities lamented that "to ward off the exterior menace one must first pacify the interior." An edict of August 16 in reply sanctioned the enlistment of smugglers through a certain leader, Yang Yung, but cautioned against the temperamental instability of such troops.[18]

Similar efforts were made to buy off the Chinese traitors connected with Hongkong. A report of August 1842 indicated the very important potentialities of secret societies, those fraternities which were secret because they were anti-dynastic. At Hongkong various leaders had set up the Lodge of United Righteousness, the Lodge of Loyal Hearts and some eight other such organizations. The allegiance of more than a thousand of these lodge members had been bought by the Kwangtung authorities in 1841. Their principal leader, Lu Ya-ching, when secretly offered a feather and button of official rank, had promised "support from within" (*nei-ying*). Unfortunately, since British protection impeded the capture of traitors, they were flocking to Hongkong in increasing numbers. The provincial authorities proclaimed a full pardon for all who returned, and rewards for their assistance. Already they had got the services of a certain Chu who was a clerk of the barbarian chief *Tsan-shun* (A. R. Johnston, acting governor of Hongkong in 1841 [?]). Since dissension was to be expected among the secret societies in the island, the court encouraged these promises as a means of embarassing the British.[19]

The type of Chinese who actually helped the enemy is indicated in the depositions of five traitors shipwrecked with the British vessel *Nerbudda* in Formosa. Huang Chou and Cheng Ah-er were both from the Hsiang-shan district north of Macao. Having been in business and become acquainted with barbarians, in 1841 they had hired several others "to act as Chinese traitors" on the English ship. They further deposed that the leading traitors on Pottinger's vessel were two Cantonese, Su Wang and Liu Hsiang, who passed upon the antecedents of all the dozen or so traitors used on each British ship. These men had written the letters in Chinese which the British, it was said, brought to Formosa to encourage a rising among traitors there — one of whom had previously confessed to such a plot.[20]

Chinese traitors were also feared as a channel of intelligence to the enemy. In July 1842 Ch'i-ying complained that the British "every day read the *Peking Gazette* (*Ching-pao*). Since the officials of Kiangnan and Chekiang all have its news, it is more difficult to estimate from what ultimate source it is circuitously transmitted to the (British) rebels." He demanded a thorough investigation and the taking of secret precautions. The emperor in reply denounced the traitors who must be transmitting the *Gazette* and ordered their seizure and execution, to keep official secrets from the invaders.[21]

Such fears at court reflected the social conditions of the late Tao-kuang period. One cannot but note the community of interest between the ruling bureaucracy and the gentry. The two groups coöperated then as later in organizing militia and applying the *pao-chia* system for the maintenance of local order. For example, when disorder seized the countryside near Chinkiang after the fall of that city, and the merchants were panic-stricken at Anking, the capital of Anhwei, the governor of that province ordered the local authorities to organize militia and the gentry to coöperate with them for self-protection. The emperor promised to reward gentry who did so. That this was not a new or one-sided partnership, desired only by the government, is shown by reference to individuals among the gentry class (*shen-shih*) who had formerly been helpful and received rewards.[22]

These fears of the Manchu court greatly complicated the task of negotiation. Through a form of guilt by association, the British connection with Chinese traitors made the court suspicious of all who had any intercourse with the barbarians. When so many lowly Chinese were in league with the British, imperial officials who seemed to hobnob with them were at once open to distrust both by their colleagues and by the gentry. This was a stumbling block in all China's negotiations until much later in the century.

An official risked his position merely by consenting to negotiate with the barbarians.

The decision to negotiate. In these circumstances of fear and uncertainty, the resumption of negotiations in 1842, after the collapse of Ch'i-shan's efforts in 1840–41, was dictated by obvious necessity, manifest in the superiority of British arms.

The second British expedition, accompanied by Sir Henry Pottinger as plenipotentiary, had come up the coast and reoccupied Tinghai, on Chusan Island, and Ningpo by October 1841. It then awaited reinforcements from England. On March 10, 1842, the British garrison at Ningpo was subjected to a surprise attack from an army of Chinese troops which had gradually been gathered nearby, and was saved only by the superiority of foreign arms. As it was, the Chinese were completely routed, losing some four hundred men without killing a single Englishman, and the British reopened the campaign by counter-attacking a few days later.[23] Reports of this disaster were read by the emperor on March 23 and, after the extensive preparations that had been made for a victory, were so disheartening as to inspire renewed interest in a policy of negotiation. In particular, memorials from Liu Yün-k'o, governor of Chekiang, portrayed the dangers of the situation in very frank terms and advocated, as he had done before, the reappointment of I-li-pu, who had been active in support of Ch'i-shan's negotiations eighteen months before.[24] The court was thus moved to reconsider its policy, and several transfers of officials took place in such a way as to indicate that it did so.

It is of interest to find, for example, that Lin Tse-hsü, although sentenced to transportation to Ili in July 1841, had nevertheless since then been assisting the grand councillor, Wang Ting, in flood control work in Honan, whither Wang had been sent in the seventh month of 1841 (August 17–September 14). Wang was degraded but left at his post in Honan in the first month of 1842 (February 10–March 11); and Lin was finally ordered to proceed to Ili on March 18, 1842, just about the time the British reopened their campaign in Chekiang. Wang Ting returned to Peking in the third month (April 11–May 9) and died on June 9, 1842 at the Chinese age of seventy-five.[25] Chinese writers say that he committed suicide in protest against appeasement.[26] On the other side of the picture we know that on March 26 Mu-chang-a was ordered posthaste to Tientsin, to manage affairs there jointly with the governor-general. About the same time two other officials were ordered to the scene of danger in Chekiang: Ch'i Shen (distinguish from Ch'i-shan), who had been assisting in the defense of Canton, on March 24; and on the twenty-eighth I-li-pu, who represented the peace party. About a month earlier, on February 24, 1842, Ch'i-ying, who was then Tartar-general at Mukden, had been made Tartar-general at

Canton. On March 24 he was commanded to proceed posthaste to his new office. But on March 28, before he had started for the south, he was ordered to hasten to Chekiang, to be acting Hangchow Tartar-general.[27]

The conclusion seems warranted that the reopening of the British campaign precipitated decisions of policy in Peking, that the party of Mu-chang-a won out, and that the close supporters of the throne, mentioned above, were sent forward as part of a supreme effort to check the British juggernaut. On April 7, 1842, Ch'i-ying was given the seal of an imperial commissioner (*Ch'in-ch'ai ta-ch'en*) and ordered to proceed at once to Chekiang. Just three days previously a partial restoration of rank had been granted to two degraded Manchu officials — I-li-pu, mentioned above, who was now given brevet rank of the seventh class, and Hsien-ling, who was given the status of an imperial bodyguard (*Shih-wei*) of the fourth class. Both were to be taken south by Ch'i-ying.[28] Thereupon on April 12 Ch'i-ying received the imperial instructions in audience, and on the fifteenth he left the capital accompanied by I-li-pu, Hsien-ling, and a suite of attachés. The party reached Hangchow twenty-seven days later, on May 9, having covered a post-route distance of 3,050 li (about 1,000 miles). Ch'i-ying's first memorial from Hangchow states once again the doctrine which his ill-fated predecessor, Ch'i-shan, had followed, and which foreshadows his own later policy: ". . . to control the barbarians, one must first know their nature. . . . It is like the men who catch tigers in Kirin province. In their hands they have no bits of iron (as weapons); they merely take a leather robe and put it over the tiger's head, and so the tiger is caught alive. This is to know their nature and then to catch them. Today, if we thoroughly know their nature, we can get hold of their minds and subdue their courage, and so all the sooner can finish the matter. This is the essential principle, which is called 'to know yourself and to know your adversary, and in a hundred battles win a hundred victories.' " This aphorism of Sun-tzu stressed out-thinking the enemy.[29]

That Ch'i-ying and his colleagues were sent south for the special purpose of opening negotiations is confirmed by an unpublished memorial of General I-ching, which urges that, since Ch'i-ying had brought to Chekiang the special command of the emperor to prosecute the war with increased vigor, he should be associated with I-ching in the military command. But the emperor refused absolutely to allow it. Even the British interpreters concluded at the time that, while Ch'i-ying and I-li-pu had duties "not unconnected with the military arrangements," still they "stand apart from" the military, "whose duties point solely to the conclusion of the war by force of arms." [30] Accordingly, after their arrival near the theatre of war, military operations continued to be under the direction of I-ching; and Liu Yun-k'o, governor of Chekiang, continued his former activities.[31] Ch'i-ying meanwhile sent I-li-pu and Hsien-ling to Chapu "to find a way of controlling[b] the British . . . to proclaim abroad the heavenly majesty and manifest great righteousness," as the memorial phrases it, "with the object of delaying the approach of the enemy."[32] Although he assisted other officials later in their military arrangements, there can be little doubt that Ch'i-ying's mission, as an imperial commissioner, was meant from the first to be a diplomatic one.

The imperial commissioner Ch'i-ying. In view of Ch'i-ying's close connection, over a period of six years, with the foundation of the treaty system in China, his career and personality are of unusual interest.

He was the son of an imperial clansman, Lu-k'ang, who appears to have typified the corrupt Manchu bureaucrat: nearly all his service was passed in Peking, where he did not lack opportunities for enrichment. In 1801, for example, Lu-k'ang had become assistant superintendent, and in 1811 superintendent, of the Hatamen octroi, under which there were taxing stations in a cordon about the capital, at the head of the Grand Canal at Tungchow, and at the city gates, which contributed to the imperial coffers every year a fixed revenue of some Tls. 370,000. Since revenue beyond that amount was kept by the collectors, the post of superintendent was one of the biggest plums in the empire, and its tenure was limited to one year.[33] In 1804 and again in 1809 Lu-k'ang was degraded because of peculation among his subordinates and finally dismissed in 1813, never again to be employed. He died in 1816. He must have bequeathed to Ch'i-ying the habit of money-making, if not wealth itself.

The imperial clansman Ch'i-ying had begun his official career in 1806. Gutzlaff, a well-informed contemporary, states that he was a bosom friend of the young prince who, in 1820, became the Tao-kuang Emperor, and was, "by his sister's marriage, related with the imperial house."[34] Other Western accounts call him a "relative" and a "cousin" of the emperor, perhaps from the mere fact that he was a clansman; Chinese accounts yield little on such relationships. In any case, Ch'i-ying certainly received unusual preferment at the hands of the new ruler. Having advanced from the ninth to the fifth rank in the first fourteen years of his service, he was suddenly raised in 1820 to positions in the cabinet and in the banner forces of the second degree of rank. In the next five years he held nine different positions successively among the various banner forces — certainly no lack of attention, whatever else it may signify. More important posts had followed: comptroller of the imperial household (1825), commandant of the Peking gendarmerie ("general of the nine gates," 1827). In the next decade he served five times as president of a Board and once as superintendent of the

[b] The phrase *chi-mi* (lit., "to put a halter on," "to restrain," "to control") is used regularly in the documents with the implication of subduing through non-warlike measures, presumably by negotiation.

Hatamen octroi. His career outside the capital, however, did not really begin until his appointment in 1838 as Tartar-general at Mukden, where he drew up defense regulations but had little to do with foreign policy during the three years of his tenure.

This bare recital indicates putative reasons why Ch'i-ying was chosen to negotiate in 1842. He was a rich man, as all accounts agree, of long experience in the capital, and a clansman close to the emperor. His only recorded experience in the provinces south of Peking had been in 1836–37, when he had investigated cases of corruption in Kiangsi and Kwangtung. He can have had few local connections with provincial interests such as that of the Canton trade. Perhaps this fact outweighed his lack of provincial experience.

At any rate, the appointment of I-li-pu as his colleague made up for such a lack. I-li-pu was an older man, likewise an imperial clansman, and a metropolitan graduate of 1801. He had early acquired a reputation in Yunnan for making use of (lit., "yoking and driving") the headmen among the aborigines. He was also well versed in provincial administration, having filled high positions in Shansi, Shensi, and Shantung and having been governor-general of Yunnan and Kweichow. In 1839, being experienced in the conduct of barbarian affairs among the tribes of these frontier provinces, he had been made Nanking governor-general, and in 1840 sent to Chekiang as imperial commissioner, where he seconded the peace policy of Ch'i-shan and was accordingly degraded in 1841. His resurrection now was no doubt for the purpose of placing at Ch'i-ying's disposal his knowledge of the provinces and particularly of the earlier Sino-British negotiations. From the documents there appears to be no question that Ch'i-ying, and not I-li-pu, was meant to be the chief negotiator. To some degree this was no doubt necessitated by I-li-pu's age and infirmity. Various British observers in 1842 describe Ch'i-ying as "about fifty-six years old, stout, and strongly built," "graceful and dignified in carriage," or, again, "between sixty and seventy . . . a stout, hale, good-humored looking old gentleman with a firm step and upright carriage"; whereas I-li-pu impressed them as "about seventy-six years old, thin, and rather infirm," or "upwards of eighty . . . and his countenance bore a sad expression of mental suffering." [35] Actually we know that I-li-pu was seventy-two or seventy-three.

Opening the negotiations. Ch'i-ying's immediate problem after his arrival in Chekiang in May 1842, lay in the fact that he had been sent to negotiate a victory or at least a compromise, whereas circumstances called for a surrender. His diplomatic efforts, desirable as they might be, could not get too far ahead of opinion at Peking. And opinion at Peking evidently vacillated uncertainly, fearing diplomatic entanglement in proportion as its hope of victorious defense rose or fell. For example, when a censor reported a Cantonese rumor that a native revolt in Bengal had seized the British stores there, the emperor at once ordered a punitive expedition against the British.[36] On May 25, 1842, two days after learning of the first efforts to negotiate at Chapu, he ordered Ch'i-ying, still as imperial commissioner, to go to Kwangtung as Tartar-general at Canton, there to report on the progress of the Bogue defenses below Canton. He was also to investigate the possibility of recovering Hongkong: "Why should the rebellious barbarians be allowed to keep it permanently?" [37] On May 25 Ch'i-ying's assistants, I-li-pu and Hsien-ling, were ordered either to be attached to the suite of General I-ching in the theatre of war or to return to Peking. Pursuant to these instructions, Ch'i-ying arranged for I-li-pu to stay in Chekiang, while Hsien-ling and his other aides brought from Mukden were to accompany him to Canton.[38] News of the annihilation of the Manchu garrison at Chapu on May 18 must have reached the court immediately after the foregoing orders had been dispatched. (In this period a memorial from General I-ching took eight days to reach the capital.[39] The first report of the Chapu disaster is recorded as received from Ch'i-ying, then in Kiangsu, on May 26.) That this report was not received sooner and was not in some way the cause of his being ordered to Canton, seems to be clear from the fact that on June 4 he was ordered to delay his departure for Kwangtung and to remain at Hangchow.[40]

While the court thus vacillated, there had been an increased interest in opening negotiations. As Ch'i-ying reported after Chapu, "Aside from getting them under control [*chi-mi*, i.e., by diplomacy], there is no other policy to follow; yet getting them under control also cannot be managed"; the chances for such a policy had grown worse since the failure at Ningpo (in March); and, as for the policy of "advancing and exterminating," he would leave that up to I-ching. I-ching, however, soon suggested peace overtures himself: "There is nothing for it but to devise means of getting them under control [*chi-mi*]." On June 4, the emperor read a memorial from Ch'i-ying reporting the first diplomatic efforts: I-li-pu had sent an emissary "well acquainted with the barbarian nature," who reached the British fleet and saw a chieftain named Kuo (the interpreter Gutzlaff), who respectfully told him that the British sought not war but trade. When an edict of June 5 asked for more details of this interview, which "certainly did not stop at two words," Ch'i-ying replied that the British had asked: What was I-li-pu's status? Could he or could he not memorialize? They feared that he was incapable of settling matters and must first see him personally. If he were an imperial commissioner, they might meet at Chusan.[41]

The next step was for I-li-pu to send the British a diplomatic communication (*chao-hui*) by the same bearer, who did not succeed in delivering it until after the fall of Shanghai (June 19). The British reply, received June 23, was that the troops were already gathered, and they could not but fight; but a place for discussions might be arranged.[42] Thereupon Ch'i-ying and I-li-pu, according to the former's memorial, replied to the British through the medium of the same emissary and suggested Chen-hai (Chinhai, the port of Ningpo) or Sungkiang (inland from Shanghai) as a place for discussions. When the court heard of these efforts on July 3 it expressed fear of English trickery and warned Ch'i-ying that "on no account should you so expose yourself as to go (for an interview). Even if the rebels come and ask to see you, it is not permissible to have an interview with them. Should there be points that ought to be discussed and dealt with, it is only permissible for (the messenger) Ch'en Chih-kang and others to go with a letter, to avoid falling into their treacherous schemes." If their demands were excessive, either they must be attacked or their progress must be obstructed.[43] All in all, it is hard to see any constructive policy behind the mixture of hope and fear expressed in these instructions.

Until late in July 1842, the court maintained its bellicose attitude while its representatives in the provinces made cautious and futile overtures for peace. On June 22 Ch'i-ying and I-li-pu were both ordered to Kiangsu to assist the governor-general, Niu Chien, who was defending Shanghai. Ch'i-ying reached Kashing, Chekiang, on June 21, where he heard of the fall of Shanghai, and then advanced to a spot on the Chekiang-Kiangsu border. By the time he received the above-mentioned order to assist at Shanghai, the British fleet was already reported to have left Wusung. He and I-li-pu thereupon went to K'un-shan, Kiangsu, on June 30 and saw Niu Chien there. On July 2 their emissary returned with a reply from Pottinger, having seen the chief British interpreter, Morrison, on June 28; the British again expressed fear that Ch'i-ying and I-li-pu possessed insufficient diplomatic powers, and refused to stop fighting.[44]

As the British pressure increased, the split between opinion at the capital and at the front rapidly widened. It had been feared that the next British objective after Shanghai would be Tientsin and Peking itself, and there were rumors of an enlarged fleet sailing to the north.[45] Soon, however, the British announced that they would first enter the Yangtze, where their ships were quickly seen, and efforts were accordingly directed to the defense of strategic points, particularly Chinkiang.[46] At this time the warlike determination of the emperor and his advisors seems to have risen to a greater height than ever. An edict of July 9 opined that, since the British refused to stop fighting, further efforts at negotiation not only would be useless but might injure the national prestige.[47] On July 14 I-li-pu was ordered to return to his post at Chapu, and Ch'i-ying was commanded to stay and defend Kiangsu with the provincial authorities before going to his post at Canton.[48]

A secret court letter (*t'ing-chi*) of July 15 seems to have marked the first acceptance of defeat[49] and after the climactic capture of Chinkiang, the crossroads of China's inland commerce, on July 21, Ch'i-ying was ordered to make peace at any cost.[c]

Pending closer analysis, the conclusion may be drawn that the court realized, as soon as the British campaign began in 1842, that a settlement must be made, and Ch'i-ying was dispatched for the purpose. But the court was extremely reluctant to acknowledge the necessity of abject surrender, which in its eyes probably involved more than the British really had in mind. Ch'i-ying's appointment as Tartar-general at Canton, just before Peking learned of the Chapu disaster, may perhaps have meaning as an effort to prepare him more fully for turning defeat into victory through negotiation; for then, as later, Canton was the seat of trade, far from the capital, and the proper point for managing barbarian affairs. (He was not formally appointed to a different post, that of Nanking governor-general; until October 1842.) At any rate, the attitude of Peking being bellicose and the fate of his predecessor Ch'i-shan being clear before him, it may be imagined that Ch'i-ying was not inclined to endanger himself by opening negotiations and beginning the inevitable process of surrender until sentiment at court was unequivocally for peace at any price.

Certainly, so long as he lacked anything approaching the full powers repeatedly demanded by Pottinger, he was wise to hesitate. His title of imperial commissioner (*Ch'in-ch'ai ta-ch'en*, "imperially-deputed great-minister") was not connected with any regular post in the official hierarchy and carried with it no ascertainable statutory powers. By custom at least, an imperial commissioner was given an official seal (*kuan-fang*) and exercised the absolute power of the emperor within the limits of his commission.[51] In July 1842, there were at least two others holding the commission of *Ch'in-ch'ai* in other parts of the empire.[52] While such commissioners had greater power than any provincial officials for the execution of certain tasks, it did not mean that they possessed what the West would call "full" or "plenipotentiary" powers. The arrangements which a *Ch'in-ch'ai* might make were not sanctioned in advance so long as they carried out the letter of his instructions, for the very good reason that he was not given anything corresponding to a Western envoy's detailed written instructions. Like any other imperial official, he received instructions in very general terms. At most he would be informed of the problem to be solved, not of specific steps to follow in dealing with it. Hence his course of action was judged not by its adherence to instructions, there being none, but by its results. Until the results were known, imperial approval remained uncertain.

[c] It is worth noting that the rice shipments for 1842, so important for the sustenance of the capital, had already gone northward from Chinkiang.[50]

The emperor's surrender in 1842 was therefore not complete until Ch'i-ying was given a Chinese approximation of full powers. The necessary step in this direction was taken on July 26, the bitter day on which Peking received the first full report of the debacle at Chinkiang. Ch'i-ying and I-li-pu were ordered [53] to "go to Ching-k'ou [opposite Chinkiang] and manage affairs in a proper fashion. If by any chance the said rebels should go to the provincial capital (Nanking) and cause trouble, it is permitted that the said ministers temporarily try to restrain them by negotiation [*chi-mi*]. If the said barbarians are hesitant and not trusting, then tell them that there already has been handed down a decree calling upon Ch'i-ying and I-li-pu to take special charge of this matter. . ." [d]

The question here arises, what sort of communications of an unofficial and personal nature may have passed between the provinces and the capital. It is difficult to believe that at such a time as this an official as close to the emperor as Ch'i-ying would not send private messages with his memorials; the reassuring tone of the edict just quoted suggests that it replied to personal, as well as official, appeals for greater authority. That such correspondence occurred is shown by the fact that on July 31 and August 1 Ch'i-ying, at Nanking, received two confidential letters (*t'ing-chi*) sent express from the palace, commanding him, with regard to matters in which he ought to "act as circumstances might require" (*pien-i ts'ung-shih*), to "act as the exigency required" (*ts'ung-ch'üan pan-li*).[55] An edict of August 7 reiterated:

"If what these barbarians discuss and request is within the bounds of reason, the ministers certainly may grant it. And they ought to say that, after they have discussed it together satisfactorily and it has been memorialized to the throne, it may be carried into effect — they need have no further hesitation. . ."

These instructions were finally sufficient to allow the imperial representatives to satisfy the British demand for plenipotentiaries with full powers. On August 3 a reply received from Pottinger had stated that he would cease hostilities if they had received "full powers (*ch'üan-ch'üan*) to settle independently according to his demands." Ch'i-ying had replied that there was no difference between the phrase used by the British for

[d] A secret edict of the same date (July 26), perhaps the one just referred to, should also be quoted: "According to a former reply of the said rebellious barbarians, apparently they suspect that Ch'i-ying and I-li-pu are not able to act as responsible parties, and so it is to be feared that their hearts are full of fear and doubt, and they are not willing to stop the rebel vanguard immediately. Let Ch'i-ying and I-li-pu give them very clear instructions explaining that 'if with true hearts you repent of your faults, and both sides are willing to cease hostilities, we shall memorialize beseeching his majesty the Emperor; we shall definitely get his consent, there is no need to be inordinately doubtful and fearful.' The said ministers were our special appointment; they must cautiously uphold the prestige of the country, patiently soothe the barbarian temperament, in order that the incipient hostilities may soon be stopped and the seacoast be released from its state of emergency; then they may be considered not to have failed their commission; they need not worry about any hindrance and accordingly harbor dread within their minds, which, after all, would be useless for their task." [54]

"full powers" and his own title of imperial commissioner. Again, on August 8, Pottinger demanded the production of full powers; and although I-li-pu prepared a "clear proclamation" in reply, the British "stubbornly would not come to their senses." [56] On August 11 they were prepared to attack Nanking when Chinese emissaries dramatically reached the river bank at dawn and announced the imminent arrival of Ch'i-ying. The British attack was therefore called off, and Morrison sent a reply which was "not at all clear or smooth in style" but which stated that, since the emperor had sent a minister with "full powers" (*ch'üan-ch'üan*, the term used by the British), hostilities would cease.[57] On August 14 Morrison examined and accepted the "imperial commission," and on the eighteenth the English formally suspended hostilities.[58]

The Manchu-Chinese side of the negotiations. The beginning of negotiations in earnest put the imperial representatives in the position more of mediators than of protagonists. They alone were in direct contact with both the emperor and the barbarians, and their fate depended upon the production of harmony. To move the court, Ch'i-ying could play upon its fears; and it is an interesting question whether his memorial received on August 17, for example, describing vividly the danger of a British advance to Anking, Kiukiang, and the Wuhan cities, was not phrased for this purpose.[59] Toward the English he already knew that he must manifest sincerity to quell their suspicions, but the way of doing this remained to be found. The most urgent necessity was to find subordinates who could deal with the barbarians face to face. They must be low enough in rank to be able to go to the British ships, and yet clever enough to do business with J. R. Morrison (son of the first Protestant missionary) and Gutzlaff, the British interpreters, without losing their heads.

Up to this point nearly all the communications sent by I-li-pu to the invading fleet had been carried by a minor military officer, Corporal [60] Ch'en Chih-kang, who was said to be "a man of moderate rank but shrewd and intelligent" and "well known in the [English] force as an occasional internuncio, who was first employed as messenger from Keshen [Ch'i-shan] when the squadron visited the mouth of the Peiho in 1840" (sic).[61] This "well-known character" had been "jocularly christened Corporal White" and was a familiar figure to all foreign observers.[62] In actual fact, the foreign observers appear to have given to this messenger, Ch'en, the name of Ch'i-shan's messenger of 1840, Pai Han-chang, whose name actually *was* "White" (*pai*); but this erroneous belief that the two men were one and the same merely strengthened the British confidence in "Corporal White." [63] The new "Corporal White" incarnate in the person of Ch'en was an intelligent conveyor of messages, but someone of higher status was urgently needed for the opening of negotiations. Such a person was now found in an experienced retainer (*chia-jen*) of I-li-pu named Chang Hsi, who left a diary which is well worthy of study as an inside account.[64]

Although Chang Hsi was a person of humble status without official rank, it took a good deal of urging to persuade him to come to Nanking and assist in the negotiations. He had helped I-li-pu in his conciliatory dealings with the British in Chekiang in 1840–41 and had been put in jail as a result. Apparently he hesitated to repeat the experience. But Chang, of all his patron's entourage, appears to have been regarded as the preëminent barbarian expert, possessed of a unique insight without which negotiations would be impossible. Ch'i-ying and I-li-pu had both consulted him in Peking in April 1842 and with some effort I-li-pu finally persuaded him to join them. Chang's ham acting as a negotiator — his calculated fits of rage, windy invocations of the right, and fondness for barbarian wine — made him something less than a diplomat.[65] His own form of diplomacy was limited to a personal approach on the basis of manners, braggadocio, and bargaining, but his diary depicts vividly some of the difficulties of Chinese-Manchu foreign policy in operation.

Travel, communication, and intelligence all presented problems. Chang Hsi, for example, had traveled from Tientsin to join I-li-pu and finally reached his superior's vessel at Wusih on the Grand Canal west of Soochow on August 5. On that very evening an express letter from the governor-general at Nanking announced that the British fleet had arrived there; so Chang was sent to Nanking on August 6 to forestall a British attack by negotiation. Chang and his party went by junk along the Canal to Tan-yang and then rode sweating horses for 90 *li* that evening. On the second day (August 7) they walked 45 *li* in the heat and rode another 45 *li* to reach Nanking by noon. (On his arrival Chang at once showed his expertness by pointing out that the expected British attack would not begin on the morrow because it was the Sabbath. His idea was sound, although the day actually happened to be a Monday.) [66] I-li-pu suffered sunstroke and did not arrive until the third day.

When Chang Hsi later opened *pourparlers* on board Pottinger's ship at Nanking, he and Morrison indulged in a bluffing contest, Morrison promising that the British fleet was prepared to go upstream all the way to Szechwan while part of it would take Tientsin and Peking. Chang countered this by consoling the British on the defeat they would sustain when the emperor finally decided to arm the countryside and rouse the populace against them till "the grass and trees would all be soldiers" (of course this would have been an extreme and dangerously double-edged move, which has been eyed askance by some administrators even in modern China). Chang then, by his own account, flew into a rage, pounded the table, and excoriated the invaders' unrighteousness until Morrison appeased him with the explanation that the English nation must have its treaty or perish, there was no alternative. This performance was much admired by Chang's speechless and perspiring colleagues.[67]

The imperial commissioner's staff work was so faulty that when Chang brought back the first version of Pottinger's demands, the document was handed to a secretary who on the next day "had gone out to visit friends," so that the document could not be recovered in time for the next conference with the British.[68]

Chang Hsi's diary also indicates the jealousy which existed between the principal Manchu negotiators. I-li-pu was old and ill, recently disgraced and anxious to "right the wrongs" that had been done him.[69] Ch'i-ying had been sent with higher rank, yet was a younger man, and had no barbarian experience. Each had his own staff, so that in their combined operations they would send two messengers or more at a time, and might quarrel over their respective agents' handling of affairs. They and the Nanking governor-general each lived in separate establishments and in order to confer would pay official calls.

In the conduct of negotiations, the principals sent forward emissaries in three or more waves: the first were mere messengers, like Ch'en Chih-kang; the second were talkers like Chang Hsi who could attempt to fathom the British intentions by drawing them out in conversation; the third were responsible officials like Hsien-ling and Huang En-t'ung whose rank [70] allowed them to discuss terms; finally, after the terms were settled and no undignified argument remained, the imperial commissioner appeared in person to sign the treaty. As Ch'i-ying put it, his tactics were to depute the minor officers "to go and have an interview with the barbarian headman, and see in what manner he disposed his phrases, and then afterward depute officers of comparatively higher rank to go and talk things over." [71] This use of subordinates unable to commit themselves (a practice traditional in oriental diplomacy) enraged the British, who vigorously denounced such dilatory tactics and demanded officials of higher rank. This demand for high rank among his emissaries, among whom the most experienced or trusted were of low rank, placed Ch'i-ying in an awkward position. He saved the situation partly by memorializing the emperor and partly by pulling the wool over the eyes of the British, who were experienced enough to demand envoys of high rank but not quite clever enough to know what they got.

All Western accounts of the Nanking negotiations, at the time and since then, have stated that both Ch'i-ying and I-li-pu were imperial commissioners. They cannot be blamed, since that is the plain statement made in the preamble of the treaty of Nanking itself in both the English and Chinese certified versions.[72] The fact remains, however, that I-li-pu was not an imperial commissioner at the time the treaty was signed. No edict can be found giving him that status in 1842 until October 17, when Ch'i-ying was ordered to transfer his imperial commissioner's seal to I-li-pu preparatory to the latter's departure to negotiate at Canton.[73] The British did not realize that for two *Ch'in-ch'ai* to manage the same affair, each embodying the imperial will, would have been anomalous.

This little deception apparently went unknown to the court, since the preamble of the treaty was not copied out and sent to Peking. Probably it was indulged in because Ch'i-ying was unknown to the British while I-li-pu had a wide and favorable reputation among them, and the first overtures were made as from him rather than from Ch'i-ying. The latter wrote his first letter to Pottinger sometime after the fall of Chinkiang but did not reveal his rank or authority to negotiate.[74] Meanwhile Chinese emissaries told the English verbally that "Eleepoo, the imperial high commissioner . . . had received orders to conclude . . . a treaty of lasting amity." [75] Later, on August 4, the British received a dispatch from I-li-pu stating that Ch'i-ying, "in conjunction with himself, was empowered to treat for peace." [76] Thus Ch'i-ying made himself known only gradually. During August the British accounts, like the treaty text, speak of the Chinese "High Commissioners" in the plural. But there is no evidence that I-li-pu's status was as high as the British assumed that it was. On the contrary Ch'i-ying memorialized about August 13, explaining that eventually personal interviews with the barbarians might be necessary, and asking, therefore, that I-li-pu be allowed temporarily, when the time arrived, to wear a first-class button and feather in order to increase English respect and confidence. This was granted on August 17.[77] I-li-pu may have acted in advance of this permission when he visited the *Cornwallis* on August 20, wearing the same insignia as Ch'i-ying and the Nanking governor-general.[78]

Ch'i-ying's relations with the emperor were almost as delicate as his relations with the enemy. Several commands from Peking had to be disregarded. For example, an edict of August 17 had ordered the imperial representatives not to see the wily barbarians until all was settled, and then only after the entire British fleet had departed; thereupon they might name a central spot and ask the barbarian chieftains to come and see them. They certainly should not rashly board the barbarian vessels. By the time these orders could have arrived, Ch'i-ying and his colleagues were already visiting the *Cornwallis* (August 20), and they did so again, to sign the treaty, on the twenty-ninth. Their excuse on the first occasion was the necessity of dispelling English suspicion.[79]

This artfulness of the Manchu negotiators at Nanking was also evident in one or two other pretensions to unauthorized rank, as when Ch'i-ying's subordinate, Hsien-ling, posed as a Tartar-general.[80] All in all it reflects quite clearly their principal aim at the time; to ingratiate themselves with the British invaders and get them out of the Yangtze just as soon as possible. In their minds this was more important than the terms of the treaty settlement and they did not scruple to commit the empire on a few points to which the emperor himself had not agreed.[e] By so doing they of course sowed the seeds of future discord.

Imperfections in the treaty agreement. To begin with, they reported to the emperor in the first instance only those British demands to which he had already given consent or at least consideration; (1) the indemnity, (2) diplomatic equality, and (3) trade at the five ports and Hongkong.[81] The emperor had objected to the first and agreed to the other two of these points as early as July 26.[82] When Pottinger presented twelve demands at Nanking on August 14, Ch'i-ying and I-li-pu reported three items which were substantially the same as the above and added, "although there were other demands, yet these were the fundamental points." The news having been broken in this gentle fashion, the rest of Pottinger's demands do not appear to have been known in Peking until August 22. They included such matters as the abolition of the Cohong and the establishment of the treaty tariff and treaty-port consuls.

In the end, Ch'i-ying, I-li-pu, and the local governor-general, Niu Chien, signed the treaty of Nanking on August 29 without having secured the imperial assent to two of its provisions: the opening of Foochow and permanent foreign residence at the new ports. The edict of August 22, on the basis of which they signed the treaty, declared that "Foochow absolutely may not be conferred" as a place for trade and that in trading at the new ports the British "must not take possession and dwell for a long time." [83] As will be noted in Chapter 16, at Foochow the export of tea, and hence foreign trade, although nominally permitted by edicts of August 31 and September 6, 1842, were actually forbidden for more than a decade after the signing of the treaty of Nanking.[84] In the meantime at Canton, the

[e] These Nanking negotiations indicate a pattern of diplomatic behavior very similar to that analyzed by Professor M. Banno for the treaty-revision pourparlers of 1854. His interesting summary shows how Chinese officials, in the effort to control the foreigners, used such tactics as politeness, delay, ambiguous promises, avoidance of issues, and citing of precedents or of treaty clauses (when convenient), as well as alleging the limitations of their capacity. They sought constantly to preserve Chinese superiority by such standard procedures as the use of unequal terms in documents and unequal ceremonial forms in interviews, refusal of interviews (or granting them only in places like warehouses), deputation of junior officers, refusal to memorialize the throne (or doing it only "unofficially"), or even handing back foreign communications. In extremity they would appeal to the foreign negotiators on a basis of personal friendship, and they could always plead that "popular feeling" as well as the imperial institutions dictated their course. Similarly, in the effort to satisfy the throne the provincial officials of 1854 used the clichés of the day, cited precedents and imperial utterances, and argued from considerations of prestige (face) and popular feeling. All this was customary, but in addition they sought to excuse their concessions to foreign demands by citing differences in foreign and Chinese customs, quoting the treaties, alleging that concessions were mutually advantageous, or glossing them over as measures of benevolence toward the barbarians, rather than subservience. In a tight spot, finally, they would simply misrepresent the facts to the emperor. Professor Banno also indicates how Ch'ing diplomacy had to keep a balance between domestic and foreign policy problems. Examples of all his points will appear below.

chief point of friction in Anglo-Chinese diplomacy hinged on the British claim to entrance to the city (see Chapter 20), a right which the Chinese did not believe had been granted in 1842.

Another concession which is generally thought to have been given England in the treaty of Nanking, albeit unwillingly, was the formal recognition, in that document, of the equality of the British and Chinese nations and rulers. In the Chinese and English originals signed at Nanking this is shown by raising their names above the rest of the text in the Chinese fashion traditionally reserved for references pertaining to the ruler. Unfortunately, the Chinese version of the treaty presented to the emperor differed from that signed on the *Cornwallis*.[85] It suppressed, throughout, the indications of national equality used in the version drawn up by the British. Great Britain is referred to simply as "England," *ying-kuo*, not as "The great English country," *Ta-Ying-kuo*, and the characters are not elevated (*t'ai-t'ou*) to equal the corresponding *Ta-Ch'ing*; the same applies to designations of the British ruler. In particular the entire preamble was omitted, including the designation of both Ch'i-ying and I-li-pu as "high officers imperially appointed to manage affairs as circumstances may require" (*Ch'in-ch'ai pien-i hsing-shih ta-ch'en*), the nearest Chinese equivalent to Western full powers — " 'plenipotentiary' in the fullest sense of the term," as Sir John Davis translated it.[86]

These imperfections are no more than the documentary evidence of a non-meeting of minds — a gap which was recognized on both sides in 1842 and necessitated another year of negotiation.[87]

CHAPTER VII

CH'I-YING'S APPEASEMENT POLICY

In the year which intervened between the treaty of Nanking and the so-called "Supplementary treaty" of October 8, 1843, the British officials in China tried to set up a system of treaty law which would take the place of the old scheme of things at Canton. Their objectives were simple: to give the British merchant access to a free market and to protect him by law in his exploitation of it. Treaty ports were to provide the market, treaty clauses enforced by consular officers were to provide the law, with gunboats at hand in case of trouble. It was equally important that trade should be free to expand within agreed limits and that the law should expand with it to see that it remained free. As it turned out, merchants of all countries were ready to join in the spread of commerce, but the British government was too often alone in its efforts to expand the rule of law.

After the conclusion of the Nanking treaty, the signers of that famous document remained on the spot for another month in order to define more fully what they had agreed to. Their most immediate concern was the resumption of trade, for which the new treaty tariff had to be established. In order to deal with this and numerous other problems not yet provided for, they decided that a supplementary treaty would be necessary. In the end the relations between China and Hongkong had also to be dealt with in the Supplementary treaty. But the opium trade, which had been the immediate occasion for war, remained a problem which could not be formally solved and required an unofficial arrangement. Each of these major problems reflected a British commercial interest which was a good deal more conscious and tangible than the primarily political interest of the Manchu dynasty represented by the imperial commissioner, Ch'i-ying.

Modern Chinese patriots have condemned Ch'i-ying's conduct of Sino-foreign relations as simple treachery. The British, who got what they wanted, admired his compliance. But few have given him credit for any kind of statesmanship. Yet the Chinese documents make it plain that Ch'i-ying himself thought he had a policy, and the British archives unwittingly describe its development. It was to be a policy of appeasement combined with personal influence over Pottinger. Unfortunately it was based on an utter misconception, and Ch'i-ying's brilliant efforts in the realm of personal relations proved abortive.

While the dynasty remained blandly ignorant of commerce, Ch'i-ying studied the barbarian invaders with a view to pacifying them and soon realized that commercial concessions would do the trick. All the while that he was helping to set up the new treaty system, however, his policy remained in the old Ch'ing tradition. His aim was to fit the novel relations with Britain into the orthodox framework of the Chinese imperial system. The outward show of tribute was gone, but the spirit remained. Ch'i-ying's memorials use the age-old terms — China was to secure the foreigners' allegiance by deigning to treat them compassionately (*huai-jou*), to get them under peaceful control (*fu-yü*) by bringing them within the Confucian order, and to subdue them (*chi-mi*) through negotiation. The foreign trade of China, considered unimportant in itself, was to be the primary means to this political end, the bait which, judiciously used, could keep the greedy Westerners in order. This system of rewards and punishments was left standing on one leg so long as China remained incapable of coercing the British, but Ch'i-ying had to act with what ideas he had inherited.[1]

He therefore developed his own policy: to mollify the British with a trade treaty and meanwhile win the confidence and friendship of their chieftain, Pottinger. This aim he consistently pursued throughout 1843, quite independently of any instructions from the emperor, and his efforts at personal friendship cast a rosy light over the whole of the negotiations. As he explained in his memorials to the throne, it was necessary to show both sincerity and condescension. With these he was often able to combine an ingratiating familiarity. At one banquet in Nanking, for example, the dignified Manchu fascinated his English guests by insisting, "as a *coup de grâce* . . . upon Sir Henry opening his mouth while with great dexterity he shot into it several immense sugar-plums." [2] Such bonhomie was added to serious promises, which greatly facilitated Pottinger's plans for the regulation of trade. It was agreed before the British departed from the scene of their success at Nanking that a supplementary treaty should be drawn up and ratified by both sovereigns. Pottinger offered to submit the outline of such a treaty,[3] and Ch'i-ying and his colleagues reported to Peking that their subordinates, meeting with the British interpreters, had drawn up eight supplementary regulations (*shan-hou chang-ch'eng*) regarding which the principals had exchanged communications to avoid misunderstanding.[4] In this way several clauses that later formed part of the Supplementary treaty of October 8, 1843, were settled almost at once. It was further agreed by Pottinger and Ch'i-ying that they should meet in Kwangtung in the tenth month (November 3–December 1) to settle the new tariff.

Ch'i-ying's desire for responsibility. Ch'i-ying's sincerity in making these plans is attested by the fact that he took measures to have himself appointed to carry them out. There is little evidence that he was animated primarily by patriotism toward the Chinese state, or ever sought to sacrifice himself on the altar of the dynasty. Yet he aspired to, and obtained, control of the Chinese side of the negotiations and in fact acted as a sort of foreign secretary for the next five years. Evidently his experience at Nanking had given him self-confidence and he hoped to gain ascendancy over Pottinger and through him over the whole British tribe. Considering that Sir Henry was the British chieftain in China, at the tremendous salary of $10,000 a year,[5] his power could hardly be small in the councils of his own people in their island beyond the seas. After his return home he might well continue to influence his country's policy in China. Meanwhile it could be assumed that, at a distance from home, the details of Pottinger's policy would be of his own invention. Therefore they might be influenced, like all things in China, by personal considerations. So while Pottinger studied how to expand the scope of British law, Ch'i-ying studied Pottinger.

Early in October, after the British departure from Nanking, he proposed to the throne, evidently with every expectation of imperial concurrence, that he should proceed to Canton forthwith as imperial commissioner. In preparation for such negotiations he emphasized in another memorial the exploits of his subordinates, Hsien-ling and Huang En-t'ung, who had saved Nanking by going to the British, and "without change of voice or countenance subdued them by means of great righteousness." He suggested that they be raised in rank, which would put them in a stronger postion for continuing the negotiations. In still another memorial Ch'i-ying and I-li-pu went even further and proposed both that they themselves should hasten to Canton and that they should be accompanied by Hsien-ling and Huang, in whom "the barbarians had the greatest confidence." [6]

The imperial response to these proposals is most significant. On October 17, 1842, Ch'i-ying was made Nanking governor-general to succeed Niu Chien, while I-li-pu was made imperial commissioner and Canton Tartar-general in succession to Ch'i-ying and ordered to take Hsien-ling and Huang with him to negotiate at Canton. The last two should be rewarded as Ch'i-ying had urged, but only after the conclusion of their work at Canton. Meanwhile Ch'i-ying himself was to discuss the tariff negotiations with I-li-pu and to communicate with the authorities of Kiangsu, Chekiang, and Fukien regarding the trade regulations for those provinces;[7] he was to have general superintendence of barbarian affairs, but no direct part in the negotiations.

This decision demonstrated that the court was still primarily concerned with defense and did not yet realize the immense importance of the commercial settlement. Far from the scene of foreign trade, the officials at Peking could not put it first in their thoughts even though the negotiators at Nanking were learning to do so. As the latter declared more than once, "in conjunction with the governors-general and the governors of the various provinces, we ought to make proper (commercial) arrangements, in the hope of perpetual peace and security." They reiterated that the British seemed entirely sincere in their interest in trade and in their readiness to help regulate it,[8] that the court's vague fears of territorial conquest were not justified in fact, and that the immediate necessity was to satisfy the invaders by completing the treaty system. But this effort was unavailing. During the next six months Ch'i-ying's talents were in large part diverted to the planning of defense measures for the Lower Yangtze,[9] while the actual conduct of the negotiations was left to I-li-pu, now handicapped by infirmities of age which had already obliged him to play a secondary role at Nanking.[10]

Ch'i-ying was thus left at Nanking, ten days from the scene of action.[a] The remarkable thing is that he was not content to be relegated to a position of power and safety as governor-general of the Lower Yangtze. On the contrary, he made persistent efforts and finally succeeded in resuming control of the negotiations, stepping into a position of the greatest danger and responsibility.

In the first place it was clearly demonstrated that the British looked to Ch'i-ying personally to settle the treaty arrangements. When the latter was detained at Nanking, Pottinger protested vigorously against that decision; and I-li-pu, who had reached Hangchow on November 6 on his way south, consequently remained there while Pottinger's protest was referred to Ch'i-ying and to the throne. The imperial reply on November 18 argued that for Ch'i-ying to arrange matters in the north while I-li-pu went south would really expedite the opening of trade. I-li-pu was instructed to wait and see how this reply affected the barbarians; if they seemed mollified, he was to hasten on to Canton.[11] Accordingly he delayed at Hangchow until November 21 while Ch'i-ying explained to Pottinger that he himself still had general control over the treaty settlement. After a slow progress through Kiangsi, I-li-pu reached Canton only on January 10, 1843.

Meanwhile Ch'i-ying's influence over the British was plainly shown. In October it had been learned with consternation that some 139 of their nationals shipwrecked in Formosa had been beheaded shortly before the signing of the treaty of Nanking.[12] "None of the barbarian chiefs know that the execution took place and daily they look for their men's return. . . . we cannot avoid mentioning it, our only course is to maintain mutual sincerity."[13] The direst consequences were feared, not without reason. In this emergency Ch'i-ying was authorized to hasten to Fukien, whither Pottinger had already gone, if such action seemed necessary to prevent a

[a] The maximum speed of correspondence normally obtainable was fifteen days from Canton to Peking and five days from Nanking to Peking; see Fairbank and Teng, "On the Transmission of Ch'ing Documents."

rupture of the peace so recently established. Ch'i-ying did not make use of this permission, but on the basis of his communications from Pottinger he did convince the court that an official investigation was necessary. As a result, after much correspondence, the cause célèbre was settled by the dispatch to Formosa of the Foochow governor-general, I-liang, whose judgment confirmed the British accusation that the Formosan officials had misrepresented the facts in order to gain merit and had executed helpless castaways rather than dangerous invaders. After this crisis it was clearly recognized by the imperial bureaucracy that the British more than ever looked to Ch'i-ying to secure fulfillment of the treaty.[14]

The latter's memorials at this time betray a lively desire to participate in the treaty making. Time after time he explained to the throne that the barbarians' entire interest was in trade, that in dealing with them it was essential to show sincerity and good faith (*ch'eng-hsin*); and he hinted broadly that there might be matters which only he could settle. Just as steadily the court failed to grasp the importance of the commercial settlement and argued that Ch'i-ying and I-li-pu could keep in touch by post: "there is no need for you both to be stationed at Canton." [15]

In the end Ch'i-ying's participation in the negotiations was necessitated by the death of I-li-pu, an event which, with all respect to that humane official, was a great relief to the British. Pottinger had reached Hongkong on December 2, 1842, and after roundly excoriating his countrymen for their contribution to the destructive riot which occurred at Canton shortly afterward, had deemed it best to conduct his diplomacy outside the atmosphere of the crown colony and nearer the center of trade. He had therefore gone to Whampoa in a steam frigate on January 19, 1843, and entertained I-li-pu and his suite and the high provincial authorities on the next day. When the tariff negotiations began it was found that both I-li-pu and the Canton governor-general, Ch'i Kung (Kekung), "elderly men of the old school . . . were entirely under the tuition and guidance of the Hong merchants; . . . had Eleepoo lived, nothing whatever would have been done, not from any evil intention on his part, but from his and Kekung's utter ignorance and impracticality." [16] In one of his last memorials I-li-pu himself confessed that the tariff question was most bewildering in its complexity (*t'ou-hsü fen-fan*). His death on March 4 soon stopped the tariff discussions. The governor-general Ch'i Kung hopefully reported that I-li-pu had just begun to get a clue (*shao yu t'ou-hsü*) to the very perplexing subject, and the court urged that Huang and Hsien-ling continue the work.[17] But the absence of an imperial commissioner who could make decisions caused the British representatives to withdraw by the middle of March to Macao and Hongkong. Thereupon, foreign cargoes continued to arrive in China, shipments were made to the new ports not yet opened, where armed vessels appeared, and smuggling flourished on the Canton River as never before. The speedy intervention of Ch'i-ying became essential to complete the tariff, and stop this growing anarchy.

Both the British and Ch'i-ying himself worked to bring it about. On hearing of the death of I-li-pu, Ch'i-ying at once gave orders for Huang and Hsien-ling to continue negotiations. The emperor commented, "though unconcerted, this is identical with the orders we have given — most commendable." Ch'i-ying also wrote urging Pottinger to continue the work, and the emperor approved this act as "even more completely proper." This general unanimity is of course understandable: negotiations were insurance against a possible renewal of hostilities; we need not infer that the court now appreciated the importance of commercial arrangements. To stimulate Chinese activity, Pottinger proposed (to Ch'i-ying) that he come north to Shanghai or Ningpo in order to save Ch'i-ying the trouble of journeying to Canton. In reply Ch'i-ying promised Sir Henry that if he should be commanded to go to Canton he could arrive by the first ten days of May; if another were appointed, such an official could arrive by the middle ten days of May.[18] This correspondence, presenting these clear alternatives, was then presented by Ch'i-ying to the emperor, with the observation that trouble might arise, and decisions could really be made only at Canton. Should he go there? [19] (At about the same time he was flatly assuring Pottinger that he would be appointed I-li-pu's successor.)[20] The correspondence was seen by the emperor on April 6 and Ch'i-ying became imperial commissioner by an edict of the same date.[21] On April 11 he received his orders to proceed to Canton; on April 17 he left Nanking, and en route to Kiangsi he received from Canton both the commissioner's seal and the news that the British had been pacified by the mere word of his coming.[22]

The friendship policy in action. Three weeks before Ch'i-ying's arrival at Canton his chief subordinates, Hsien-ling and Huang En-t'ung, on May 11, 1843, had set a precedent by visiting the barbarian establishment at Hongkong. There they stayed an entire week, during which they were made familiar with Pottinger's proposals for the tariff, "so that they will be ready to communicate their opinions to Keying as soon as he comes." [23] They lived in the best houses obtainable, were given the use of carriages on the island and were taken around it in an iron steamer. They saw the 98th regiment under arms, lunched with the officers, watched artillery practice, visited the charity hospital and the Morrison Educational Society, and in general appeared much impressed with British "power, customs, and character." [24] On their return in a British steamer to Whampoa, the chief interpreter, J. R. Morrison, accompanied them to explain further aspects of the tariff.

In continuation of this policy, Ch'i-ying himself visited Hongkong, after arriving at Canton on June 4. This was the high point of the year's negotiations. It resulted in the speedy settlement of the tariff and general regulations of trade and throws much light on Ch'i-ying's technique for the management of barbarians.[25]

On June 23, he and his suite were brought from Whampoa at his own request in two British gunboats. They were saluted and escorted by a band to two of the best houses on the island. Early the next morning Pottinger called. Ch'i-ying "embraced me with all the warmth and sincerity of an old friend and was even visibly affected by the strength of his emotion at our meeting again." He praised the gunboat *Akbar* and its captain and "laughingly hinted at applying to me for one to carry him back to his government at Nanking." The festivities of the next five days centered about the imperial commissioner. Ratifications of the treaty of Nanking were exchanged on June 26, and tariff negotiations were continued by Morrison and Huang. Meanwhile Ch'i-ying was shown the sights; he visited the admiral's flagship, received the calls of the British officials, and was the life and soul of every banquet.[b] Supported by his suite, he sang operatic airs, played "guess-fingers," drank everyone's health, and overwhelmed Sir Henry with spontaneous expressions of irrepressible affection.

The latter recounted them with a pleasure not unmixed with amazement. Seeing a miniature of Pottinger's family, for example, Ch'i-ying explained that, having no son himself, he wished to adopt Sir Henry's eldest boy. On being told that the boy must first finish his education in England, Ch'i-ying replied, "Very well, he is my adopted son from this day"; henceforth his name should be "Frederick Keying Pottinger." Having obtained the son's miniature, he then made bold to ask for that of his mother and offered a portrait of his own wife in exchange. After some hesitation Sir Henry gave up Lady Pottinger's picture also. Ch'i-ying received it in elaborate Manchu fashion and ordered it borne home in his chair of state. Next he gave Pottinger a gold bracelet, receiving in return a sword and belt brought specially from England. Finally Ch'i-ying declared that in three or four years he expected to go to Peking, when he would send for Sir Henry and the emperor would give him a double-eyed peacock feather — so great was Sir Henry's reputation in all of China. Meantime they must correspond regularly.

Pottinger wrote to Lord Aberdeen, with a touch of awe, that the visit of Ch'i-ying had "thrown a perfectly new light on the character and habits" of the Chinese authorities. Ch'i-ying himself, in his detailed report to the emperor, explained that the picture of Lady Pottinger had been pressed

[b] Lord Saltoun recorded that the visitors "did very well with the soup and fish, but when it came to the meat, they could not use the knife, so we cut it up into small pieces for them, I feeding the Tartar [Hsien-ling] as if he had been a tame sparrow." [26]

upon him: "the English barbarians think much of women and little of men," and "the barbarian chiefs who understood Chinese" had all assured him that such gifts were a mark of "sincere regard and respectful confidence." In general Ch'i-ying argued as he had done on previous occasions that his condescension had been necessary to remove suspicion; as in their interviews with the barbarians at Nanking, he and his small suite had worn informal dress. His memorial belittled the significance of the occasion.[27]

It need hardly be remarked that Manchu officials were normally capable, and in the habit, of suppressing their emotions. The imperial commissioner's histrionics — his parting from bluff Sir Henry with tears in his eyes, pressing him "long and fervidly" to his breast — must be regarded as part of a settled policy, evidence of which is visible throughout 1843. For example, it was after Ch'i-ying's appointment to Canton that the Chinese negotiator had begun to send private and personal notes to Pottinger. In May a letter of Huang's begins, "When I received your fragrant words I thought that I was in your sweet presence," an hyperbole typical of Chinese personal letters but not of state papers. Ch'i-ying sought to carry this intimacy into the barbarian tongue by asking Morrison how to express in English the idea of a close or familiar friend. Morrison suggested the word "intimate," which Ch'i-ying thereafter used in private letters to Pottinger, writing as a transliteration four Chinese characters, devoid of meaning but sounding *yin-ti-mi-t'e*.[c] The spirit of this approach was immanent in the imperial commissioner's parting letter to Sir Henry, written after the conclusion of the Supplementary treaty of October 8, 1843, in which he asked him to take China's part vis-a-vis other Western powers.[d]

This policy had the effect of making the imperial commissioner highly coöperative in the settlement of many disputed points. There are numerous examples to justify the unanimous testimony of the British negotiators as to his "reasonableness." Yet there is no indication that Ch'i-ying could profit personally in most of these cases, and it is plain that they seldom re-

[c] "I respectfully hope that my 'intimate friend' may be happy and in prosperity.

"When I was lately at Hongkong, you honored me with a large measure of your valuable friendship, and at the same time bestowed upon me a precious sword, which whenever I gird it on, inspires me with the idea that you are by my side. As we shook hands and parted in a hurried manner, I could not repress my anxious thoughts regarding you; and I was just proposing to write you a letter to thank you for all your kindness, when on the instant, I received your note, which seemed as if we were talking face to face. At the same time you address me in words of truth and sincerity and require equal truth and sincerity on my part; by this it may be seen that we two men have alike our hearts pointing to our country's good; surely the Supreme Ruler must look down and behold our faithfulness and truth! Doubtless our two countries will now enjoy the blessings of peace for ten thousand years!

"Mr. Woosnam's [the British doctor's] cutaneous medicine is most efficacious. . . . Do not, I pray you, indulge in any anxiety on my account. . . ."[28]

[d] "We two have now been engaged in the same work for upward of a year, and have alone been known to each other as men whose hearts are entirely devoted to their country; thus actuated by no selfish motives, influenced by no wish to deceive, in speaking or transacting business, our hearts appear to be stamped with each other's impress, so that there is nothing which we may not consult about; in fine, it may be said of us, tho' our persons seem *two*, yet our hearts are absolutely as *one*.

dounded to China's advantage from an economic point of view. (A sound economist, which Ch'i-ying was not, could hardly have subscribed to such things as the treaty tariff.) The inference seems logical that his coöperation was a political move, to keep the British in a good humor — not merely a passive measure of defense to ward off barbarian ire, but also a positive part of his general program to capture the friendship of Sir Henry and his colleagues and by trifling favors of trade bring them into a kind of psychological subjection. This was a traditional Chinese technique toward the barbarians.

This policy of personal friendship, while it contributed to the elimination of friction at the time, was fruitless in the long run. There is no evidence that Pottinger ever modified his instructions in China's favor.[e] Versed

---

"The great business of commercial intercourse being now for the most part arranged and settled, I ought immediately to return to Kiangnan, where the commercial affairs of Shanghai will come within my superintendence: the time of parting is at hand, and I know not in what year or in what spot, I may again have the pleasure of meeting you face to face, the thought of which is almost insupportable; but what concerns our country, is of the utmost importance, and we may not, for any dislike to part, loiter in the slightest degree in the discharge of our duty, which might cause people to remark, that our sense of the public good had been sacrificed to feelings of private friendship. I shall therefore take certain parting words, and without reference to good arrangement, write them out one by one as they come uppermost in my heart. —

"First — I beg to present you with a trifle at parting; it is however the choicest production of our Northern Regions (i.e., ginseng) and will suffice to manifest the strength of our attachment to each other and afterwards, looking at this trifling present will be as looking upon him who gave it; when we have parted you will think of me, and that will be some small consolation.

"Secondly — The climate in these seas, now hot, now cold, is most variable; you are a single individual from whom many most important duties are required; you must therefore from the time of rising till going to rest, be attentive to your comfort, be more guarded in your diet and particularly careful in all that concerns you. This is most important.

"Thirdly — After that we shall have shaken hands and parted, you must write to me frequently through the Consul at Shanghai, who will give your letters to the resident Taotai to forward; in your letters you will tell me all the news after parting, and, in like manner, my replies will be sent through the consul at Shanghai.

"Fourthly — Kiangnan is a long way distant from Canton; if anything should happen which I cannot promptly attend to as if on the spot, you must make allowance for my distance; indeed, there is almost no need to mention this. *Also in the case of foreign nations; if they have any differences of opinion with us (or if their ideas of right and wrong jar with ours) I hope that you will act the part of peacemaker, and set the matter at rest* [italics added], thus avoiding the evil of losing *that* while we are taking care of *this* (i.e., of making enemies of one country, while we are trying to conciliate another country). By acting in this way it will show that we two men consider all hostile boundaries as broken down (i.e., that our two countries form as it were but one large family). I do most urgently enjoin this upon you.

"Fifthly — If there is anything that you may have forgotten to tell me, or I may have forgotten to tell you, let either party, at any time, or at all times, immediately address the other a letter, without any ceremony.

"Sixthly — If you should have a favor for any of the productions of our northern regions whether articles of food, or clothing, or anything else, just send me a letter and let me know and they will be immediately sent to you; you must not look upon me as a stranger, or in any way different from yourself." [29]

[e] Pottinger was not a little impressed by his own remarkable success in making friends in China. In December 1842 he wrote to the foreign secretary:

"The most gratifying and important part of Mr. Thom's [see Ch. 8] letter, however, is that H. I. Majesty has recently given express orders that all documents coming from me (The Barbarian Eye Pottinger) shall be presented to H. M. for perusal without a letter being changed, — a command which I look upon to be so pregnant with benefit to the lasting friendship and amicable relations of the Governments of England and China, that it affords me unfeigned gratification to make it known to Her Majesty's Government. Mr. Thom adds — The Emperor has accustomed himself to them (my Papers) like physics, and that some of my statements have already caused

neither in economics nor in Western law, the Manchu administration hardly realized what it gave away.

In November 1844, at the height of his success, Ch'i-ying summarized to the emperor his methods of dealing with the barbarians. This was the famous memorial which the British years later discovered at Canton and with which they laughed the aged diplomat into his grave when he tried again to save the dynasty, and himself, in 1858. His conclusion was that, "with this type of people from outside the bounds of civilization . . . if we adhered to the proper forms in official documents and let them be weighed according to the status of superior and inferior . . . truly it would be of no advantage in the essential business of subduing and conciliating them. To fight with them over empty names and get no substantial result would not be so good as to pass over these small matters and achieve our larger scheme."[31] Unfortunately this general approach, which might have got results with a border tribe, left Her Majesty's Government unaffected.

---

the downfall and degradation of Yih-shan (the late Imperial Commissioner at Canton), and Yih-king, (the "Terror Inspiring General and Imperial Commissioner in Chekiang.")[30]

CHAPTER VIII

THE TREATY SETTLEMENT OF 1843

In the opening of China to the West the "unequal treaties" have been the subject of much praise and blame, as symbols and safeguards of a politico-legal system in turn admired by old China hands and denounced by young Chinese patriots. In this chapter we are concerned primarily with the mechanisms which the first British treaties created for the expansion of foreign trade with China. Each of these arrangements — the low treaty tariff, the status of Hongkong as a free British port, all the terms and procedures by which Sino-foreign commerce was to be conducted — were expressions of a new order imposed upon the Chinese empire by British power. Yet these treaty provisions, by and large, were compromises. British desires had to be modified in the course of being realized. Sir Henry Pottinger finally settled for what was feasible, taking into account the inertia of old custom in the China trade and particularly the limitations of British capability. The drawing up and carrying out of the treaties required much thought and effort on the part of both parties, not of the British alone. This may be seen in the year-long negotiations which produced the treaty tariff and general regulations of July 22, 1843, and the Supplementary treaty of October 8.

The treaty tariff versus transit taxes. From the first there were seen to be two aspects to the problem of taxing China's foreign trade. It could be done by customs duties levied at the ports. It could also be done by transit duties levied on goods passing through the interior to and from the ports. In 1843 only the first of these forms of taxation was really fixed within statutory limits and the second was left uncertain, to haunt the minds of an entire generation of treaty-port consuls. By 1852 the Shanghai consul could see an entire "custom house cordon . . . like a wall of brass across our path."[1] Most of it was imaginary.

At Nanking Pottinger had got it accepted in principle that the Cohong should be abolished and a single revised tariff be published for all the new ports. It took many months for Peking to accept this idea, but there was never much doubt that it would have to do so. Transit duties were a different matter. Pottinger clearly foresaw that a low treaty-port tariff could be nullified by inland exactions. Yet he felt it unwise to demand a lowering of transit duty rates, since such dictation in China's internal affairs could not be easily enforced. He felt the best course was to forestall any raising of the moderate rates then prevailing. But the actual scale of these rates was not known. Pottinger's demands at Nanking had therefore included a transit duty clause that "British merchandise having once paid the Import Duties on entering any of the above mentioned Ports are to be allowed to pass to any part of the Empire on a further payment of moderate Transit Duties which shall not under any circumstances exceed —— per cent." [2] This demand had been accepted in principle but without specifying a percentage. Sir Henry had thereupon suggested how this duty might be administered, preferably at the treaty port in the case of imports: "The goods might be stamped, or furnished with a certificate showing their quality, quantity, etc., and exempting them from further demands." This plan foreshadowed the eventual transit-pass system set up in 1858; but in 1842 it was vitiated by the blank space left in article X of the treaty of Nanking, which stated that the transit duties "shall not exceed —— per cent on the tariff value." This anomaly was noted by the Foreign Office and Pottinger was instructed either to insert in the ratified copy of the treaty the words "a moderate rate," rather than leave it blank; or he might sign with the Chinese a special declaration respecting transit duties, for which the Foreign Office sent him a draft form.[3]

Meanwhile, unknown to Pottinger, Chinese officials had been considering the question of transit taxes, led by the Shantung censor, Lei I-hsien. This was the fiscal specialist who, a decade later, was to introduce the famous likin tax which bolstered the imperial finances during the Taiping Rebellion and hampered China's domestic trade for a lifetime thereafter.[4] His proposals in October 1842 were logical and yet somehow academic, and are worth noting as an example of the best economic thought of the period.[5] To begin with, Lei asserted the prime importance of customs duties as a source of revenue. Foreign purchases of tea, rhubarb,[6] and silk totalled annually, he declared, some fifty or sixty million silver dollars; [7] and the barbarians had caused trouble not because of reckless greed but in order to get a grip on these economic interests (this was a note seldom struck by memorialists of this period). Though now pacified, they must be paid more than Tls. 20,000,000, as specified at Nanking. But in the present state of the country the utmost exertion would not suffice to raise this sum from contributions; hence it was all the more necessary to find a way of getting it from the customs.

Lei I-hsien then speculated rather naively upon the method of taxation to be adopted at the treaty ports. If the Chinese authorities levied duties, he wrote, the barbarians might do so too, but this would be too much for the merchants to bear. If the barbarians levied customs duties, then the Chinese authorities could not levy an additional duty — and this would let the barbarians grow steadily richer and the authorities poorer. If the barbarians permitted the payment of duties to the Chinese authorities (as was the British intention throughout), there would be unforeseen difficulties over the question whether to pay duties in silver or in opium (*sic*), and over the evasion of duties (as was later actually the case). Lei therefore proposed that an increased levy of duties be considered at (1) areas of tea, rhubarb, and silk production, (2) customhouses passed by such goods en route to the ports, and (3) warehouses of licensed brokers where the goods were stored. Thus the Chinese authorities would tax the Chinese merchants, these would raise their prices accordingly, and the foreign merchants in the end would repay to the Chinese government the indemnity exacted from it. Against the objection that this increase might lead to trouble, Lei adduced the confidence which the barbarians had long placed in the good faith of the hong merchants; nor could foreigners penetrate the interior, and there the Chinese merchants could be told to recoup themselves from the barbarians.

This proposal for transit taxes appealed to the emperor as "not without discrimination" (*pu-wei wu-chien*). It was passed on to Ch'i-ying, who agreed in December: "for the barbarians there should be no appearance of added duties, but for the customs duties there should be the reality of an increase." I-li-pu was told to investigate the possibilities,[8] and so, even before they met with the British to discuss the treaty tariff, the Manchu negotiators had agreed to increase the inland transit taxes. Their object, it should be noted, was merely to maintain the existing transit duty revenue, which otherwise would be reduced by the shorter haul from the areas of production which were nearer to the new ports than to Canton.

When the negotiations began about January 23, 1843, transit duties were at once taken up by Huang En-t'ung, who made the straightforward proposal that the customs tariff at the new treaty ports should be raised slightly to make up for the expected falling off in inland taxes on the old route to Canton. I-li-pu also made the rather broad promise that such taxes would "on no account be permitted to impede internal communication or consumption." But Pottinger was adamant in oppositon to higher rates of any kind and offered to demonstrate that there would be a great increase in collections of both the maritime customs and the inland transit duties.[9]

The misunderstanding here seems to have lain in the fact that Pottinger foresaw a great increase in trade and therefore in the Chinese revenue, while the Chinese officials regarded the foreign trade as a fixed quantity which would now be dissipated among five ports instead of being concentrated at one. Huang and his colleagues decided that coöperation on this point was hopeless, and the data on transit duty tariffs which had been promised to Pottinger were not delivered before the conclusion of the treaty settlement.[10] When the maritime customs tariff was finally completed in the summer of 1843 Pottinger decided to wait no longer regarding transit dues. On June 26 he signed with Ch'i-ying the innocuous declaration which had been drafted by the Foreign Office, that transit duties "shall not exceed the present rates which are upon a moderate scale." [11] Meanwhile the Chinese government took unilateral action, as of course it had every right to do, and as will be described below (Chapter 16). British efforts to prevent the inland taxation of foreign trade had been a complete failure.

The tariff negotiations. When it came to the treaty port tariff Pottinger felt himself on firmer ground.[12] The foreign merchants naturally desired a low scale of duties, but the British officials had a double criterion: the Chinese tariff must be low enough to make evasion unprofitable, yet high enough to support an efficient customs collectorate. From their experience in England the British government were well aware that high duties provoked evasion. Conversely, because of their ignorance of China, they were perhaps too ready to disregard the interests of the Hoppo, of the hong merchants, and of the customhouse underlings who profited from unofficial charges not included in the tariff. Would rates low enough to suit the British actually be high enough to satisfy the Canton community? How far such local interests should be regarded was the real problem of the tariff negotiations.

The problem was complicated by the fact that the officials of both sides were in the dark as to the amounts actually levied on the Canton trade.[13] In January 1843 I-li-pu stated that he had asked the hong merchants for a complete return of all fees and charges, but, if he got it, he never produced it for British inspection. A committee of British merchants which had met at Pottinger's request under the chairmanship of Alexander Matheson, when asked for a similar statement, failed after ten days of "the most diligent inquiry" to secure a complete list of duties, which were "believed frequently even to have differed at the same time in different hongs" — a logical result of the fact that the hong merchants paid them.[14] In short, the chief object of attack, the Cohong, held the whip hand because of their unique knowledge of the trade. Their leader, the aged Howqua, who died on September 3, 1843, was violently opposed to the new treaty regulations.[15] Meanwhile his son, Howqua IV (Wu Ch'ung-yueh), had been designated by the Canton authorities as early as July 1842 to assist in the treaty negotiations [16] and was no doubt active behind the scenes. Both the Hoppo and the Kwangtung provincial treasurer, the two officials in closest touch with the trade, took little formal part in the negotiations, the ancient "Canton interest" evidently being highly suspicious of the Manchu negotiators sent from Peking. At the beginning of March 1843, I'li-pu submitted a plan for duties with a scale so high that the British interpreters declared Pottinger never would accept it; they were told that the imperial commissioner had been "obliged to shape *his* ideas according to those of the Hoppo and local Officers, that he was quite aware some of them were impracticable, and you might abrogate them or amend them in any way you please."[17] From Nanking Ch'i-ying had also indicated his awareness of the difficulty: he explained to the emperor that all the British wanted was to get rid of the accumulated malpractices at Canton; but I-li-pu could only work out the general principles, for he was new to Canton and could not himself superintend the details; Ch'i-ying had therefore corresponded with Pottinger and sent an able subordinate from Nanking to keep himself informed of the situation.[18]

During the pause in negotiations which followed the death of I-li-pu on March 4, 1843, goods from England had continued to arrive and the trade at Canton had suffered from the confusion of an interregnum. Ch'i-ying therefore joined in urging a speedy settlement of the new tariff system,[19] and Morrison secured from the Hoppo some ten or twenty passes under which vessels might ply between Canton and Hongkong.[20] By the time Ch'i-ying came to Hongkong in June to exchange ratifications of the treaty of Nanking, both sides were under severe pressure to finish the tariff.

Pottinger had been resolved to prove "that England has no intention of asking anything . . . that shall not be mutually beneficial to both Empires," and Morrison described the Chinese negotiators as "perfectly satisfied" that Sir Henry's scale of duties would be on liberal terms.[21] Nevertheless, the actual drawing up of the tariff was entrusted to Jardine's former piece-goods man, Robert Thom, who had been brought out by the firm in 1833 and had learned some Chinese in his spare time, before becoming one of Her Majesty's interpreters. The scale of duties which Thom drew up was "in almost every instance . . . more advantageous to the importer than even the merchants themselves" had dared to suggest, so that Pottinger feared Chinese objections and authorized a small increase if necessary. ("But of course unless the Chinese do start objections there will be no occasion to allude to my sentiments.") Similarly on exports "the rates proposed by Mr. Thom are considerably lower than those of the merchants," so much so that Sir Henry again authorized an increase, if it should be made necessary by Chinese obstinacy.[22]

Thus prepared, Messrs. Thom, Morrison, and Malcolm, Pottinger's aide, followed Ch'i-ying to Canton on June 30.[23] By July 9, 1843, Ch'i-ying and his colleagues, including the Hoppo, had agreed to the tariff, apparently with compromises on both sides. Pending its necessary formal publication by the Board of Revenue, they also agreed to open the port of Canton to trade under its terms on July 27, a consummation for which some thirty British ships were already waiting.[24] The English version of the tariff was published at Hongkong on July 22.

The trade regulations. Meanwhile, as a further element in the new system, the "General Regulations under which the British Trade is to be conducted at the Five Ports" were also published at Hongkong on July 22, 1843. They outlined the procedure to be followed from the time a merchant ship reached the coast of China until its return cargo was purchased and taken away. Like the tariff, they were largely a British creation, the Manchu-Chinese authorities confining themselves to the protection of the emperor's interests rather than those of Canton. For instance, they had tried to preserve the old system of measurement fees, but capitulated in the face of Thom's explanations of British tonnage registration. When confronted by Chinese objections, the British gave up provisions for erecting hospitals or stationing subordinate consular officers on shore at ship anchorages like Whampoa, and allowing them to exercise judicial functions.

Finally Morrison's first draft of the regulations, in thirteen articles, was rewritten by Thom and submitted to the Chinese authorities, who found the Chinese version "in some parts wanting in perspicuity" and sometimes incomprehensible, and so rewrote the thirteen articles with minor changes to form sixteen. This Chinese version having been translated back into English, Thom drew up a commentary either agreeing or objecting to each article, and on the basis of these papers, which Morrison and Thom brought back from Canton, Pottinger penned some "Remarks." On July 15 he wrote Ch'i-ying enclosing fifteen regulations as finally amended, which Ch'i-ying at once submitted to Peking.[25]

In effect, besides providing for extensive consular supervision and protection of the British merchants, the general regulations of trade struck a heavy blow at the miscellaneous charges and commissions by which the customhouse underlings had formerly been supported. So far as possible the customs subordinates were to be prevented from profiting even indirectly from pilots' fees, or from the stationing of customs guards on foreign vessels, or from an official monopoly of cargo lighters, or from measurement or port fees other than the moderate tonnage duties of five mace (Tls. 0.5) per register ton. Charges for differences in measurements of weight or for the assay of silver or its transportation or smelting were also to be eliminated. Meanwhile the perquisites of the Hoppo were seriously jeopardized.

Only two clauses in the general regulations appear to have been inserted at the request of the Chinese authorities, and each illustrates the confusion which attended the negotiations. The first concerned debts due by Chinese to foreign merchants, which had accumulated in spite of official prohibitions because many Chinese had operated on borrowed foreign capital. As a result of various bankruptcies, three million dollars had been demanded at Nanking on account of hong debts. With this in mind, the imperial government had from the first shown a lively interest in avoiding official responsibility for the future.[26] In January 1843 I-li-pu and his colleagues had hopefully proposed that debts be prevented thereafter by requiring that ready cash or ready produce be paid immediately for all goods exchanged in Sino-British trade. All sums lent or borrowed should be confiscated.[27] Pottinger had rebuffed this. Such rules were "unknown in the whole universe . . . would render the makers of them the laughing stock of all the world . . . The merchants of both countries are not children who require to be taught how to walk with a gocart and will take care to their own interests." [28] I-li-pu had dropped the subject. As he said,[29] the details of trade were "exceedingly minute and troublesome." [a] Ch'i-ying and Huang now solved the difficulty by adding article IV to the trade regulations, disclaiming any responsibility on the part of the Chinese government or of the Chinese merchants collectively for debts due by Chinese to British merchants.

The other addition was article XV, which was intended to ensure that the British consul should take the place formerly occupied by the security merchant. Since foreign vessels had been regularly secured by the members of the Cohong in rotation, this was an effort to substitute the consul in part for the Cohong in the Chinese scheme of things. The wording of the regulation has perpetuated among numerous writers the myth that British consuls were themselves to collect the Chinese customs revenue.[31] This was not the case. It is true that in his original demands at Nanking Pottinger had stipulated: "All hong merchants to be abolished and British merchants to trade with whom they like, paying the just dues of the Chinese Government through the Consular officers." [32] But this first bald statement was soon modified. In January 1843 the British idea was that the consul "will on the arrival of a ship at any particular port, see that security is given for the payment of all dues, and he will not restore the manifest and other sailing papers till he is satisfied that everything has been settled, or at least provided for." Pottinger expected consuls "to see that the duties and other charges are regularly paid" [33] but in March he stoutly denied that he meant to make them "personally responsible for the realization of the Chinese duties." [34] By the time he was instructing the first consul at Canton in July 1843 he was ready to brand as "equally erroneous and absurd" the impression that British officers were bound "to supply in some measure the loss of the agency of the abolished hong merchants." [35]

The seeming contradiction in these statements arises from the confusion between the hong merchants, who had done a multitude of things, and the security merchants, who were hong merchants as viewed in only one of

[a] Pottinger himself confessed that questions of trade "are strange to me, owing to my never having had to look much into commercial matters." He reported that I-li-pu and his colleagues at Canton were "confessedly in the dark as to the commonest principles of commerce." Being traditionally omnicompetent, on the basis of a literary training, the Chinese authorities were in fact "utterly ignorant" of such matters as tariffs.[30]

their capacities, namely, that of guaranteeing the payment of foreign customs duties. For the security merchant and his liability to the Chinese government, as a means of ensuring payment, there were now substituted the consul and his instructions from Pottinger to withhold a ship's papers until her duties had been paid. But consular activity was not substituted for all the other traditional duties of the hong merchants, and the problem of consular interference for the prevention of smuggling had not yet assumed its later proportions.

These documents having been submitted to Peking, within a month the ministers of the Grand Council headed by Mu-chang-a memorialized recommending approval of both the tariff and the regulations of trade and the issuance of imperial orders for the opening of the four new ports. Imperial approval was granted on August 16, 1843.[36] Ch'i-ying received it on September 2 and notified the officials at the five ports accordingly.[37]

The Supplementary treaty of 1843. The keystone of the legal arch supporting the new British order was the Supplementary treaty signed by Pottinger and Ch'i-ying on October 8, 1843, at the mouth of the river below Canton and sometimes called for that reason the treaty of the Bogue or of Hoomunchai (*Hu-men-chai*, "the tiger's-mouth narrows," from which the Portuguese had derived the more picturesque Boca Tigre or Bocca Tigris, converted in China coast parlance into Bogue). This document dealt with the most difficult points in the general settlement — the restriction of foreign trade to treaty limits (art. IV), residence and travel at the ports (art. VI, VII), the most favored nation clause (art. VIII), extraterritoriality and the extradition of criminals (art. IX), stationing of gunboats at the ports (art. X), rendition of the islands of Chusan and Kulangsu after payment of the indemnity (art. XI), prevention of smuggling (art. XII), the status of Hongkong (art. XIII–XVI), and the local Hongkong-Canton trade in lorchas and small craft (art. XVII). On the enforcement of these crucial provisions hinged the success of the treaty of Nanking.

It is consequently of some interest to see how this treaty was actually negotiated. The hardest problems having been left till the last, they ought naturally to have received the best attention of the British government. But unluckily the summer climate of South China played havoc with the overworked British staff. Pottinger was in poor health. His chief interpreter, John Robert Morrison, died at the age of twenty-eight after nine days' illness on August 29, 1843,[38] the anniversary of the treaty in negotiating which he had played so large a part at Nanking. Morrison had combined an unusual knowledge of the Chinese language and people with an understanding of trade and diplomacy. There is little doubt that he would have risen to the top in the British service in the Far East, and his loss was a very serious blow. His death occurred, like that of his father who had been interpreter to Lord Napier, as a result of overwork during a critical period. It left Pottinger dependent upon Jardine's former piece-goods man, Robert Thom, an amiable but much less able individual who, in September 1843, was himself "a severe sufferer from fever and ague." [39]

The drawing up of the treaty got under way after the settlement of the tariff and general regulations, when Ch'i-ying on July 25 sent Pottinger a list of the points proposed at Nanking for inclusion in the later agreement. Sir Henry made a rough draft and on August 10 hoped "in two or three days" to send it back. About the middle of the month he had given it to Morrison to translate into Chinese, but the latter died without beginning the task. At Ch'i-ying's request [40] Thom was finally sent to Canton on September 4 for that purpose, while Pottinger remained in communication with him from Macao. At Canton, in the midst of his chills and fever, Thom "gave every day's work to the Mandarin Wootinghien" (Wu T'ing-hsien),[41] whom Ch'i-ying had detailed to assist him. According to Thom's later testimony, Wu after a few days "brought me back the Supplementary Treaty entirely rewritten in the form of a pamphlet with a remark that my translation had been found exceeding harsh and stiff and that H. E. Hwang [Huang En-t'ung] had been at the trouble of writing it over again in more idiomatic Chinese." When informed of this, Pottinger typically remarked that "it did not matter to him what Chinese the treaty was written in so long as the spirit and meaning of his original were truly represented; that they might keep their Chinese and he would keep his English, etc." Thom proceeded to retranslate Huang's version back into English, and at length early in October the British negotiators met at Macao and compared Pottinger's original with Thom's retranslation. After making a few minor changes they had the respective English and Chinese versions fair-copied and bound together; "but I do not remember," wrote Thom, "any comparison between the English and Chinese after this; indeed I was without a colleague or fellow student to assist me and stood entirely alone in my department, a circumstance which I much regretted at the time." [42]

The identity of the English and Chinese texts of the treaty in this way came to depend upon one man, who was none too well and who, although he published about this time a Chinese-English vocabulary for use at the northern ports,[43] was certainly no sinologue. It is not surprising, therefore, that the Chinese text was later found to contain a few key points which were not in the English text.

Ch'i-ying opposed any formal ratification of the treaty on various ingenious grounds — that it impugned the validity of the first treaty, or that once ratified it could never be changed [44] — but Pottinger demanded the imperial assent, which was granted on November 15, 1843.[45] After Huang had refused to bring the ratified copy to Hongkong, H.M.S. *Proserpine* went to Canton to get it in December. The other copy which had meantime been sent to England was anxiously awaited there, since Pottinger had been too rushed even to send the Foreign Office a summary of its contents. When the two versions — ratified by the queen and the emperor, respectively — were compared in London, discrepancies were discovered in their English wording.[46] This was only a foretaste of the English-Chinese discrepancies which will be noted below. The treaty was formally proclaimed at Hongkong on July 10, 1844.[47]

The commercial status of Hongkong. Fully one quarter of the new document (articles XIII through XVI and part of XVII) referred to Hongkong and the problems raised by the establishment of this crown colony on the Chinese coast. The idea of an island base in Chinese waters was an old one which had been mooted by the East India Company almost a century before. The deep-water harbor of Hongkong, protected against typhoons and accessible from both ends, had early attracted the notice of mariners.[48] At the beginning of the war, in February 1840, Palmerston had demanded the island as "a place of residence and of commerce." [49] A year later in the abortive Chuenpi convention Captain Elliot had begun to arrange for its cession to Britain and (somewhat contrarily) the establishment of a Chinese customhouse on it.

In 1842 Pottinger had inherited Hongkong as a base of operations. British merchants had begun building there without waiting for the confirmation of British sovereignty. But Palmerston's successor as foreign secretary, Lord Aberdeen, did not regard the island "in the light of a permanent conquest," foreseeing that its possession would be "attended with great and certain expense," and involve political complications with the Chinese.[50] In obtaining it at Nanking, Pottinger was therefore obliged to exceed his instructions. His original demand there had been for the cession of Hongkong "as an atonement for the insult offered [at Canton] to Her Majesty's Crown and Dignity." To save the emperor's face this was changed in the treaty to the euphemistic explanation that British merchants needed some port "whereat they may careen and refit their ships, when required, and keep stores for that purpose. . . ." [51]

Aberdeen acquiesced in Pottinger's *fait accompli* and instructed him, as first governor of the colony, to make it a free port and raise revenue chiefly by leasing the crown lands, although, to be sure, "a duty levied on wines, spirits, opium, and tobacco imported into the island for the use of the inhabitants would, as in other colonies, produce a considerable revenue." The Colonial Office from the first expected the colony to be self-supporting.[52] The mercantile community welcomed it as a protective stronghold and a bit of home, and also as a warehouse where goods could be cheaply stored. During the war, crowded with troops and warships, with merchants from Canton and Chinese purveyors, it was also envisioned as a great commercial center, "the grand emporium of Eastern Asia . . . another Carthage, with a population equal to that of ancient Rome." [53] But in 1843 when the troops departed and commerce returned to its ancient grooves at Canton, the boom collapsed. "The whole trade of Hongkong consisted in transshipping those articles which the smugglers would engage to carry for less than the duty." Even this activity was ruined when the low treaty tariff went into effect in July. "Shipping which used to resort to Hongkong to put two or three cargoes into one bottom for the purpose of lightening the heavy port charges at Canton now proceeded at once to Whampoa." [54] It therefore became one of Pottinger's chief objectives in the Supplementary treaty to nurture the trade of the new colony, particularly the Chinese junk trade from all the ports along the coast.

The argument between the Manchu diplomats and Pottinger over this Chinese trade at Hongkong illustrates very well their respective views of commerce and its regulation in China. The Englishman wanted Hongkong to be a free port, "a sort of bonding warehouse"; duties should not be levied there but at the Chinese port of origin or destination on the mainland. Not comprehending the doctrines of the Manchester School, I-li-pu and his colleagues commended Pottinger's willingness "not to regard his own private interest, or to profit himself." But to them free trade meant lawlessness. "Hongkong is surrounded by water on all sides, boats of every description may touch at every place . . . unprincipled native merchants may induce the English merchants to carry on a smuggling trade." [55]

To the British plenipotentiary this view was "inexplicable. . . . The very fact of Hongkong being surrounded by water is the surest preventive against smuggling since no articles can reach it . . . or be carried from it to the mainland without the duties being paid on them, unless indeed the Chinese custom house officers fail in their duty and connive" at smuggling.[56] This righteous statement implies that Sir Henry either was so ingenuous as to suppose that such connivance was unlikely, or was content to let it occur so long as it cast no reflection on the British name. His remark that the Chinese revenue could not be injured "so long as the Chinese custom house officers are men of honesty and integrity" must probably be set down as a failure in understanding of Chinese revenue personnel problems.

Ch'i-ying tried another tack in June 1843, proposing that Chinese trade with Hongkong be allowed under a system of passes. When Pottinger, in the spirit of laisser-faire, asked him to proclaim unrestricted trade between Hongkong and all the ports of China (not merely treaty ports), Ch'i-ying did so readily enough but added the clause that Chinese merchants were to report at the customs and pay Chinese tariff duties, "obtaining a pass before they quit port to commence their traffic. Any who may dare to go and trade without having requested such a pass, on discovery, shall be dealt with as offenders." [57] This meant that by withholding passes the Chinese customhouses could, in practice, choke off the Chinese junk trade with Hongkong.[b]

In the end Ch'i-ying secured the insertion in the treaty of the famous thirteenth article, the English and Chinese versions of which may be compared as follows:

TABLE 3. ARTICLE XIII OF THE SUPPLEMENTARY TREATY (OCTOBER 8, 1843)

British version	*Chinese version* (translated)
All persons whether Natives of China, or otherwise, who may wish to convey Goods from any one of the five Ports of Canton, Fuchowfoo, Amoy, Ningpo and Shanghai to Hong Kong for sale or consumption, shall be at full and perfect liberty to do so on paying the duties on such Goods and obtaining a Pass or Port Clearance from the Chinese Custom House at one of the said Ports. Should Natives of China wish to repair to Hong Kong to purchase Goods, they shall have free and full permission to do so, and should they require a Chinese Vessel to carry away their purchases, they must obtain a Pass or Port clearance, for her at the Custom House of the Port whence the Vessel may sail for Hong Kong. It is further settled, that in all cases these Passes are to be returned to the Officers of the Chinese Government, as soon as the trip for which they may be granted shall be completed.	Hereafter all such persons as Chinese merchants who desire to convey goods to Hongkong for sale shall first at the various customhouses of Canton, Foochow, Amoy, Ningpo, and Shanghai, according to the new regulations pay the customs duties, (whereupon) the superintendent of customs will issue a pass to enable them to proceed without hindrance. If there are Chinese merchants who wish to go to Hongkong to deal in produce, it is also permissible that they go to the yamen of the Chinese authorities at Canton, Foochow, Amoy, Ningpo, or Shanghai and ask for a pass (allowing them) to come and go. On the day when they bring their goods into port, the duties shall be paid. But Chinese merchants from the time when they have bought their produce must make use of Chinese vessels on which to lade it and bring it back. There shall be no distinction between these Chinese vessels asking for a pass at Hongkong in order to leave the port, and their being given a pass at the various ports of Canton, Foochow, Amoy, Ningpo, and Shanghai in order to go to Hongkong. All merchant vessels and merchants which have received this type of pass, each time they come or go, must take the pass originally received and present it to the Chinese officials to facilitate their examination and prevent the rise of evils of false representation. As to the various other provinces and places in the four provinces of Kwangtung, Fukien, Kiangsu, and Chekiang such as Chapu, none of them are places for trade. It is not permitted that Chinese merchants unauthorizedly request passes for intercourse with Hongkong. And the sub-district magistrate of Kowloon is charged with the responsibility in conjunction with the English officials from time to time to make an investigation and report to the higher authorities.[59]

[b] The reasoning of the Chinese authorities on this score was garrulously recorded by Robert Thom as follows: "After having been urged repeatedly to throw open the whole coast to our colony of Hong Kong, they answered, that Hong Kong had certainly been ceded to the British

Both the clause of the Chinese version which required the use of Chinese vessels only, and the last three sentences, which effectively cut off all the coast of China except the treaty ports, were apparently quite unknown to Pottinger in 1843. He believed that the article was "obviously introduced by the Imperial Commissioner with the object of checking smuggling and I was very glad to accede to any plan for doing so." The Foreign Office did not learn of the discrepancy until a year later, in October 1844. When an explanation was demanded, Consul Thom asserted that it was "neither a surreptitious insertion nor a mere overlook" and that, whatever the treaty had said, "the effects upon our Colony would have been exactly the same." [60] His basis for this argument was the phenomenal growth of the carrying trade under the British flag which was already beginning to supplant the junk trade on the China coast.

Meanwhile the Canton consular records indicate how the pass system of article XIII was used to stifle Chinese trade with Hongkong. When the first British consul, shortly after the conclusion of the treaty, requested passes on behalf of Chinese merchants, the Hoppo quite properly rebuffed him: passes were not the business of the British authorities. Meanwhile such high fees were demanded by the customhouse underlings that Chinese applicants appear to have given up the effort. A year later, in August 1844, a Chinese boatman appealed to the governor of Hongkong who had the Canton consul again request a pass from the Hoppo. In the interests of peace, that official sent a pass good for one trip and promised that his clerks would demand no fees. Later the fee was fixed at two dollars a trip, but few

---

Crown, there it was, we might take it and make what we liked of it, but Hong Kong was not characterized in the Treaty of Nanking as a port of trade . . . They then proceeded in the following strain. How are we to view Hong Kong? Is it part of England? Or is it part of China? We answered, Hong Kong is now an integral part of the British Empire. Upon which they said, if Hong Kong be part of the British Empire, a little England, in short, we must regard it as a foreign country, and must put it on the same footing as all other foreign countries. We can allow Hong Kong to trade at the five ports, but we cannot, we dare not do more. [The Chinese authorities then delicately hinted that if Hongkong were put in the same status as Macao, with a Chinese magistrate and customhouse within its borders. an arrangement might be made; but this the British refused.] Upon the unlimited intercourse of Hong Kong with the coast being again urged, they met it by another argument. We have but lately, they said, been engaged in drawing up a tariff and trading regulations by which the imperial duties are to be fairly paid at the five ports; do you now call upon us to countenance a smuggling depot at the mouth of the Canton River, having for its very object the evading of those duties? Would not that be to . . . nullify our own tariff? When we called their attention to the fact of junks being allowed to trade with other foreign countries, such as Siam, Singapore, Borneo, Manila, Loochoo, Japan, etc., from other than the five ports, from Chaochoufoo in Quangtung, from Chincheu in Fokien, from Taichow and Chapoo in Chekian, etc., and urged that the same privileges might be conceded to Hong Kong, they answered that . . . they did not dare lay such a proposal before the throne, that H. E. Keying would be accused by the opposite party of opening more ports to the foreigners than he was authorized to do by the treaty, that if the English at Hong Kong were permitted to trade with these ports, all other foreign nations would be claiming the same privileges, that such interference with the native trade was a thing not anticipated in the treaty of Nanking, and if this point were to be urged it would unquestionably compromise the Imperial Commissioner Keying and the whole of his party, etc." [58]

From this colloquy and the documents of the time one cannot avoid the conclusion that the Chinese authorities saw more clearly than the British themselves the implications of Hongkong as a point of entrance into the whole Chinese coasting trade in Eastern Asia.

passes appear to have been issued. The original twenty passes which had been issued for supply boats between Canton and Hongkong in March 1843 before the drawing up of article XIII were not renewed a year later, the Hoppo claiming[61] that several of the vessels had been caught smuggling.[c]

British sailing letters. Legal intercourse with Hongkong under the Chinese flag being thus inhibited, it was natural that it should develop under the British flag. The intricate waterways of the Pearl River delta formed a series of connecting links between the metropolis of Canton, its anchorage twelve miles downstream at Whampoa, and the foreign community perched on the outer edge of the delta at Macao; and an incessant stream of small craft — fast-boats, luggers, cutters, lorchas, and passage boats of all sorts — had for centuries plied these waterways to maintain contact between Canton and the sea. The establishment of Hongkong added another focus for this traffic, and article XVII of the Supplementary treaty under the heading, "Additional article relating to British small craft," gave it encouragement to use the British flag through the medium of sailing letters.

As will be noted below (Chapter 17), these documents were a unilateral British invention, sanctioned by the government in England without reference to China. But now by a treaty agreement with the Chinese authorities they were given a special value at Canton. Article XVII concerned only local craft plying between Hongkong, Macao, and Canton, and its original object was not to inject the British flag into the delta traffic but merely to free the British vessels then in service from the payment of heavy tonnage dues every time they went up to Canton. As late as August 1843 British merchants were told that not only would goods sent to Canton in British lorchas have to pay regular duties but that the vessels would have to pay regular tonnage dues of five mace (half a tael) per ton each time they entered. On August 20, however, Pottinger sent Thom the draft of a special article concerning small craft for insertion in the treaty.[62]

In its final form this treaty clause freed from tonnage dues all small

[c] The following data on the trade of Hongkong lorchas at Canton are compiled from the British consulate records: the lorchas averaged about 60 tons each (as compared with some 450 or 500 tons average measurement of British ships at Canton) and carried about 5½ per cent of the British imports into Canton but less of the exports, probably because they took non-taxable supplies to Hongkong more than trade goods.

Table 4: Proportion of Hongkong Registered Lorcha Trade to British International Trade at Canton 1844–47

Year		*British vessels*		*Hongkong lorchas*	
		no.	*tonnage*	*no.*	*tonnage*
1844	imports	206	104,322	96	5,774
1845	"	158	78,823	60	3,508
1846	"	182	85,937	100	5,510
	exports	175	78,374	58	3,450
1847	imports	184	78,763	73	4,285
	exports	176	74,664	66	4,211

British vessels which carried only passengers, letters, and baggage, while vessels carrying dutiable goods and not over 150 tons burthen were to pay at the rate of one mace (one-tenth of a tael) per ton; vessels under 75 tons would be charged for 75 tons, and vessels over 150 tons would be charged the regular rate of five mace per ton. Every such British "schooner, cutter, lorcha, etc.," should have a sailing letter, to be obtained at Hongkong and deposited with the British consul while in the port of Canton.

This article, inserted at the very end of the treaty almost as an afterthought, provided the excuse for the entrance of the British flag into the Chinese coast trade, for which certain Hongkong ordinances later gave a firmer legal basis. The last sentence of the article therefore takes on significance as an index either of Pottinger's lack of imagination or else of Ch'i-ying's foresight: "Fuchow and the other ports having none of this kind of intercourse and none of this kind of small craft, it would be unnecessary to make any arrangements as regards them." Within a few years exactly this type of British craft, with sailing letters from Hongkong, was active along the entire southeast coast.

Chinese in Hongkong. A final question, the control of Chinese residents at Hongkong, was worked out in much the same way as the control of Chinese trade: faced by new problems, the British administrators at first contemplated their solution with the aid of the Chinese government, and then changed their minds. At Nanking and again in February 1843 the Manchu-Chinese negotiators had suggested that the Chinese population of Hongkong should be governed by Chinese law administered by a sub-district magistrate (*Hsun-chien*) stationed at Kowloon. Pottinger acceded to this suggestion in principle. But by the end of March 1843 he argued that the British authorities at Hongkong must have police jurisdiction over Chinese residents merely to keep order. Chinese litigants might apply to the Kowloon magistrate if they liked; "when foreigners are parties in disputes of course the British Officers must in all cases investigate and where the Chinese are found to be in the wrong they will be sent with the evidence to Kowloon to be punished according to the Laws of the Empire."[63] Ch'i Kung, the Kwangtung governor-general, agreed to this after the death of I-li-pu.

This arrangement would have amounted, in effect, to a reciprocal extraterritoriality. It was a logical enough compromise on paper, but would have weakened the enforcement of British law in the island. The British government in London therefore countermanded it. When Ch'i-ying reached Canton in June he was told that the home government had decided that, Hongkong having been ceded, its inhabitants could no longer come under the jurisdiction of China in any way. Ch'i-ying quite rightly found this inconsistent with the earlier agreement. He argued that for the Chinese populace to be unwilling to obey the laws of England was "a thing of the same nature as the refusal of the English merchants and people to be forcibly ruled by the laws of China." The treaty, he contended, had referred to the cession of the ground for British use; it had not provided that the Chinese inhabitants of Hongkong should become British subjects. Since Pottinger had been given "full powers to act and decide according to his own judgment, how can he be ruled from afar by the Ministry of his own country!" Judging by Pottinger's earlier agreements, Ch'i-ying had the better of the debate, which therefore came to an end. Robert Thom summed up the situation in a confidential memorandum: "Jurisdiction at Hongkong — Being now English ground and Sir Henry being Governor of it, he may do with the people on it just as he likes. Keying cannot *put upon paper* any more or other than what he has done. Why have any further correspondence about the matter?"[64]

In practice it was found necessary in April 1844 to ask the governor of Kwangtung to station at Kowloon a magistrate who could coöperate with the Hongkong magistrates in controlling Chinese evildoers coming from the mainland. Governor Ch'eng replied that police officers had already been established at Kowloon for this purpose, although as yet unacquainted with the British authorities.[65] By that time the Chinese authorities had dropped all idea of claiming jurisdiction in Hongkong. By the end of 1844 Governor Davis finally obtained from Ch'i-ying a written acknowledgment of British sovereignty over the whole of the island and its people.[66]

Enforcement of the treaty tariff. In 1843 British hopes were high and great innovations seemed possible. Conscious of his historic role at the meeting point of two civilizations, Pottinger declared "now that peace is made, I consider myself to stand as it were in the light of an Umpire between the Empires. . . . I am resolved that all Commercial arrangements shall be reciprocal as far as it is possible to make them."[67] To this end he sought to ensure to the Chinese government the same moderate revenue from foreign trade which any British government would deem proper. More important, he sought to give the British merchant the security of a printed tariff scrupulously enforced on all competitors alike. To combat the lawlessness which had already accompanied the expansion of trade, he formulated conjugate policies — to throw the burden of preventing the evasion of duties squarely upon the Chinese authorities, on whom in the last analysis it always had to rest, and at the same time to discipline British subjects to the full extent of his powers.

As the year 1843 wore on, however, it became evident that the customhouse at Canton was a chief participant in the smuggling which flourished there. In April tea was being shipped off at a private payment of one tael per picul instead of the reduced Cohong rate of six taels. There was at least one pitched battle on the river when troops of the governor-general and governor attacked a fleet of tea cargo boats guarded by men from the Hoppo's office. British merchants complained of the smuggling openly carried on at the foreign factory stairs along the waterfront, "with the avowed assistance and countenance of the Hoppo and his people." Pottinger responded by writing an open letter to the governor-general, in which he denounced these illegalities and asserted that "the suppression of smuggling must depend on the activity and integrity of the Chinese Custom house officers; . . . neither British officers, nor people, nor vessels, can be employed in it." [68]

On April 15, 1843, Sir Henry also published a proclamation expressing his "unmitigated disapprobation" of British merchants' complicity in an evil which, if continued, would destroy all efforts to put the trade "on a firm, regular, and respectable footing." To the best of his powers he would aid the Chinese in stopping it. Smugglers should expect no shelter at Hongkong. The governor-general's reply made no denial of the facts and asked Pottinger to be "more stringent than ever" in preventing his countrymen from listening to "the seductions of the Hoppo's clerks and followers." For a time the situation improved, but two months later Sir Henry was still outraged "by the public and undisguised system of smuggling, which is not only winked at but encouraged." [69]

In accordance with British principles the general regulations of trade provided in article II that "the Chinese Superintendent of Customs at each port will adopt the means that he may judge most proper to prevent the revenue suffering by fraud or smuggling," and the Supplementary treaty contained under article XII the following forthright provision for what later became known as "Consular interference for the prevention of smuggling in China":

"A fair and regular Tariff of duties and other dues having now been established, it is to be hoped that the system of smuggling which has heretofore been carried on between English and Chinese merchants — in many cases with the open connivance and collusion of the Chinese Custom house officers — will entirely cease: and the most peremptory Proclamation to all English merchants has been already issued on this subject by the British Plenipotentiary, who will also instruct the different Consuls to strictly watch over, and carefully scrutinize the conduct of all persons, being British subjects, trading under his superintendence. In any positive instance of smuggling coming to the Consul's knowledge he will instantly apprize the Chinese authorities of the fact, and they will proceed to seize and confiscate all goods, whatever their value or nature, that may have been so smuggled, and will also be at liberty if they see fit, to prohibit the ship from which the smuggled goods were landed, from trading further, and to send her away, as soon as her accounts are adjusted and paid. The Chinese Government officers will at the same time, adopt whatever measures they may think fit with regard to the Chinese merchants and Custom House officers who may be discovered to be concerned in smuggling."

In later years aggrieved traders interpreted this clause, in the light of consular enforcement of it, to mean that the consuls were made the protectors, and hence, because of Chinese apathy, the sole protectors, of the imperial revenue. This interpretation was then denied by British officials, who argued that the treaty documents did not pledge them "to any crusade against smuggling," but merely provided that "in so far as there is a reserved jurisdiction over British subjects, this privilege" should not handicap necessary Chinese measures to protect the revenue.[70] This is not the only possible interpretation, however, and it must be confessed that in 1843 it could not be foreseen how article XII would work out in practice. It epitomized in a single phrase the impracticability of the treaties when it assumed that, after the consul informed the Chinese authorities, "they will proceed to seize and confiscate."[d] In its application, the British consul's theoretical assistance in the cause of the emperor's "just duties and other dues," soon became actual interference in the private arrangements of the foreign traders and corrupt Chinese authorities, as will appear below (Chapter 20).

The legal settlement of which the Supplementary treaty was the formal conclusion contained numerous other provisions which will be touched upon below, but certain generalizations may be hazarded at this point. The negotiations were, first of all, an education for the authorities of both sides, who had reached the scene largely ignorant of the details of the China trade. In the commercial settlement the advantage was with the British not only because of their military victory but also because they had a clear objective in mind, the expansion of British commerce. Yet Pottinger

[d] On the same day that the general regulations were published, July 22, 1843, the plenipotentiary wrote to Consul Lay at Canton: "Should you obtain positive and incontrovertible proof that any British Merchant ship in the River has been or is, engaged in smuggling or evading the payment of the just dues of the Chinese Government, as laid down in the Tariff and Regulations of Trade, you will take immediate measures for intimating the same to the Chinese High Officers and Officers of Customs, in order that they may, if they think proper, put a stop to such vessel either landing or shipping further cargo as the case may be, and you will likewise apprize the master, owner, or consignee of such ships of the steps you have taken, and will acquaint them, that any attempt to carry on their smuggling practices, or to trade in any shape, in opposition to the wishes and directions of the Chinese authorities, will oblige me to have such ships removed from the River." These instructions were also published in a government notification of the same date.[71]

On January 17, 1844, when he had received word of silk smuggling at Shanghai, Sir Henry wrote to Consul Balfour: "Should you have subsequently obtained any certain information of this disgraceful proceeding I depend on your having scrupulously denounced the parties engaged in it to the Chinese Authorities, and it would afford me great satisfaction to learn that they had not only obliged the vessel receiving the smuggled goods to leave the port, but that they had further refused to admit any vessels belonging to the same persons (or Firm) to entry in future at the Port of Shanghai."[72] Stricter instructions than the above could hardly be desired.

gave up the transit duty problem as hopeless, he failed to perceive the imminent growth of the British coasting trade, and his treatment of the smuggling problem implied some rather naive ideas of mandarin honesty. Ch'i-ying and his colleagues showed an even greater lack of prescience because commercial arrangements in their view were merely a means to the pacification of the barbarians. When they accepted a fixed treaty tariff and the most-favored-nation clause, they were hardly aware of what they were giving away. They affected, at least, to believe that the volume of Sino-foreign trade was a fixed quantity which could not be expected to grow.

Meanwhile Peking lagged far behind the imperial commissioner in its appreciation of the importance of the commercial settlement. Ch'i-ying reported in a memorial received December 1, 1843, that having completed the negotiations at Canton he was coming north again by the Mei-ling pass to Nanking, bringing Hsien-ling with him, in order to arrange matters at Shanghai. He raised the question whether he should not return to Peking for an imperial audience so as to report fully and in person on his arrangements. The emperor, however, took a very different view of the urgency of foreign affairs. Now that Ch'i-ying had returned to his post at Nanking, he was ordered to hand over all unfinished business concerning Canton to the Canton governor-general, Ch'i Kung, who should superintend their management by the Hoppo, Wen-feng, in the usual way. Since the post of Nanking governor-general was an important one, in charge of all post-war reconstruction arrangements and trade matters at Shanghai, Ch'i-ying was ordered to wait one or two years more and then request an imperial audience.[73]

In the end Ch'i-ying's innocence of economics, combined with his shrewdness in the art of personal relations, let him coöperate in the later settlement a good deal more fully than has been realized. Its terms were not dictated. In fact the incapacity of the British at the time left it up to the Chinese negotiators to draft the final Chinese version of the Supplementary treaty.

The sincerity with which both sides attempted to establish a permanent basis for peaceful commerce proved least effective, of course, in the case of opium, for the entire treaty structure remained incomplete so long as it omitted from its purview the major part of the import trade. This has rightly been singled out as the most glaring defect in the first treaty settlement. But further study shows that Pottinger and Ch'i-ying actually did regulate the opium problem in 1843, even though they did not advertise the fact in the treaties.

CHAPTER IX

THE OPIUM SETTLEMENT OF 1843

THE OPIUM TRADE on the China coast a century ago has had the glittering fascination of evil, and much ink was at one time used in moral judgments upon it. There is no question that it was a social evil, like the great contemporary institution of human slavery in the United States of America. But, as with slavery, its economic value for many decades outweighed its moral turpitude. During the middle decades of the nineteenth century as many as 100,000 slaves a year were still being exported from Africa in a smuggling trade which had been contraband in the British empire since 1807.[1] In the case of opium in China the ethical situation was complicated by the facts of Chinese public demand, mercantile coöperation, and official connivance which we have already noted. In examining the settlement of 1843 we are necessarily concerned with the actual function of the drug trade in Sino-foreign relations, not with its ethical status in retrospect.

By 1843 the opium question which faced the British treaty makers was an intensely practical one — not whether to permit the trade but how to regulate it. When persistent efforts failed to secure Chinese legalization, it became even more urgent to work out some form of unofficial regulation, some accepted rules of the game within which the regularity of the trade and the security of its valuable cargoes could be assured. This was accomplished, but not on paper. In the end the various schemes for joint Anglo-Chinese regulation put forward both by Pottinger and by Ch'i-ying could not be worked out. Sir Henry had to arrange his own system of limitations on the opium traffic — not without much hesitation, double talk, and misapprehension in the process.

The British opium establishment. The formidable proportions which the opium trade had already assumed may be seen by another glance at the history of Jardine, Matheson and Company in its decade of growth between 1832 and 1842. In its early days (see Chapter 4) this leading firm had acted in China chiefly as agents for owners of opium in India. They would charge a commission of 3 per cent on sales and 1 per cent on returns, and clear about $20 on each chest sold. This had freed them from the necessity of gambling on the widely fluctuating prices, which in the case of Bengal (Patna) opium varied in the early period all the way from $550 up to $1375 per chest (the price of Malwa was about a third less). The ramifications of the trade can be seen in the fact that these price fluctuations were due to at least five factors: "the amount of Patna and Benares sold at Calcutta, the quantity and quality of Malwa exported from Bombay and Damaun, the stock of both in India and China, the activities of market speculators, and the attitude of the mandarins toward the native dealers." In their expansion after 1832, to which we have already referred, Jardine's had built up a considerable fleet. The *Sylph* with the Rev. Charles Gutzlaff aboard had gone on a six months' exploratory voyage as far north as Tientsin. This unheralded testing of the opium market followed immediately after the better known voyage of the Company's agent, Lindsay, in the *Lord Amherst*, noted above (Chapter 4). By 1836 Jardine's had a fleet of a dozen ships and were using half a dozen small vessels for work on the coast.[2] Their first vessel built to order, the brig *Fairy*, 161 tons, was completed at Liverpool in 1833. In 1835 the firm became sole owners of the early clipper *Red Rover*, 254 tons, which made a record of 18 days from Calcutta to Lintin Island and completed three round trips in one year.[3] In 1834 Jardine's had also led the way in entering the direct tea trade to London, and had become a leading element in the Canton community. During the subsequent crisis at Canton the firm had continued business there through neutral American agents, and on the coast through a partner in Manila.[a] But in this new period, instead of acting as agents and encouraging large sales at low prices as formerly, the firm bet its funds on the continuation of the opium trade and bought opium itself, taking advantage of the cheap market which Commissioner Lin's vigorous action at Canton had temporarily demoralized. As a result of this foresight they were soon able to sell their cheaply bought stocks at virtual monopoly prices with immense profit. Increasingly, through their superior fleet, larger capital, and faster communications they were able to freeze out minor competitors, even by lowering prices if necessary.[b]

[a] Letters of partners and ship captains illustrate the firm's views and arrangements. Thus the firm wrote on October 16, 1839: "We shall modify the arrangements of our firm so as to prevent our drug operations at Manila being interfered with by Captain Elliot's views, should they be carried into effect — which however we much doubt. We cannot believe that the British Government will adopt the novel and unheard of principle of acting against its own subjects to enforce the fiscal regulations of a foreign power; unless far larger concessions can be got from the Chinese than have yet been thought of . . . ."[4]

[b] "The plan we adopt is to credit them [i.e., the firm's constituents] at the period of its dispatch [i.e., of opium from Manila] with a net sum regulated by our opinion of what the state of the market on the coast will enable us to obtain for it, after deducting the charges incurred by our numerous flotilla, and a reasonable allowance for the heavy risks of all kinds run by ourselves and our commanders . . . .

"Our sales will in general be far more favorable than those of our rivals, not only from our superior resources, but from the desire we always have to act with liberality to our constituents . . ., and the advantage of sending accounts and remittances at once without risk, in place of having to wait the result of a two or three months cruize on the China Coast, the risk of which as regards the Chinese Government is not covered by insurance." (Private Letter Book, Nov. 24, 1839.)

"Agreements with ships of other parties to divide sales were very well so long as the trade was confined to a few individuals, but of late so many have entered it with trifling capital, for whose advantage it is to make such arrangements, that we have determined to discontinue them in future. We request therefore that you do the best you can without dividing. . . . We do not however pro-

By 1843 Jardine's alone had five clippers on the Indian run and six on the coast, with receiving ships at Whampoa below Canton (under the Swedish flag), the Six Islands outside Amoy, Chusan off Ningpo, Wusung below Shanghai — that is, at all the new treaty ports except Foochow — and in addition at Chinchew (Ch'üan-chou), Namoa (Nan-ao) on the Kwangtung-Fukien border, and Tienpak southwest of Macao. Dent and Company had a similar establishment, and appear to have had a very similar record of rapid growth.[6] The post-treaty marketing system was already established and the treaty-makers faced a fait accompli. Since Pottinger and his assistants were well aware of this development and its commercial and financial importance, they could see no alternative but to seek from the Chinese court a legal recognition of the opium trade which would bring it within the new law of the treaties.

The principle of bilateral regulation. Their original negotiations over opium at Nanking had quickly reached an impasse. In brief, the Manchu-Chinese side would not consent to formal legalization of the opium trade, while the British would not undertake to suppress it. The British argued, with much reason, that the supply of drug was bound to continue from somewhere and by some means as long as the Chinese demand continued; the trade could not be stopped by Britain and had best be regularized by China; an irrepressible evil was best regulated by moderate taxation. The Chinese met this stock argument with their own stock answer, that the emperor who had once prohibited the traffic could not now reverse himself. No agreement was reached, and the Chinese negotiators did not refer to the future status of opium in their memorials to the emperor.[7] Only one step was taken toward a solution. This was a written statement to Pottinger from Ch'i-ying and I-li-pu in which they promised not to interfere with the foreign side of the trade. The Chinese officials, they said, would confine their attention to Chinese subjects. "Whether the merchant vessels of the various countries bring opium or not, China will not need to inquire, or to take any proceedings with regard thereto."[8]

This Chinese proposal significantly foreshadowed the eventual solution, a bilateral (or parallel) system of informal regulation. But its acceptance would mean a continuation of the old precarious arrangement whereby the trade was illegal by Chinese law and yet winked at by Chinese officialdom. This ran directly counter to one of the chief British objectives, the protection of commerce by the establishment of the rule of law. Pottinger was therefore extremely loath to accept bilateral regulation. He made repeated

---

hibit your exercising your own judgment in the matter, in which case we want the division of sales to be made according to the cargoes of the different vessels.

"We consider the Chusan market as an exception, where we hope to have the market to ourselves for some little time longer, and to keep the price at least 100 dollars above those at Chinchew." (Coastal Letter Book, Mar. 10, 1841.)[5]

proposals for formal legalization, which were later described in a special blue book,[9] and on his way south in November 1842 he urged his view upon the Foochow governor-general, I-liang [10] — all to no avail. By degrees he was forced to accept the original Manchu proposal and take a series of steps in the direction of informal parallel regulation.

His first step was to brand as illegal all British trade in China at ports other than the five to be opened by treaty. This was requested by Ch'i-ying and I-li-pu at Nanking, where Pottinger promised to issue a proclamation and enforce it with British warships. Ch'i-ying reported to the emperor the written statement from Pottinger that "English vessels will not be permitted to proceed to the region of the Chinese seacoast aside from the five ports," on penalty of seizure and confiscation by the Chinese authorities.[11] Sir Henry on his part asked the Foreign Office to secure an order in council, if it should be necessary, to restrict his country's merchantmen accordingly. "I think it is due to the Chinese Government to enforce the prohibition." Later, in January 1843, he published at Hongkong his promise above noted, that British merchants and their servants would not be allowed to go into the country or away from the seaports to trade and that no British ship would be allowed to visit any other ports than those opened by treaty.[12]

By that time a further step had become necessary, for shortly after the treaty of Nanking was signed it had become apparent that the four new ports (Amoy, Foochow, Ningpo, and Shanghai) could not be opened for many months. Until the legal trade at those places could be properly regulated, it must be prohibited. In line with the promises that he had already made and again at the request of the Chinese authorities, Sir Henry issued a proclamation at Chusan on November 14, 1842, "that no British merchant vessel can be allowed to go to any of the ports, Canton excepted, . . . until the tariffs and scale of duties shall be fixed and consular officers appointed." In the meantime the ports of Tinghai (Chusan) and Kulangsu (Amoy) would remain open, they being the seats of British garrisons.[13]

To complicate the situation, this initial effort to control the movements of ships under the Union Jack was handicapped by the doubtful adequacy of Pottinger's legal powers.[c] His authority stemmed from an order in council of 1833 which was now supplemented by another order of January 4, 1843,

[c] Mercantile opinion at this time was reflected in a letter of James Matheson of December 6, 1842: "Uncertainty prevails as to opium. Sir Henry Pottinger thinks it must be legalized eventually, but when it is impossible to say. Meanwhile it is evident that the new system will tend materially to increase the difficulties under which the coast trade is carried on. Vessels found in the new ports with opium on board will be liable to confiscation, and the Plenipotentiary has engaged . . . that British vessels shall be forbidden from trading anywhere else along the coast.

"This stipulation, if strictly adhered to, will confine the opium trade to Hongkong, and cannot fail to check the consumption very materially. Under these circumstances we consider it extremely hazardous to purchase drug at high prices in India, and imprudent to hold a large stock on hand here. No doubt some expedient will be fallen upon in the course of time for conveying drug to the northern ports, in spite of any regulations of the Government. But the trade may before then receive a serious check." [14]

transferring the British criminal and admiralty court from Canton to Hongkong.[15] But it was ruled that "the crown possesses no inherent prerogative of imparting a legislative authority over British subjects within a foreign state or on the high seas," and so without another act of Parliament Pottinger's legal control over his countrymen would be confined to Hongkong. In an effort to carry out his proposal to restrict trade to the treaty ports, the law officers in London drew up an appropriate notification for Sir Henry to issue, but they confessed that they doubted whether it would have any legal validity. Without further authority from Parliament the British government could issue an order that trade should be confined to the treaty ports; but could it impose penalties to enforce this order? The answer was as yet uncertain.[16] In official circles this uncertainty clung to the formal order in council which was finally issued on February 24, 1843. It supported Pottinger's position by forbidding British subjects to resort to China for purposes of trade at any places other than the five treaty ports,[d] but it remained in doubt whether it could really be enforced.

The immediate result of this order in council, which created a sensation on the China coast, was to drive the opium trade under cover of the American flag, which had been found so useful for it during the recent hostilities at Canton. Jardine, Matheson and Company, for example, now purchased three American "running vessels," the *Ariel*, *Mazeppa*, and *Gazelle*, the first two being nominally owned and operated by an American citizen, George Frazer. The practice became general. Since American ships, particularly those of Russell and Company, were already competing in the carriage of opium from India, this boded ill for the British carrying trade.[18] Thus Pottinger had to consider that his prohibitions restricting the movements of English vessels might either be successfully defied by British merchants or on the other hand, if obeyed, might damage the carrying trade of English ships on the China coast.

His position was made the more precarious because the opium trade had been under fire in England. A memorial of more than two hundred merchants and manufacturers not connected with the opium trade was presented to Peel in July 1842; it denounced the drug as the rival of English manufactures in the Chinese market.[19] It was contended that increasing sums of Chinese capital had been diverted to pay for opium imports, leaving none available for English goods. By this time, however, the trade had become too useful to the British government to be lightly attacked for, quite aside from its value to the treasury of India, it had now become the chief source of specie for the expeditionary force in China. The two leading firms, Jardine's

[d] James Matheson commented on April 21, 1843: "The Plenipotentiary has published a most fiery proclamation against smuggling, but I believe it is like the Chinese edicts, meaning nothing and only intended . . . for the gratification of the Saints in England. Sir Henry never means to act on it, and no doubt privately considers it a good joke." [17]

and Dent's, had expanded in the wake of the British campaign to the north, combining when necessary to freeze out competitors, and the silver which they took in from opium sales was regularly sold to the comptroller general of the British forces.[20] In these delicate circumstances the British plenipotentiary was forced to a decision by the "rash action" of a literal-minded young British naval captain.

The rashness of Captain Hope. The naval officers at Chusan, not impressed with the special status of opium, had long been convinced that the drug fleet operated in contravention of the navigation laws.[e] Capt. Charles Hope, the senior officer, had received Pottinger's proclamation of November 14, 1842, in good faith. In retrospect he considered that he would have been liable to court martial if he had not accordingly prevented the resort of British vessels to the four new treaty ports which had not yet been formally opened. Although he had no orders from his superior at Hongkong, he could not "for a moment suppose that a British minister would issue proclamations without he intended to act upon them." When he heard of efforts to open trade at Wusung in March 1843, he took action.

On April 4, 1843, he instructed the vessels under him to detain ships under British colors which could not produce a port clearance from the marine magistrate of Chusan specifying their destination.[22] The British commander-in-chief at Chusan coöperated by ordering the harbor master not to grant port clearance for any place on the coast of China except Kulangsu, Hongkong, Canton, and Macao. A port clearance was therefore refused to Jardine, Matheson and Company's schooner *Vixen* when she

[e] Robert Thom, now interpreter to the Chusan garrison, wrote to his former employer, James Matheson, on November 24, 1842:

"During the last month I have been living on board Men o' War, and being thus thrown into the society of Naval officers . . . the opium trade and the ships engaged in it have of course been discussed . . . I have heard only one opinion expressed, which is that these vessels are navigating expressly in the teeth of the Navigation Act.

"This Act they tell me provides that every ship shall have a license to show for the arms she carries and a port clearance, which if a vessel have not she is liable to capture . . . What makes me feel particularly anxious on your account is that I have since been told that the Admiral himself entertains somewhat similar views, and should he be tempted to put forward the strong hand of power, I tremble for the consequences. I have urged that these vessels are actually collecting the Indian revenues; that neither could the government of India be carried on nor even the expenses of this expedition be paid for without them; that they are all provided with passes from the Bengal government; that they arm themselves for defense with the express connivance of the Indian government; that they carry letters, examine the enemy's coasts, and survey unknown seas etc., etc.

"To all of this they have replied that no circumstance can palliate an infraction of the law, that no Colonial government can give passes in contravention of the Navigation laws, and they have borne me down by quoting innumerable cases, where such and such an Admiral has seized such and such a vessel with Colonial passes, but not navigating on terms of the Navigation Act. As they knew much more about these matters than I did I could only assent and hold my tongue . . .

"What I dread is that when the Admiral is at Macao, some of these affrays may take place, and stories may be circulated about piracy, murder, cutting off of tails, etc., and the old gentleman may all of a sudden give orders to have all the opium vessels detained, and this would be a calamity indeed.

"Be good enough, my dear Mr. Matheson, not to let the contents of this letter go further, as it may compromise me in a number of ways. But at the same time I would strongly recommend you to give the subject of it your most serious consideration. Remember the seizure of the *Anna* by Captain Smith last year, and let me assure you that Naval men never miss any opportunity of making prize money when they can."[21]

dutifully applied for one for the Rugged Isles, situated in the mouth of the Yangtze. It was the *Vixen's* misfortune that she sought official sanction for an irregularity which the Chusan commander, on his part, would have continued to wink at.[23] Not so Captain Hope, however. When the *Vixen* cleared on April 10 for Kulangsu, he "strongly suspected" that she was bound for Shanghai and ordered the vessels under him to detain her on sight and to seize other ships if they would not produce their log books. After some delay he sent the sloop *Childers* and the steamer *Medusa* to Shanghai, with instructions to order all British vessels out of the Shanghai River within twenty-four hours, to seize any that remained, and thereafter to take up a position about twenty miles below Wusung and prevent any more entering the Yangtze. There can be no doubt of Captain Hope's motives. He conceived that "those opium gentlemen hitherto have been allowed to go along the coast between this and Macao without port clearance and no questions ever put to them. As the higher power allowed them to do this I never interfered, as long as they confined their smuggling operations to the south of this — and did not go near any of the five prohibited towns . . . but when they went to the *Yangtze-Keang* and above all to *Shanghai*, I thought it high time to put a stop to such lawless proceedings — more especially as those vessels are manned and armed more like men of war than merchantmen, and are well known to commit all kinds of irregularities, and to[o] often great excesses to promote their own selfish ends. . ."[24]

To make doubly certain, Hope had the Rev. Mr. Gutzlaff put into Chinese a letter to the chief official at Shanghai, the local taotai. In this the captain, on behalf of his admiral, denounced all British vessels appearing at Wusung or Shanghai, outlined his instructions to the *Childers*, and offered to apprehend British evildoers at the taotai's request. On April 20 the *Childers* found four English vessels at the mouth of the Yangtze, made them leave within twenty-four hours, and delivered this letter.

What followed was an object lesson of unmistakable significance; for the merchants and officials of both England and China united in condemnation, and Captain Hope was explicitly disavowed and recalled from his post. Before his ill-fated proceedings had begun, a correspondent of Pottinger's "in no way connected with trade" had reported from Chusan that "the governor of Shanghai had appointed an anchoring place near Wusung for the British merchant vessels, that the most friendly feeling existed, that trade was exceedingly brisk, that not only numbers of the people but many inferior mandarins had visited the ships, and that the authorities and merchants of Ningpo were constantly and anxiously inquiring when the trade with their port was to commence."[25] Indeed, as proof of this the *Childers* had received a petition from "all the merchants of every province now at

Shanghai," expatiating on the friendly relations which had accompanied their trade with the English vessels since March 3. "The merchants look forward that your precious vessels will come in crowds to Shanghai . . . and all classes anticipate with joy their commerce and the building of the factories." [26] Chinese complaints against the trade, if any, were not voiced.

On the other hand, the British traders were most outspoken. Jardine, Matheson and Company's *Vixen* had in actual fact returned to Hongkong, and the firm lost no time in bringing Captain Hope's proceedings to Sir Henry's notice. On April 20 the latter received from Macao a private letter in the name of all the principal houses engaged in the opium trade remonstrating against Captain Hope's interference with their vessels. They stated that they were "unwilling, for obvious reasons, to address me officially on a question on which they are aware that I am beset with difficulties, that they are chiefly acting for others, that I will understand the value at stake by the admitted immense profit which has accrued to the East India Company's Government by the first two opium sales of this year, that if any further restrictions or great changes were contemplated by the British government, they feel that they have a right to expect and *demand* previous intimation; that they will be always ready to obey, as far as their duty to their constituents and themselves will admit [*sic*!], any legal regulations that may be laid down, but that they humbly submit, that whilst the local officers all along the coast of China not only permit, but actually encourage the trade in opium (doubtless, I may here remark, for their own private benefit) it can hardly be expected that they (the merchants) will desist from it, and leave it to be taken up by others (which I may further observe it would be *instantly*, by less scrupulous dealers who have not the same means and capital and who would therefore probably grasp at greater gain, at all risks)." [27]

Sir Henry's reaction summarized the rationalizations, both sound and unsound, of his day and generation. He informed the Foreign Office that the most extended inquiries completely refuted the opinions that some had set forth as to the pernicious and baleful effects of opium. He had already [28] convinced the Chinese authorities of "the utter impossibility and hopelessness of suppressing the trade so long as the people of China *will* have and *will* use opium." [f] He was acutely conscious also that the law officers in England had doubted whether British vessels could be *legally* prohibited from going to other ports than those opened by treaty. He was loath to

[f] Matheson wrote on September 10, 1843:

"Sir Henry Pottinger gives me to understand that in all his dispatches . . . he reprobates in the strongest terms any interference with the storing of drug at Hongkong, or its sale on the coast of China. He denies *in toto* the assertions of Lord Ashley respecting the atrocities committed by the opium traders, or the evil effects of smoking on the Chinese — having never witnessed either the one or the other. Kiying, the Imperial Commissioner, declares that on the swampy banks of the Yangtze Kiang and other large rivers they would all die of fever and ague, if they had not opium to smoke." [29]

give the appearance of officially approving the opium trade — not because it was evil, the evil was "very trifling," but because it was prohibited by China. But anything was better than to leave matters as they were — "leading the Chinese government to fancy that we can stop the trade whenever we like." Accordingly Sir Henry declared [30] that his proclamation of November 1842 on which Hope had acted, "had no sort of reference to the opium trade, which has never been recognized by me, nor will be so, unless I can succeed in obtaining its legalization." [g] He requested the admiral to have Captain Hope rescind his orders at Chusan and recall the *Childers* from the Yangtze. The captain had assumed authority which he did not possess, he could be sued by the owners of vessels he had detained, it would be best to recall him from his command. Henceforth the naval officers in their correspondence with Chinese officials should abstain from all reference to political arrangements. Similar views were expressed [32] for the guidance of the army.[h] Meanwhile the opium trade continued undiminished, partly under the protection of the American flag.

The Chinese reaction. The British minister's struggles with his Anglo-Saxon conscience seem to have had little interest for the Chinese higher authorities. In their memorials, a conspiracy of silence now cloaked the opium trade. The court at Peking betrayed a very imperfect idea of the situation on the southeast coast. Thus, for example, the effort of an American-flag vessel (probably British) from Chusan to open the legal trade by selling piece goods and paying duties at Ningpo at the end of November 1842 was entirely misunderstood. The attempt was rebuffed and reported by the Ningpo authorities.[34] But at Peking it was wrongly identified with the recent request of the American, Commodore Kearny, who had asked at Canton for equal privileges for American traders in China.[35] Again, Chinese officials reported to Peking that in January 1843 two foreign vessels had appeared at Shih-p'u on Hangchow Bay and had tried to procure pilots to take them, respectively, to Foochow and, so it was said, to the port of

[g] James Matheson wrote to Captain McMinnies, April 22, 1843:

"Sir Henry . . . not only disapproves of what has been done, but the steamer *Vixen* is sent to Chusan with orders that everything shall be placed precisely on the same footing on which His Excellency, the Plenipotentiary left the opium and all other questions, when he quitted Chusan on November last.

"We beg to impress on you most earnestly the necessity of conciliating the good will of those in command at Chusan as much as possible, and above all that you will not on the present occasion make any demonstration indicative of your having obtained a victory over them.

"We feel assured that we need not caution you against incurring more risk than necessary in carrying on trade in the Yangtze Kiang. Let every effort be made to please the mandarins, such as moving from one anchorage to another when they require it, and not approaching too near to their towns. The opium trade is now so very unpopular in England, that we cannot be too cautious in keeping it as quiet and as much out of the public eye as possible." [31]

[h] Captain Hope knew well that "the whole mercantile world in the east . . . will be up in arms against me . . . I expect to be 'shown up' in Parliament if some of the members connected with the opium trade hear what I have done." He appealed indignantly to friends at the admiralty and to the foreign secretary himself, as an "English nobleman." The general at Chusan wrote to his superiors, and the Duke of Wellington wrote to Aberdeen. But the latter approved Pottinger's course.[33]

Teng-chou, Shantung. Since Shantung was beyond the new treaty limits for British trade, this report provoked the liveliest suspicion and speculation at Peking, until it was finally established that the mysterious craft in question were merely British surveying vessels of whose mission Pottinger had already given warning; and that the fear of their going to Shantung had arisen purely from faulty translation.[36] This was of course a chronic source of mystification and misunderstanding.

In the midst of these misapprehensions and uncertainties, Ch'i-ying tried to reassure the court with an impressive recital of statistics of barbarian ship movements, as reported by the coastal authorities. This was evidently an effort to conceal the real situation, for we find him reporting disingenuously, for example, that a two-masted vessel had approached Wusung (the opium receiving station for Shanghai) from the south on February 7, 1843, that an official investigation had been ordered, but that the vessel had gone away southward on February 9 before it could be interrogated! From such watchdogs the opium trader had little to fear. About this time a censor reported barbarian buildings and various depredations in the region of Nan-ao (the receiving station at Namoa Island, on the Kwangtung coast), but again there was no reference to opium; and an official investigation declared incorrectly that the barbarians who once landed there had all departed.[37]

In this atmosphere of tacit agreement to avoid the facts, the Chinese authorities, far from rejoicing at Captain Hope's action of April 1843, had been mystified and alarmed by it. Already an English vessel in March 1843 had tried to open trade at Shanghai in legal goods, and Ch'i-ying had had it ordered back to Chusan to await the official opening of trade, but he had taken no further action.[38] After Ch'i-ying's departure for Canton in April, his successor at Nanking apparently felt obliged to report the situation at Shanghai, lest ensuing events undo him. His memorial recounted meticulously that three American vessels had arrived on March 3, were refused trade, and anchored outside the port "for repairs," where they were joined by a fourth American ship; subsequently an English steamer had arrived on April 20 with orders to send these ships back to Chusan lest they cause trouble.[39] Soon afterward the Nanking authorities found that the acting Shanghai taotai (evidently in response to Captain Hope's communication to him) had issued an ill-advised proclamation which openly referred to the unauthorized trade then going on at Wusung and forbade it until publication of the tariff. Yet in spite of this ban proclaimed by the taotai, five British and American vessels reappeared at Wusung on May 8, two of them the same as those of March. The taotai's recent proclamation therefore became "muddled and unclear"; the provincial authorities suggested that it might even lead the populace into relations with the barbarians and they urged that the unfortunate acting taotai be removed from office. The emperor did so and ordered an inquiry.[40]

When Captain Hope heard of his reversal, and before he received full instructions, he complicated the situation still further by addressing the Shanghai taotai a second time in a dispatch delivered on May 18, explaining that "in the present altered condition of things" his warship must be withdrawn from below Wusung and could no longer stop British vessels entering the river. His dispatch unfortunately referred to the "Chang-kiang" (*Ch'ang-chiang* or "long river") and "Yangszekiang" (*Yang-tzu-chiang*), names used by the Chinese for the main stream of the Yangtze above Harvey Point in the region of Chinkiang. This led the Chinese authorities into terrified speculation that British vessels could be kept from Wusung as first announced but not from the Yangtze proper as now indicated. An explanation was demanded of Pottinger.[41] This was forthcoming both in person and by letter, and Hope's actions were disavowed. Pottinger declared "it depended on the Chinese local officers to enforce my proclamation by preventing the people of the country from trading with the vessels, in which event they would come away of their own accord."[42]

In these terms, by the public disavowal and disgrace of the British captain and the Chinese taotai who had conscientiously taken action in their respective spheres to enforce their superior's ban on trade at unopened ports, the opium trade was assured of practical immunity for the future. It was made evident that official proclamations about "trade" did not apply to it. Meanwhile the British traders at Wusung had continued to do a brisk business in opium, piece goods, yarn, and cotton. They sold their goods "to Chinese boats which come alongside, and which either smuggle the goods on shore, or make the best bargain they can with the local custom house officers." Thus the receiving station at Wusung was a flourishing mart six months before the opening of the treaty port of Shanghai. Pottinger reported that "a similar system appears to be in force at several ports along the eastern coast of China, and will no doubt continue until the consular officers are established and the five ports regularly opened by proclamation."[43] He did not foresee that "the system" was to plague his successors for another fifteen years.

The Hope case ushered in a second phase in the treatment of the opium problem by making it plainer than ever that the trade would continue even if illegal. More vividly than any amount of generalization it demonstrated the essential point, that opium had become useful to too many people, both Chinese and foreign. Statements of good intention on the part of the British Foreign Office were therefore as unavailing as the edicts of the emperor of China.

In reply to Pottinger's dispatches concerning opium the foreign secretary,

Lord Aberdeen, on January 4, 1843, had sent very proper instructions. After urging legalization by China, he took the position that while Great Britain could not prevent its subjects from trading in opium, at least it could refuse to assist them. To that end Pottinger could by various measures "prevent the island of Hong-kong from being a resort and market for the British smuggler." This high-principled declaration of policy was approved by Queen Victoria and has been widely quoted,[44] although it never had much vogue at Hongkong: Matheson had understood at the time of the British occupation in January 1841 that "so independent will Hongkong be that it will be even allowable to store opium on it as soon as we build warehouses there." [45] Sir Henry offered to the Chinese authorities to issue a proclamation "calling on all British vessels trading in opium to quit the harbors and inner waters of China on pain of seizure and confiscation." But the British government, he added, could not assist in such seizure and confiscation; consequently the proclamation would only draw attention to the fact that the Chinese government could control neither the foreign traders nor its own corrupt officials.[46] The plenipotentiary therefore realistically continued his efforts to secure for opium a recognized status, or as Aberdeen put it, "to place the trade, even as a smuggling trade, on a less discreditable footing." He sought an extra-treaty agreement, and was soon obliged to disregard the foreign secretary's instructions regarding Hongkong.

Pottinger's proposal and arrangements. When Ch'i-ying visited Hongkong in June 1843, Sir Henry as a practical measure suggested "confining the opium vessels to one or two points on the coast. This would at all events limit the trade and bring it into something like a tangible and controllable form." [47] From his brief references, it appears that the solution which Pottinger had in mind was to obtain the informal consent of the Chinese authorities to the establishment of Namoa and Chinchew (Ch'üan-chou) on the Kwangtung-Fukien coast as opium distributing centers — under the British order in council of February 24, 1843, he could prevent British vessels from going elsewhere than to the five ports; by a gentlemen's agreement he could allow them to visit the opium depots; on its part the Chinese government could authorize Chinese buyers to go there also.

"This arrangement would have the advantages of keeping the legal commerce and contraband trade (in opium) entirely distinct. It would be, in reality, a direct sanction to the opium trade. It would remove from Her Majesty's subjects the obloquy of being engaged in absolutely smuggling the opium into the country, and would prevent as far as practicable, all risk of collusion between our vessels and the Chinese government cruizers." [In this way Pottinger hoped to have] "the trade (if not legalized) put on a defined and respectable basis; and though the prices to be obtained at a fixed point may be less, and the profits thereby be reduced, when compared with the present plan of our vessels carrying opium to all parts of the coast (even beyond the limits of the five ports to be opened by treaty), yet that is a matter which I should not consider to be worthy of a moment's consideration, nor could those who speculate in the trade offer a complaint. . . ."[48]

The Chinese response to this proposal was not one of moral indignation. Ch'i-ying had already stated to the emperor the traditional principle that foreign traders could be best controlled at certain fixed ports.[49] He and his colleagues had also agreed to the doctrine that smuggling should be prevented and revenue assured, in the case of a valuable commodity, ginseng, by lowering the duty.[50] Even from the Chinese point of view, Pottinger's plan was the nearest approach yet made to a practical solution of the administrative problem presented by opium; but it now died stillborn when Ch'i-ying refused unconditionally to allow any points on the coast to be set aside for the contraband trade, on the ground that the imperial prohibition still existed.

The practicality of the Manchu approach to the problem was demonstrated by Ch'i-ying's counter-proposal. He asked Pottinger to guarantee on behalf of the British opium-traders that the 30,000-odd chests of opium imported each year [51] would pay a tax to the Chinese government of three million dollars or Tls. 2,100,000 in silver. He suggested that this amount be paid in advance for five years, the whole arrangement to last for ten years, and he offered to lay the proposition before the throne in his memorial regarding the new tariff. Pottinger refused to consider it, and Ch'i-ying's memorials on the tariff made no reference to the idea.[52] But his proposal indicates again that to the Manchu administration opium was primarily an economic and political problem. There was no aversion to taxing the evil, provided dynastic prestige suffered no further lowering in the process. A money guarantee from the British government would provide definite revenue and might be disguised from the populace. It could also, no doubt, profit the imperial commissioner.

Having rejected Ch'i-ying's proposal, which would have put moral responsibility too directly upon the British government, Pottinger was obliged to make his own arrangements. He had become convinced that, in spite of the permission given him to do so, it was "neither desirable nor necessary to exclude our opium trading ships from Hongkong Harbor or its waters." [53] On July 8, he informed the imperial commissioner that he proposed not to exclude opium vessels from the British colony, because such exclusion would only intensify the evils of the situation. At the same time he prepared, chiefly from Aberdeen's instruction of January 4, 1843, a memorandum for submission to the emperor setting forth the arguments for legalization. This gesture had been proposed by Ch'i'ying himself. In view of "the extraordinary friendship and kindness" of the imperial commissioner, Pottinger felt he should not refuse, whatever difficulties of etiquette might be involved.[54]

Without waiting to see the result of this appeal to the throne, the British plenipotentiary took what steps he could to put the opium trade on a secure and regular basis. His measures concerned both the carrying vessels and the places of storage at Hongkong and on the coast.

Clippers, lorchas, and small craft owned by British subjects and plying in Chinese waters plainly needed papers of registry to entitle them to the use and protection of their national flag. In July 1842 Aberdeen had sent out a form for sailing letters to be issued by the plenipotentiary as chief superintendent of British trade.[55] But this opportunity to acquire British registry had not been widely used until Commodore Lawrence Kearny, commanding the United States squadron in the East Indies, provided a stimulus in May 1843 by seizing the opium schooner *Ariel* in Amoy harbor. This vessel was really owned by Jardine, Matheson and Company but now flew the American flag and carried a bill of sale certified by John P. Sturgis of Russell and Company, U. S. vice-consul at Macao. In March 1842 Commodore Kearny had already denounced the opium trade and forbidden American protection of it. On May 18, 1843, he now issued another notice cautioning all persons against shipping goods "on board any vessel in the 'opium trade' sailing under the flag of the United States." As a result the British-owned vessels similarly situated to the *Ariel* had forthwith applied for British sailing letters, which Pottinger had granted them. In this way the opium distributing trade from Hongkong came further under his protection and control.[56]

At the same time he took measures to keep the contraband opium trade distinct from the smuggling of legal goods (on the latter, see Chapter 19). This was an important step in the development of British policy. As the foreign secretary put it, in approving Sir Henry's denunciation of the smuggling countenanced in the Canton River, "the perserverence of the Chinese officers in conniving at contraband [i.e., opium] trade might . . . induce the chief authorities to interfere with legal trade."[57] The legal trade in teas and silks must be kept free from the dangers which might be brought upon it by association with opium. With this object in mind. Sir Henry issued a proclamation on August 1, 1843, warning all merchants that the importation of opium was illegal under Chinese law, that opium was therefore not in the class of articles which passed at a duty of 5 per cent *ad valorem* because unenumerated in the new treaty tariff, and that persons taking it into the treaty ports would do so at their own risk and would receive no consular protection.[58] (By implication, this was a charter assuring immunity to the receiving stations outside the treaty ports.) Ch'i-ying gave it his blessing in a communication of August 24, which urged that the British and Chinese authorities should prevent incidents and altercations both by excluding opium from the treaty ports and by asking consuls of other nations to do the same.[59]

Finally, Anglo-Chinese coöperation to regulate the trade in an unofficial manner was stimulated by the appearance of foreign (presumably British) traders on the coast of North China. On August 18, 1843, the emperor received a report that two foreign vessels had attempted to open trade in opium and other goods at Teng-chou in Shantung. His resultant edicts on the subject, although they referred to the effort to sell opium, inveighed not at all against the opium traffic but instead levelled their condemnation at the resort of foreign ships bearing Chinese traitors to places other than the five treaty ports. Two similar foreign ships, with "over 20 Cantonese and 50 or 60 white and black devils" aboard, subsequently sought trade off Tientsin. Again the edicts in reply were wholly concerned with the illegal place of their attempted trade, not with the nature of their goods.[60] To the ruling dynasty at least, the barbarian was more hateful than his opium. The two cases just mentioned, of foreign vessels appearing on the coast of Shantung and Chihli in August 1843, were referred to Ch'i-ying and led to immediate action. He and Pottinger proceeded to lay down the limits for foreign merchant-adventuring. Opium was of course the staple of such adventuring, and unofficial limitation of the opium trade resulted.

The unofficial solution of the opium problem. Because of its extra-legal nature, this solution is indicated by what the documents leave out, rather than by what they say. By article IV of the Supplementary treaty signed on October 8, 1843, British traders were restricted to the five treaty ports, Chinese were forbidden to trade with them elsewhere, and the Chinese government was to be at liberty to seize and confiscate both vessels[61] and cargoes of British subjects acting "in contravention of this agreement and of a proclamation to the same purpose to be issued by the British plenipotentiary." Pottinger's forthcoming proclamation was thus to be an integral part of the treaty settlement. It was issued on October 24, 1843. With it was republished the order in council of February 24, prohibiting trade elsewhere than at the five ports, although that document had been published less than three months before, on August 1. The new proclamation now interpreted the order in council. Its main point was to make a distinction between vessels which disobeyed the order south of the mouth of the Yangtze (32° north latitude) and those which did so north of it. The proclamation stated that, in view of the long seacoast, the winds, and other difficulties of navigation, "it will not be . . . a breach or violation of the said order in council, should British vessels approach and anchor for safety . . . near the coast of China . . . southward of the embouchure of the Yangtsy' kiang"; although of course all British subjects must realize the risk they would run by trading elsewhere than at the five ports. In sharp contrast to this, the proclamation stated that "any British merchant vessel that may be positively known . . . to have visited any part of the seacoast of China higher up than the 32d degree of north latitude (unless she should be forced by absolute stress of weather) will be assumed" to have violated the order in council; she would be detained if possible by H. M.'s vessels, "with a view to her being sent to Hongkong for inquiry and adjudication." [62]

On the surface it is true that the above warnings could have been intended solely for traders in legal goods; but when taken in the context of the times, the conclusion of this proclamation of October 24, 1843, can only be regarded as an injunction intended directly for the opium trade.

"In conclusion, her majesty's plenipotentiary, etc., most especially and solemnly warns all her majesty's subjects against any act of violence — no matter what the alleged cause or pretext may be, towards any of the officers or people of China. *If merchant vessels will go to trade at any of the ports of China not opened by treaty for purposes of trade or commerce* [italics inserted], it is self-evident that they voluntarily expose themselves, after the oft repeated warnings, to the chances of being attacked or driven away, or seized and confiscated, and in either case not only will they receive no protection or countenance from her majesty's ships of war or other authorities in China, but they will if they attempt to defend themselves, and loss of life or bloodshed should ensue, be seized as pirates, and brought to Hongkong to await the decision and commands of her majesty's government." [i]

An equally significant distinction between trade north and south of the Yangtze was made by Ch'i-ying in his report to the emperor. Though veiled in vague terms this may be construed as giving notice to Peking that the drug trade was going to continue south of the Yangtze.[j]

[i] Pottinger regarded this proclamation as perhaps "the most important step that my complicated duties have required me to take since I came to China," and he suggested that it might be better applied to British subjects than merely to vessels under British colors. "I really do not believe that the Officers of the Chinese Government or even H. M. the Emperor himself would much care for our vessels going to trade at the few remaining ports (not opened by treaty) to the south of the Yangtze-kiang, but vessels penetrating into the Yellow Sea, or proceeding north of the limit I have laid down, excites the alarm and offends the prejudices and dignity of the Imperial Government, and therefore I should be very glad to see it prevented even by what might be considered in any other part of the world, an arbitrary act of power."

Pottinger's suggestion to Ch'i-ying was that "any persons landing from such vessels ought to be seized and not released until they pay a fine of $1,000 each person." If forceful efforts should be made to rescue such persons, "I shall order the offending vessel wherever she may be found in China if under English Colours to be seized as a pirate and brought to Hongkong." [63]

[j] After recounting Pottinger's request for Chinese coöperation to prevent trade outside the five ports, Ch'i-ying requested instructions to the authorities of the coast provinces to seize all vessels so trading with their cargoes; those refusing to be seized should be reported to Canton for reference to the British. But he then made a distinction. Since 1830 vessels had, occasionally, gone to the north. But in the south on the coast of Fukien and Chekiang they were constantly active, in league with traitorous natives and indulged by the minor officials. There was no help for it. Ch'i-ying quoted the Confucian maxim, "As for law, one must first govern oneself and then one can govern

Chinese opium policy in 1843 is further revealed by Ch'i-ying's memorial raising the question of legalization, which he had agreed with Pottinger to present to the court. After reporting the completion of his treaty arrangements, in a secret memorial received at Peking on December 1, 1843, he proceeded to quote Pottinger's arguments: the British government could only prohibit the opium trade to British merchants, they could not control those of other countries; if opium smuggling continued, legal goods were bound to become involved in it and trouble would result; it would be better to levy a duty. Ch'i-ying then stated that he had replied to the British that there should be Sino-foreign coöperation to suppress the traffic in the hope that it would collapse, but that a just duty would probably be difficult to agree upon. To the emperor, he observed that in all things "one first should purify the source"; in suppressing opium, one should first cut off its circulation. Yet wherever there was profit to be gained, traitorous natives would be attracted to it, whatever the hazards. To act severely against so many would be most difficult; but to be hypocritical about it would provoke the derision of the barbarians, and lead to improper intimacy between them and traitorous natives. At this time when barbarian relations were just being put on a new basis, there was no way either to relax the prohibiton or to tighten it up. After most anxious consideration, Ch'i-ying and his colleagues had no policy to propose, although they dared not keep silent regarding the situation which thrust itself upon their attention.[66]

The imperial reaction to these reasoned proposals was just what the imperial commissioner had prophesied. The emperor agreed as to the difficulty of the problem:

"Although opium comes from the outer barbarians, yet generally the people of this country acting in their own interest make sport of the law and voluntarily commit suicide, with the result that the spreading poison daily increases. But if we actually give orders to carry out the prohibition and do not allow two-faced evasion of it, the custom of smoking will be broken off, and the opium dealers will have no profit to scheme for."

The emperor therefore commanded Ch'i-ying to order strict punishment

---

others. If the prohibition of traitorous natives leaguing with [the barbarians] is not strict, if the evil of soldiers indulging them is not checked — whither there is profit, men necessarily will tend; so when things are putrid, worms are bred. Our administration therefore will be much impeded. Also it is to be feared that the customs duties for this reason will show a deficiency." [64]

The imperial response on this topic followed the same line. Referring only to the provinces south of the Yangtze, the emperor ordered that "if there are traitorous natives, who, when barbarian vessels arrive at a port, coerce or obstruct them with the result that merchant goods cannot circulate," then the provincial authorities should with secrecy seize and punsh them. Barbarian vessels found at non-treaty ports should be seized and confiscated according to treaty. This order was issued to all the officials concerned.[65] Pending the discovery of further evidence we can assert no more than that the first part of these highly ambiguous instructions was an innocent paper command to prevent the causing of trouble by native racketeers in foreign trade; yet these orders may equally well have been inspired in the first instance by Ch'i-ying's purpose to give the drug trade carte blanche as long as it remained in recognized channels and caused the officials no trouble.

of dealers, divan keepers, and smokers, and also the prevention of extortion by officials. Thus the smoking habit and the opium dealers would both gradually cease to exist.[67] From all this it seems plain that the court had no solution either, and no recourse but proud and empty commands.

Meanwhile Pottinger proceeded with his extra-treaty arrangements. At the beginning of November 1843 the British community at Hongkong was notified of the form of sailing letter which had been prepared "for the better regulation and security of small craft, as cutters, schooners, lorchas, etc.," which had already been granted reduced tonnage rates at Canton by article XVII of the Supplementary treaty; while the British naval forces were publicly ordered by the admiral to enforce the proclamation of October 24 above quoted. Vessels having no flag or register or sailing letter were to be sent into a British port for a breach of the navigation laws.[68] Simultaneously in England the Foreign Office considered the whole of Pottinger's arrangements up to the end of July. Aberdeen concluded that the plenipotentiary had best be allowed, if he wished, "to suspend for the present any measures for the exclusion of opium vessels from the waters and harbor of Hongkong." Lord Stanley of the Colonial Office concurring, Pottinger was so instructed.[69] In this manner Hongkong became, as it was to remain for a generation, the recognized receiving point for opium supplies from India, the great warehouse from which schooners and small craft under the British flag supplied the Chinese mainland.

In retrospect it is plain that the real opium question at issue between Britain and China in 1843 was whether the opium trade should be regulated, and so protected, in a Western manner. The British government tried to secure regulation through legalization. We must assume that they were thwarted not only by the emperor's unwillingness to countenance the evil but also by the vested interests of the drug trade — the petty Chinese officials, the "traitorous natives," and the great foreign monopolists mentioned in their various roles above, all of whom stood to profit more by a continuation of the old contraband system. Thus the extra-treaty arrangement finally achieved was a defeat for Western methods of regulation and for the rule of law which the British officials were trying to establish. As a second-best substitute these officials finally subscribed to the view of the British opium monopolists, that the trade "should be carried on by parties of respectability as at present, and not be driven into the hands of desperadoes and pirates; as would inevitably be the case were Lord Ashley and his friends [leading the anti-opium crusade in England] to succeed in carrying their measures." [k] Similarly, the extra-treaty arrangement appears

[k] Alexander Matheson, letter of July 31, 1843. He continued: "No one is more conscious of this than Sir Henry Pottinger, who of course communicated his sentiments to Sir Robert Peel." Under date of September 10, 1843, he epitomized the situation: "All hopes of legalization of the drug

to have had the acquiescence and support of the Manchu authorities in charge of foreign affairs.

The result was to split the foreign trade of China into two parts, legal and illegal. Two sets of foreign communities, two channels for trade, two codes of conduct grew up as a consequence. In the words of one unhappy British consul, the officials of both countries were expected to acknowledge the presence of one of the Siamese twins and forget all knowledge of his brother. This dichotomy between the contraband drug traffic and the legitimate trade in teas, silks, and foreign manufactures continued until 1858 and colored the whole intervening period.

If we now put the opium settlement of 1843 into the context of the general treaty settlement described in preceding chapters, we can conclude that by the end of October 1843 Pottinger had succeeded in setting up a framework of regulations within the protection of which British trade with China might proceed to expand. Four aspects of these arrangements may be particularly noted:

1) British merchants knew the duties they would have to pay by the treaty tariff at Canton, even though they did not know how much prices might be raised by Chinese transit taxes in the interior or by the squeeze of local authorities. 2) Hongkong was their own free port, even though not an emporium of legitimate Chinese trade.[71] 3) By general agreement among officials of both governments and the opium merchants, the drug trade could flourish within certain known limits, even though it remained beyond the reach of the law and the official tax-collector. 4) British small craft in the coast trade from Hongkong, finally, were licensed to carry the British flag; under article XVII of the Supplementary treaty they were allowed to pay reduced tonnage dues at the port of Canton, if not elsewhere. In general the treaty system was neither complete nor perfect, but it was firmly outlined and ready for application at the ports.

---

trade are . . . at an end and you may rest assured that if ever it is legalized, it will cease to be profitable from that time. The more difficulties attend it the better for . . . us. We shall always find ways and means to carry on despite every obstacle."[70]

PART III

THE APPLICATION OF THE TREATIES 1843–45

CHAPTER X

THE TREATY PORTS AND THE BRITISH CONSULS

THE OPENING OF THE TREATY PORTS in the early 1840's, like the contemporary opening of the American West, was adventurous pioner work on a frontier. The problem of the frontier in China, however, was not how to overcome nature but how to deal with the ancient Chinese way of life. Like his cousins on the Great Plains, the Western frontiersman in Shanghai had to adjust himself to the local scene while still pursuing his expansive and acquisitive ends. The treaty ports were the answer to this problem; they can also be fruitfully compared with the trading posts and mining camps, the forts and pony express stations of the American West. One of their major problems, for instance, was in the realm of "law and order"—not so much how to make the treaty port community law-abiding in general but rather how to secure Chinese compliance with the Anglo-Saxon type of law. Getting the treaties drawn up, signed, and ratified had been only the first steps on a long road.

During the year-long process of treaty making in 1842 and 1843, Western trade with China had continued as best it could, at Canton and on the coast. Canton had been opened to trade on July 27, 1843, and the Supplementary treaty was signed on October 8. But the opening of the new treaty ports took several months thereafter and was not completed until the middle of 1844. The official dates of opening were: for Amoy, November 2, and Shanghai, November 17, 1843; for Ningpo, January 1, and Foochow, in June, 1844.[1]

The treaty port community. The early treaty ports were not picked by chance, much less created *de novo* by the blessings of European trade. They were shrewdly chosen as points of entrance into the avenues of Chinese maritime trade which already existed. Amoy had long rivalled Canton as the chief center of the junk trade with the Straits. Foochow was the port for tributary trade with Liu-ch'iu and also with Formosa, as well as the chief city of Fukien. Ningpo was the traditional home of the great native commerce from Chekiang to the north of China and the coasts of Japan and Korea. Shanghai, far from being the insignificant village adjacent to a mud-flat pictured by treaty port writers of later years, had been for centuries a recognized port at the mouth of the Yangtze.[a] The promi-

[a] Situated in the Yangtze delta where new land has been forming century by century, Shanghai was the youngest of these trading centers. Edwin O. Reischauer's study of T'ang sea routes indi-

nence of these ports had long been known to the East India Company and to the opium traders who explored the coast, and British arms had appeared at all of them except Foochow during the war. Indeed, the natural configuration of the China coast has given certain places like Namoa and Chusan a continuing strategic importance — whether for the rebel Koxinga in 1660, for British admirals and opium captains in the 1840's, or for Chiang Kai-shek in 1950.

The morphology of the British commercial penetration of China may be likened roughly to a long arm stretching through India and the Straits to Hongkong, from which five fingers clutched the Chinese mainland. In the cases of the consular service and opium trade there is some verisimilitude, for the superintendent of British trade, who was concurrently H. M.'s minister plenipotentiary to China and governor of Hongkong, was the administrative head to whom the consuls looked for instructions, while the beautiful harbor of Hongkong and its city of Victoria were the entrepôt where opium cargoes from India were stored to await shipment to the receiving stations. Although legal cargoes from the ports seldom were transshipped at Hongkong, nearly all of them passed through it as a port of call.

That Hongkong and the five ports were alike in being advanced positions for the British commercial invasion was indicated by certain topographical features which they had in common. In each case the foreign settlement became established not only on the water but behind a defensive screen of water. Hongkong illustrated this principle — the British community on its mountainous island was separated from Kowloon on the Chinese mainland by a harbor which had two entrances and could not easily be blockaded. At Amoy the foreign settlement gravitated of its own accord to the island of Kulangsu which was separated from the walled Chinese city

cates that the Lower Yangtze was less important than the mouth of the Huai as a focus of foreign contact in that period; records of travel between Japan and the Lower Yangtze, in any case, mention Soochow rather than Shanghai.[2] The route from the sea to Soochow through the Sung-chiang (Sung River), also known as the Wu-sung-chiang and called Soochow Creek in modern times by foreigners at Shanghai, antedated the rise of Shanghai as a port. One account is that this stream had originally been cut out to provide a direct passage from Soochow to the mouth of the Yangtze and "flowed independently of the Whangpoo into the sea near Woosung." Early in the Ming, however, the broad Wu-sung-chiang silted up and became less important than the Whangpu, which now forms the main stream at Shanghai.[3] Although Shanghai had been established as a market town at the end of the Sung and became a *hsien* city early in the Yuan period, it was for long unimportant: under the T'ang, Yang-chou had served as a great emporium and under the Sung and Yuan its place was taken by Ch'üan-chou, Hangchow, and Ningpo. Shanghai began as a fishing port and became a center of trade only by degrees, probably through its connection with Soochow; yet the Soochow Creek was shallow and Shanghai did not stand out before the nineteenth century, either as a center of domestic trade or as a focus of heavy junk traffic by sea. Up to 1840, says one Chinese scholar, Chusan Island had been considered as important as Shanghai.[4]

In 1843 the mouth of the Soochow Creek was still wide enough to accommodate part of the British fleet. But after the barque *Hotspur* went aground in 1866 and was lost off the bund at the junction of Soochow Creek and the Whangpu, silt accumulated and soon formed the "Consular mud flat," which was transferred to the Shanghai Municipal Council in 1868 and eventually became a public garden. Soochow Creek is now reduced to a width of 40 yards.[5]

by the harbor between them. The same thing happened later at Swatow. At Foochow the foreign community grew up on the island of Nantai (*Nan-t'ai*) across the river from the walled city, nine miles above Pagoda anchorage and twenty-five miles from the sea. The same pattern was followed at Ningpo and Shanghai. In both cases the foreign settlements were situated outside the Chinese walled cities on the banks of navigable rivers, the Yung and the Whangpu, and some eighteen and twelve miles, respectively, from their mouths. At Ningpo the confluence of the river's two branches formed a point on which the foreigners settled, across from the city. At Shanghai the settlement was bounded on the east by the Whangpu and on the north by Soochow Creek and separated from the Chinese city on the south by still another creek; yet within ten years it became necessary to enlarge another watercourse on the west, "called Defence Creek, running north and south and connecting the three others. The English and French settlements united thus occupy a strong strategical position for defence, and together form what may be called an irregularly shaped island."[6] (This was said as late as 1900.)

At Amoy, Foochow, and Shanghai it was the merchants, not the consuls, who sought this protection. The first consuls at those ports, for purposes of prestige and in order to assert their claim to enter the administrative cities, had begun by obtaining consular sites within the city walls. Only later did they follow the example of the foreign merchants in moving out nearer the waterway on which trade was conducted. After 1858 this pattern, spontaneously developed in the northern ports, was applied to Canton by the construction of the artificial island of Shameen (*sha-mien*, "sandbank"), where room for expansion, accessibility by water, and ease of defense were all provided.

The similarity between the ports was more than topographical. The anchorage, the bund, the club, the church and cemetery, the consulate, the race-course, all can be regarded as integral manifestations of an early "treaty-port culture," which in ethnological terms may be said to have been closely affiliated to the British-Indian culture of the day. This culture produced its own substantial style of square colonnaded or arcaded architecture, its own type of local and vitriolic personal feud, its own form of scholar (the sinologue who took all Chinese learning for his province), and its own idea of China — that intransigently disillusioned view later termed "the Shanghai mind." Cut off as the early ports were in the period here spoken of, when the telegraph reached only from England to Italy and steamers and mails were infrequent, it was natural that the foreign communities in China should be thrown upon their own resources. Commercial partners and assistants, as well as consular officers and to a less extent missionaries, were transferred periodically from port to port. As

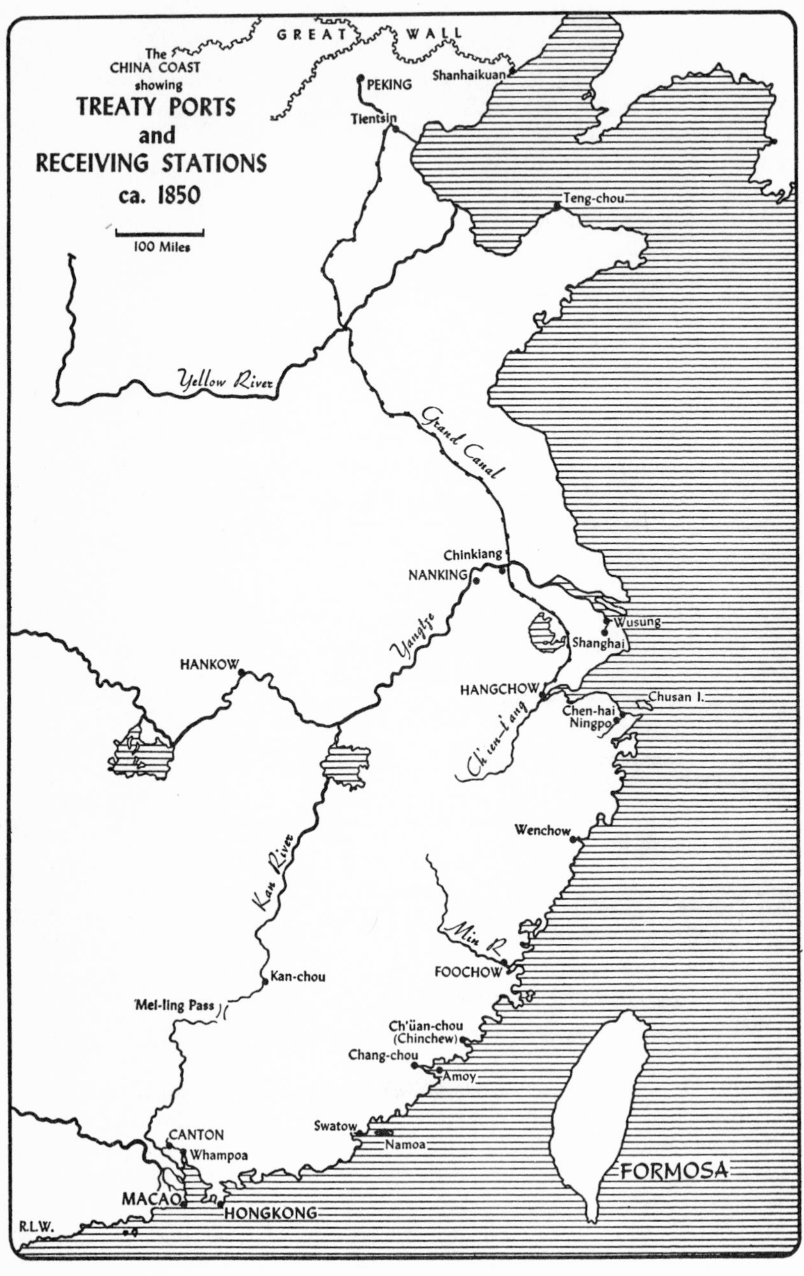
The CHINA COAST showing
TREATY PORTS and RECEIVING STATIONS ca. 1850
100 Miles
GREAT WALL
PEKING
Tientsin
Shanhaikuan
Teng-chou
Yellow River
Grand Canal
Chinkiang
NANKING
Wusung
Shanghai
Yangtze
HANKOW
HANGCHOW
Chusan I.
Chen-hai
Ningpo
Ch'ien-t'ang
Wenchow
Kan River
Min R.
FOOCHOW
Kan-chou
Mei-ling Pass
Ch'üan-chou (Chinchew)
Chang-chou
Amoy
Swatow
Namoa
CANTON
Whampoa
MACAO
HONGKONG
FORMOSA
R.L.W.

late as 1850 many of the leaders in trade and evangelism were still of the pre-treaty generation who had once lived crowded together at Canton and Macao. This made the early ports really one community, as they remained to some degree throughout the century. Their position also, on the very edge of a teeming continent, exposed to a hostility which was more cultural than political but at times none the less plain, created an underlying solidarity among the foreign residents.[b]

After the first expansion when the new ports were opened, the size of the treaty port population remained almost constant at Canton for a decade (305 in 1846 and 321 in 1854), while it grew mainly at Shanghai (108 in 1846 and 214 in 1854). The ports in between remained outposts — in the same years Amoy grew only from 23 to 29, Foochow from 5 to 14, and Ningpo from 11 to 19. (These figures for settled foreign residents are only approximate; records vary widely because so much of this population was transient.)

Since Shanghai was to become so rapidly the central emporium of the China trade, its early history and administration have received a good deal of attention.[8] The foreign settlement had to be built from the ground up. Consul Balfour picked the site in October 1842 and fixed the boundaries on his return a year later. During its first year only 44 foreign vessels arrived, the foreign community (by one count) "consisted of 23 residents and families, there were only 11 merchants' houses, 2 Protestant missionaries, and 1 Consular flag"; the bund was just being built, out of the old towing path, new streets were barely 25 feet wide, and large areas were still swamp and tide-water, waiting to be filled in. The first sewer was not built until 1852.[9]

In such a place the foreign establishments had to grow up as self-contained units, somewhat like a Chinese official's yamen, or the old factories at Canton. An English or American firm's hong might cover an acre or two of ground within the walls of its compound. This area would be filled with the big residence of the taipan (*tai-pan*, firm managers or partners) and junior clerks, the business offices (usually in the same building), quarters for servants, compradores, and shroffs, a stable, and various godowns (warehouses) for tea, silk, or piece goods. As the ports developed, a big hong would have a junior mess distinct from the resident partners' senior mess. A big firm would be organized in departments to handle tea, silk, piece goods, shirtings or other imports, shipping, insurance, and some-

[b] In 1844 there were some 94 commercial firms or agencies represented in the treaty ports, with almost 300 partners or assistants listed under them. Of this total, 19 were parsee firms from India with about 64 members. Roughly 33 firms from Western countries were represented by single individuals. Under the remaining 40-odd British, American, and European firms were listed 226 partners and associates, a few of them absent in England. Jardine's was the largest, with 5 partners and 20 assistants. Dent and Co. had 5 partners and 8 assistants; Russell and Co. (American), 6 partners and 4 assistants; D. and M. Rustomjee (Indian), 15 partners.[7]

times even "muck and truck" — miscellaneous Chinese exports. Its key staff members would include a silk inspector ("grub," in local slang), a bookkeeper ("books"), and a tea-taster ("expectorator"), who might get £300 to £600 a year for his gustatory ability and the abstemious life which preserved it.

News from home came spasmodically, chiefly by a monthly mail. News within the treaty port community circulated by gossip, supplemented by a weekly press. In Hongkong the *Friend of China* began in 1841, and the *China Mail* in 1845; in Shanghai the *North China Herald* began in 1850 — all supplementing the monthly *Chinese Repository* at Canton (1832–1851).

By the early 1850's the Westerners in China ran some two hundred business concerns engaged in trade or connected with it. (To make such a total one must include ship-chandlers, bankers, watchmakers, storekeepers, physicians, architects, publishers, steamship agents, and the various branches of firms, many of which were represented at all the three larger settlements.) Of this number usually half were English and almost a quarter were Parsee or Indian, making the "British" share almost three quarters of the whole. Among the remaining fifty-odd, Continental and American firms were about equal in number; but the ships of the latter carried a third, and at Shanghai almost half, of the foreign trade, while the French and Swiss monopolized chiefly wine-selling and watch-making and the Scandinavians seldom even had their own nationals to represent them as consuls. The British set the style. The Americans were their chief competitors, particularly in the carrying trade. A dozen British firms dominated the insurance business, as agents for companies in London, Calcutta, and Bombay. The large tea and silk exporters maintained their own fleets, while the smaller chartered vessels for single voyages or acted as local consignees and agents for correspondents in London, Liverpool, and New York, making profit both through commissions and through investment in cargoes. Thus the merchants actually in the treaty ports were but the forward echelon of those concerned in the China trade.

Treaty port life in the middle of the century followed the general routine of Company days, in that periods of leisure were punctuated by the feverish activity attendant upon the arrivals and departures of the mail and of vessels bearing consignments. Since correspondents and senior partners were usually at a distance, at Hongkong or in England or America, local agents of big firms bore responsibilities and took decisions on a scale which the telegraph was later to make unnecessary. They maintained baronial establishments and upheld a tradition of hospitality. Table-boys, chair-bearers, and other servants were cheap and living was sumptuous. Shanghailanders of the period used to "begin dinner with rich soup, and a glass of sherry; *then* one or two side dishes with champagne; *then* some beef, mutton, or fowls and bacon, with *more* champagne, or beer; *then* rice and curry and ham; *afterwards* game; *then* pudding, pastry, jelly, custard, or blancmange, and *more* champagne; *then* cheese and salad, and bread and butter, and a glass of port wine; *then* in many cases, oranges, figs, raisins, and walnuts . . . *with* two or three glasses of claret or some other wine." In view of the illness resulting from a diet appropriate, if at all, to the English winter, an experienced Shanghai physician counselled moderation,— "for breakfast a mutton chop, fresh eggs, curry and bread-and-butter, with coffee or tea, or claret and water.[10]

Foreign women remained in a great minority and male social life centered about the strenuous regimen of sports — rowing, rackets, fives, cricket, bowling, riding, pheasant-shooting — such exercise being considered essential every day just to "shake up your liver." Otherwise, everything was business. As one Shanghailander put it,[11] "Commerce was the beginning, the middle, and the end of our life in China; . . . if there were no trade, not a single man, except missionaries, would have come there at all."[c] It was this concentration of the treaty port community upon its commercial enterprises that gave such importance to the rules of trade and their consular enforcement.

The British consular staff. The treaty ports were designed to revolve around the British consul. In his person, as in the person of a Chinese magistrate, were vested nearly all the powers of government, and the consular functions listed in the treaties make impressive reading. Under the general regulations of trade the British consul had a full time job looking after commercial matters alone. He settled pilots' fees (art. I), received a ship's papers and notified the customs of its arrival (art. III), returned a ship's papers on its departure (art. VI), requested the examination of goods and heard appeals over duties (art. VII), coöperated in settling the standard of coinage (art. VIII), kept standard sets of weights and measures (art. IX), gave certificates for transshipment of goods (art. XI), controlled British seamen (art. XII), heard grievances against both Chinese and British subjects and punished British criminals (art. XIII), notified the Chinese authorities of the movements of British cruisers (art. XIV), and acted as security for all British merchant ships. To these the Supplementary treaty had added numerous other duties regarding the enforcement of port limits, renting of ground and houses, extradition of criminals, prevention of smuggling, and control of sailing letters.[13]

[c] "In two or three years at farthest I hope to realize a fortune and get away," confessed a Shanghai merchant to his consul, "and what can it matter to me if all Shanghai disappear afterwards in fire or flood? You must not expect men in my position to condemn themselves to prolonged exile in an unhealthy climate for the benefit of posterity. We are money-making, practical men. Our business is to make money, as much and as fast as we can: — and for this end all modes or means are good which the law permits."[12]

Able men were needed in 1843 to put this new legal machinery in motion, and Pottinger's first problem was one of personnel. He could not open a treaty port until he had found an officer capable of applying the treaties, and an adequate interpreter to go with him. The process was consequently a slow one, much as the merchants might chafe.

The first five British consuls included two men of long experience in China who could act as their own interpreters but had little administrative background, a military man chosen on the spot, and two administrators of proven ability who had never seen China before. Only one of these men eventually rose to the top of the service. (For a table of British consular officers at the ports, see Appendix A below.)

George Tradescant Lay, who opened the consulates at Canton and Foochow and died at Amoy in 1845, had been successively a naturalist with the Beechey expedition in 1825–28, an agent of the British and Foreign Bible Society in China after 1836, and a British interpreter during the war — a mild man who got on so well with the Chinese people that he proved incapable of pounding the tables of the mandarins. Jardine's former employee Robert Thom, the unhappy co-author of the Supplementary treaty, who opened Ningpo and served there until his death on Sept. 14, 1846, was a faithful servant of British trade but scarcely a diplomat. Captain George Balfour of the Madras Artillery was chosen from Pottinger's personal staff and presented to Ch'i-ying in September 1842 as the future consul for Shanghai. Sir Henry recommended him to the Foreign Office as having already acquired a tolerable knowledge of Chinese; fortunately he was never obliged to rely upon it.[14]

Of the administrators sent out from England, Francis C. Macgregor, the first substantive consul at the key port of Canton, had been for many years H. M.'s consul at Elsinore and retired from China after four years' able and unspectacular service. Rutherford Alcock (1809–1897), later minister in Tokyo and Peking, on the other hand, found in the treaty ports a career which exemplified the best of Victorian imperialism. He was a truly philosophic man of action, singularly gifted with a sense of duty and almost religiously devoted to the interests of British trade. As a young man he had studied surgery, in fact modelled artificial limbs in Paris to pay for his medical education. In 1832 he joined the British foreign legion fighting in the internal struggles in Portugal and Spain, and as surgeon to mercenary troops for whom slight provision was made he saw at first hand the medical chaos on which Florence Nightingale was to begin her attack twenty years later. On returning to England in 1838 Alcock rapidly became a promising man in his profession, lecturing and writing on surgery, apparently headed for a chair at King's College. Suddenly his career was ended when at thirty-five he lost the use of his thumbs through a mysterious rheumatic fever. Almost at once he secured appointment as a consul in China, and in the new ports of Amoy, Foochow, and Shanghai began a second career.[15]

A temporary appointee, Captain Henry Gribble, was made officiating consul (as a second choice) [d] to open the port of Amoy; he had been in the Company's service and in trade at Macao, but he became so confused in his new and strange duties that he was shortly removed.

As vice-consuls and assistants there was sent out from England a miscellaneous group of younger sons and recipients of patronage. One was a former Canton tea-taster, another a London barrister, and several bore names famous in the British bureaucracy. Temple Hilliard Layton, for example, after leaving Corpus Christi College, Cambridge, in 1832, had become a tea inspector in the Company's factory at Canton with a salary of £500 per annum, a house at Canton, another at Macao, a monthly allowance of £10.10, and a seat at the public table of the Company maintained at their expense. After 1834 he remained in the Company's Canton agency at a salary of £600, £1200, and finally £2400 per year, and later served the private foreign mercantile community. Having tasted samples of nine or ten million pounds sterling worth of tea in his seven years at Canton, Mr. Layton returned to England in 1839 with a small independent fortune. Appointed vice-consul at Ningpo, he sailed from Portsmouth on the *City of Derry*, Feb. 8, 1844, and reached Hongkong on June 18, with his wife, their only daughter, aged 5, her governess, his wife's sister, a Chinese female servant and her son, aged 15, and an English female servant, paying the government £206 extra for their passage.

Another man sent out as vice-consul was Henry Charles Sirr, whose father of the same name (1764–1841) had been the much-hated chief agent of the Dublin authorities in the suppression of the Irish rebels at the turn of the century. The father made a collection of five hundred paintings and one of his sons became a rector and author of minor religious works. Henry Charles became a barrister at Lincoln's Inn. Having taken an appointment to China, he reached Hongkong in May 1844 and ran into difficulties. The boarding house was as expensive as a first class hotel in London, with the rain pouring in the windows and his wife the only woman resident. He heard that the British gunboats were to be removed from the consulates, felt unprepared "to sacrifice my wife's life or liberty," and resigned. In August 1844 he and his wife both were fined $10 for assault and beating their landlord.[17] He eventually became Queen's advocate for the southern circuit of Ceylon, having written two books: *China and the*

[d] Pottinger's first offer was made to William Davidson, "a very respectable and well-informed merchant who has lately come to Hongkong from Batavia." The latter declined the temporary honor, since it would cut short his business career.[16] He figures below in the coast trade of Ningpo (Ch. 18).

Chinese, their History, etc. (London, 1849) and *Ceylon and the Cingalese, their History*, etc. (London, 1850).

The other original vice-consuls included D. B. Robertson, later consul at Shanghai and Canton, G. G. Sullivan, a master of the Royal Navy whom Pottinger found at a loose end in Hongkong after twenty-two years in that service,[18] and Robert Belgrave Jackson. Another man picked up in China was Charles A. Sinclair, "a gentleman who was five years in the Bank of Belgium"; he began as an accountant at Canton and later became a vice-consul. Among the assistants were several names of note in the British civil service: Frank Parish, Hertslet, C. F. Giles, Backhouse, Patrick Hague, Frederick Harvey.

These consular officers were both servants of the Queen and members of the treaty port community. Their social contact in these early years was necessarily with British merchants, they lived in the same fashion, and made up in social prestige for their relatively more modest incomes.

The language problem. Interpreters were the essential link without which all the treaties and regulations would remain ineffective ideas in the mind of the consul. A prime object lesson was supplied at Amoy, where there was at first no British interpreter. At this port on the Fukien coast there was no backlog of pidgin-English-speaking natives through whom to do business as at Canton. There was moreover a native dialect to deal with in addition to the Cantonese spoken by merchants and the Pekinese dialect of the mandarins. When Captain Gribble arrived as officiating consul he had with him as interpreters two Cantonese linguists, Ah-foo and A-ping, who had been engaged at Hongkong for $40.00 and $30.00 a month, respectively. They proved incompetent both at the local Fukien dialect and at the mandarin necessary for official interviews. Mistakes were "so frequent from the incompetency of my interpreters" that Gribble had to lean heavily upon the services of the local American missionary, the Rev. David Abeel, who was very busy with his own flock and lived at some distance from the consulate.[19] Even Mr. Abeel, although he understood "a good deal" of what was said in mandarin, could not speak it. Captain Gribble therefore engaged the services of two more Chinese: an intelligent native of Amoy who had learned some English at Singapore and received $20.00 a month and Ton-jee, a writer, who could interpret and translate between Fukienese and mandarin. He received $12.00 a month, while the luckless Cantonese linguists, A-ping and Ah-foo, had their salaries cut to $20 apiece in order to balance the budget (within $2). They remained essential as the only members of the consular staff who knew the names of the articles of trade. Meanwhile the only medium for communication with the local authorities, the ill-paid Ton-jee, remained unable to communicate with the consul.

In his negotiations Captain Gribble prepared for his meetings with the Chinese authorities on the evening before, drawing up a list of questions with memoranda. On the following morning he would communicate these to his Chinese linguist-interpreters, who would copy down his questions. In the interview itself, the Captain would address in English the Chinese educated at Singapore who would then convey the statement in Fukienese to his assistant, Ton-jee, who would express it in mandarin to the officials. Gradually, the consul began to suspect that his Chinese assistants were in the pay of the madarins, particularly after it was found that some of his memoranda had found their way to the Chinese authorities who proceeded to quote them for their own purposes.[20]

The Chinese language remained at all the ports a constant though minor source of trouble. When Gutzlaff was transferred from Chusan to take the place of J. R. Morrison as Chinese secretary in the superintendency of trade at Hongkong,[21] the military government of Chusan was left without an interpreter; and when Chinese authorities came to take a register of fishing vessels late in 1843 the British army officers in charge drove them summarily away under the Anglo-Saxon misapprehension that they were trying to hold court and flout the Queen. When translated at Hongkong, their communications were found to be both polite and innocuous. Mere contact had produced misunderstanding.

In the conduct of trade there was similar room for confusion since the name of a British vessel might be translated into one set of Chinese characters at one customhouse and into entirely different characters at another. Thus the ship *Stalhart* was given the Chinese name *Shih-te-ko* at Amoy and the name *Shih-to-chi* at the Bogue, to the subsequent confusion of the Hoppo's office at Canton. Sometimes, in fact, the Chinese names of foreign ships invented by the customs and those thought up at the consulate in their reports to the customs could not be identified and left the Chinese authorities in a quandary as to the exact volume of trade.[22] A Dutch vessel, the *Ho-lun-ti*, was reported in January 1845 to have visited Ningpo. The captain's name was *Mo-ta-man*. It afterwards proceeded to Amoy and at the end of February the report from that port gave the captain's name as *Hu-fu-te*. The identity of the vessel being well established, the discrepancy in names was attributed to the local dialects.[23]

The Chinese documents do not confirm the traditional American pride in the linguistic abilities of our early missionaries at Canton. As the American treaty negotiations got under way in 1844, Ch'i-ying's assistant, Huang En-t'ung, found that the Americans were even more difficult to instruct than the British. Where the British had had Morrison and others with some knowledge of Chinese writing and speech, the Americans had only the missionaries Parker and Bridgman, whose knowledge of Chinese characters was slight and who could understand only Cantonese. Communicating with them was very laborious.[24]

The interpreters' key position in the conduct of business gave opportunity to men of talent who were willing to make the necessary investment in language study.[e] Many British ministers and consuls in the Far East during the third quarter of the century were drawn from the interpreters' ranks. The meteoric Harry Parkes (1828–1885), who saved the situation at Amoy as interpreter there after June 1844, was only the most spectacular of this group. Later minister in Japan and China, he had come out to China at the age of thirteen, begun Chinese under Gutzlaff and J. R. Morrison, witnessed the signing of the Nanking treaty, and by January 1844 was able to act as interpreter at the farewell interview between Pottinger and Ch'i-ying. The confusion of tongues also gave an opening to Lieut. Thomas Francis Wade of the 98th regiment, a young man of great linguistic aptitude who at the end of the war was "already moderately qualified in the Court language, and willing to devote himself" to the study of the Fukien dialect. After sick leave in England he became interpreter at Amoy in July 1847.[26] (The influence of this Amoy experience upon the Wade system of romanization, still standard, is an interesting question.)

At Shanghai the first consul was greatly aided by the presence of Dr. Walter Henry Medhurst, one of the pioneers of the London Missionary Society and a translator of the so-called delegates' version of the New Testament. His son, Walter Henry Medhurst, aged twenty, became official interpreter at the consulate; father and son together formed a combination to which the foreign settlement became much indebted. The son was later consul at Foochow, Shanghai, and Hankow.[27]

Consulates and their health. The first consulates were set up on a lavish scale. The original salary budget for the five ports totaled some twenty thousand pounds sterling a year, since each was thought to require a consul, vice-consul, interpreter, and surgeon, plus British assistants where necessary and a number of Chinese clerks and writers. Even Ningpo began with a staff of these proportions and, although the absence of trade soon re-

[e] John A. T. Meadows followed the example of his famous brother, Thomas Taylor Meadows, and set out to become an interpreter in the China service. After arriving in Canton, where Thomas Taylor was consular interpreter, in January 1845, he at once began to study the Peking dialect with a teacher at $20.00 a month, reading the *Hung-lou-meng* (Dream of the Red Chamber) and writing an hour a day with a brush. After a year of this he began to study Cantonese and read official documents with a second teacher, also at $20.00 a month. From September 1846 to November 1849 he served as a public translator for the Canton community, doing all sorts of commercial documents into and out of Chinese and also acting as interpreter for the consular representatives of Holland, France, Belgium and Prussia, and translating from the *Peking Gazette* for the *Hongkong Register*. For the first half of 1850 he acted in place of T. T. Meadows in the British consulate, and finally became acting interpreter at Ningpo from August 1, 1850. After seven years at the language he still worked with a teacher every day out of office hours, and had paid his teachers all told the sum of $2517.[25]

duced the British personnel, the Chinese staff in 1847 totaled ten persons: a writer, linguist, messenger, porter, two boatmen, two watchmen, and two coolies, all of whose salaries totaled $59.50 a month. If we estimate families at five persons and cousins at only three more, this makes some eighty residents of Ningpo dependent upon the Queen. The numbers were greater elsewhere.

The personnel proposed for Amoy and actually employed at Canton was as follows: [28]

TABLE 5. STAFF AND SALARIES PROPOSED FOR H. B. M.'S CONSULATE AT AMOY, SEPTEMBER 1843

consul (officiating)	£ 1500	
vice-consul	750	
interpreter	800	
surgeon	600	
		Total £ 3650.
head clerk	$ 1800	
2nd clerk	1200	
2 Chinese linguists at $30 a month each	720	
	$ 3720	(say £ 845)
approximate grand total for salaries		£ 4495

TABLE 6. STAFF AND SALARIES FOR H. B. M.'S CONSULATE AT CANTON, JUNE 1844

consul	£ 1800
vice-consul	750
assistant interpreter	600
1st assistant	405
2nd assistant	324
3 Chinese writers at $30 a month each	243
total salaries	£ 4122

Once these British staffs had been installed at the ports, their health became a major cause of concern, to them if not to the Foreign Office. By order of the latter, the medical officers were withdrawn from all the consulates as from March 31, 1844, for budgetary reasons.[29] Whether their presence would have made a difference is of course uncertain.

In any case, the mortality rate in the first years of the China service was heavy, and discouraging to the survivors. Amoy may serve as an example. Early in 1844 new houses had not yet been built there for the consular staff. It was damp and cold. A clerk, Mr. Mitchell, was ill with fever. The other clerk and all in his house had fever and ague. Vice-consul Sullivan had been near death for several weeks. A Chinese servant had died from "malignant Kulangsoo fever"; Consul Gribble had an inflammation of the eye which had destroyed his sight for ten days. By August Sullivan's extreme illness necessitated his being sent to Chusan, and the newly arrived assistant, Frank Parish, had been taken ill. By November interpreter Parkes, who had arrived with Parish in June, was given six weeks sick leave because of a return of fever. Consul Lay arrived on April 19, 1845, from a nine months' solitary sojourn at Foochow. He had a compound fracture of one metacarpal of his right hand, had not seen his wife at Hongkong for nearly four years, and was low in spirits. On November 6, he died of the fever after a seventeen-day illness, leaving "a wife with helpless offspring" and not enough money to return to England. Vice-consul Sullivan died at Amoy in July 1852 and vice-consul Jackson (of Foochow) in July 1854. The record of the other ports was not much better. Of twenty-five young men appointed as student interpreters in China in the ten years from 1847 to 1858, thirteen were still in the service in 1872, four had resigned from ill health and three had died at their posts.[f]

Communications and finance. Not the least demoralizing feature of consular life in these early ports was its separation from the European world. Ship passages to England still took about four months. Government dispatches via the new overland route across the Isthmus of Suez usually took three months. For example, twenty monthly overland mails between October 10, 1841, and May 6, 1843, averaged eighty-nine days. The side-wheel steamers of the Peninsular and Oriental Company maintained a schedule of thirty-five days from London to Ceylon. In September 1843 the company proposed to add a service of twenty-four days between Ceylon and Hongkong, which would cut the time between London and Hongkong from three months to two.[31] But it was not until the middle of June 1845 that the mail reached Hongkong under steam in the *Lady Mary Wood* (553 tons gross). Regular steam communication with England on a fifty-four day schedule was inaugurated the following August with two or more vessels on each of three sections: Hongkong to Ceylon, Ceylon to Suez, Alexandria to Southampton. Passengers crossed from Suez to Cairo by van in twenty-four hours and proceeded thence to Alexandria by river steamer and canal boat. During their first eighteen months of operation the P. and O. steamers actually

[f] Consul G. T. Lay's letters of 1842–45 to his son, H. N. Lay, then a schoolboy at Mill Hill in London, testify repeatedly to his bodily discomfort: he was wounded in the head and face during the capture of Wusung, June 16, 1842; in June 1843, he professed himself "very unwell though I move about as if nothing were the matter"; in November he was "seldom without some pain or disagreeable sensation"; in March 1844, he was having insomnia from about one to five every morning — "I cannot work so hard as I once did"; by May 1845, "hardship is grown familiar and comfort is something more than I expect."[30]

averaged 55 and 3/4 days between England and Hongkong. A gentleman's berth in the general cabin including all fees and food cost £185.[32] In 1850 the *Lady Mary Wood* began a P. and O. service between Hongkong and Shanghai. Although these early paddle-wheelers were capable of averaging about seven knots, their trips were not so frequent as to make sailing vessels unnecessary.

Opium clippers for several years continued to be the fastest means of communication between India and China, and the government made no bones about using them for mail. In 1842 Pottinger had forwarded dispatches to India by the *Cowasjee Family* and in 1843 he used the *Red Rover*, *Petrel*, and *Kelpie*. These aristocratic vessels, however, carried their owners' drug and his firm's market reports as their specialty and the government mail only by way of courtesy. In 1843 Dent's opium schooner *Zephyr* sailed from Bombay four hours ahead of schedule and a mail boat sent after her "reached within a short distance of the vessel" but was disregarded, so that the dispatches for the plenipotentiary and the admiral in China had to wait and proceed slowly via Calcutta. Both officers inveighed against the "system of evading the conveyance of mails" which was practiced by shipowners in order to send their friends or business associates exclusive news of the home market; they proposed a law requiring the formal dispatch of all mail vessels by the post office.[33]

In China, during the negotiation of the treaties, naval steamers such as H.M.S. *Proserpine* had been used to communicate between Canton and Hongkong. When the new ports were opened Pottinger arranged with the admiral for a bi-monthly naval steamer service between Hongkong and Chusan, to begin with a large steamer going south from Chusan in January 1844, returning in February, and so on. Reports from the consuls at Shanghai and Ningpo would meanwhile be collected each month by a steamer from Chusan, for transmission to the south. But the use of naval steamers for the conveyance of consular dispatches, especially from a dead port like Foochow, to which no British vessel had yet gone at the end of 1844, was too extravagant to be continued. Pottinger had already made use of clippers like the *Zoe*, which he had asked to wait over a day in April 1843 in order to take dispatches to Chusan.[34] The consuls soon followed his example.

At Amoy Consul Gribble arranged to use the facilities offered by the opium clippers which called outside the port on their swift journeys north and south. He explained in July 1844 that these running vessels frequently anchored among the shipping for hours at a time, but their agents would not notify their arrival until after they had left, while the masters would not think of the mails until it suited their own convenience. Thus mail for Foochow from England had often been taken nonchalantly up to Chusan. While regular mails might arrive at intervals of three weeks or a month, the running vessels called outside once or twice a week. He therefore proposed that a small consular police cutter, useful for harbor work, might be equally useful to make contact with the opium fleet.[35]

At the northern ports, particularly Ningpo, the facilities of the drug trade were used almost from the beginning. Because of the great delay through regular post office channels, the Ningpo consul in 1847 asked that government dispatches be sent to him through Dent and Company, Hongkong, who would "kindly forward any packages or letters to my address through the Opium Clippers to the care of the Capts. of their vessels at Lookong [the early opium station outside Ningpo] or Wusung." [36] Foochow in 1848 received dispatches via *Zephyr*, *Audax*, and *Gazelle*, all of them famous names on the coast.

Equally important was the service which the opium trade rendered to Her Majesty's government in the matter of banking. Sir John Davis, when governor of Hongkong and superintendent of British trade in China, complained at the end of 1844 that he had difficulty in sending cash or public funds to the three northern ports for want of public conveyance.[37] Here again it became natural to use the facilities so obviously at hand. A letter from Matheson to his agent, A. G. Dallas, later the firm's representative at Shanghai, remarked that "Captain Balfour, the consul for Shanghai, and Mr. Thom, the consul for Ningpo, are particular friends of ours, and will give our vessels as little trouble as they can, but it will be advisable to keep entirely out of sight of these ports . . . You will of course oblige Captain Balfour or Mr. Thom by cashing their bills or otherwise." [38] The Ningpo consul noted casually in 1850 that the funds of the consulate were all supplied by Capt. Hall of the *Ternate*, Dent and Company's receiving ship at Tinghai twelve miles down the river. When the consulate officers in 1846 wished to send to Hongkong a subscription of $100 for the widow of Consul Lay, they sent an order on Jardine, Matheson and Company. The consulate was still using Jardine's agent, Capt. Dan Patridge, as a means of remitting fees to Hongkong in 1855.[39]

In South China, however, the British authorities did not have to rely entirely on a trade of whose existence they were officially unaware. Between Hongkong and Canton Sir Henry Pottinger originally intended to have weekly postal communication, and nearly that rate must have been maintained for in 1849 a total of 245 dispatches was addressed to the plenipotentiary and superintendent of trade from the Canton consulate. Such dispatches in 1844 were forwarded by lorcha and fast boat on the Canton river, a fee being paid to the bearer, sometimes Chinese, on delivery at either end.

When the Fukien ports were first opened and Pottinger and Ch'i-ying were on terms of affection, it was arranged in July 1844 that British dispatches from Hongkong to Foochow should be forwarded, in the temporary absence of trade, through the Chinese authorities at Amoy. Ch'i-ying promised to arrange with the Fukien governor-general for an overland service, presumably by the imperial post, between Amoy and Foochow. Early in 1845, however, an overland courier service under British control was set up between Canton, Amoy, and Foochow. This was continued in operation up to 1850 or later to form a line between Hongkong and the Fukien ports. In May 1845 this service was functioning once a month. The fees paid to the Chinese courier, as quoted at different times, were between $20 and $26 for a round trip: $8 or $10 on leaving Canton, another $8 or $10 on arrival via Amoy at Foochow, and the remaining $4 or $6 upon return to Canton with dispatches from Foochow in a locked bag. The time taken, probably on foot or by chair, was 32 or 34 days round trip. In July 1849 the Foochow consul instructed Canton to pay the courier $7 if he arrived within 17 days — since one could not go faster in the hot season. Consul Alcock proposed in 1846 that this service be extended to Shanghai and Ningpo, but the probable cost, estimated at $100, was prohibitive.[40]

Local dispatches from Ningpo to Shanghai were also taken, occasionally, by courier. In December 1851 the Ningpo consul hired one Tsai-sze-te to carry dispatches to Shanghai; Tsai was delayed by illness, wind, and tide and took ten days, reaching Shanghai after another courier had been sent back. He returned to Ningpo on the sixteenth day but was afraid to report to the consulate. The quickest mail communication with Shanghai was of course by boat. In 1855 the Ningpo consulate mail was delivered to Capt. Baylis of Jardine's receiving ship *Folkestone* at Wusung, for delivery to Ningpo by a J. M. and Co. lugger. Jardine's appear to have had the official contract for carriage, Capt. Patridge's *Erin* taking the mail from Ningpo to Wusung.[41]

By these various means the consulates managed to keep in monthly touch with Hongkong. It was decidedly unusual, for example, when Foochow received no dispatches for seven weeks in the summer of 1849.

After the first hopeful years when naval vessels delivered the new consuls to their posts, cheaper and more humble services were used to convey consular officers from port to port when transferred or on leave. Such travel was done frequently by the use of coastal lorchas, small craft which battened on the drug traffic in particular. Vice-consul Sullivan reached Ningpo from Amoy in 1846 on the 75-ton brig *St. Antonio*, for a fee of $500. Interpreter Gingell got a lorcha passage from Amoy to Foochow in June 1849 for $100, and Assistant Parish then proceeded from Foochow to Ningpo by Portuguese lorcha.[42] All these services of communication, finance, and travel provided by the opium traffic, which were used also by the foreign merchants and sometimes by missionaries, merely illustrated the importance of the drug which energized the advance of Western civilization along the China coast.

Sir John Davis made a tour of the new ports in September and October 1844, to inspect the consulates and appraise the promise of trade. He found that opium at Shanghai was "carried openly about the town and publicly sold," and the receiving ships outside Amoy were well known to the local authorities, "to whom they paid fixed dues." There were already 15 English residents at Shanghai, including half a dozen females, and a foreign community was growing up on Kulangsu at Amoy. But the ports of Ningpo and Foochow were still dead to legitimate trade.[43]

The British consular approach to China. As protagonists of British commercial expansion, the early consular personnel had behind them a long tradition inherited from the East India Company and strongly colored by British experience in India. The examples of Clive and Hastings, Cornwallis and Raffles, the faith in Britain's innate superiority and the white man's burden, the code of personal rectitude and the belief in meting out justice, even if mixed with contempt, to the natives — all shaped the attitude of these new officials in the treaty ports. In China they found themselves in the position of reformers who conducted a daily battle against Chinese ways. Faced with the complex and never-ending task of enforcing the new treaties, they had to meet all a reformer's problems — whether to attack at once a small irregularity or to wait for overwhelming evidence to accumulate against it, whether to demand the fulfillment of the treaty even when it seemed impossible or to accept a momentary compromise and renew the demand later. The old Chinese methods of conducting foreign relations continued to be used under the thin veneer of treaty formalities, and the consul was often in a position of influence but not of power, uncertain of the facts and unable to control Chinese conduct. As a final recourse he could appeal to the Royal Navy. But gunboats were not always at hand and when used might be a damaging admission of diplomatic failure. Warships could maintain order or punish disorder, when the Chinese authorities were incapable of doing it themselves, but they seldom could substitute for diplomacy. Instead of coercing his Chinese opponent the consul had first to try to outmanoeuvre him.

For this it was soon found that there was only one method — to take a definite stand based on a clear right, and inexorably maintain it. Firmness of will was the priceless ingredient. The successful consul must have genuine insight into the Confucian ethical code, a sense of the logic of his position in Chinese eyes such that he could base it on accepted moral principles and so make it invulnerable. Wilful or headstrong acts, like the unjustified use of force, were likely to fail. A stand based on rational principles might win Chinese acquiescence. In the final showdown it was the consul's determination, his reputation for sticking to his guns through thick and thin, that would be most likely to gain his point; for his determination implied the ultimate possibility of an appeal to Britain's superior force, and no Chinese official could desire such an eventuality.

Behind a British consul's diplomatic firmness there was usually moral fervor, a real faith in the transcendent civilizing value of British commerce and British law. Consul Alcock looked upon commerce as "the true herald of civilization . . . the human agency appointed under a Divine dispensation to work out man's emancipation from the thralldom and evils of a savage isolation." He believed also in "a natural and moral law which governs the life, and growth, and decay of nations, as clearly as it does the life of man. . . . Man's efforts at civilization invariably — when the race to be benefited is inferior and weaker, intellectually and physically, than the nation civilizing — have had but one result: the weaker has gone down before the stronger." (This was written some four years before the publication of *The Origin of Species.*) Alcock believed that "China may linger . . . in her agonies," but must surely succumb in the end. This faith both in the cause of commerce and in the decadence of China, inspired Alcock's ambitious proposals for the forcible opening of the Chinese market; it sustained him in a debilitating climate, and combined with a rich administrative experience to give him strong convictions as to the proper manner of dealing with the Chinese. "No policy can be a good or successful policy in China which has not a special adaptation to the traditions, character, and prejudices of the nation, governors, and people; . . . there must be no *ko-towing* to them — the one besetting sin of the past — but rather an assertion, in proper time and place, and with all temper and discretion, of the dignity and rights of other nations immeasurably their superiors in all that constitutes a nation's worth, or a people's strength . . . truckling and temporizing will never have any other issue than to add insolence to arrogance, and impracticability to conceit." [g]

The classical method for maintaining British prestige was demonstrated by Consul Balfour in a tiff with the local authorities at Shanghai in August 1844. It appears that the sub-prefect and district magistrate, minor officials, sent the consul a dispatch in improper style and at the same time seized a Chinese Christian named Yao who had helped Medhurst in translation work during the war. Balfour sent Medhurst at the hour of 8 P.M. to the

[g] Alcock's colleague, the American merchant-consul at Shanghai, Edward Cunningham of Russell and Co., echoed this view: ". . . the exercise of self-restraint and the practice of justice are not consistent with the treatment of a nation of the 17th century in knowledge and policy as if it were one of the 19th, with the treatment of a child as if it were a grown man. The civilized world, moved by philanthropic feelings, is too apt to consider any attempt to procure further advantages of trade with Eastern nations, though equally advantageous to them as to us, except by simple request, as unmannerly and unchristian. The sentiment is founded on a noble principle, but overlooks the childish character of the people with whom we have to deal, and whom it may be considered our mission to guide and enlighten . . ." [44]

yamen to declare that Yao must be released in one hour or the consul would embark on a British vessel and leave Shanghai. Yao was released. At 6 A.M. the next day Balfour called upon the taotai with a memorandum demanding apologies from the sub-prefect and district magistrate. The taotai was friendly. At 3 P.M., no apologies having come, Medhurst called on the taotai again to demand them. At 9 P.M. arrived the original improper dispatch, now corrected, but no apology. At midnight Balfour therefore wrote the taotai that he intended to close the consulate. The taotai replied at 1 A.M. asking for a delay. At daybreak the consul informed the taotai that the *Vixen*, hired from Jardine's for the purpose, would be sent to Chusan at noon, without asking a port clearance, to obtain the help of the British military there. The taotai replied that he would call at 1 P.M. Balfour replied that the *Vixen* would depart at noon. The taotai called at noon and produced the letter of apology, not yet completed. Balfour consented to rehoist his flag as a mark of confidence in the taotai. The letter of apology later arrived and the case was closed, the taotai having promised that the lower Chinese authorities would address the consul only through him thereafter. Davis approved Balfour's proceedings, although dubious as to the advisability of threats to withdraw, which should not be made on the consul's initiative.[45] It soon became evident that this type of diplomatic blitzkrieg would almost always succeed. Consul Alcock's famous stoppage of the grain junk fleet to secure redress for assaults on Englishmen in the Tsingpu affair at Shanghai in 1848 was only another illustration.[46]

As an alternative to demands, threats and action, a consul could appeal to the Confucian code of conduct, providing he knew enough about it. Thus Consul Thom at Ningpo wrote to the magistrate in the following vein: Ningpo was famous as a place where the "rules of politeness are understood," but unfortunately "a gang of ill-bred rude boys" habitually saluted foreigners "with all kinds of abuse and filthy language," encouraged by the bystanders. Now "foreigners from the Western Ocean are exceedingly hot and hasty in their temperament"; trouble was to be feared. Should not the magistrate therefore issue a proclamation so that "fathers will instruct their sons, and elder brothers their younger brothers," to be civil to foreigners?[47] This appeal to the magistrate to preserve face, avoid trouble, and inculcate Confucian principles in the people was not particularly successful. The old order could not be changed merely by invoking its own rules.

Alcock and Parkes were the most effective treaty port proconsuls because they combined vigorous action with a certain degree of understanding of Confucian principles, especially the apothegm that moral prestige flows from right conduct which not only *is* right but also *looks* right. In their year as consul and interpreter together at Foochow (March 1845–August

1846) they developed a keen eye for Her Majesty's prestige. After a certain incident they demanded that the local authorities post proclamations forbidding insults to foreigners and they secured a list of nineteen places where this would be done. Parkes made a tour of these places and found only eight proclamations. Eventually, when written complaints had little effect, Alcock wrote to Hongkong for a gunboat. Later when Parkes was stoned, he got three culprits put in the cangue.[48] He had learned that eternal vigilance was the price of British prestige and that to resent one insult, vigorously and in time, would forestall nine insults later.

CHAPTER XI

THE CHINESE RESPONSE TO WESTERN CONTACT

The new "barbarian experts." The Chinese response considered in this chapter is not that of the Chinese populace in the countryside nor even that of the towns. It concerns only the small fraction of the Chinese-Manchu élite which got into the business of being "barbarian experts." No doubt these men were roughly representative of the official class, but they were few in number — a group of individuals. Similarly the British "impact" which roused them was mainly in the realm of material things — warfare and trade, weapons and goods. It did not involve, as yet, many conscious questions of cultural values or even of institutional change. The mandarinate's reaction to the British victory was first manifested on a material and practical level.

The new specialists in barbarian-taming appear to have been tolerated by their colleagues: they did an odious and distasteful job, like sewer-inspectors, but in the mid-1840's it was generally acknowledged to be a necessary service. (A few years later this treating with the British would be denounced as simple treachery.) In previous periods Chinese sailors, pilots, merchants, and linguists had sailed the seas and sometimes left accounts of the Westerners, as noted in Chapter 1 above. Now it had become necessary for individuals of the upper class, persons of scholarship and official status, to look into the barbarian problem, discuss it in proper language, and achieve an understanding of the barbarian nature — for it was generally recognized that "if you know yourself and know your opponent, in a hundred battles you can get a hundred victories." [1] To perceive the motivation of the enemy was half the struggle — he could then be led, by adequate means, into a state of harmlessness.

This Chinese situation of the 1840's is not unlike a reverse situation today, in which the American people, finding themselves vitally concerned with new social movements among certain Far Eastern peoples of whom they have long heard, listen hopefully to the political utterances of "Far Eastern experts" whose function it is to explain all aspects of East Asian civilization and thus reassure their audiences. Like their present Western counterparts, the "barbarian experts" in China were likely to discover unpalatable truths, displease the more conservative members of their class and generation, and suffer suspicion and condemnation accordingly. In such cases they frequently succumbed to the contemporary climate of opinion and repeated the stock phrases of the day — traditional terminology which illustrates what the early Chinese "barbarian experts" were up against in their own background.

One striking phrase which flowed constantly from the brushes of yamen writers was *i-ch'ing p'o-ts'e*,[2] "the barbarian nature cannot be fathomed," in modern parlance, Western psychology cannot be understood. Like the more recent occidental belief in oriental inscrutability, this feeling was based on the same sort of ignorance that makes things Chinese still unfathomable to the West. It inspired in China a fear of the unknown Western menace comparable to the later Western fear of the Yellow Peril. Added to the barbarian's inscrutability was his cunning. *I-ch'ing kuei-chueh* — "the barbarian nature is treacherous and deceitful." Barbarians were fickle and greedy opportunists. They were full of trickery and fraud, prone to prevaricate. This constant reiteration that "the barbarian nature is crafty" and "cannot be fathomed," indicated simply that Chinese officials were uncertain of Western motives. Western conduct did not spring from the *li* according to which all persons of Confucian culture might be expected to act.

In one respect there was universal agreement — the barbarians' chief desire was for the profits of trade.[3] The Canton governor-general reiterated to the emperor in 1850 that "the whole country of England relies for its livelihood on the trade of its crowd of merchants. Superiors and inferiors compete against each other. There is none who does not look only for profit. If that country has some undertaking afoot, they turn around first to listen to the commands of the merchants." [4] Chinese memorialists frequently pointed out that "barbarians consider the merchant important, and the official unimportant. Everything they wish to undertake must first be schemed out by the crowd of merchants." [5]

In these circumstances the Manchu-Chinese officials were inclined to give the British their trade if only they would keep quiet. Their reactions were almost entirely defensive, as may be seen in a few more stock phrases. In imperial instructions from Peking one of the commonest commands was to avoid complications, *pu chih ling-sheng chih-chieh*, act in such a way that no other difficulties will branch off from those already grown. The chief object in managing barbarian affairs was to prevent trouble, *mien-sheng shih-tuan*, to keep altercations, issues, and incidents from arising; particularly to keep out of situations where the barbarians might make demands or exactions, *yao-hsieh*, *hsieh-chih*, which would be equally hard to comply with or to refuse. To that end the officials in the provinces and at the capital wrote constantly of *fang-fan*, taking precautionary measures. To their subordinates they wrote *pu tung sheng-se*, "keep a calm exterior, changing neither voice nor countenance"; and of course, take precautions and prevent complications from arising. Perhaps this general policy of resistance, non-coöperation, delay and avoidance of issues reflected the unconscious insecurity of scholar-officials who were beginning to lose their self-confidence in the face of British gunboats. But we cannot be sure how far those officials who became specialists in barbarian affairs had as yet begun to feel themselves up against the irresistible attack of an incomprehensible invader.

The terms applied to the British continued to be stock phrases from the Confucian repertoire. The Western barbarians, like their ancient Hun and Mongol predecessors, displayed the unpredictable and avaricious "nature of dogs and sheep," *ch'üan-yang chih hsing*. The British were called *Ying-i*,[G] "English barbarians," in time of peace and *Ying-ni*, "English rebels," in time of war. This assumed that, like all barbarians, they recognized the supreme position of the Son of Heaven in normal times, and in time of warfare became genuine "rebels" against the acknowledged order of mankind. Thus at the beginning of 1843, when the British had only just been "pacified" by the treaty of Nanking, it was entirely natural for the imperial commissioner to refer to the possibility of further Anglo-Chinese hostilities as *fan-hsun*, "disobedience," in the sense of rebellion against the suzerain power. (Used of persons, the phrase referred to disorderly conduct, unbecoming on the part of inferiors toward elders or superiors.)[7]

Western contact at this time, though it might absorb the attention of a "barbarian expert," was too slight to give him much genuine understanding. A Chinese official could have little direct contact with Western merchants or missionaries. Consular officers were his immediate antagonists. With none of these three types of foreigners could he normally develop a personal or friendly relationship. Consequently it remained for a few pioneers, who seem to have felt relatively more secure in status, to take the lead in study and understanding of the West.

The Lin-Wei foreign policy. As the first Chinese of modern times really to grapple with the barbarian problem, Lin Tse-hsü exerted a unique influence both by his bold example at Canton and through certain writings ascribed to him. Among the latter, the *Hai-kuo t'u-chih* (Illustrated gazetteer of the maritime nations) is justly famous for its reflection of his views. Its influence in the period after the first war is indicated by the fact that it was originally published in 50 *chüan* in 1844, while a second edition in 60 *chüan* appeared in 1849, and a third in 100 *chüan* in 1852.[8] The author was Wei Yuan, a scholar noted for his interest in current governmental problems as well as history, who had already helped compile in 1826 the first of the much-imitated *Huang-ch'ao ching-shih wen-pien* (Collected essays on administration [or "statesmanship"] of the reigning dynasty). Wei Yuan was one of the few scholars of the day who ventured to look the barbarian problem directly in the face. He had long been acquainted with Lin Tse-hsü and during the Opium War finished another famous work, the *Sheng-wu chi* (Record of imperial military exploits). The latter was a rather conventional account of Ch'ing dynasty campaigns, which Wei Yuan completed in August 1842 about the time of the treaty of Nanking. His preface to the *Hai-kuo t'u-chih* was dated late in 1842.

As Chinese scholars have pointed out, the two works differ so thoroughly in point of view and in style that there is a strong presumption that Wei's connection with some parts of the *Hai-kuo t'u-chih* was less as author than as editor. Whether or not Lin actually did any of the writing, both contemporary testimony and internal evidence indicate his close connection with the book in its early stage of compilation. His interest while at Canton in translating Western geographical data and his curiosity about Western armament are well recorded. The preface to the *Hai-kuo t'u-chih* states that it is based first of all on a work called the "Gazetteer of the Four Continents," which had been written by Western barbarians and translated by (i.e., for) Lin Tse-hsü.[9]

The *Hai-kuo t'u-chih*, although well known for its study of geography and Western arms, has not been appraised from the point of view of Ch'ing foreign policy. Its chief significance is that it attempted to apply traditional Chinese conceptions to the new relations with the Western barbarians. Its essential idea was the ancient one of using barbarians to control barbarians. The author's application of this conception led him to advocate the use of foreign arms. But this was only part of his argument. The major portion of the book is a description of the world, recounting its peoples with their cities, religions, and general characteristics. The author's information, collated from Western sources, is not used for mere purposes of geography but to describe the West so that China may successfully deal with it. The essential interest is in politics, not in mechanical devices or geographic lore.

As the preface makes plain, the author's purpose is to utilize the barbarians' learning and their points of superiority in order to achieve stable relations with them. This implies the use of the cognate principles of attack and conciliation, force and persuasion. The preliminary argument is very simple — whether you intend to oppose an adversary by force or win him over by cordiality, it is a hundred times more advantageous to know his circumstances and feelings than not to know them. Chinese officials must look at the barbarian menace realistically and study the facts. They must stop "eating painted cakes to allay hunger" and avoid being misled by their own wishful thinking. Only then can they have the intellectual flexibility to take advantage of the barbarians' circumstances and use them to China's advantage. The breadth of this approach, which considered attack, defense, trade and concessions as parts of a general pattern, is apparent in the book's concern to keep out both barbarian opium, as an economic menace, and the barbarian religion, as an ideological threat.

Wei Yuan's ideas (or Lin's) on foreign policy are stated most cogently in four essays on "Policies for maritime defense." [10] The first essay castigates those Chinese policy makers who have urged extremist courses, either to exterminate the barbarian root and branch, or to appease him helplessly. In contrast to these narrow views, it urges a dual policy which would use both attack and appeasement to achieve final control of the barbarians. For purposes of attack, it urges a twofold program: first, to stir up other countries which are enemies of the British; and secondly, to imitate the superior devices of the barbarians and use these against them. For purposes of appeasement it also urges a dual program: first, to permit the development of trade relations with the other countries; and second, to stand by the treaty already made with the British.

How to use barbarians against barbarians is developed in the third essay.[11] The author argues that using government troops to attack pirates is not as easy as to use pirates to attack pirates. How much more should this be the case with pirates who are many thousands of miles across the sea! Specifically, there are three countries which the English barbarians fear: Russia, France, and America. There are four countries subordinate to China whom they fear: Nepal, Burma, Siam, and Annam. These are the countries to use. The British in their conquest of India have come up against the Gurkhas in Nepal and the Russians across the mountains in Central Asia. Only recently the Gurkhas have asked the Chinese resident in Tibet to support their attacking India. In short, if Chinese foreign policy makers had only permitted the Gurkhas to disturb India on the east and got the Russians to attack on the west, then India would have been in a state of disorder and the British expedition in China would have had to think about its Indian base. The same approach is then applied to the Americans and French:

"There is no better method of attacking England by sea than to use France and America. France is very close to the English barbarians, being separated only by an arm of the sea. America and the English barbarians, on the other hand, are separated by a great ocean. Beginning from the period at the end of the Ming and the beginning of this Dynasty, France colonized the northeast territory of America. Cities and towns were built, markets and ports were opened. The British barbarians suddenly attacked and seized them. Thereupon the French barbarians and the English barbarians became bitter enemies. Later on the British barbarians levied numerous and heavy taxes which caused the thirteen parts of America to start a righteous revolt to drive them out. At the same time the Americans asked France to help them. Several hundred warships of the three countries, and several hundreds of thousands of soldiers and seamen were kept on duty for several years. The Americans cut the British supply lines. The British soldiers were in hunger and distress, and the British ceded territory and asked for peace. The Americans then entirely recovered the twenty-seven parts of their original land, and the British barbarians only retained the four parts in the northeast corner [i.e., Canada]. They did not dare invade the United States any more.

"Even the land of India was also opened by Holland and France but was taken over by the British barbarians. At the beginning of the Ch'ien-lung period [1736–1795] the local Indian chiefs invited the two countries, France and Holland, to unite with them to resist the British barbarians. After several years of continuous warfare, India was finally partitioned, the eastern part to the British barbarians, and the southern part to the various barbarians of the Western Ocean [i.e., Europe] and trading ports were established. This is the condition of the various countries.

"As for commerce at Canton, the British barbarians are the most fierce and arrogant while France and America are the most amicable and obedient. After the stopping of trade, the British barbarians even used warships to prevent other countries carrying on a trade with us. The various countries were all resentful and said that if the British barbarians did not withdraw their troops for a lengthy period, they would each be obliged to go home and send ships of war to dispute the issue with them. Last year [1840] after the General for Rebellion Pacification [I-shan] had mobilized his troops, the barbarian headman among the Americans at Canton immediately came to mediate. Thereupon, Elliot submitted a document saying that he was only asking that he might carry on trade as usual. He dared not make demands even regarding the cost of the burned opium and the status of Hong Kong. This is the third opportunity [in addition to the Gurkhas and Russia] which might have been used. Unfortunately, when the peace negotiation had not yet been settled, our troops suddenly attacked the barbarian factories and unexpectedly injured several Americans by mistake. Thereupon, the American headman no longer made an effort to mediate."

Such passages expressed traditional principles which were to remain second nature for Chinese diplomats for a century afterward. The seemingly novel idea of using barbarian methods against the barbarians was merely an extension of this ancient use-barbarians-against-barbarians principle, as the following passage makes plain: "Even when the Gurkhas dutifully volunteered their services to attack India, it was refused; when France and America showed their willingness to help us with warships and to negotiate peace for us, they were suspected. Regarding these countries, with which we have had trade relations for two hundred years, we indeed know neither their locations nor their interrelations of friendship or enmity. Can it even yet be said that we are paying attention to frontier affairs? . . . From ancient times those who tried to control the outer barbarians only prevented their alliance with our enemies to plan against us, but did not prevent their alliance with us to attack our enemies; they only prevented the leaking of Chinese intelligence to the outside but we have not heard that they prohibited the conditions of foreign countries being revealed to China. Thus, he who wishes to control the outer barbarians must begin by understanding their circumstances, and he who wishes to understand their circumstances must begin by establishing a bureau for the translation of barbarian books. . . . Before the peace settlement, it behooves us to use barbarians against barbarians. After the peace, it is proper for us to learn the superior techniques of the barbarians in order to control them. The superior techniques of the barbarians are three: (1) warships, (2) firearms, and (3) methods of maintaining and training soldiers."[12]

Judged by these principles stated at its inception, the whole "self-strengthening" movement of nineteenth century China — all the arsenals, dockyards, woolen mills and Western studies — were no more than modern variations on an ancient defensive theme; further study should make plain that no revolutionary institutional changes were contemplated.

A survey of the Western religions. The *Hai-kuo t'u-chih* did not, however, confine itself to strategy and material defense alone. In an effort to provide an understanding of the psychology of foreign parts, it presents among many other things a table of the religious faiths of the various countries of the southern and western oceans.[a] This explains that the Western Regions before the time of Buddha all had the religion of Brahma (*P'o-lo-men chiao*), from which were derived both Christianity and Mohammedanism. Like Buddhism, they are each divided into three sects. For the Christians these are Catholicism, Protestantism and the Orthodox Church. Among these sects there is great variety. Some do not worship statue-images but still worship painted-images. Some worship the cross and some do not. Only the British disputed the religion of the Lord of Heaven [Roman Catholicism]. Consequently when the English king ascends the throne, his people all have to promise him to turn their backs on Catholicism and follow Protestantism.

The conclusion is reached that, unlike the Chinese, the barbarians generally struggle to adhere stubbornly to one religion. There are all sorts

[a] "From the Eastern Sea to the Western Sea and from the North Pole to the South Pole, there are countries for tens of thousands of *li*, and hundreds of thousands of people as innumerable as the sands of the Ganges . . . they have their eminent men and their tyrants, their moral laws and their annals, their periods of separation and of unity."[13]

and degrees of differences among them. The author of the *Hai-kuo t'u-chih* sees no way in which China could unite them in a universal brotherhood. The Ch'ing, for example, had been able to establish unified control over the Moslem tribes, but not to make them change their religion and submit to Confucianism. It had been able to subdue the Mongolian dependencies, but could not make them give up the Yellow Sect of Lamaism. Neither the Russian encroachments in the northwest nor the British in the southeast could make these people accept the religion of the Lord of Heaven.[b] From this analysis one gets the impression that, as part of China's defense, Wei Yuan was seeking, but not finding, some means of exerting an ideological influence over the West.

China's post-war defense program. The adoption of Western armament was particularly urged in the *Hai-kuo t'u-chih*, and during the war of 1840–42 the Chinese made efforts to purchase large numbers of foreign cannon, as the British eventually discovered in combat and recorded in various Western accounts. Casting of foreign-style cannon and building of foreign-style ships were also attempted.[15] Crude efforts to catch up with Western armament by attaching paddle-wheels to the new-style war junks continued until the end of the war. The outstanding innovator in this defense movement was a Cantonese literatus, P'an Shih-ch'eng, a wealthy descendant of the hong merchant Puankhequa (P'an Chen-ch'eng). He developed a ship with a Western-type hull and Chinese masts and sails.[16] This was

[b] In surveying the peoples and religions of the world, the *Hai-kuo t'u-chih* had to harmonize Chinese traditional lore concerning foreign countries with the new information presented in Western geography books available in the 1840's. This called for making identifications between new and old terms. In listing the island countries of the southeastern ocean (*Nan-yang*), it records the Philippines as Catholic (*Chia-t'e-li*), great Java (Sulu and Borneo) and small Java (Java proper) as both formerly Buddhist and now Moslem. The same is true of Achin (Sumatra). Under the five Indias are listed Eastern, Southern, and Central India as Buddhist, Western India (Persia and Arabia) as formerly Buddhist and now Moslem, and the same for Northern India (Kashmir).

In the countries of Europe confusion arises occasionally through duplication. Portugal, France, and Italy are Catholic. Holland and England are Protestant (*P'o-lo-t'e-shih-tun*). The 27 "tribes" of Germany are half Catholic, half Protestant. Austria also has both religions. Poland is Catholic, but the country of *P'u-lu-she* (Prussia) is either Jewish (*Yu-ssu*) or Lutheran (*Lu-ti-lan*) or Catholic or Protestant. Russia is divided into various sections, Great Russia, Western, Eastern, Lesser, and South, totaling 42 tribes, all Orthodox (*O-li*). In North America the 27 tribes of the country of America are Catholic and Protestant.

In summing up these data taken from the "Gazetteer of the Four Continents," the editor lists the following totals of persons living under various faiths:

Catholic	116,000,000
Orthodox	70,000,000
Protestant	42,000,000
Jewish	about 40 or 50,000
Mohammedan	120,000,000
Taoists and Buddhists, various sects, total	253,000,000
Total of all religions:	(sic) 671,000,000

The editor makes a final note that the Westerners who compiled these figures may have some basis of knowledge concerning the Western religion of Christianity. But as to Buddhism, Lamaism, Mohammedanism, and the Taoists of the various continents, "from what did the English barbarians get the record of these numbers of people?" [14]

essentially the same principle as that of the lorcha, applied to warships. P'an also experimented with the casting of ordinance, and encouraged the pioneer gunnery specialist, Ting Kung-ch'en, who produced a famous work, *Yen-p'ao t'u-shuo* (Drawings on gunnery). Ting had gone abroad as a merchant and learned something of foreign mathematics and engineering. His book described not only Western guns and their carriages, but also the manufacture of explosives and Western principles of fortification, military training, combat between ships and forts,[17] and the use of the steam engine in Western steamers and railways.

By the end of the war the court was convinced of the need to develop new Western-type arms, but their nature remained still a mystery. Imperial edicts ordered the provincial authorities to build stronger ships and forts and heavier guns. By the time of the treaty of Nanking the court was actually inquiring about Ting Kung-ch'en. In succeeding months an effort was made to reform and rebuild the entire defense system in the southern coastal province.[18]

Unfortunately, after the stimulus of foreign invasion ceased, the provincial authorities were too enmeshed in the old ways to make radical changes. Programs for strengthening the coastal defenses were vigorously developed on paper. Memorials and edicts of the years 1843–47 give long lists of new forts and guns installed at strategic spots. It seems evident, however, that behind this flow of paper, little was accomplished. Public defense works were primarily problems of finance. They suffered both from the lack of funds in the provincial treasuries and from the corruption of officials who squeezed the funds available.

In October 1843 the Chekiang governor, Liu Yun-k'o, sponsored twenty-four regulations to reorganize the coast defense of Chekiang. The proposed measures included the transfer of provincial commands to take up coast defense duties, strengthening of the forces at Chen-hai, Shih-p'u and Chapu as well as Kan-p'u, Hai-ning and other strategic points, and a reduction of garrisons at various inland places. Three-tenths of all the troops in the province should be selected for training with firearms. Naval vessels should regularly put to sea on patrol duty. The military authorities should make regular inspections. Warships should be built, crews recruited, the batteries strengthened at the mouth of the river to Ningpo and elsewhere, and ammunition supplied them. An edict of October 26 ordered these plans to be carried out.[19]

In May 1844 Governor Sun Shan-pao took over from Ch'i-ying responsibility for the coast defense program in Kiangsu. A naval force was being trained and ships tested. Batteries were being built according to regulations already decreed, although in the preceding year construction had been delayed by lack of funds in the treasury.[20] In August 1844 the Nanking governor-general, Pi-ch'ang, reported his inspection of key defense works on the Lower Yangtze along a stretch of 600 *li* from Chiang-ning to Fu-shan. He submitted nine regulations for defense preparations in this region, principally the establishment of batteries.[21] Later, in February 1846, a trusted military administrator, Sai-shang-a, and a senior secretary of the Board of War, Chou Tsu-p'ei, were specially deputed to inspect the Lower Yangtze defenses at Wusung and similar places. In May Sai-shang-a and Chou reported in gratifying detail the specifications and numbers of newly installed batteries and cannon along the Lower Yangtze. He and Consul Balfour, although they did not meet (owing to Sai-shang-a's deliberate avoidance of the British consul), expressed deep suspicion of each other's actions. On June 6 Sai-shang-a submitted a memorial on secret measures desirable to provide military security against the foreigners at Shanghai, including the more rigorous training of troops and increased armament. In the following October the provincial authorities followed this up with a joint memorial full of preventive stratagems and secret arrangements.[22]

One or two examples will indicate what happened to the movement for Western armament. The Foochow governor-general, Liu Yun-k'o, reported in February 1844 that his predecessor, I-liang, had received from Ch'i-ying four drawings of gun carriages (by Ting Kung-ch'en) and had considered how to imitate them. However, the provincial authorities had found on investigation that the Western-style gun carriages suitable for Western ships were inappropriate for Chinese vessels and had accordingly given up the project. By using a Cantonese model they had made some seventy carriages suited to their needs.

British subjects at Shanghai imported gunpowder and more than twenty fowling-pieces and pistols for sale. The governor-general ordered that these arms already on hand be bought up, and considered whether to forbid further importation as was customary. Import of foreign arms, however, had not been forbidden at Macao and Canton lest the arms trade be driven outside the ports and become a smuggling trade to the pirates. The Shanghai taotai accordingly bought these Western guns and tried them out, with impressive results, and the provincial authorities proposed issuing them to their own troops.[23]

Until the end of Ch'i-ying's regime at Canton, certain members of his staff like P'an Shih-ch'eng maintained their curiosity about foreign arms,[24] and used their opportunities to investigate them when visiting Hongkong. British observers noted that Ch'i-ying brought with him to Hongkong on his visit in November 1845 his "commissioner for naval and military affairs, Pwan-tze-shing" (also "Pwan-sze-ching"), who took special note of Western armament. Ch'i-ying himself fired the *Vixen's* great stern gun, showed a special interest in the engine room, inspected the gun deck of the *Agincourt* and at the review in Hongkong [25] scanned the arms of the troops narrowly and had much discussion regarding them with his staff.[c]

Nevertheless, the persistent impetus to the use of Western arms proved ineffective on the level of government activity. Foreign-style guns and ammunition were appreciated both by Chinese and Manchu military officials and by their opponents — the pirates, banditti, and rebels of South China. As disorder increased toward the middle of the century, the Western arms trade developed and made ready converts both in government and antigovernment circles. But this trade did not rouse Chinese officialdom generally to the need of modern arms production. Ch'i-ying's successors at Canton included, in their dislike for the foreigner, a dislike for all his works.

Ch'i-ying's staff. Against the background of these various attitudes concerning the barbarians — suspicious ignorance of their motives, hope of using one against the other, recognition of the power of their arms but a mighty distaste for the whole problem — it becomes a very interesting question what manner of men stepped forward as China's first "barbarian experts."

In opening the treaty ports Ch'i-ying faced a personnel problem comparable to Pottinger's. From the treaties he was well aware of the central role given to each British consul as the personal embodiment of the new system. His memorials of 1843–44 indicate his efforts to match the consuls with competent and reliable men. At the signature of the Supplementary treaty in October 1843, Ch'i-ying described how Pottinger was accompanied by Robert Thom and a retinue of twenty-two others, — the British all voiced their deep gratitude to the emperor, swore never to infringe the treaty, and stated that they had already sent Lay to Canton, Gribble to Amoy, and Balfour to Shanghai to manage trade and control the foreigners. Thom was to go to Ningpo, but had been temporarily filling the post of Chinese secretary vacated by Morrison's death; as soon as Gutzlaff came from Chusan to take over this job, Thom would proceed to Ningpo; but the British had no one to send to Foochow. Ch'i-ying replied to them that trade should not begin there in the absence of a restraining official. He informed the appropriate provincial authorities of these British arrangements,[27] and was now under pressure to match them from the Chinese side. He had particularly to consider that, judging by the sole available example of the Canton trade, the Chinese officials in charge of Western relations at the new ports would have opportunities for private revenue comparable to that of the Canton Hoppo. This seems to have produced

[c] Ch'i-ying's own report to the throne mentioned only casually that he had inspected the troops on his arrival at Hongkong.[26] P'an told the British on this occasion that the Chinese were manufacturing artillery shells at Futshan (Fatshan?) but that "many years must elapse before they can use them with effect."

competition between Ch'i-ying, an imperial commissioner sent especially from Peking, and the provincial authorities as to which would get their own nominees into these posts.

In November 1843 Ch'i-ying reported to Peking that at the new ports north of Canton the Chinese and foreigners were not acquainted with each other and all their arrangements would have to be made according to the local circumstances. But the barbarians were naturally very suspicious. If there were no Chinese officials of comparatively high rank who had their confidence and could thereby get them under control, it would be necessary for the high authorities to go and arrange all sorts of things in person. Yet it was not feasible for the governor and governor-general to have constant dealings with the foreigner. Some matters they could not handle personally. Therefore it was of the first importance to send to the ports special officials who could manage negotiations. (On this the emperor observed, "These views are very true.")

The imperial commissioner then put forward his slate of candidates, several of whom had already figured in the negotiations.[28] His nominee for Canton was the provincial treasurer, Huang En-t'ung, who had been his right-hand man throughout the treaty making. Surprisingly little is known about Huang. He had been a metropolitan graduate in 1826, served for many years as a judge in Jehol (where he was punished for bribery), and in 1840 had become salt taotai at Nanking. By 1842 he was provincial judge and acting treasurer and seemed to the British "a remarkably fine, intelligent-looking fellow," some 42 years of age.[29] I-ching had first used him in barbarian work and Ch'i-ying found him invaluable. He showed marked diplomatic ability and rapidly became *persona grata* to the English, one of whom declared,[30] "I do not remember ever having met, even in my own country, a person of more gentle and polished manner or courteous breeding than this Chinese, so different from the majority of his countrymen in their intercourse with foreigners."[d] Pottinger regarded Huang as "warmly interested" in promoting the Anglo-Chinese "alliance" (as Sir Henry liked to call it), and reported his appointment as treasurer at Canton late in 1843 as proof of the emperor's general satisfaction. Huang finally became governor of Kwangtung in 1845, while Ch'i-ying was governor-general at Canton. He was accused of improper conduct in December 1846, was eventually forced out of office and spent the last thirty-odd years of his life in retirement in Shantung.[32]

For the most difficult post, at Shanghai, Ch'i-ying picked his most trusted subordinate, Hsien-ling, a Manchu whom he had brought with

[d] One of the French diplomats of 1844 found in Huang "un esprit assez élevé par l'habitude des généralités métaphysiques pour tout comprendre et assez mûri par celle des affaires pour tout apprécier sans préjugés."[31]

him from Peking.[e] In November 1843 Ch'i-ying touted Hsien-ling as a man of quick and perspicacious understanding, not afraid of dangers, able to withstand hardship and take advantage of opportunities. The barbarians all had the greatest respect for him. Since Ch'i-ying had found it expedient to use officers of the rank of taotai and prefect, he asked that Hsien-ling be given the status of an expectant taotai and left at his disposal in Kiangsu where, should there be an opening for a taotai or a prefect, he would ask for a substantive appointment. Edicts of November 7, 1843, made Hsien-ling a taotai in Kiangsu awaiting appointment.[36] They ordered that foreign affairs in Canton be handled by Huang under the governor-general and governor, and in Kiangsu by Hsien-ling and the taotai at Shanghai, Kung Mu-chiu. Hsien-ling accordingly assisted in the opening of Shanghai, was taotai there at least in 1848 and was taotai at Ningpo in 1850. There he was caught in the resurgent xenophobia of the new Hsien-feng reign (1851–1861) and was accused and tried for his many years' intimacy with foreigners.[37]

Li T'ing-yü (1792–1861), Ch'i-ying's nominee to handle the barbarians in Chekiang, was not accepted. The provincial military commander and son of the famous pirate-suppressor, Li Ch'ang-keng, he had suffered reverses in the recent war and was under indictment. Ch'i-ying praised him for having controlled the British at Tinghai on Chusan for a year already and for having gained their trust and confidence. But this was not enough — the Chekiang authorities were merely ordered by the court to send competent barbarian experts to assist the local officials, and to prevent smuggling or the connivance of traitorous Chinese with the barbarians. Since it was the governor-general, Liu Yun-k'o, who had impeached Li T'ing-yü for his part in the war, Liu was now ordered to find a substitute but he failed to do so. On January 12, 1844, an edict ordered him to consult Ch'i-ying, proceed with his case against Li T'ing-yü, and secretly

[e] Hsien-ling had been in Kirin in 1835–38 and in Peking at the end of 1838; he was listed as imperial agent at K'e-la-sha-erh (Harashar) in 1839 and 1840, but had been degraded in June of the latter year.[33] In April 1842, at Ch'i-ying's request, he was made a fourth-class imperial bodyguard (see ch. 6) and in August was of the fifth rank (and therefore entitled to wear a crystal button). He was first dispatched to interview the British at Nanking on August 14, when a supreme effort seemed necessary to forestall an attack on the city and the chief British interpreter, Morrison, had demanded the appearance of emissaries of authority. Hsien-ling sought to fill the role and succeeded in masquerading as an official of higher rank. In the British dispatches he is referred to as a "Tartar Lieutenant General" and in contemporary British accounts as a "Tartar General." [34] The latter (*chiang-chün*, rank 1b) would have ranked with, but before, a governor-general; in actual fact, at this time Ch'i-ying himself held the post of Tartar-general at Canton.

An English witness wrote, "The General was a portly old veteran about sixty, wearing a little grey tufted beard, a plain dress, crystal ball, and peacock's feather. His red ball [i.e., first or second rank] had been taken away for some offense shortly before our arrival." He was most "loquacious . . . and pretended a great interest in, and examined with a critical inquisitiveness, everything appertaining to the art of war." As another English officer explained it, "the Tartar General had been disgraced by the Emperor and yet (a common case here) not deprived of his command [*sic*]. It was droll to see three men of superior decorations [blue buttons, i.e., third or fourth rank] attending on him . . . This disgraced Tartar was the only fine-looking man in visage of the whole party." [35]

recommend a naval or military officer to take his place. The arrangement finally made for Chekiang appears to have been a compromise between the imperial commissioner and the provincial hierarchy. Governor-general Liu discussed the problems of foreign intercourse with the taotai, Ch'en Chih-chi, and the Ningpo prefect, Li Ju-lin. However, since these men had had no experience with the barbarians, it was proposed to make use of a former Ningpo taotai, Lu Tse-ch'ang, who had been cashiered after being defeated in the war but had been recalled to Chekiang in the ninth month of 1843 to render an account of military expenditure. He had worked with Hsien-ling and Huang in the treaty negotiations with Pottinger, who had confidence in him. Therefore he had been sent to Ningpo and was already on duty. An edict at once confirmed this arrangement: Lu was to work with Ch'en and Li as a team.[38]

Ch'i-ying and Liu Yun-k'o appear to have continued at loggerheads over the management of foreign affairs in Chekiang, most of which concerned the British garrison left on Chusan Island. To handle Sino-barbarian relations at Tinghai, Ch'i-ying, in December 1843, suggested Shu Kung-shou, the former Ningpo prefect, a man of probity much admired by the gentry and populace, who also possessed that apparently priceless asset, the confidence of the barbarians. The British had captured Ningpo in 1841 and exacted a ransom of $250,000, but at the time of the Nanking treaty settlement there had been no mention of deducting this sum, until Shu had argued the point. Pottinger had then acknowledged it and the sum had been subtracted from the current year's indemnity payment. Although Shu had been judicially condemned in connection with the loss of Ningpo, nevertheless able men were needed for post-war reconstruction and Ch'i-ying implored the emperor to send Shu to Tinghai. An imperial rescript stated that this was very difficult to permit.[39] An edict of the same date stated that pardoning Shu would be quite outside the law. Since Chi'i-ying needed personnel he should consult the provincial authorities, namely Liu Yun-k'o, and select able officials.

In a memorial of June 1844, the governor of Chekiang, Liang Pao-ch'ang, referred to the correspondence of Ch'i-ying and Liu Yun-k'o with the throne concerning personnel for Tinghai. For four months no one had been found, since the mixture of foreigners and Chinese created very difficult administrative problems. The best man they could find was the former Ning-Shao-T'ai taotai, who had been removed from office but deputed to assist in the management of foreign trade, Lu Tse-ch'ang. He had been ordered to concert action with his subordinate, the Tinghai sub-prefect, and manage matters on the spot with full responsibility, though in consultation with the local taotai and prefect. Governor Liang had kept Lu under careful observation. An edict of June 2, 1844, confirmed Lu Tse-ch'ang as the responsible officer at Tinghai.[40] But this was not the end of it.

In December 1844 Ch'i-ying suggested that when the indemnity to Britain was paid up and Chusan recovered, there was sure to be trouble unless the Chinese officials concerned were well acquainted with barbarian affairs. After much thought he had observed that the cashiered sub-prefect, Shu Kung-shou, was a man whom the barbarians and the populace commonly trusted. He had recently reached Peking and an edict had ordered that he need not be sent on to Sinkiang. Since officials for Sinkiang were numerous whereas at Tinghai there was only the cashiered taotai Lu Tse-ch'ang, Ch'i-ying proposed that Shu be retained there to help manage the populace and the barbarians. He could be sent to Sinkiang later without any change in his punishment. An edict accordingly ordered that Shu be sent back to work with Lu at Chusan.[41] Thus the imperial commissioner got his man appointed after a year's delay.

From the documents it is not possible to decide how far these appointments reflected the rivalries of official cliques. The one constant theme is that "barbarian experts" must be men toward whom the barbarians had that magical feeling, "confidence." Lu Tse-ch'ang and Shu Kung-shou, like Hsien-ling and Huang, had participated in the original Nanking negotiations. Shu had been a metropolitan graduate and became district magistrate of Ningpo in 1838. He had an imperial audience in 1839 and was promoted to sub-prefect at Ningpo early in 1840, where the British victory brought him degradation.[f] But in the negotiations he had become "a universal favorite among the officers of the British expedition, especially . . . Pottinger,"[43] which was enough to save him from exile. Of Lu Tse-ch'ang little is known except that he had been Ningpo taotai during the war, had dealt with the British, and so was summoned to Nanking by Ch'i-ying in August 1842.[44] All in all, it seems less likely that Ch'i-ying was seeking to install his own clique at the new ports for purposes of power and corruption than that he was up against the problem of finding men who

[f] A British missionary who saw a good deal of Shu at Ningpo in 1842–43 described this barbarian-expert as "a short thickset man; his head is large; his face round; his features very marked and deep; his countenance intelligent, cheerful, agreeable; his eyes large, black, quick, expressive; his beard jet, long, and pointed, and over his lips hangs a pair of heavy mustaches. Upon his head he wore an official cap, topped with a transparent crystal knob, and flourishing from behind a thick plume of peacock-feathers. His dress was not gaudy, though of rich dark-colored satin; around his neck was slung a string of elegant beads, which fell over a square breast-piece of beautiful embroidery, a duplicate of which was sewed upon his tunic, the one in front, the other behind, and on which was depicted the . . . silver pheasant, the badge of his order. His voice is musical. When he speaks, it is with an air of authority. To me his utterance was indistinct, partly from not being used to hear him, partly from his talking with a strong accent peculiar to Kiangsi his native province, and partly from his being rather toothless, although only 53 years of age. In his deportment, there was much to please one. He was dignified but not supercilious; bland and affable, but far from being familiar. I left him with a very favorable impression of the character of an officer, who is held in high reputation among his own countrymen, and is often spoken of among the English, as 'a fine old fellow.' "[42]

would take the onus of foreign contact and who were favorably known to the British as Ch'i-ying's men.

In this way by persistent effort during 1844 the imperial commissioner got his representatives installed at the main points of barbarian contact. Meanwhile at Canton he had also built up his own staff, concerning whom we know little more than their names. In July 1844 Ch'i-ying explained to the throne that the attachés who had accompanied him south in 1843 to manage barbarian affairs (namely, Hsien-ling, Ch'en Po-ling,[45] Chang P'an-lung, and Ch'en Chih-kang) had not now accompanied him on his second trip to Canton. Of the officials at Canton, aside from the treasurer, Huang En-t'ung, only the sub-prefect T'ung-lin and Wu T'ing-hsien, a dismissed official retained for service, were well acquainted with the barbarian temperament. We know that Wu T'ing-hsien was a provincial graduate from Shantung and former district magistrate of Shang-yuan near Nanking; he had taken a minor part in the Nanking treaty negotiations and acted as host, for example, when Parkes and others visited the Porcelain Pagoda. As seen in Chapter 8, he is chiefly to be remembered as the Chinese who rewrote the Supplementary treaty.[46] On his way south in 1844 Ch'i-ying had also met at Nan-hsiung the former prefect of Chao-ch'ing, Chao Ch'ang-ling, who was then an expectant second class secretary. Since he knew from his previous year's experience that Chao had unusual ability, he had brought him to Canton.[47]

Another valuable barbarian expert whom Ch'i-ying praised to the emperor was P'an Shih-ch'eng, the wealthy scion of a hong merchant family whose interest in Western warships has been noted earlier in this chapter. Ch'i-ying described him as a native of eastern Kwangtung who understood the local dialect, without referring to his hong merchant ancestry. In the post-war reconstruction period, he had bought foreign cannon, hired foreign workmen, invented the water-thunder (*shui-lei*, a type of mine) and become well acquainted with the American merchants, by whom he was greatly respected. Since P'an was available, Ch'i-ying brought him into his office to work with Chao Ch'ang-ling as an assistant to Huang En-t'ung in handling British and American affairs. Later, in July 1844, when the French were seeking a treaty and the Chinese wanted to discover their intentions, the expectant sub-prefect T'ung-lin was dispatched to see them and found that what they said was mainly unreliable. P'an Shih-ch'eng was therefore instructed on successive days to make secret inquiries of the Frenchmen living at Macao.[48] Subsequently, P'an served as Ch'i-ying's chief expert in Western geography. When the trade of Macao was reported in September 1844 to be suffering from the competition of Hongkong, P'an Shih-ch'eng investigated the situation. To keep an eye on Cushing and the French, P'an and Chao later went to stay at Macao. In dealing with the

French there, Ch'i-ying relied on P'an and Chao as his emissaries. A leading part was also played by the Macao district magistrate and by Wu T'ing-hsien. When Ch'i-ying saw the French envoy, Lagrené, at Macao, he took with him Huang, P'an, Chao, T'ung-lin, and Wu.[49]

It is evident that most of these men were bona fide scholar-officials, who became barbarian experts by virtue of their acceptability both to the foreigner and to their own colleagues in the Manchu-Chinese bureaucracy. How far this acceptability depended upon their adeptness in securing private revenue from sources of wealth like the opium trade is a pure speculation, on which the documents are silent.

Among all these men, Hsü Chi-yü (1795–1873), who took the main burden of barbarian contact in Fukien, was by far the most substantial figure. He was a native of Shansi and belonged to a family of scholars and officials. In 1826 he became a metropolitan graduate and later was a compiler in the Hanlin academy. After becoming a censor in 1836, he subsequently served as prefect in Kwangsi, taotai in Fukien, salt controller of Kwangtung-Kwangsi and judge in Kwangtung. In 1843, when not yet 50, he became Fukien treasurer. Having been nominated by Ch'i-ying, in November 1843 he was appointed to handle foreign relations and in the line of duty began his active study of the West, which was to produce in 1850 the famous *Ying-huan chih-lueh* (A Brief Gazetteer of the oceans roundabout).[50] The steps by which Hsü gradually took charge of the foreign problem in Fukien make an interesting story, although somewhat confused by the activity of minor officials.

When Amoy was opened on November 2, 1843, the local authorities concerned comprised the Hsing-Ch'üan-Yung taotai, the acting coast defense sub-prefect, and the district magistrate of T'ung-an. They found the acting consul, Gribble, "extremely respectful" and helped him get a house. But they were not foreign trade specialists. The Foochow Tartar-general, who in Fukien had charge of the customs, and the Fukien governor affected to ignore the edict designating the provincial treasurer, Hsü Chi-yü, and put forward their own candidate, an acting taotai named Tai Chia-ku. On December 14, the court received their report that Tai had gone to assist in superintending the Amoy trade. An edict immediately reversed the Tartar-general's arrangement and repeated that Hsü was to be in charge, under the governor-general and governor.[51] Acknowledgment of this edict was received at Peking four months later, in April 1844, when Fukien's receipt of the customs tariff (proclaimed by Pottinger on July 27, 1843) was also confirmed. Meantime Tai Chia-ku had begun dealing with Gribble, up to the point where interpretation of the treaty regulations was required. At this point, Hsü Chi-yü as provincial treasurer finally emerges in the record. He visited Amoy from his official residence at Foochow.[52]

By February 1844 Gribble was corresponding both with Hsü and with the Amoy taotai, Heng-ch'ang.[53] When Sir John Francis Davis visited Foochow on his tour of inspection in October 1844, he was visited on board H. M. S. *Proserpine* by "the provincial treasurer accompanied by the praefect of the city"[54] — a visit which Hsü naturally did not report to Peking. It was in this period that Hsü met at Amoy Gribble's occasional interpreter, the American missionary, David Abeel, who showed him an atlas of the world[55] and inspired Hsü's own compilation, to be described below.[56]

Handling the barbarians at Shanghai. Shanghai was from the first recognized as the most important of the new ports. Late in 1843 Ch'i-ying called Canton the head and Shanghai the tail of the new order: Amoy, Foochow, and Ningpo could all follow the example of the arrangements to be made there. Since Kiangsu had formerly had no foreign intercourse, no one knew the classifications of foreign ships and the populace were a prey to all kinds of suspicions and fears. The early arrival of foreign ships at Wusung had caused a panic. Barbarian vessels were assembling like clouds, yet in the whole province of Kiangsu there was no official so acquainted with foreigners that he could gain both their confidence and that of the populace. Ch'i-ying had felt such great concern that he had come north late in 1843 over the Mei-ling pass and down the Yangtze so that the populace on the waterways might all know that he had settled the barbarian problem and that barbarian vessels from the sea would not enter the River. This, he said, was all done to calm the public mind and stop disquieting rumors.[57]

Meanwhile the provincial officials in Kiangsu outlined in interesting detail the philosophy with which they approached the barbarian problem at Shanghai. The governor-general at Nanking was a Mongol named Pi-ch'ang who had seen service among the Moslems of Sinkiang. It was his observation that the problem of getting the outer barbarians under control was first of all a matter of bringing their hearts into submission (*che-fu ch'i hsin*), by making them conscious of their reasons for gratitude and the fear arising from it. In this way one could both strengthen the frontier defenses and show reverence for the emperor. He proposed to manifest sincerity and justice and purposely defer to the barbarians' tendency to seek profit, while making plain to them the various ranks and distinctions (of the civilized social order), so as to display the fundamental institutions of the dynasty. Now that the English barbarians had been brought to order, and Shanghai was to begin its first trade with barbarian vessels, said Pi-ch'ang, he had wondered whether, before trade was opened, either the governor-general or governor should not go to Shanghai temporarily to superintend matters. But he feared that after the British consul arrived, if he learned that a high official was there, he might raise small problems so as to involve this high official in relations with him. As it had turned out, various communications from Pottinger had all been handed to the Shanghai taotai. From persons well acquainted with the Canton trade the governor-general understood that the person given the official title of consul (*ling-shih*) was merely the head man among the barbarian merchants. His status was very far below that of the chief, Pottinger. So the governor-general concluded, with great protestations of his sense of loyalty and responsibility, that the opening of Shanghai should be handled by the taotai, while the governor-general kept busy with examinations and the governor stayed nearby at Soochow. Since dike works being finished at Pao-shan near Shanghai required the governor's personal inspection, he would be near the taotai for conference. He could decide later whether to give the consul an interview.[58]

After his arrival at Shanghai on November 8, 1843, Consul Balfour accordingly saw nothing of these high provincial authorities. He was received by the Su-Sung-T'ai taotai (Kung Mu-chiu), the sub-prefect (Shen Ping-yuan), the district magistrate (Lan Wei-wen), and other local officials on the following day and proved himself "extremely respectful." Together, with Medhurst as interpreter, they compared their respective copies of the trade regulations and tariff and arranged to open the port on the 17th. The fact that the Chinese authorities returned his call by visiting the British warship *Medusa* was glossed over: the court was assured that Balfour "tremblingly obeyed" in the traditional fashion of barbarians, and was kept from "stirring up the local populace." It was learned from Medhurst that Balfour's captaincy was a decidedly minor rank. The Chinese officials ordered him to forbid the sailors of foreign ships to come ashore or wander about, or use force in purchasing goods, and the consul acted accordingly. The Chinese officials reported that they also sent a number of competent officers, on the excuse that they were to send and receive documents, to keep an eye on things in the neighborhood of Balfour's temporary residence.[59] (There is no evidence, however, that any of these eavesdroppers understood English, as did the innocent-looking Japanese menials who welcomed Commodore Perry in 1853.)

Subsequently the Kiangsu governor, Sun Shan-pao, visited Shanghai to confer with the taotai and local officials and also with the provincial commander-in-chief, who had been ordered to move closer to the port. The consul did not try to see either of these high officials and had been scrupulously observing the treaties. The governor reiterated that the soothing and control of barbarians was essentially a matter of getting them to have feelings of both gratitude and fear. He concluded by recommending Kung in the highest terms as a manager of barbarians, who could work with Ch'i-ying's nominee, Hsien-ling.[60] From the British records it appears that Balfour's early contact was mainly with the taotai ("Kung Mooyun," i.e., Kung Mu-chiu), the sub-prefect ("Shin Ping Yuan," whose activity preceded that of the taotai), the district magistrate ("Lan Yue-wan," who became taotai a decade later), and only from February 1844 with Hsien-ling.[61]

In the case of Ningpo the governor-general, Liu Yun-k'o, had made a special trip to the city before its opening to advise the Ning-Shao-T'ai taotai, Ch'en Chih-chi, concerning local preparations. The Chekiang authorities put the responsibility on the local taotai and prefect but deputed the cashiered taotai, Lu Tse-ch'ang, to be their active partner. When Consul Thom arrived, he was granted an interview by Ch'i-ying's original nominee, the Chekiang provincial commander-in-chief, Li T'ing-yü. Li found Thom to be conversant with Chinese speech and writing but so filled with a cunning obstinacy and suspicion that he could not reach decisions. Trade had been opened at Thom's request on the barbarian New Year's with Lu Tse-ch'ang to superintend it, while the provincial commander had assembled a force of troops and ships to maintain order.[62] Consul Thom's early contact continued to be with the taotai ("Chin Chekee"), the district magistrate ("Leejoolin"), and Lu Tse-ch'ang, whose enthusiasm for barbarians was found to be considerably dampened by his degradation as a result of the British capture of Ningpo. It was said that he had been sentenced to serve eight years at Ningpo without pay.[63]

The fact that the new foreign relations in the treaty ports had to be handled by barbarian experts, of the sort described above, was a portentous development of specialization within the normally omnicompetent Ch'ing bureaucracy. From the very opening of the ports there seems to emerge a new type of "treaty port mandarin," who makes his career outside the regular official system. He is comparable to the new type of Chinese merchant-compradore who was developing at this time among the foreign firms.

The most-favored-nation principle: the American and French treaties. One facet of China's response to the British invasion was visible in the American and French treaties of 1844. Since these later documents were little more than summaries of the Sino-British agreements already negotiated, with certain improvements, the chief diplomatic feat in securing them lay in the establishment of the most-favored-nation principle. The British treaties were secured by fighting and the French treaty was secured by copying the American — praise has therefore been given the Americans for establishing the rule that other Western powers might obtain peacefully the privileges for which the British had had to wage war. Ill-informed American writers have claimed for Commodore Lawrence Kearny the honor of first securing equal rights for Americans in China, a principle which eventually was to figure largely in American state papers as the predecessor of the Open Door doctrine.

These claims are not well founded, for the ancient idea of equal treatment of all barbarians was applied by the Manchu negotiators of 1842–44 of their own accord. Since the emperor was accustomed to viewing all men from afar with equal compassion, his ministers almost instinctively decided to extend the British treaty terms to the Americans. Their aim was to prevent the British themselves admitting the Americans to these privileges and so winning for Britain the gratitude which ought really to be felt by the Americans toward the emperor. Specifically, Commodore Kearny's claim to have inaugurated the policy of equal treatment for the United States rests chiefly on his dealings with the Canton governor-general, Ch'i Kung, in 1842, when the latter at one point replied to him (in words of the consular translator) "decidedly it shall not be permitted that the American merchants shall come to have merely a dry stick." Professor Swisher has pointed out that this reply, instead of constituting a genuine promise as alleged by some writers, "must be interpreted as a noncommittal evasion."[64] Neither Ch'i Kung nor Kearny was really commissioned to negotiate, nor did Ch'i Kung secure an imperial edict, which alone could have granted the concession.[65] On the contrary, equal treatment of the Americans was suggested by both I-li-pu and Ch'i-ying, apparently independently, and it was carried out by Ch'i-ying as a part of his general policy of appeasement. It had always been welcomed by the British.[66]

As a result of this Manchu policy, the American merchants were admitted to trade on the same terms as the British, with British appproval, even before the American envoy, Caleb Cushing, left for China. By the time he arrived in 1844 his primary objective had already been realized. The latest and most thorough study of the negotiations leading up to the American treaty signed by Caleb Cushing and Ch'i-ying at Wanghia (Wanghsia) near Macao on July 3, 1844, comes to the conclusion that they were throughout "an exhibition of shadow boxing." Far from vindicating Yankee shrewdness by outwitting his oriental antagonist, as American biographers have liked to believe, Cushing's chief tactic consisted in coercing Ch'i-ying (as he thought) to sign his treaty by threatening to go to Peking to present the President's letter. In actual fact, Cushing did not have "any serious intention or necessity under his instructions to go there" and would have been embarrassed if his bluff had been called. Meanwhile Ch'i-ying was ready to sign the treaty all the time, having the most-favored-nation concept already in mind. He used the "threat of refusal to negotiate, or of breaking off negotiations once started, or of refusal to sign and seal the treaty after it was negotiated, to get Cushing to abandon his trip north and deliver his credentials at Macao." In this contest the Manchu won and the Yankee lawyer got nowhere. As soon as Cushing abandoned his trip, he was given his treaty.[67]

On the other hand, Cushing, like Pottinger, had definite objectives, in that he wished to establish by treaty certain commercial privileges already enjoyed in fact, while Ch'i-ying was on the defensive and wished merely to limit the treaty to commercial matters and avoid ceding another island or opening more ports. The American diplomat was therefore able to profit by Pottinger's errors and a year's experience. He saw the British authorities on more than one occasion and took their advice and that of American merchants also in securing certain further concessions. By special agreement the provisions of the American treaty came into effect on October 1, 1844, without waiting for the exchange of ratifications. On the application of Consul Macgregor at Canton, these provisions were extended under the most-favored-nation clause to British trade also.[68]

The Chinese belief in equal treatment of barbarians was applied without difficulty to the French in the treaty of October 24, 1844. Lagrené, like Cushing, had been sent to China to keep up with the British by getting a commercial treaty, but he found on his arrival that his aim was already accomplished. The French consul at Canton, Ratti-Menton, had been assured that France would enjoy all the privileges accorded England. Lagrené's expedition thus "had no real objective which could justify the considerable expense which it had caused the French government." A recent student of the Lagrené-Ch'i-ying negotiations of 1844–46 finds in this fact the main reason why Lagrené championed the toleration of Christianity, which had not been in his original instructions but which became the main function of his mission. Like Pottinger, Lagrené was amazed at the "extremely friendly disposition" and indeed profuse affection manifested by Ch'i-ying and his chief assistants, Huang En-t'ung and P'an Shih-ch'eng. The French were mystified by the Chinese insistence (due to the similarity of *Fo-lang-chi* and *Fo-lan-hsi*) that France had been China's first friend from the West, "sincere friends for over three hundred years." Ch'i-ying's memorials actually show the liveliest suspicion of French intentions, but on the basis of experience with Pottinger and Cushing his entourage had worked out impressive methods of barbarian-soothing, which found a ready response from the Lagrené mission. Few diplomats in China had had such pleasant dealings.[69]

The Chinese idea of equal treatment was applied again in 1845 in the less-known case of Belgium. A joint memorial from Ch'i-ying, the Canton governor, and the Hoppo, received on April 10th, noted that aside from the barbarians of the Great Western Ocean at Macao, those formerly allowed to trade with China had totalled twenty countries. But in recent years only France, Holland, Spain, America, England, and India had sent ships annually to trade. Others like Austria (*Shuang-ying*, lit., the Double-Eagle Country) and Belgium (*Pi-li-shih*) might come once in several years or not for many years. The countries formerly permitted to trade had thus been reduced by 60 or 70 per cent. But now came a consul named Lan-wa (Lannoy) of the country of *Pei-er-jih-k'o* who said that his country had traded a century ago but had fallen on evil times and ceased it. Hearing of the emperor's benevolence, the country's king had now sent him to share in the trade of the five ports. A letter also came from the French minister, Lagrené, on his behalf. While formerly there had been no such country name as this, it was like "Belgique" in sound. On secret enquiry, P'an Shih-ch'eng found it was indeed Belgium and, like France, one of the places (*pu*, tribes) of Europe. Ch'i-ying therefore concluded that trade could be allowed. But the emperor ordered further investigation.[70] He was not certain whether trade should be permitted to Belgium in these circumstances.

Ch'i-ying and Huang replied in July 1845 with a further explanation that Belgium was a small and weak country, between France and England. Its merchant ships were neither numerous nor important. Its emissary now was respectful and obedient. It would be inconvenient to refuse him. They explained that only France, England, and America had regular consuls. Other countries like Holland, Spain, Denmark (*Ta-ni*), the Yellow Flag country (*Huang-ch'i*, also Denmark ?), India, and Sweden, when their merchant ships arrived, commonly had their duties paid through the consuls of the first three powers. These minor barbarians were all very much alike in dress, speech, and deportment and there was no way to find out what countries they actually came from. If this Belgian were thwarted he could still hide behind other countries and trade anyway, unbeholden to the emperor's benevolence. Since the French sponsored him, this was a chance to get him under control and win barbarian gratitude. He was now in Manila and proposed to come to Canton with the French minister. An edict in reply finally approved the application of the new trade regulations to Belgium, in order to manifest compassion toward the foreigner.[71]

It is ironic that the Chinese-Manchu policy of equal treatment of the Western nations, although intended to keep them divided and facilitate playing off one against another, had the opposite effect of consolidating them. Because China was the weaker side and on the defensive, the most-favored-nation clause proved to be a one-way street — any concession or privilege gained by one Western power at once accrued to all. China could never reverse the tide and, by abolishing the privileges of one power, eliminate those of others. Treaty privileges steadily accumulated against her interest.

The implications of this legal ratchet, working irreversibly, were not foreseen by Ch'i-ying and Mu-chang-a in 1844. They thought they were applying to the Western nations a principle long tested by successful application to the tribes of Inner Asia. Their error lay in not recognizing that the Middle Kingdom was no longer the suzerain and center of the world.

CHAPTER XII

PROBLEMS IN THE APPLICATION OF THE TREATIES AT THE NEW PORTS

THE DAY-BY-DAY TEXTURE of Sino-Western contact in China has always been an interweaving of Chinese and Western ways and values. Even in periods of the greatest foreign domination, the foreigner's conduct in China has been profoundly and subtly influenced by the Chinese environment. It has taken constant effort, and a degree of insulation from Chinese life, to preserve in the treaty ports even the hybrid semi-foreign patterns of treaty port life. The two sides were equally involved in creating these patterns. What follows is a selection of incidents from the various ports, each of which may be viewed as an illustration of the foreigners' general problem, whether to seek Chinese conformity to the Western scheme of things, or modify the Western scheme to suit Chinese conditions.[a]

Problems of consular residence. The first task of each British consul was to establish his consulate, and the first sites were chosen not with a view to convenience or comfort but in order to maintain British prestige by hoisting the British flag within the walls of the administrative cities. This policy at the new ports reflected the famous "city question" at Canton, the issue of foreign entrance to the walled city, which was to occupy so many pages of blue books and contribute directly to the outbreak of the second Anglo-Chinese war.[1]

In the exchange of documents effected at Nanking before the signing of the first treaty, the trade of British merchants and the residence of consuls had been provided for, but not the residence of merchants.[b] The English version of the treaty, article II, provided that "British Subjects . . . shall be allowed to reside . . . at the Cities and Towns of Canton," etc. But

[a] The account which follows is based on the British consular archives. If it should seem unduly picturesque, as though the accumulated excitement of years had been condensed into a few pages for amusement — a dubious procedure in history writing — it should be remembered that the circumstances were in fact unusual and adventurous. On the other hand the reader will be well aware that there was generally nothing more dull than port life, unless it was consular life. Consular dispatches tended to epitomize all the real or imagined excitement available; personal feuds were intense and chauvinism rampant in a treaty port, partly no doubt because of the boredom between mails. The steady and soothing bustle of Chinese life formed a background for all early consular activities and the incidents cited below are chosen to show the types of crises that arose, not that a crisis arose every day.

[b] An English memorandum at Nanking declared that "the demand for Hongkong as a residence will of course be complied with; and commercial intercourse be opened at the five places, Canton," etc. The Chinese responded: "at Hongkong where England has already built houses, it is proper to allow that she still retain a dwelling place. And at these five ports . . . England will be allowed to carry on trade and commercial intercourse and to appoint subordinate officers to reside there."[2]

the corresponding part of the Chinese version, which was of course the only one intelligible to Ch'i-ying and his colleagues, called only for temporary residence of British subjects at the "harbors" or "anchorages" (*chiang-k'ou*) of the five port cities, and residence of the British consuls at the corresponding "walled cities" (*ch'eng-i*). On the basis of this treaty terminology, Ch'i-ying, I-li-pu, and Niu Chien on September 1, 1842, had put forward the argument that it would be proper to build foreign factories at the new ports, to which the merchants and their families might come; "but after commercial affairs are at an end, they should return again on board their vessels and go home; it will be unnecessary that they should remain throughout the year residing in the factories." [3] In effect this would have preserved the old system, allowing foreign merchants to live at Hongkong and trade at the new ports, just as formerly they had (nominally) resided at Macao and traded at Canton. Pottinger rebuffed the argument at once. Evidently not realizing the ambiguity of the Chinese version of the treaty and its distinction between "ports" and "cities," he replied that it was "impossible to make any alteration . . . even supposing it to be desirable, but that is by no means admitted." The English object being "a free and unrestricted trade," no such restrictions on the merchants could be allowed.[4] This terminated the discussion although it did not settle the issue. A year later the Supplementary treaty retained the same terminology: for "Ports" and "Cities and Towns" in the English version, it read merely "harbors" or "anchorages" (*chiang-k'ou*) in the Chinese version. This left the whole question really unsettled, but the British authorities recognized only their own interpretation and strove to establish it.

At Amoy the officiating consul who opened the port on November 2, 1843, Captain Henry Gribble, first considered setting up his consulate on the site of the Long (or Two Hundred Gun) Battery ("Hoomunkong"), that "monument of art and folly" built to resist the British in 1841,[5] near the present Amoy University.[6] This was objected to by British merchants as being half a day's trip from the waterfront. In fact, Gribble's plan for the new consular buildings was "totally unintelligible to [Pottinger] and everyone else that has seen it," [7] and he was censured for assuming that the consulate needed a godown and jetty for handling merchants' goods as in the days of the Honorable Company. For a consular office he finally rented from a man named Wu an empty establishment situated "next the Hae Kwan's office," that is, the customhouse on the waterfront, for $400 a year. Soon, however, he found this district very crowded and continually subject to fires, and his house uncomfortable. Gribble therefore asked to live on the island of Kulangsu ("drum-wave island") in the harbor, which was still held by a British garrison. He reported to Pottinger that on February 19, 1844, he had got a promise from the local authorities that Kulangsu could be used for foreign residence.[8] This would merely have recognized a fact, since Jardine's agent, Captain Forbes, a resident of the port since the end of 1841,[9] had already built a house on the island and set up his office in Amoy, and other merchants had followed suit. But the officials of both sides were unconcerned with the comfort of merchants. The Fukien authorities in their memorials made no mention of any promise to Gribble: barbarians were residing on Kulangsu until the indemnity should be paid up, but formal permission for permanent consular residence was another matter, which they referred to the imperial commissioner. Pottinger supported Gribble's request, but Ch'i-ying throughout 1844 consistently and strongly supported the provincial authorities in objecting to the threatened use of Kulangsu for residential purposes after its military evacuation, fearing that this would really prevent Chinese recovery of the island.

Hsü Chi-yü, on his arrival at Amoy in charge of foreign trade relations, held long arguments with Gribble and reported that he had shut him up with logic but still could not get him to agree to live at a site in Amoy. The emperor supported Ch'i-ying and Hsü.[10] Meanwhile Pottinger's successor, Davis, replied to the imperial commissioner's "tiresome" and "childish" objections in sharp terms, while Gribble got local Chinese acquiescence to his living on Kulangsu until his house was built in Amoy.[11] Davis finally left the decision for Gribble's successor, Alcock, threatening that if decent accommodations were not arranged, Alcock would have to live on a warship or return to Hongkong,[12] neither of which alternatives was likely to please Ch'i-ying.

When Alcock took charge at Amoy on November 7, 1844, however, he was from the first concerned to maintain British prestige by hoisting his flag within the city walls. Early in 1845 he agreed with the taotai that a consulate should be built with Chinese capital on the old site of the taotai's yamen, which had been ruined during the late war. Pending its construction, the consular staff continued to stay on Kulangsu.[13]

In January 1845 Davis proposed to restore Kulangsu to Chinese control by removing the British garrison ahead of time, before indemnity payments had been completed. He also proposed that the consular officers be allowed to continue living there temporarily until their houses were completed in the city. This proposal provoked Chinese misgiving as a possible opening wedge of some sort, and the local authorities were happy to refer it to Ch'i-ying. In February 1845 when Ch'i-ying reported to Peking the arrangement for the early rendition of Kulangsu and Gribble's choice of a consular site in Amoy, he remarked that the barbarian temperament was truly unfathomable: the rendition of the island ahead of time was a beautiful idea but did not accord with the treaty. If Kulangsu was restored early then might not Chusan be restored late? It would be best to wait until the time specified by treaty and get them both back together. To Davis, Ch'i-ying argued that Kulangsu was not a trading port and should be restored to the original inhabitants. The emperor supported this course.[14]

When Kulangsu was evacuated by the British garrison at noon on March 22, 1845, Consul Alcock was urged by the taotai either to leave the island himself or to keep a consular guard there. Looting of doors and windows and everything portable did indeed begin as soon as the troops were in their boats, but Alcock remained, unguarded, putting upon the Chinese the responsibility for his safety. Finally in August 1845 his successor, Consul Lay, moved from Kulangsu into the new consular residence in Amoy. Since it was half an hour's walk from Gribble's original hong on the waterfront, Lay proposed to get rid of the latter and combine his office with his residence, avoiding the necessity of traversing the filthy streets of Amoy in the heat and leaving that pleasure to British shipmasters and merchants.[15] It is interesting to note that the final memorial of the Fukien authorities, on the conclusion of this long wrangle, reported that on July 1 the taotai and local officials had gone with Consul Lay to inspect his new establishment. The consul "danced with joy" (*ku-wu*) and gratefully installed his office in the new buildings at the appointed time, withdrawing all his staff from Kulangsu, where not a barbarian was left (*sic*) and where the local populace had resumed their residence. The court approved this benevolent concern for the populace.[16] Years later, the point of residence in the city having been gained, the British consulate was moved back among the pleasant breezes and vistas to be enjoyed on the island, which formally became an International Settlement in 1903.

British experience at the other ports was similar. At Shanghai Captain Balfour, after his arrival in the beginning of November 1843, for $400 rented a house for the consulate inside the city and close to the wall between the east and west gates, and did not move out into the new settlement until several months later.[17] At Ningpo, on the other hand, Consul Thom preferred to keep his eye on the trade, and the consulate was established on the bank of the river across from the walled city.[18] But when the taotai proposed that British subjects be restricted to certain areas outside the city, Mr. Thom firmly refused. "All Englishmen from the time of infancy to old age," he explained, "are accustomed to take active exercise without a single exception," and he proposed complete access to the city and limits of ten *li* (say three miles) in all directions outside.[19]

When Consul Lay opened Foochow in the middle of 1844 he was aided by Hsü Chi-yü and his colleagues in finding a common house (*min-fang*) on Nantai Island, accessible to the shipping. Hsü reported that Lay seemed grateful and happy, but Governor Davis on his tour of inspection soon afterward found his consul in "a miserable dwelling built upon piles over a mud bank" and practically flooded at every high tide.[20] To maintain British prestige he demanded that Lay seek a place inside Foochow city. This prompted Hsü to observe (in a memorial of May 1845) that the Nanking treaty had not clearly provided for foreign consuls at the five ports dwelling within the city walls. Since the Foochow gentry had already petitioned to stop Lay's entrance, Hsü had found a big residence with which to entice him to stay on Nantai. But Lay refused and demanded to live in the White Pagoda temple (*Pai-t'a-ssu*) in a populous section of Foochow. Finally he settled for another more remote and dilapitated Buddhist temple on Wu-shih-shan (Black Rock Hill).

Hsü's idea throughout was to "manifest sincerity in the hope of getting control" over the British through the treaty provisions. Even though the treaty did not settle whether residence was to be inside or outside the city walls, Hsü tried to give the British no excuse for alleging a Chinese treaty violation. He remarked that the British were crafty and perverse by nature, hard to bring under control whether you resisted them or acted humbly.[21]

After Alcock took over the temple consulate in March 1845, he complained to the governor of Fukien because the "rains that have poured in from every roof and in all directions through the thin plank walls" were undermining the health of the staff. Walls built for Lay at a cost of $300 were blown down. The next year after much negotiation it was finally agreed that the local authorities for a sum of $2980 would repair the main building and build a three room cottage, the district magistrate to be repaid at the rate of $298 a year. This tenant-landlord relationship proved to be a strain on Anglo-Chinese relations. The repairs were long delayed and made with weak materials, and the authorities never appeared to supervise them, although they were reputed to be withholding some of the funds. (For some time after the opening of the port a consular assistant had lived on Nantai near the head of shipping in expectation of trade. When none developed he was brought up to the consulate.) [22]

In all these cases it is significant that Her Majesty's professional servants, Balfour and Alcock, pursued prestige and were generally considered successful, while Gribble and Lay followed expediency and received repeated censure.

Problems of treaty application: a) tonnage dues. In opening the ports for trade it was necessary to interpret and apply a multitude of treaty regulations, and this could be done only in coöperation with the Chinese local authorities. Of the many altercations which resulted a few may serve as illustrations.

At Amoy the presence of the British garrison on Kulangsu had put out of action the customhouse normally established there. The customs superintendent, through I-li-pu, had therefore asked in February 1843 either that the Kulangsu customs be allowed to reopen or that a station be recognized on the nearby island of Sinsea, and Pottinger had agreed to the latter alternative.[23] After the opening of the treaty port, the authorities sought to invoke article XVII of the Supplementary treaty and levy a tonnage duty of one mace per ton on all vessels which merely called at Amoy without discharging cargo.[24] The real issue here was how to tax the opium clippers which regularly called at Amoy without entering for trade. The British contention was that vessels entering to trade should pay five mace per ton, according to article V of the regulations of trade, but that those which landed only letters, loaded no more than water or supplies, and stayed not longer than forty-eight hours, need pay no tonnage dues whatever. The Foochow governor-general asserted that Consul Gribble had consented to the Chinese interpretation, but Hsü Chi-yü and the Canton governor-general finally agreed that vessels calling only for letters or treasure should pay no tonnage dues. Meanwhile Pottinger agreed that to allow such vessels to load supplies would facilitate smuggling, and he even suggested the imposition of tonnage dues upon them after twelve hours in port instead of the leisurely limit of three days which the Chinese were ready to allow. The amount of correspondence required to effect this compromise can be imagined. In October 1844 on Hsü's initiative the Chinese authorities at Amoy finally published ten regulations for foreign trade.[25] But three years later the consul reported that they had never been acted upon nor made a source of annoyance.[26]

b) *The shroff shops.* One of the most perplexing features of the China trade, to foreign merchants accustomed to standardized national currencies, was the matter of exchange. According to article VIII of the general regulations, foreign coins tendered for customs duties were to be evaluated in terms of "standard or pure silver" (an ambiguous phrase) and accepted at that value by the Chinese authorities.[27] The application of this rule, however, was left in the hands of licensed banking establishments or shroff shops whose business it was to act as the agents of the Chinese government and make their own living at the same time. At Canton the shroff shop (forerunner of the Customs bank) for the receipt of customs duties was set up in No. 13 Hong near Tang-lung street by two men who gave bonds for each other and deposited as security Tls. 6000 to be held for two years in the Hoppo's treasury in silver ingots stamped with their name and the date. They were guaranteed by the previous shroff shops and were then given licenses and seals by the Chinese authorities and proclaimed open for business by the imperial commissioner. At Shanghai the government bankers were a firm of six partners, each of whom could give receipts valid at the customhouse. Their shop was first located outside the walls on the street from the Little East Gate to the riverbank.[28]

The question of "meltage fees" (payments required nominally to make up for loss in handling silver) soon arose and affords an example of the working of the new diplomatic "alliance," as Pottinger called it. The correspondence was as follows: Balfour at Shanghai refused to agree to a meltage fee of 1.2 per cent being added to all payments made to the Chinese government in silver. The Shanghai authorities wrote to Ch'i-ying at Canton, who ascertained that the Fukien and Kwangtung customhouses had agreed with Consul Lay on the fee of 1.2 per cent. This he explained to Davis under date of November 24, 1844. Davis wrote to Balfour accordingly. Balfour issued a circular to the British community dated December 25 and reported to Davis who had meanwhile replied to Ch'i-ying.[29] The whole process took about two months, first to last.

At Amoy the exchange business was operated for several years as a racket. Consul Gribble had early arranged with the local authorities to reduce "the relative value of different coins to sycee [silver ingots or "shoes"] at par for the paying of imperial duties." [30] Early in December 1843 the Amoy district magistrate and the superintendent of customs notified the consul of the appointment of four men to assay and receive money for foreign duties. They, their families, their village headmen, and their neighbors had all made themselves responsible. A month later it developed that these new government bankers had obliged the English firm of Gibb, Livingston and Company to pay duties in chopped Spanish and Mexican dollars at a high discount, in addition to a high meltage fee. Sycee properly tendered through Consul Gribble was refused, and Pottinger censured Gribble for allowing this "indirect infraction of the treaty," for, by treaty, merchants could always pay sycee or dollars as they preferred. To this the superintendent of customs at Amoy agreed, but the shroffs continued to refuse to take sycee except at a discount plus a meltage fee. The taotai protested his inability to coerce the shroffs on the ground that they were chartered to receive duties in coins but not in sycee. Gribble offered to test the various types of impure sycee in circulation to determine how far it fell below the government standard of purity, but to no avail. Governor Davis thereupon applied as usual to Ch'i-ying,[31] and in August 1844 the Fukien provincial authorities proclaimed a set of regulations, based on Canton practice, which they asserted should prevail at all the ports. In this they recognized sycee of 100 touch [32] as legal payment for duties, plus a meltage fee of 1.2 per cent. Sycee of inferior touch was to be fairly evaluated as a substitute. But the Amoy shroffs, nothing daunted, continued to evaluate inferior sycee at their own arbitrary rates, levying, for example, a discount of 4.3 per cent on Tientsin-*pao* silver rated by the Canton shroffs at 98 touch — a profit of 2.3 per cent.

Consul Alcock found this racket continuing on his arrival at Amoy in

November 1844 and set out to break it. In December he got the superintendent of customs to agree verbally to the assay of samples of all sycee offered by merchants. The superintendent when written to, however, affected to misunderstand the agreement. Alcock then pressed him to accept the standard rates of discount for various types of sycee which were used at Canton. The superintendent in another conference in January 1845 agreed to this verbally, but refused to take the responsibility of committing himself in writing. Alcock thereupon announced that he would direct British merchants to proffer sycee at the Canton rates and, if refused, to lodge it in the consulate pending a decision. This amounted very nearly to a temporary stoppage of duty payments, a technique which Alcock was to use later at Shanghai. The superintendent then proposed a reference to Ch'i-ying and to Davis. Alcock agreed but stated that he would follow his plan pending the reference. This put the shroffs in a dilemma, and a few days later the superintendent of customs agreed to have Tientsin-*pao* silver accepted at 98 touch as at Canton — which Alcock had desired in the first place. But when Alcock sent him the agreement in writing, he again found an excuse for not committing himself beyond a statement that the shroffs acknowledged that their previous assay had been incorrect and would thenceforth demand a discount of only 98, instead of 94 or 95. Alcock still refused to accept a settlement of this sort covering only one kind of sycee, and the superintendent at length sent him a formal letter comprising the whole settlement previously agreed upon. The rates in use at Canton were now obtained and demonstrated what an "enormous imposition" had been practiced at Amoy.[33]

This whole proceeding is an interesting example of the tenacity required of treaty port consuls, and the success which usually attended it. As proof of Alcock's low opinion of the Amoy shroffs, his successors uncovered further extortions. It appeared that the government shroffs were really a large mercantile firm which traded chiefly with Malaya under the name of "Ty-Chaong [T'ai-ch'ang?] and Co." They were accustomed to boarding vessels from the Straits and using their official position to induce the Chinese merchants from Penang and Singapore to appoint them consignees of the cargo. Indeed, their power was so great that they could control the growing and illegal coolie trade by threatening to expose those traders who failed to coöperate. Their wrath was turned against Mr. Syme, the chief Amoy agent for trade with Manila, and they also tried to obstruct the activity of British merchants in the Singapore trade. While British Straits vessels under the Union Jack paid duties, those under the Dutch flag were allowed to evade them. The British consulate therefore again set out to break the power of the shroffs by an appeal to Ch'i-ying. The latter agreed that "these gainseeking and vile merchants, who receive the duties for us, cheat us of our customs." He wrote to the Fukien authorities, and the Amoy consulate also sent a copy of his letter directly to the Amoy customs. In February 1846 the shroffs were dismissed.[34]

Effect of the American treaty of 1844. The early British consular establishment in the treaty ports did not receive much reinforcement from the treaty relations with China entered into by the United States and France, for neither of these governments was as much interested as the British in the regulation and fostering of trade. The Americans used a cheap system of merchant consuls in the new ports, while the French confined their consular work mainly to Canton and Shanghai. The two treaties of 1844 made certain important additions to the British structure, however, and so formed part of the same treaty settlement.

Cushing's treaty has been extolled as showing how a Yankee lawyer could improve on British diplomacy. It did indeed provide a more thorough legal framework for Sino-foreign relations, gathering up into one document nearly all of Pottinger's treaty clauses and regulations, and adding in particular certain very important provisions regarding extraterritoriality (arts. XXI, XXV, XXVI and XXIX). At first glance, which has sufficed for many writers, the treaty also seemed to be more fair to China, for it outlawed American participation in the opium trade. But by the treaty the United States did not assume any obligation to bar Americans from the opium trade which flourished chiefly under the Boston firm of Russell and Company, whose members acted as American consuls at Canton and Shanghai.[35] Meanwhile the treaty provisions for extraterritoriality increased the difficulty of Chinese action against possible American opium smugglers. No one need be blinded by the fact that this fundamentally unilateral treaty was phrased in many places equilaterally. To say (in art. XXI) that "justice shall be equitably and impartially administered on both sides," does not change the nature of extraterritoriality.

The chief point about the American treaty, in its application, is the fact that it was not backed up, until a decade later, by a genuine consular administration. As a result, the much-advertised provisions favorable to China were generally not enforced, while the provisions favorable to the foreigner were avidly taken up and enforced by the Birtish consuls, if not also by the Americans. Cushing had in fact foreseen that his treaty would be enforced if at all by merchant consuls only. He therefore expressly omitted Pottinger's provisions for consular interference for the prevention of smuggling and to this extent weakened the British effort to reform the Chinese customhouse. On the other hand, Cushing inserted a number of provisions which facilitated foreign entrance into the coastal trade and so accelerated the Western economic penetration of China. From this point of view his treaty added to the Western charter of privileges.[36] There were also some favorable changes in the tariff. Behind all these provisions[c] the most important aim was to give encouragement to American interport trade in order to offset the advantage which the possession of Hongkong might give to British trade.[d]

Ingenious merchants were not slow to invoke the most-favored-nation clause. The reduction of tonnage dues on vessels of 150 tons or less, gained in the American treaty, was claimed for British vessels at Canton six months later in January 1845. In September of that year the provision of the French and American treaties was invoked, whereby vessels coming to China from foreign countries should pay tonnage dues only once. In 1848 the enterprising firm of Murrow and Company claimed that by this clause their vessels on the coast of China, having come from abroad and once paid tonnage dues, were thereafter exempt for as long as they stayed in China. Although this was obviously not the idea of the French treaty clause, the merchants at Canton appear for a time to have secured a tacit compromise whereby the Hoppo agreed to levy tonnage dues on foreign vessels in China only once a year. The enjoyment of this arrangement was then claimed at Shanghai, where several foreign coasters early in 1849 were able to avoid tonnage dues by proving that they had paid elsewhere in China within the preceding year. Consul Alcock finally looked into the matter. Reference to Canton gave no proof of the Hoppo's formal sanction. The American consul agreed with the British that there was no treaty basis for it, and the whole claim was exploded.[39]

Restriction of foreign excursionists and hunters. Enforcement of local

[c] The following concessions were obtained in the American treaty, sometimes merely as a codification of practices already grown up:

1. Tonnage dues on vessels of 150 tons or under were reduced from 5 mace (Br. gen. reg. 5) to 1 mace per ton (art. 6).
2. A vessel which had paid tonnage dues at one port in China and which then went to another port should not pay tonnage dues a second time (art. 6).
3. Boats conveying passengers, baggage, letters, provisions, or articles not subject to duty might go to or from any of the five ports without paying tonnage dues (art. 7).
4. A vessel which had entered port but had not broken bulk might depart within 48 hours without paying tonnage dues (art. 10).
5. Imports which had paid duty at one port might be re-exported to another treaty port without further payment of duty (art. 20). It was specified that the superintendent of customs should "make a memorandum in the port clearance of the goods and the amount of duties paid on the same, and deliver the same to the merchant, and shall also certify the facts to the officers of Customs of the other ports."

The following provisions settled matters which had been disputed:

6. A vessel should pay duty only on the part of its cargo which it discharged (art. 10).
7. Import and export duties should be paid when the goods were discharged or loaded, respectively (art. 13).
8. Duties would be received either in sycee silver or in foreign money at the rates of exchange then in force (art. 13).[37]

[d] Some of these new provisions, however, took years to become established in practice. Until July 1849 the exemption from duty of re-exported goods was proved, at Canton at least, by production of a special re-export or exemption certificate. This was in spite of the fact that the American treaty (art. 20) provided that the facts regarding re-export should be noted in the port clearance. The Hoppo finally asked that this practice be followed, five years after it had been provided for. The two documents were therefore combined, and the practice extended to other ports.[38]

regulations upon foreigners was just as difficult as upon Chinese merchants. By treaty the limits of British travel into the interior at each port were to be fixed by the authorities of both countries. Usually the limit was a half-day's journey, so that the traveler could return to the port by nightfall. With the passage of time and the growth of the receiving stations as communities outside port limits, it became nothing uncommon for foreigners to appear all along the coast at the small ports and harbors not opened by treaty. The exploration of the interior was undertaken more gradually and in part by missionaries.[40]

At Amoy the question of inland travel arose even before the opening of the port. In October 1843 a party of Americans made an excursion to the metropolis of Chang-chou, a day's journey up the estuary of the Chiu-lung (Nine Dragon) River, and an account of it was published in the *Chinese Repository* at Macao. The Chinese authorities complained to the British, and after verifying the facts Pottinger published a notification on November 27 condemning such trips and warning both British subjects and those of "all other states" in China. This he hoped would have more effect than anything that the American merchant-consul at Canton, Paul S. Forbes of Russell and Company,[41] might do, for Pottinger regarded the latter's consular function as "a mere name, so far as the wholesome control of his fellow citizens extends."[42] Shortly afterward it was complained, however, that a party of British officers from Amoy had made a similar expedition: they had applied to the Amoy taotai, who had sidestepped their request by referring them to the Amoy magistrate, and so they had left without waiting for a permit. Eventually in July 1844 the emperor was told, when he asked why the acting British consul, Captain Gribble, had been withdrawn from Amoy, that the Captain had not been very bright; he did not understand Chinese speech or writing, nor could be control his merchants; his reports to Pottinger were full of errors; and he had secretly allowed some ten men to go without a pass to Chang-chou, where they had disported themselves outside the city walls. All this had been reported to Ch'i-ying, who demanded that Pottinger forbid it.[43] In the end Pottinger had duly complained to his British colleagues, the general and the admiral, they had all apologized to the Chinese high authorities, and Gribble and Thom at Amoy had told the local officials that they were at perfect liberty to employ force to prevent such expeditions. These apologies were accepted.[44] The result was that foreign excursions did not cease but became more circumspect. A year later, for example, Chinese magistrates at Amoy complained that a party of two whites and four blacks had terrified the natives by landing and shooting ducks in a nearby harbor.

Foreign hunters at Shanghai produced the first real "incident" in the history of the port almost as soon as it was opened. After Consul Balfour arrived early in November 1843 in H. M. S. *Medusa,* as noted above (Chapter 11), port limits were fixed to include all the river between Shanghai and the Yangtze estuary. H. M. S. *Wolf* arrived on November 14, the port was proclaimed open as from the 17th, and six merchant vessels entered almost immediately. Among them the American ship *Valparaiso* had arrived on November 16, chartered by and consigned to the British firm of Dent and Company. On the day the port opened, Kung Taotai asked Balfour to restrain the men of this vessel from wandering on shore. The American master accordingly next day gave a bond to obey the regulations and surrendered the ship's register to the agent of Dent and Company, Captain John Wade of the *Island Queen* (a famous opium vessel in its day). Balfour explained to the taotai that he had no authority over Americans but that the British consignees would be responsible for them.

On the day following, November 20, an American from the *Valparaiso* (probably the mate) with two Chinese went on a hunting expedition a mile and a half into the Shanghai countryside. Curious crowds followed him and he accidentally shot two Chinese boys who were behind a "hedge which surrounded their dwelling." The populace became angry. Three days later the Shanghai magistrate cautiously informed Balfour that a boy had been wounded. The consul was unable to find the two Chinese concerned, by whom to identify the foreign hunter. He warned British subjects not to leave their ships with arms, and succeeded in having both wounded boys brought to the consulate and put under the care of Dr. Hale, the consular surgeon. It was feared that one would lose his sight. In this situation the Chinese authorities had recourse to the treaty and at once quoted article XII of the regulations of trade, according to which the mate of a vessel should always accompany the crew ashore. Balfour replied that the hunter was doubtless the mate himself, since the crew would not have had fowling pieces. He took no further action, although Pottinger would have approved his using H. M. S. *Wolf* to discover the offender by forcibly searching all the ships in port. Pottinger also pointed out that the British consul should not have become security for a non-British vessel. A month after the accident Balfour lifted the ban on hunting, with the restriction that hunters must get a consular permit and a police escort and not try to *learn* how to hunt in Shanghai. The boy's eyesight seemed likely to recover and the British merchants arranged to give both boys a purse and find jobs for them later, when it should not appear like "blood money." Meanwhile the *Valparaiso* had left port, and the taotai again demanded that hunters should be accompanied by the mate of their vessel.[45]

This first case at Shanghai epitomized many aspects of Sino-foreign relations. The foreigners probably showed throughout a greater concern for the individual welfare of the wounded boys than did anyone else on the scene. But this same respect for the individual, as expressed in Western law, made it impossible to find the culprit without witnesses to identify him positively. The Chinese authorities clung to the Chinese view of responsibility, that in all situations it should be squarely placed on someone, and the taotai also clung to the letter of the treaty, regarding the sanctity of which the foreigners had been so emphatic. A fundamental evil appeared in the inadequacy of British law to cover a situation in which irresponsible Americans were involved.

Chinese sensitivity to foreign excursions inland was soon manifested at Shanghai, after Consul Balfour's brother, a lieutenant in the 28th Madras infantry, went up-river and made soundings. The Chinese authorities objected. In May 1844 the consul notified the community that river surveys had already been made but pointed out that all governments were jealous of such activity: "the Chinese government is as independent as any other nation," and he therefore would defend "the just rights of China, the government of which is not empowered to punish the offending persons." [46] This appreciation of the responsibilities of extraterritoriality, so well stated in this case, tended to diminish with time, as the treaty port community grew accustomed to its privileges. By April 1851 it was nothing unusual when three Americans from Canton, one of them Mr. King of Olyphant and Company, made an expedition from Ningpo to Shanghai through the interior via Hangchow. Their trip having called attention to the practice, the masters of the Chinese boats which conveyed them from Ningpo were seized by the district magistrates and punished at Hangchow; and a proclamation of the Ningpo taotai in June 1852 forbade such expeditions.[47] Again, at Canton in March 1854 three Englishmen (the Rev. Mr. Cox, M. C. Morrison of the consulate and Johnson) went to the hills, 25 or 30 miles from the city. They asked for police runners to accompany them but set off without waiting for a reply to their application, and on the way were attacked by villagers. Since they were on a journey which could not have been completed roundtrip in the usual 24 hours — in short, out of bounds — the foreign community generally regarded it as an indiscretion. Other such cases became famous through British blue books.[48]

The problem of British control over other foreigners. The control of non-British foreigners, as demonstrated in the *Valparaiso* shooting case at Shanghai, early became a problem for both the British and the Chinese authorities. The Chinese view of responsibility required that all foreign vessels should be secured by some local authority, just as the British consul went security for all British ships. After the opening of the ports British consuls were several times asked to secure non-British foreign vessels. In some cases they did so, feeling themselves to be the representatives of all the West, as indeed they were. Moveover, when foreign vessels were chartered by British merchants, it was a great convenience to have the British consul act as security. Pottinger himself late in 1843 allowed Consul Lay at Canton to be security for a Chilean vessel on receiving a written undertaking from the charterer, Jardine, Matheson and Company, to be responsible for all dues and for the good conduct of the crew. About the same time Consul Thom at Ningpo secured the American barque *Oscar*, "on the captain and supercargo addressing me officially and engaging to obey my orders as if she were a British vessel." A few weeks later Gribble acted as security for the Danish brig *Danesborg* at Amoy. In May 1844 Lay confessed that at Canton he had two or three times become security for Dutch vessels, taking their registers and promises to pay duties and obey the consular authorities while in port. This practice, however, had dangerous implications, for the British consuls lacked legal jurisdiction over foreign subjects. In case of serious trouble they could not have lived up to their responsibility. At Pottinger's order the practice was therefore stopped.[49]

This paved the way for the practice which soon became general, by which resident British merchants received commissions from foreign governments to act as consuls or vice-consuls on their behalf. Soon each port had its array of foreign officials in the persons of British merchants, who naturally derived from their official status a very pleasant degree of prestige in Chinese eyes. At Amoy James Tait, a pioneer in the coolie trade, who had a godown adjoining the customhouse, became Spanish vice-consul and consular agent late in 1846 through the commission of the governor of the Philippines and with the permission of Palmerston. In January 1847 the Amoy taotai and customs superintendent reported to Peking that on December 7, 1846, an Englishman, James Tait (*Te-ti*), had come to Amoy in a ship of Spain and asked the officials for an interview, which they gave him. This barbarian official was extremely courteous and said that since he had formerly traded in Spain, the Spanish had asked him to come to Amoy and be their consul. He wanted to rent buildings for his consulate. The authorities helped him lease the house originally rented by Gribble. Tait was delighted, arranged with the owner, named Wu, to pay $400 a year, and then moved in. The Fukien governor-general observed that if the English had trade and consuls at the ports to manage custom affairs, it was hard to prevent other countries sending consuls too. With Tait as consul, Spanish ships at Amoy would now be under control.[50] In 1851 Tait became Netherlands vice-consul at Amoy, again with the permission of the British government. Both his offices were naturally of use to him in trade with Southeast Asia. In 1848 he was reported by his enemy, Consul Layton,[e] to be using his official status to coerce and

[e] Layton wrote to James Tait, Esq., Spanish consul, Jan. 11, 1848: "As your two assumptions, as

insult the Chinese authorities. In 1852 he became Portuguese consul, again with British permission. Four years later he illegally appointed a Spanish consular agent at the unopened port of Swatow, the center of the illegal coolie trade, in which he had meanwhile been a leading pioneer.

Meantime another English merchant, John Connolly, had become French consul at Amoy in 1849 and later tried unavailingly to become Peruvian consul, much of his trade in coolies and other goods being to that country. In 1851 Tait and Company included an American, Charles W. Bradley, LL.D., who was also United States consul at Amoy. The British community at Canton in the years 1853–55 included consular officers of Belgium, Peru, Denmark, Spain, and Portugal. Shanghai had an equally brilliant international array.[51]

The British government maintained its hold over these Englishmen who became consular representatives of other powers by the treaty provision that its subjects, unless formally recognized as consular representatives, could have access to the Chinese authorities only through the British consul. Thus the foreign country concerned was customarily expected to request of his government in London that a certain British subject be allowed to serve as consul. William Walkinshaw of Canton, a British merchant, received a letter from the King of the Belgians and proclaimed himself Belgian consul in 1853 but failed to observe the usual formalities. Two years later he was therefore forbidden as a British subject to have direct dealings with the Chinese authorities. He subsequently moved the Belgian government to follow the usual diplomatic procedure. Usually the British government gave its consent only after the permit or exequatur of the Chinese government had been received. Thus Alexander Stuart at Foochow was not at first accepted as Hamburg consul in 1857 because the Chinese authorities did not recognize the Chinese characters he used for the name of Hamburg.[52]

The evils of the merchant consul system were also mitigated by allowing British vice-consuls to act as the consular representatives of foreign powers. Thus Vice-consul Robertson at Shanghai became Danish consul in 1855 and Vice-consul Winchester of the Canton consulate became Peruvian vice-consul at Whampoa in 1854.

There is little doubt that the system of merchant consulships tended to confuse still further in the Chinese mind the at-best-shadowy distinction between one Western nationality and another. When the British consul at Amoy patiently explained that he had no authority over foreigners of other nationalities, no matter how they might break the peace, the sub-

---

you call them, are founded upon your own presumption, I will spare you the consumption of time and paper by refusing to receive any resumption of your eccentric correspondence." This is a good example of intra-treaty-port relations.

prefect was genuinely aggrieved. He pointed out that the consular representative of Holland and also of Spain (Tait) and that of France (Jackson) were both in reality British merchants. "From this it might be considered that the countries were virtually the same, and that there was no distinction between them." He asked for the names of the nationalities subject to British jurisdiction at Amoy.[53] The dominating position of the British in the treaty ports naturally encouraged such an effort to class all other Westerners under them.

Britain's control over her Chinese subjects. Problems of nationality became still more confused when Chinese became British subjects. This was particularly the case at Amoy, where the already flourishing native junk trade with Malaya and the British trade with the Straits, which was grafted onto it, had encouraged the migration of Chinese to Singapore and Penang, where they had acquired British nationality. Straits produce soon became a chief foreign import at Amoy, and coolies a staple export, and a considerable Anglo-Chinese community grew up to assist in both. The degree to which the Straits-Chinese flocked to Amoy appears in the consular registers, where they outnumbered the natives of Great Britain. In 1846 a total of 53 persons registered, of whom 27 were Anglo-Chinese from Malaya who returned thence at the end of the season. In 1847 the total was 35 Britsh subjects, of whom 16 were Anglo-Chinese who left at the close of the season. At the end of 1848 the British subjects present at Amoy included 13 natives of Great Britain, 4 of British India, and 26 of Chinese race from Singapore, Malacca or Penang.[54]

Like the protégés of other powers more recently — the Formosan-Chinese who used to claim Japanese nationality in China or the Filipino-Chinese who claim American nationality — these Englishmen by adoption were largely the descendants of emigrants from Amoy, if not actually natives. As such they blended perfectly with the local population except when it suited them not to do so. True to its legal principles, however, the British government undertook to protect them, when they could be identified. As one step in the spread of English law, a Hongkong ordinance of March 1844 extended the jurisdiction of the Hongkong courts over all British subjects in China or within one hundred miles of the coast, and this naturally came to include Anglo-Chinese from Malaya. The governor at Hongkong requested the governor of Singapore, Malacca, and Penang to give British-born Chinese a certificate of British naturalization whenever they departed for China, for presentation to the British consul on arrival at a treaty port. In accordance with the request of the Chinese authorities, who gave up jurisdiction over them, these British subjects should strictly avoid wearing Chinese dress while in China.[55] Foreign clothes thus became a cheap and easily obtainable symbol of foreign protection, the badge of the Chinese "traitor." The best smugglers were native Chinese in Western garb.

The right to protect these semi-foreignized Chinese involved the British consuls also in the duty of controlling them. For example, they were not supposed to enter China beyond the treaty limits of a half-day's journey (or thereabouts) prescribed for Westerners. By September 1846 it became necessary to have the consuls notify all Chinese who were natives of British colonies that (1) they could not claim British protection unless they brought proof that they were British subjects and unless they registered at a consulate on arrival, (2) they would forfeit British protection if they penetrated the interior beyond treaty limits, and (3) they were liable to all the treaty regulations regarding smuggling and the like. This order was occasioned by the Amoy consul's difficulty in rescuing certain Anglo-Chinese from Penang who were going inland with their household goods and had been seized by the local authorities as smugglers. In 1849 the legal authorities in England reaffirmed that persons of Chinese parentage born in British settlements were to be treated as British subjects in the treaty ports. They were not entitled to protection if they resided in other parts of China, providing they were recognized as Chinese subjects by Chinese law.[56]

A typical instance of the trouble caused by this dual nationality occurred in 1847, when an Anglo-Chinese originally of Amoy and now from Penang named Lee Shun Fah, who had evidently acted as a crimp (procurer) in the coolie trade, was seized by local villagers. They held him responsible for the death of sundry coolies below hatches in a typhoon on the emigrant ship *Sophie Frazier*. The Chinese authorities were dilatory about securing his release but at length Mr. Lee was recovered and handed over to the British consul. In the end the taotai paid him $605 compensation as a British subject. In other cases the dénouement was not so simple. The Amoy authorities seized an employee of Jardine's, Ch'en Ch'ing-chen ("Tan Keng-chin," "Tan King Chin"), a British subject from Singapore used by that firm as an English clerk, who was also the organizer of the Amoy branch of the anti-dynastic Small Knife Society. For this reason (as will be noted in Chapter 22 below) he was seized, and he died under punishment in prison, in January 1851. Governor Bonham applied to the imperial commissioner for redress and meanwhile revived Davis' order of 1844 that British subjects from the Straits make a point of wearing foreign dress while in China. He also ordered lists of all such British subjects to be supplied to the Chinese authorities, and all new arrivals to be presented at the taotai's office by a consular linguist for identification, so as to obviate all pleas of ignorance thereafter. Although this case drew from Palmerston the opinion that it was "neither necessary nor expedient" to press it further, the superintendent of customs at Amoy in February 1851 eventually was brought to promise not to arrest Chinese in British employ "without previously demanding them in due form" from the consul. On the other hand, the Amoy taotai, who was also titular provincial judge of Kansu, denied that Chinese born in British territory ceased to be Chinese when they returned to China. It was not stated in the treaties; the children of Englishmen born in China did not become Chinese, nor remain so after their return to England. He suggested, however, that the two nationalities should be distinguished by their clothing and by wearing shaved heads for Chinese and long hair for Englishmen; since the British subjects listed at Amoy dressed as Chinese, shaved their heads, and lived in Chinese villages, they were to be considered Chinese. This opinion was undoubtedly more scholarly, but did not prevail.[57]

As a result of the Straits-Chinese practice of identifying themselves by wearing Western dress, Cantonese at the other ports were inspired to adopt that garb whenever evil was afoot or when they were on the business of their foreign employers in the interior.

The early trade in coolies. No foreign activity on the coast of China was more spectacular than the coolie trade. This "buying of men," as the Chinese called it, became a flourishing business at Amoy in the late 1840's and developed later at the unopened port of Swatow. The dilemma faced by Consul Layton at Amoy was eloquently set forth by that staunch supporter of Victorian moral standards in mid-1848. The leading member of the British community of less than half a dozen persons, Mr. James Tait, complained to his consul that the Chinese authorities had arrested a Chinese named Vicente, a Roman Catholic convert, who was known to have been crimping coolies on Tait's behalf. Consul Layton had Mr. Tait put his complaint in writing and then approached the taotai, who offered to release Vicente if the consul would admit that British subjects were involved in the illegal coolie trade and take responsibility for it. Mr. Layton rejoiced that he had discovered Tait to be the offender but when he summoned him for trial, James Tait, in spite of his own written confession, defended himself on the ground that there was no evidence against him.

Consular investigation disclosed that Tait had made agreements of indenture with 100 Chinese coolies and 21 Chinese boys, who had been shipped to Sydney on the *Nimrod* on account of Captain Thomas Larkins, formerly of the East India Company fleet and now resident at Hongkong. The 100 men and 21 boys had agreed to serve Captain Larkins or his assigns for five years in New South Wales at $2.50 and $1.50 per month, respectively, receiving as weekly provisions 10 pounds of meat, 10 pounds of wheat, ¼ pound of tea, 1 pound of sugar, and such other provisions as might be agreed upon. Eight dollars was advanced to each emigrant on leaving Amoy. This was the sum that might be received by his family in compensation for his departure. He would repay it to his employers at the rate of 50 cents a week in Australia. The shipment was well known in Amoy and aroused much discussion, the populace conceiving that the men had been bought by Tait. Since they came from the lowest, poorest, and most vicious classes, the consul could not but consider that the community had been benefited by their removal: the departure of 10,000 a year would be a great boon, and continued shipments might serve to raise many vicious characters in the scale of civilization and place them in the way of an honest living. On the other hand, the situation was complicated by the fact that the Chinese authorities studiously avoided the whole matter, while the consular interpreter, Mr. Gingell, witnessed the signing of the agreements and seemed to be supervising the trade. As a result the consulate received petitions from parents who bewailed the enticement of their sons.

Consul Layton was uncertain of his legal position, and put questions before his superior. "How could he influence a slippery supercargo and avaricious agent or a cunning consignee? 'The consul is not authorized to detain the ship,' says the Queen's attorney general. 'Give me my papers and let me sail,' says the supercargo. 'Give us our sons,' say some agonized parents. 'Do not place any impediment in the way,' says Sir J. Davis. 'Take care of yourself and pacify those people,' would be the language of the Taoutae, 'to keep my own head from tumbling off is enough for me. I know nothing of emigration; I only connive at it when all goes smoothly; you had better restore all the people or the consequences may be bitter to you.' . . ."[58]

Ill-feeling engendered by the coolie traffic at Amoy came to a head in November 1852. The taotai asserted that three drunken Englishmen had bullied Chinese soldiers outside a yamen over some coolies whom the "English had purchased," and a fight ensued. As a result the taotai received a petition from the "entire community of the gentry and tradespeople of Amoy," protesting against his leniency toward Chinese coolie brokers, "who under false pretenses and delusive offers have succeeded in a number of instances in enticing (Chinese) from their homes, when these unfortunate people are entrapped and sold to the English." When the taotai took action, a British merchant attempted to rescue a Chinese coolie broker who had been seized. In retaliation Chinese soldiers seized Mr. Mackay, clerk in Tait and Company, gave him a talking to, and hit him over the head with a spear. Other Englishmen were stoned and a guard was landed from H. M. S. *Salamander*. The shops closed, a mob gathered, more stones flew, men poured in from the countryside scenting plunder, and eventually the British guard fired into the crowd, killing or wounding a dozen persons. "The missionaries, possessing nothing to tempt the cupidity of marauders, [were] safe from attack." (Eventually, in 1855, the Chinese Passengers Act was enacted by Parliament to curb such abuses.)

The Cantonese as British allies. This brings us to the final and most difficult question of all, the degree of British protection which was to be given to Cantonese servants. It cannot be too much emphasized that the real shock troops in the British invasion of China were not the Scotch and English merchants on the coast and in the ports but their Cantonese assistants — Chinese traders and "traitors" (*han-chien*), crimps, compradores, and opium salesmen from the south. The opening of the new ports was the signal for the expansion of the Cantonese to the north, for only the Cantonese, with their knowledge of pidgin English and of the mysteries of foreign trade and foreign ways, could provide the necessary link between the barbarian and the Middle Kingdom. Just as at Canton in pre-treaty days, so now it was they who provided in the new northern ports the managers, shroffs, clerks and linguists who were indispensable to the foreign merchant in the conduct of his business. As each port was opened there were set down among the local population not only a handful of barbarians but also a considerably greater number of their Cantonese hangers-on. Since the barbarians were, as at Canton, not inclined to study the local dialect, and since the local knowledge of pidgin English was at first negligible, the Cantonese appear in some cases to have been quite as necessary to the native merchants as to the foreign. To the Chinese of Fukien and the north, however, these Kwangtung men were foreigners and troublemakers.[f]

In a sense the British merchants merely financed and coördinated the expansive activities of these people, with the British consul bringing up the rear. The invasion came in waves: Cantonese merchants with opium and other goods, then British prospectors with Cantonese assistants, followed at length by treaty port settlements and British consuls, still with Cantonese clerks and servants. At Canton the foreigner had been helpless without his local servants, to whom he gave orders in pidgin and who often knew many aspects of his business, usually the less savory, better than he did himself. At the new ports he remained for some time dependent upon them because of the lack of any language in which the natives of Kiangsu and of Glasgow, for instance, could communicate. The foreigner

[f] In 1847 the Chinese correspondent at Shanghai of Hongkong's leading paper, the *China Mail,* declared that "the Canton fellows that have followed the English to Shanghai as hired servants are very great blackguards and ought to be under more strict and severe discipline, as they create every kind of mischief . . . The people of Shanghai not understanding the English language, but being deeply interested (in the foreign trade) they have received linguists from Canton who have caused much confusion and injury. They have been with us several years so that our affairs have become mixed up with theirs and our original wealth greatly diminished."[59]

was inclined to ascribe it simply to imbecility on the part of the northern natives, who appeared to him to be "as nearly devoid of intellect as is compatible with the existence of a human conformation," and quite different from "the brisk and handy natives of the South."[60] When Consul Balfour reached Shanghai he found Cantonese merchants already there. They had moved north along the coast with the British expeditionary forces. British trade at Shanghai was initiated with the help of a Canton broker named Alum, a merchant well known to the foreign community as an energetic business man, long connected with the tea and silk trades from the interior. At Shanghai "he at once broke down the barrier of exclusiveness, taught the Chinese the principle of barter trade and by creating a demand furnished a supply. He pushed the British manufactures up country and by his influence induced the tea and silk growers to consign their products to the Shanghai market." According to Vice-consul Robertson, who evidently worked with him, Alum was chiefly responsible for the sudden flourishing of trade at Shanghai, which at first centered in him from the Chinese side. Within a few years losses and debts forced his flight and bankruptcy. But in 1851 Robertson helped him to enter the tea trade at Ningpo, where Alum became established as a leading member of the rapidly growing Cantonese community.[61] At Ningpo, however, he lacked capital and succeeded chiefly in collecting old debts, in the end becoming the chief front man for the disposal on the Shanghai market of the ill-gotten gains of his fellow-provincials, the notorious pirate brothers, Apak and Alumtay (see Chapter 18).[62]

Cantonese were equally useful in the consulates. Gribble took Cantonese linguists with him to Amoy, and Thom did the same at Ningpo. The Chinese authorities described the latter's arrival with an entourage of some fifteen persons including Cantonese servants and two linguists, Chiang-pin and Yuan-hua, who were natives of Hsiang-shan (Heung-shan, the district of Macao), and had once been licensed by the Hoppo.[63] In 1845 Alcock at Foochow[g] vigorously intervened between the Chinese authorities and Cantonese employees of the consulate. He admitted that he had no legal jurisdiction over them but argued that such servants were part of the "establishments" allowed British subjects by article II of the Nanking treaty. (The Chinese treaty phrase was *so-shu chia-chüan*, a phrase equivalent to wife and family, perhaps including servants, but certainly more narrow than in the English version of the treaty.) Alcock demanded that

[g] Shortly after opening the port, his predecessor, Consul Lay, had publicly stated "his determination that no Cantonman speaking English shall enter the consulate on any pretext whatsoever. Any aid in the way of shroffing money, purchasing provisions, or communicating with the people the Officiating Consul will provide himself. Merchants and Captains are warned by him against bringing up men who are mixed up in a well organized system of fraud and villainy and who by oppressing the natives and contracting large debts have reduced themselves to objects of fear and detestation."[64]

consular employees when accused of crime should first be sent to the consulate, and Davis backed him: the consul should deliver them up to their own authorities only "on fair presumptive proof of their guilt." Davis agreed that the first war had begun with attacks on foreigners' servants, which must therefore be prevented.[h] (This virtual extension of extrality became an established feature of British policy even though the case which gave rise to it at Foochow had had its darker side: the Cantonese originally accused there in November 1845, while shooting cranes in a suburb, had actually killed a boy and confessed the fact.) [68]

It is important to remember that from the point of view of the populace of Fukien, Chekiang, and Kiangsu, the Cantonese with their peculiar spoken dialect were really strangers, if not actual foreigners. They had different tastes in food and all those subtly varied physical and cultural characteristics which distinguish major regions of China. Compared with Chinese residents of the northern ports, these Cantonese invaders had a more coöperative attitude toward the foreigner and his trade. Since they were more numerous than their European and American employers and more closely in contact with the local people, they were even more hated than the foreigners who employed and protected them. At Foochow, for example, an English merchant, Mr. Glen, became active in the opium trade and conducted it out of bounds, actually bringing drug up to his hong for sale. Consul Alcock warned him not to do so in November 1845 and issued a public notice against the practice. Against this background a series of sanguinary riots erupted on Nantai during the four days March 28 — April 1, 1846, involving Fukienese, Cantonese, and Englishmen. This brought Consul Alcock and Hsü Chi-yü face to face as official protagonists.

[h] The British home government did not support this view very strongly. The question whether Chinese servants of foreigners should be surrendered when accused by their own authorities, when it arose at Canton in August 1849, was settled by Palmerston in the affirmative: the right of the Chinese government to exercise its authority over its own subjects could not be questioned by refusing to deliver up such persons, unless the Chinese acted purely for vexatious purposes. Extreme caution was advised in such matters.[65] In both 1854 and 1857 Bowring followed the dictum, "I cannot take Chinamen under British protection." Thus when Jardine, Matheson and Co. informed him of the arrest of one of their servants at Foochow, he told the consul to secure the man's release but avoid threats in doing so.[66] The treaty port view was expressed by Consul Meadows to the Ningpo taotai in 1854: "Should the local authorities at any of the five ports seize the servants of British subjects without entering first into communication with the Consul, would that be allowing foreigners 'to live without molestation or restraint'? . . . the Shanghai Taoutae's police secretly carried off from the Foreign Factories the Compradore of a British Indian subject for selling powder to the Rebels. The British subject petitioned the Consul; and two armed Boats from the British war ships were dispatched to the Taoutae's war vessels where the Compradore was supposed to be confined. The Compradore not being there the officer in charge of the British war Boats seized two mandarins in the Taoutae's war vessels — one the Shaohing Chefoo [Shao-hsing prefect] — and took them on board the British war vessels for examination. The compradore having however before anything was done further on the affair, been released, the two mandarins were allowed to return to their vessels.

"I mention the above," concluded Meadows, "merely for the purpose of showing you that the foreign governments will not permit the servants in the employment of their subjects to be apprehended by the local authorities; but that a communication must, in accordance with Treaty Rights and civilized customs, be sent to the Consul to request his investigating the case and the delivery of the servants, if sufficient evidence be found of their being guilty of the crime imputed to them." [67]

Their extensive reports to their respective governments offer an interesting comparative study. In general Alcock made plain the evil influence which emanated from an opium trade which had overflowed its normal channels. He reported that on March 28, 1846, a Chinese servant of Capt. Miln of the opium ship *Vixen* was assaulted and a general free-for-all broke out in Nantai between the populace and the Canton element. A pockmarked Cantonese named Le, who understood English and ran the "Eho shop in Chungchow at Nantae, a small establishment for the secret sale of opium," fired a musket among the Fukienese and wounded two persons.[69] He then found concealment with Mr. Glen's shroff and linguist, who were the acknowledged leaders of the local Cantonese. On April 1 occurred a second affray in which Glen himself was badly wounded. He and Captains Hackett and Roper later had to run for safety, abandoning their hongs to plunderers. Roper for a time occupied a local island in self-defense.

The Chinese official version of these riots covered up the whole question of opium and dealt at length with the temper of the local populace and of the British — two groups whom the Manchu-Chinese authorities would rather see at odds than united. Hsü Chi-yü presented such an impressive wealth of plausible detail that his report is worth summarizing below.[i]

[i] Hsü Chi-yü's memorial to the emperor stated that Sino-barbarian relations had been completely peaceful in Fukien until March 28, 1846, when a small British ship anchored off Nantai and its sailors went to market to buy fish. Because the speech used on both sides was not understood, they did not pay the full price and made off with the fish. All the shopkeepers were upset by this forcible purchase. A commoner named Lin went out in the street to make some purchases and met a white English barbarian accompanied by a Cantonese linguist, and, because the street was narrow, accidentally struck the barbarian on the shoulder-blade. The barbarian was displeased and accordingly used a wooden cudgel which he carried in his hand to beat Lin about the head. Lin was afraid and fled into the Yang-huan-chih oil shop for refuge, pursued by the barbarian and his linguist. Although the oil-shop people exhorted him not to, the barbarian proceeded to shatter their oil jars. At this time neighbors and passersby, hearing the noise, crowded about. Some say the Englishman and the Cantonese reviled them too harshly and they would not take it. They wanted to argue with the barbarian. At that time there happened to be passing the barbarian merchant, Glen (*Chi-lien*). The crowd suspected that he had come to help. A man named Lin Ch'i-ch'i, who was later seized, took a wooden stick and injured Glen in the left ribs. A man named Wang Ch'i-ch'i seized a rock and hit him on the right side. Another picked up a piece of tile and wounded him on the back. Two servants of the barbarian merchant Miln (*Mi-lun*) were also wounded. The local authorities restored order and the merchant Glen, the other white barbarian, and the linguist were escorted by the troops back to the barbarian hong.

Because the barbarians had beaten a man and relied on a show of force the Nantai populace were much disturbed and a clamorous crowd gathered in a noodles shop next to the barbarian hong. Several linguists who were there fired off fowling pieces in an intimidating manner, in the hope of scaring the crowd away, but their bullets flew through the air and wounded two men, Ting and Chou, who happened to be passing on the street. Both men fell to the ground. The local inhabitants at this became even more unsettled and surged toward the barbarian hong in a displeased manner. They happened to meet a black barbarian, and beat him severely.

Meanwhile the barbarian merchant Roper (*Lo-pa*) became frightened and ordered his linguist to take the silver in his hong elsewhere for safety. Local gangsters led by one Huang K'un-k'un, seeing the silver chest, conceived the idea of seizing it. Others entered the hong to loot miscellaneous goods and another group outside picked up some of the stolen clothing. One silver chest was carried off and opened. In it were found 2,300 foreign dollars. One man took a thousand. Another was given forty because he had been injured, and the assisting coolies received two dollars apiece. Another took three hundred, another eighty, and another eight, and they all ran away.

(In the Chinese judicial settlement, reported to Peking six months after the event, it was noted that robbery of Tls. 120 or more was banditry; the various crimes that had been committed were punished by various amounts of beating with a heavy bamboo according to minute statutes and various assign-

On the British side the opium merchants' reaction was to make claims against the Chinese government, Glen demanding $50,000 for "frustration of plans, . . . loss on commission of goods about to have been sent," . . . and passage to England for the recovery of his health. Sir John Davis heard privately that Chinese feeling against Glen was caused by violent and unjustifiable conduct, and allowed only the claims for tangible loss — 302 bales of cotton worth $2260. The gunboat *Pluto*, the only steamer small enough to ascend the Min River, was sent to Foochow express, while H. M. S. *Espiègle*, already there, anchored as close up as possible. But the claims for compensation and for punishment dragged on without much result in spite of the presence of the gunboats. In the end Mr. Glen departed for good [71] and the opium captains, Roper, Miln, and Hackett were all transferred, the last two being succeeded by Captains Roope and Hely, who proceeded to live on their ships. A year later Davis ordered the names of all Cantonese in English employ to be given to the Chinese authorities with a disclaimer of responsibility for all others. Captain Hely reported a linguist, A-ping (of the same name as Captain Gribble's linguist at Amoy in 1843), and a caretaker, A-kwang, and Captain Roope had none in his employ.[72]

The ill-starred triangle of British-Cantonese-native relations produced

---

ments of penal servitude. Those who stole clothing were given a hundred blows and three years. Evidently punishment was meted out for stealing property a good deal more than for breaking bones.)

The Chinese officials reported their troops' success in restoring order and seizing the culprits. But they also felt it necessary, at this time when the anger of the crowd had not yet been assuaged, to issue a clear proclamation so that the ignorant villagers might not say that the local authorities were shielding the barbarians and did not love the common people. Accordingly they posted a proclamation to the populace saying in effect, "you have been moved to mass indignation by incidents with barbarians and Cantonese. Originally this was on the part of honest citizens but gangsters took advantage of it to loot the barbarian hongs, which was really not your intention. If we do not severely deal with this, the gangsters will have their way and subsequently loot your goods too. Our dealing severely with the bandits is in order to give you protection. The barbarian consul, Alcock, is now within the city and the local authorities of course will make the facts clear to him so that there will be no trouble. You need not get excited." By this perspicacious admonition the local mob was mollified.

The authorities also considered that, since the barbarians' deceitful ways were clearly apparent, this provided an opportunity to get them under control so that they would be both grateful and fearful. So they sent a deputy to Alcock's residence on Wu-shih-shan. Alcock was disturbed and very fearful and requested that the high authorities immediately provide protection. The officer replied, "This riot originally was started by you. Now the populace of Nantai in vast numbers are all moved to righteous wrath. Although the high authorities have already admonished them to disperse and sent troops to the foot of Wu-shih-shan to protect you, hereafter if you do not restrain the barbarian mob from stirring up popular anger, then the protection of the officials will be inadequate." Alcock recognized he had no ground to stand on and said that thereafter they should frame regulations ordering the men of all colors in the ships and hongs to stir up no more trouble.

On April 8 Alcock came for an interview accompanied by Harry Parkes (*Hsia-pa*). Hsü Chi-yü told them that thereafter they must severely restrain the barbarian mob. The Chinese officials likewise would control the populace. If on both sides they were impartial then they could have permanent peace. Alcock was acquiescent and sincerely submissive. He gave prompt respectful answers and went away (*wei-wei er ch'ü*). Finally, Hsü observed that the barbarians now realized that when the mob was angry it was difficult to withstand and hereafter would be more careful.

The imperial edict in response to this report approved the Fukien officials' conduct of affairs. Where foreigners and Chinese were mixed in together, quarrels were bound to occur. The provincial authorities should see that the local officials exercised a restraining influence and handled disputes with an even hand, so as to keep the people quiet and not give the barbarians any pretexts.[70]

similar incidents all along the coast. At Shanghai in 1845 a British subject obtained consular approval to build a "pleasure boat," which proved to be a 26-foot lorcha of 60 tons burthen. It appeared that a former Canton shroff named Fowqua planned to use it to levy blackmail (in the form of "protection fees") on Chinese boats smuggling opium up the river. The local authorities, hearing of this, seized and tortured Fowqua, who implicated more than 100 others in the scheme.[73]

In May 1847 the Shanghai magistrate issued proclamations against the Kwangtung and Fukien vagabonds who had opened gambling houses and brothels and seduced the young men of good families.[74] Six years later it was this same element which seized the city of Shanghai under the aegis of the Triad Society (see Chapter 21).

One more example of Cantonese-Fukienese relations may be cited. On December 17, 1855, a coolie carrying a timber through the street at Nantai accidentally knocked down a Cantonese, who kicked the coolie in the stomach and killed him. A mob seized and bound the Cantonese, the wife of the deceased drove nails into his eyes and temples, others made various incisions and he lingered for some time before dying. The local Cantonese armed themselves in perturbation and the authorities called out troops, but a riot was averted by compromise. Fortunately the dead Cantonese had not been connected with a foreign firm. In May 1856 the high authorities announced that all Cantonese boats coming to Foochow must be secured by a merchant of their own province; the crews should not be allowed to go about with knives and swords.[75]

Friction between the local populace and the foreign residents, particularly of the smaller treaty ports — Amoy, Foochow, and Ningpo — was engendered partly by the fact that the foreign community in these early days was never large enough to be self-contained. Far from the self-sufficient social life typical of the treaty ports at a later date, there were at this time almost no social amenities. The community usually contained few foreign ladies and almost none for long unmarried, and, what was equally important, no social body large enough to exert the influence of a public opinion. The white man's sense of superiority and the strong moral code of the Chinese populace both served to check overt relationships. On the other hand, it is plain that not a few of the young men in their twenties and thirties, who made up the great majority of the foreign population, made their own prudent and unadvertised domestic arrangements.[j] This tied them into the Chinese community in a way that occa-

[j] One vice-consul succumbed after prolonged immersion in the backwash of Ningpo. The Bishop of Victoria accused him in 1853 of having seduced a Chinese girl from a Church of England missionary school (Miss Aldersey's), taken her and her family to Foochow on his transfer there in 1850, and lodged them in a monastery, with the result that the church was besmirched and disgraceful notoriety was caused at Foochow. Even a consular colleague agreed that the man of this Chinese family was a notorious vagabond; popular feeling eventually necessitated their being sent back to Ningpo.[76]

sionally produced trouble, usually through the claims of the Chinese family system upon all those connected with it.[k]

[k] In 1857–58 gangs of Cantonese at Foochow, mostly servants in the foreign firms, formed the habit of "annoying such of the foreigners as have Chinese women living with them, by tempting the women to infidelity and maltreating or extorting money from such as are obstinate in constancy to their masters. In two cases . . . this maltreatment amounted to a severe beating given at night by the gang in a body when the foreign masters happened to be absent. The majority of the community has been more or less interested in putting a stop to these proceedings, and various plans have been formed . . . for taking vengeance upon the ruffians. Unhappily for one of these and for our own good name, they were discovered a few nights ago feasting in an empty house belonging to one of the aggrieved, accompanied by some of their female friends. A body of foreigners proceeded to the place forthwith, and having routed the whole party and made the leader a prisoner, they carried him off to one of their hongs, flogged him severely, and I am sorry to say shaved his head [i.e., cut off his queue, a serious matter] and sent him on board one of their receiving ships at the anchorage, intending to ship him off by the mail steamer. I first learned the fact from a relative of the captured man." The consul at once secured the release of the hapless Cantonese from the receiving ship and offered to entertain charges against his captors. This emboldened the gang who had so far been under the censure of their own community as well as the foreign one, "and they became so noisy in their demands for redress, and reports were so prevalent that they talked of attacking the Hong where the deed was done," that the consul felt obliged to have a boat's crew landed from the British warship in the harbor. He feared the foreigners concerned would be liable to "secret and severe revenge, indeed it is given out that they are to be assassinated."[77]

CHAPTER XIII

THE OPIUM SETTLEMENT IN PRACTICE

The Western side of the drug traffic in the interim decades between the two Anglo-Chinese wars has been vividly recorded in numerous works — picturesque, matter-of-fact, or denunciatory, as the case may be. The system of production and official sale in India, the storage of opium cargoes at Hongkong, and their distribution thence in the famous opium clippers to the receiving ships at a dozen stations on the China coast are fairly well known. In this early period of growth, the trade verged upon armed monopoly, for the coastal running vessels and receiving ships were both heavily armed and had fighting crews constantly on the alert to repel pirates; while the two leading British firms, Jardine's and Dent's, had outstripped all others in the thoroughness of their transportation and importing mechanisms. Commanded by able and conscientious Anglo-Saxons, some of whom were the sons of leading families at home, the opium fleet set a high standard of seamanship, elegance, and efficiency. American clippers such as those of Russell and Company, and the early paddle-wheel steamers of Britain's Peninsular and Oriental Steam Navigation Company, provided the chief competition for the leading British firms. The P. and O., however, engaged only in transporting opium, not in selling it, while the Americans, though they did the best they could, conducted only about one-tenth of the total trade.

This American participation in the drug traffic, being less than the British, has gone relatively unstudied. It began as early as 1805 but was at first handicapped by the necessity of procuring drug supplies from Turkey (Smyrna) and Persia. The Boston firm of Russell and Company (successor to Perkins and Company) eventually set up their own network of clippers and receiving ships and also handled British Indian opium on consignment. In the 1840's American policy and opinion were against the trade, but the American flag continued to give it cover and protection. American vessels were chartered to British firms, as noted above (Chapter 9). Augustine Heard and Company of Boston began to act as Jardine's agents in Canton in 1840, and soon were distributing Indian opium on their own account.[1]

The economic role of this unlegalized trade continued to give it impetus, for "opium was still inextricably bound up with the triangular system of trade. China was the creditor of England, England of India, and

India of China, and opium was the biggest single item in enabling India to discharge her debt to England and England hers to China." [2] During the first decade after the treaty of Nanking, the Middle Kingdom continued to suffer a net drain of silver in payment for opium imports. As China's tea and silk exports increased, however, the drain of Chinese silver to India was eventually more than covered by British shipments of silver specie to China. About 1851 the balance of trade appears to have shifted back to China's favor. Meanwhile imports of British manufactures into that country continued to find a small and limited market. This was because China had little need of Lancashire textiles, although the British manufacturers contended that it was because opium purchases exhausted her purchasing power. Thus the chief economic role of opium continued to be the balancing of China's foreign trade.

What happened after the drug chests from India left the foreign merchants' hands at the receiving stations has remained obscure. Some 50,000 chests a year (an average of 37,000 during the 1840's and 68,000 during the 1850's) were shipped from India and disappeared into the East Asian distribution network, the bulk of them going to China. But almost no one has tried to trace the development of the undocumented opium trade of the Chinese interior. The Western administrator wracked his brains and the Christian reformer was tormented by his conscience for a whole generation before the 1860's, but all with reference to the wholesale commerce from India to the coast, with little or no knowledge of the retail trade in Chinese hands. The historical scene is so brightly lit in the foreign foreground that shadow engulfs the Chinese background.

Smuggling opium — light in weight and high in value — was of course an ideal occupation to flourish in a period of disorder such as China was now entering. The growing social chaos of the times undoubtedly increased the number of demoralized individuals ready to take up smoking and also persuaded officials to seize quick profits by connivance. Once under way, the trade was further stimulated by an irreducible and growing Chinese demand, steadily increasing British-Indian supplies, the accumulating capital resources of the Chinese merchants and the mounting dependence of local officials on their illicit opium revenues. Finally, where the trade could not buy its way, it could use force. The heavy armament of the foreign vessels on the coast was symptomatic of the Chinese domestic situation, in which armed bands, including defensive "local corps," were becoming more active year by year while piracy along the coast increased roughly in proportion. Since piracy cannot flourish without pickings, further research should show its close connection with the domestic channels of opium distribution.[3]

British exclusion of the opium trade from the treaty ports. Against this background of growing lawlessness, the British consuls had to seek the security of British trade. It had already been decided that their concern was with the legal trade alone — the import of English manufactures and Indian cotton, the export of Chinese tea and silk. When the first ports were opened late in 1843, the special status of opium had still to be established in practice. Since the contraband trade could neither be legalized nor suppressed, it must be officially ignored. But within what limits was it to be ignored? If it were invisible at the receiving stations, was it also to be invisible inside treaty port limits? How long could the consul avert his eyes when opium was thrust under his nose? This very practical question was not settled until the spring of 1844.

At the new ports the consuls were handicapped by the fact that opium had long preceded their arrival. When Amoy was opened the Chinese superintendent of customs informed Consul Gribble of the presence of four British ships in the harbor, all unreported at the customs. These vessels had all been anchored on the west side of Kulangsu trading in both opium and legal goods. An officer of H. M. S. *Serpent* now boarded them and secured their registers but reported that none had manifests.[4] As Matheson had foreseen and written to his agent, Capt. D. Forbes of the receiving ship *Mahamoodie*, "it will be necessary for you to move your vessel out of the harbour to some anchorage where you cannot be seen from the town. Otherwise the consul, as soon as he enters upon his duties, will have to call on you for your manifest, which of course you cannot give" (because of having opium on board).[5]

The result was that the opium vessels moved outside the port limits, and the larger firms took the lead in keeping the legal and illegal trades separate and distinct. Matheson's letter had continued, "Since this may interfere with your sales of cotton . . . we think it will be necessary for you to have a godown on shore near the consulate, in which you can store [legal] goods when unable to sell them off at once. In this way you can dispense with a receiving ship in the harbour. You might live and keep your money close by the godown in the house you are building. When you have accumulated any amount of dollars they might be sent to the *Mahamoodie* outside the port under the charge of your clerk . . . in a ship's long boat, there to remain for the first of our opium clippers coming down the coast. It will never suit to pay freight on our treasure to other vessels. After you have fixed on a proper anchorage for the *Mahamoodie*, we shall direct all cotton and other vessels for Amoy to call there first, so that any portion of their cargo required for Chinchew [the nearby opium emporium] may be put on board and sent up as required. It will not do to send a vessel with cotton or other lawful cargo to Chinchew, as it would be talked about and might lead to the drug trade being interfered with. Supplies must therefore be in small quantities to any other than the five ports. . . ."[6]

In spite of this coöperation from the leading firms, it took some time to shunt the opium trade into a special channel. Opium boats at Amoy still plied back and forth like ferry-boats. The drug was carried openly through the streets and the mandarins were said to get about fivepence sterling per ball. Some 150 chests a month were consumed and paid for in ready money. At Chinchew (Ch'üan-chou), 80 miles away, at nearby Chimmo, and at Namoa 70 miles to the south, the demand was in each case greater than at Amoy, so that in this region the British consul believed the balance of trade was definitely against China.[7]

At Shanghai the opium trade was already a year old when Consul Balfour arrived. Some 8000 chests of drug, valued at nearly six million dollars, had been disposed of in the Shanghai market by the three to six vessels at Wusung, which dealt with Chinese purchasers who came alongside. The receiving ships had "remained during this winter outside, exposed in the open sea to the rough and inclement weather and gales for the sake of selling this drug." For some time after the opening of the port under the treaties, opium was publicly carried past the customhouse and through the streets, as at the other ports.[8]

While both the British opium monopolists and the consuls were interested from the first to confine the drug trade to a separate and safer channel, it required a resounding object lesson to impress this point upon the smaller fry who imported opium, and also upon the Chinese authorities who were not accustomed to Anglo-Saxon legal distinctions. After Shanghai had been opened the taotai complained to the consul that five foreign ships had been found outside the river and port limits at Wusung, unreported and presumably smuggling. Since their presence had long been obvious, the crews regularly coming up to Shanghai, this action by the taotai indicated his desire to enforce treaty regulations. But he overlooked the fact that the consul was deaf, dumb, and blind outside port limits. Balfour replied, "These vessels must then be at sea outside the port and cannot yet have entered . . . This certainly is not disobedience of the regulations." He promised to act if the ships entered port.[9] This was in December 1843. Two months later occurred a famous case which established the distinction for all to see.

The British barque *Maingay*, 281 tons, George Brown, master, and the brig *Amelia*, John Rogers Alexander, master, cleared from Singapore for Shanghai with opium aboard. The vessels were owned by British firms resident in Singapore and Calcutta, respectively, and carried among other cargo a total of 128 chests of drug worth perhaps $64,000. "Without inquiring at the mouth of the port [Wusung] where information could have been obtained," as the consul phrased it (and that was the real crime), these two vessels "unhesitatingly steer direct for the anchorage and moor off the town." [10] At the consulate on February 1, 1844, the master of the *Amelia* declared one chest of Turkey opium, evidently to see what the consul would think of it. The consul told him to throw it overboard, he pretended to do so, and thereupon began to trade in the usual fashion. (Later the consul did not make public that this had been his advice.) On the following day the master of the *Maingay* reported at the consulate with papers so confused and irregular that the consul felt obliged, after several days had brought no rectification of them, to hold an investigation aided by two British merchants as assessors. Meanwhile both masters had become frightened. On the night of February 7–8, they transhipped their opium cargoes to a British vessel which had already received its clearance for leaving port, the *William the Fourth*. Hearing of this act on the following evening, Consul Balfour had naval officers detain the vessel. The opium was then thrown off the luckless *William the Fourth*, some of it into the muddy waters of the Whangpu and some of it into native boats which took it out of port. Lieutenant Harvey, R. N., found a mad scramble going on among a crowd of boats searching for floating chests. He seized several which had loose opium aboard and fished one chest out of the water himself. This haul he turned over to the Chinese customhouse.

Consul Balfour now seized his chance to drive the drug trade out of port. He took action under the treaty regulations for legal trade, which had been flagrantly broken, and levied fines totalling $3200 for the various crimes of irregular papers, false manifest, breaking bulk without permission, and transhipping without permission. He penalized the opium smugglers in this indirect way, without reference to the nature of their cargo, because he was in doubt as to his policy on opium. "So long as the parties who are at present employed in the traffic in opium have almost the entire monopoly along the coast, I do not anticiptate many cases occuring difficult of management, but I do certainly expect most serious evils to arise from other parties engaging in the traffic and not having the same inducement to carry on the traffic free from collision with the Chinese authorities." Between the cupidity of the opium dealers and the apathy of the local authorities, the consul was in an anomalous position. The Chinese authorities at Shanghai had known of the opium transhipment long before he had, but had done nothing. Where should he draw the line between maintaining the British treaty system in the port and enforcing the laws of China on the coast? [11]

The British government was now obliged to define its policy toward a commodity which was contraband by the laws of China but not by those of Great Britain. In order to allow his superior every opportunity to review the case, Balfour had detained the *Amelia* and *Maingay* at Shanghai and sent the *William the Fourth* in charge of a naval officer to Hongkong, whence it was going anyway. Pottinger took a half-way position: he approved the fines for breaking bulk and for false manifest (total $1500), and later for irregular papers ($200), since such fines were clearly prescribed by treaty, but he suggested remitting the fines for transhipping (total $1500), because such matters were primarily the responsibility of the Chinese authorities. The consul should have recommended to the customs officers that the vessels be forbidden to trade and be turned out of port. By going further, he had acted as an excise officer for the Chinese government. In fine, he should tell the Chinese that "whatever is on record in the treaties . . . will be rigidly enforced by myself and all officers under my authority, but that whether with regard to the forbidden trade in opium, or to smuggling transactions or transhipments in legal merchandise, the great remedy lies in their own hands, and that unless they administer it, they must abide the consequent loss of revenue." [12] In short, the consuls were to enforce the treaties and nothing but the treaties. Opium not being mentioned in those documents, they could do nothing about it.

Balfour's notification to the Shanghai community stated that opium was "an article which being forbidden by the laws of [China] must necessarily involve the established good faith of Great Britain." [13] Kung Taotai, who had broken off a trip to see Ch'i-ying at Nanking and hastened back to Shanghai to deal with the case, agreed with Balfour and told him, in effect, that "so long as opium is kept on board our British vessels, it must be dealt with according to our laws; and that it necessarily falls under the laws of China when landed or purchased by natives of the country." [a] Kung therefore argued that if a British vessel entered port with opium but did not land it as cargo, the Chinese authorities could punish the Chinese involved and ask the consul to fine the British vessel. In support of this view Ch'i-ying tried to stimulate the consul's activity by sending his special approval of Balfour's course and proposing that the fines levied be used for public purposes, one-half by the taotai and one-half by the consul, without whose help the Chinese authorities could not have prevented the smuggling system in the port of Shanghai "from growing up into settled practice." [15]

Consul Balfour, in a very able review of the problem to Pottinger, was inclined to sympathize with the taotai in his hope that "violations of the

[a] Mr. Stanley Wright points out that "in other words, China did not then claim the right, common to every sovereign state, of searching for and seizing contraband carried in foreign vessels, even when such vessels were admittedly within the territorial waters of the prohibiting country. Had the Superintendent been alive to the legal implications involved he would have claimed that sovereign rights not definitely yielded by treaty are just as definitely retained." This is an excellent example of the paralyzing effect of Chinese ignorance as to how to interpret the treaties.[14]

laws of China committed by our people would be redressed by us." Pottinger having refused to do so, the taotai was "now at a loss how to act, doubtful as he feels regarding the authority he may exercise over British subjects and British property, for hitherto he had looked to me as placed in a positon to remove from the Chinese officers that heavy responsibility which rests upon them, not only to repress but to prevent the occurrence of acts done in violation of the laws. . . He hesitates as to taking the Chinese law as his guide, or to act under Your Excellency's proclamation. . . He fears going too far lest he should involve himself with our government, or doing too little, and thus be implicated with his own government . . ." Opium was already so delicate a question that Chinese officials feared to have any connection either with permitting it or with suppressing it, lest jealous and anti-foreign gentry and literati attack them. If a British opium vessel entered port the consul would expect to receive queries from the authorities which could only embarrass his relations with them, for they would consider him as "not effectually performing his duty." He therefore desired some way of keeping the opium ships outside.[16]

Agreeing as they did on the necessity of keeping the opium trade out of Shanghai, the consul and the taotai began joint measures to that end. Early in April 1844 the taotai pointed out that two British vessels, the *Urgent* and the *Thomas Crisp*, had remained outside the port of Shanghai anchored at Wusung for an entire month, obviously engaged in the opium trade, and then had come into port to load teas. The consul issued a notification stating the taotai's intention to prevent such conduct in future, and warned British merchants to do nothing contrary to the rights of China.[17] A few days later Ch'i-ying had the taotai convey to Balfour the strict instructions which he had delivered to the Shanghai authorities to check their tacit permission of the trade at Wusung. Ch'i-ying hoped that Balfour would restrain British vessels from anchoring there, while the local authorities would keep Chinese merchants away.[18] This was a frank effort to secure Anglo-Chinese coöperation against the trade at Wusung. The question was, whether the Chinese authorities could really take action. A few weeks later, in May 1844, the taotai sent Balfour a formal statement reiterating the official stand taken by the Chinese authorities and calling upon the consul to issue notifications similar to those already issued. The consul thought it advisable not to send any reply, for it already seemed evident that the Chinese officials were having recourse to the policy of empty paper denunciation which had been used in previous decades at Canton.[19]

The dual system of trade. The fundamental issue in the *Amelia* and *Maingay* case was whether the opium trade which had grown up at the receiving station outside the port was now to be allowed to invade the treaty port itself. The dangers of such an invasion were obvious both to the Chinese officials who would thereby be involved in a fatal responsibility for the flouting of Chinese prohibitions, and to the British consul who would see the legal trade under his supervision demoralized to the level of smuggling and general irregularity. The result of the case was to establish more firmly than ever the nascent system of receiving stations. Full details were spread up and down the China coast, and it was made crystal clear by the British authorities that opium within the ports would be in danger of British action, while at the stations outside it would have only Chinese action to fear. This separation of the legal and the contraband branches of the foreign trade required that separate fleets be used. No longer could the consul allow a vessel from India, Singapore, or Hongkong to bring its opium cargo to the receiving station, and then take away teas and silks from the treaty port. This in turn tended to throw the drug trade more than ever into the hands of the great Hongkong monopolists, the firms of Jardine and Dent, for only they, with occasional competitors, were able to operate the dual system now demanded, using one fleet for opium imports and another fleet for tea and silk exports. The small adventurer was thereby cut out, and the trade placed in responsible channels. This tendency toward monopoly was approved and encouraged by the British government, on the same practical grounds which have usually made the distribution of opium or liquor a matter of government monopoly or control. On the China coast these big firms were the best equivalent to the East India Company's opium monopoly in India.

In keeping with this new doctrine of separation, the British consuls studiously refused officially to recognize the existence of the receiving stations. The inefficiency of the one-eyed jurisdiction which resulted is typified in the following entries of correspondence between the consul and the opium captain at Foochow: "From Capt. Hely, June 27, 1849, the officers at Mingan have seized property belonging to him from a Bumboat." "To Capt. Hely, June 28, will lay his complaint before the Supt. of Customs." "To Capt. Hely, July 6, Statement of Supt. of Customs. Consul must decline further notice of the affair." [20]

The solution which had been reached at Shanghai was soon imitated elsewhere. At first, true to their instructions to enforce the treaty, the Chinese magistrates in districts near Ch'üan-chou had complained (in February 1844) that foreign ships were still coming and going. In March the Amoy taotai had informed Gribble that the presence of two foreign vessels in Mei-lin Bay had been reported to Ch'i-ying, who had ordered the taotai to order Gribble to order them away: why were they still there after the opening of Amoy? [21] But by the middle of 1844 the status of opium at Amoy was better understood. The depot ships lay outside the Six Islands at the eastern limit of the port, supplied by the coastal clippers. Native boats, well-armed against pirates, brought the drug in, landed it at all hours of the day, and carried it calmly through the city, where the opium shops were said to pay a present of $16 a month to the coast defense sub-prefect. About seven chests a day were consumed at Amoy, say half in the city itself, in the following proportions: Patna 60 per cent, Benares 20 per cent, Malwa 20 per cent. In six months the trade had increased perhaps 40 per cent.[22]

At Canton the establishment of recognized and separate channels for opium took longer than at the new ports. After the *Amelia* and *Maingay* case Consul Lay reported to Pottinger his clear arrangement with the local authorities, that the latter were unable to touch the trade and that the consul would not do so if it remained distinctly separate from the legal trade.[23] For a year all went well and opium pursued its own course nominally separate from dutiable goods, although both used the same anchorage and transportation facilities. The opium receiving ships lay unmolested in Blenheim Reach at Whampoa, and delivered to mandarin boats which brought the drug up the river to Canton, under the cloak of their official status, for a fee of $15 a chest. But unofficial small craft — 12-oared boats, schooners, and cutters — had begun to take advantage of the resulting demoralization by competing with the official boats, offering a rate of $5 a chest, and landing cargoes at the customs station on the waterfront of the Old Company's hong.[24] By degrees this smuggling service had been made available for teas and silks outward bound to Western ships at Whampoa. The sizable community of Parsee merchants at Canton became involved in it, a dozen small craft on the river began to transport opium consignments directly to the factories, and the receiving ships at Whampoa increasingly served the legal trade as convenient floating warehouses where cargoes of all kinds might be stored on demurrage.[25] The danger foreseen by Consul Balfour at Shanghai was at hand, that "our entire trade with China become . . . really a smuggling one,"[26] and the Canton consul therefore took action in the spring of 1845.

In February 1845 the British vessel *Sir Edward Ryan*, 320 tons, entered the river, anchored at Blenheim Reach, and remained there for a month selling opium in the usual fashion. But on March 18 this vessel delivered 138 bags of saltpetre (14,232 catties) to certain Chinese merchants authorized by the Chinese authorities to receive this special commodity (saleable only to the Chinese government). The Hoppo, Wen-feng, complained to the consul because the *Ryan* had not been reported and had not allowed customs examiners to come on board. Since the vessel had now taken part in the legal trade of the port, Consul Macgregor investigated through his harbor master at Whampoa, Mr. St. Croix, and secured a confession that the saltpetre had been discharged. He therefore levied a fine of $500 and ordered the ship to enter port formally and pay the regular tonnage dues and duties, which was done.[27]

But because the *Sir Edward Ryan* case had called attention to the semi-official Chinese opium market at Whampoa, the consul felt obliged to clear the river of opium vessels. The foreign community generally regarded this latter action as officious, since the Chinese authorities had been content with the payment of duties and had not even demanded the levy of a fine.[28] Mr. St. Croix reported that of the vessels at Whampoa nine flew British colors, one the American flag and another the Swedish flag. The consulate warned these British vessels on April 21, 1845, to leave the river within three days or else report and pay fines, for non-payment of which they would be prosecuted. The British ships accordingly left the river, their owners at the same time demanding that vessels of other nations, particularly the Portuguese, be obliged to leave also. The American ship *New Lintin* changed to Danish colors and with the Swedish opium vessel *John* delayed its departure. But in general the British merchants removed their vessels willingly and without cavil, except for "some of those of the inferior class," and established themselves at the old anchorage of Cumsingmoon near Hongkong. The Canton authorities expressed their great appreciation and sent their experts in foreign contact, Wu and T'ung, to expel the minor vessels still loitering about; but from the British records it would appear that they were chiefly concerned to avoid responsibility for a malodorous situation from which they and their underlings had profited. At Cumsingmoon the Sino-foreign opium trade continued on as regular a basis as it had two decades earlier at the romantic site of Lintin Island across the bay.[29]

Hongkong and the receiving stations. Hongkong's function as an opium distribution center was as unpremeditated, on the part of the British government, as the growth of the receiving stations. Since the colony must pay its way, the Colonial Office gave Pottinger's successor, Davis, wide latitude in determining his fiscal policy. At least £25,000 would have to be raised by local taxation, inclusive of land rents. For this purpose local rates were suggested and certain licenses, consumption taxes, and perhaps tonnage dues. In this context, the status of opium became a chief concern. The British government still wished to keep Hongkong from becoming a smuggling base, and were opposed to the "unrestricted import and export of opium into and from the colony," which China might justly consider an unfriendly act. But in view of the large Chinese population local opium consumption could hardly be prevented. Therefore it might be best to levy a moderate duty on opium imported into Hongkong and grant no drawback on re-exportation, so as to discourage the importation of opium solely for re-export.

This hopefully humane yet hard-headed point of view illustrates the conflict between the dictates of legal principle and of commerce, which typified British opium policy.[b] To these instructions Davis, who was still in England, at once replied that he would canvass the views of the Chinese authorities and then "adopt the best course in my power." Preferably he would follow out some sort of agreement with them, in the hope of moving, in that way, toward eventual lagalization.[31] The effort to secure legalization of the opium trade, pursued by Pottinger in 1842 and 1843, was continued in 1844, as has been recorded in blue books and elsewhere. It was unavailing and need not detain us.[32] No equivalent effort seems to have been made to lessen the dependence of Indian finance upon the opium revenue, since it was firmly believed that China would get opium from other sources if not from India.

Meanwhile Hongkong developed into a cheap and convenient warehouse for the opium brought from India. In 1850 an experienced local official, W. H. Mitchell, at the governor's request, drew up a memorandum in which he estimated that "fully three-fourths of the entire [Indian] Opium Crops from 1845 to 1849 inclusive were deposited in and reshipped from

[b] Lord Stanley at the Colonial Office instructed Davis to proceed in all directions at once, as follows (February 8, 1844): ". . . the newly acquired Colony of Hong Kong should not be made subservient to the object of carrying on a trade in Opium with China so long as that drug continues to be prohibited by the Laws of the Chinese Empire. . . . it would not be consistent . . . to permit the unrestricted import and export of Opium into and from the Colony, even altho' no immediate and direct advantage were derived to the Local Government from its transit. The Establishment of an Opium Depot close to the Coast of China, affording facilities for its warehousing and contraband introduction, might justly be complained of as an unfriendly action. . . . On the other hand, adverting especially to the large number of Chinese settled on the Island and to the general principles which regulate our Commercial system and the adoption of which we have repeatedly pressed upon the Chinese Authorities, it would not appear to be politic to attempt, even if it were practicable, to effect the total exclusion of Opium for purposes of consumption. It appears to Her Majesty's Government that the objects of friendly relations with China, of adherence to sound Commercial Principles and to a certain extent, of local Revenue, may all be attained by the imposition upon Opium, imported into Hong Kong, of such a moderate duty as may not defeat its own object through the means of the Smuggler and by granting no drawback upon its re-exportation. Considering the existing facilities for carrying on the Contraband trade, without entering Hong Kong, a very moderate rate of duty would probably have the effect of turning the balance against its introduction into that Colony for purposes of re-exportation, while it is obvious that the many opportunities for smuggling an Article of so much value as compared to its bulk renders it necessary to be very cautious as to the amount of duty charged upon consumption. . . . Your aim must be not to prohibit or impede consumption on the Island; to raise as large an amount of Local Revenue as you can realise, and to impose such a duty as shall have the effect of discouraging the import for purposes of re-exportation.

"It is of the first importance not only that the Treaty should be acted upon by us in the most entire good faith in Spirit as well as in Letter, but that the Chinese Government should feel and know that it is so; and it is hardly less important that we should take the means, so far as we consistently can, not only which are, but which they believe to be, the most efficacious, for discouraging an extensive smuggling trade from our newly acquired Colony. We cannot of course prohibit the importation of Opium for the consumption of the Island, we believe that a moderate duty without drawback will check its Warehousing for re-exportation, but their Authorities may take a different view and if you should find that by acceding to their wishes on this subject, you are enabled to promote even indirectly the main object of the legalization of the Trade, you have full discretion, either on the one hand absolutely to prohibit the Warehousing of Opium, or on the other to permit its ingress and egress (except for internal consumption) without notice or duty. . . ."[30]

this harbour."[33] He took the total shipments from India to be 220,717 chests. At $500 a chest the value of the three-quarters (say 165,537 chests of opium) stored at Hongkong during these five years would be some $82,700,000 or £18,450,000.

From this the colony benefited indirectly through an increase in the shipping which used the port and spent money in it, while the opium firms made equally tangible savings. Protected by the Murray battery at Hongkong, Jardine's receiving ship, the *Bomanjee Hormusjee*, could dispense with the crew and armament it had formerly needed at Cumsingmoon and save almost $2000 a month in salaries alone. Dent and Company had begun to store their opium in a godown on shore. Jardine's followed suit and used Sepoy guards to protect it.[34] Minor firms receiving from India no more than fifty chests at a time could save money by storing them in the colony, instead of in another firm's receiving ship on the coast at a charge of five dollars a chest every month.

Within the colony, meanwhile, the retail trade disposed of some 250 chests a month, worth about $125,000. These were successively handled by the merchants licensed by the government to sell opium, the brokers who supplied the refiners, and the retail merchants who sold to the Chinese consuming public, leaving a fraction of profit with each. At first the colonial government had given an opium monopoly to the highest bidder, who sought to profit by monopoly prices and to maintain them by limiting the supply. Under ordinance 21 of 1844, the exclusive privilege of retailing opium in any quantity less than one chest within the colony for one year was auctioned off at 2 P.M. on February 28, 1845, to George Duddell and Alexander Martin Mathieson (the latter gentleman, of the firm of McEwen and Company, died six months later). The monopolists soon found it difficult to enforce their privilege because competing sellers caught with opium on hand could claim that they intended only to sell it outside the colony. Colonial ordinance No. 5 of 1845 was therefore passed to confer a monopoly on all sales under one chest, whether for consumption within the colony or otherwise, and the privilege was auctioned off again on August 1, 1845. This opium farm, however, did not prove profitable to the farmer and Chinese opium merchants in Hongkong also petitioned against it. Revised regulations of July 1847 finally substituted a licensing system under which licencees must make monthly payments in advance as follows: for keeping an opium smoking shop, $10; for preparing and selling prepared opium, $20; for selling new opium below the amount of one chest, $30. Quarterly reports were also required of the amounts of opium smoked, prepared, or sold, respectively. Smoking shops must be well provided to serve their customers, must display their licenses, sell opium only for money, keep out armed persons, and close at 10 P.M.[35] The effect of this new system was that licensees could profit only in proportion as they increased their sales.

As the supply increased at Hongkong, opium in small amounts had become the chief mode of remitting funds to the nearby ports on the mainland. The official above quoted described how "the passage boats ply unceasingly, carrying to and fro the shopkeeper, the artizan, the coolie, and the adventurer, together with those endless small wares which a Chinese population requires. The capital upon which the shopkeeper is trading here is probably borrowed at interest in his native village, and in paying up either the interest or principal, he remits opium instead of money — the same of all the other working classes as to the mode they prefer of sending home their savings: and the same of the remittances for the small wares alluded to above." [36]

Profitable as it might be to develop a market for opium at Hongkong, however, the two leading firms preferred to restrict it in favor of the market on the coast which they could more easily monopolize. Their policy was to retard the growth of the opium trade at Hongkong in order that it might flourish more profitably elsewhere. Accordingly, if too great a number of smugglers ventured to come from the coast to buy their opium supplies at Hongkong, instead of at the receiving ships, the Jardine-Dent duopoly would proceed to flood the market with cut-rate opium as soon as the coast smugglers had departed, and by lowering prices would so ruin their ventures that they would remain content to buy from the receiving ships as before.[c] Similarly they had been able at times, through their subsidiary insurance companies, to embarrass competition by withholding insurance from rivals' vessels.[d]

Eventually the power of these houses came to be challenged, largely through the growth of a regular steamer service. In 1850 the P. and O. Company's steamer *Canton* and another steamer, the *Juno*, began "to

[c] As W. H. Mitchell put it in 1850, "Really it is a matter of immense surprise to me how Hongkong has any trade of any kind whatever. Here we have these two powerful Houses making heavy pecuniary sacrifices every other month, *to beat back to the Coast*, any trade which may try to force its way down to this Colony, and thereby utterly shutting out the sugars and coarse drugs, such as Camphor and Alum and similar stuffs, which the native coasters would otherwise bring down to us. This in itself would be hard enough for any young Colony to contend with. But, when in addition to this, our Treaty with China limits all Junk traffic with this port to Junks clearing out of the Five Ports, and places even these under the most vexatious restrictions — my repeated wonder is *that the Colony has any trade at all.*" [37]

[d] In 1848 the *Amoy Packet*, built at Hongkong by Murrow and Co. for the coast trade and judged by a competent surveyor to be "staunch and tight and fit to carry a dry and perishable cargo to any part of the world," was refused insurance from Hongkong to Amoy by the local insurance offices at Hongkong and therefore by the agents of companies in India. Murrow and Co. asserted that the local insurance offices represented "the two leading firms deeply interested in the coast trade, in the operation of which they have coalesced"; and cited the fact that opium was selling at Amoy for $100 per chest more than at Hongkong. The *Friend of China* remarked that "the integrity of these houses is unimpeachable but that for years they have coalesced to obtain a monopoly of the opium trade at some of the ports . . . is notorious . . . The *Amoy Packet* is not the first instance of such refusal." [38] Out of 25 marine insurance agencies in China listed in 1844, the Jardine and Dent firms held eleven.[39]

throw heavy opposition supplies into the Amoy Station, so that it will likely absorb into itself all the trade of the neighbouring anchorages, including that of Namoa; the effect of which would be to give this Colony the supplying of the immediate line of Coast between Namoa and this place, and to raise up a productive barter in Sugar and Indian produce." [40] These intestine struggles in the contraband trade constitute one of its most intricate aspects. By degrees the trade grew more diversified, monopoly became less feasible, and with the inauguration of a steam packet service to Canton, swifter and safer than lorchas, Hongkong at last began to fulfill its intended function as a bonded warehouse for legal merchandise. By 1850 its prospects were becoming brighter as a result of trans-Pacific trade inspired by the gold rush in California and the beginning of coolie emigration to both North and South America.

Meanwhile the receiving stations became twice as numerous as the ports. In their shipping lists the *China Mail* and other papers, beginning in late 1846, devoted a separate table to receiving ships. Some forty of them, with their flag, tonnage, owners, and captains, would commonly be listed and divided among the following stations: Hongkong; Cumsingmoon, "a fine bay . . . about twelve miles north of Macao, from whence it may be reached overland"; [41] Macao, where there was only a Portuguese vessel; Namoa off Swatow; Amoy; Chimo or Chimmo, a little to the north of Amoy; Chinchew (Ch'üan-chou) in the middle of the Fukien coastline; Foochow; Tinghai, the port of Chusan Island, later shifted at the desire of the local Chinese officials to Lookong, 12 or 15 miles away and closer to Ningpo; [42] and finally Wusung. It is significant that only two firms had receiving ships at as many as eight of these stations — Jardine, Matheson and Company and Dent and Company. Their nearest competitors were Gilman and Company, who at first maintained five vessels but later dropped out of the running. No other firm was represented at more than two stations, and these two were usually Cumsingmoon (for Canton) and Wusung (for Shanghai), where there were, respectively, some 8 and 12 vessels in all. Elsewhere, on all the coast between, the two ships of J. M. and Company and of Dent and Company, with perhaps that of a third firm, were at each port the sole permanent purveyors of drug.[e]

The quiet, respectable life of the major receiving stations is exemplified in the uneventful history of the island of Namoa, which had early been used by the opium clippers and remained one of their chief points of call.[44] The Kwangtung authorities inveighed against the foreign settlement

[e] As the Hongkong paper *Friend of China* put it in 1848: "We do not believe that if the question were put to the partners of either firm they would hesitate to admit that at several ports the commanders of their respective receiving ships arrange prices in the morning and divide sales in the afternoon, and that should a stranger drop into the bay, prices are reduced $50 to $100 until he is forced to seek another market." [43]

on Namoa in February 1844. In a long dispatch they overwhelmed Sir Henry Pottinger with details as to the number, location, and dimensions of the houses which had been built there contrary to treaty. Pottinger replied that it was for the Chinese authorities to drive the foreigners away: they remained only because the local officials connived at the settlement, having received large bribes for ten years past from the agents of the large mercantile houses. He suggested that a Chinese officer be deputed to give the English community on Namoa a time limit, say six months, for their departure. The governor at Canton fell in with this suggestion, and Pottinger published the correspondence as a warning to his countrymen. The expectant prefect ("Neshow") was ordered to investigate, with a linguist.[45] At his conference with Davis two months later Ch'i-ying reported that the residents of Namoa had requested a time limit of ten months, when they would then "deliberate about the removal." He accordingly granted them until April 1845, after which time the authorities would pull down their houses.[46] This was never done but it was one of the few occasions on which the treaty provision against resort to other than the five ports was even halfway invoked.

Ch'ing anti-opium policy. Thus within two years of the treaty settlement of 1842–43 the contraband drug trade had carved its own channels beyond reach of the law. From the point of view of the British government, this was a perilous makeshift. In February 1844 the Foreign Office had agreed with the Colonial Office that legalization was essential, to "get rid of a system pregnant with so much danger and so thoroughly demoralizing." They urged Davis to lose no opportunity to press for this, against either "the personal sentiments of the emperor or . . . the intrigues of Chinese officers who find their profit in the continuance of a smuggling trade." For a year or more the Foreign Office remained hopeful. Pottinger in April 1844 still felt sure that the open growth of the trade would lead to its legalization.[47] He failed to realize that Chinese law was not the scaffolding which in the West necessarily accompanied the growth of new commercial structures. There is no evidence in any of the documents that Ch'i-ying, much less the emperor, was in any way moved by the British suggestion that a trade which undeniably existed should be legally regulated.

The real attitude of the Manchu court toward the "spreading poison" (*liu-tu*) may be surmised from cases recorded in the Grand Council archives. In 1841–42 the Board of Punishments had been ordered to present for imperial inspection a list of the persons arraigned each year both at Peking and in the provinces for smoking opium.[48] During 1842 censors at Peking reported seizure of 40 ounces (*liang*) of opium in February, some 18 ounces in March, and 282 ounces in July.[49] A detailed return of such cases was made to the emperor in at least the four years 1843, 1846, 1848, and 1849. In 1843, 24 offenders against the opium laws were reported as held for either the provincial or the imperial assizes. Of these there were 6 cases, one of a woman, brought up because of smoking in Hu-Kwang (Hupei and Hunan), 2 each in Kiangsi and Yunnan, and 1 each in Feng-tien, Szechwan, and Anhwei. There were 8 other cases, one of a woman, held for the imperial assize at Peking. Of the above, all but two, who had been arrested for selling opium, stated by way of extenuation that they had taken to smoking in order to cure an illness. In addition there were reported during the year the cases of an official seized for smoking in Chihli, of a smuggler caught at Shanhaikuan, and of another smuggler seized in the capital.[50] In 1845 British observers gleaned from the *Peking Gazette* that about 60 persons had been convicted of smoking opium, among them a palace eunuch and others attached to the court. When the Board of Punishments asked whether to apply the legal death penalty, the emperor countermanded their execution pending his perusal of a further report on these cases.[51] The Nanking authorities reported in 1845 that reports of armed opium smuggling in the Shanghai hinterland, around Soochow and Sungkiang, had proved on investigation to be utterly false.[52] In 1846 only 2 men were reported as held for the provincial autumn assizes and 7 for the imperial assize. During the year there were also reports of two opium cases in Peking, one of smoking and one of selling. Of 6 cases concerning commoners reported in 1848, 5 were in the metropolitan prefecture, Shun-t'ien-fu. There were two cases of officials; and one of an imperial clansman, reported by the Imperial Clan Court. The clansman also had smoked in order to cure an illness. Before the imperial assize of 1849 there were 7 cases, one of an official, involving ten offenders.[53] No report appears to have been received from the provinces.

In commenting on this Chinese judicial activity the *China Mail* in July 1848 asserted that lists of smokers had been sent to court annually just "to keep up appearances." Culprits sentenced to death were "mostly reprieved and those strangled were chiefly such as had committed other crimes deserving of capital punishment." In 1848, however, the practice of listing condemned opium smokers, "amongst criminals of the deepest dye" to be sentenced at the autumn assizes, was discontinued. Thenceforth accused opium smokers were to be listed separately, which may account for their disappearance from the records after 1849.[54]

The Hsien-feng Emperor on his accession in 1850 preserved the policy of his predecessor by issuing in August of that year an edict prohibiting the use of opium, allowing smokers five months in which to reform, and increasing the penalty from strangulation to decapitation.[55] The reports of cases preserved in the records became steadily fewer. In 1851 a gioro (*chueh-lo*) or collateral relative of the imperial house, was arrested for smoking in Fengtien; and in that year and province also appeared one of the first cases mentioned during this period concerning the domestic production of opium. The Fengtien authorities remark that the opium poison is spreading and that although there are as yet few smokers in that province, the arrests are nevertheless frequent. They fear that the habit will sweep the country if not severely dealt with. To which the vermilion pencil replies, "Examine strictly, judge, and report." For the year 1852 there is no available report, but in 1853 two censors announce the seizure of three men hiding opium in Peking. In 1854 a riot over opium occurs in a Manchu garrison in the metropolitan prefecture.[56] After this date the archives appear to be silent.

From this fragmentary evidence the conclusion may be drawn that the pretense of enforcing the opium prohibition was maintained more actively in the north, particularly in the capital itself, and until a later date. In the southern provinces, however, where the importation of opium rapidly mounted and where cultivation was already beginning,[57] repressive measures, even *pro forma*, became steadily fewer. As opium spread, it silenced its opposition.

The British records contain a more explicit account of the nascent production of poppy within China. In 1848 the government of India instituted an inquiry concerning the danger of increased Chinese production, which would affect Indian sales. The original motivation came through a letter from Alexander Matheson to C. B. Skinner of Jardine, Skinner and Company, Calcutta, in November 1847 describing the increase of poppy cultivation in China. This letter found its way through the Board of Customs, Salt, and Opium to the Earl of Dalhousie, Governor of Bengal. Six months after Mr. Matheson had expressed his private fears, the government of Hongkong, at the request of that of Bengal, was seeking full information from the treaty-port consuls, who naturally had no better sources of information than Matheson's original informants. The picture painted by the consuls was vague but not too alarming. Opium production in China was said to be confined almost entirely to Yunnan, Kweichow, and Shensi — Yunnan being the chief center. It had been introduced about twenty years before by Chinese from Cochin China who had been to India and learned the methods in use there. Production had been stimulated by the anti-opium crusade of the 1830's, which promised to cut off Indian supplies and so give a free field to the Chinese product. For 1847 the crop was estimated at 8 to 10,000 piculs (say 10,600 to 13,300 pounds). The quality was comparable to that of the foreign drug, but the adulteration with other substances was higher, perhaps 35 per cent as compared with 15 per cent or less (and sometimes none) in the foreign drug. Thus the best quality sold in Yunnan at $400 a picul and in Canton for $500, while the adulterated grade cost as little as $250 at the source and $300 at Canton. It reached Canton by irregular means, including the bribing of the officials en route.[58] Meanwhile the Canton consulate estimated by 1850 that China's annual opium consumption of some 50,000 chests from India (32,000 Bengal, 18,000 Malwa) represented a capital of thirty million dollars. Three-fifths of this importation came into South China, in exchange for silver; two-fifths went to the north (i.e., Central China), much of it by barter.[59]

The Chimmo Bay piracy, 1847. That the opium trade was a cause of disorder, as well as facilitated by it, hardly needs to be emphasized, and the subject may be dismissed with the citation of one or two outstanding and yet not atypical cases. The first was the famous Chimmo Bay piracy, in which the two local receiving ships, the *Caroline*, Capt. Chamberlain (J. M. and Company), and the *Omega*, Capt. MacFarlane (Dent and Company), were simultaneously attacked at eight o'clock on the evening of February 5, 1847, by two Macao lorchas, painted black below and brightly varnished above and carrying about forty men apiece as well as 24-pounders, fire-balls, and other armament. These vessels had hovered about for three days, arousing little suspicion, and attacked so suddenly that defense was impossible. The foreign captains and mates on both ships, plus 13 men on the *Caroline* and some 15 on the *Omega*, were killed outright, 13 of the *Caroline*'s crew escaping only by climbing into the rigging and staying there. The total value of opium and silver on these receiving ships may be taken as typical of the trade: an Amoy correspondent of the *China Mail* reported that the *Omega* had on board 60 chests of Patna and 40 of Benares worth altogether $70,000, plus $40,000 in treasure, while the *Caroline* had 40 chests of Patna and 39 of Benares, out of which 59 chests were lost, worth $41,000, together with $19,000 in treasure. This private source estimated the total loss at $160,000. The official report [60] was that the pirates got away with $75,000 to $100,000 in cash and 114 chests of opium, leaving 67 behind. These amounts of treasure and of drug were not unusual and indicate the financial importance of the receiving stations, in their collections month by month. In April 1845, for example, the running vessel *Ariel*, after narrowly escaping seizure by mutiny, returned to Hongkong with over $100,000 on board.[61]

The opium traders, nothing daunted, took the *Omega* and *Caroline* to Hongkong for refitting and heavier armament prior to continuing the trade. The Amoy consul feared only that they might attack Chinese government ships as an indirect retaliation. The Chinese authorities were chiefly concerned because the case had called attention to the receiving stations which flourished within their jurisdiction. The naval and civil authorities at Amoy expected degradation or imperial censure, and so demanded the removal of all the other depot ships along the Fukien coast. In brief, according to the British consul, they were now ready to sacrifice their interest in the opium trade in order to avoid responsibility for piracies which they could not prevent.[62] They captured eight of the pirates and sentenced the leader to death by slicing and three others to decapitation, while three died in prison. Rewards offered by Jardine's and Dent and Company brought several alleged pirates into the Hongkong courts but most of them escaped sentence through legal flaws in the indictment, while some of those sentenced were found to have been victimized and were later pardoned.[63]

Since this is one of the few opium cases that were ever reported to the emperor within his palace in Peking, its treatment in the Chinese documents makes interesting reading. In a memorial received on April 12, 1847, more than two full months after the incident, the Foochow governor-general, Liu Yun-k'o, stated that Consul Jackson (*Jo-sun*) at Foochow had reported the piracy to him on February 11. He had thereupon inquired of the Amoy taotai, Heng-ch'ang, who replied that he had been just on the point of investigating the case when he had received details of it from Consul Layton (*Lieh-tun*) at Amoy. The taotai then gave an accurate account of all the circumstances, naming the vessels (*Chia-no-lai* and *A-mi-ko*) and stating the numbers killed, except that no word was said about opium. He also described the exertions of the provincial naval commander-in-chief in combing the seas. Meanwhile "the Consul gazed upon the officers and men who had been deputed by the Taotai and his colleagues, searching and seizing in all directions (*fen-t'ou ch'a-na*), and expressed his thanks in the highest terms." The Chinese authorities were continuing to search for the junks and the pirates, and to fish out the victims' corpses. They regarded this attack on foreigners as particularly bloodthirsty and of serious import because if unpunished it would provoke others to emulation and also increase the danger to Chinese merchant vessels.

Having left out the whole point of the story, namely opium, the governor-general was now obliged to ask numerous rhetorical questions: "How did it happen that on that one day the barbarian ships came to anchor in the ocean and the pirates plundered them? And what goods were they that were plundered?" The other southern coastal provinces had been informed and also the imperial commissioner at Canton. The imperial edict in response to this memorial agreed that it was a serious matter when foreigners began to be attacked by pirates. It approved the deprivations of rank and the blows with the bamboo meted out to the officers and men in whose jurisdiction the affair occurred. The fact that opium had precipitated this bloodshed was finally announced to the court only by Ch'i-ying and Hsü

Kuang-chin from Canton on August 2, 1847: the cargoes, valued somewhere between $70,000 and more than $100,000, were foreign opium; of the pirates captured, some had died in prison, others would be executed by slicing. It seems evident that the case had been too hot for anyone but the imperial commissioner to handle; but he had done a conscientious job of pirate-punishing.[64]

The stand taken by the British authorities is equally instructive. Consul Layton considered the receiving ships generally to be the "resort of Thieves, Robbers, Pimps, and Prostitutes with few exceptions . . . there is a close connection between the vilest of the vile Chinese population and our opium ships." Moreover, they provided smuggling stations for camphor, crockery, and other articles, to the detriment of legal trade at Amoy. He would be glad to see them all withdrawn. But Sir John Davis at Hongkong expressed a more responsible view. "You are mistaken in supposing that the smuggling ships in question by using force against the Chinese Government can in the least involve H. M. Government. They will only involve themselves and become liable to all the consequences. This consideration will show the importance of your disavowing all connection whatever with these vessels and stating to the Chinese authorities . . . that they must be left to them, to be dealt with according to the treaty by the Chinese government. The open connivance which has been afforded by the authorities of China, ever since the peace, to the trade in opium (rendering it in fact illegal only on paper) deprives that Government of all right of complaint, and under no circumstances could it expect Her Majesty's government to adopt measures for the prevention of smuggling on the coast of China." [65] This effectually disposed of the consul's naive observation that "the Chinese Mandarin Government is in some cases perfectly powerless, and the seizure of two British vessels of 200 tons each by the force of arms would be a great and possibly an impracticable undertaking for the Admiral of Amoy." [66]

As a result of the Chimmo Bay piracy, several receiving ships sought safety at Amoy. With the consul's permission and the private consent of the mandarins, they moored at the back of Kulangsu within the consular port limits but outside the area used by Chinese shipping. Since Sir John Davis had just renewed his assurance to Ch'i-ying that he "would not offer any shelter or protection to smuggling vessels," he informed the consul that to sanction his acts at Amoy "would be a direct violation of my engagement. . . . You therefore admit these vessels within the port limits on your own responsibility and must be answerable to the Chinese government for any unlawful proceedings on their part." [67] Needless to say, this extraordinary hypocrisy, unusual even in the opium business, was not reported to the Foreign Office. The opium ships at Foochow at once applied for a similar degree of protection. Sir John thought better of it, and a fortnight later ordered the Amoy consul not to permit "any opium vessel under any pretext to anchor within the consular limits of the port." [68] He did so just in time to prevent the opium trade from moving in on the consulates.[f] Two years later Palmerston repeated the standing instructions of the Foreign Office, that consuls should "take great care not to afford any facilities for smuggling and not to give the Chinese any pretext for saying that you abet and encourage it." [70]

The common assumption that the foreign opium smuggler remained on his ship and let the Chinese come and get it, is only partly borne out by the consular archives, as may be indicated by a case at Ningpo. Captain Isaac Gutsell of Jardine's receiving ship *Hellas* at Lookong outside Ningpo made a practice of sending his lascars, black British subjects, in the boats of his Chinese customers to provide protection against the Chinese authorities on the route into Ningpo. Mr. Gutsell was a man of action, inclined to take the law into his own hands. He was not registered at the Ningpo consulate after an entire year's service on the *Hellas*, and in 1847 he had recovered stolen opium through a direct appeal to the Ningpo magistrate.

At the beginning of March 1848 Gutsell and his mate, John Dallin, again called upon the Ningpo magistrate, without reference to the consul, for help against a Ningpo man who had stolen 60 catties of opium from a Chinchew man, one of Gutsell's clients. Without waiting for the doubtful efficacy of this appeal, they sent two lascars with the aggrieved Fukienese dealer up to Ningpo, where they seized four men at the shop of the accused, beat them, and transported them to Lookong for confinement. A few days later they handed the four men over to the Ningpo (Yin) district magistrate for examination, and the British consul then heard of the matter for the first time. Consul Sullivan at once obtained the release of the four victims and hailed Gutsell and Dallin into court. With the commanders of H. M. S. *Childers* and *Espiègle* and Mr. Davidson as assessors, he sentenced Gutsell to a month in jail with bond of $500 for a year's (later four months') good behavior. This attack on Jardine, Matheson and Company was hotly resented. Mr. Robert A. Brine of Ningpo offered the consular linguist $50, and each of the four victims of assault $5, to stay away from the trial. Mr. B. Waterhouse, another local merchant, wrote to "one of Gutsell's employers" describing the severity of the solitary confinement which allowed the Captain to see his friends only three hours a

[f] Frightened by the Chimmo Bay piracy, Captains Roope (of the *Vixen*) and Hely (of the *Denia*) outside Foochow asked permission in March 1847 to move their receiving ships up into the consular port, to avoid an attack planned on them. Six months earlier they had asked without success to be permitted to move their vessels up to the Mingan Pass, the narrows on the Min River, part way up to Pagoda anchorage. Under Davis' orders they were now again refused, although the consul on their behalf wrote to the governor-general asking that he take precautions to protect them against piracy.[69]

day. The consul stood his ground, however, and Gutsell served his month in the consular jail. This encouraged his tailor and grocer to come forward and complain that he beat them when they sought payment, and a certain Ahnew to depose that he also had been seized, beaten, and confined at Lookong by Gutsell's men. To Consul Sullivan it became all "too apparent that Capt. Gutsell had long aided the opium smugglers in committing a series of assaults upon the people of this neighborhood." The Captain on his release swore he would continue to use his crew to help his customers, and the consul issued a notification [71] that the crews of receiving ships found assisting Chinese smugglers would be punished.[g]

All in all, the mixed pattern of China's bifurcated foreign trade, legal and contraband, under the first treaty settlement, was hardly designed to smooth the path of diplomatic intercourse. The conscientious British administrator who took a stand for law and order found himself perched precariously between the powerful British opium duopoly, which was discreetly permitted to be a law unto itself, and Chinese authorities who were unacquainted with Western law of any sort. The British consul could not even count on the support of the other foreign consuls, who were often themselves merchants dealing in opium. The whole treaty system stood precariously on one leg only.

[g] Gutsell was accidentally struck by a falling yard and killed in June 1851 while en route from Wusung to Lookong in a large Chinese boat which he had built for himself.[72]

CHAPTER XIV

THE REORGANIZATION OF THE CANTON SYSTEM

THE INTERESTING QUESTION as to how the treaties affected the old Canton system of trade regulation has been deferred to this chapter. What was the effect of the treaty tariff on Ch'ing fiscal arrangements? How were the hoary institutions of Hoppo and Cohong adjusted to the new order? These problems are so confusing that it has seemed desirable to approach them only in the context of the general post-treaty developments described above. In brief, Canton seems to have shown great inertia — the old ways persisted even longer than the foreigner realized. This appears from an examination both of the actual conduct of trade and of the unpublished Ch'ing documents on customs administration.

Hong merchants and Hoppo under the treaties. The treaty provisions for free private trade in a free market according to a low fixed tariff expressed the British ideal of free trade, which was just rising to its ascendancy in Great Britain. But it was not easy to carry out these treaty principles in the stratified and bureaucrat-ridden society of Canton. The merchant-gild monopoly of the Cohong was formally abolished, but the hong merchants continued as before to act as private brokers to the foreign merchants, a practice to which Pottinger had from the first raised no objection.[1] As I-li-pu had cogently pointed out, the members of the Cohong had provided a guarantee against the falsification or adulteration of export goods, they had conducted the actual selling off of imports while assuring the foreign importer of his sales price, and they had provided vast warehouses and capital for trade.[2] For the foreign merchant they obviated the need of bonded warehouses and insurance charges. Their horde of shroffs, linguists, compradores, boatmen, runners, coolies, warehousemen, and attendant hangers-on were as indispensable as ever to the conduct of the Canton trade. When commercial operations were resumed in the summer of 1843 each foreign vessel proceeded to place itself in the hands of one of the former hong merchant establishments.[3] The *Chinese Commercial Guide* listed them as shown in Table 7 on the opposite page.[4]

These ex-Cohong firms continued to play major roles in the Canton tea trade and also continued to be mulcted by the imperial government year after year.[5] The working of the traditional rewards and punishments as a milking mechanism is laconically recorded: in 1834 Kingqua owed the government Tls. 420,000, defaulted on payment several times and was

TABLE 7: FORMER HONG MERCHANTS AND THEIR ESTABLISHMENTS, AS OF JULY 27, 1843

Individual names		*Hong names*	*Official names* [a]
Foreign	*Chinese*		
Howqua	Wu Hao-kuan	I-ho hang	Wu Shao-jung
Mowqua	Lu Mao-kuan	Kuang-li hang	Lu Chi-kuang
Ponkhequa (or Puankhequa)	P'an Cheng-wei	T'ung-fu hang	P'an Shao-kuang
Goqua (or Gowqua)	Hsieh Ao-kuan	Tung-hsing hang	Hsieh Yu-jen
Kingqua	Liang Ching-kuan	T'ien-pao hang	Liang Ch'eng-hsi
Mingqua	P'an Ming-kuan	Chung-ho hang	P'an Wen-tao
Saoqua	Ma Hsiu-kuan	Shun-t'ai hang	Ma Tso-liang
Punhoyqua	P'an Hai-kuan	Jen-ho hang	P'an Wen-hai
Samqua	Wu Shuang-kuan	T'ung-shun hang	Wu T'ien-yuan
Kwanshing	I K'un-kuan	Fu-t'ai hang	I Yuan-ch'ang

therefore deprived of his honorary ("brevet") rank of taotai. In 1837 Puankhequa owed a sum to the East River conservancy and was deprived of his purchased brevet rank of sub-prefect. By 1842 both had paid up and on the Hoppo's recommendation their ranks were restored.[6] But the war had brought new burdens. The hong merchants complained in 1843 that the authorities were trying to recover from them the five million dollars which had been paid the British in 1840 as the "ransom of Canton." They were asked for annual instalments of Tls. 600,000. For this reason their trade was paralyzed and they refused to lease their godowns to foreign merchants, as Pottinger had requested.[7] The British took up their cause and urged Ch'i-ying to restrain such taxation at least until after the trade had begun. In February 1844 Huang explained to Pottinger that the hong merchants must pay their debts to the government in proportion to the size of their trade in foreign goods, but he contended that this would not increase the market price they demanded nor hurt foreign trade.[8] As late as July 1846 the ex-Cohong merchants were still seeking to escape from these debts to the government.[9]

[a] These names of 1843 were only the final remnants of the long and intricate genealogy which a modern scholar, Liang Chia-pin (a descendant of "Kingqua") has laboriously worked out. In brief, the name in the leftmost column, used by the Western community, was usually derived from a corruption of the name of the original founder with the honorific suffix *kuan* ("official," in Cantonese pronounced *qua*) — thus Howqua, from Hao-kuan. The "hong name" was used like that of any firm. The "official name" according to S. Wells Williams (editor of the *Chinese Commercial Guide*) was "the title of the individual in whose name the license is held in the government records." For simplicity, historians refer to the successive heads of a hong by number — thus in the I-ho or Ewo hong the succession was Wu Kuo-ying (1731–1800, Howqua I), Wu Ping-chien (1769–1843, Howqua II), Wu Yuan-hua (1801–1833, Howqua III), and Wu Ch'ung-yueh (1810–1863, Howqua IV), who adopted the name Wu Shao-jung when he took over the firm in 1833–34. Some 34 hong names, first to last, figure in Cohong history, variant spellings abound in the East India Co. and other records (e.g., Puankhequa, Pankhequa), and the whole subject is a rich green pasture for the genealogist.

As the Chinese counterpart of British merchant princes who bought their way into the peerage, several descendants of Cohong families played important public roles after 1842. P'an Shih-ch'eng, the descendant of Puankhequa, has been mentioned above (Chapter 11). The former head of the Cohong, Howqua IV (Wu Ch'ung-yueh), inherited and maintained a special position in the Canton community. Even in British dispatches he was referred to respectfully as "Mr. Howqua."[b] Land for British merchants was leased from him through the consulate, rent being payable to him half-yearly. At the end of 1849 Dr. Bowring conversed with him during a reception at the latter's residence, the place generally used by the Canton authorities for interviews with foreigners. The reception room contained many pictures, including an engraving of the marriage of the queen. Howqua said that he was not a merchant, when the Doctor tactlessly raised the question. He said his father had long acted as go-between with foreigners for the Chinese authorities, and he still did the same. Through him, for example, had gone the negotiations for the return of the head and hand of Governor Amaral of Macao, who had been murdered that year. On January 17, 1850, Howqua came to the consulate to call on Bowring, accompanied by Teen Paou (i.e., Kingqua), Gowqua, Samqua, and Footae (i.e., Kwanshing), all former hong merchants, wearing blue buttons (third or fourth rank). A month later the *Peking Gazette* reported that Howqua had been made government agent for the conveyance of rice to alleviate the famine in Chekiang. When the imperial commissioner soon announced that the taotai, Wu (i.e., Howqua), had been deputed to assist in handling foreign affairs, Bowring vigorously protested. He refused to deal with a mere merchant and in 1854 demanded that an appeal to him from Howqua and others be forwarded through the imperial commissioner. This care for the British official position involved no animus against Howqua personally. In 1855 he won a case in the British consular court against Jardine, Matheson and Company and was sustained on appeal to Hongkong.[11] In 1857 he led the hong merchants' effort to intercede with the British. In the world of Chinese letters he had already earned a place of respectability as the patron of several collectanea.[12] Earlier Howqua had been known as the great and good friend of the American firm of Russell and Company. It is therefore a curious fact that his ancestral Cantonese hong name, Ewo (*I-ho*), by 1861 had become that of his ancient enemy,

[b] On his arrival at Canton in June 1849 Consul Bowring found that the British government had used a hong of Howqua's for three years without paying rent. The original occupation had been considered temporary, rent had been refused, and thereafter ejection had been impossible, according to custom. Her majesty was therefore much indebted. Bowring suggested presenting a gift — a service of plate or a small steamer. Palmerston agreed and made the offer to Howqua, but the latter refused all but a gold snuff-box or similar portable present of not over $400 or $500 value. He feared to receive presents from foreigners, but came to the consulate to receive a $100 snuff-box in October 1850.[10]

Jardine, Matheson and Company, who used it as their own Chinese firm name at Shanghai and Tientsin, and later at Kiukiang and elsewhere, although Jardine's did not use it originally in South China.[13] The role of the former hong merchants in the new trade of the treaty ports will reward further research.

The tariff and the Hoppo. The Hoppo as an institution survived the inauguration of the treaty system without much difficulty. The treaty tariff was designed to destroy his customary perquisites from foreign trade, but the British principle of free trade did not extend so far as to include the coercion of foreign governments. *The Economist* opined in 1844 that "it would be contrary to the principles on which all international negotiations are conducted for one state, under any circumstances, to dictate to another the amount of its duties." Sir Henry Pottinger on his return to England gave credit for the low treaty tariff to Ch'i-ying, who was therefore hailed in the West as a paragon among statesmen.[14] In China, however, the effect of the low tariff was not very evident. A number of adjustments (noted below) were quietly made to compensate for the victory of free trade to which Ch'i-ying appeared in England to have been a party. Although these adjustments were kept from the knowledge of the British, their object seems to have been relatively innocuous: the Chinese authorities did not consider the taxation of commerce to be the foundation of the state and merely wished to assure themselves by one means or another of the customs revenue of former years. Their documents betray little or no desire to increase the total revenue. As seen in chapter 8, they assumed, at least on paper, that the total volume of foreign trade would not greatly increase. After all, they had never seen the mills of Lancashire.

Ch'i-ying argued in a memorial that, even though revenue at Canton might decline a little, the new tariff at all the ports would produce a larger total revenue because the rates of duty on the chief exports, tea and cotton goods,[15] had been practically doubled, and this would more than make up for those rates which had been lowered. On the other hand, the most expert modern student of the Chinese tariff (Mr. S. F. Wright) has concluded that the new rates were "based on those of the old Imperial tariff of regular duties, exclusive of local charges and fees, and were in the great majority of cases for both exports and imports much lower than those formerly prevailing."[16] The widely reiterated statement that the rates were worked out on a 5 per cent ad valorem basis is not correct. Many rates on imports were over 5 per cent, while those on most categories of exports were below that figure. On the great staple of tea, however, the export duty of Tls. 2½ per picul was really about 10 per cent ad valorem. This was about 25 per cent higher than the old imperial and customary local charges combined (although it was still less than the total which was estimated by British merchants at the time to have been actually levied).[17] For 1844 and 1845 the British consul at Canton calculated that duties on imports averaged about 5.33 per cent ad valorem and on exports between 8.2 and 9 per cent ad valorem.[18]

The apparent contradictions in these judgments — that the new tariff would provide the same imperial revenue as before, and that the duties to be collected on foreign trade would be lower than before — is of course explainable by the fact that Peking received only a fraction of what Canton collected. The record would indicate that the Chinese negotiators concentrated their efforts on the two export staples of tea and cotton goods (not realizing that the latter had now become a net import) and raised the duty on them, while the British secured lower duties on imported manufactured goods and on some miscellaneous exports. Presumably the British hope was to stimulate the trade in legal goods in general, in order to offset the concentration on tea and opium. At any rate, the first responsibility of Ch'i-ying and Huang in 1843 was to protect the imperial revenue against loss, and this was done. The fate of those vested interests of Canton — the Hoppo and his retinue of customhouse underlings — is a different question. Several memorials of 1843 shed light on it.

Contemporaneously with the settlement of the treaty tariff in July 1843, Ch'i-ying and his colleagues at Canton, including the Hoppo, proposed to the throne under nine headings a complete rearrangement of the customs accounts. The Grand Council under the leadership of Mu-chang-a recommended [19] the adoption of several of these changes, for which imperial sanction was received on August 31, 1843 (see Appendix B, sec. 1). It would appear that the Hoppo had been responsible each year for regular duties (i.e., an official quota, *cheng-o*) and a fixed surplus (*o-nei ying-yü*) which together totalled Tls. 899,064, plus an unfixed surplus (*o-wai ying-yü*) which varied between Tls. 100,000 and Tls. 400,000. In addition, the Cohong had been responsible to Peking for about Tls. 200,000 a year, which they had paid the Hoppo under three heads: for annual purchases of tribute objects (Tls. 55,000), for ginseng [20] to be sent to the court (about Tls. 100,000), and for charitable purposes (Tls. 40,000 to 50,000). Finally, the Hoppo had set aside about Tls. 100,000 a year to pay for tribute objects. Thus the total reported collections from the Canton trade, as listed by these officials in Peking, had been somewhere between Tls. 1,300,000 and Tls. 1,600,000 a year.

After 1842, of the payments formerly made by the Cohong, about one-half (Tls. 100,000 for ginseng) was to continue to be paid by the former hong merchants for at least four more years, while the other half was to be paid by the Hoppo. But to help him meet this and his other payments to Peking, the unfixed surpluses of the collections at the new ports were to be made available to the Canton customs. In short, the Hoppo would not suffer from the new dispensation, for it was promised that the Canton customs would receive assistance from the collections elsewhere. The Grand Council archives reveal that the new treaty port customhouses remained for some time mere appendages of the Hoppo, added to his fiscal domain.

Before surveying the fiscal arrangements at the new ports, let us look briefly at the fate of the customhouse underlings at Canton. Were they left in a position both to obey the treaties and to survive? The imperial representatives saw clearly the need of reconciling the interests of the barbarians, who opposed all extra-tariff charges, and of the little people of Canton (boatmen, shroffs, runners, *et al.*), who by immemorial custom lived upon just such charges and had no salaries or other means of support. As Ch'i-ying explained to the emperor, the regular duties at Canton originally had not been great, but customary fees had gradually accumulated until in the eighteenth century on several occasions the customary fees had been made into regular payments due to the government, some of which were retained at Canton to meet expenses of administration. Gradually, however, illegal fees had again accumulated, until in 1842 the abolition of excess fees (*fou-fei*) was demanded by the British. In June 1843 Ch'i-ying recorded the British proposal to remove all official sanction from such charges.[21] In July the general regulations of trade confirmed it. Accordingly the ninth of Ch'i-ying's proposals for readjustment at Canton in August 1843 dealt with the sustenance of the customhouse underlings whose former means of revenue (a percentage on all goods handled) had now been made illegal. In the view of the authorities at Canton it was not feasible to have these government runners *et al.* "do business on an empty stomach" (i.e., serve without salary); hence it was proposed and decided to give them workmen's rations (*kung-shih*) [22] which they had not formerly received. The imperial commissioner and the Hoppo expressed a most sincere desire to eliminate the old evils.

Before regulations could be drawn up for this purpose, however, the amount of trade at Canton had increased to such a degree — 53 vessels in the first forty days of trade, in the off season — that more runners were needed.[23] On October 15, 1843, the Canton governor-general and the Hoppo dispatched a memorial outlining the new preventive service. There had been seven customs barriers in the Canton area. At each of them the Hoppo would now station the following personnel, at the indicated allowances per month: one man from his own household (Tls. 5), one clerk (Tls. 5), one constable (Tls. 5), ten watchmen (each Tls. 3.5), a cook and a water carrier (each Tls. 2), and a patrol-boat crew of eight men (each Tls. 2). Funds for the repair or building of the stations and boats would be contributed by the Hoppo himself, Wen-feng. For payment of the staff it was proposed to use some Tls. 5,000 formerly spent in the collection of measurement fees and as bonuses.[24] The scale of monthly pay just listed hardly seems munificent, although it appears to have been an innovation.

At the same time proposals were made for the support of the clerks and runners of the Canton customhouse who formerly had received their sustenance and even writing materials from a percentage levied on foreign trade by the hong merchants. In a busy season some twenty to sixty of these men had daily to be sent to oversee activities on the river, even down below Whampoa. Action must be taken lest they now be forced to live on bribes, and so again rouse the ire of the barbarians. Since the duties collected by treaty tariff were all to be remitted to Peking, it was proposed to support these clerks and runners by taking from the unfixed surplus collected at Canton each year (presumably on non-treaty trade) a tax of 1 mace 8 candareens (Tls. 0.18) per picul of goods.[25] The underlings included 20 head clerks of various types already provided with support; 182 assistant clerks, of whom 47 had been formerly supported at the substations, and 135 left unprovided with support.[26]

It has long been realized that for many years after 1843 the treaties had only a nominal and superficial effect upon commercial and customs practice at Canton. That the new system should cloak the old vices was to be expected. After the trade was reopened, foreign merchants frequently complained of customhouse delays: customs officers on duty only from 4 P.M. to sunset, steamers detained from 30 hours to 5 days awaiting examination, lighters forbidden to make round trips to Whampoa and back in one day, and the like. The inquiring British consul, Thomas Taylor Meadows, cast light on this institutionalized procrastination by finding out that office routine in the customhouse involved the following steps: a communication on its receipt was sent to the clerk's room for the drafting of a reply; usually on the same day, the draft reply was presented for the Hoppo's examination; on the second day a decision was made on the draft and it was sent out in final form for fair-copying; it was then presented again to the Hoppo; and on the third day it was sealed, marked and dispatched. Matters requiring consultation would of course take more time.[27]

The post-treaty customs reform at Canton proved to be only skin-deep. For another two generations the Hoppo retained his key position as a tax-farmer sent from the court, and his post was not abolished until 1904. One scholar concludes that the changes of 1842, by restricting the Hoppo's opportunities for profit at Canton, made his administration more corrupt than ever and fostered a labyrinth of tax stations and barriers with special charges, fees, duties and taxes, collected by a swarm of functionaries each of whom had his customary and private, as well as his public, responsibilities and emoluments. Throughout the remainder of the nineteenth century the Hoppo profited both by his control over these persons and also by his manipulation of the confused and inadequate system of reports, some of which were delayed up to eight years. When the Board of Revenue in 1904 finally demanded a unified reporting system, its investigation disclosed discrepancies of some Tls. 200,000 a year.[28]

Insertion of the treaty ports into the Ch'ing customs administration. Against this background at Canton it is of interest to trace the steps by which the new treaty port customs collectorates were set up under the wing of the Hoppo. Needless to say, the multifarious complexity of Ch'ing fiscal practices makes a clear statistical summary out of the question, at least for the present writer — the very terms used in the accounts have now become frequently unintelligible[29] to scholars of the post-Ch'ing generation. Changes of the 1840's went largely unrecorded in official compendia of the late nineteenth century and the following summary is based on month-to-month reports in the Palace Museum archives in Peking.[30]

Without encompassing too many ramifications, let us note first the network of customhouses in the Ch'ing empire of the 1840's.[31] Customs stations for the taxation of trade were established at 29 key spots, mainly on the routes of China's domestic commerce. Of these stations the 5 under the Board of Works were of somewhat less importance, as revenue sources, than the 24 stations under the Board of Revenue (for a list, see Table 8). The latter dominated the waterways of the Yangtze valley at such cities as Huai-an and Yang-chou on the Grand Canal in North Kiangsu; Nanking, Soochow, Hangchow and Shanghai in the Lower Yangtze region; Wu-hu and Feng-yang in Anhwei; and Kiukiang and Kan-chou on the route to Canton through Kiangsi. Other stations embraced Peking and key points on the trade and caravan routes coming into North China: Shanhaikuan, Kalgan, and other spots in Shansi. It is significant that the maritime customs collectorates (*hai-kuan*) of the southern coastal provinces, located at Canton, Foochow, Chen-hai (the port of Ningpo), and Shanghai, respectively, were merely elements in the general structure. As indicated above in Chapter 3, the Chinese state had lacked any conception of a protective tariff. No great distinction existed between overseas and domestic trade, both of which were conducted mainly by Chinese merchants and neither of which was relied upon for the major revenue of the state.

British administrators versed in the tariff and trade policies of European nations were ill-prepared to believe that the government at Peking, chronically hard-pressed for funds and averse to foreign intercourse, would fail to erect tariff barriers against British goods. As they learned of the

TABLE 8: QUOTAS AND REPORTED COLLECTIONS OF 29 CUSTOMS ADMINISTRATIONS UNDER THE BOARDS OF REVENUE AND OF WORKS IN THE 1840'S.[1]

1. Under the Board of Revenue (in taels)

Name and location of customs offices[2]	Fixed annual quota (*ting-o*)[3]	Actual collections (*shih-cheng*) reported 1841	1842	1845	1849	Allotment retained for annual expenditure
Ch'ung-wen-men (Hatamen octroi, Peking)	102175	323166	315061	315627	323739	35103
Tso-i (E. Peking)	10000	12108	11317	11788	10633	8632
Yu-i (W. Peking)	10000	11200	10738	10813	10582	8662
Tso-liang-t'ing (Tungchow, Chihli)	12339	12387	12383	12389	12419	8914
Huai-an kuan (Kiangsu)	328679	255760	250594	181022	146916	146916
Hu-shu kuan (mainly Soochow)	441151	272540	251982	322364	340280	340280
Yang-chou kuan (Kiangsu)	164790	163808	118752	118049	118453	118453
Wu-hu kuan (Anhwei)	229919	272947	248639	274117	274329	243043
Hsi-hsin kuan (Nanking)	74376	42616	41437	41481	41892	full amount
Feng-yang kuan (Anhwei)	107159	107179	96431	107278	106303	full amount
Chiang-hai kuan (Shanghai)	65980	57046	73685	79820	72997	full amount
T'ien-chin kuan (Tientsin)	68156	83618	83248	82528	53547	44894
Lin-ch'ing kuan (Shantung)	48376	55095	25436	59739	85441	68397
Chiu-chiang kuan (Kiukiang)	539281	562932	536816	451740	579013	full amount
Kan kuan (Kan-chou, Kiangsi)	85470	93048	82711	93184	93771	85314
Pei-hsin kuan (Hangchow)	188053	188566	188218	188525	188498	158955

[1] These figures are taken from Wang Ch'ing-yun, *Shih-ch'ü yü-chi*, ch. vi, and stated by him to have been based on the *Collected Statutes* (*Ta-Ch'ing hui-tien*).

[2] For location of these customhouses, see the following: *Che-chiang t'ung-chih* (Yung-cheng ed.), ch. lxxxvi; *Chiang-nan t'ung-chih*, ch. lxxix; *Chiang-ning-fu chih*, ch. xv.

[3] The "fixed quota" (*ting-o*) was the total derived by combining the "regular quota" (*cheng-o*) and the "surplus" (*ying-yü*, presumably, in fact, the "fixed surplus"). The "actual collections" (*shih-cheng*) were the sums reported to have been remitted, within the general category of the land tax, in the years in question.

Che-hai kuan (Chen-hai, Chekiang)	79908	79908	18839	78018	79908	full amount
Min-hai kuan (Foochow)	186549	199465	127479	185955	193012	186012
T'ai-p'ing kuan (Shao-chou-fu, Kwangtung)	128175	135245	135724	135253	118643	15063
Yueh-hai kuan (Canton)	899064	864232	1128240	2362164	1429766	807768
Shan-hai kuan (Shanhaikwan)	111129	61760	61730	61702	61695	41494
Chang-chia-k'ou (Kalgan, Chihli)	60561	20004	20004	20004	20004	20000
Sha-hu-k'ou (Shansi)	32333	16919	16919	16919	16919	1188
Kuei-hua-ch'eng (Shansi)	16600	23565	24036	23418	22749	6050
Total Board of Revenue 24 offices	3,990,223	3,915,110	3,880,419	5,243,897	4,401,499	2,345,178 [4]
2. *Under the Board of Works*						
Lung-chiang kuan (Nanking)	112607	95740	90599	100900	120937	
Wu-hu kuan (Anhwei)	136853	101021	70547	117190	117081	
Su-ch'ien kuan (Kiangsu)	56684	59426	58543	26934	27648	
Lin-ch'ing chuan-pan-cha (Lin-ch'ing, Shantung)	8372	6155	6289	7271 (for 1844)	7453	
Nan-hsin kuan (Hangchow)	49469	30247	30247	30247	30247	
Total Board of Works 5 offices	363985	292589	256225	282542	303366	
Grand Total 29 offices	4,354,208	4,207,699	4,136,644	5,526,439	4,704,865	

[4] Adding this column without reference to the entries listed as "full amount" (*chin-shu*), gives a total of Tls. 2,345,178. If for "full amount" is substituted in each case the average reported collection of the four years noted in the preceding columns, the total comes to about Tls. 3,158,972.

taxation of trade effected at "inland custom houses" (the very name seemed anomalous), they developed a phobia about "transit taxes" which could reimpose in the interior the charges which had been lightened by the treaty tariff at the ports. To a generation who saw the advent of Free Trade as the chief harbinger of Progress, it was almost incredible that any government would be so "anti-commercial" as to tax its own domestic commerce as heavily as its foreign trade. Yet this was the Chinese fiscal practice at the time when the ports were opened: as shown in Table 8, the Hoppo at Canton (Yueh-hai kuan) was the greatest revenue producer of all (Tls. 2.3 million reported for 1845). But the second largest producer was the Kiukiang customs (ca. Tls. 0.5 million), followed by Soochow and the famous Hatamen octroi in Peking (each ca. Tls. 0.33 million). Thereafter, in descending order, came Wuhu, Foochow, Hangchow, Huai-an on the Grand Canal and Shao-chou on the route to Canton. Except for the bonanza provided by tea and silk exports at Canton, foreign trade played a minor role. This is more obvious if we look not at actual collections but at the quotas expected from each station — on this basis the order of importance was Canton (Tls. 0.9 million), Kiukiang (0.5), Soochow (0.4), Huai-an (0.3), Wuhu (0.2), Hangchow, Foochow, Shao-chou, and Shanhaikuan. It seems plain that Ch'ing customs arrangements were not oriented toward the taxation of maritime trade any more than inland trade. No basic distinction was made between them. Collections listed in 1845 show that the revenue at inland customs stations (Tls. 2,537,950) was roughly equal to that at the four "maritime customs" collectorates at the seaports (Tls. 2,705,947). The great predominance of Canton is of course very obvious.

Since the taxation of Western trade had been the prerogative of the Hoppo for generations past, the duties collected from Western trade at the new ports after 1843 continued to be reported to Peking through that official.

At Canton all revenue from Chinese and Western maritime trade was classed as before under the single category of "customs duties" (*kuan-shui*). But at the four new treaty ports, the revenues from Chinese and Western trade were kept in separate accounts. The latter apparently covered imports from and exports to Western countries and goods carried in Western bottoms and were called "barbarian duties" (*i-shui*). Levies on the Chinese coastal trade, on the other hand, continued to follow long-established practices and were called either "customs duties" or "regular duties" (*ch'ang-shui*). The funds were kept in separate treasuries.

Keeping separate customs accounts at one taxing station was not a practice confined to the treaty ports. At Tientsin two accounts were kept by two different officials: (1) an account for the regular customs, supervised by the Ch'ang-lu Salt Administrator (*Ch'ang-lu yen-cheng*), which dealt with the trade of Chinese merchants from Kwangtung and Fukien; (2) an account for the "sea duties" (*hai-shui*), levied mainly on rice shipments and in charge of the Tientsin taotai, which were reported to Peking by the Chihli governor-general. Each of these categories had its own quota and customhouse.[32]

After 1843 the customs administrations of Fukien, Chekiang and Kiangsu retained their old designations (Min-hai kuan, Che-hai huan, Chiang-hai kuan, respectively) in all matters concerning the "regular duties." Each of these administrations consisted of a network of larger and smaller stations, with the chief ones located in or around the emporia which now became the new treaty ports.[33] In inaugurating the treaty system, Peking ruled that the collections of the new "barbarian duties" at the four newly opened ports were to be reported to Canton, and thence forwarded to Peking by the Hoppo. The purpose of this procedure was evidently to keep the new Western trade revenue in the channels of the traditional quota system. But actually it resulted only in the Hoppo's making annual statements of the amounts collected at the four new ports.[34] By various ways and for various reasons the treaty tariff revenues, contrary to the Grand Council's original promise, seem to have been retained by the individual customs authorities concerned. Canton exercised no firm jurisdiction over the other ports. Since the Canton quota could always be comfortably met because of the large volume of Western trade, the Hoppo evinced little interest in the revenue of the other treaty ports — probably because such an interest on his part might lead eventually to an increase of his financial responsibility to Peking.

On the other hand, no suggestion seems to have been made that the four new ports should become independent units, as Canton had been before the war and as all the old-established regular customhouses were, each directly accountable to the Board of Revenue and the throne. (The fiscal year for the four new ports was identical with that of Canton, a uniformity that did not exist among the regular customs administrations.) There was no central organ to oversee Western trade, just as there was lacking any government agency or foreign office to deal with the West in general. Seen in this light, Canton's nominal headship over the other treaty ports appears to have been an administrative rather than a financial arrangement.

The working of the quota system. Each of the old-established customhouses (called by foreigners the "native customs") had its own annual quota to fulfil. By the early nineteenth century these quotas usually consisted of two parts, as we have already seen at Canton — the official or "regular quota" (*cheng-o*), and the "surplus quota" (*ying-yü*). The latter had been added at a later date, had undergone changes in amount and generally exceeded the official quota by a large sum.[c] If the amount actually collected fell short of the full quota, the gap was to be made up by the

Table 9: Examples of Regular and Surplus Quotas[35]

Customs office	*Regular quota*	*Surplus quota*	*Total*
Yueh-hai kuan (Canton)	Tls. 43,560	855,500	899,060
Che-hai kuan (Chen-hai, Ningpo)	36,508	44,000	80,508
Min-hai kuan (Foochow)	73,549	113,000	186,549

customs superintendent, theoretically by his own efforts. But even before the treaty tariff came on the scene, there were signs of the breakdown of the quota system.[36] In spite of the customs superintendent's personal responsibility for meeting the quota, he did not always produce the required sum. Instead the records show an accumulation of large backlogs of unpaid deficits, caused either by individual cases of inability to pay within the prescribed time, or by the practice of cancelling the obligation by "contributing" a certain sum to a public works project (usually said to be only 10 per cent of what was owed as the customs quota).[37] These deficits in the customs revenue sometimes became quite large. One official incurred an obligation in 1843 to pay up Tls. 136,349 after he had been ten months in office overseeing three customs stations in Anhwei. From 1830 on, the surplus quotas of the Chekiang (Che-hai kuan) and Kiukiang customs offices were divided into two classes, the "fixed surplus" (*o-nei ying-yü*) and the "unfixed surplus" (*o-wai ying-yü*). This action was probably induced by repeated reports of short collections. The deficits in both kinds of surplus were still to be paid by the official in charge, but defalcation on the unfixed surplus would not involve him in punishment.[38]

The court at Peking saw little need for changing the old system to accommodate the new Western trade. The edict which consented to the treaty of Nanking had remarked that at each prospective treaty port a tariff was already in force — it had taken some time to realize that innovation was necessary.[39] In 1843 no quota was fixed for the revenue from Western trade, on the ground that the amount of this trade was yet unknown. It was decided that after a three-year test period the amount realizable at the new treaty ports should be incorporated into a revised quota for Canton,[40] which was still regarded as the center of foreign trade. After revenue began to flow from Western trade at the new ports it constituted a body of unattached wealth, much as though the local officials had begun working private gold mines on government property. In general the new revenue either served to make up the deficits in the regular customs quota, or was retained in the province instead of being sent to Canton. In Fukien, for example, in 1845 the Board of Revenue let the treaty tariff receipts be kept for military expenses in the province. In 1848 it was decided that Tls. 25,000 of the treaty tariff revenue were to be transferred annually to the account of the regular Fukien customs to make up deficits in its quota.(Even after this transfer the regular customs was still often short of its quota.) The treaty tariff collection, as reported, was certainly truncated. In 1849 it was reported to be less than Tls. 25,000, and therefore was all thrown into the regular customs. In 1852 after the transfer of this sum, there remained only Tls. 9,618. After the outbreak of the Taiping Rebellion the Fukien customs superintendent asked to have all treaty tariff revenues transferred to the regular customs account until peace should be restored, on the ground that warfare was producing a complete stoppage of the regular revenue.[41]

Similarly the Kiangsu authorities in 1849 asked for permission to retain in the province Tls. 10,000 out of every Tls. 100,000 collected under the treaty tariff. At Canton the annual intake far exceeded the quota. The officials opposed a revision of quotas when the three-year test period ended in 1846. They received permission to postpone it for another year or two.[42]

In order to avoid an increase in the quota payments expected of them, there is little doubt that the Chinese customs authorities failed to report fully the new collections on Western trade. As we shall see in later chapters, this non-reporting of revenue was an integral part of the corruption which was overtaking the Ch'ing regime. One idea used by the customs collectors to sanction their malpractice was the conception that foreign trade was a static quantity which should be expected to produce a fixed amount of total revenue. Thus difficulties in meeting the quota at Canton in 1846 and 1847 were explained by the diversion of trade from Canton to Shanghai. Shortcomings in the collection at Amoy were explained by the "encroachment" of "barbarian duties" on "regular duties." (For the confusion between the treaty tariff and "native" tariff, see Ch. 17.) Ch'i-ying and his colleagues justified the postponement of the date for fixing quotas on the new Western trade revenues by arguing that, since the Canton quota was being met, no further arrangement was necessary.[43]

The following table shows maritime customs collections, both regular ("native") and foreign (Western barbarian), reported to Peking in the first dozen years of the treaty period, 1843–1855.[44] It will be noted that this table is incomplete and the figures are not generally comparable. In any case, it shows only the reported, by no means the actual, collections. Considering the known volume of foreign trade at Shanghai, the low returns are amazing. From 1853 they were cut down by the rebellion there (see below, Chapters 22–23).

Investigation of the Ch'ing customs administration in the first decade of the treaties could be pushed a good deal further by persistent monographic research. Yet the feeling is inescapable that the figures, in addition to the confusion among them created by discordant collection periods, are essentially window dressing. Since the reported collections were frittered away by a great variety of allocations and transfers of funds for provincial purposes, we can have little confidence that much of this revenue reached Peking. We therefore lack final evidence as to how the funds were actually used. The accounts take on a ritualistic character, as though the officials at both ends of the paper-chain of fiscal accounting wore that "secret smile" appropriate to an elaborate game of literary make-believe.

TABLE 10: CUSTOMS COLLECTIONS REPORTED FROM THE FIVE TREATY PORTS, 1843–1855 (in taels)

	Canton	Amoy		Foochow		Ningpo		Shanghai	
		collections under							
Year of collection [1]	*total collections* [2]	Treaty tariff	Regular customs	Treaty tariff	Regular customs	Treaty tariff	Regular customs	Treaty tariff	Regular customs
Gross quotas (from Table 8)	899,064		90,000 [7]		96,549 [7]		79,908		65,980
1843–44	2,030,543	15,134 [3]	38,040 [3]	.... [4]	92,679	6,264 [3]	77,037	41,933 [3]	70,423
1844–45	3,360,832	48,132	79,078	143	90,082	24.735	78,018	172,922	70,612
1845–46	2,186,530	31,734	72,620	4,045	81,894	7,086	78,020	480,239	70,649
1846–47	1,972,089	35,783		1,213		2,196	76,542	662,467	69,049
1847–48	1,825,223	29,132		4		1,571		628,274	69,619
1848–49	1,424,045	24,568	(76,589) [5]	31	(76,590) [5]		78,376	540,970	
1849 [6] (Regular)			(78,045) [5]		(78,046) [5]				
1849–50	1,471,318	29,932	(73,365) [5]	732	(73,365) [5]		76,546	704,612	
1850 [6] (Treaty)	1,476,867	32,098		1,585		117		1,203,395	69,855
1850–51	1,636,574	31,203		3,415				1,243,165	
1851–52	1,666,811	31,170	(66,175) [5]	11	(66,176) [5]		76,336	545,687	
1852–53	1,274,129	8,174	20,942	41,416	52,578		62,698	591,941	
1853–54	1,166,492						62,321		
1854–55	342,043 [3]	45,370		220,106			62,522		

[1] The "years" here listed were really fiscal 12-month periods according to the lunar calendar. For exact dates see Appendix C, sec. 2, "Tables of Collection Periods."

[2] The accounts submitted for Canton did not distinguish the regular customs and treaty tariff revenues.

[3] This return includes only a part of the year.

[4] Blank spaces indicate that the available sources lacked data.

[5] Reports from Fukien for these years are made as over-all totals for the province. For the purpose of constructing this table the sum for each year has been divided arbitrarily into two equal parts and entered half under Amoy and half under Foochow.

[6] In these instances the 12-month fiscal year fell within the Chinese calendar year; see Appendix B, sec. 2.

[7] We have arbitrarily split the Fukien provincial total between its two ports.

This chapter and the four preceding it have indicated certain steps taken on both sides to put the treaty system into operation. The selection and dispatching of British and Chinese personnel, the establishment of forms of contact between them at the ports, the misunderstandings, delays, frustrations, suspicions, stratagems and remonstrances which occupied the official life of either side — all these novel and confusing experiences were part of a meeting of two civilizations which now, after a century of contact, have again altered their relationship. These chapters have dealt chiefly with the creation of new institutions for Sino-Western trade, a process full of human contretemps, wasteful and inefficient, which nevertheless was to form a major chapter in Chinese and world history. Viewed through the consulate archives, this process often seems like a British crusade for law enforcement, in which Chinese mandarins occasionally helped but usually proved a hindrance. Seen through the Chinese official records, this crusade of the British consuls shrinks to a mean and uncouth posturing, ominous, to be sure, but far less important than the domestic affairs of an empire heading into a great rebellion. Even in fiscal matters, the Westerners and their trade had less influence upon China than they supposed. The chief "impact" in the treaty ports was the jar experienced by the foreigners when they confronted Chinese life. Considering the superficiality of many of the arrangements noted above, the persistent gap between treaty theory and treaty port practice, it is hardly surprising that the British consular effort to set up a new order on the coast of China was almost a failure. Judged in the general view of history, the British opening of China was inevitably a bright chapter of the Victorian epic, as well as the first grim warning for the Confucian state. Judged in its own terms, however, by what it was supposed to do, the first treaty system began to fall apart within a few years after its inauguration.

PART IV

THE PROGRESSIVE BREAKDOWN OF THE TREATY SYSTEM 1845–51

CHAPTER XV

ANGLO-CHINESE FRICTION

THE DETERIORATION of Anglo-Chinese relations after the first treaty settlement was due to many subtle causes. British advocates of gunboat diplomacy believed that Chinese truculence increased as the memory of the late war became dim. Particularly after the British garrisons withdrew from the islands of Chusan and Kulangsu, following the completion of China's indemnity payments in 1846, the British sensed a decline in their prestige. Contrary to their expectations, the import trade in English manufactured goods did not prosper. They suspected that Chinese officials were quietly frustrating the intent of the treaties by erecting secret impediments to the flow of British goods into the interior. Meanwhile there was a similar disenchantment on the Chinese side. By March 1848, when Ch'i-ying finally departed for Peking, the "Canton city question" had become a focus of popular Chinese feeling and unresolved diplomatic conflict. The British seemed steadily to be getting the worst of it. In 1851 Palmerston finally contemplated the necessity of another use of British force in China, and the second Anglo-Chinese war was delayed for seven years thereafter only by a series of circumstances — rebellion in China, war in the Crimea, and the mutiny in India.

This steady deterioration after the Ch'i-ying-Pottinger "alliance" of 1843 was plainly marked in the decline of personal amicability between the British and Chinese representatives. Pottinger's successors, Davis and Bonham, were progressively less interested in a policy of friendship and more aware of shortcomings in the treaties, while Ch'i-ying's successors, Hsü and Yeh, were anti-foreign Chinese who were fundamentally opposed to the Manchu policy of conciliation. Each change in personnel on either side was marked by an increase in hostility.

The end of the diplomatic honeymoon. The honeymoon period of the new treaty relations came to an end when Sir Henry Pottinger was succeeded by John Francis Davis in the middle of 1844. Pottinger had come to China from India, without bitter memories of the past, and had succeeded in his negotiations beyond all precedent, he being the first European to negotiate in China at the conclusion of a successful war. His unparalleled intimacy with the imperial commissioner, Ch'i-ying, had been most gratifying, as well as the G. C. B. given him by the Queen at the end of 1842. Not sharing the merchants' preoccupation with profits, he was in a position to indulge in magnanimity and to view the treaty system with a degree of perspective. For the enforcement of the treaties on British subjects, he declared in July 1843, he was "resolved to take the most decided measures."[1] Such vigor might be contrary to Western international law but it was "indispensably required in our commerce with a weak and powerless . . . Empire like China, which . . . we have *forced* into the close commercial arrangements which are now on the eve of taking effect." In a long dispatch in March 1844 the plenipotentiary summed up his thesis that China could not be dealt with by the rules of international law applicable to Western states. He suggested that the British government must guard against the constant tendency of foreigners to take advantage of this situation and infringe upon Chinese rights in a way that would not be tolerated elsewhere; British officials in particular must be cautioned against this tendency; since the war, Chinese officials had been deterred by apathy or dread from remonstrating, beyond a personal appeal to Pottinger. They had put up with things that no other country would have suffered, and if this continued it would inevitably undermine Chinese confidence in British justice and moderation. The Foreign Office agreed and urged the Colonial Office, Admiralty, and India Board to urge this view upon their subordinates.[2]

From this point of view, the appointment of Davis to succeed Pottinger was a step backward. J. F. Davis (1795–1890) was the son of an East India Company director formerly active in India. He had entered the Canton factory at the age of eighteen and eventually became one of the earliest British sinologues.[3] He was with Lord Amherst during the uncomfortable fiasco when that envoy was sent away from Peking without an audience in 1816. He had been second superintendent of trade under Lord Napier during that emissary's discomfiture at Canton in 1834, remaining in charge for a year after the latter's death. More than any other British official in China, Davis was aware of Britain's past humiliations, having been frequently, as an interpreter, the actual transmitting medium. Under the Company he had been trained as a prince of commerce rather than as a diplomat. In July 1845 he was made a baronet. There clung to him inevitably something of the Anglo-Indian attitude toward the natives of the East and also vestiges of the old mercantilist order under which he had grown up.

Appointed early in 1844, Davis carefully went through the "voluminous mass" of Pottinger's correspondence and received his instructions from Lord Aberdeen.[a] These instructions expressed an orthodox free trade point

[a] Davis confessed himself "rather a novice on the subject of patronage and by no means desirous of any undue share of it. 'One ungrateful and twenty discontented is the usual result.' " Being "happily independent," he offered no candidates for appointment in China. Under the Foreign Office, indeed, he would probably have few appointments to make, except linguists and menials. He took only one private secretary with him and a governor's uniform of blue turned up with red, with silver epaulettes; fortunately linen trousers could be worn with it.[4]

of view, that legal commerce in China was "likely to flourish in proportion as it is . . . unfettered by minute regulations and untrammeled by official interference." It was true that the "peculiar character of our intercourse with China calls for a certain degree of supervision on the part of British authorities," but that supervision should be aimed merely at preventing the rise of "discussion or dissension" between the British traders and the Chinese authorities.[5] In other words, if the Chinese did not object, nothing need be done. In fine, Davis was to coöperate in enforcing the treaty but at the same time to point out that such coöperation was useless unless the Chinese authorities really controlled their own people.

Such instructions were orthodox and proper, but they failed to express the view of Pottinger, which came closer to the concept of trusteeship for native peoples then being developed by British administrators elsewhere.[6] The significance of Pottinger's view lay in the fact that he realized the harm which would come to the Chinese state if it were treated as an equal, and therefore as fair game, in international relations with the Western powers.

Davis reached Hongkong on May 7, 1844, and took charge the next day, although Pottinger stayed on for another six weeks to smooth his path. Ch'i-ying and his colleagues were particularly concerned over the change and showered Sir Henry with communications asking that Davis be apprised of all his arrangements. Accompanied by three war steamers, the two British diplomats met Ch'i-ying and his suite at the Bogue on June 12–13 and were elegantly banqueted. Ch'i-ying had an hour's interview with Davis and spent two hours with Pottinger. He pursued his usual tactics, asking for a life-size portrait of Sir Henry for presentation to the emperor, who approved of Sir Henry's conduct. This high compliment was "totally unexpected" by Pottinger, who nevertheless felt he could not refuse and promised to sit for a likeness on arrival in England and have it sent out. "Keying particularly begged that the picture might be as large as life." [7]

Davis was not amenable to the same treatment, although Ch'i-ying tried for a time to make him an "intimate friend" also.[b] In August 1844, Davis

[b] Cp. Ch'i-ying to Davis, rec'd Dec. 28, 1844: "Yesterday I opened your answer, and learned that my various communications had come to hand. I may suppose, that you the Honorable Envoy are happy, and in the enjoyment of tranquillity, and enjoy every success, which greatly consoles my mind . . . The severity of the winter is now close, and I hope you will take care of yourself. As a proof of my affectionate regard I send you four boxes of preserves, four hams, and four jars of Shaouhing wine, which I trust you will receive with a smile, and drop an answer. I wish you every happiness and have nothing to add."

Davis to Ch'i-ying, Dec. 29, 1844: "I have had the pleasure to receive your two letters, and am happy to find you are well and prosperous. As to the articles of provisions which you have been so kind as to send, Consul Macgregor informs me that they are on the way and I shall soon receive them. They will be valuable to me as marks of your friendship. Whenever a vessel of war goes up to Canton for the Treasure [i.e., indemnity payment] I hope to return your kind recollection of me by some articles of the production of my country, which I shall take the liberty to send, and in the meanwhile wish you all happiness and prosperity." [8]

commented on the inveterate Chinese "inability to comprehend the observance of good faith on the part of the strongest." By the end of the year he was finding Ch'i-ying's rather long-winded interpretations of minor treaty points "tiresome" and "childish." [9]

When Ch'i-ying paid his final visit to Hongkong in November 1845, the festivities were a trifle repetitious. Accompanied by the chief magistrate of Hongkong and by Dr. Gutzlaff as interpreter, the imperial commissioner and his suite were brought from Whampoa to the new city of Victoria in H. M. Steamer *Vixen* and received on landing both the British naval salute, due to a minister plenipotentiary, and an outburst of three gigantic firecrackers in Chinese style. A procession of Chinese guards and coolies, British military staff officers, mandarins borne in chairs, and Sepoy troops with a band escorted Ch'i-ying to a new building adjoining the harbor master's wharf which had been donated by the Parsee firm of D. and M. Rustomjee and Company, wines, cherry brandy, and beer being supplied at public expense and the entertainment continuing for four days.[c]

Ch'i-ying's own report to the emperor on this visit explained that, since he had gone to Macao to see the American and French ministers and to

[c] On the second day, Ch'i-ying exchanged calls with the governor and major-general, receiving and embracing them "with his accustomed graceful urbanity." He reviewed the troops and in the evening attended a state dinner and ball at which several of the mandarins joined in the spirit of the occasion "keeping time with head, hands and feet and waggishly ogled the ladies." On the third day there were further conferences and another ball, aboard the warship *Agincourt*. On the fourth day Ch'i-ying was taken by ship around the island, getting seasick in the process. At a banquet that evening he was toasted as an enlightened statesman "who, alike the friend of England and of China, has taught us to respect him as much for his political talents, as we value him for his social qualities." The *China Mail* felt that "nothing could exceed the affability and good humor of Keying, accompanied by the highest tact and good breeding. He was jovial at dinner but without excess; and . . . volunteered a Mantchow Tartar song, which he gave with great spirit." He offered his hand to each of the ladies "with the utmost blandness," gave some of them little presents of purses or rosaries, and held a small child on his knee.

As the climax of these festivities Ch'i-ying gave a sumptuous Chinese banquet. The half-hour before dinner, so "proverbially dull" in England, was enlivened by entertainers and tea and followed by a four-hour feast during which the imperial commissioner "with the most refined Chinese politeness, more than once took a tid-bit from his own dish and with his chopsticks conveyed it to the mouth of the honored guests beside him." Both Ch'i-ying and Davis sang songs, as did the major-general, the chief justice of Hongkong, and the editor of the *China Mail*. A son-in-law of the emperor excused himself on account of hoarseness but a Tartar descendant of Genghis Khan "chanted a wild lilt."

The *China Mail* described Ch'i-ying's "tall and majestic form (as) being graced with manners at once dignified and courteous . . . but for his dress and language he might have been taken for a fine specimen of an old English gentleman of the highest class . . . His bland countenance was beaming with good humoured benevolence but it is of an intellectual cast and lighted up with a twinkling eye which as the occasion demanded would be equally expressive of penetrative shrewdness as of social glee." [10]

The foreign community's regard for Ch'i-ying as their patron made him a temporary vogue. A few months later the "spacious and commodious premises" of a new British hotel on Queen's Road were christened "Keying House." [11] In December of 1846 the famous Chinese junk *Keying*, purchased at Canton by Douglas Lapraik and other English entrepreneurs, sailed for England with a crew of 30 Chinese and 12 Englishmen and with a salute from the British fleet at Hongkong. Captain Kellett rounded the Cape of Good Hope, visited New York and Boston, and reached London in March 1848, 477 days from Canton. This junk was built of teak and measured 160 feet in length, 25½ feet in breadth of beam and 800 tons burthen, with a mainmast reaching 85 feet from the deck. She crossed the North Atlantic in 21 days, "a short period even for the American Packet-ships." [12]

Hongkong to see Pottinger but thus far had seen Davis only at the Bogue, he had decided to accept the latter's invitation. Chusan was still to be restored and other aspects of foreign affairs had been regulated satisfactorily for three years past, so that a personal interview with Davis might reinforce these good relations. Huang, Chao, and P'an accompanied him and they were all treated very respectfully. When Davis wished to talk business, Ch'i-ying with his aides went to his foreign-style house. Davis dismissed all his underlings except Gutzlaff. They discussed the completion of the indemnity payments and the rendition of Chusan (against which British merchants had been agitating). Ch'i-ying offered assurances that the natives of Chusan, whom the emperor regarded as his children, would not thereafter be penalized for their contact with the British. He also agreed that a high Chinese official should be sent to supervise the rendition and suggested for this task his man Hsien-ling. At this Davis was delighted. Davis then, according to Ch'i-ying's memorial, presented his request for an imperial edict promising that Chusan would not thereafter be given to any other foreign power. His only explanation for wanting this unusual arrangement (better known in later decades as a "non-alienation agreement") was that an imperial rescript would quiet the hearts of his countrymen.[d] Ch'i-ying argued in reply that Chusan after its recovery would be Chinese territory. Why need this be formally stated? If he proposed it, the emperor would rebuke him, and other countries on hearing of it would conceive suspicions inconvenient to the British. Chao and P'an also explained these difficulties to Davis and he temporarily dropped the matter.[14]

In reporting the exchange of banquets, Ch'i-ying noted that the barbarians were all delighted at his speeches proclaiming the imperial benevolence and China's lack of ulterior motives toward England. When told they had only to trade peacefully according to treaty and there would be nothing to worry about, Davis and the other chiefs were all grateful. During the banquets they raised their wine cups and danced about, wishing long life to His Majesty and seeming very sincere. The imperial commissioner concluded from this observation of the barbarians' temperament that they seemed inclined to restore Chusan without stirring up any further trouble concerning it. But they were naturally crafty and would probably make further demands. Although the barbarian mind was hard to fathom, they always gave away their stratagems whenever they wanted something. The

[d] The Chusan problem became complicated, at least in Ch'i-ying's mind, by his lively suspicion not only that Britain might retain it but that France also had covetous designs upon it (as confirmed by the fact that Lagrené seldom mentioned it!). Ch'i-ying sought French intervention to secure British rendition. When Davis hesitated, pending orders from home (between the last indemnity payment of Jan. 22, 1846, and the actual rendition of July 25), Ch'i-ying was ready to seek French help, but Lagrené precipitately left China (Jan. 9 or 11, 1846) to avoid involvement. Eventually Britain got her non-alienation agreement (on Apr. 4, 1846), combined with the promise of future entrance into Canton city. See below.[18]

essential thing was to be prepared ahead of time and prevent their making use of pretexts. For example, when Davis wanted to restore Kulangsu ahead of time, Ch'i-ying had been clever enough to perceive that he wanted an excuse for restoring Chusan later than had been agreed. So he refused to take Kulangsu back until the barbarians had set a definite time for restoring Chusan. Later when the barbarian troops withdrew from Kulangsu and the foreign merchants wanted to stay there, he feared that they were plotting to keep it and vigorously forbade their staying by invoking the treaty. Davis still knew that he must preserve the treaty. The only course for China was to manifest confidence outwardly and inwardly to be on guard.[15]

In the end the effusive popularity bestowed at Hongkong upon Ch'i-ying, as the barbarians' friend at court, was not enough to offset the disillusionment which followed the opening of the treaty ports. Governor Davis's unsentimental attitude was apparent in his later communications. During 1846 Ch'i-ying gradually gave up the effort to "get him under control" by cordiality. The honeymoon was over, and there have been two views of Chinese affairs among foreigners — the sentimental and the cynical — ever since. The cynical view became gradually concentrated at Canton.

The British community at Canton. From the foreign point of view, the inauguration of the treaty system at Canton had been attended with such success that the complaints recorded in the British consular archives in the early years after 1843 seem significant chiefly for their unimportance. The consular office in which George Tradescant Lay opened the port on July 27, 1843, was burned in October. A month later a twenty-five year lease was signed with six of the former hong merchants for the use at $6000 a year of the Old Company, Dutch, and Creek factory sites, then in ruins. They were to be divided into three areas for the consulate and the British firms of Lindsay and Company and Jardine, Matheson and Company respectively. Sixteen lots were subsequently rented to merchants, of whom three were Parsees and at least two Americans.[16] The quarters enjoyed here by Mr. Lay and his successors were not lavish. Dr. John Bowring on his arrival in 1849 found that the consul's house did not even contain a bathroom, "an accommodation so especially requisite in this climate." The large room on the first floor had been used for a year as a place of public worship and the upper story in 1847 as quarters for the Ceylon Rifle Corps. The whole place was dirty and in need of repair.

In Canton the British merchants organized their own community agencies. The Associated Gentlemen Volunteers obtained arms and ammunition from the British government. Two fire engines were brought out from England in 1846 for the protection of the factories. In 1847 a public meeting of 53 persons, David Jardine in the chair, at the request of the consul and Governor Davis considered the use of Whampoa as a recreation ground but decided that it was too far from Canton. In 1849 John Dent, chairman of the Canton Regatta Club, was still complaining "against the egress of pullers and others who go out of an evening to enjoy the breeze in the passage" and got in the way of more serious sportsmen. Others in the community sought the removal from the river of more than twenty flower-boats, which impeded traffic and inconvenienced the merchants because "their servants spend whole nights there drinking and whoring." They were dispersed only to collect again.

The Parsee merchants from India were a considerable element in this British community, for these Zoroastrians of Persian origin, still active today in the foreign trade of the Indian subcontinent, played a leading role in the country trade. In September 1847 the Parsee community leased a hill at Whampoa from the Chinese government for 100 years at Tls. 25 a year to be used as a cemetery. At the burial of Dhunjeebhoy Dossabhoy Satna in 1849 there were 78 Parsees on hand. The burial ground rent was paid to Howqua.

By 1851 after slow accretions the British community at Canton was totalled as follows: [17]

TABLE 11: BRITISH COMMUNITY AT CANTON 1851

	Male	*Female*
British residents	72	9
Anglo-Indian subjects	149	1
At Whampoa (of whom only 10 were residents)	96	3
	317	13

The Canton British Chamber of Commerce was established in February 1847 to promote British commercial interests, collect information, and assist the arbitration of commercial disputes. (The Board of Trade in London saw little need of giving it official recognition, but in 1849 Palmerston did so for the Foreign Office.) Each member firm contributed $50 a year. Under David Jardine as the first chairman,[18] the new organization at once began to agitate for local reforms, particularly to get more space for the foreign community. Thus it sought to remove a row of Chinese shops in back of the factories on the east side of Old China street, to buy up ten shops in Hog Lane in order to close the street and erect a church, and especially to procure land on which British warehouses might be erected. The disadvantage of storing British goods in Chinese godowns had recently been demonstrated by the failure of Minkee's hong, when British owned goods had passed into the hands of Chinese pawnbrokers in a most inconvenient fashion.

This reflected the fact that the Canton trade was still handled almost entirely by Chinese: imports were taken from the ship at Whampoa into Chinese boats, and stored at Canton in Chinese packhouses, where they remained in charge of Chinese until sold. Teas and other exports were shipped in boats from the warehouse of the Chinese seller and remained in his possession usually at least one night after being examined, weighed and marked, and were then sent down to the ship at Whampoa in Chinese boats. As a result, the foreign merchants were obliged to trust absolutely in the Chinese with whom they dealt, and had no means of inspecting or supervising their goods in transit or in storage. Fraud naturally occurred. About the beginning of 1847 it came to light that one of these warehousemen, Ahming, had regularly raised money upon the foreign property entrusted to him by pledging it to native bankers. His failure and the resulting scandal destroyed foreign confidence in the system, which was a holdover from pre-treaty days, with the difference that the Chinese authorities were now in no way responsible for it. The system had continued because the foreign community lacked space in which to store their own goods. In this predicament Hongkong was really no remedy because of the trouble and danger of transportation thence to Canton. The Chamber of Commerce therefore under their treaty rights demanded more land.[19] Sir John Davis quickly offered to have the British government pay half the cost of buying out Chinese shops at the end of Hog Lane. Interest soon shifted, however, to the Honam side of the river, where David Jardine with the usual prescience of his firm got an option on the choicest site a month before the public meeting on the subject.[20]

Another foreign complaint concerned the lack of aids to navigation in the river. Of 25 junks sunk at the First Bar below Whampoa to form a wartime barrier, 17 were still in the way; the pilots charged for the upkeep of boats moored to mark them. Other sunken junks still reposed in both channels of the river between Whampoa and Canton, and the same obstructions existed in the Macao Passage. There were two rocks abreast of the factories and much dangerous rubbish. Meanwhile the lack of water police left the shipping at Whampoa endangered by pirates. The British Chamber of Commerce argued that such evils should be remedied by the Chinese government out of the sums collected as tonnage dues, as was done in Western countries. Port charges (tonnage dues) at Canton in 1848 had totalled over $66,000 (i.e., $46,870 British, and about $20,000 American), with no value whatever received for them. The consul complained to the imperial commissioner, who denied the existence of all the obstructions to navigation cited by the merchants. The latter concluded [21] that he was hoodwinked by his subordinates.[e]

The "city question" and the Davis raid. In all the long controversy at Canton between the small but aggressive British community and the Cantonese among whom the English were asserting a new and unprecedented status, the officials of both sides did not hold the initiative. Palmerston supported Davis in censuring the young British taipans who "amuse themselves by kicking over fruit-stalls and by making foot-balls of the Chinese." [23] The ill-will and bloody affrays which characterized the increase of sino-foreign contact at Canton were publicized at the time in British blue books. Yet the question of foreign entrance within the city walls, the famous "city question" which became the bone of contention, still awaits thorough study from the Chinese side.[24] How far xenophobia sprang from the people's hearts, as the Chinese officials alleged, and how far it was stirred up and exacerbated by gentry-official efforts, has been debated. But a contemporary first-hand account, like the *I-fen chi-wen* (Record of the barbarian miasma) by Liang T'ing-nan, that highly reputable scholar who helped to organize the anti-foreign Cantonese militia in the late 1840's, leaves little doubt that the active dislike of the British while fomented particularly by the gentry (through their placards, pronouncements, and organization of local militia, especially), was widely shared by gentry and villagers alike.[25] Without going into this important subject, we can note that this period at Canton saw the stirrings of a genuine nationalism of the modern type.[26] For this reason Manchu officials like Ch'i-ying, caught between the Cantonese and the British, were very much on the spot, subject to a disastrous pressure from both sides. Continued research should show that Ch'i-ying tried persistently to carry out the treaties and meet the British half-way. From the first, however, the imperial commissioner's effort to do so laid him open to the charge of sacrificing Chinese interests and yielding to barbarian threats — a charge which has not ceased to be laid against him down to the present day.

The British attempted to obviate the ambiguity of their treaty right to enter the Canton city walls (see above, Chapter 12) by securing a formal written convention, which was signed by Davis and Ch'i-ying on April 4, 1846. Its Chinese text stated in rather general terms that the Chinese high authorities had received an imperial edict permitting entrance to the walled city after mutual tranquillity had been long established, but that since the populace could not easily be controlled at present, entrance, though not abandoned, was postponed and permission for it would be given again

[e] In February 1949 a fund of $110,000 from the United States Economic Coöperation Admnistration was being used to reopen the main channel of the Pearl River which had been blocked since 1840. Some 9,000 tons of rock had already been removed and the channel would eventually take ships of 3000 tons.[22]

later.[27] In order to thwart the rumored designs of the French to occupy Chusan, this convention also promised that that island would not be given to any other power after the British withdrew.[28] On the Chinese side this appeared to be its more important aspect.

Since the stoning of English excursionists and similar "incidents" continued during the following year at Canton, Sir John Davis at the beginning of April 1847 staged his famous "raid." Within thirty-six hours a British force of 900 men in three steamers and a brig had captured the Bogue forts, spiked 827 cannon, and occupied the Canton factories. By an agreement of April 6, 1847, Ch'i-ying met a long series of British demands, and promised to permit entrance to the city at the end of two years. Such concessions naturally weakened his public position at Canton, while the withdrawal of the British raiding party detracted from its prestige. The exploit also caused alarm over the defenses of the Bogue, which had proved signally inadequate. Ch'i-ying forwarded to Peking the report of the fortress commanders, who complained that the barbarians had brought ladders and small boats and scaled the batteries with cunning methods. This defeat required a good deal of explanation but little from the technical point of view was offered, although the unpreparedness of the batteries was admitted. Stimulated by this event, in November 1847 Mu-chang-a and the other grand councillors gave their approval to the secret defense program of the Nanking governor-general, Li Hsing-yuan, to increase the defenses at Mao-hu which adjoined Soochow and the Whangpu. This program called for the secret installation of batteries and an increase of garrisons near Shanghai.[29] Chinese intransigence at Canton meanwhile increased, Ch'i-ying and his conciliatory policy having been discredited.

The new protagonists of 1848. In March 1848 Ch'i-ying departed for Peking, his post as imperial commissioner and governor-general being taken by Hsü Kuang-chin (*ca.* 1785–1858).[30] In the same month Sir John Davis was succeeded as plenipotentiary, superintendent of trade, and governor of Hongkong by Mr. (Samuel) George Bonham (1803–1863). These new protagonists had a great deal less in common than their predecessors.

Bonham was a youngish man, still in his forties, only recently married. His father had been captain of an East Indiaman and he himself had grown up in the environment of the Eastern trade. In 1830, while yet in his twenties, he had become resident councillor of Singapore, at a time when the Straits and the East Indies still consumed more Indian opium than did China. In 1837 he had succeeded to the governorship of the Incorporated Settlements of Prince of Wales Island, Singapore, and Malacca,[31] where British administrators had first dealt with Chinese communities. At one time "the more ambitious among them, like Mr. S. G. Bonham, devoted themselves to the study of the Chinese language and the mastery of Chinese habits and customs."[32] But in the end it was not Chinese studies which chiefly facilitated Bonham's rapid advance: "Lord Palmerston subsequently stated that Sir George's 'practical common sense' was the chief cause of his appointment to the governorship of Hong Kong."[33] After taking up his new duties he enrolled leading merchants as justices of the peace and in various other ways recognized the new commercial aristocracy of young men, among whom his own comparative youth and bonhomie made him a popular contrast to the hauteur of Davis. "From the very commencement of this administration, Hong Kong society began to take its tone from, and was henceforth held together by, the spirit that prevailed at Government House."[34] That spirit was through and through practical, cautious, and devoted to the interests of British trade.

Bonham's chief antagonist, Hsü Kuang-chin, had become a metropolitan graduate (*chin-shih*) in 1820 and a compiler in the Hanlin academy, that center of Confucian indoctrination. His rise as an administrative official had been unspectacular: he had attained taotai's rank only in 1836, about the age of 50, and became governor of Kwangtung in 1846. On the other hand, his career had included from the beginning positions of trust, as a supervising censor in the provinces as early as 1830 and as chief examiner in provincial examinations. He had served in all the ranks of higher provincial administration and in half the provinces of the empire, and from his biography he would appear to have been certainly a man of scholarship and of Confucian morality.[35]

Whatever Hsü lacked in fire was fully made up by his colleague, the new governor of Kwangtung, Yeh Ming-ch'en (1807–1859). This stubborn diehard xenophobe put his impress on the situation at Canton for a full decade, until the British eventually captured him and shipped him to Calcutta in 1858. Unlike the new governor-general, Yeh had risen rapidly. After becoming a metropolitan graduate in 1835 and a member of the Hanlin academy, Yeh had quickly climbed the rungs of prefect (1835), taotai (1839), judge (1841) and treasurer (1842). After a statutory interval of mourning (1843–46), he reached Kwangtung as provincial treasurer in 1847. He was a more vigorous man than Hsü; and became the dominant partner in the combinaton of Hsü and Yeh, when the two of them moved upward in 1848. The policy followed while he was governor at Canton (1848–52) was similar to that which he pursued as governor-general (1852–58), and the decade he spent there may be considered a single phase in China's foreign relations.[36]

The new cast of personnel was completed early in 1849 by the arrival at Canton of the new British consul, Dr. John Bowring (1792–1872), a man of great vigor and literary industry, who was a virtual embodiment of the spirit of Free Trade. Bowring was not a career official, but a versatile man of affairs. He came to China at the age of fifty-seven after an unusually varied experience in the literary and political life of England and the continent. Having shown linguistic precocity as a boy, he had developed it while clerking in a commercial house, and after setting up his own business had traveled widely and mastered most of the languages of Europe. The result was, as he confessed, that in the course of his life he "spoke with ease and fluency" French, Italian, Spanish, Portuguese, German and Dutch," had a "fair acquaintance with Danish and Swedish, . . . a book knowledge of Russian, Servian, Polish and Bohemian, . . . studied Magyar with some success, . . . learnt a little Arabic, . . . and mastered a good deal of that difficult language, Chinese."[37] This virtuosity was attested by his numerous anthologies of continental poetry translated into English, and by his receipt of honors, diplomas, or certificates from some thirty societies, representing over a dozen countries and ranging all the way from Abo University to the Sociedad Economica de Guatemala and the Hull Literary Association of the Friends of Poland.

Bowring had made his chief contribution, however, as a parliamentary radical. After meeting Jeremy Bentham in 1821, he had advanced £4,000 toward founding the *Westminster Review*, for which he often "wrote the political articles" and eventually became editor. He had later "for many years . . . lived in Bentham's house, and acted as his private secretary,"[38] and in 1843 completed the editing of Bentham's *Life and Works* in eleven volumes. In parliament in the years 1835–7 and 1841–9 he had advocated reform and Free Trade with all the idealism and ardor of his reforming generation. He had even been stigmatized by Wellington as a dangerous radical. As author of the report of Hume's committee on imports, and in his own report as British representative at the Zollverein meeting of 1838, he had shown more than ordinary ability in matters of fiscal reform.[39] Among a host of writers, scientists, and diplomats, he had known George Villiers (later Earl of Clarendon and foreign secretary) as his partner on the commercial mission of 1831 to France, and with him "maintained for many years a close intimacy." Finding himself, toward the close of a long career and after ten years in Parliament, suddenly in financial straits ("his devotion to literature prevented his concentrating his mind on business"),[40] he applied to his friend Palmerston and was commissioned consul at Canton in January 1849.

In his memoirs, published posthumously, Bowring printed a "Memorandum of a conversation with Lord Palmerston on 18th December 1848," during which, although not yet formally commissioned as consul, he had suggested that he visit the five ports in China with an eye to reforming the consular establishment where necessary. Palmerston had mildly replied that this perhaps had best be done in concurrence with his superior; but "he wished me to write him privately on . . . any . . . matters of interest." This Bowring proceeded to do. At Canton he was fascinated by Chinese civilization and energetically set about mastering the details of the trade. But he found little in common with the mercantile community and chafed at his intellectual isolation and the lack of any recognition from the Chinese authorities. His mind, however, formed strong convictions rapidly and expressed them with force and enthusiasm. He felt himself Palmerston's proconsul in China and from the first seems to have looked forward to becoming British plenipotentiary. To a young American missionary, W. A. P. Martin, Consul Bowring in 1850 "expatiated on the principles of the Peace Society. . . . Who could have imagined that this apostle of peace would be the author of the next war!"[41]

Growth of anti-foreignism. The diplomatic struggle which ensued at Canton between strong-willed officials like Bowring and Yeh has been justly celebrated and cannot be detailed here. Seen through the correspondence printed later in blue books on "Insults in China," the British consul's problems seem more grim and even dire than the consulate archives would indicate. Yet there emerges from the humdrum records of daily correspondence an underlying theme of concern over Cantonese anti-foreignism, which came to preoccupy the consular mind and produce that final frustration which precipitated the second Anglo-Chinese war. By 1849 venturesome foreigners had been stoned and even killed, insulting and inflammatory placards had heaped insult upon injury, and the tiny English community felt that its prestige was diminishing and that the danger of its position was therefore increasing. Moreover, the sale of British manufactured goods had failed to develop as expected, and to free-traders for whom commercial expansion was a natural and almost divine law, this could be explained only as a result of Chinese political interference — which again could be combatted only by asserting British superiority and maintaining the prestige so established. For this reason the question of entrance into Canton city retained its importance. Commercially it was non-essential, foreign trade centering about the factories outside the walls. But politically the city question became an unavoidable matter of face. The British could not afford to disregard it.

In August 1849, the time for foreign entrance to the city having again arrived, Bonham was obliged by the menacing attitude of the Cantonese community to accept a continued frustration. His acknowledgment to Hsü Kuang-chin that "the question must rest in abeyance," as he put it in his English draft, was interpreted by the latter as a complete capitulation. Hsü and Yeh reported to Peking that, "chief Bonham's communication in reply states that it has now been agreed that hereafter there will be no further discussion of entering the city." This seemed to be confirmed by British acquiescence. The emperor was delighted.[42]

Thus by 1850 Anglo-Chinese relations had come full circle and were again in the state of unresolved tension which Lin Tse-hsü had found at Canton in 1839. This tension shows a sharp rise from the early part of 1848, even before Ch'i-ying left Canton. Its manifestations seem too widespread to have been solely a product of Chinese policy. The Chinese official record of foreign relations for the years 1848 and 1849 becomes suddenly briefer by half. The little that is reported concerns attacks on Englishmen at Canton, Shanghai (the Tsingpu affair, March 1848), and Foochow, together with the imperial commissioner Hsü Kuang-chin's success in giving the brush-off to successive envoys of Britain, France, and the United States. The officials show increasing concern over the connivance of Chinese "traitors" with foreigners at Wusung, Canton, and Amoy; Hsü and Yeh in particular manifest real hysteria over the dangers of Chinese disloyalty and treachery from within, especially among the troops, and the eventual combination of domestic rebellion with foreign invasion.[43] Their spies in Hongkong, who read the local newspapers, tell them that the colony has been losing money and yet increasing its garrison. They order the Bogue batteries to fire only in self-defense, fearing some further British move, but adhere nevertheless to the orthodox doctrine of *chi-mi* — keeping the barbarians under control by diplomatic means (a euphemism for concessions).[44] Chinese concern is heightened by the increasing reports of foreigners in disguise penetrating such inland centers as Soochow and the tea and silk districts.[45] Thus fear of the foreigner kept pace with the onset of domestic revolt.

No official of this period inveighed more vigorously against the menace of Chinese traitors in league with barbarians than the governor of Fukien, Hsü Chi-yü. When he moved up from the post of financial commissioner in Fukien to that of governor at the beginning of 1847, he and the governor-general, Liu Yun-k'o, were still confronted with the disorders provoked at Foochow by the Cantonese element in the British opium trade (see Chapter 12 above) and similar barbarian problems; they secured the services of Lu Tse-ch'ang, the former Ningpo taotai who had taken charge on Chusan in 1844 (see above, Chapter 11).[46] By imperial decree Lu was deputed to Fukien in 1847. With British consular coöperation, he set up a system for the registration of the linguists in foreign trade so as to catch Cantonese racketeers who masqueraded as linguists or were otherwise associated with foreigners as compradores. When Lu and his posse seized such men as opium smugglers, they often asserted their reliance on the foreigners, whose wrath would protect them. But if they were not on the consul's list of linguists, the consul would keep silent and Chinese justice had free rein. Four such Cantonese freebooters were put out of business in this way.[47]

Governor Hsü's new view of the world. This contemporary background of anti-British feeling makes doubly interesting Hsü Chi-yü's famous geography of the world, *Ying-huan chih-lueh*, which was printed in 1850. The prefaces to this work, dated 1848, include one by his handy-man Lu Tse-ch'ang, another by his successor as Fukien financial commissioner, both of whom read the proofs, and another by P'eng Yun-chang (1792–1862), who was then commissioner of education in Fukien but later became a grand secretary at Peking (1856). The plates were preserved at the governor's yamen; it was a semi-official work. This "Brief description of the oceans roundabout" was destined to survive as the leading world atlas for a whole generation of Chinese literati (it was reprinted in Japan and in 1866 by the Tsungli Yamen, after its author had entered that new organ for foreign affairs).[48]

Hsü's first inspiration was derived from the American evangelist, David Abeel (1804–1846), who had first come to Canton in 1830 with the pioneer American missionary Elijah C. Bridgman. In spite of poor health he had traveled in the East Indies, Siam, Europe and America as a missionary. Returning to China in 1839, Abeel inaugurated the Dutch Reformed Church mission at Amoy, until forced by ill health to return home in 1845.[49] In his preface Governor Hsü explains how in 1843 he met at Amoy an American named *Ya-pi-li*, who could speak the Fukien dialect and who had an atlas of the world. He got Abeel to translate parts of the geography book, and the next year through a Chinese friend, Hsü obtained a more comprehensive Western work in two volumes, and also several accounts of the West written in Chinese by Westerners. The style of these tracts, he says, was decidedly vulgar and unliterary, but to him this merely proved that they were genuinely barbarian in origin, and so more reliable. "Whenever I met Westerners," he says, "I unceremoniously opened the volumes," and compared notes with what the Westerners had to say. Bit by bit, over a period of five years from 1843 to 1848, he thus compiled a general account. Abeel wrote, "He is the most inquisitive Chinese of a high rank I have yet met."

Governor Hsü's treatment of this material is critical and courageous. He points out, first, that the countries and island kingdoms of Southeast Asia, which had been tributaries of China since Han times, had now become trading centers of the Western countries. This was a cataclysmic change, and he therefore treats Southeast Asia in detail, relying on the accounts of contemporary writers and not repeating the outmoded traditional names to be found in Chinese classical works on the subject. For India he relies on British works. Ancient names he subordinates to names now in use. For the Western countries he relies upon Western books, including monthly journals — several dozen items. In cases of conflicting evidence, he chooses the source of later date.

Hsü Chi-yü also takes cogent note of the phonetic problem involved in foreign place names. Foreign countries, he says, have few words sounding alike, while Chinese speech has many words that sound the same. Using Chinese characters to represent foreign place names is therefore not easy. Moreover most foreigners have studied the Cantonese dialect, which is not the Chinese language proper and sounds quite different. Consequently Persia, for example, may be represented by characters sounding *Po-ssu, Po-hsi, Pao-she, Pa-she,* or the like, whereas it really sounds like *Po-er-she.* Hsü therefore includes the many variant transliterations he has come across — like the confusing versions for France — *Fo-lang-hsi, Fa-lan-hsi, Fo-lang-chi, Ho-lan-hsi,* etc. Westerners, he points out further, do not distinguish tones. For example, they make no distinction between *shih* 4, *shih* 2, *hsi* 1, and *su* 1: or between *t'u* 3, *tu* 1, *tu* 4, *to* 1, and *t'u* 4. Again, the transliterations of the English and the Portuguese vary widely. The English call the state of Maine, *mien.* The Portuguese call it, *mai-nei.*

It is an amazing commentary on the backwardness of Chinese studies that no serious modern student, Chinese or foreign, seems as yet to have made an over-all study of the two great geographies of Wei Yuan (1842) and Hsü Chi-yü (1848), much less a comparison of them. Even a cursory examination shows that Wei's treatment of the West in the *Hai-kuo t'u-chih* is under orthodox Chinese headings. The result is that he gives rather meaningless lists, for example, of the ancient British tribes or of the various "yamen" of the British governmental system, arranging his foreign data in a Chinese pattern.[f] Hsü, on the other hand, gives a simpler summary, with fewer transliterations, evidently following Western sources more directly. Again, the *Hai-kuo t'u-chih* of 1842 (see Chapter 11) had added little to Chinese cartography of the West, which seems to have been largely marking time since the days of Ricci and his successors in the seventeenth century. Hsü Chi-yü's work therefore opened a new era by copying directly from Western atlases,[50] which he says are much more reliable than the usual Chinese sketch maps because the men of the West

[f] Wei Yuan had arranged his 50 chapters of material by a conventional Chinese scheme in 10 major parts: *chüan* 1–2, preliminary discussion of defense, Chinese maps: 3–12, the eastern southern ocean (*tung-nan-yang*), i.e., Southeast Asia and Japan; 13–19, the western southern ocean, i.e., India and Moslem states; 20–23, the small western ocean (*hsiao-hsi-yang*), i.e., Africa; 24–35, the great western ocean, i.e., Europe; 36–37, the northern ocean, i.e., Russia; 38–42, the farther great western ocean (*wai ta-hsi-yang*), i.e., America, North and South; 43–44, tables of religions, calendars, etc; 45–48, general discussions, of maritime and geographic matters; 49–50, appendices, on barbarian source materials and foreign arms.

In comparison, Hsü Chi-yü divides his briefer work on standard Western lines in 10 *chüan*; 1–3, Asia, including the Far East, Southeast Asia, and India, etc.; 4–7, Europe, by countries; 8, Africa; 9–10, North and South America.

excel at traveling far over the four seas, mapping as they go. Using Western sources of a more purely geographic nature, his treatment is more simple and concise and omits the accumulated Chinese lore concerning maritime barbarians — it is genuinely a world atlas.

In selecting from the material available to him what was important and what was unimportant, Hsü Chi-yü naturally betrays his own evaluations. In his chapter on North America, for example, he likens its shape to that of a flying fish, and concludes that the three continents Asia, Europe, and Africa are on the face of the earth, while America is on the back of it. In the United States he likens the great central river, the *Mi-shih-shih-pi*, to the Yellow River in respect to its devastating floods, while the river *Ya-ma-sun* in South America is as big as the Yangtze. The plethora of cities obliges him to suppress from his maps all but the capitals of states, which he assumes to be dominant in their districts, like the administrative centers of Chinese provinces.

In Hsü's account of American history several pages are devoted to one person, the leader of the people, *Hua-sheng-tun* (also *Wang-hsing-teng*). Having established Washington's name, Hsü thereafter calls him *Tun*, or as we might say, Ton. Ton was asked by the local villagers to lead them, but refused and retired, Chinese fashion, until the populace in desperation rose against the British. Ton then led them, through many trials, and by his courage wore out the oppressors.

Hsü also pays great attention to the capital of the United States, which is called *Ko-lun-mi-ah* (Columbia). It is a small district south of *Ma-li-lan* and northwest of *Wu-erh-chi-ni-ah*, and the elders of the country meet there. On the west of the capital is *Ch'a-chih-tang* (Georgetown) containing an arsenal and school, and on the east is *A-li-shan-t'e-li-ah* (Alexandria) containing an arsenal and orphanage. These clumsy transliterations, in a description of the cities upon the banks of the *Po-to-mo*, may be a consolation to those who find place names in China confusing.

Not content with mere geography, Hsü briefly and accurately describes the fire-wheel-carriage, which goes 100 miles a day, burning coal; the system of elections, the banks and currency, and similar aspects of American life. It is evident that he is doing more than merely translating Western accounts but his summary has the unreal quality of things perceived only through books.

This Chinese account of the West is almost exactly contemporary with S. Wells Williams's monumental two volumes, *The Middle Kingdom*, a compendious work which describes with great detail and no little understanding all aspects of Chinese life and history, and is today still a work of primary value. Governor Hsü studied the West in China from secondhand tracts and in his leisure time over a period of five years. Wells

Williams had studied China at first hand continuously for twenty years using the Chinese language.

We should not infer that Governor Hsü, from his greater factual knowledge of the West, became pro-foreign. "Foreign mud" (opium) and the foreign religion seem both to have remained anathema to him. One of his anti-opium essays concludes that the British, who enrich their country from a drug that robs China of her strength, are a race of "dogs and sheep," ignorant of good faith or right principles, intent only on material profit.[51] In 1850 he was still repeating, at least in official writings, this phraseology of the 1830's: though relatively peaceful at the moment, he says, the barbarians have a beastly, unpredictable nature.[52] Yet on December 7, 1850, in an interview at Foochow with the Bishop of Victoria he tried to help that worthy gentleman decide upon the proper Chinese equivalent for "God" and so settle the acrimonious "term question" which had been agitating the missionary translators of the Bible.[53] In his handling of the Chinese agitation at Foochow in 1850–51 against missionaries who tried to rent a temple, Hsü Chi-yü showed sensible moderation but expressed no greater belief in toleration than did his xenophobic colleagues.[54] Whether or not he was ahead of the times in his view of the world, he considered the West and Western trade in China with evident mistrust, which was steadily intensified by the ingress of foreigners and their goods. Although dismissed from office in the general purge of 1851, he was briefly reëmployed by the new Hsien-feng Emperor before being forced into retirement. His service in the Tsungli Yamen in the years 1865–1869 was an epilogue to a career which deserves futher study.[55]

We must conclude, I think, that the increase of Sino-foreign contact in the 1840's brought increased hostility, which the treaty system could not obviate. China's foreign trade grew amazingly, but as we shall see below, less and less of it remained within a framework of law and order. Neither the old Chinese way nor the new British way was now dominant. Inland on the tea routes, along the China coast, and in the treaty ports themselves, the influence of the West became ever stronger as foreign trade expanded and the stirrings of domestic rebellion became more violent. But this growth was a victory neither for free trade nor for the rule of Anglo-Saxon law. By 1850 the treaties stood on shaky ground. Their major tenets were challenged and some of their major provisions inoperative.

CHAPTER XVI

GROWTH AND TAXATION OF THE LEGAL TRADE

SINCE THE TREATY PORTS with their consuls, missionaries, and merchants had all become established on the coast of China in the wake of the China trade, it is time that we examine briefly some of the economic factors which lay behind the commercial growth and frustrations of the 1840's and early 1850's. In general, historians have thus far given us a foreshortened view of the old Canton trade, out of perspective because not seen in its Chinese economic context. Canton, the hong merchants, and the East India Company provided merely the point of contact between the enormous domestic commerce of China and the diffused international trade of South and East Asia. Mainly because of the preservation of the Company's records (as well as Dr. H. B. Morse's masterly summary of them in five volumes as *The Chronicles of the East India Company trading to China 1635–1834*,[1] the commercial activity at Canton has been known and studied while the more complex trade of the Chinese interior remains still shadowy. As we have already noted in the case of opium (Chapter 13), the foreigner's wares entered China before him and were distributed in native channels long before the opening of treaty ports. The governor of Kiangsu in 1843 described how the big Kiangsu trading junks (*sha-ch'uan*) regularly took colored cotton cloth (*hua-pu*) to Shantung and Kwantung (i.e., Manchuria) markets, to exchange for soy beans. Foreign cloth ("calico," "shirtings," "piece goods"), woolens, and camlets had all entered this trade via the emporium of Soochow, west of Shanghai. The treaties gave the British merchant his chance both to accumulate trading capital in Hongkong and to press more Western goods into these established channels of distribution, with a resulting cycle of boom and bust in the market.[2]

Political circumstances created two periods of expansion in the China trade, before and after the Opium War, respectively. The opening of free trade in 1834 had been followed by a first rush of British manufactured goods to China and a glutting of the market, which was limited by China's small capacity to pay for foreign imports. Opium imports, however, as noted in Chapter 5, grew so rapidly during this period that they exceeded the legal imports of cotton piece goods and woolens, and equalled in value the tea and silk exports. In order to balance the total trade, including the import of legal goods, treasure had to leave China.

After the opening of the new ports in 1843, a second rush of British goods into China almost doubled the import trade. The slowing down of legal trade during the war had created a backlog of demand that inspired a trade boom after the inauguration of the treaty system. In August 1843, Pottinger had received glowing reports from Chusan, where the harbor was full of ships, and where foreign sales of Straits produce, English cotton manufactures, and opium were estimated to be taking in $600,000 a month.[3] At Canton in January 1844, Consul Lay reported an enormous demand for English goods — long ells sold out, camlets bringing good prices, and the desire for British goods steadily increasing.[4] Other reports corroborated this. The Canton market was so strong that British cargoes were sold sight unseen even before their arrival at Hongkong. Vessels consigned to other ports were held back and discharged their cargoes into small craft for delivery to Canton. Some suspected that this betokened a Cantonese effort to keep trade from developing elsewhere. Yet merchantmen at Chusan were also swept clean of cargo and Chinese junks from the mainland were forced to go away unsatisfied. Merchants admitted their error in thinking that the market might be overstocked by excessive speculation.[5]

By the beginning of 1845, however, the Canton market had become definitely overstocked, the trade of the port was declining, and imported goods were being shipped out for sale at Shanghai. Prices for British manufactures dropped and imports in 1845 were valued at only two-thirds of the total of 1844 — in fact, the trade of Canton in the four years after 1844 never equalled that season of hope.[6] In view of the stagnation of legal trade, the British government felt obliged to add to the gloom of the treaty port community by retrenching at the consulates and placing the offices at Ningpo, Foochow, and Amoy under vice-consuls who received half the salaries of the former consuls.

In order to improve the Chinese market for British imports, a special committee of the House of Commons in 1847 urged that tea consumption in the West be increased so as to increase China's purchasing power. They urged a reduction of the profitable British tea duties of about 200 per cent; for the Western tea consumption of 72 million pounds, as estimated in 1847, was concentrated in the United Kingdom, where 45 million pounds of tea paid £5,000,000 in revenue. (Indian tea shipments to England by 1851 had reached only 250,000 pounds.)

Since the Chinese demand for Western goods continued to be limited, British imports in 1850 showed little increase over 1843, and were even less in 1854. The difficulty was that these imports were largely Lancashire textiles placed in direct competition with the old-style Chinese textile production, and Lancashire long cloths did not compete successfully with nankeens. After the rapid growth of tea and silk exports in the 1850's had eventually outstripped the growth of the opium trade, so that the flow of silver again became favorable to China, silver shipments from India and the Straits were still preferred in China over the British textiles which might have taken their place. For example, at Shanghai in 1857 exports including Chinese tea and silk valued at about £10,000,000 were paid for by importing legal goods worth £3,000,000, treasure worth £4,500,000, and finally opium worth £4,500,000. The limiting factor in legal imports was again the lack of Chinese demand for British textiles.[7] The growth of China's exports had served only to expand the Anglo-Indian opium trade.

Domestic trade and capital. China's tardiness in buying British textiles testified to the strength of the native cotton industry, which the British had failed to recognize. Cotton had been grown and used in China for at least five hundred years before the nineteenth century. The plant grows best in the central river basins of the Yangtze, the Hwai, and the Yellow Rivers, rather than in the damp Southeast or the dry Northwest. Since rainfall in North China is variable, the best growing region is in Central China between Hangchow on the east and the Tungting Lake on the west. Because of China's early experience in cottage silk culture, cotton production had been fitted easily into the relatively self-sufficient farm economy. After an early spread under the Yuan dynasty in the thirteenth century, cotton production received vigorous official encouragement from the first Ming emperors.[8] "These energetic measures made China one of the great cotton growing areas of the world by the fifteenth century."[9] The Ming army alone required something like five or six million bolts of cloth and two or three million catties of cotton wadding a year, much of which was secured in the form of a cotton tax on the surplus production of the countryside.[10] Government commutation of land tax quotas from grain to cotton cloth had the effect of forcing wider cultivation of cotton. Thus by the time Western trade began, the Chinese farmer was traditionally accustomed to meeting his needs for cotton cloth with his own simple but effective methods and machinery. Foreign trade, indeed, had at first called forth an export of Chinese nankeens and calicoes to meet the European demand. This export reached a height of over 300,000 bolts in 1819. Not until 1830 did China's imports of cotton goods begin to exceed her exports.[11]

So well established were the Chinese cotton spinning and weaving industries in this period that they created a steady demand for raw cotton imports. Raw cotton from Bombay had been one of the few articles of Indian produce for which a market could be found in China in the late eighteenth century before the rise of the opium trade.[12] This Indian cotton was used in the native Chinese production of nankeen cloth for domestic consumption, and continued to be a major item of import from India to China until 1864, when the Civil War obliged England to monopolize Indian cotton supplies in place of American. During the 1830's and 1840's Indian raw cotton imports totalled annually as much as half the value of the Indian opium imports, amounting to about one-third of the country trade.[13]

British observers found in 1845 that cotton was "the staple summer production of the country" around Shanghai. It was harvested in August, September, and October, and the crop partly sold to merchants and partly used on the farmer's own spinning-wheel and small hand-loom.[14] Further research on the Chinese economy of a century ago should make it plain that the lack of demand for British textiles reflected the low purchasing power which accompanied a self-sufficient and "unmonetary" economy: cotton cloth could be produced in a subsidiary rural industry, using the surplus labor power of the farm household; it could not be purchased.

British officials of the 1840's were also aware that the enormous growth of the tea trade had created a great vested interest at Canton. But they were unable to trace clearly the pervasive influence within China of this "Canton interest" which represented the first big accumulation of modern Chinese commercial capital.[a] Historians have had little better success, since the records of domestic commerce are more diffuse and scattered than those concerning the treaty ports and the coast. The first British consul at Amoy, for example, found that local Chinese trade appeared to be carried on by brokers from the larger center of Chang-chou. Easy inland water transport between Canton and Chang-chou meant that the latter place was supplied in large part from Canton. It appeared also that the merchants of Amoy and nearby places obtained credit from the wealthier merchants of Canton, who never charged more than 1 per cent a month but were able to maintain partners on the coast so as to keep a lien on goods or otherwise represent their interest until their loans were repaid.[15] This gives us a brief insight into the practices by which Chinese capital, formerly concentrated at Canton, was now diffused to Amoy and Shanghai. Pending further monographic research, we can only highlight a few of the major elements in the picture: the steady increase in volume of tea and silk exports, the position of tea and silk production in the farm economy, the transport routes and commercial methods by which these crops were exported, the vested interests which grew up as a result.

Tea exports in the early 1830's had been over 50 million pounds a year. After the opening of Shanghai in 1843 they at once reached 70 million pounds and for the next six years were between 76 and 84 million pounds annually. In 1851 they reached a new peak of 99 million pounds, and

[a] The Jardine, Matheson archives indicate how the Canton shopmen, under hong merchant protection, put capital illegally into the staple trade in silks and teas. The private foreign traders fostered this business with merchants "outside" the Cohong. "In 1817 over 200 'outside' shops were closed down and their goods confiscated," but their operations continued to develop (Greenberg, *British Trade*, 53–57).

climbed to 130 million in 1856 after the sudden commencement of the tea trade at Foochow. Exports through Shanghai eclipsed those through Canton only in 1852, as an obvious consequence of the Rebellion. Meanwhile silk exports had been about 12,000 bales a year in the middle thirties and did not exceed this figure until 1845, after which they rose to about 20,000 bales in the late 1840's, spurted suddenly to 32,000 in 1852 and 63,000 in 1853, and rose even higher in the late 1850's.[16] This silk was shipped almost entirely from Shanghai.

The striking fact here is that tea continued to leave Canton in larger amounts than Shanghai for a full decade after the opening of the new ports — certainly a *prima facie* evidence of the persistence of old commercial channels. This was in spite of the fact that the tea trade roughly doubled in volume in the decade after the treaties. Chinese silk exports meanwhile increased at least five times over. The economic significance of these increases can be appreciated when we consider the enormous investment of farm labor which they represented and the place they must have occupied in the livelihood of South China.

The silk and tea industries. Silk culture is a handicraft industry dependent on large seasonal applications of manpower such as the Chinese farm economy can provide. Aside from the yellow silk production of Szechwan, some white silk from the Canton delta, and scattered production in other provinces, China's main center of this industry had for long been the region of south Kiangsu and northern Chekiang, within a radius, as it happened, of about 150 miles inland from Shanghai.

A Chinese manual available in the 1840's gives minute instructions as to the cultivation, transplanting, grafting and clipping of mulberry trees, and as to the rearing and care of silk worms. Since the worms belong to the *yang* rather than the *yin* side of nature, they love fire and hate water, eat without drinking, and require warmth without dampness. They abhor smoke, vinegar, musk, loud noises, and pregnant women. Silk culture involves these stages: washing the eggs left from last year's cocoons, drying and wrapping them, and waiting for the grubs to hatch out; removing the newly hatched grubs from the egg cards and spreading them out over shredded mulberry leaves; and feeding them fine-cut leaves five or six times every twenty-four hours while maintaining an equable temperature in spite of hot or cold weather, so that the worms will have neither constipation nor diarrhea but retain healthy young appetites. When the worms fall into a torpor, revive, and resume eating, their excrement must be carefully removed every day. After three or four periods of torpor, they become mature and are put upon prepared receptacles where they can spin their cocoons — "should the weather be cold or rainy, place a fire under the frame and heat them well." This Chinese handbook then offers instruction on how to select male and female seed moths, arrange their propagation, collect the eggs and preserve them. There follow twelve rules for winding the silk off the cocoons, twelve more rules on how to run a silk farm, and descriptions of 32 tools and appliances used in the process.[17] It is ultra-important that a generation of worms be kept together in their life cycle (with a minimum of individualism), while the unfit are constantly weeded out. One can imagine that a series of three crops a year, each requiring daily if not hourly care for about five weeks at a stretch, keeps a family busy. One estimate [18] is that a crop of 700,000 worms weighs about one pound at birth but after eating steadily and shedding their skins four times they will weigh at maturity nearly five tons — an almost explosive phenomenon. By this time they will have actually eaten twelve tons of mulberry leaves and will eventually produce "between 116 and 175 pounds of raw silk." [b]

A similar application of man power was required by the tea industry. Contrary to Western belief in the early nineteenth century, the black teas of Fukien and the green teas of Chekiang were produced from the same bush; black teas were blacker because they were more extensively fermented and oxidized in the course of their preparation. In general the finest teas, black or green, were produced from the earliest spring leaves and by more careful heating, rolling, and sifting processes. The coarsest grade of black tea was Bohea (*wu-i*), named for the famous Wu-i hills of Fukien, where the tea leaves were gathered generally three times a season, from mid-April to the end of September. Tea leaves were picked and extensively processed by hand, being first heated ("tatched") in a shallow iron pan for five minutes, then rubbed and rolled by hand to make each leaf curl, then heated for an hour or so, and finally picked over by hand and sorted. Any but the coarsest tea, however, required a good deal more attention than this. In ascending order among black teas, Congo or Congou (*kung-fu*, i.e., requiring care or labor) was a superior kind of Bohea, of larger leaf; Souchong (*hsiao-chung*, "small sort") was made of the first and youngest leaves of selected bushes, the leaves being whole, fine, and curly; and Pekoe (*pai-hao*, "white down") was the finest of all and very scarce, consisting mainly of young spring-buds gathered just after blooming. There was a similar progression from coarse to fine among the green teas: Twankay (*t'un-ch'i*), named for T'un-ch'i chen, a center of green tea production southwest of Hui-chou on the Chekiang border of Anhwei, was

[b] The collapse of China's silk exports in the last years of the Taiping Rebellion is variously attributed to the destruction of the mulberry trees in the main producing area, which was fought over in the years 1860–64, and to the loss of man power in the countryside necessary to maintain the industry.[19] As a result, while China produced over half the world's silk in 1854, she was producing only one-twelfth of it a decade later and her export trade gradually succumbed to the competition of Japan and Italy.

"the Bohea of green teas," produced in the largest volume and with the least care. The various kinds of Hyson (*hsi-ch'un*, "blooming spring") were proportionately finer, Gunpowder being a superior grade.

The incredible amount of hand labor required for tea production can hardly be imagined by modern Westerners. To make the finest green tea, for example, the tender leaves were first carefully picked, then tatched over the fire, rubbed by hand to roll them, spread out to divide them, tatched very dry, spread on tables to be picked over (a quick girl could pick five pounds a day), then tatched in the pan again, tossed in flat baskets to eliminate dust, spread out, picked and tatched a fourth time, collected in parcels and tatched again, stored in baskets, and finally tatched a last time before being packed in chests or tubs, into which they must be shaken and pressed by hand.[20]

The non-opening of Foochow. The Bohea (Wu-i) tea-producing district, famous since Sung times, is a region of valley farming with rice terraces on the slopes of the hills. There is a good amount of local timber production in the Fukien mountains, and the region is served by three streams tributary to the Min River, some of the waters of which originate in Kiangsi. These streams provide small-boat transportation[21] directly down the Min to Foochow, the natural outlet for the whole region.[c]

It appears that tea exports through Foochow were prohibited by the Chinese government for a decade after the nominal opening of the port in 1844. From the Wu-i hills in northern Fukien, about 150 miles up the Min, the British learned that "a cargo of tea may be brought in boats in four days down the stream to Foochow; while the expensive route . . . of more than 600 miles to Canton . . . occupies almost as many weeks."[24] In 1845 the British consul was assured of "the anxious desire of the tea growers to obtain a market here in preference to Canton."[25] From every practical point of view, Foochow was the logical outlet for Bohea teas. But it appears that the vested interests of Canton prevented its being used. Pottinger at Nanking had sensed the existence of a "scheme of the 'clique' connected with Canton to force us to continue to carry on the Black Tea Trade at that port,"[26] and this supposition receives some tacit support from the Chinese documents.

In 1842, as noted in Chapter 6 above, imperial consent to the opening of

[c] The eclipse of the Fukien tea export trade has been even more spectacular than its rise in the 1850's. Until 1860 Chinese tea exports to the United States, for instance, supplied 96 per cent of the American consumption, while the nascent exports from India and Japan provided only 3 and 1 per cent, respectively. Chinese exports steadily lost this position, however, in 1870 providing 67 per cent, in 1880, 44, and in 1901, 26.5 per cent. By 1907 Chinese tea sales in the United States had dropped to third place with only 12.5 per cent of the total.[22] A similar shift occurred in the large English market. A survey of the Wu-i hills recently conducted by the Nanking government and the Fukien provincial government found large areas of the earlier tea plantations gone to waste because of the effects of warfare in recent years; their resuscitation was proposed through plant and water control.[23]

Foochow had not been granted before the signing of the treaty of Nanking. The emperor's argument against it (expressed on August 17, 1842) had been specious and unconvincing: Foochow "is connected with the interior by a land road and the mountain paths are crowded and confused; traveling merchants will not find it convenient, and inasmuch as the province of Fukien has Amoy as a trading mart, they need not also seek Foochow." [27] The inclusion of Foochow among the treaty ports was finally sanctioned on August 31, two days after the treaty had been signed. This *fait accompli* of the treaty was accepted by the emperor without enthusiasm.[28] Among the new ports, Foochow was the only provincial capital, and its scholar-official class reacted vigorously against the prospect of their city becoming another Amoy or Shanghai.[29]

The imperial negotiators had explained their disobedience in a long memorial received on Sept. 6, 1842. They argued that Foochow was near the main depot for Bohea teas, possessed a maritime customhouse, and had long been used for trade with the Liu-ch'iu Islands; it was, after all, a port like Canton, on the far southeastern seacoast. Borrowing the strategy which the British had just used at Nanking, they pointed out that if Foochow were refused, Tientsin would be demanded as an alternative. The barbarians already had been pacified, and it did not seem worth it "to insist stubbornly on one point, with the result of impeding a general settlement." Ch'i-ying and his colleagues were therefore pardoned [30] for having opened Foochow by treaty, but it is a matter of record that practically no tea was exported through Foochow for twelve years thereafter.

During that time some foreigners attributed the stagnation of trade at Foochow to the absorption of local capital by opium sales, others to the supposed conservatism of Chinese business practice. For 1848 the consul reported no British or other foreign (legal) trade at Foochow whatever. In the first half of 1849 the only foreign imports were some woolens and cottons transshipped from Amoy in a Portuguese lorcha in charge of a "Chinaman." In June a British merchant finally arrived from Canton, Mr. Charles S. Compton, who found to his surprise that tea prices at Foochow were higher than at Canton. The consul could account for this only by assuming that 1) the local merchants were ignorant and did not stock the Canton types of tea, or 2) they deceived Compton for their own mysterious purposes, or 3) they deceived him at the behest of the local authorities. In 1853, however, the British vice-consul reported that a letter from the provincial treasurer of Fukien had urged his superiors to ask the emperor for "the temporary suspension of the prohibition to export tea by the way of Foochow. From the words used it is plain that neither natives nor foreigners had been before at liberty to do so." In confirmation of this, a memorial of the Fukien governor-general and governor which appeared in the *Peking Gazette* under date of May 25, 1856, stated that "ever since the proposition to remove the restrictions on the export of tea was submitted to the Throne, some years since, the merchants of Kwangtung have been one and all bringing funds to Foochow."[31] The previous existence of such a prohibition was also confirmed by H. N. Lay in 1857.[d]

Deprived of the tea trade, Foochow in the late 1840's became like Ningpo a center for opium, missionaries, and little else. Three English merchants attempted to open a legitimate trade and failed. One of them remained only by trading in contraband. The captains of the opium receiving ships hired houses on Nantai, their vessels remaining outside port limits. Four years after the opening of the port there were four American missionaries living on Nantai, plus a Spaniard who had built a chapel outside the city gate. The British consular staff comprised all the rest of the foreign population.[33]

Exploration of the tea and silk routes. The mysterious stagnation of foreign trade at Foochow was only one facet of the great *terra incognita* of the Chinese interior. Newly lodged on the periphery of China, the British consuls took pains to learn the geography of the Chinese market. They were told that the teas of northern Fukien were shipped out mainly by boat, on a route that went circuitously north, west, and then far south to reach Canton or else east to reach Shanghai. Specifically, according to consular accounts, the city of Ch'ung-an (Tsungan) on the headwaters of the Min close to the southern border of Kiangsi served as the starting point, whence the tea route led northward into the watershed of the Poyang Lake, to Yuan-shan in northeastern Kiangsi, and thence downstream to Ho-k'ou on the Kuang-hsin River. Ho-k'ou was the point of departure for either Canton or Shanghai. To Canton the route lay southwestward through Kiangsi so as to pass through the Kan customhouse at the headwaters of the Kan River. (The latter flows through the center of Kiangsi from south to north as the backbone of the province.) From the Kan customs the route crossed the famous Mei-ling Pass to the headwaters of the North River flowing to Canton. This pass was about one thousand feet high, with a portage of only 24 miles separating the water communication system of the south from that of the Yangtze valley.

From Ho-k'ou the tea route to Shanghai went northeastward through the city of Yü-shan (Yuh-shan) over the hills into Chekiang, toward the

[d] Lay reported: "Ever since the opening of the Five Ports this foreign trade at Foochow has been secretly interdicted by the Peking government, it being its policy to restrict our intercourse as much as possible to Canton. Our admission to Foochow at all was obtained from the Emperor with great difficulty, as can be proved from the *Peking Gazettes* of the period (1840–41). Greater facilities of trade were allowed at Shanghai, as I learned from a Chinese official of high standing, in the fear that we might otherwise be seeking it at ports farther north. The same policy and possibly its financial difficulties induced the Government to open Foochow when rebellion affected the trade elsewhere." [32]

headwaters of the Ch'ien-t'ang River which empties into Hangchow Bay. Like the Kan River in Kiangsi, the Ch'ien-t'ang forms the backbone of the northwest half of Chekiang and provides a trade route of major importance. Fukien teas going northward for the Manchurian or Russian markets also used this route. These were the channels to which Britain sought access.

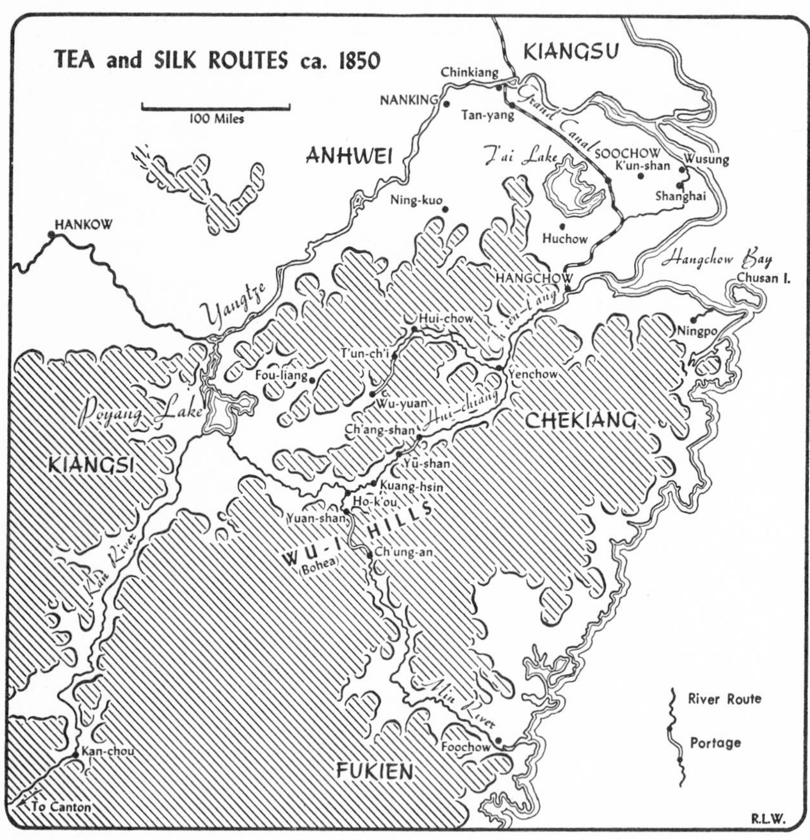

Leadership in the active exploration of the interior was taken by missionaries like W. H. Medhurst, who donned Chinese dress and spent seven weeks traveling inland from Shanghai through "the silk and green tea districts" in the spring of 1845.[34] His careful record describes the dress, diet, accommodations and modes of travel by land and water in that period. Medhurst went fully disguised, in defiance of "existing political regulations . . . yet in dependence on the divine guidance," and also on a

Chinese guide interested in Christianity. Their aim was to visit certain Chinese "reformers" who were curious about barbarian philosophy and lived in the hills of Fou-liang hsien (near Ching-te chen) in northern Kiangsi. En route they proceeded by canal boat from Shanghai, Medhurst wearing a false queue and lying hidden. They proceeded from Kiangsu into Chekiang and reached Huchow on the T'ai Lake. From the west of Huchow they proceeded on foot with coolies carrying their baggage and slept in the dirty crowded inns along the way. Medhurst wore dark glasses but was in constant danger of detection as a barbarian, especially when he talked Malay in his sleep. Nevertheless he made copious diary notes on the bustling life about him. Like a true foreigner he counted his paces while walking around the walls of Ning-kuo hsien, and collected geological and sociological data and statistics on commerce and finance. They traveled by chair from Ning-kuo, Anhwei, through Hui-chou to the tea emporium of T'un-ch'i. Though an unwalled town, it had "at least 100,000 inhabitants, among whom are the most extensive tea dealers." Their exports were sent either by water via Hui-chou to Shanghai or by land westward over the hills to Wu-yuan and thence south to Canton. Medhurst found that "700 or 800 chops [brands] of tea" were sent out every year in this manner and that T'un-ch'i merchants had an accurate knowledge of business conditions in Shanghai.[35] Having crossed the hills to Wu-yuan, Anhwei, some 240 *li* southwest of Hangchow, they entered Kiangsi and reached their Chinese hosts near Fou-liang. The missionary found them admirably intent "to carry out the system of Confucius in its genuineness, free from that atheistic gloss which the commentators of the Sung dynasty have put upon it."[e]

The most spectacular job of exploration was done by the pioneer botanist, Robert Fortune (1812–1880), who made four trips to China in the years 1843–46, 1848–51, 1853–56, and 1861–62, each time writing voluminously on his travels and observations. He produced half a dozen books, sent thousands of tea plants and several Chinese tea-growers to the East India Company's plantations in the foothills of the Himalayas, and introduced some 190 varieties of plants into England — one of the few Western scientists who took full advantage of the opening of China.

By 1848 the novelty of foreign contact had worn off somewhat, and

[e] Wrote Medhurst: "Some of their observations and sentiments regarding self-examination, victory over evil desires, constant vigilance, searching after their own errors, and ingenuous confession of them when ascertained, were tolerably good, and would not have disgraced a Christian moralist. But while they had some sense of sin, they had of course no idea of an atonement, and were utterly in the dark as to the manner in which their sins could be pardoned, or the Divine Being reconciled. Their prevailing errors appeared to be, too great a veneration for the sages, whom they actually idolized, and in many instances put upon a level with the Author of wisdom; as well as too high an estimation of their deceased parents and ancestors, to whom they paid divine honors, and from whom they expected protection and every blessing." [36]

Fortune was able to visit the Hui-chou green tea district of Chekiang, dressed as a Chinese but known to his boatmen and other travelers as a genuine "foreign devil." From Hangchow he went up the Ch'ien-t'ang River and its tributary, the Hui-chiang, all the way to the emporium at T'un-ch'i, "a thriving, busy town" about 20 miles from Hui-chou of which it was the port. "All the large Hang-chow and Yen-chow boats are moored and loaded here. . . . Nearly all the green teas which are sent down the river to Hang-chow-foo and then onward to Shanghae, are shipped at this place. The green teas destined for Canton are carried across a range of hills to the westward, where there is a river which flows in the direction of the Poyang lake." The population of T'un-ch'i was reported to Fortune as 150,000, mainly "supported by the foreign tea trade" and including both the large tea dealers who bought up teas, refined and sorted them and made up chops for shipment, and the carpenters who made the tea chests.

The size and growth of the new Fukien-Shanghai tea export was vividly confirmed by Fortune's journey of 1849 from Ningpo to the Wu-i hills and back. With one servant and wearing "a glossy black tail, which had been grafted on my own hair, and . . . hung gracefully down nearly to my heels," this Englishman passed for an oriental from "somewhere beyond the Great Wall." He again ascended the Ch'ien-t'ang by boat to Yenchow but from there took the southern tributary, instead of the Hui-chiang to the west, and passed through Lan-ch'i, Lung-yu, and Ch'ü-chou, to the head of navigation at Ch'ang-shan. The river became narrow, shallow, and rapid but continued to form the main highway. Fortune found Ch'ang-shan to be a tea transport center "full of hongs, inns, tea-shops, and warehouses."

Thence he set out by chair southwestward on a road "well paved with granite, about twelve feet in width, and perfectly free from weeds," on which he met long trains of coolies carrying teas to Ch'ang-shan or returning with loads of raw cotton, cotton goods, lead, and other articles of coastal or foreign origin. This portage brought him to another head of navigation at Yü-shan across the border in Kiangsi, whence he again embarked on a river boat to Kuang-hsin (Shang-jao) and Ho-k'ou, "one of the most important inland towns in the empire . . . the great emporium of the black tea trade. Merchants from all parts of China come here, either to buy teas, or to get them conveyed to other parts of the country." There were large inns, tea-hongs, and warehouses everywhere in the town. The river boats included large passage-boats for the public, mandarin boats gaily decorated with flags, and large cargo-boats for tea shipments either eastward to Yü-shan and Shanghai or westward to the Poyang Lake and Canton.

To reach this division point at Ho-k'ou the Fukien teas were brought down a mountain stream in small boats from Yuan-shan, Kiangsi. Here

Fortune found himself again on "the great tea highway," a paved mountain road crowded with coolie trains which led over the divide from Kiangsi south into Fukien. Chests of the finer teas on this route were carried on bamboo frames on the coolies' shoulders and never allowed to touch the ground lest they be damaged. After crossing the mountains by chair this forty-niner of the tea trade at last reached his objective, at Ch'ung-an, the chief collecting and packing center in the Wu-i hills, at the head of the forbidden navigation to Foochow.

Robert Fortune's careful account of Chinese inns and their meals, coolies and their altercations, and the natural beauties and human dangers of the open road include several significant economic observations:

1) At Ch'ung-an he found Cantonese merchants in great numbers, "as they carry on a large trade with foreigners both at Canton and Shanghae." At one inn he feared detection by a Cantonese merchant whom he had "frequently seen at Shanghae."

2) On the northern slope of the Wu-i mountains, the side closer to Shanghai, he found that "many of the tea-farms had been but lately formed, and the cultivation of the shrub in this district is evidently on the increase . . . apparently the greater part of this land had been cleared and planted within the last few years."

3) He met several opium addicts and found that opium was kept in all the inns for sale to the guests, "just as a London innkeeper retails tobacco." Thus drug distribution followed the main routes of the tea export trade.

4) The capitalism necessary in tea marketing was obvious: tea production was a cottage industry. "No single farm which came under my observation could have produced a chop of 600 chests." Actually a tea merchant would buy up small quantities of tea from "all the small towns, villages, and temples in the district," and mix them together to make a chop of 620 or 630 chests, all of uniform quality. The chop (brand name) was affixed last, to facilitate sale, and the merchant then had to finance its transportation to the coast.[37]

Another glimpse of these tea middlemen can be obtained from the Canton end of the trade. Traditionally the hong merchants at Canton had dominated the local scene, including the shop-merchants (who at first had supplied only the daily necessities of the foreign community), the compradores (who until 1842 had been merely licensed agents engaged in purchasing the foreigner's daily supplies), and the linguists (who at first had learned Portuguese and only gradually added some English to their patois of pidgin). To control all these people and their functions, the responsible Chinese authorities required that the hong merchants guarantee the linguists, the linguists the compradores, and the compradores the servants and workmen, all in an interlocking hierarchy. But the contact between this tightly knit community and the chief tea and silk producing areas south of the Yangtze was supplied by another class of traveling merchants or middlemen (*k'o-shang*), who handled the bringing of goods from the interior. These included merchants from Anhwei, Chekiang, Fukien and other provinces, even some from Shansi, who operated large transport enterprises on the routes from the lower Yangtze to Canton. Their main route had been through Kiangsi to Kan-chou and thence over the Mei-ling Pass to Canton.[38] Over this same route in the reverse direction there had flowed a smaller volume of British imported goods. We may guess that the men Robert Fortune met on the "tea highway" of northern Fukien included not only agents of Cantonese merchants but also independent operators. As the Canton consul reported for 1845, Cantonese firms had been "grievously disappointed at the paucity of orders and the non-appearance of many of their friends from the north, who had hitherto made their purchases in the Canton market." [39]

When these independent middlemen brought their wares to Shanghai they found a freer market than at Canton. Barter deals quickly concluded on the spot could often substitute for big capital investments. As Consul Thom explained it, the treaty port trade at Shanghai was conducted on the fiction that it was a cash trade, although actually it was a barter trade. It was like the pre-treaty trade at Canton where the foreign merchant had seldom known the real market prices but had traded foreign goods and silver for teas and silks. By barter the British merchant selling imports at Shanghai would get a higher *nominal* price than if he had sold his goods for cash at the local market price of the day. This was possible because the tea and silk merchants would add an equivalent or greater sum to their export prices, thus recouping themselves. Consequently, when the English sales agent sent home his account, an increase of 5 cents a yard in the sales price of woolens would please the eye of the exporter in London or Liverpool, and meanwhile the importer in England would not be displeased by an increased purchase price of $10 or $20 per picul of silk, providing such an increase were consistently maintained. On the Chinese side, the silk or tea merchant who received foreign funds would send them inland for further purchases. But if he got goods by barter, instead of funds, and sent them to Soochow for sale and distribution — having in his barter arrangement charged a good deal more than the current Chinese market price — he could afford to pay the costs of inland transport and still make a profit. As a result, foreign goods imported through Shanghai could appear on the Ningpo market in Chinese hands and sell for less than the foreign importer must ask, if he brought them in himself directly from England.[40]

In effect, in order to gain a nominally better price for himself, and so a bigger commission as a sales agent, the British merchant really gave the

Chinese teaman a better bargain — this was a division of form and substance pleasing to both parties, which also tended in a mild way to equalize standards of living in England and China more rapidly than cash sales in a competitive market would have done. This manner of barter trade made British conceptions of free trade and moderate taxation difficult to apply.

"Transit taxes" from the Chinese side. British exploration of the interior in the late 1840's only confirmed the suspicions of the first consuls, that the vested interests of the Canton trade and of Chinese officialdom along the trade routes inhibited the free expansion of commerce to which Britain was dedicated. This suspicion became focussed on the twin questions of transit duties, which had been left unsettled by Pottinger and Ch'i-ying (see Chapter 8), and trade monopolies, which were the alternative method of Chinese taxation.

Without immersing ourselves in the intricate variety of Ch'ing taxes on trade, let us distinguish between a) the regular customs transit duties levied at inland (as well as maritime) customs stations (as totalled in Table 8 on p. 256) and b) the likin tax, which grew up after 1853 as a local tax on the transit of goods, collected under provincial auspices. Later in the century likin in its many forms would produce some fifteen million taels a year for the provinces, which may be compared with a total revenue, before the period of likin, of some forty million taels a year recorded as imperial income in Peking. Students of the origin of likin point out that under the Ch'ing, as under the Sung and Ming in their early periods, the taxation of trade had been rather light, but increased as financial difficulties multiplied toward the end of the dynasty.[41] The eventual rise of likin fits such a pattern. But although various proposals to tax the merchants' goods, capital, and transactions began to be made as early as 1843, no active policy seems to have been initiated before the outbreak of the Rebellion. We are here concerned, therefore, only with the regular customs transit duties (briefly noted above in Chapter 8).

However, it must be confessed that the Ch'ing fiscal records included such a variety of different charges that it will require further monographic research to unscramble them. Within the general category of customs collections on goods passing fixed points, which were known to the British generically as "transit duties," there were various taxes on commercial transactions and on the types of goods sold, as well as taxes on boats and goods passing the numerous barriers and sub-stations of the customs collectorates. Pending the unscrambling of the terminology by such scholars as Professor Yang Lien-sheng,[42] we may conclude that the British faced a hydra-headed fiscal monster — British goods carried into the domestic market by Chinese merchants would be subject to various and multiform "transit taxes," to which would be added the far greater levies exacted as squeeze by the mob of parasitic tax-gatherers at each station. To illustrate this latter evil, when the modern Chinese Maritime Customs through a foreign commissioner took over the Kiukiang "native" customs in 1913 it was found possible to reduce the staff from 249 to 89. The sums of squeeze by which staff members had customarily paid for the privilege of fleecing the boatmen and merchants are instructive: the eight treasurers had each paid the taotai and his staff Tls. 10,000 on assuming office for a limited number of years; the chief assayer paid Tls. 10,000, the chief raft-measurer Tls. 7,000, a duty-calculator Tls. 3,000, a chief examiner Tls. 1,000, and so on. The official salaries of such functionaries — a few taels a month —[43] were purely nominal. Similarly the tax rates listed by tariff were inconsiderable, compared to the unofficial exactions, fees, charges, "presents" and other forms of squeeze. Both types of charges were a normal part of Ch'ing fiscal practice and not aimed especially at excluding foreign imports. Indeed, as we have noted, the distinction between "maritime customs duties" collected at the ports and "inland transit taxes" levied along the trade routes of the interior was more distinct in the British mind than in the Chinese. This made it all the more difficult for British consuls to object to the intricate, impalpable and organized irregularities of the Chinese transit duty system.

Unknown to the British (see Chapter 8), the question of transit duties had been dealt with at Peking in August 1843. Mu-chang-a and the rest of the Grand Council sought to make up for the customs transit duties that would be lost when trade went to the new treaty ports instead of over the long old road to Canton. On this point Ch'i-ying and his colleagues had argued that the transit duty revenue quotas on tea and rhubarb need not be protected against loss because the export duties had been raised; but on raw silk they noted that the export duty had been lowered,[44] and therefore Chinese merchants carrying raw silk to the new treaty ports, in proportion as they passed through fewer taxing stations than they would have passed en route to Canton, should pay more duty. They also believed that collections at the inland customs stations had been falling off because heavy unofficial exactions there had stimulated shipments by sea. To ensure the revenue quotas of these inland stations, it was proposed and agreed that teas, raw silk, and silk goods should not be allowed to be transported by sea, unless they paid export duties according to the new treaty tariff (instead of by the old "native" tariff of the regular customs stations). Finally, it was proposed and agreed that except for teas, raw silk, and silk goods, native goods not affected by the new treaty tariff for foreign trade should continue at the new ports to pay the old established rates of duty.[45] In line with this general principle, the Shanghai maritime customs was given the joint task of 1) collecting export duties according to the treaty tariff and also 2) acting on behalf of the inland customs stations to collect the duties which the silk exporters would formerly have paid on the inland route from the silk districts to Canton. These inland stations were the famous "three customs," *san-kuan*, at Hangchow in Chekiang (*Pei-hsin kuan*), Kan-chou in Kiangsi (*Kan-kuan*), and Shao-chou-fu in Kwangtung (*T'ai-p'ing kuan*). The Shanghai customs collector dutifully reported his silk-duty collections on their behalf and his remittances to them, in addition to his regular task of enforcing the treaty tariff.[46]

This clumsy method of protecting the traditional revenue of old established customs collectorates, without regard for the trade or traders, would have been more exasperating to the British if the taxes had been heavy; but they were not. In February 1844 Pottinger published at Hongkong and circulated to all the consulates a translation by Gutzlaff of an extract from the regulations of the Board of Revenue (*Hu-pu tse-li*, Chapters 30–31), giving the rates of transit duties levied at the "three customs." These rates were seen to be moderate. For instance, a picul of first quality raw silk paid Tls. 0.8576 at Hangchow, Tls. 1 at Kan-chou, and Tls. 1.432 at Shao-chou-fu, which compared favorably with the export duty of Tls. 10 to be levied by the treaty tariff.[47]

Licensed merchants and trade monopolies. The chief complaint of the British was not so much against the statutory amount of these duties as against the manner in which they were levied, by the standard operating procedure of setting up licensed monopolists. The application of the decision taken secretly at Peking in August 1843 became apparent at Shanghai, where Consul Balfour reported on December 6, 1843, that the Chinese authorities had licensed some of the silk merchants, who were to control the others, contrary to treaty; the silk exported from Shanghai would be obliged in this way to pay a duty of about 5 per cent in addition to the export duty fixed by treaty. The licensed merchants were to report to the authorities all the teas and silks arriving from the interior, and all the exports, and were to be responsible for the payment of all the transit and export duties.

Consul Balfour regarded this as an effort to extend the old Canton system. Cantonese had arrived at Shanghai in numbers before the port was opened, bringing with them the worst habits and ideas of the south, including the desire to organize combinations for the control of trade.[48] He had tried to discourage this movement by explaining to the local Chinese merchants "the danger to themselves of having peculiar privileges"; on December 19 he pointed out to the taotai how undesirable it would be to have one class of merchants able to "pry into" the affairs of others. This anarchic Anglo-Saxon doctrine naturally left both merchants and taotai unmoved, for order in China was in large part maintained by having some persons pry into the affairs of others. The consul's further arguments no doubt seemed equally strange. He pointed out that the licensed merchants, not being paid for their pains, had already begun to collect a percentage from the unlicensed; that this squeeze and the height of the combined transit and export duties would encourage them to evade the duties; and that meanwhile the great power of the licensed merchants had already allowed them to smuggle. In these arguments the consul was assuming that the Chinese authorities wanted to secure and report a formal official revenue from trade and provide equal opportunity for all merchants: it may be questioned if either of these assumptions hit the mark. The taotai promised, however, to withdraw the licenses and establish a government office to collect the revenue. Balfour suggested that transit duty payments could be scrutinized when application was finally made to the consul for permission to export the goods. But he refrained from recognizing the Chinese right to levy a transit duty, pending a reference to his superior.[49]

This dispute was reflected in memorials of the Kiangsu authorities which were received at Peking on December 29, 1844. They reported their arguments with Consul Balfour, who vigorously opposed any increase of silk duties to make up for the lack of a taxing station on the silk route to Shanghai. Balfour had wanted to have the high authorities memorialize the throne, but the taotai told him the regulations could not be changed and he "withdrew without a word." An edict of the same date confirmed this extra taxation at Shanghai as the only way to preserve the customs revenue.[50]

It is interesting to note that at this early date Pottinger specifically recognized transit duties as justified by the lowered export duty rates of the treaty tariff and by the fact that merchants' transportation costs to Shanghai were less than to Canton and that, in general, the British government had no right to interfere with Chinese internal taxation. In the light of his successors' complaints against transit taxes, these views of the author of the treaty system are worth noting.[f] They were approved by Lord Aberdeen in June 1844. But by the beginning of 1846 Consul Balfour was beginning to object to this silk transit tax on the ground that it had not formerly been levied on silk brought to Shanghai and "to this date it is only levied on silk actually sold for exportation." He was aware of Pottinger's original agreement, and he also admitted that the amount of

[f] "I consider not only that the large reduction made on the Export Duties on Silk and Silk piece goods is a sufficient bonus to the trade, but cannot forget that that bonus is greatly added to by the saving in expense and risk of land carriage . . ." Pottinger reported in April 1844 that he was certain no transit duties were being levied in excess of, or contrary to, the interests of foreign trade. "Not a single farthing has been unjustly taken" from merchants in the provinces, he said, both the people and the emperor being averse to such encroachments.[51]

the tax, Tls. 3.2896 per picul, "cannot be said to be high on so valuable an article as the finest description of Hoochow silk." But he felt it should be lowered on cheaper grades of silk.[52]

In the meantime regulations had also been instituted at Shanghai for the export trade in tea. Chinese merchants transporting cheap grades of tea to Shantung, Tientsin, and Manchuria complained of the new transit duty of Tls. 2.5 per picul which they were now required to pay. When first bought by the merchant these coarse teas cost only Tls. 2.5 or 2.6; transportation and duties together brought this cost to about Tls. 4.[g] They therefore wished to pay according to the old "native" tariff, some Tls. 0.2. In support of this petition, the Shanghai local authorities pointed out that tea cargoes for north China could easily be distinguished from those for the south, or for foreign purchase, because vessels trading to Shantung and northward were of a type entirely different from those which voyaged in deeper seas to Fukien and Kwangtung. Voyages in these opposite directions were made by different crews and at opposite seasons. On the basis of this difference, the sea transport of tea to the north had previously been sanctioned, while that to the south had remained illegal. After consultation with the imperial commissioner, the Kiangsu authorities therefore arranged to let the northward tea trade continue under license as before, paying the old rate of duty.[54] The merchants were ordered to establish at Shanghai northern and southern tea warehouses, at which the two categories of tea exports would respectively be delivered, stored, and taxed.

In June 1844, by a proclamation of the Ningpo district magistrate, a system of supervision through licensed tea godowns was established there, similar to that first set up at Shanghai.[h] There were only three tea godowns,

[g] As of 1849, Robert Fortune summarized the distances and costs on the tea route to Shanghai as follows:

Table 12: Costs on the Tea Route to Shanghai from Fukien

stage	*transportation*	*distance*	*days*	*coolie or boat hire in cash*
Ch'ung-an to Ho-k'ou	by land	280 *li* *	6	800 per chest
Ho-k'ou to Yü-shan	by water	180 "	4	150
Yü-shan to Ch'ang-shan	by land	100 "	3	400
Ch'ang-shan to Hangchow	by water	800 "	6	200
expenses for coolies at Hangchow				10
Hangchow to Shanghai	by water	500 "	5	180
	Total	1860 *li*	24 days	1740 cash per chest

* Approximately one third of a mile.

His final estimate was that the small tea farmer sold his common product at about 80 cash a catty, equal to Tls. 4 per picul (say roughtly $5.33 for 133 lbs.). Finer teas would bring twice this price (say Tls. 8 per picul), but in any case it was little enough. When the teas were finally sold for export, however, the Chinese merchant had paid about Tls. 5.773 for packing, transport, and customs charges (making a total expense of Tls. 14 at most), and stood to get a price from the foreigner of about Tls. 22. This meant a clear profit of Tls. 8 per picul, more or less.[53]

[h] The consul at Ningpo reported the inauguration of a new arrangement for the control and taxation of tea exports from Fukien, outlined in a proclamation of the Ningpo (Yin) district magistrate,

run respectively by a Cantonese, a man from Ningpo, and another from Chen-hai below Ningpo at the mouth of the river. These three would now make minute, detailed semi-monthly reports, in stamped ledgers, to the local authorities. The tea-boat firms were likewise to report monthly their carriage of tea cargoes. This system for the control of teas coming to Ningpo from the distributing center in northeastern Kiangsi at Ho-k'ou, had all the earmarks of a normal Chinese arrangement; but the consul feared that it was the beginning of a thorough tea monopoly system reminiscent of Canton.[56]

It is not easy to tell how far the British fears of official trade restrictions were justified. A proclamation by the Kiangsu governor, Sun Shan-pao, under date of January 27, 1844 (based on a dispatch received from the Kiangsi governor on December 31, 1843) stated that certain Cantonese tea merchants, Le Taoufung (Li Tao-feng?) and others, now desired to transport their teas for the foreign market by way of Yü-shan (i.e., on the route to Hangchow and Shanghai). Under the new regulations, this was permitted, and merchants might take their teas to Shanghai or Ningpo. But the boat firms must be required to make detailed monthly reports of the tea transported, the merchants involved, and their destination, to aid in the prevention of smuggling. At Shanghai the south and the north tea warehouses already established would likewise make a monthly report to the taotai, for purposes of comparison.[i]

Six months afterward, in July 1844, Balfour complained to the Shanghai authorities that the officials at Ho-k'ou had ordered that certain teas, destined to come north to Shanghai, should be taken south to Canton, and had otherwise impeded the exports of tea. The sub-prefect at Ho-k'ou, Koo Linche, and the district magistrate of Yuan-shan, Wu Lin-kuang, replied to this charge through the Shanghai taotai. They said that in the fourth month (May 17 — June 15, 1844) they had received orders transmitted from the emperor to search for teas going by clandestine routes, and to have the tea establishments report monthly on tea shipments. Accordingly they had ordered the tea-boat firms to make "double checks", serially numbered, of which one part was to be given the tea merchant and the

---

Ye-kwan, on June 30, 1844. This was along the same lines as a proclamation by Sun Shan-pao, Governor of Kiangsu, issued on Jan. 27, and reported by Consul Balfour in September 1844. From these and similar documents it is possible to reconstruct the functioning of the tea export trade.[55]

[i] Later in 1844 Kung Taotai at Shanghai in reply to Balfour's complaints explained that to control the tea trade via Shanghai for the north there were four "duty-protecting hongs" whose job it was to find the amounts of tea exported and see that customs duties were paid. Now that teas were to go from Shanghai to the south, there had already been established seven tea warehouses where the Chinese and English merchants might trade, and new warehouses might freely be set up. The procedure for the prevention of smuggling was as follows: tea dealers on arrival recorded their names at the government post station, and stored their goods in the warehouse, where they were recorded in sealed ledgers examined monthly. When the teas were shipped, the dealer went to the government bank and paid the export duties.[57]

other to be retained by the boat firm (see copy below).[j] But beyond this they contended that there was not the slightest restriction of trade.[59]

The British authorities were quick to see Cantonese influence at work behind these arrangements. Consul Balfour understood that Wu Lin-kuang, magistrate of the key city on the tea-routes, was a native of Nan-hai hsien in Canton, the district in which the foreign factories were located. He was related to the great hong merchant Howqua, having a sister married to Howqua's second or third son, and he also had several brothers in the government, one of them a former governor-general residing at Fushan (Fo-shan, i.e., Fatshan?) near Canton; another brother was now assistant magistrate at Shanghai, a position he had obtained by the merit of assembling militia during the late war, with the help of a fortune acquired while employed by Howqua to collect teas in the Wu-i hills.[60] The consul naturally feared this Cantonese influence would stifle Shanghai.

Although the Chinese official explanations of these regulatory activities sounded proper and innocuous, they appeared to Governor Davis to afford "ample proof of the iniquitous attempts to divert the tea trade from Shanghai." He protested to Ch'i-ying against this interference "with the free progress of commerce," and repeated his protest twice at weekly intervals. Ch'i-ying in reply on Nov. 11, 1844, admitted that a Chinese merchant also had petitioned regarding teas held at Ho-k'ou, but he denied discrimination. "As the statutes of the Central Empire are multifarious, the old laws cannot instantly be changed." Dealers had been timid, but now were going to Shanghai in numbers. Davis accepted this explanation as satisfactory.[61]

The *Peking Gazette* of December 5, 1844, as translated in the *China Mail* at Hongkong, offered a further explanation: Shanghai tea merchants had complained that the Yü-shan magistrate had forbidden the conveyance of teas to Shanghai, Ningpo, and Chapu and ordered them to be taken to

[j] W. H. Medhurst's obviously rough translation of one-half of a duplicate "Boat Check": "To be preserved at the boat Office for reference [duplicate to be held by merchant as proof]. The Boat Office of the ______ Military Station of Hokow, in the district of Yuenshan, in the prefecture of Kwangsin has received the commands of the ______ Officers, prohibiting Fukien teas passing by a secret way, and being incorrectly ______ reported, and instructing the boat ______ establishments to engrave and set on foot numbered checks for issue. That when any tea merchants arrive in the town the conductor of the conveyance establishments where they put up must go in person to a boat establishment, and enter clearly the place, the designation, the place of birth, the surname, the number of piculs of tea brought, the real destination for sale, that there is no passing by a clandestine way, no incorrect report of quantity, no underhand conveyance and such like villainies — in order to be held as proof to take to the place of delivery of the goods, where the check given will be examined, received, and that at the passes examination may be made and permission given to proceed and this check, printed in obedience to these orders, is therefore given to the merchant as a proof. ______ province ______ prefecture ______ district ______ village ______ constabulary. Tea Merchant ______ designation ______ hired ______ boats ______ in number, calculated to have carried peculs of tea to take to ______ to be delivered for sale at ______ Do not on the way take a clandestine route, to the consequent involving of the Conveyance and Boat Establishments in disgrace and punishment. Taoukwang ______ year ______ month ______ day. ______ Boat Establishment ______ conveyance place of their stay. Fair winds and good luck."[58]

Canton as before. This was contrary to the explicit orders of the governor-general of Fukien and Chekiang, who had agreed that Fukien teas should be transported to Ningpo and Shanghai for sale. The Shanghai taotai investigated and reported that the Yü-shan magistrate had demanded the transport to Canton only of 1000 catties of tea already reported as destined for Canton, in order to keep the accounts straight; some 8000 piculs of tea had actually been permitted to go to Shanghai without hindrance. Nevertheless, an imperial edict ordered the trial of the local officers concerned.[62]

At Ningpo, Consul Thom had immediately sensed the existence of trade monopolies in iron, tea, and silk, and had objected to them. The taotai's reply in extenuation described the normal Chinese situation: Chinese wishing to deal in iron were regularly obliged to get certain firms to become security for them before they could obtain permits to deal in iron from the provincial treasurer. If this system were applied to foreign trade also, the taotai admitted that an iron monopoly would result. He therefore had arranged that Chinese merchants buying foreign iron should be allowed to sell it wherever they wished. The silk firms, for their part, were set up to report on the trade, not to trade themselves. Similarly tea merchants were free to sell as they wished, but the tea warehousemen were obliged to report the details of the trade to the customs. No monopolies, he promised, would be permitted.[63]

At Canton trade monopolies similarly provided a main battleground for English and Chinese ideas of trade regulation. As one example of this, September 1844 saw the beginning of a long controversy over the activities of a certain Tseay-wei-chuen (Ts'ai Wei-ch'uan?) who was granted by the Chinese authorities the right to levy a tax of Tls. 113 on every 10,000 catties of cassia (a variety of cinnamon) passing through Chao-ch'ing-fu, west of Canton, en route from the production area in Kwangsi. Official regulations required the Chinese merchants transporting cassia over this route to obtain permits and pay transit duties to the tax-farmer, Tseay. This was of course the usual Chinese system of farming the duties to an individual who would undertake to collect them at a certain taxing station. The Chinese cassia merchants, however, complained to the British merchants, and the consul therefore accused Ch'i-ying and his colleagues of breaking art. X of the treaty of Nanking. This treaty clause referred to the published tariff for taxing exports at the treaty ports. Since it made no reference to transit duties on export goods, the law officers in London later held that it gave no basis for objections such as were now being made. But meanwhile the Chinese authorities gave way to the consul and agreed to abolish Mr. Tseay's obnoxious tax-monopoly and collect the transit duties on cassia themselves. Their new procedure would give each merchant who desired to purchase cassia in Kwangsi and export it through Canton an equal opportunity to state his detailed intentions to the Canton authorities. He could present security bonds, secure a certified permit, have it further stamped and certified at five places in the interior en route to the cassia district, and on his return register and store his goods at the Canton custom house pending their sale. Infractions of this procedure would be punished as smuggling.

By this time (May 1845) Consul Macgregor at Canton also had to complain against an apparent iron monopoly: for notices posted at the factories had required foreign purchasers of iron to buy only from certain Chinese sellers. This seemed to be directly contrary to article V of the treaty of Nanking, which allowed British merchants to trade with whomever they pleased.[64]

The cassia tax system continued. In 1848 the the Canton consulate received a complaint that 1500 piculs of cassia to be delivered to a British merchant, Wardley, were held up by the authorities because the Chinese dealers had no licenses. The imperial commissioner refused to modify the tax system and the acting-consul therefore stopped the payment of customs duties on British vessels — a move which his superior countermanded. It appeared that in addition to the transit dues and export duty on cassia, there had grown up a levy of Tls. 0.8.1.7. per picul, of which Tls. 0.7 was paid to the customs authorities by the licensed Chinese merchants, who got the money back from the foreign traders. Cassia exports to India and England in 1844 had been 21,000 piculs in 228 ships, but in 1847 had declined to 5,920 piculs in 176 ships, and the consulate blamed the added tax. Wardley claimed $4,660 from the Chinese government because his cassia was held up. When he later tried to move it, certain coolies who claimed a monopoly to transport it staged a riot which the local authorities seemed helpless to prevent. Chinese merchants informed the consul that the original tax farmer, Tseay, although nominally deposed by the authorities, had connived with a clerk in the customhouse to set up a system whereby only thirty firms were licensed to trade in cassia, and had thereupon exacted payments from them. To transport 300 piculs of cassia he would make a merchant pay Tls. 350 for a permit, plus incidental fees. Finally, Tseay had set up another monopolist with exclusive rights to sell cassia and collect profits for him. The Hoppo, without apparent consciousness of guilt, also confessed about this time that the buying and transporting of cassia was restricted to thirty firms which had permits; he refused to give permits to a merchant not guaranteed by these thirty firms. By November 1848 the consulate calculated that the charge for permits and incidental fees collected by the customhouse equalled about Tls. 0.7 per picul, in addition to the Tls. 0.7.5 fixed as export duty by treaty. Fortunately in 1848 the export of cassia increased again and the consulate let the matter drop, at the same time that the Chinese authorities gave up the licensing system — or so they reported to Peking.[65]

It is apparent that the British consular officers throughout this altercation had been siding with Chinese merchants against the Chinese government, objecting to a system which, though annoying, was normal in China, and though contrary to the spirit of the treaty, was not contrary to its letter. In May 1845 Dent and Company had complained of a cotton broker's tax on raw cotton which was additional to any previous tax. The consul admitted there was no treaty stipulation directly against such a practice but asked Ch'i-ying to check the exaction. The latter had agreed to do so.[66] It was increasingly plain, however, that the conflict over monopoly was not so much between official policies as between the British and Chinese systems of economic administration.

The Hangchow customs. A more prosaic type of hindrance to trade — the Chinese system of squeeze — was described by certain Chinese merchants. Petitioning the Shanghai taotai late in 1845, they stated that in the old trade from Canton their British cotton goods (long cloths) had always paid duties at the Kan-chou and Shao-chou (T'ai-p'ing) customs stations, but had never passed through the Hangchow customs. Having transferred their trade to Shanghai, they now found that Hangchow was the bottleneck through which British cotton goods flowed to their broad market in Anhwei, Kiangsi, Chekiang, and Fukien.

The *Pei-hsin kuan* or New North Customs (named for the New North bridge) had its main office on the river about 10 *li* north of Hangchow. To tax the traffic passing by boat between the watershed of the Ch'ien-t'ang River and the Yangtze delta, this office had developed a wide network of sub-stations on the numerous canal routes of the region. By the end of the Ch'ing dynasty these totalled 15 taxing stations and 20 examining stations, some as far as 120 *li* distant. A Ming inheritance, this lucrative office had finally been put under the Ch'ing superintendent of the imperial manufactory at Hangchow, an official specially deputed from the court, like the Canton Hoppo. Early in the dynasty the main station was assigned some 130 officers and clerks, and the first seven sub-stations more than 100 further personnel. The administration of these customs barriers reflected the endemic struggle between the interests of the emperor and of his tax-gatherers. As an edict of 1723 put it, "the country's establishment of a customs tariff is to promote trade, not to embarrass the merchant — to aid the people, not to injure them"; but the customs collectors used their office to squeeze the public — a complaint reiterated year after year.[67] So strong was the vested interest of these tax officers that they were able to protect the Hangchow customs revenue by an unofficial "veto on sea communication by native craft" between Shanghai and Ningpo, which Vice-consul Robertson alleged in 1856 had been instituted in 1843.[68]

Since the foreign trade at Shanghai was conducted by barter, the inflow of foreign cotton goods was essential to the outflow of teas and silks. The Chinese merchants who petitioned in 1845 asked for a definite tariff on cotton imports passing through Hangchow. They stated that numerous small taxing stations had been established purely to levy fees along the route, and the total of these exactions now hindered trade. The standards of measurement were also uncertain. Balfour calculated from reports reaching him that the transit duty was as high as Tls. 0.3 per picul, which with the necessary bribes and tips would amount really to Tls. 0.5 or Tls. 0.7 — more than one-third of the value of the goods, and of course much higher than the import tariff levied at Shanghai by treaty. The fact that a group of merchants formally petitioned was the best proof of the evil.[69]

The dilemma of the Chinese tea and silk exporter appears to have been very real. In the barter trade at Shanghai he was obliged to take large quantities of cotton manufactures, and if the transit taxes as they went inland through Hangchow were too high, he had only two alternatives — either to invest in opium and go into the contraband traffic or to smuggle his cotton goods into the interior. Merchants at Ningpo early in 1846 described to Consul Thom how they evaded the duties of the Hangchow customhouse and its annoying sub-stations. They took their foreign long cloths from the inland market at Soochow to Kashing, and thence to the maritime customs station at Kan-p'u near Hai-yen on the north shore of Hangchow Bay, where they paid a duty of 100 cash per piece. From there they came to Yü-yao (between Shaohing and Ningpo), evidently by junk, and thence to Ningpo. In this way some 200,000 pieces of white and grey long cloths had passed through Ningpo in the year 1845, most of them on the way to Fukien.[70]

In short, the real hindrances to trade were not the statutory transit taxes but the officials who used them as an excuse for their private exactions. The organized corruption of the Chinese fiscal system applied to foreign imports as much as to the land tax or other aspects of internal economy.[k] On his secret journey to the tea districts in 1845, Medhurst

[k] Medhurst found in 1845 that the Hui-chou gazetteer in its account of the land and poll taxes for the Wu-yuan district listed an income of Tls. 34,031 together with 6,586 piculs of rice and 365 piculs of peas. "Only 31,504 taels are forwarded to the provincial capital from this district." Official salaries totalled only Tls. 1432. But "it is not to be supposed that the magistrates of such an extensive and rich district as Woo-yuen should be content with 60 and 45 taels annually; neither are they. The way in which they make their money is by charging for inferior officers and assistants without paying them; by concealing from the government the amount of cultivated fields; by exacting from the cultivators more than the amount sent in; and by levying toll on articles, and in a way, not specified in the tariff. To instance only one thing: it is well known that Woo-yuen produces large quantities of the best green teas. And yet in the statistical account of the district, published and intended for the eye of government, there is not one word said about tea. Judging from this record, a stranger would not imagine that a single leaf of tea was exported from Woo-yuen.

found that the "troublesome custom house at Hangchow" was the chief obstacle on his route. "The officers stationed there are said to be most annoying, examining every part of a traveler's baggage . . . (their) ill-fame had spread all over this part of the empire."[72] The *Peking Gazette* reported the Hangchow (*Pei-hsin*) customs collection for 1847 at Tls. 179,843, which was Tls. 8,200 less than for 1846.[73] But both these sums were inconsiderable compared with the volume of trade which suffered unofficial taxation.

Given these inveterate tendencies of the Chinese tax-gatherer to batten upon the commerce of the interior, it was inevitable that foreign traders should find a great opportunity in the sea-borne trade along the China coast.

The English merchants in Shanghai best know how many chops of tea they obtain from this district every year; and the writer has been informed on the spot, that upwards of 20,000 taels are annually extracted from the tea-merchants as they export this article from the district, by regular levies of so much per pecul. If however this were to be complained of to the Chinese Government, as an improper levying of transit duties, they would reply that according to the information before them, there was no such thing as tea grown in Woo-yuen."[71]

CHAPTER XVII

THE FOREIGN INVASION OF THE COASTING TRADE

HISTORICAL INTEREST IN THE TWO "lost decades" [1] which intervened between the first and second treaty settlements has so far neglected a significant development which occurred during this period on the China coast, a growth which went almost unrecorded except in the consular archives — this was the invasion of the coastal trade by vessels under the British flag, which presaged the eventual British domination of the carrying trade in Chinese waters. This British participation amounted to 60 per cent by 1894 and remained for a century one of the chief foreign stakes in China; it began at this time on the eve of the great Rebellion and in the midst of growing disorder, piracy, and official demoralization. The way for it was paved by the work of British consular officers in gaining legal privileges which facilitated, or perhaps more accurately, kept pace with, the expansion of British commercial activity. The whole development is the more striking because there was no specific legal basis for it in the treaties of 1842–44.

The Chinese junk trade. Despite its obvious importance, the native junk trade has been little studied. What follows is culled chiefly from consular reports.[2] In 1852 the junk trade at Canton, for example, was said to total 850 arrivals of trading junks a year from all quarters, while between 300 and 400 salt junks operated locally in fleets, largely from the neighborhood of Tienpak (*Tien-pai*) on the far southern coast. The average size of the sea-going junks was about 150 tons, but there were many variations ranging between 50 and 1000 tons. The crew usually numbered 10 to 15 men per hundred tons. Thus a large junk might have 160 to 180 men aboard, divided into several different categories: the captain, who was really the supercargo, carrying the responsibility for final decisions as to commercial dealings and route of the voyage, although he had nothing to do with the navigation; clerks, who assisted the captain and kept all the accounts; the pilot, together with one or more deputies, who navigated without instruments save for the compass, from one headland to another, sometimes running for several days out of sight of land before picking up the next landmark (in time of trouble the pilot usually suffered from a personal responsibility for the acts of nature); the helmsman (*to-kung*), who gave the commands regarding sails, anchors, and such things; the compradore (*mai-pan*), who bought all provisions; and finally the priest, who burnt incense near the compass, propitiated the gods of the junk, and performed numerous rites day by day. The crew would include barbers and cooks, the sailors being divided into headmen, who managed the sails, and shipmates, who pulled and hauled generally.[3]

Detailed sailing directions for the established coastal routes of these junks are available, still awaiting study. A work like the *Hai-wai chi-yao* (A record of essentials concerning the outer seas), which has a postface dated 1828, describes the itineraries of vessels sailing from Canton to Shanghai, from Amoy to the Straits, etc., with data concerning 23 sheltered harbors, how to choose a pilot or fight a pirate, and much other useful knowledge for sailing captains.[4]

When bound for the Southern Ocean, junks from Canton would usually clear at the Canton customs for Hainan or the west coast of Kwangtung, and enter from there on their return, in order to avoid squeeze. Generally, however, these Cantonese vessels voyaged less far afield than those from Fukien. They were usually chartered by the voyage, unless the captain (supercargo) was himself the owner. Thus a junk of 6000 to 8000 piculs capacity (say 400 to 533 tons), for a seven or eight month voyage would bring $8,000. Junks sailed on long voyages only with the monsoon, departing in November or December and returning in July or August. They sometimes got pilots at Macao, who might be paid $100 a month and have also an allotment of cargo space for themselves. An average cargo might be worth $30,000 and some as much as $150,000. At the ports of destination Chinese merchant firms acted as agents, handling the import cargo and lading the junk for its return; they received a remunerative commission of from 7 to 10 per cent, as well as presents.[5]

In the north the Ningpo junk fleets in 1844 were said to make three or four voyages annually to the coasts of Shantung, Tientsin, or Tartary (i.e., modern Manchuria), taking chinaware, salt fish, silk, cotton cloth, and paper to the value of some $200,000 a year. From the north they brought back much more valuable cargoes of fruits, bean cake, and skins, to a value of some $2,000,000 annually. Ningpo junks returning from Fukien and Formosa brought wood and timber, rice and paddy, oranges and other fruits, worth about $3,000,000 a year. They took back raw cotton, cotton cloth, and silks worth perhaps $2,000,000 a year, making two or three voyages annually. This trade was balanced partly by the transfer of specie and partly by bills of exchange. In the Ningpo junk trade generally, promissory notes were used for large sums and copper cash for smaller, and there was a dearth of silver in circulation. This Ningpo native trade, however, was estimated to be far below that of Shanghai, where annual imports from North China were roughly $10,000,000 a year and from the south perhaps twice as much.

As the British trade developed at Amoy, its most distinctive feature was the high proportion of it conducted with the Straits: by 1845 more than one-quarter of the British imports at Amoy were from Malaya, and most of the British exports went there. By 1847 most of the Straits trade carried in non-Chinese vessels at Amoy was in British hands, with very high freight rates being paid.[6] In this way the British flag was invading the most ancient and well-established avenue of the Chinese junk trade overseas. It was but another step to expand along the China coast itself.

Re-export. The British invasion of the established native trade routes was made by almost imperceptible stages, and had to begin with the five treaty ports becoming interchangeable as parts of a single market for foreign shipping. This elementary provision had not been made in the British treaties, where it was unconsciously assumed that Western trade would move into and out of the treaty ports as it had done at Canton, without stopping at another port en route — as a staple trade on a seasonal basis. Accordingly no opportunity was allowed the British merchant to shift his goods from port to port in China in search of the best market. But under the treaty provisions it became the common practice for merchant vessels loading in China to commence loading at a northern port, usually Shanghai, and then drop down to Canton (really Whampoa) to complete their cargoes, sometimes stopping at Foochow or Amoy en route. In the same way a great part of the vessels in the China trade called at Hongkong, perhaps both on arrival and on departure. When a vessel entered more than one treaty-port in this manner, she was to be treated on the same basis at the second port as she had been at the first: that is, she must pay tonnage dues, report to the consul with her papers and a manifest, get from the Chinese superintendent of customs a permit to discharge, and pay duties on her cargo; or else leave within forty-eight hours. This was a clumsy basis for inter-port trade.

In fact, the treaties had not even provided for the bonding of imported goods so as to defer the payment of duties on them, a convenience generally expected by merchants in the West. Thus the general regulations of trade, article VI, provided in their English version that "all duties incurred by an English Merchant vessel, whether on goods imported or exported, or in the shape of tonnage dues, must first be paid up in full, which done the Superintendent of Customs will grant a Port Clearance" for the vessel's departure. Consul Thom confessed that the Chinese version of this clause "certainly implies that the hold should be swept (i.e., everything discharged out of it) and duty paid upon all of it." [a]

[a] "The weakness of my ground . . . deterred me from referring too much to the General Regulations in my correspondence with the Mandarins. I tried rather to put the question on a footing of reasonableness and expediency, and to effect this I was obliged to go into very lengthy and prolix details." Nevertheless, he finally arranged for unlanded cargo to leave port free.[7]

As a result of this lack of foresight the issue was soon raised by the local authorities at the new ports as to whether duties were due upon all goods entering port, or upon all goods discharged from the vessel, or only upon goods actually sold. At Amoy in November 1843 the Chinese authorities contended that merchant vessels on entering port should pay duty on their entire cargoes. Consul Gribble argued that duties should be paid on foreign imports as they were sold.[8] The issue also arose at Ningpo and at Shanghai, where Kung Taotai magnanimously agreed in February 1844 that goods not sold, need not pay duties.

Unknown to the British, this problem was carefully laid before the throne. Ch'i-ying forwarded reports from the Shanghai taotai which reached Peking on February 8, 1844, describing the new difficulty: goods once imported at Canton in the old days had never been sent away, but foreign merchants at Shanghai now wanted to do so. The British consul strongly urged the taotai to accept duties on all imported goods, whether destined for Shanghai or elsewhere, so as to preserve the treaties. Ch'i-ying was therefore instructing all the treaty port authorities to follow the same course and take care to prevent smuggling. The emperor enjoined careful management.[9] After much correspondence it was finally settled in March 1844 that foreign cargoes should pay duties only as landed. Memorials from the Fukien authorities reached the throne in April, describing the inability of foreign merchants to sell their entire cargoes at Amoy: since the taxation of goods only as landed and examined would not be according to treaty, reference had been made to Ch'i-ying, who had finally replied that the practice in Kwangtung and Kiangsu was now to tax only goods reported for examination or discharged from a vessel. Goods unexamined or undischarged could be shipped elsewhere. Hsü Chi-yü therefore followed this Canton-Shanghai precedent at Amoy, to preserve uniform practice, and an edict of April 25 confirmed the arrangement.[10] This was reinforced by Davis' circular in May that piece goods should pay duties only when opened at the customhouse, as had been the practice at Canton.[11] Caleb Cushing incorporated these arrangements for re-export in article 20 of the American treaty in July 1844: foreign imports paying duty at one treaty port could be re-exported free to another treaty port.

This was a relief to the British merchant but it still did not approach the convenience of Western practice. Consul Balfour at Shanghai moved to introduce a bonding system and persuaded the taotai and the local authorities, and also Hsien-ling, who was then at Shanghai as Ch'i-ying's representative, to establish a bonded warehouse. Certain English merchants selected by the consul were to be in charge of this warehouse, where goods entering the port might be registered and stored at fixed rates, until released by application through the warehouse superintendent, the consul, and the superintendent of customs in turn. Pottinger heartily approved the innovation as the most important commercial gain since the published tariff.[12]

This proposed bonding system might have been a fruitful experiment in Anglo-Chinese regulation of trade, for British individuals would have acted as quasi-agents of the Chinese customhouse — a possibility later realized in the Inspectorate of Customs. But like the latter, it met the initial difficulty that to be just and efficient it must be universal, and Pottinger therefore had to try to extend it to the other ports. Unfortunately Ch'i-ying was unable to agree to it. He cited the precedents already on record, in which goods had paid duties on landing, as reported to the emperor, and he also cited the regulations. But he gave his real reason in a private reply to Pottinger: bonding was impossible at Canton because the government was not strong enough there to carry through so great an innovation.[13] The hong merchants, as noted above, had a vested interest in the use of their warehouses, which bonding might obviate.

At Amoy the superintendent of customs rejected the idea of bonding on the grounds that it was contrary to treaty, and that it could be done only through the Tartar-general of Fukien, head of the Fukien customs; foreign trade at Amoy was not, as at Shanghai, in charge of officials on the spot who could make their own arrangements. When Consul Sullivan at Ningpo in November 1846 revived Balfour's original idea of a bonded warehouse, the taotai demanded that the consul be the superintendent of it. Sullivan refused to play the part of a customhouse and the suggestion was dropped.

In the end the equivalent of bonding was provided partly by the use of Hongkong as a warehouse, and partly by the practice of re-export as provided in the American treaty. Under this latter arrangement imports which had entered one treaty port and paid duty there might be re-exported and taken into another treaty port without paying any further import duty. Instead of being bonded, imports had to pay duty on arrival, but at least they did not have to moulder in one port if they could find a market at another. This privilege of re-export under an exemption certificate from the customs (the document necessary to exempt the goods from a second payment of import duty) was duly extended to British merchants and greatly aided interport trade. Its application, however, varied greatly at the different ports and gave rise to all sorts of ingenious interpretations.

Ch'i-ying argued that goods once imported could be re-exported and enter a second port free *only* if they were taken in the same ship. But this interpretation was generally disregarded. Foreign goods coming to Amoy, for instance, were usually carried in large vessels which first entered port at Canton; the goods paid import duty there, came out under an exemption certificate, were transshipped at Hongkong into smaller coastwise craft, and entered Amoy duty free in these small vessels. When unsaleable at Amoy, the local authorities even allowed them to be transshipped to a departing vessel without entering the customs, thus sidestepping the whole question. At the other extreme, British merchants tried to convince the Hoppo that an exemption certificate, given for British goods re-exported from Canton to Hongkong, might be used to cover the importation, duty free, of substitute goods brought up from Hongkong to Canton. The Hoppo refused.

The principle of re-export was soon quietly extended, by the persuasion of consular logic, to China's international trade, at some if not all of the treaty ports. When the unfortunate Mr. Mackenzie, in attempting to liquidate his investment in the market which failed to materialize at Ningpo, had tried to re-export his goods to Singapore in July 1845, Consul Thom had been unable to secure a refund of his import duties. In March 1847, however, Alcock at Shanghai arranged that when unsaleable imports were re-exported to places other than the five ports, a duty-credit might be given at Shanghai for the import duties already paid there. This duty-credit was really a refund (drawback) and could be used to meet later import duties. When the Ningpo consul applied for equal treatment, both the Shanghai and the Ningpo authorities carefully refused to put the concession in writing, but the practice nevertheless was allowed at Ningpo also. Meanwhile the use of exemption certificates became well established. In August 1847 a memorial from the governor of Chekiang reported that goods coming to Ningpo in foreign ships were mainly from Canton where they had paid duties to the Canton customs and received a *yen-tan* (exemption [lit., examination] — certificate), so that whether they were sold at Ningpo or carried on to Shanghai, duties would not be levied again. Consequently in the current month only some Tls. 400 had been collected at Ningpo.[14]

The British Chamber of Commerce at Canton asked for the same privilege. In February 1848 an extension of the drawback system already in use at Shanghai was proposed to Ch'i-ying in these terms: (1) that the exporter, on re-exporting goods to a foreign port, should submit a bill of lading in proof of shipment from Canton, (2) that the fact of entry into the foreign country should be proved by certification, and (3) that the amount of the orignal import duty should then be deducted from the next payment of duty due by the exporter. This proposal hung fire, however, and in September Governor Bonham advised the consuls not to push at one port for the privileges of re-export granted at another port, because such privileges were not all written in the treaties and might be curtailed if too much publicized.[15] In 1852 Alcock warned the Shanghai community that the securing of drawback certificates was not a treaty right but an "extra-treaty privilege . . . to be used solely for future duty payments."

Such documents were to be obtained "only for duty-paid imports re-exported abroad." [16] In fact, of course, they had become an extra-treaty convenience sanctioned by custom, similar to the exemption certificates already used in foreign inter-port trade in China.

Native shippers and the native tariff. A further stimulus to the foreign carrying trade in Chinese waters was given by the confusion which now resulted between foreign and native trade. By sending Western imports from one treaty port to another, the foreign merchants were in reality entering the coastal trade of China on a limited basis. When Englishmen dealt in Chinese produce and Chinese merchants shipped their cargoes in British vessels, the former clear-cut distinction between foreign and native trade began to break down. This in turn confused the application of the tariff, for there were two tariffs now in force — the Chinese "native" tariff as of old, and the new foreign treaty tariff. This produced four pairs of variables — "native" and "foreign" vessels, goods, shippers, and tariffs.

Under the Chinese tariff, native produce on leaving a port paid export duty; on entering a second port it paid import duty, and if it left the second port it again paid export duty. The law was simple and of course operated for the convenience of the customs collector rather than of the Chinese merchants: each collector counted on taxing all goods that entered and left his port, and that was all. The old customs administrations of the coastal provinces were not unified and efforts to coördinate their activities were likely to be resented, because all such efforts seemed to involve someone in loss of revenue.

By way of contrast, the foreign treaty tariff, although its rates were usually higher than those of the native tariff, was now being applied to suit the convenience of the merchant, who might move his Western importations from port to port indefinitely without paying more than a single import duty. The stage was thus set for disputes over borderline cases. By which tariff were goods to be taxed when in the hands of a Chinese merchant lading on a British vessel? The combinations and permutations devised by the merchants of both countries left the consular archives littered with correspondence, much of it as confusing to the Chinese customs as it is to the historian. In general, practice varied from port to port and from time to time at the same port, as a few examples will show. The object of the merchants in most cases was to enjoy both the privileges of the foreign tariff and the lower rates of the native tariff, while the customs collectors as consistently tried to fill their own coffers.

Thus in August 1845 British merchants at Canton sought to pay the native export duty on Chinese produce when they took it out of Canton, and claim a return of this export duty at the port of discharge. The Hoppo refused.[17] In April 1848 Murrow and Company brought to Canton certain

Chinese produce from Shanghai, and the Canton customs demanded certificates proving payment of export duties at Shanghai and also levied import duties of 5 per cent, as on articles unenumerated in the treaty tariff. This led to an investigation in which the consul ascertained that native vessels from the other ports, having paid export duty there, did not pay import duty at Canton according to the native tariff but only a small charge per picul levied on cargo without reference to its nature. Shortly afterward a Parsee merchant revived the claim for a certificate exempting his Chinese produce from import duty at Shanghai after it had paid export duty at Canton. On this principle the consul also asked that native produce which had paid export duties at Shanghai, and received a certificate exempting it from all further payments of duty, be allowed to enter free at Canton. The Hoppo refused both requests, his receipts having fallen below normal. But it is plain that the tendency already existed to extend the foreign privileges to Chinese produce.[18]

In January 1849 the question was temporarily shelved by the circulation of an opinion from the advocate general in London that the Chinese government had not by treaty granted the right to import Chinese produce at one port free, if export duty had been paid at another, and therefore could act as it pleased in the matter.[19]

In the spring of 1847 the Amoy authorities warned Chinese merchants not to ship their goods on British ships. This was a blow aimed at the British carrying trade between Amoy and the Straits, and Governor Davis immediately rebuffed it. To Ch'i-ying he repeated an argument used by Pottinger four years before, that the restrictions placed by treaty on the foreign trade of Chinese merchants had referred only to Hongkong, and that necessarily when one thing was specifically restricted, all other things were thereby left unrestricted. This sophistry was accompanied by a veiled threat. It got the desired result. In September 1847 Ch'i-ying agreed that there should be no interference with Chinese shipments in British vessels. The Amoy authorities were told that such interference would contravene the "conventional rights" of England as well as the interpretation agreed upon by the imperial commissioner.[20]

The concession thus extorted from the higher authorities now remained to be extracted from the lower. The British claim under it was that Chinese might ship Chinese goods on British ships and pay duties according to the Chinese tariff, rather than the treaty tariff. This amounted to full British participation in the coastal carrying trade. Whether Ch'i-ying had actually granted the use of the native tariff was uncertain, but the consuls took it for granted. In 1848 the Amoy customs in the presence of a consular officer levied duties at the Chinese tariff rate on 170 baskets of sugar shipped by a Chinese merchant on the British vessel *Sophie Fraser* to Shanghai.[21] It was hoped that this would form a clear precedent, and the report of the consular interpreter, Mr. Medhurst, who happened to be a passenger aboard the vessel, was eagerly awaited. But the reception of the shipment at Shanghai was disappointing. Ch'i-ying's supposed concession of 1847, that native goods owned by Chinese shippers should pay duty at the native rate, was inoperative, the high authorities of Kiangnan having decided [22] that the new treaty tariff should apply.[b]

In June 1848 Syme, Muir and Company, British merchants at Amoy, sought to improve their fortunes by shipping locally produced sugar on their vessel the *Amoy Packet* to the Shanghai market, claiming it to be Chinese owned and therefore dutiable by the Chinese native tariff (Tls. 217) instead of by the treaty tariff (Tls. 567). By an agreement between Davis and Ch'i-ying of the previous year, the names of Chinese shippers on British vessels were to be given to the customs. It soon appeared that Syme, Muir and Company, although they indulged in "the most disgraceful and disgusting falsehoods and prevarications," were themselves the owners and shippers of the sugar. The customhouse finally checked them by declaring that Chinese-owned sugar would have to pay an export duty at Amoy, and an import duty at Shanghai, plus the usual fees collected from Chinese junks — all in all a good deal more than would be due by the treaty tariff itself.[24]

Parkes' inconclusive victory at Amoy. By 1854 (to look ahead for a moment) the principle of re-export had been applied to Chinese produce taxed under the treaty tariff — in effect, native produce which paid the treaty export duty at one treaty port was freed from paying import duties on entering a second treaty port. Thus the treaty tariff for China's foreign trade was being applied to Chinese produce carried along the China coast. The result was that the customs collector of the first port levied duties by the higher foreign tariff (apparently with enthusiasm) and issued a duty certificate to exempt the goods from further payments, and the customs collector of the second port got nothing. This opportunism was practiced particularly at Amoy, where the staple tea and silk exports destined for England under the treaty tariff were inconsiderable, and the miscellaneous

[b] Foochow was the slowest of all the ports in the development of this coasting trade. As late as December 1849 a Portuguese there, Pedro Nolesco da Silva, appealed for British consular advice because his lorcha, the *Taoukwang*, laden with 1000 tubs of oranges for Ningpo, was detained by the customs on the grounds that shipping Chinese produce from one Chinese port to another in a foreign vessel would interfere with the Chinese coasting trade — as indeed it would. The customs would not object to his shipping to Macao or another foreign port. Even if he left Foochow altogether, it was asserted that da Silva's oranges could not be admitted at Ningpo; the customs there had strict orders from the Tartar-general of Fukien. Apparently this strictness manifested at Foochow expressed not only the usual antiforeignism of the Fukien administration but also the more uncompromising spirit of Ch'i-ying's successor as imperial commissioner. Bonham at any rate thought it best not to appeal to Commissioner Hsü lest it "induce that functionary to introduce modifications at the other ports" where all was going well. As a result, the foreign lorches at Foochow in 1850 were kept busy acting as convoys for Chinese junks but did not themselves carry Chinese produce.[23]

items of native produce destined for other ports in China consequently formed the chief cargo of outbound ships. Contradictions therefore developed most strikingly at Amoy; they were brought to a head in 1854 by the British brig *Kitty* in which Tait and Company sent to Foochow a mixed cargo all owned by Chinese merchants. The vessel being foreign, export duties were levied by the foreign tariff and a duty certificate was issued exempting the cargo from further payments of duty. The cargo passed through Foochow successfully and the *Kitty* reached Ningpo on May 16 with 188,000 catties of sugar which had paid Tls. 300 as export duty at Amoy and so claimed exemption from import duty at Ningpo. To this the Ningpo authorities strenuously objected: "the custom house of the whole province of Chekiang is completely dependent on the duties levied on the sugar and other native produce of Fukien for its annual stipulated sum of customs revenue." Piracy had decreased the trade and the revenue already; duty exemption certificates connected with foreign vessels could not be allowed to decrease it still further. The sugar importers in this case, two Chinese merchants, therefore presented a request (acting on the instigation of the unfortunate customs superintendent at Ningpo) that native goods in foreign vessels should pay duties by the native tariff and receive no exemption certificates. In view of the delicacy of inter-provincial relations, the superintendent at Ningpo forbore punishing the merchants, while giving them all the blame, and merely forwarded their petition with a few strong remarks of his own to the Amoy superintendent. Since the merchants had had to pay an additional Tls. 160 as import duties by native tariff at Ningpo, they therefore appealed through Tait and Company and the Amoy consul for a refund of the extra amount paid at Amoy according to the foreign tariff, which was higher than the native. This request was refused by the Amoy customs on the grounds that the sum collected had already been handed over to the local authorities.[25]

The use of a double standard in this case put the consular officer at Amoy, Harry Parkes, in a strong logical position. He pointed out that both tariffs could not be applied to one single shipment. Sugar in the British lorchas *Eliza* and *Mary Ann* had paid export duty at Amoy by the foreign tariff (Tls. 492) but on arrival at Ningpo had been obliged to pay in addition an import duty under the native tariff (Tls. 224). Either Amoy must refund the difference between the foreign and the native export duty or Ningpo must recognize the foreign tariff exemption certificate and refund the native tariff import duty. Using this logic in September 1854 Parkes was able to get an agreement from the Amoy customs which confirmed the participation of foreign vessels in the coastal carrying trade. On September 21, he announced his coup to the foreign community: native produce for Foochow and Ningpo in foreign vessels, either Chinese or foreign owned, would henceforth pay export duties at Amoy under the native tariff and import duties at Ningpo also by the native tariff. (Foochow being in the same province, under the native tariff a second duty would not be levied there.) Since the foreign duties had been about 12 per cent and the native rates on coarse sugar were only 2 per cent, a considerable saving would result.

The motivation of the Chinese customs collectors in taking this loss was evident: duties collected by the foreign tariff were supposed to be reported to Peking as collected, whereas the native customs duties were farmed out to the collectors. They had to pay a fixed sum and could keep whatever else they took in. The decline of coastwise shipping in Chinese junks and the increase of trade in foreign vessels under the foreign tariff had seriously injured their takings under the native tariff. The collectors therefore "replenished their own incomings at the expense of those of the foreign tariff, which should belong exclusively to their imperial master."[26]

Now the permission extorted from Ch'i-ying in 1847 that Chinese might ship goods on foreign vessels (presumably according to the native tariff) had at various times been refused acknowledgment at Canton, Amoy, and Shanghai. Parkes had therefore been careful to wait for official confirmation of his coup from the Fukien Tartar-general himself. The new ruling was now "enforced by his express direction." A month later, however, after several cargoes had left under it, the Tartar-general appears to have calculated the loss involved and suffered a change of heart. The Amoy customs superintendent informed Consul Parkes on October 22 that native duty payments had been allowed "only as a measure of temporary convenience"; the whole question had been referred to the imperial commissioner at Canton. Parkes met this tergiversation by quoting the previous correspondence at length, and, a fortnight later, sending copies of it to the Foochow consul for delivery to the Tartar-general, directly.[27]

A week later the Amoy customs added to its record of inconsistency by demanding foreign tariff duties on a cargo of Chinese sugar in the British vessel *Crisis* destined for Foochow, on the ground that the late ruling applied only to Ningpo. Parkes objected and got a deferment of duty payment until the issue of foreign versus native tariffs should be finally settled, meanwhile laying this further correspondence before the Tartar-general at Foochow. By this means he hoped to aid British penetration of the coasting trade to Foochow, which appeared to be a lucrative one, especially in the comparative absence of any genuine foreign trade. In the year 1845–46, for instance, native trade to Foochow by junk had carried $237,000 worth of sugar from Amoy and its neighborhood, $134,911 worth of native cotton from Shanghai, and $218,665 worth of cotton cloths from Soochow via Shanghai.[28]

At this point Parkes was prepared for a showdown between the British minister and the imperial commissioner, but the former at once pointed out that he could not repeat an application to the commissioner which was grounded on no treaty right and which had already been refused by him. He urged that the matter be soft-pedalled, since the commissioner could overrule provincial arrangements if he wished. At the end of 1854, the Fukien Tartar-general, evidently avoiding a reference to Canton which would indicate his own inconsistencies, gave in, and the Amoy customs removed its objections to the agreement of September. Parkes therefore claimed that he had finally won for British shipping "the right to participate in the coasting trade of China." [29] But this concession which Parkes dramatized at Amoy was a purely local concession. Bowring repeated in February 1856 that "British ships have no treaty right to convey . . . Chinese produce shipped from one port to another in China . . . and I am sorry to say the Imperial Commissioner has distinctly prohibited its conveyance . . . Nothing beyond a tacit non-interference has been hitherto accomplished, and I am quite unable to give any official protection to a trade which stands upon no lawful foundation." [30]

Since this concession at Amoy — for a coast trade in native produce carried in British bottoms and taxed by the native tariff — was purely a local matter without legal foundation, difficulty was experienced in extending it to other ports. At Ningpo goods arrived from Shanghai under exemption certificates (i.e., foreign tariff) and the consul naturally felt it his duty to demand exemption from the native tariff import duty which the customs tried to levy. He asked that the duty certificates issued at Shanghai state distinctly under which tariff, native or foreign, the duties in each case had been levied. The Ningpo customs were particularly opposed to letting Chinese produce owned by Chinese enter port duty free; while the consul was equally opposed to having such produce be carried in British ships and yet pay (1) export duty on leaving Amoy, (2) import duty when transshipped at Shanghai, and (3) import duty at Ningpo.[31]

Sailing letters. Underlying the administrative battle over tariffs lay a more significant development, the use of foreign flags in coastwise shipping. British vessels in Chinese waters, as already seen in Chapter 8, were required to carry sailing letters entitling them to the use of the British flag. This gave them a recognized status in British law, but their status under the treaties was less clear.

Of the seven treaties and agreements made between England and China in the years 1842–58, only the Supplementary treaty of 1843 made any reference to the possibility of a local trade, to be conducted solely between ports on the coast of China. Article XVII provided specifically for the regulation of British-owned small craft plying between Hongkong, Canton, and

Macao only, and concluded as already noted, with the famous brush-off: Foochow and the other ports "having none of this kind of intercourse, and none of this kind of small craft," needed no similar arrangement. Aside from this one article, the first treaties provided that vessels (as distinct from small craft) owned by foreigners could trade between any of the five ports opened by treaty, but not at any other ports or places in China on penalty of confiscation of ship and cargo by the Chinese government (Hongkong and Macao were foreign ports). This was provided by article IV of the British Supplementary treaty (1843), and was reiterated in articles III and XXXIII of the American treaty (1844). Article III of the latter states explicitly that American vessels "shall not unlawfully enter the other ports of China, nor carry on a clandestine and fraudulent trade along the coasts thereof." The French treaty (1844) and the treaty of Canton with Sweden and Norway (1847), both of which were modelled on the American treaty, repeat the interdiction.

The first appearance of British small craft in the north had been due to the occupation of Chusan, where the British marine magistrate issued sailing letters to British schooners and other craft so as to entitle them to the use of the flag in their necessary work of transporting supplies from the mainland. This was a proceeding of limited legal value, however, as the magistrate's sailing letters themselves made evident.[c] When British vessels of this type arrived at Ningpo, the Chinese authorities allowed them to enjoy the concession gained in the American treaty, that merchant vessels of 150 tons or under should pay only one mace per ton as tonnage dues; but a year after the opening of the port they pointed out that the Supplementary treaty had forbidden such craft at Foochow and the other ports and asked for the facts of the case. The consul appears to have side-stepped the question and let the small craft continue their operations on an uncertain basis.[32]

The foreign coasting trade remained on this basis for the next decade — a *de facto* activity like the opium trade, which actually needed no basis *de jure*. When that ardent Benthamite, Sir J. Bowring, in his effort to make

[c] These documents issued at Chusan were very circumspect indeed, headed "*Sailing Letter*, to be renewed yearly to the privileges of British Ships duly registered and Navigated" and reading in part: ". . . The said Ship, or vessel, 'Owners Delight,' is the property of a British Subject, and She is therefore entitled to the protection of the Laws of England in all matters relating to the rights of property. But I do at the same time make known that by this Sailing Letter, there are given to the said vessel no rights of Trade, or Navigation, which are by the Laws of England confined to British Ships properly so called, and provided with certificates of British Registry; which is the only legal evidence of their title to that Character; nor to exercise any priveledge of Trade or Navigation, which is by the Law of England confined to the ships of any Foreign Country, owned, and navigated by the subjects of such country; But in as much as the British Laws of Navigation, and registry do not preclude British Subjects from employing other than registered ships, in voyages between Foreign Countries between which they Trade, nor in certain other cases, this sailing letter is granted to the said ship or vessel 'Owners Delight' in order that she may be duly protected as British property, while employed in any such unrestricted voyages, and for the more certain identification of the said Vessel for which this letter is granted, I do hereby certify that she has, . . ." etc. (BN).

the regulations fit the facts, described his licensing of the British coasting trade in a dispatch to the foreign secretary, Lord Clarendon, the latter remarked in pencil, "approve. I conclude he (Bowring) is legally empowered to give sailing licenses." Nevertheless it was a question whether the British superintendent at this time possessed legal power to grant sailing licenses, under a strict interpretation of the treaty, especially in view of the fact that the law officers of the crown later decided against the legality of the coasting trade as it was conducted before the treaty of 1858.

So far as the British community alone was concerned, both the opium receiving ships and the running vessels were careful to qualify for the right to fly the British flag, usually by being registered in the name of the captain. Thus James Miln requested a sailing letter from the Amoy consul for the *Aurora* in 1848, naming himself as her owner, resident at Amoy. As a matter of fact, she was part of the opium fleet, newly purchased and transferred from the Spanish flag. Governor Bonham refused to grant a sailing letter *in absentia* for the first time, and the *Aurora* was required to come to Hongkong in order that the proper bond might be signed and fees paid.[d]

On the other hand, once a vessel had received a sailing letter, its owner might renew it from a distance without presenting either himself or the vessel for further formalities. The general result of this practice was that each of the opium captains on the coast was listed as owner of several vessels, and sometimes as master of two at once. The same James Miln in July 1848 obtained a renewal of the sailing letter of the barque *Mahamoodie* and asked also for a renewal of that of the *Gazelle*. The consulate at Amoy asked that the actual master of the *Gazelle* be designated

[d] The form of sailing letter bond used in the 1850's at Hongkong was a formidable legal document: "Know all Men by these Presents, that______ of______ British Merchant and Owner of the______ called the______ and______ Master of the said Vessel, are held and firmly bound to ______ Her Brittanic Majesty's Chief Superintendent of Trade in China and Governor of Hongkong, in the full Sum of______ Dollars of the lawful currency of Hongkong, to be paid to the said ______ his Assigns or Successors in the Offices last aforesaid, for which Payment to be faithfully made we bind ourselves, and each of us jointly and severally, and our and each of our heirs, Executors, and Administrators, and everyone of them, firmly by these presents; in witness we have hereunto put our respective Hands and Seals the______ day of______ 185______ Whereas a Sailing Letter of even date with these Presents has been granted for the______ called the______ to the within bound______ by the said______ Now the Condition of this Obligation is such, that if the aforesaid Sailing Letter be not sold, lent, or otherwise disposed of to any persons whatever, and that the same be solely made use of for the service of the said ______ the ______ and in case the said ______ the ______ be Lost, or taken by the Enemy, Burnt, or Broken up, or otherwise prevented from returning to Hongkong aforesaid, or shall have been taken in Execution for Debt, and sold by due process of Law, or shall have been sold to the Crown, or shall under any circumstance have obtained a fresh Sailing Letter or in case of any new Master being appointed to the said Vessel, or in case of the said Sailing Letter being demanded from the within bound______ by the said______ or his Successors in Office, — then if the said Sailing Letter be delivered up to the said______ or his Successors in Office, within One Month from the time of the happening of any of the first mentioned events, or shall be delivered up forthwith on its being demanded by the said______ or his Successors in Office, then and in such case this Obligation shall be void and of no effect, but otherwise shall remain in full force and virtue. Signed, Sealed, and Delivered at Victoria, Hongkong, this ______ day of______ One Thousand Eight Hundred and Fifty-______ " (BA).

in the application, and Miln accordingly named his colleague Mr. Crawford. But it developed that Crawford was already the commander of the brig *Harlequin* which lay in Chinchew Bay and received her supplies from the *Gazelle*. The consular officers believed that this double mastership was irregular. The superintendency officials at Hongkong agreed with them and refused to renew the sailing letter of the *Gazelle* until a master should be expressly named for her.[33] (It is interesting to note that the laws of England prevented the irregularity of one man signing as master of two vessels on the coast of China but could not take cognizance of the fact that both man and vessels were professionally engaged in breaking the laws of China.) Although sailing letters were taken out for the receiving ships in most cases, it was not always necessary to renew them, since the vessels remained permanently on the coast. Jardine's *Harlequin* received a sailing letter in 1844 at the inauguration of the sailing letter system. It expired on August 6, 1845, but the brig continued in business until her sale in March 1858 — almost thirteen years under the British flag — without applying for a renewal.[34]

Outside the opium fleet, the number of British small craft registered at the northern ports under sailing letters from Hongkong during the late 1840's was still inconsiderable, the chief growth being at Canton. Here we find mention of at least eight lorchas and schooners in the years 1847–49. Some, like the *Wild Irish Girl*, were used as supply vessels ("bumboats") at Whampoa and Cumsingmoon, but most of them were in the delta trade.[35] The chief problem which they presented to the authorities arose from the fact that they could not easily be differentiated from the Portuguese lorchas based on Macao. These latter craft were to be a thorn in the side of the British government for more than a decade both at Canton and on the coast.

The Portuguese lorchas. The Portuguese at Macao occupied a position somewhere between a "Chinaman" and a "barbarian." After almost 300 years, the Macao population were in fact interbred with Chinese. They had taken on a certain protective coloring which made them fit more easily into the Chinese scene than Anglo-Saxon newcomers from the West. Macao was in some respects a backwater, where a previous century was preserved. But during the first treaty period an effort was made there to come up to date and join in the Western penetration of China. The attempt to spread the rule of law, to establish the Portuguese claim to sovereignty over Macao, and to place Portuguese consuls in the treaty ports, plus certain internal reforms during this period, all indicate that a degree of regeneration occurred in the ancient settlement *pari passu* with the British invasion of the China coast.

Until March 1849 when the Portuguese successfully asserted their independence at Macao, the status of that settlement was a perplexing legal problem. If Portuguese sovereignty were recognized, the rights gained by the British treaties with China would not be valid there. But if Chinese control were recognized, then it would be possible for the Chinese authorities, supposing they knew international law, to argue that Macao was not a treaty port and hence that British rights of trade were equally invalid. In 1844 the facts were somewhere in between. The Chinese assistant district magistrate issued licenses to Chinese residents and gave orders to the "head of the soldiers," the Portuguese governor. A Chinese customhouse collected duties at Macao. The Portuguese on their part taxed their own foreign trade, and also the opium trade. But their exactions on the latter in 1822 ($40 a chest) had driven it to Lintin, just as later exactions had driven out rich Portuguese merchants. Foreign residents had increased after the expulsion of the British from Canton in 1839, but had again declined with the growth of the free port of Hongkong. In general, the Portuguese population appears to have degenerated in proportion as it became assimilated to its Chinese environment. After much puzzling over the confusion of sovereignty at Macao, the Foreign Office decided in November 1844 to sidestep the question if possible, avoiding any recognition of Portuguese sovereignty and yet not allowing the Chinese to object that it was not a port open by treaty.[36] Meanwhile on November 26, 1844, by an Anglo-Portuguese agreement made at Macao, the port had finally been opened again to the trade of British vessels which had been expelled during the late war. Even so, British merchants continued to be hampered by the bias of the Macao courts, where a Portuguese who, as an attorney, had lost a case might later decide it in his own favor as judge.[37]

In May 1844 the Chinese local authorities of Hsiang-shan, the district of Macao, proposed three rules for the control of Portuguese lorchas: (1) that they should not be rented to Chinese, (2) that they should be numbered and clearly marked for identification, and (3) that they should not be allowed to enter the inner waters without authorization. The high provincial authorities conferred and agreed to these proposals and asked British coöperation. Since the proposed regulations accorded with the Supplementary treaty, except for the numbering of the lorchas, there was no British objection.[38] But it remained practically impossible for Chinese minor officers, who spent their days chiefly in the avoidance of trouble, to coerce these heavily armed vessels from Macao; and they continued to come and go unchecked. Chinese efforts at regulation were impeded by the fact that foreign lorchas were under two or more categories, according to the flag they carried: British lorchas with sailing letters from Hongkong were entitled by treaty to come up to Canton, whereas Portuguese lorchas from Macao, each of which bore a number registered with the Chinese authorities, were supposed to come only as far as Whampoa.[39]

Early in 1845 "bitch-bellied" lorchas appeared on the West River to the west of Canton (i.e., inland), asserting that they were selling salt and were *Hung-mao* ("red hairs") of Portugal and England, deputed by their "great naval officer" to go everywhere and sell goods. A military officer of low rank was sent to warn them away and Ch'i-ying appealed to Consul Macgregor, who effectively disclaimed them. A few months later foreign lorchas were smuggling so flagrantly under the very noses of mandarin boats off the Canton factories that the consul arranged to enforce against British lorchas the treaty procedure applicable to larger vessels. With Davis' concurrence it was agreed that small craft under British colors would be given port clearances by the Hongkong harbor master and the Canton consul, respectively, as they came and went, and would report their inward and outward cargoes at the consulate. It was hoped this would stimulate Chinese action against the Portuguese.[40] Ch'i-ying and Huang took up the problem and with consular concurrence published in June 1845 eight regulations for small craft.[41] But these regulations were really effective for only a few weeks. In August 1845 small craft were reporting to the consulate as coming and going in ballast, while actually carrying opium from the receiving station at Lintin and smuggling as before. The new system of port clearances from Hongkong merely served as a cloak for this, and irregularity continued.[42] Thus the lighter *William* produced a sailing letter from Hongkong in its English version only, raising the question whether the Chinese half had not been taken for fraudulent use on another vessel. Again the *Therese*, 44 tons, owned by a Mr. Lane of Canton, sailed under a register issued at Calcutta in 1840 which lacked notations of ownership since that date. A lorcha caught smuggling 20,000 catties of contraband salt had a sailing letter made up of sections in English and Chinese pasted together. Ch'i-ying and Huang applied to the consul to see if the lorcha were English, but the master was named Antonio (*An-tun*).[43] In February 1846 the Canton authorities issued a notice requiring Macao lorchas to report for examination or be treated as smugglers. "Upwards of 100" such vessels had been flouting the regulations.[44]

Portuguese consular control over this activity was for long a minus quantity. In July 1847 the Canton Hoppo put forward the idea that a Portuguese lorcha which brought goods from Hongkong should be reported through the British consul. The consul privately feared that if Portuguese lorchas entered the Hongkong-Canton trade it would greatly increase the smuggling problem. Since Hongkong was a free port, Portuguese lorchas must be welcomed; but he urged that in the absence of a Portuguese consul, the masters of lorchas should report directly to the customs.[45] The Portuguese had already found it to their advantage to have consuls in the ports, usually a British merchant. Thus John Dent became Portuguese consul at Canton as early as 1849.[46] T. C. Beale of Dent, Beale and Company at Shanghai likewise became Portuguese consul there. Governor Amaral as one move in his assertion of independence at Macao in April 1849 announced a decree of his home government of the preceding December, that all Portuguese anywhere in China were under the jurisdiction of the Macao courts, as of old.[47] At the same time Governor Bonham ruled that the British consular court at Canton would be open to the plaints of all Portuguese subjects.

But these efforts were insufficient. At Amoy the Portuguese played their customary role as disturbers of the peace, importing cannon for lawless natives or transporting Chinese subjects in irons to Macao in defiance of the local authorities.[48] At Foochow Portuguese lorchas passed themselves off as English, carrying papers of *Ta-Ying-kuo*, the "Great English Nation," in Chinese and Portuguese. The local populace and the magistrates being totally unable to distinguish foreign nationalities, much hard feeling against the British was engendered along the coast. On the other hand, when an honest lorcha master felt he had to fire into a mob, in the process of rescuing his crew from a house of ill-fame, at least one British consul was not averse to helping "an European without friends" in a far country.[49]

It was at Ningpo, however, that the Portuguese problem became most acute. Their early activity there had long been a matter of legend, and Professor Pelliot has concluded that the early Portuguese settlement of Liampo described by Mendez Pinto and others was probably Ningpo. The old settlement was perhaps downstream toward Chen-hai, near the fort which was found to have Portuguese arms engraved on it. No proof has yet emerged of Pinto's story of this settlement's sudden destruction in 1542, and it appears to have died slowly.[50] In the 1840's the Portuguese connection with Ningpo arose purely from their participation in the coasting trade, which apparently began soon after the opening of the port.

CHAPTER XVIII

NINGPO: PIRACY AND CONVOY

ALL THE DEVELOPMENTS noted above finally became concentrated at Ningpo after 1847. It was a center for the junk trade but its only commerce for Westerners was the coastal interport trade, in which native produce, Chinese merchants and the native tariff all became involved; and the chief foreign vessels using the port were small craft under the flags of Britain and Portugal. The concentration of this activity at Ningpo betokened one main fact, that Ningpo had become an outport, cut off from the main flow of tea and silk in international trade. This trend emerged early in the history of the port.

When they opened Ningpo the British had high expectations. An early traveler to the five ports noted in 1845 that "Ningpo has the reputation of being the finest city on the coast of China open to foreigners . . . inferior only to Soo-chow and Hang-chow in the refinement and taste of the people." He was told that one-fifth of the population belonged to the literary class.[1] It is indeed noteworthy that more than half of the 500 private libraries of note during the Ch'ing period were situated in Chekiang and Kiangsu, Chekiang alone having had some 267 individual book collectors; and the outstanding private collection in the country was in fact the T'ien-i-ko of the Fan family at Ningpo, whose catalogue in 1808 listed over 4000 valuable works. Its editions were housed in a fireproof building under strict control, and had been taken as standard sources during the great literary compilation work of the late eighteenth century.[2] Yet this very concentration of Chinese literati created a xenophobic barrier to the early growth of Sino-foreign contact.

Commercially Ningpo was an equally prominent center, both for the junk trade north and south along the coast, and for the fishing industry in Hangchow bay. The Maritime Customs estimated in 1890 that in the Ningpo area including the Chusan archipelago there were "at least 10,000 fishing-boats and at least 80,000 fishermen."[3] Given this flourishing cultural and commercial background, the torpid development of Sino-Western intercourse at Ningpo proved a great disappointment to missionaries and merchants alike.

Consul Thom had entered upon his duties auspiciously, arriving at Ningpo in H. M. S. *Medusa* on December 19, 1843, and presenting his credentials to the taotai on the following day, accompanied for the moment by a suite of British officers from Chusan.[4] Save for a brief trip to Shanghai, Thom did not leave Ningpo again before his death at the age of 39 on September 14, 1846. For much of that time he acted as his own translator and interpreter, which inevitably lowered him in Chinese eyes. Indeed, he confessed himself "as yet quite a novice in Government employ." It seems quite plain that his commercial background hit the eye of all beholders. For an official in China he knew far too much about trade. With the Chinese authorities he soon drew up and published regulations for governing British subjects, and for British merchant vessels, together with various circulars, and a paper of "Hints" to British merchants. His consulate was established in a building formerly occupied as a wood yard by the Tung Sang (*T'ung-sheng*) firm, in the region known as San-kuan-t'ang ("Hall of the three officials") on the east bank of the river. A customs examining shed was erected on ground leased on the north bank of the other river (two rivers meet at Ningpo) opposite the consulate at a place called locally Lee-kea-taow-tow (*Li-chia-tao t'ou*, lit., "head of the street of the Li family"). The river bank at that place was known as Shang-pih-sha (*Shang-pai-sha*), and British ships were to anchor between it and the opposite river bank in front of the consulate.[5]

All these preparations and hopes were nullified when foreign trade in legal goods failed to develop at Ningpo. Consul Thom reported that the native green tea men at the beginning were prepared for big shipments. But the only purchaser at the new port was the British ship *Nautilus*, 232 tons, which obtained 246,695 lbs. of tea for the small sum of $33,000 and made a 75 per cent profit in London. Meantime teas were in great demand at Canton and prices higher. After keeping several thousand chests of tea on hand for two months or more in vain, the tea men removed in disgust to Canton. So brief was the direct overseas trade of Ningpo. It lent support to the contemporary theory that the Cantonese were striving to eclipse trade elsewhere than at Canton; even so, competitive bidding among English buyers at Ningpo might have encouraged the tea market there.[6]

In the end, however, Ningpo was bound to be eclipsed by Shanghai on the single score of communication facilities. As Thom explained, Shanghai was "Sze tung pa-ta ti" (*ssu-t'ung pa-ta ti*, open to communication in all directions), while Ningpo was cut off from all but its immediate hinterland by rivers. Hangchow, Kashing, and such cities were supplied from Chapu. Taichow and Wenchow on the Chekiang coast farther south supplied themselves, "and a considerable amount of illegal traffic is carried on at a place called Shippo" (*Shih-p'u*), later to become famous as a pirate den. By the end of 1845 he reported that "Shanghai has drawn everything to its centre, it has flooded this market with its superabundant importations." The green tea merchants complained that the consul did not compel British merchants to come to Ningpo, nor compel them to accept fair prices. The situation was hopeless and continued so. For the first half of 1848 the trade returns of the port totalled: imports, 17 bales of grey shirtings; exports, 3 piculs of ginseng and 300 piculs of sandalwood.[7]

The Chekiang authorities themselves analyzed the failure of trade and hence of customs revenue at Ningpo as due to poor communications. In June 1844 the Chekiang governor, Liang Pao-ch'ang, reported that while the foreigners on Chusan took their exercise and secured provisions on friendly terms with the populace, the opening of trade at Ningpo had not produced much commercial activity; in two months only six ships had come; customs duties had totalled only Tls. 16,000. Consul Thom said these ships had brought goods from Canton and others might come in the autumn. But the governor feared these goods could not be sold, Chinese merchants would be few, fewer foreign ships would come to Chekiang, and customs collections would be small. He observed that for various reasons there was little market for foreign goods in six of the eleven prefectures of Chekiang, while in the five prefectures of Hangchow, Kashing, Huchow, Ningpo and Shao-hsing the population was larger, foreign broadcloth found a market, and the chief exports, silks and satins, as well as tea, were also produced. But although seven-tenths of the trade was with these prefectures, unfortunately they were all connected with Kiangsu by waterways. Their imports for daily use and their silk and satin exports could all pass through Shanghai, on a route where porterage was cheaper than to Canton. Yet even Canton was an established emporium to which merchants came with quick transportation and no obstruction of goods or profits, while the port of Ningpo was off in a corner. It was over five hundred *li* from Hangchow across two big rivers. At Shao-hsing the river was narrow and shallow, boats could not carry much, porterage was very expensive. Ningpo could expect to be a port only for eastern Chekiang. The Huchow silk reaching Ningpo from western Chekiang had amounted to only about 4000 catties, and its future supply at Ningpo was uncertain.[8]

Features of outport life. In the absence of all real business, Consul Thom developed the choleric temperament peculiar to lonely outposts. In October 1841 shortly after the occupation of Ningpo by the British forces he had become the patron of a young Chinese traitor named Lo Luhming, a native of the district, of prepossessing appearance and about 26 years of age, who offered his services in return for friendship and protection and became Thom's right hand man. His mother was immediately removed from Ningpo to Chusan and put under the care of the British magistrate. In the spring of 1844 the Chinese authorities succeeded in extraditing Lo Luhming from Chusan on charges of extortion and brought him to Ningpo. The British magistrate at Chusan had complacently made no investigation. Consul Thom rushed to the rescue. In the process he felt obliged to establish himself in a Chinese police station in Ningpo with the British flag hoisted over the doorway. Luhming was finally released on the consul's security, but Lord Aberdeen and others expressed their "entire disapproval" of actions so likely to degrade the consular office.[9]

Thom's commercial sense of values involved him in a similar lowering of the flag the following year. In March 1845 two trunks were irregularly landed from the British schooner *Owners Delight*, on the riverbank between Ningpo and Chen-hai. The master, whose name was Thompson, and an English-speaking Cantonese went to the Chen-hai customhouse and demanded them back, with threats. The authorities appealed to the consul, who conducted a joint investigation, and found in one trunk 57 balls of Patna opium — over half a chest. It also appeared that the *Owners Delight* flew the British flag under a sailing letter granted by the British magistrate at Chusan, but the bill of sale to a British subject was irregular and executed before an American merchant, Mr. Bates, who possessed no legal authority. The opium was owned in part by the Chinese firm of Tung Ha, to whom Mr. Bates always consigned the vessel. In short the British flag was being used by an American for opium smuggling. Thom took away the flag and sailing letter and for some reason brought the 57 balls of opium up to the British consulate for storage, where 27 balls were mysteriously stolen. He therefore issued a public notification offering a reward for the opium stolen from the British consulate but no thief was ever convicted.[a] His superiors censured him.

A year after his arrival the British community at Ningpo consisted of three persons, a merchant named Charles D. Mackenzie who struggled for a year and a half to develop a trade and finally left; a missionary, Miss Mary Ann Aldersey, who became a sort of local saint and by the time of Robert Hart's arrival in 1854 was ensconsed in a local temple; and another missionary lady from Batavia. The Reverend George Smith on his tour of the treaty ports visited Ningpo in the summer of 1845 and found the houses of the foreign residents forming a little suburb on the north bank of the river across from the city. In order to prosecute his missionary labors he rented a house at $9.00 a month within the city between the East Gate and the Salt Gate, visited the various Buddhist, Taoist, and Moslem establishments to observe his competitors, and began to study the local dialect and pass out Protestant tracts. At a religious service held by some American missionaries he found "about sixty persons, consisting principally of Chinese servants, teachers, and pupils . . . Boys could be

[a] Thom to District Magistrate Ye-kwun, June 15, 1845: "On the 5th of April last my consulate was robbed of a chest containing 27 balls of Patna opium on which occasion I issued public notices offering a reward for the conviction of the offenders but without result."[10]

obtained from their parents without difficulty, for a term of years, to be educated by the Missionaries." But since the local Chinese were willing to entrust little girls only to an unmarried female, Miss Aldersey's school already had a head start.[11]

At the end of two years this number of British subjects had grown to eight missionaries, with two Indian servants and one from England, and three merchants with two clerks. A year later the British residents outside the consulate still numbered only fifteen; no American or French merchants arrived, and the port took on the Janus-faced character which it was to maintain for a generation. It became a flourishing center of missionary good works within the city walls and of opium smuggling, piracy, extortion and petty violence outside the port limits.

Ningpo saw little of the opium trade until 1846. In March of 1844 the *Mazeppa*, Captain Fraser, had tried to begin a trade off Chen-hai at the mouth of the river, but had given it up after a week's trial. Meanwhile the three to five receiving ships nearby at Chusan delivered regularly 100 to 200 chests a month, which went to Taichow, Wenchow and such places on the Chekiang coast. In 1845 one-tenth of the total China drug trade was estimated to have passed through the Chusan station, viz., 1000–1200 chests of Bengal, 2500–3000 chests of Malwa, and 150–200 chests of Turkey opium.[12] The consul estimated the local Ningpo consumption at about one chest of Patna and 30 of Malwa a month. Until the case of the *Owners Delight* in March 1845, mentioned above, he had had little evidence of the Chinese official connivance in drug smuggling, on which Sir John Davis was piling up evidence. The evacuation of Chusan in the middle of 1846 and the breaking up of the foreign community there meant an increase of activity at Ningpo. Mr. Davidson, the highly respectable merchant who had turned down Pottinger's offer of an officiating vice-consulship at Amoy, shortly after his removal to Ningpo reported to the consul confidentially that in August 1846 he had imported 38 chests of opium from Chusan to Ningpo with the assistance of three Chinese, one of whom was a white-button (i.e., sixth-rank) mandarin named Chang Kia-tsin. These three men divided a bonus which they received after the arrival of the drug. Their presence was the "best possible protection for its safe entry into Ningpo." [13]

Further evidence of official corruption at Ningpo was seen in the taotai's purchase of saltpetre. According to the British consul, the military authorities bought their saltpetre for the manufacture of gunpowder by sending to the production centre in Honan and paying a fixed government price on delivery at Ningpo. By the treaty tariff, imported saltpetre was "to be sold to Government agents only." When the American schooner *Boxer* imported 36 bags in 1844, the taotai bought it at $12 a picul in the market.

This new market became overstocked, however, when two British vessels in June brought in, respectively, 25 bags and 348 bags of saltpetre, and 426 bags of brimstone, "expressly designed for the government," that is, the taotai. That official was unable to do business on so large a scale, but a deal was finally patched up by the commercially gifted consul, who arranged a price of $8 per picul and so allowed the merchants to make expenses. He urged that Ch'i-ying be asked to forbid further importations, lest a flood of cheap Calcutta gunpowder supplies arrive at the treaty ports. Ch'i-ying in October 1844 did request that no more cargoes be taken to Ningpo, on the ground that storage facilities were lacking. This request was repeated in July 1845 by the Chekiang authorities on the ground that Chinese production would be upset by foreign importations. In September of the following year an exception was made when Mr. Davidson wished to bring in 20,430 catties of saltpetre stored at Chusan, following its evacuation a few weeks before. Mr. Davidson made his own deal with the authorities, without reference to the consul.[14]

In these circumstances of stagnant foreign trade and official corruption which facilitated the opium traffic, Ningpo offered opportunities for the foreign coaster, and the confusion of native and foreign trade began early. In July 1844 the arrival of a Chinese from Malacca, a British subject importing goods in a British vessel, moved the superintendent of customs to express the nostalgic hope that British subjects would use only British ships and Chinese would ship only on native junks as of old. It was too late. Native boats were soon being used for foreign cargo. In October 1845 the consul discovered that the American merchant, Bates, had chartered a Chinese boat at Chusan to carry goods in foreign trade, on which duties had been levied according to the treaty tariff. The same privilege was claimed for British merchants, and the authorities acquiesced, by permission of Ch'i-ying. They agreed that goods destined for Ningpo in the cargo of a ship going to a larger port might be transshipped into native boats outside and made to pay duties only on reaching Ningpo. In the following month Davidson brought goods into Ningpo from Chusan by native boat, and at the end of the year he re-exported them to Canton, again by Chinese boat. This was all done under Consul Thom, although his successor, G. G. Sullivan, also claimed to have secured the "concession of introducing British merchandize in native boats, . . . a privilege enjoyed at no other port."[15]

When Ch'i-ying in September 1847 conceded the right of Chinese merchants to lade their goods on English vessels, Consul Sullivan at once claimed the right at Ningpo. The taotai waited for instructions directly from Canton, and Sullivan issued a notification by himself, to the Chinese mercantile community. In this he did not fail to point out that "our British vessels are strongly built and sail swiftly with all the winds, they carry goods with safety and without fear of pirates." Chinese merchants would themselves pay duty at the customhouse on their cargoes according to the Chinese (native) tariff, while the tonnage dues would be paid as usual either by the English captain or the consignees, the consul being a guarantor of both. The consul reported the Chinese merchants pleased at the prospect but hesitating for confirmation from their own authorities.[16]

The growth of piracy. Chinese use of British vessels was hastened by the growth of piracy, which became marked after 1847. In the last analysis this growth of disorder was a symptom of social ills which were soon to become manifest in the great Rebellion. We need not therefore assume, however, that piracy was a direct result of economic want along the coast. On the contrary, it may have been a recognition, by the adventurous riff-raff of the coastal provinces, that the coasting trade under the stimulus of foreign commerce now offered fatter pickings. More must be known of the economic and social situation of the 1840's before piracy can be seen in full context.

Opium appears to have been one strong incentive towards piracy. In the middle of 1847 pirates increased their forays against the opium boats which brought in drug from Lookong, the station outside and to the east of Ningpo. The receiving ship captains at the station in August took charge of a large West Coast boat (junk), which was found to be armed with three large 12-pounders, several swivels, some 400 lbs. of gunpowder, pikes, swords, 12 stink-pots, and false papers. The vessel and its crew of 25 men were delivered over to H. M. S. *Daedalus* and taken to Hongkong.[17]

The pirate lairs were concentrated off the coast of Chekiang half way between Shanghai and Amoy, particularly in the neighborhood of Shih-p'u (Shihpoo) and the Hei-shan ("Hieshan," "Sie Shan") Islands about 25 miles to the southeast. No large administrative centers adjoined this stretch of coast, and it contained valuable fishing banks. In the Chusan archipelago as a whole, during four months of the year, the pursuit of yellow-fish and cuttlefish supplied an important article of diet for the poor of the coastal area and employed some 4000 boats.[18] Chinese fishermen were soon appealing for British assistance. In May 1848 a poor woman living near the Ningpo consulate petitioned the consul for assistance in rescuing her son, a fisherman captured by pirates near the sacred island of P'u-t'o. The taotai had excused himself from employing the local Chinese naval vessels on the ground of the admiral's ill-health and an anticipated visit of inspection from the governor; he suggested that Captain Campbell of H. M. sloop *Espiègle* undertake the task. According to the consul, the admiral and his Chinese war-junks were afraid to leave port, being in every respect less efficient, less well-armed, and less numerous than the pirates. On the following day the crews of the fishing fleet, some eight or nine thousand men in all, gathered at Chen-hai. A month of the fishing season had already expired and, having obtained no help from their own authorities, they proceeded in a body to the customhouse and the magistracy and demolished a considerable part of them. When the Ningpo taotai appealed for the help of Captain Campbell, the consul seized the chance to demonstrate foreign prowess and good will, and the *Espiègle* was forthwith towed down the river to Chen-hai by forty Chinese boats sent by the taotai, followed by the admiral's junks with a great fanfare of guns and gongs. The chief magistrate of Chusan and another mandarin stood on the forecastle of the British sloop and harangued the mob, with assurances of British protection. The fishermen responded by showing contempt for their own officials but respect for the British sloop, which thereupon put to sea with them.[19]

By mid-1849 the Amoy consul estimated that at least 3000 pirates were operating off the Fukien coast. The British navy expanded its anti-pirate program. In a little over two years, between March 1847 and July 1849, Commander Loring of H. M. S. *Scout* and his successor Commander Lyons of H. M. S. *Pilot* had brought into Amoy and handed over to the Chinese authorities a total of 499 pirates. They were delivered in batches of 40, 60, and 80 at a time, after a series of eight pirate-hunting voyages. The Chinese officers at Amoy did little enough to help in the extermination, being at times unable even to provide "efficient pilots" for the British warships; but they formally tendered their thanks on each occasion. On a cruise in May and June 1849 H. M. S. *Pilot* captured 123 pirates alive and 60 dead, and freed 45 innocent persons who had been held, in many cases for nine months, awaiting ransoms of from $300 to $3,000. No British casualties were sustained.

The problems of pirate hunting were extremely intricate. It was often impossible to obtain proper assistance from the Chinese authorities, without which British naval officers were practically blind and tongue-tied. The mandarins themselves were uninformed regarding the coast and averse to losing face by accepting foreign help, while the native pilots were often unreliable and unable to handle all the dialects necessary, which included those of all the coastal provinces. Some foreigners were therefore inclined to take the easiest way and class all junks as pirates. The British lorcha *Victoria*, the property of Shaik Moosden ("Sic-me-deen") of Hongkong, on a seven weeks voyage up to Foochow with a Portuguese crew, fired consistently at everything that came within gunshot. Distinguishing friend from foe was sometimes impossible because Chinese vessels themselves were not sure of their own status. The British schooner *Aurora*, convoying 50 junks from Amoy to Foochow in January 1848, left her convoy briefly to get provisions; on her return she captured a pirate and found it manned by a crew from the junks of the convoy. At the beginning of February 1848 the Foochow consul reported that for the last year junks had been allowed to carry arms, contrary to the Chinese law usually in force.[20] This increased the difficulty of distinguishing the hunters and the hunted. It also meant that British naval vessels were more likely to make mistakes, and eventually their activities were curtailed for this reason.[b]

The convoy business. The natural antidote to piracy was convoy. Both fishing and cargo junks sought the protection to be got from sailing in fleets. But like all fleets of commercial vessels, they required fighting ships to deal with their attackers. Heavily armed foreign schooners and lorchas found a growing market for their services as professional private warships. In November 1847 the new 140-ton schooner *Amoy Packet*, aided by a Portuguese lorcha, brought a convoy of 120 junks safely into Ningpo from Chinchew with only two men wounded en route. Returning with a group of 30 junks, the *Amoy Packet* received $5,000 for the round trip. The British lorcha *Ann* of Ningpo contracted in January 1848 to convoy a fleet of junks from there to Shanghai for the fee of Tls. 536, payable on arrival. The British consul gave her a document to prove her legitimate occupation. In May Mr. Davidson's vessel *Spec* was hired by Ningpo merchants to protect Shantung junks between Chen-hai and the mouth of the Yangtze, while his *Dido* was on hire as a guardian at the fisheries north of Kintang.[22]

Defensive convoy work not unnaturally gave way at times to actual pirate-hunting. The *Dido* of Ningpo in May 1848 chased and captured a pirated junk and 16 pirates. Six got away overboard. The prisoners were handed over to the Chinese authorities at Ningpo and Davidson thereupon claimed a reward. The consul held up the claim because he feared it illegal for the *Dido* to be heavily armed as a cruiser, and its activities might lead to unexpected collisions. Three weeks later the *Dido* captured another pirate ship, twenty-seven members of the crew of which went overboard or were killed, leaving but one survivor.

When this private armed convoying under British colors was referred to Hongkong, Davis issued a warning against it in May 1848 but in June the attorney general gave a pussy-footing decision, that it was permissible if the Chinese government did not object; the consul should warn the British merchants so engaged that he "equally declined either to sanction or to interfere with their employment."[23] It remained for Palmerston to settle the matter with the remark that he saw no reason why convoy work

[b] This was not done until 1868, after the British government had paid out £149,243 in bounties. Dr. Grace Fox, *British Admirals and Chinese Pirates*, lists data concerning a dozen British pirate hunts in the four years 1847–50, which captured some 139 vessels and obtained head money for some 7325 pirates, most of them killed or captured, at the rate of £20 apiece. A total of £56,238 was awarded British naval ships for services against pirates 1851–68.[21]

"should be interfered with by any British authority." Later he went further: "there can be no evil but much good in this practice of giving convoy"; he demanded only that the competent Chinese authorities approve and that proper bargains be made beforehand with the Chinese employers; British consuls might then interfere to see that the bargain was lived up to.[24] This view expressed in London was perhaps simplified by distance, for the business of convoy and pirate-hunting on the China coast entailed considerable risk. The mere identification of a Chinese junk as merchant, mandarin or pirate was not easy and not always attempted by a foreign vessel of superior armament. This may be illustrated by the case of the schooner *Spec*.

Mr. Wm. Davidson purchased the *Spec* at Shanghai in February 1848 and hired it out to a group of Chinese merchants at Ningpo for convoy duty against pirates. It was a vessel of 105 tons, 70 feet long, 19 feet wide, and 8 feet deep, with one deck and two masts, and carried a sailing letter dated Sept. 4, 1847, which had been issued by the governor of Hongkong on an annual basis. It had an armament of nine guns, of which two were four-pounders, two were six-pound carronades, two were four-pound carronades and three were half-pound swivels. It also carried 23 muskets, 5 pistols, 10 cutlasses, 4 pikes and 5 spears for a crew, on this occasion, of 11 men.[25]

The *Spec* carried articles dated Dec. 19, 1846, which described her as from the port of Hongkong "on a voyage to Amoy and other ports and places on the northeast coast of China for a period of 6 calendar months." Of the 23 crew members listed on these out-of-date articles, the mate was an Englishman from Exmouth and the gunner from Teignmouth, nine men were from Manila with ages varying between 20 and 29 years, one from Goa, the Portuguese colony in India, the cook was from Calcutta and the rest not stated. Seamen were to receive $12 a month and the 3 gunners each $20. In actual fact, however, the *Spec* carried a master, mate and three other persons not on the articles and one English seaman with no register ticket. Her actual master was William Cole of Pembrokeshire and the mate was George Johnson of London. The gunner, Ephraim Francis, "a tall man with light hair," of Meldon, Essex, was not on the articles. Altogether the crew members had served previously on the following ships: *Coquette*, *Lyra*, *Eagle*, *Anglona*, *Dido*, *Time*, *William*, *Clown*, *Dart*, and *W. Hughes*, all of them well known in recent years along the China coast.

On June 20 the *Spec* sailed from Ningpo in search of her sister vessel the *Dido*, with a cargo of powder and shot for delivery to her. This included 100 pounds of loose powder, 150 round iron shot for the half-pounder swivels, 27 bags of grape shot, 9 one-foot lengths of chain to be used as shot, 210 percussion caps for rifles, a considerable supply of cartridges, and other miscellaneous weapons.

On the next morning the *Spec* sighted a junk near the Rugged Islands. This vessel was a fisherman of some 900 piculs burden which carried 4 boats and a crew of 24 men.[26] The owner, Kwo-kin, was aboard and the vessel's catch of fish was consigned to a Chinese firm at Chen-hai, from which it secured its provisions and with which it settled accounts periodically. The junk carried papers from a Chinese customhouse and an armament of two matchlocks and two three-foot guns of 1 inch bore, as protection against pirates. Its crew was partly from Fukien. A net-thrower fisherman among them received $4 every three months as pay. They were able to make about two trips to the fishing banks each month.

The pilot of the *Spec*, named Kew-Tsae-Kin, a native of Ningpo, had been put aboard it by a body of Chinese merchants at that port and was not paid by the master of the *Spec*. He suggested that the fishing vessel should be investigated; and when the *Spec* came up to her about 9 A.M., he declared her to be a pirate. On being hailed, the junk did not lower its sails and the *Spec* therefore fired a single gun and a number of muskets, killing the owner, Kwo-kin, and breaking both legs of one crew member. Some of the fishermen ran below and others lifted up the owner's dead body to show the foreigners what they had done. The Englishmen continued firing, however, and then closed and boarded the junk, tied the crew up on deck and threw the owner's body overboard. Since the fisherman with the broken legs was "calling for someone to put him out of his pain," the *Spec's* gunner, Ephraim Francis, cut at him with his sword and threw him overboard too. The *Spec* then towed the junk back toward the Ruggeds and anchored there, confining the remaining crew of 18 men and one boy in her own hold, five having been killed and others being badly wounded.

On June 22, Captain J. C. Pitman of H. M. sloop *Childers*, standing up for the Ruggeds, found the *Spec* alongside the junk discharging all her cargo. Captain Pitman asked the master, Cole, for an explanation and the master of the *Spec* replied that he had taken the junk as a pirate, on the word of his pilot, and volunteered the further information that several of the junkmen had been killed or wounded. Pitman asked him if he was aware of the serious consequences of such action. Cole replied, no, that he saw no harm in it and the same thing had been done before. He was also unaware of the fact that he ought not to be sailing the high seas without a destination. Cole had no papers to show what he was doing. He admitted that he had made no effort to call on the *Childers* or on Chinese war junks nearby to investigate the alleged pirates nor had he attempted to go alongside her for boarding without firing into her.

Pitman then inquired of a Chinese mandarin junk in the neighborhood and the commander replied that he had known the fishing junk to be a fisherman and not a pirate but he had taken no action because he did not like to interfere with the British flag.

Captain Pitman then boarded the *Spec*, had the junk crew released, took depositions from them, had his surgeon examine the wounded and sent one to Shanghai for treatment. He then took the mate of the *Spec* and two junkmen to the mandarin boat, whose commander declared the junk's papers to be perfectly in order and the junkmen innocent of piracy. He also contended that the *Spec* had no right to act as she did but that English vessels were constantly doing so. The junk crew were sent to report to the Chinese authorities at Chen-hai, and Captain Pitman decided to take the *Spec* to Shanghai. "Mr. Cole then turned to the pilot and said, 'What a nice mess you've got me into.' "

Consul Alcock at Shanghai having taken further evidence, the *Spec* was sent to Hongkong in July in charge of a British naval officer. Captain Cole and his crew were jailed on a charge of piracy. The *China Mail* editorially regretted making such an example of the *Spec* and her commander, "so long favorably known in China." In September a grand jury was instructed that the evidence was inadequate and after two hours' deliberation returned a finding of "No true bill." The prosecution had based their evidence mainly on Cole's voluntary statements, but the latter had not been warned that his statements might be used against him. None of the junk's owners had appeared to claim their property nor had any of the wounded been produced as witnesses. The defense attorney denied that he had seduced the key witness, a wounded junkman, who had absconded. Unfortunately Captain Pitman had assumed that the evidence of his own log book and that of the *Spec* and its master, which might have been adequate for a naval court martial, would suffice before a Hongkong grand jury.[27] It appeared, in any case, that the British flag and British armament had been used as a pawn in the internecine rivalry of Chinese fishing interests, and that Chinese and British activities on the China coast could not be controlled by the rules of Whitehall.[c]

[c] On May 12, 1849, Peter Lawry Laen, master of the *Spec*, and his mate and gunner, Charles Vitale, with some twenty armed sailors entered the house of a fisherman near the fisheries at Tae-shan (Tai-shan) for the purpose of carrying off his daughter-in-law. Five Chinese were wounded, one seriously. Laen pleaded guilty at the consulate, but with the approval of the mandarins the case was compromised out of court. Bonham himself urged the consul to state that either the case must go to Hongkong for trial or, if the witnesses did not appear, be dismissed; this might make the accused pay more to the injured, and would avoid the appearance that British subjects in the British courts always got off with a fine. The owner of the *Spec*, Davidson, got a new captain and at the end of the year renewed his sailing letter as usual.[28] It appears, however, that he began to hire out his convoy vessels in order to avoid involvement for their use. Under a contract signed in the summer of 1850 the *Dido* together with her British master, J. Leitch, was chartered by King-na-quong, a man in the Ningpo customhouse, at $450 a month for a period of two months and nine days. In the consular court Davidson claimed $1,039, of which only $900 had been paid. In November 1850

Portuguese competition. British enterprise in the convoy business also met trouble from the Portuguese of Macao. By the middle of 1848 there were "no less than a dozen" Portuguese lorchas in the Ningpo river. Two years later there was a community of some twenty foreigners of dubious origin, from Macao, Goa, or Manila, deserters from lorchas, smugglers and blackmailers, who lived outside Ningpo and at Chen-hai without honest support. They made their living partly by the collection of alleged debts from Chinese merchants. Juan and Botado, for example, and a few of their friends would appear at a dried-fish shop and demand payment of a bogus bill for 12,000 cash which bore the forged seal of the shop. The British consul could not intervene against Portuguese and the local authorities feared they would get into trouble if they acted against foreigners. The racketeers thus made a fine living and at times even succeeded in ousting Chinese from their houses by means of forged documents and braggadocio. It was not by any means unusual when Luis Brazillia, Patactoo, and half a dozen Fukienese broke into a house in Ningpo, beat up the four families within, raped a daughter, and later rescued one of their number from the jail where the local police had succeeded in putting him.[30]

Portuguese conduct was of direct concern to the British because they bore the odium of Portuguese misdeeds; for the Chinese made no great distinction between one barbarian nationality and another. At times the Foochow and Ningpo consuls felt it necessary to use their good offices to save their fellow Westerners from Chinese law. In 1849 Governor Amaral of Macao promised that he would deal with all of his countrymen whom they might send there for trial. On another occasion the Ningpo consul, in trying to keep the opium trade outside the port, chastised some of the local Portuguese riffraff and exacted from the brothers da Silva a written promise "not to serve on board Chinese boats again," they having been used to protect native vessels from the authorities.

In answer to British complaints, the Council of Macao observed bitterly that "foreigners in these parts . . . call by the name of Portuguese everyone whose country is unknown," especially if he spoke a romance language. Thus Italians, Spanish Manilamen, and the dregs of Asia generally, were all attributed to Macao. The Council went on to agree that "the imbecility and weakness of the Chinese government is so superabundantly notorious as to preclude the hope of its being able by itself to repress the excesses" on the coast.[31] In April 1851 the Macao government sent the corvette *Dom Joao I* to Ningpo and in August the armed lorcha *Adamaster* under Lieut. Barrancho of the Portuguese navy. The lieutenant ordered

---

he also received with the consul's help a repayment of $496 principal and $56 interest as the result of lodging a claim against Yaou-heen-mou, the master of a wood junk.[29]

five lorchas to Macao for trial and together with the Chinese authorities [d] prevailed upon Patrick Hague, in charge of the British consulate, to act temporarily as Portuguese consul. Mr. Hague consented and about the first of December issued a notification requiring all Portuguese lorchas to report and lodge their papers at the consulate in accordance with the practice of British vessels. This was approved in Hongkong and by Palmerston,[33] and the arrangement continued for nine months.[e] Lieut. Barrancho had drawn up with the Ningpo authorities a set of regulations for the control of Portuguese subjects at Ningpo, which were approved by Commissioner Hsü at Canton and given Consul Hague by the taotai in February 1852. One of Hague's chief problems was to prevent Portuguese buying Chinese boats for $300 or $400 at Ningpo, converting them into lorchas of a sort, and obtaining from Macao the right to raise the Portuguese flag over them.[34]

During 1851 and 1852 Davidson's *Dido* under British colors fought a long battle with the Portuguese [f] — especially with lorcha No. 23, J. dos A. Xavier, master. This illustrated in miniscule the nature of the protective work done by foreigners for the Ningpo fishing fleets. It is significant that Xavier won out, there being fewer things that he would stop at, but that Davidson collected from his investment anyway, through the help of the British-Portuguese consul. Both contestants for the right of protection made agreements. Xavier went into the country and made a solemn arrangement with an assembly of more than 400 fishermen, who agreed to take his flag (as the mark of his protection) on their junks; a feast was prepared and "three days sing-song was made." He notified the British consul, who refused to recognize his monopoly. Davidson meanwhile had agreed with other members of the fishing fleet that they should take his flag (a favorite trick of the convoy blackmailer was to throw his flag aboard a junk in passing and then allege breach of contract if it was not used and paid for). The rival parties were thus at loggerheads before the fishing began. Some of the fishermen wished to petition the district magistrate, "but fear the squeeze which they will have to pay." The British consul therefore did so for them, whereupon the magistrate after five days

[d] In 1850 the Ningpo authorities had more than once appealed to the British consulate to take care of cases involving Chinese and Portuguese. Vice-consul Robertson repeatedly explained his legal inability to act but he consented to take evidence and send a statement to Hongkong for transmission to Macao, declaring "Ningpo people are polite to foreigners, and I am sorry to find foreigners not polite to them." [32]

[e] Palmerston's decision to allow British consuls to act as security for ships of other nations was made known to the Ningpo authorities in the latter part of June 1851. Bonham had readily concurred.

[f] In March 1851 the *Dido* with a convoy of junks for Ningpo, on leaving the mouth of the river at Wenchow, met lorcha No. 8, which proceeded to detain some of the junks. The *Dido's* master, J. Leitch, threatened the Portuguese with his fowling piece, whereat lorcha No. 8 cleared for action, called on lorcha No. 28 which was nearby, and challenged Leitch to fight it out on sea or land. Being outnumbered, he withdrew, losing $46 per junk.[35] Similar Anglo-Portuguese disputes occurred from month to month.

cogitation came down precisely on the fence: some fishermen had subscribed money to pay the *Dido*, some to pay the lorcha, and some had not subscribed; litigation and trouble would result and the magistrate could reach no decision.

The fleet put to sea, lorcha No. 23 and *Dido* both providing protection and attempting by threats, the pulling down of rival flags, and in the case of the lorcha, at least, the seizure of both nets and fishermen, to establish an hegemony over the fleet. The record of the case is particularly interesting because Patrick Hague, in charge of the British consulate and acting also as Portuguese consul, had some difficulty in dividing himself. To prevent future trouble he drew up with the district magistrate a set of "regulations for Portuguese vessels employed for the protection of Chinese merchant vessels and fishing boats," dated Sept. 5, 1851. But these paper regulations made little difference. In support of Xavier, Portuguese lorcha No. 8 joined the fray, cudgeled fishermen who flew the *Dido's* flag, ejected Davidson's men from the thatched houses they had rented on the Saddle Islands — barren places "except for small patches cultivated by the fishermen for potatoes" — and wounded a few persons seriously. Consul Hague warned both sides repeatedly but had trouble in getting his advice respected on the Saddle Islands.

Davidson eventually withdrew, claiming payment for two months and seven days' protection at $450 a month as originally agreed. Two years later (April 1853) the consul was still pressing for payment of this debt of $1005 due from 20 fishermen. Meanwhile Davidson secured a new group of fishermen through the medium of Encarnacao, "one of the principal leaders in levying blackmail on Chinese boats," thus acknowledging that only Portuguese could beat Portuguese at their own game.[36]

Cantonese versus Portuguese. With the beginning of the Rebellion in the interior after 1850, piracy on the southeast coast received a new stimulus and was raised to a higher level of efficiency. The leaders in this, as in so much of the coast trade and opium traffic, were Cantonese, the most successful of whom were the notorious P'u brothers, generally known by their names in the Macao (Hsiang-shan) dialect as Apak ("Poohingyew," P'u Hsing-yu) and Alumtay ("Pooleangtae," P'u Liang-t'ai). Late in 1851 a fleet of 17 of their pirate vessels with one to two thousand men aboard was reported near Ningpo. The Chinese authorities as well as the British community asked that H. M. brig *Contest*, which arrived with dispatches at the end of November, be kept at the port until the Chinese navy could be collected. The brig stayed for a time, but trade remained paralyzed and the port virtually blockaded by pirates. A fruitless offer of $6000 a month was made to the P. and O. Company for the use of two steamers; but at the crucial moment H. M. steamer *Sphinx* arrived, as well as the governor of Chekiang from Hangchow, and after mutual feasting and compromise, a settlement was at last effected with the pirates in January 1852. The luckless merchants of Ningpo were obliged to pay $25,000 ransom for some 400 boats, while each pirate leader received $1000 and a button (i.e., official rank) and each sailor $30.[37] The totals reported to the consul were: $63,000 to the leaders who received official rank, $24,000 to the crews plus the blackmail rights (worth another $20,000) on merchants' junks which they had detained.[38]

Evidently this bargaining for the surrender of the pirates and their enrollment in the emperor's navy underwent the usual ups and downs. Juy (Jui) Taotai on January 28, 1852, earnestly entreated Captain Shadwell of the British navy to help against Apak's fleet at Chen-hai, whose intentions were "hard to fathom"; but on the following day he explained that the pirates were so inextricably intermingled amongst the merchant junks that attack would be impossible without harm to the innocent, and he requested that the Captain "on his passing Chen-hai on no account attack and destroy the pirates." [39]

The final bargain gave Apak the fifth Chinese rank and an appointment as captain in the imperial navy. Three of his 24 vessels were made into warships, under Apak's command, and the taotai proceeded to make the best of the situation by keeping the outraged populace in check with the help of the pirates. The latter assisted early in 1854 in the beheading of 64 persons charged with plotting a revolution in favor of the Taipings. The port was practically taken over by Apak and his relatives and the Cantonese element in general. The Canton broker Alum, who had helped the British merchants begin their trade at Shanghai a decade before, now became a chief confederate [40] in the disposal on shore of his fellow provincials' takings at sea.[g]

This situation at Ningpo was only moderately improved when a real Portuguese consul, J. F. Marques, arrived on June 22, 1852, and took over from his British colleague. Senor Marques was allowed to engage in trade and his salary was correspondingly low: an office allowance, including rent, of $50 a month, plus a salary of $150 a month out of the fees collected on Portuguese lorchas, collections beyond that sum going to his government.[41]

In this way by 1852 two gangs of desperadoes had become established at Ningpo, the Cantonese pirates under Apak in the imperial navy, and

[g] Cp. Winchester's 85, Aug. 15, 1855: "No sign can be more indicative of the utter prostration of the Chinese government than the position occupied by the Apak at Ningpo. Eight or nine of his armed commantines are anchored in the Tszi-ki [Tze-ki] branch. He and his people occupy a large hong in the city close to the salt gate where some scores of them are constantly knocking about. Here he directs the operations of his gang, sending out vessels to reinforce those outside or receive the plunder they have taken." Apak was also suspcted of using American sailing letters obtained from the Shanghai consulate.

the Portuguese lorchas in the coast trade under the nominal jurisdiction of Consul Marques. For the next few years a bitter rivalry ensued between these two groups over the pickings of blackmail and convoy work, with the British usually sitting respectably on the sidelines. In the summer of 1854 Consul Marques demanded of the taotai a Portuguese monopoly of the convoy business. Friction between the taotai's new Cantonese "volunteers" and the lorchamen had resulted in various deaths on either side and hostilities between small groups of ships at Chen-hai. The amount of convoy money paid out in 1853 was said to have been $180,000 nominally, and $220,000 in fact. The British consul understood that Marques received as part of his salary 4 per cent of the earnings of the lorchas — hence the monopolistic impulse. The situation was complicated by the fact that Marques knew no Chinese and had no interpreter: "I once thought of employing a proper person to translate, but the languages being very different, I was afraid errors might be made which would impede affairs." Consequently he communicated with the taotai verbally through a messenger, and it was not easy to pin him down.[h] The murder of a Portuguese in April 1854 and the killing of two Cantonese about the same time led Consul Marques to send to Macao for the corvette *Dom Joao I*, which eventually arrived and fired upon the town in an affray with Apak's fleet on July 10, 1854. Marques demanded reparation and indemnity, punishment of Apak and the murderers of the Portuguese, and a promise signed by Apak and Alumtay that their men would no longer tax the fishing vessels sailing under the convoy of the Portuguese lorchamen.

In this troubled situation Tuan Taotai used barbarians to control barbarians with great success. He communicated the demands of the

[h] J. A. T. Meadows as interpreter in charge, with a staff consisting chiefly of Robert Hart (who arrived as a language student on Oct. 19, 1854), grew gradually more and more anti-Portuguese as he watched their proceedings at Ningpo and became submerged himself in the petty emotions of treaty port life. These complicated circumstances came to a head on Christmas Day 1854 when a Portuguese subject of Ningpo named Bemvindo (Benevindo da Razor Baptista) struck a Chinese boy, and Messrs. Meadows and Hart and all their Chinese staff in retaliation pulled Bemvindo from a sick bed, dragged him to the consulate, tied him to a post, and had the head consular servant administer 35 lashes with a rope. This procedure was unlawful and accusations flew from all sides, the Portuguese deposing that the Chinese boy was sent to provoke Bemvindo and was the brother of the British consul's "paramour." Meadows retorted that the woman in question was the wife of the head consular servant, had been nurse to the family of his predecessor, Hague, and had never been touched by him. The Portuguese asserted that Meadows struck Bemvindo (this was denied) and that Hart went him one better by doing it with a pistol and drawing blood. Robert Hart denied this in a single though somewhat lengthy sentence containing seven negatives.[42] The voluminous British archives accord the Englishman the better of the argument. Meadows' functions were immediately suspended and when Vice-consul Winchester arrived from Amoy to take charge on April 1, 1855, he resigned "temporarily," aggrieved at being judged without a hearing. This resignation was accepted by Lord Clarendon as the best way to mollify the Macao government and on the ground that Meadows had been "unnecessarily violent." His services as interpreter at Ningpo were so useful, however, that Clarendon allowed him to be employed at Ningpo "temporarily." This decision arrived a year and a half after the beating of Bemvindo. By this time J. A. T. Meadows had become interested in trade; he left government employ sometime after the middle of 1856 and later played a leading part in the mercantile community at Tientsin. His brother T. T. Meadows took charge at Ningpo in January 1857.[43]

Portuguese consul ("whose country is not even mentioned in the treaties") and his own grievances very fully to the British and American consulates, which were naturally jealous of the activities of another foreign power and particularly suspicious of the half-caste Portuguese as unscrupulous rivals in foreign trade. The rights of the case are not easily found on any side, the interest of the British consulate being chiefly to see that its own countrymen were not cut out of the convoy business themselves. The repeated assertion that a Portuguese convoy monopoly had been demanded was hotly resented at Macao, where the British acting consul was accused of planning the pirates' strategy for them. An offer of mediation put forward by Bowring and McLane, the British and American ministers then at Shanghai, was indignantly refused. Meanwhile the British position was complicated by the fact that the U. S. S. *Powhatan* arrived from Shanghai on July 20 and landed 75 men to protect foreign interests, giving such aid to the taotai that the British consul feared the Americans, if they asked for it, might get the convoy monopoly themselves.[44]

In this context of extortion and piracy on the coast and in the outports, the legal trade with China after 1850 also began rapidly to fall into a state of chaos and insecurity.

CHAPTER XIX

THE EVASION OF LEGAL DUTIES

By 1850 the British effort to safeguard their commercial expansion through the rule of treaty law was an admitted failure in respect of most of the opium import trade and much of the coasting trade. A similar failure was now threatened in the export trade carried on within the treaty ports themselves, where the evasion of legal duties on tea and silk foreshadowed a final collapse of the treaty system altogether.

In retrospect it is plain that the system of commercial regulation which the first treaties sought to establish was an experiment. The treaties themselves were utopian. They were based, as they had to be, on the assumption that the Chinese authorities would for some reason coöperate in their enforcement. The experiment was to see whether this coöperation could be obtained short of a further resort to force. Within ten years the effort had admittedly failed, and the enlarged commercial opportunity desired by the West was secured in the end not through treaty clauses so much as through elements extraneous to the treaties — including events connected with the Taiping Rebellion, the Sino-foreign hostilities of 1856–60, and the introduction of Westerners into the customs administration.

The smuggling problem at Amoy. Smuggling was a complex administrative problem which arose from a fundamental contradiction in the treaty system itself. If the trade was to be regulated according to the tariff and general regulations, there must be a full and impartial collection of the Chinese customs revenue. Smuggling flourished, however, because of the weakness of the Chinese customhouse, which was in turn caused partly (but only partly) by extraterritoriality. By treaty the British consuls had a responsibility of uncertain extent to interfere for the prevention of smuggling. But the competition of merchants of other countries made it undesirable for them to do so. They faced the alternatives either to substitute for the Chinese authorities and enforce the treaty tariff (which would handicap British ships and merchants in their competition with other foreigners) or to let the tariff collapse into a smuggler's free-for-all (which would abandon the original objective of the treaty tariff and subvert the rule of law including the legal safeguards of commerce).

Consular interference was at first invoked in literal terms. In March 1844 Consul Lay at Canton levied a fine of $500 upon the vessel *Carthaginian* for breaking bulk without a permit. Actually the goods landed were opium and the consul was attacking the opium trade in this manner. To ensure collection of the fine, he directed further that cotton goods on the ship be landed subject to his orders. All this was done on his own initiative, the Chinese authorities having made no complaint to him. It was exceptional action, seldom if ever taken by a British consul thereafter. Lay explained that he "did not appeal to the Chinese Authorities in this matter since they deemed it to be my province to keep British subjects from offending against the regulations, and because they had no will or power or judgement to act on such occasions with propriety and effect." [1]

The dilemma inherent in any consular initiative to defend the emperor's revenue soon was highlighted at Amoy. In the spring of 1844 Consul Gribble ill-advisedly became security for the Danish barque *Danesborg*, the supercargo, an Englishman, having promised to abide by the regulations of trade. It soon appeared that the *Danesborg* had loaded 678 chests of tea on a chop (i.e., certificate) for 20 only. After the customs officers, at the consul's insistence, had tried to investigate by themselves and been "obstructed," the British vice-consul investigated and proved the fact of smuggling. The Chinese officers then asked British assistance in confiscating the smuggled tea, were refused, and did nothing. The Danish captain insulted the consul and sailed away, tea and all, whereupon the Chinese authorities recovered their composure by punishing severely the Chinese merchants involved in the case. Pottinger censured the consul for securing the *Danesborg* in the first place; he should not become responsible for ships under foreign colors, even if they were British-owned. Pottinger's purpose in this decision was to avoid trouble with other Western nations.[2] Yet in the end the avoidance of such trouble led to still greater dangers in China.

Amoy became a smuggling port from the end of 1845, after Consul Lay moved into the new consular residence in the old taotai's yamen in August and subsequently removed his office from the waterside. The key to the smuggler's success lay in avoiding the use of British vessels, so that the British consul had no direct supervision over them. Instead foreign ships were chartered. Ships under the Spanish flag from Manila came under the control of the Spanish vice-consul, Mr. James Tait, who was thus able to lead the way in defrauding the Chinese revenue, being in most cases the merchant consignee of Spanish vessels as well as the local official responsible for them. In effect, he had his own smuggling fleet. While the foreign trade of the port was almost entirely British, almost none of it came under the British consul's supervision.

In facing this problem the British consul had to deal with the superintendent of customs at Amoy. But the incumbent of this post was required to be changed every year and seemed to the British actually to be changed every six months or so, when the Fukien Tartar-general would appoint another Manchu brigadier or colonel to take his turn at the revenue. This type of customs superintendent knew little of trade and less of its regulation. In 1846 it was a Manchu named "Kah-ur-sah . . . so aged as to be altogether incapable . . . fast sinking into utter childishness . . . therefore at the mercy of a large body of hungry retainers."[3] In 1848, Lt. Colonel "Heaou," an eccentric given to wine and very lax; in 1849, "a corrupt, venal, and obstinate old man," between 60 and 70 years of age.[4] Consul Sullivan in August 1851 had to outline the entire structure of the treaties to the newest arrival in the post.

Consul Layton estimated that in 1846 about 13 per cent of the whole trade of Amoy was smuggled (i.e., £40,000. smuggled, in addition to £261,240. reported). The observed decline in the exports from Amoy could hardly be explained on any other basis. He was determined to claim for British shippers all advantages illegally enjoyed by others, but he feared that if the treaty tariff were not enforced, the advantages of the treaty would be lost together with the profits of British trade. In 1847 the daily fraud upon the imperial revenue, as estimated by the superintendent of customs himself, was Tls. 22 a day. For many small persons with little capital "smuggling is the chief source of subsistence." The Chinese naval officers occasionally informed the consul of English boats being found at night in questionable circumstances, but the consul could not "trace out these proceedings or discover the parties engaged in them."[5] For 1848 Layton estimated the whole trade at £292,416. worth of legal goods (and £250,000. worth of opium); yet the *Peking Gazette* reported customs collections at Amoy totalling only £7,108 (Tls. 24,568) for the year.[6] To save the British reputation he denounced to the customhouse eight non-British foreign ships the tonnage of which had been falsely reported by the British consignees. "But it is somewhat difficult to define the occasions upon which a British Consul should interfere with the smuggling of his own countrymen or denounce their conduct." To assist them in smuggling could only lower him in the eyes of "a suspicious, weak, and jealous government and . . . an observing and inquisitive people." Under the pressure of the non-British smugglers' competition, however, the consul had felt obliged by 1849 to abolish the treaty requirement that merchants obtain from the consulate a landing- or shipping-off-chop for all goods landed or shipped on British vessels. He did this because 1) merchants shipping under other foreign flags were not required to do so, 2) the applications made to him were untrue as to quantity, weight, etc., and 3) the chops issued by him implicated the consulate in the bribery and corruption practised at the customhouse, where the superintendent could take refuge if necessary in the possession of documents under the consular seal. Consular chops could again be required whenever desired by "an honest Haikwan (if such a man can be found at Amoy)." [7]

Similarly at Foochow the consul refused to assume the burden of protecting the imperial revenue. In August 1846 Alcock was firmly unwilling to oblige the superintendent of customs, a Manchu military official, by reporting to him not only the entry of a British vessel but also the amount of its tonnage dues and duties. The levy of duties, he explained, was the "sole and particular" task of the customhouse, and he would not do their examining for them.[8]

As Sino-foreign relations worsened in the period after Ch'i-ying's departure in 1848, the British consuls found that almost their only hold upon the customhouse was their ability to stop or delay the payment of duties due on British vessels. Consul Layton made use of this tactic at Amoy in July 1849 in order to recover debts of $2300 due from Chinese to an English merchant, Jackson. He detained at the consulate "dues and duties to the amount of $1700." The customs reported this to the higher authorities, and the governor-general at Foochow censured the Amoy taotai for the Chinese reason that he "ought not to have allowed the matter to go so far." Two and a half months later Mr. Jackson received $1100 due on his debt and an official promise of the rest. The consul was delighted with his new-found power of coercion, even though his superior at Hongkong refused his approval on the orthodox ground that the consul should only persuade, not appear as a creditor's agent.[9]

Corruption at Canton. At Canton the immemorial struggle continued between the private and public interest, which were represented respectively by merchant-official corruption and by full collection of the imperial revenue. In April 1845 the imperial commissioner and the Hoppo tried to set up a customs station at Shih-lung (Sheklung) some 30 miles outside Canton to prevent smuggling of tea and silk coming from other provinces for export. The first building erected for this purpose was burned in a local disturbance apparently directed at the preservation of the old system of smuggling.[10]

Within the treaty port of Canton the evasion of full duties by the linguists went on out of the public gaze. The most obnoxious and demoralizing malpractice in the legal trade was that carried on by small craft in the Canton River. In May 1845 the Hoppo was officially requested by the British consul to put a stop to the smuggling carried on in front of the factories. He replied that the two examining stations located in front of the factories would take action if the consul could make all the foreign vessels in the river stop there. The consul accordingly reminded all British small craft that they must deposit papers and report cargo at the consulate on arrival at Canton, according to article XVII of the Supplementary treaty. But small craft under foreign flags not represented by consuls at Canton must still be dealt with by the customhouse itself.

Not perceiving any subsequent diminution in the smuggling, Consul Macgregor proceeded to stop the landing of ships' boats on the shore front rented as a building ground by the British government. But this had the sole effect of concentrating the smuggling traffic at the Hog Lane and "Se paou tae" customs stations. He appealed to Ch'i-ying and Huang, who replied expressing gratification at his measures: they on their part had deputed a reliable officer to cruise up and down the river. They framed eight regulations to deal with the evil and, through their deputy Wu, asked Macgregor confidentially if these agreed with the treaty. To overcome the handicap imposed by Chinese ignorance of foreigners and foreign vessels, they proposed to employ the Macao pilots, who were experienced in such things, as reporting agents. To secure control over small craft under foreign flags not represented by consuls, they framed a regulation requiring that they also report.[11] These new regulations were announced to the foreign community on June 27, 1845, but had no real effect.

Official customs collections, judging by British consular records, steadily declined at Canton. China's revenue from British trade there was recorded as follows (taking the dollar as 72 per cent of a tael):

TABLE 13: CUSTOMS DUTIES PAID ON BRITISH TRADE AT CANTON [12]

Year	*Levied on*	*Amount*	*Annual total*
1844	Shipping	$ 85,351	$ 2,468,784
	Imports	821,882	
	Exports	1,561,551	(or Tls. 1,777,524)
1845	Shipping	$ 58,404	$ 2,312,245
	Imports	551,632	
	Exports	1,702,209	(or Tls. 1,664,816)
1846	Shipping	$ 61,873	$ 1,850,880
	Imports	528,362	
	Exports	1,260,645	(or Tls. 1,232,134)
1847	Shipping	$ 56,828	$ 1,810,785
	Imports	475,182	
	Exports	1,278,775	(or Tls. 1,303,767)
1848	Shipping	Tls. 33,746	
	Imports and Exports	Tls. 920,325	Tls. 954,072

A comparison with the volume of British exports, which declined only slightly in this period, yields prima facie evidence of increasing customs laxity.[13]

The decline of customs revenue at Canton in 1848 led the Hoppo to bestir himself and propose to the consul that joint measures be taken against fraud. This afforded the consul a happy chance to lecture the Hoppo. He explained that the revenue declined partly because the inefficiency of the customhouse was driving trade to Shanghai. Smuggling was encouraged by the customs officers, who failed to investigate the many small craft which illegally hoisted the British flag. To capitalize on this sorry situation he reported to the imperial commissioner the exact amount of the Hoppo's recorded collections on British trade, which in 1848 fell about a third of a million taels short of the preceding year.[14] Davis had already advertised the British way of taxing a regulated trade by sending Ch'i-ying in 1847 a summary of the British government's budget for 1846, in which customs duties accounted for some $97,000,000 out of a total of $254,000,000, while the land tax and assessed taxes totalled only $20,000,000.[15] But none of these British demonstrations sufficed to remake the Ch'ing fiscal system.

In the end the evasion of duties at Canton proved less of a problem than at Shanghai (see below) because of the foreign merchant's insulation from contact with the Canton customs. Customarily, after a foreign merchant vessel had come to Hongkong harbor, or as less frequently happened, to Macao Roads, and had engaged one of the twenty-odd river pilots licensed by the Chinese authorities [a] she would proceed to the mouth of the Pearl River at the Bogue (*Hu-men*), where the precipitous and fortified heights of Anunghoi and Ch'uan-pi rise from the deltaic plain and guard the approach to Canton. There the vessel would report to the customs. On proceeding toward Second Bar, the vessel would hire boats to mark the passage, and by that time the services of a compradore (*mai-pan*) would also have been accepted, to accompany the ship, furnish provisions, hire workmen, make purchases, and in general act as clerk and local purveyor at Whampoa. A ship consigned to or owned by a firm established

[a] On the resumption of British trade in July 1843, Ch'i-ying proposed that vessels be allowed to hire their own pilots, either fishermen who possessed ship-passes or some of the originally licensed pilots; these pilots need no longer report to the Chinese prefect at Macao, but a foreign vessel on arrival at the Wangtong fort (on the northern of the two Wangtong or "Bar-the-way" Islands at the Bogue) [16] should report to the garrison commander, who would send out "registering tide-waiters" to take the particulars of the vessel and report them to the governor-general and governor in Canton, and also to the Hoppo through his customhouse guards. Orders would then be given to allow the pilot to bring the vessel up to Whampoa. Meanwhile customs guards would stay on the ship to prevent smuggling.

The days of delay which would be involved in such a cumbersome procedure were obviated by Pottinger's proposal that British vessels be supplied with blank forms for reporting their arrival, obtainable from the British consular agent at Whampoa or the harbour master at Hongkong, which should be filled up and delivered to the Hoppo's officers before the vessel passed Wangtong. Pottinger thought that smuggling would be sufficiently prevented by the trade regulations already in effect. This solution brought the entrance procedure at Canton into line with the regulation that pilots should be allowed to take vessels "immediately into port." Pilots' licenses and a public notification were accordingly issued.[17]

at Canton would naturally be attended to by that firm's compradore, assisted by his own shroff and staff of servants. In this way when the vessel anchored at Whampoa, all matters connected with her maintenance would have been provided for [b] and attention could be centered upon the unloading of cargo and its passage twelve miles up to Canton and through the customs.

In this operation under the treaty system it was the linguists (*t'ung-shih*) who enlarge their activities and so helped the new foreign element, represented by the consul, to fill the gap left by the security merchants of the old Cohong. British vessels would now open two accounts, one at the consulate and one at the customs, to record the fees and duties incurred while in port. At the consulate the captain of the vessel would deposit his papers and manifest according to treaty, and a consular report, summarizing the manifest, would be sent by the consulate to the customs who would then permit cargo to be discharged into lighters, or chop boats, and delivered to Canton for customs examination and deposit in the warehouse or godown. It was the linguist [c] hired for the vessel, Young Tom, Alantsai,

[b] A British consular agent was established at Whampoa under article 12 of the general regulations of trade; on the British side he derived his authority from the Merchant Seaman's Act (7 and 8 Vic. cap. 112). Nicholas de St. Croix was made British "Marine Magistrate and Consular Agent at Whampoa" by Pottinger's appointment on August 8, 1843. He had formerly commanded an East Indiaman in the Company trade and was now sworn in as a justice of the peace and took up his residence at Whampoa aboard his own vessel, the *John Laird*, which was hired from him by the government. In the eighth month of 1843 (August 25 — September 23) he received through Consul Lay an appointment from the Chinese local authorities, which increased his power to police the Whampoa community. At the beginning of 1848 St. Croix resigned, amid plaudits for having completely stopped the sale of "samshu" (*sanshao*, "thrice fired," i.e., distilled spirits) to sailors and for having established the village called Bamboo Town where sailors could buy supplies at Whampoa without going up to Canton. He was also credited with having checked theft on the part of compradores, by the expedient of licensing them.[18] Alexander Bird succeeded to the consular agent's duties.

Mr. Bird's life was not an easy one. In a busy season there would be 700 sailors in port and he was kept occupied rowing from one ship to another all day. When the crews were on shore leave, as on Sundays, bloody affrays often resulted from their over-indulgence in samshu. In 1847 several lives were lost in pitched battles between the men of Danes Island and those of French Island, the waterfront residents at Whampoa. In the first six months of 1848 Bird levied $233 in fines, paid over to the Seamen's Hospital Society. In times of trouble he called upon the Chinese authorities for assistance, asking them to make arrests which were beyond his province. Both English and Chinese prisoners were at times incarcerated on his vessel. In 1848–49 there were frequent complaints of Mr. Bird's being over-strict, as in levying a fine of $20 when a small schooner sailed away in ballast without first hoisting the blue peter.

[c] In the early 1840's the number of head linguists formally licensed was between 4 and 6, each of whom maintained a large establishment of clerks. After the war the fee for chop boats was fixed at $15.00, of which the boatmen required $10 or $12 and the remainder went to the linguist. By 1844 there were 5 licensed establishments.[19]

In May 1846 the Hoppo publicly invited competent persons to present themselves and their securities for positions as linguists: the annual customs collections had grown to more than two million taels, levied on more than 200 foreign vessels and an even greater number of Portuguese and Hongkong lorchas. Between 170 and 180 Chinese firms were engaged in the foreign trade of Canton, and the 5 linguist establishments had grown inadequate. Linguists no longer had time to come in person to the customs and sent incompetent inferiors to do their business. To obviate this the Hoppo proposed to license another 5 linguists.[20]

In July 1848 Chinese merchants at Canton complained that the linguist establishments (of which there were still only 5) were charging exorbitant fees. They estimated that the linguists' fee of $6 on each of 5000 boatloads of imported goods brought them in some $30,000 annually. On a total of or another, who took charge of this most important operation: by him the chop-boats were hired, at fixed rates, and by him the coolies were paid, at any rate he pleased. By him also all cargo bound to or from the ship was passed through the customhouse, by the simple process of presenting there the delivery orders signed by the senders and receivers of goods and presenting also the corresponding items of cargo, which the customs officers could count, weigh, evaluate, and assess as they wished. This done, the linguist sent chop-notes to the consul stating the amount of goods and duties connected with each chop-boat. But by that time the evasion of duties could already have been effected.[22] The treaties were no stronger than their weakest Chinese link.

The usual method of evasion was a systematic falsification of accounts. Each lighter of three hundred packages might be entered at the customs as two hundred, three bales might count as two, heavy packages as light ones, or valuable goods as cheap, with the result that the official record of goods and duties might be reduced by one third or more. To the merchant, the linguists could then present a bill for less than the amount of duties legally due, but for more than the amount actually paid. The difference between the sum paid by the merchant to the linguist, and the sum paid by the linguist to the customs, might be considerable, but still not more than enough to pay the linguist's overhead — his gratuities to the lightermen and coolies, to the warehouse-men, and not least, to the customhouse guards and examiners who regularly connived with him. To "economize his duties" in this way, all that the foreign importer need do was to falsify his manifest and leave the rest to the linguist.

In the export trade the foreigner need do even less. Usually he bought his teas and silks at "long price," that is, free on board, delivered at the ship duty paid, if at all, by the Chinese broker. Since the export trade was far more valuable and lucrative than that in imports, it is plain that in the greater part of the commerce at Canton the evasion of duties might go to any lengths without involving the foreigner. Since the Hoppo was responsible only for sums officially reported and paid to the Chinese government banker designated by him, he was often less concerned to stop irregularities than to participate in them. Only by so doing could he derive a personal revenue sufficient to maintain his establishment in the style to which Hoppos had for generations been accustomed. So much could be made by arranging for the short payment of duties that linguists at times would offer foreign traders several hundred dollars for the privilege of

2500 boatloads of exports per year, their fees were estimated to total $10,000. For these payments the linguists' sole services were to arrange lighterage from Whampoa to Canton, report imports and exports at the customs, and calculate import duties. The Chinese merchants objected because the linguists without consulting them had got the foreign merchants to agree unilaterally to a higher table of fees.[21]

putting their cargoes through the customs. In the face of such avid coöperation the consul could do nothing and the treaty law remained only partially enforced.

The presence on the Canton river front of the old "native" customs, which was separate from the new maritime customs, made the situation more complex. The collectors of native customs dues farmed the duty in the old fashion, promising the government a fixed sum in return for the rights of revenue collection over a certain stretch of river frontage. On all native goods that passed through their area it was to their interest to collect full duty according to the native tariff. But for the commodities of foreign trade they were not responsible, and when foreign lorcha-men brought opium and manufactured imports in small craft up the crowded river to the areas under their control, the native revenue farmers found it profitable to land cargoes at less than the treaty tariff, perhaps half-duty on bulky goods or a few dollars a package on smaller. This lesser and more vicious smuggling system brought the worst element of foreign lorcha-men directly into contact with the Chinese and produced numerous petty squeezes and disputes. The famous *Arrow*, that provided the *casus belli* in 1856, was a lorcha of this sort.

In the teeming waters of the Canton river, where chop-boats, bumboats, flower boats, tanka boats, and their population of several hundred thousand constantly circulated, where traffic with the interior mingled with that to the Southern Ocean, and boatmen, fishermen, and pirates were often indistinguishable, it would have been miraculous if no irregularities had occurred. Yet it was neither remarkable nor serious when they did. All persons connected with the foreign trade sought from it their shares of sustenance, licit and illicit. Each class was set by circumstances to watch the other, be it the boatmen, the linguists, or the official underlings. In a sense the consul who invoked the treaties really created disorder by his attempt to impose Western methods.[23]

This was forcibly brought home to Dr. John Bowring soon after he took over at Canton in April 1849. For some time the *Mayflower*, master Bellamy, a British subject, had been doing an active smuggling business in front of the foreign factories. Consul Bowring, with the zeal of a newcomer, on finding that she had neither flag, register, nor papers, and never reported at the consulate, had her taken into custody by H. M. S. *Phlegethon* on August 22nd, 1849.[24] He then asked the Hoppo for a personal conference, in order that they might "enter into some general arrangement for the prevention of smuggling." The Hoppo, however, saw in the barbarian's officiousness only a covert desire to break down the precedent of exclusiveness; for no Hoppo had ever met a consul. He replied, "This gives ample evidence of your friendly cultivation of amity, . . .

which affords me inexpressible delight," but he deputed minor officers to investigate. A slow joint investigation revealed that at the time of seizure the *Mayflower* had been loading tea and silk, value $1800, on which a British Indian subject, Sapoorjee Dhunjee, deposed that he had paid $60 by way of duty to one of the sixty or so officials and underlings present, as was customary. The consul fined the captain $200 for being without a sailing license (Supplementary treaty, art. XVII) and notified the Hoppo. "An expectant assistant district magistrate," delegated in return by the Hoppo, told the vice-consul that no one at the scene of the shipment confessed to having received sixty dollars and asked for names. Finally, having received not the slightest coöperation, on September 5 the consul proposed to punish the British subject by making him pay three times the amount of the duty.

The Hoppo replied, "This gives ample evidence of your very satisfactory and suitable manner of transacting business, which really affords me much delight." [25]

Mr. Bellamy was a God-fearing English citizen who had been 13 years in China and had supported his father, mother, and one sister by remitting £5 monthly during the past seven years. It was his misfortune, not that he smuggled opium, but that he began to undercut the prices of some of his Chinese competitors. Whether these were pirates or mandarin boats was never quite ascertained, but it mattered little: one night late in September 1849 the *Mayflower* was fired into without warning by a forty-oared craft which wounded the crew of four Manila-men and the master, removed 12 chests of opium, and burnt her to the water's edge. H. M. S. *Medea* effected a rescue and Mr. Bellamy claimed $3000 compensation. The consul suspected that this vengeance had been exacted by one of the mandarin boats, which smuggled opium into Canton for British owners at the price of $20 a chest; in any case he was alarmed for the safety of all British craft if the river remained crowded with armed vessels which were neither recognized nor disowned by the Chinese authorities.[26] No satisfaction could be obtained from the latter source. The imperial commissioner, when appealed to, said he had heard that the *Mayflower* had spontaneously blown up. Lord Palmerston refused the master's claim for compensation because he admitted having opium aboard at the time.[27]

A full century later, a very similar situation was reported from the Canton delta.[d]

[d] Correspondent Henry R. Lieberman reported from Canton to the *New York Times* on March 27, 1947: "Canton has managed to keep its economic head above water on the proceeds of smuggling. The fantastic traffic in illicit goods has been stimulated by stringent economic controls, and the proximity of Canton to the free port of Hong Kong. Hundreds of sampans are said to be engaged in smuggling in banned foreign goods, especially canned goods, cloth, nylons and cosmetics and smuggling out rice, firewood, wolfram and silk. Aided by a number of corrupt officials, the smugglers are said to have accounted for at least 50 per cent of the total volume of foreign trade."

"Chiseling the emperor" at Shanghai. In contrast to the well-worn grooves at Canton of a system as old as the China trade and only slightly modified by the treaties, Shanghai presented a *tabula rasa* where the foreigner could assist in making his own precedents. A trade rivaling that of Canton had grown up in less than a decade. By 1850 it had attracted the most active, if not always the most scrupulous, of the foreign traders in China, who were captained by a vigorous British consul. To oppose the trading strength of big foreign firms like Jardine-Matheson, Dent, or Russell, whose receiving ships at Wusung already assisted in the importation of some twenty thousand chests of opium a year, the Chinese merchants at Shanghai had at first neither the requisite capital and experience in foreign trade nor the diplomatic support which the presence of high provincial authorities, as at Canton, might have lent them in cases of dispute with the foreign community. Nor could the local authorities rely, as was done at Canton, upon the tradition that foreigners were excluded from the city and that the violence of the populace might resist all foreign encroachments, in defiance even of the emperor's commands. The barbarian could not be confined to a ghetto at Shanghai where none existed. He could not be insulated, but had his own settlement and conducted his own trade, and dealt through his own Cantonese staff directly with the customhouse. The adventurous and energetic temper of the foreign community, who sometimes responded too avidly to the challenge of their position as pioneers, made them from the first difficult to control. Their own self-confidence, the peace-loving spirit of the Shanghai populace, and the fact that on both sides there were fortunes to be made, all combined to let the young British and American merchants play a central part in the daily conduct of foreign trade and in the smuggling that grew within it.

Since there can be few secrets in a populous country like China, anyone who speaks of smuggling must give the term its widest meaning. The opium trade, for example, was technically clandestine. Foreign newspapers published the participants' names every week and Chinese officials

---

Correspondent Frank Robertson reported from Canton to the *Christian Science Monitor* on August 12, 1949: "Smuggling — with piracy and extortion as sidelines in some cases — has been one of the principal occupations of the people living in this part of China ever since Hong Kong was established as a trading center. The racket is not restricted to the small-time runners who carry sacks of groceries, cosmetics, or tobacco, nor is it limited to the armed gangs. The provincial government of Kwangtung Province also is generally understood to be a big operator. The government is believed to smuggle valuable shipments of vegetable oils out of Canton in order to get money to pay its troops and employees. Since many cargoes are well protected by strong troop detachments, there is little that customs officials can do to prevent it. It is reported that when the national government's finance minister complained of this recently, the provincial officials asked him to make funds for the troops and other expenses available from the national treasury. When the finance minister said this was not possible, the provincial officials are said to have shrugged and replied that they would have to continue smuggling. Smuggling between the free port of Hong Kong and China is so well established that in Canton today there are 34 shipping and forwarding agencies which guarantee to move goods to and fro without paying duty."

occasionally dined on the receiving ships. But still it could be called a smuggling trade, legally in the dark, as long as the British consul and his Chinese colleagues were afflicted with an official myopia which prevented their seeing it. Likewise the evasion of duties due on legal goods could be called smuggling in the sense that the Chinese customs authorities and the foreign merchants connived in keeping their mutually profitable arrangements hidden from the eye of the emperor. Senior partners of firms at Shanghai, young men about thirty, would speak of "chiseling the emperor" or "taking it out of Taou-Kwang," but they did not need to operate on stormy coasts under cover of night. They were smugglers only in that they flouted the treaty tariff, which was a foreign creation, and assisted in the preservation of what they regarded as an old Chinese custom. As in the opium trade, too much publicity would oblige the responsible Chinese authorities to appear to take repressive measures. But usually the evasion of duties was achieved by a process of coöperation and compromise, in which the violence of the rougher foreign merchants was certainly no greater than the venality of the minor Chinese officials, imbedded as they were in the Chinese administrative tradition.

The Chinese maritime customs at Shanghai had been established in 1685. At first under the control purely of the local officials of the district city of Shanghai, it had acquired greater importance as the trade of the port increased, and in 1725 had been put under the control of the governor at Soochow, who three years later appointed the taotai of the Su-Sung-T'ai circuit to exercise immediate control over it and for that purpose reside at Shanghai.[28] This official, one of the eighty-four intendants of circuit or taotais in China proper, was the chief military and administrative officer for the area comprised in the prefectures of Soochow and Sungkiang and the independent department of T'ai-ts'ang, a sizable area containing a dense population of several millions. Thus the collection of duties on foreign trade was but one of his manifold duties and responsibilities. The foreign trade of Shanghai since 1843 had grown suddenly to unprecedented proportions, yet no corresponding administrative changes had been made to provide for its supervision.

About 1848 the customs office, formerly within the Chinese city, had been moved outside nearer the foreign shipping. Directly to the north of the walled city and on the left or west bank of the Whangpu lay the godowns and residences of the foreign settlement. First came the narrow French area, then the Yangkingpang (*Yang-ching-peng*), a waterway in the region of the later Avenue Edward VII, and across it the area of the English and Americans. Here along the newly built bund there now stretched in a thin line to the northward, in the following order, the establishments of Russell and Company, Dent, Beale and Company, the

P. and O., Jardine, Matheson, and finally the British consulate, where it still is. Sandwiched into this row next to "the large umbrageous compound of Messrs. Dent and Company" stood the red and white customhouse, "occupying a Chinese temple, the fantastic roofs and curved gables of which constitute the only break in the line of European architecture." [29]

In this customs establishment the smallness of the employees' salaries made irregularity a foregone conclusion. The Su-Sung-T'ai taotai, as a class 4a official, received a nominal salary of Tls. 105 and at his post a further allowance (*yang-lien,* to "nourish incorruptibility," also translated "anti-extortion allowance") of Tls. 3000.[30] As superintendent of maritime customs he got a further allowance of Tls. 1800 [31] — making a total of Tls. 4905 per annum. Yet he was collecting duties at a post from which his predecessors had once been asked (1764–99) to remit nearly Tls. 100,000 to Peking every year and at which over Tls. 2,000,000 were to be collected in the year 1854–55.

The salaries of the underlings who actually conducted the business of the customhouse were proportionately a great deal less than the taotai's — for clerks, under Tls. 2 per month; for watchmen, not even one tael. Obviously they could not do otherwise than follow the immemorial custom which expected them to get their living from squeeze rather than salary. When in 1844 the taotai, Kung Mu-chiu, set up a series of new substations, with an added number of customhouse personnel,[32] he could hardly lessen the incidence of corruption. In the well worn grooves of trade at Canton squeeze had flowed for generations in channels fathomless to the foreign merchant. But at the new port of Shanghai the chronic corruption of the Chinese employees inevitably infected the British and American traders.

Early customs procedure at Shanghai had been worked out by the consul and taotai together. In January 1844 Balfour published regulations which *inter alia* permitted personal baggage and stores to be passed by the customs without examination. His notifications during 1845 cautioned British merchants to restrain their "Canton men" from presuming upon these liberal regulations; he asked for "kindness and forbearance" toward the Chinese customs officers and threatened to act vigorously upon the latters' complaints. The consulate was closed and commercial business strictly forbidden from 4 P.M. Saturday to 10 A.M. Monday; to facilitate business, however, the taotai agreed that a consignee, having declared his desire to land or ship an entire cargo, could have any number of boat passes without repeated applications (such as were required at Canton). Moreover shipping passes from the customs were to bear full details of both goods and duties, while the consulate would issue "general duty statements" on which the customs would certify all items of duty and the total to be paid before a ship departed. The consulate's participation in the routine of trade developed so far that by September 1845 it began to issue landing and shipping off "chops" (passes) directly to the British applicant.[33] Consul Alcock by mid-1847 had carried this coöperation a step further and secured the taotai's agreement that ships might leave the Shanghai anchorage as soon as they had paid all duties and filed their customs duty receipts at the consulate — that is, they might drop down to Wusung without waiting for the customs' "Grand Chop" (final clearance), which ship agents could subsequently pick up at the consulate. This would speed up the dispatch of tea vessels.[34]

The principle that the evasion of duties would injure British trade was expressed by Consul Balfour at Shanghai as early as December 1844 in the case of the *Mary Ann Webb*. This British vessel first tried to export 320 piculs of rice, to which the taotai with consular support objected as contrary to Chinese law. By making false statements to the customs underlings, she then managed to ship 274 cases of tea before notifying the consulate and getting a shipping-off chop from the customs. The consul regarded this as opening the way for bribery and corruption and also as damaging his prestige in Chinese eyes. The *Mary Ann Webb* was fined $200.[35]

In spite of the British consul's assistance, the Shanghai customs had soon developed a vested interest in squeeze. According to foreign sources its laxity was increased by the newness of the port and the rapid increase of the trade. The foreign community soon got the news that the emperor had delayed farming the customs revenue in 1843, in order to have monthly returns of the foreign trade for the first three years, and the proceeds, sent to Peking. This arrangement was renewed in October 1846 for another three years.[36] But the transmitting of a large sum of silver was expensive to the local authorities and also raised the probable amount at which the duties might be farmed to them. Hence their desire to report small receipts, which could be achieved either by conniving at evasion or, as was alleged, by complete apathy. Certainly the latter method entailed less work.[37] It was also reported that the Shanghai authorities wished to mask the increase of foreign trade, which might prove distasteful to Peking; or again, that they wished to establish the habit of evading duty in order to profit by it in time to come. At any rate by 1850 the legal trade at Shanghai had been demoralized, partly perhaps by the example of the opium trade, partly by the venality of the Chinese officials and the less responsible foreign merchants, whose profits forced their competitors to follow suit. The same methods of short reporting and undervaluation were followed as at Canton,[38] except that here the foreigner did not act through linguists but was directly concerned and responsible. This differentiated Shanghai from the other ports.

Indeed by 1850 the evasion of legal duties had become everywhere so great as to invalidate completely the consular returns of export trade; for in cases of evasion the outward manifest seen by the consul usually agreed with the reports made to the customhouse, and on these two sources the consul had to rely for his information. Ningpo estimated one-half the small trade there to have been smuggled. Amoy reported that a comparison of merchants' receipts and consul's returns from the customs showed that the superintendent of customs had pocketed several thousand taels.[39] The treaty tariff, in short, was losing its validity at the very time that circumstances outside China were combining to test it to the utmost.

The threat of American competition. Until 1850 a monopoly of the direct tea trade to England was secured to British shipping by the navigation laws. Their repeal in June 1849, as a crowning act in the apotheosis of free trade, threw the British tea market open to American clippers after January 1, 1850. Since the United States had adopted a similar law in 1817, this effected a reciprocal situation, described in a State Department circular as follows: "all goods whether of [British] growth, produce, or manufacture, or that of any other country, may, after the 1st of January next, be carried in American bottoms to any port in the United Kingdom; and British vessels may carry goods of the growth, produce, or manufacture of any part of the world to our ports, but they cannot participate in our coasting trade, nor we in theirs. An American ship may carry a cargo of goods of any country to a port in a British colony, and from that to a port in another British colony; but not from one port in such a colony to another port in the same colony. In other words, the British intercolonial trade is open to our vessels, but not the colonial coasting trade." [40]

While British and American merchants now had an equal right to invade each other's home trade, the latter were the real gainers, for their new opportunity chanced to coincide with the designing in America of the fastest sailing vessels yet constructed. The American clipper *Oriental*, on her maiden voyage, sailed from China on the 30th of January, 1850, and ran home to New York in the record time of 81 days with 1,118 tons of tea. Fortunately the navigation laws had expired only as the season ended. But the first Aberdeen model British tea clipper (Jardine's *Stornoway*) was yet to be built; and since American ships already carried almost half the trade of Shanghai, and had been rapidly improving their position,[e] this

[e] Cp. these "Consular returns of American trade with Shanghae" (in Marshall's 13, April 28, 1853, China 8):

	Imports			*Exports*		
Year	*Vessels*	*tonnage*	*value*	*Vessels*	*tonnage*	*value*
1849	24	9,829	$ 757,259	24	9,877	$1,358,182
1850	37	15,308	830,318	34	14,464	2,100,506
1851	54	27,634	1,216,922	53	26,697	4,615,533
1852	66	38,760	2,094,971	70	40,592	7,980,747

taste of future American competition was most disquieting. British ship-owners were in "absolute despair."[41] All that was needed to make American competition a serious danger to the British carrying trade was to penalize British shippers by the threat of consular interference for the prevention of smuggling, a possibility which under the American treaty could not equally threaten American shippers. This danger, latent ever since the signing of the American treaty, was first made real by the two cases of the *Lady Mary Wood* and the *John Dugdale*, which occurred at Shanghai at the beginning and end of the season of 1850–51, i.e., in June, 1850, and in January, 1851.

The case of the Lady Mary Wood. As has never been pointed out, the first of these cases had its origin in the opium trade.

In March 1850, the P. and O. put their wooden steamer *Lady Mary Wood* on the Hongkong-Shanghai service. As the directors of the P. and O. euphemistically expressed it, "The Company's agents in China had adopted the same arrangements for the *Lady Mary Wood* in respect to her using the anchorage at Woosung for receiving cargo etc. as were practised by her competitors the sailing vessels."[42] Or as the British consul put it more baldly eleven months later, the above named competitors of the P. and O. steamer were "the opium clippers, five or six in number, belonging to three of the principal firms in China [Jardine, Dent, and Russell and Company]. The clippers bring opium to the receiving ships. The steamer also brings her supplies of opium. If the clippers are required to take down Chinese produce, they *come up to Shanghai*, complying with the usual forms. But the steamer, contrary to this general practice, after discharging her opium at Woosung, came up to Shanghai, and then cleared out *in ballast*, by this avoiding (according to a local regulation) the payment of any port dues; and subsequently when returned to Woosung took in a full cargo of silk, duty unpaid. . . . It was only when the steamer, in converting this Station into a *loading anchorage* for goods in the legalized trade and on which no duty was paid, brought into peril these major interests [opium], that proceedings were taken by the parties aggrieved, . . . and she was no doubt brought under the official cognizance of the British and Chinese authorities, by the owners of one of the opium clippers."[43] In short, Jardine's consciously took the initiative in smuggling on the P. and O. steamer, so as to involve it in difficulties, check its competition, and preserve the distinction between the opium trade at Wusung and the legal trade of Shanghai.

On the surface, the motives of the case were less apparent. On June 10, 1850, the Shanghai taotai, Lin Kuei, notified Consul Alcock that on the previous evening raw silk had been shipped without a consular shipping-off chop. The Chinese in charge had offered the excuse that it was "inexpedient to apply" for a chop on Sunday; one would be sent next day. It had not arrived, however, and the taotai asked the consul for the name of the ship. Alcock at once replied that it was up to the customs to seize the ship. Nevertheless he investigated and found that while the vessel was within the limits of the port and subsequent to the issue of the grand chop and port clearance by the taotai and consul, respectively, — which had been granted upon the declaration that "the said ship should leave the Port in Ballast" — A. G. Dallas, resident partner of Jardine, Matheson and Company, had shipped 519 packages of raw silk and 180 bales on board the *Lady Mary Wood*, without a permit "on the morning of the 10th June at Shanghai and the same afternoon and next morning (the 11th) at Woosung."[44] Consul Alcock thereupon told Dallas that he would be fined $200 to the Queen for a breach of article VII of the general regulations, and must pay duties. The consul told the taotai of this decision, upbraided him for the laxity of his officers, and disclaimed all future consular obligation to repeat such active steps.

Here the case might have ended. But on June 14 Jardine, Matheson and Company reiterated to the consul that they had no objection to the penalty but they wanted all the other guilty parties to be fined, like themselves. "Several shipments have been made subsequently to ours, by the same vessel, of which the Chinese must be well aware, and of which they have taken no notice." The taotai, when asked by the consul, could obtain no information about these other alleged shipments. Alcock replied to Jardine's that he needed evidence. To this, Dallas replied on June 17 that by his own admission he had already given conclusive evidence against the *Lady Mary Wood* but no steps had been taken against her. "By the infraction of the treaty Regulations on her part, shippers were in a manner forced to commit irregularities which they would have in some cases very willingly avoided . . . the same vessel took away from Woosung on the 15th April about 150 bales and on the 13th May about 350 bales raw silk, besides a quantity in addition to our shipment on 12th instant." Alcock, however, was slow to get the point and still thought Dallas was accusing other shippers by the P. and O. steamer. Hence on June 24 the firm explained that, "the parties to whom we alluded [as smugglers] were the representatives of the *Lady Mary Wood* steamer; and not the shippers by that vessel." They then gave details.

With this to go on, Consul Alcock brought the master, Tronson, before a consular court on July 4. Dallas presented bills of lading with Tronson's signature; "defendant admitted the shipment of the silk within the limits of the port," and was fined $200 to the Queen for a breach of article 6 of the general regulations ("all duties . . . must . . . be paid up in full" before departure) and ordered to pay tonnage dues for the last voyage.

On a cargo of some $240,000 value, the customs thus recovered Tls. 5,664 in duties as well as Tls. 148 in tonnage dues, equal in all to $8,107.[45]

From the foregoing it is plain that Jardine, Matheson and Company acted to bring the P. and O. into difficulties: first, by shipping their silk openly and without a permit and making Tronson inevitably a party to this proceeding. Second, probably by arousing the Chinese authorities to appeal to the consul, and probably also by bringing the transaction "particularly to the notice of the Consul." Third, by calling the consul's attention explicitly to the guilt of the *Lady Mary Wood*. In presenting the bills of lading in evidence on July 5, they gave the coup de grâce by request. Their motive was chiefly to defend their opium monopoly from the amateur competition of the P. and O. steamer. In addition it was to their interest that the opium station at Wusung should not be contaminated by the evasion there of legal duties, a proceeding which if unchecked might lead the Chinese authorities either to denounce officially what went on there or to demand higher fees for their indifference to it. This was equally apparent to Alcock who recognized the "major interests" of opium, which "vitalizes the whole of our commerce." In his official notification to British merchants at Shanghai on June 23 the consul warned them that goods smuggled within the port were liable to confiscation by the Chinese, "and if any shipment be effected at any other ports or places, not only the goods, but also the ship, may be seized and confiscated by the Chinese authorities, in like manner. As regards indeed the latter class of smuggling operations especially [e.g., at Wusung], it may be well to bear in mind that if the Chinese be driven to extremities, questions may at any moment arise from such illegal shipments not limited in their application to the case more immediately under consideration, but taking a wider range, and involving in a common danger interests of greater magnitude." [46]

The case of the *Lady Mary Wood* [f] further established the consul's attitude toward smuggling. When first appealed to, Alcock had refused to get information for the taotai and could only recommend him "vigilantly to

[f] This case had an instructive sequel. The P. and O. appealed against Alcock's decision to both Palmerston and the supreme court at Hongkong. They claimed that Alcock's unfair discrimination had obliged them to withdraw the *Lady Mary Wood* from the Shanghai service (in February 1851). Palmerston supported Alcock.[47] But the supreme court on March 14, 1851, reversed Alcock's decision, on what the attorney general and governor at Hongkong regarded as an obvious technicality although the law officers in England thought it right on the whole and recommended no appeal.[48] At that time Governor Bonham and the chief justice were engaged in a feud, one issue of which was the division of powers to be made between the consular courts, which reflected the influence of the governor in his capacity as superintendent of trade, and the colonial supreme court at Hongkong. Bonham confessed himself "much plagued by the interference of our Supreme Court in consular matters." The chief justice's attack on Bonham's judicial influence as superintendent of trade may have become, in the case of the *Lady Mary Wood*, an attack on the influence of Bonham's friends, the big trading companies. But this remains an untraced thread in the tangled skein of Hongkong politics.[49] The case at least indicated how the large firms like Jardine's, interested in opium as well as in legal goods, were naturally more opposed to the evasion of duties than the small trader, who was interested only in the legal trade or the carrying trade and had no larger interests at stake.

exercise" his right to "seize all goods shipped without authority." Later the consul declared that his intervention in imposing fines had been merely a favor, to keep the taotai out of a difficulty incurred (so the taotai said) by passing the goods from a "friendly consideration for the British authorities." The consul's intervention could not be drawn into a precedent— "In future for any smuggling the remedy in such cases made and provided by Treaty, is in the hands of the Chinese authorities exclusively, and consists in the stoppage or seizure of the goods according to circumstances." The consul further clarified his position in his notification of June 23. He had refused to "take upon himself the proper business of Chinese Custom House officers. . . . Two parties being injured, the Government which is defrauded of its revenue, and the fair trader of his profits, to both it is equally open to appeal to the laws." The former could seize smuggled goods, the latter could inform against smugglers. "But the Consul is not authorized to act except upon positive information, and then his first and chief duty is to report. The remedy lies not with the Consul but with those who are the chief losers." Bonham entirely approved Alcock's "denying the pretensions of the Taotai to call upon H. M.'s Consul to obtain evidence of smuggling by British subjects . . . and disclaiming all right on the part of the mercantile community to look to the British Consular officers for protection against smuggling amongst themselves, unless proper evidence of such smuggling were lodged at Her Majesty's Consulate." Palmerston also approved.[50]

The British government thus agreed that the official role of the consul with regard to smuggling should be a passive one. His intervention could only respond to the action of the defrauded Chinese authorities, or the aggrieved British merchant. Yet the *Lady Mary Wood* had made it evident that the consul nevertheless had an active interest with regard to smuggling, namely, to keep it from endangering the safe regularity of British trade, including that in opium.

The case of the John Dugdale. Roused by the public attention given to the *Lady Mary Wood*, the taotai revised the Shanghai port regulations in order to tighten up his surveillance, especially at the four public jetties which the consul had succeeded in adding to the customhouse wharf as places for the landing and shipping of goods. These revised regulations gave the consul less of a part to play in customs procedure. "Export goods will be reported *direct to the Custom House for examination*, by the shippers or consignees, through their respective linguists, as they are shipped day by day, without the necessity of applying for shipping-chops to the Consul. A memorandum will be kept at the Custom House to be compared with the Export manifest sent in by the Consul." This modification of the treaties, together with the threats and promises of the taotai's notification, was approved by Alcock: "I am quite ready to coöperate with you. But if the Custom House officers do not exercise more vigilance than heretofore, neither these nor any other Regulations can possibly supply the place of an effective Custom House Establishment." [51] Likewise, the American merchant consul, J. N. A. Griswold of the firm of Russell and Company, assured the taotai of his readiness to afford every facility for the proper examination of goods; but privately he could see "no remedy for smuggling except in an efficient custom house staff to take account of the goods as landed and shipped, which has never yet been done." [52]

Regulations, in short, were idle. Honest merchants were demoralized by less meticulous competitors. When one of those as yet uncorrupted, Wm. Hogg, partner in Lindsay and Company, appealed to the consul, the latter summed up the dilemma: "Smuggling can only be stopped by the Chinese and . . . they will not. In the first place, you cannot stop it at Canton. Suppose you could stop it here, you place the trade of Shanghai at a great disadvantage as compared with that of Canton. You could only stop it here by an English staff of officers (tidewaiters) [sic]. Suppose the British Consul could stop it under the British flag, smuggling would rage more freely than ever under foreign flags."

Whereupon the merchant continued, "I brought the subject before the Chamber of Commerce. They would have nothing to do with it and for some time I was the most unpopular man in Shanghai. I wrote to the Consul that I had netted a loss of 20,000 dollars in the first three months of this season by *not* doing only a half of what my neighbours were doing. I cannot now look upon it as dishonest and I told Mr. Alcock distinctly that I would smuggle as heavily as anybody and he said there were two courses — to do so, or to give up business . . . at the same time the danger is great, the revenue must fall away so immensely that [the Chinese] will then bestir themselves." [53]

This latter danger however was but one horn of the dilemma — the other being the danger of American competition. Of thirteen American clippers launched in 1850–51, "no less than six . . . invaded the English tea trade, and caused great commotion amongst the owners of British tea ships by making passages which at that time were considered to be impossible." [54] British shipping agents, whose inefficiency had been protected too long by the navigation laws, much as the East India Company had once been protected by its monopoly, felt themselves menaced and required only a scare to be filled with panic.

On January 4, 1851, the consignees of the British ship *John Dugdale* on looking at the receipts for duties paid by the four parties shipping in their vessel, found that she was about to clear, fully laden, with a declared cargo of only half the quantity she had taken on her previous voyage.[55] They formally protested to the consul who already held the grand chop issued from the taotai's office, which cleared the ship and declared all duties to have been paid. He at once informed the taotai of the consignee's protest, and ordered the ship back to the loading anchorage, hatches sealed. On January 7th the taotai was to unload and weigh the cargo, but "after repeated and careful consultation" consul and taotai on January 8th agreed to call upon each shipper to declare the actual amount of tea shipped and accept a fine. This was done. Of 458,651 lb. of tea shipped, at least 257,251 lb. "in open day had been put on board at the anchorage opposite the Custom House, effecting a fraud on the Chinese revenue of more than 4,000 Taels, no notice whatever having been taken of the proceeding."[56] To record the guilt of the Chinese authorities, Consul Alcock wrote to the taotai on January 8th that "the illegal shipment has not been more thoroughly established than the criminal negligence and worthlessness of the Custom House officers. The manifest brought to the Consulate, though in itself false, agreed in every respect with the duty accounts passed by the Custom House. It is notorious that scarcely a foreign vessel leaves the Port without frauds nearly as large as in this case." To this the acting taotai, Wu Chien-chang, on January 12th suavely replied that he had been "on the point of sifting the matter to the utmost," just when the consul raised it.[57] He refrained from any acceptance of responsibility.

The *North China Herald* estimated that the *John Dugdale*, with so much cargo smuggled, "still paid in respect of her tonnage more export duty than ¾ of the vessels recently cleared." For a time her example discouraged others from smuggling — "even in American ships," as the British consul put it. Nevertheless he was "thoroughly satisfied that either some means must be devised of placing the British and Foreign trader on the same footing with respect to each other, in the payment of Custom House Duties, or we must be prepared to see the whole export trade transferred, and at no distant date, to foreign bottoms; . . . everyone *must* smuggle on the same wholesale scale, or all must be alike prevented. . . . It is essential something be done before the commencement of the next tea and silk season in June."[58] Alcock formulated the issue succinctly: "it is for Governments, who make treaties, to take care their subjects are not, under its provisions, reduced to so cruel an alternative as *ruin* or *fraud*." If smuggling became prevalent, "the *chief penalty* and the *greatest loss* would fall upon the foreign trade by its total demoralisation — the introduction of an element of uncertainty into all commercial transactions, and the absence of all security against the most unequal levy of duties as regarded either individuals or flags." As "An Anglo-Saxon" complained to the *North China Herald* — "what good has it done? Is it not a notorious fact that by this pernicious system produce has been enhanced in value to the *full* extent of the saving effected by it?"

The problem was thus fairly put. Over the Chinese authorities the British consul had no control. From the American merchant consul he could expect little or no coöperation. As a result he could enforce the treaties and penalize British smugglers only at the expense of the trade which the treaties were originally designed to foster. The laxity of the Chinese and American authorities, who saw little reason to suppress the evasion of duties, put the British consul on the spot. Enforcement of the British treaty would surely drive British goods into the safety of American ships and destroy the British carrying trade; not to enforce it would just as surely subvert that regularity and security, that published tariff equally enforced upon all, which the treaties were meant to ensure.

Behind this dilemma lay the contrasting social institutions of China and the trading West: the Anglo-Saxon rule of law was necessary to provide a secure framework within which British entrepreneurs could carry on their competition — without such universally accepted rules, individual traders could not play their commercial game. Chinese institutions on the other hand gave fewer legal rights to the merchants, yet left them at the same time more free to make their individual deals with the official guardians of the law. Handicapped by the limitations imposed by extraterritoriality and Sino-foreign friction, as well as by its own tradition of corruption, the Chinese customhouse was unable to function in a Western manner. By 1851 the treaty system of 1842–43, never complete in design nor wholly effective in practice, faced the prospect of a total breakdown.

PART V

THE CREATION OF THE FOREIGN INSPECTORATE OF CUSTOMS AT SHANGHAI 1850–54

CHAPTER XX

PALMERSTON ABANDONS THE TREATY TARIFF 1850–51

THE FAR-REACHING historical significance of the Foreign Inspectorate of Customs set up at Shanghai in July 1854 has been briefly noted in Chapter 1 and adumbrated elsewhere. In this and the following three chapters this event is analyzed in some detail as a case study illustrative of a theme — that the treaty system finally established in China had to be a joint Sino-foreign arrangement, a compromise or hybrid device, to which both parties had to contribute and which neither could control alone. While this thesis is in many ways a truism, expressive of China's "semi-colonial" situation, it nevertheless has interesting implications today and even some points of comparison with the Manchu-Chinese relationship noted in Chapter 3.

Seen in the immediate context of the times, the inauguration of the Shanghai Customs Inspectorate on July 12, 1854, coincided with the extension of the municipal and land regulations. These were issued on July 5, and out of them grew the International Settlement of Shanghai. Clearly, the Customs Service and the International Settlement were born of the same circumstances and formed parts of the same general solution to the problem of Sino-Western relations. This solution was one which gave special privileges to all foreign nations in China and yet, by the same token, stopped short of the dismemberment or actual foreign administration of the country.

Three factors contributed to the creation of the Inspectorate: first, the long-continued British effort to set up a rule of law under which trade might prosper. The British assumed that government and commerce were separate activities, that government should enforce rules by which individual traders could freely compete and should then sustain itself by equitable taxation of their trade. When the first treaty system was seen to have broken down, Palmerston in London decided in 1851 to give up the effort to prevent smuggling in China. But Consul Alcock at Shanghai in 1852–53 found no alternative but to keep on seeking the enforcement of Western regulations by which British trade could be fostered. Committed as they were to the principle of free trade, the British in China had to make this effort.

The second factor in 1854 was the readiness of the Chinese authorities at Shanghai to accept Alcock's solution of the customs problem. This compliant attitude resulted from two propitious circumstances: the peculiar capacities of the Shanghai taotai, Wu Chien-chang, an *arriviste* and commercial-minded opportunist who was uninhibited by orthodox Confucian training; and the unusual combination of responsibility and helplessness which the imperial officials faced at Shanghai. Having been ejected from the Chinese city by local rebels, their authority was recognized only in the foreign settlement, but on sufferance alone. They were still held accountable by Peking for customs administration at Shanghai, but they could act there only with foreign concurrence.

Finally, a fortunate meeting of minds was possible in 1854 among the superior authorities of China, Britain, the United States, and France because competent personnel happened to occupy those positions. Sir John Bowring and the American commissioner, Robert M. McLane, were both men of broad views and imagination. The Nanking governor-general, I-liang, was an experienced and trustworthy official placed by the Rebellion in a precarious position which called for desperate measures. With their subordinates, these men could bring to bear on the Shanghai customs problem a higher degree of statesmanship than had yet been seen on the China coast. Even the Americans and Englishmen coöperated.

It is significant however that Whitehall contributed rather little to this statesmanlike solution, for the institutions created at Shanghai in 1854, hybrid products of cultural miscegenation, could not be invented from a distance. This was made perfectly clear by the general frustration which overtook Palmerston's approach to China in 1850–51, and which led him to abandon all British responsibility for the enforcement of the treaty tariff. In 1851 this negative step was practicable, indeed, only because Palmerston was by that time contemplating a second show of force. Truly constructive action was possible only on a joint Sino-foreign basis and only in China; it could not be master-minded unilaterally from London.

The trend of British policy in 1850. To understand the impasse to which the Foreign Office came, let us first quickly survey the official structure through which its policy in China was now being executed. By 1850 the China service consisted of some thirty British personnel, of whom four were consuls, four vice-consuls, and ten assistants. The "Chinese" (i.e., Chinese-reading) secretary and his assistant secretary at Hongkong and the five British interpreters at the ports formed a network which ran parallel with that of the minister plenipotentiary and his consuls. In each office the Chinese writers who handled Chinese documents were often as numerous as the English staff, although this did not spare the latter the drudgery of copying dispatches in longhand sufficiently legible to satisfy Lord Palmerston.

The United States had nothing comparable to this British establishment.[1] In the American service, for lack of a political appointee, a missionary often acted as chargé d'affaires and secretary of legation, resident at Canton, while the partners of Russell and Company, the largest American firm, usually held the merchant-consulships in Canton and Shanghai and left the honor at the other ports to anyone who might apply or consent to act. The French legation had a staff of a dozen persons, including a consulate at Shanghai and two Englishmen as consular agents at Amoy and Hongkong. Since French trade was negligible this number was more than sufficient. To complete the list of foreign officials, a Spanish legation had been established and a dozen leading merchants at the various ports, usually British, now acted as consuls for the Netherlands, Chile, Peru, Denmark, Portugal, Prussia, Saxony, Austria, and Brazil. Finally the government of Macao continued its inbred existence, governing a community of some seventy merchants with the help of a large proportion of their number.[2]

The British consular staff was responsible to the Foreign Office but also reported to the Board of Trade, just as their chief was at once minister plenipotentiary, chief superintendent of British trade in China, and governor of Hongkong, enmeshed in the finances and politics of his colony and answerable to the Colonial Office. The isolation of these officials added to their responsibilities. The minister at Hongkong was head of the consular service and he alone corresponded directly with the Foreign Office. Yet he was six days or more away from Shanghai and a day from Canton, while the mail to London via Suez even by the new steamer service still took seven weeks or more, in each direction. He must make decisions that would stand for four months. Similarly the consul at Shanghai in any emergency had to devise his own program and receive his superior's opinion upon it two or three weeks after it had been put into execution. Usually he had to act first and report afterwards.

The Foreign Office in Whitehall was a clearing house for many opinions, as to fact, law, and policy, and took its decisions within limits laid down by others. For the facts of the case in China it relied chiefly upon the reports of the consuls as filtered through, or enclosed in, the dispatches of the minister. To guide it in matters of law, before the institution of legal advisers within the department itself, the Foreign Office referred questions to the Queen's advocate and the law officers of the crown; in matters regarding the colony of Hongkong, it deferred to the Colonial Office; in plans envisaging the use of force — to the Admiralty; and in a multitude of detailed questions concerning shipping and commerce — to the Board of Trade. Limits set and opinions expressed by these departments could not well be disregarded by the foreign secretary. Finally, and perhaps most important, the Foreign Office was spurred in time of crisis by the memorials and individual representations of the China merchants in England and their spokesmen in Parliament.

These merchants were usually either the senior partners of firms in China, who had retired to enjoy their strenuously earned profits and manage the English end of the trade, or else members of firms in England who exported textiles and other manufactured goods to China, sometimes through other firms as agents. The former, interested primarily in the tea and silk trades as their source of profit, were corporately articulate chiefly through the East India and China Associations of London and of Liverpool.[3] The latter, who were mainly exporters of Lancashire products, were organized in the Manchester Commercial Association, and the Chamber of Commerce and Manufactures, also at Manchester.[4] The interests of all four associations were sufficiently wrapped up in the fortunes of the China trade as a whole to make them act in concert on nearly all questions. This they would do with vigor upon receipt of important news from China, and thus the Foreign Office sometimes heard the mercantile point of view before they heard that of the British officials. In any case it would follow close upon the heels of the dispatches, and sometimes be personally presented by a delegation at the Foreign Office.[5]

The internal organization of the Foreign Office in the 1850's was an anachronism; the principle of the division of labor had not yet been applied to diplomacy, and the foreign secretary saw in person a tremendous mass of routine documents. His under-secretaries sent him "everything upon which any question can arise which is personal to any man, when there is any application for employment, or a question in which any man's feelings are concerned . . . whatever a man represents on behalf of himself, anything that may arise in matters of trade, anything about questions which may be mooted in Parliament, questions of general policy and commercial business." [6] The annual total of dispatches received and sent had risen from 11,500 in 1830 to 30,725 in 1849, while the staff had remained almost the same.[7] As late as 1855–56 the total of regular dispatches [8] passing to and from China was only about 650 a year; this was double the number of 1850, even so. It is plain that affairs in China could not bulk large in the foreign secretary's daily grind.[a]

[a] In these circumstances the under-secretaries had an important influence on policy, particularly, in the case of Chinese affairs, the permanent under-secretary, to whom the dispatches from China, as from all countries save a dozen or so in central Europe, were first sent, and whose minutes therefore accompanied them when they came before the foreign secretary.[9] Palmerston's permanent under-secretary in 1850 was Henry Unwin Addington, who had been in the Foreign Office intermittently since 1807 and in his present position since 1842.[10] In the partition of the world in which the under-secretaries indulged for expediency, China fell to Mr. Addington. But he was nearing retirement and matters connected with the Chinese department were left more and more to the chief clerk, Mr. Edmund Hammond. This extraordinary bureaucrat, ex-fellow of University College, Oxford, had entered the Foreign Office in 1824, and by the middle of the century had advanced half way in a career of nearly fifty years of indefatigable service which was to reach its climax in historical notoriety in 1870, three weeks before the outbreak of the Franco-Prussian war, when he told the foreign secretary "that he had never,

In August 1849, goaded by the obduracy of Hsü and Yeh at Canton and the mounting Anglo-Chinese friction there, Palmerston initiated an effort to reinvigorate the British position in China. In April Bonham had advocated the necessity of another resort to force. Palmerston now sent him under sealed cover a formal protest addressed to "the Minister for Foreign Affairs at Peking," which was to be transmitted to the capital over the head of the imperial commissioner at Canton.[13] In brief, the line of diplomatic communication with Peking offered so much resistance at its Canton terminal that Palmerston sought to effect a shorter connection through Shanghai and, later, through the Peiho (the river at Tientsin). This effort produced a further dispute as to the channels through which Sino-foreign relations could be conducted and so formed one chief focus of British policy in 1850–51. In September 1849, in view of the absence of British trade at both Ningpo and Foochow, Palmerston had asked Bonham to suggest other ports that might profitably be substituted. This opened up a second question long imminent, as to what changes were desirable in the British access to China. Thus at the beginning of 1850 British policy was following two closely adjoining paths, one leading toward direct communication with Peking as a last possibility between the extremes of coercion and the acceptance of defeat at Canton; the other leading towards the formulation of an ideal commercial basis for British trade in China. As the year went on, it was to become finally evident to Palmerston that direct protest to Peking was quite as difficult and unavailing as all dealings with Canton. At the same time Alcock and Bonham painted a dazzling picture of the commercial results obtainable by a slight expenditure of force.

Rutherford Alcock was now 41 and had spent six years in the treaty ports. In a dispatch of February 13, 1850, he voiced the true spirit of commercial imperialism. In spite of China's commercial self-sufficiency, he argued, British goods could invade with the greatest profit the enormous inland trade on the Yangtze and the Grand Canal. The British position on the coast, as well as customs barriers raised by the Chinese, prevented the great extension of British trade which would follow the introduction of British goods into the vast continental basins. The trunk lines must be tapped, because tea and opium might not always remain the staples of the trade and carry foreign manufactures in their train. To tap the trunk lines, said Alcock, the British should take Soochow as a trading centre, "to be flanked and guarded by positions at Chinkiang and Hangchow. What

during his long experience, known so great a lull in foreign affairs, and that he was not aware of any important question that he (Lord Granville) should have to deal with." Though obviously a bureaucrat to his fingertips, Hammond was in no sense a sinister power behind the scenes: he believed that the under-secretary, whose duties he formally assumed in 1854, "has no business to give a decision upon any point; he is merely the channel and ministerial officer, who is bound to advise and to recommend . . . but has no independent action at all."[11] Certainly in 1850 he could excel the foreign secretary neither in energy nor in experience.[12]

prevents us? Our treaty? It has been broken. The refusal of the Chinese government? They are in our power." The prejudices of the people he considered an imaginary obstacle. The same coercion necessary to gain anything would gain everything desirable. In three months a small squadron blocking the Grand Canal at Chinkiang as in 1842 could dictate terms.[14]

The brilliant enthusiasm of this program quite inspired Bonham. In passing it on to the F. O. he confessed that the existence of customs barriers must remain unproved until access to the interior allowed further investigation; but in general he was "more than ever convinced of the policy of obtaining a secure footing upon the inner line of traffic. . . . Our primary consideration in China being our commerce, we must have the means to defend it against any tendency to impede its legitimate development." Bonham repeated enthusiastically and almost verbatim Alcock's thesis: demand access to Soochow, Hangchow, and Chinkiang; negotiate at Peking, or at Nanking "with a respectable force anchored opposite to Chinkiang." The question was merely one of time; and in 1854, "when we can claim to have our treaty reconsidered, . . . the Chinese will no more readily agree than at present." Should we act at once or wait until 1854 "*at the latest*?"[15]

Palmerston's appeal to Peking. The immediate cause of Palmerston's abandonment of the treaty tariff was his frustrating experience in trying to communicate with the Chinese government. On January 2, 1850, he had approved Bonham's proposal that if the formal protest of August 1849 was not certainly reported to have reached Peking, then Bonham should himself take a copy to the north.[16] Three weeks later he approved Bonham's further expedient, that Alcock should try to deliver a copy of the protest through the Shanghai taotai and his superior, the governor-general at Nanking.[17] Toward the end of March however he learned that the Shanghai taotai refused to receive barbarian messages and so Bonham would go to the Peiho; but this could not be done until March or April.[18] At the end of May it was reported that all efforts to induce the Shanghai taotai or his superior at Nanking to receive Lord Palmerston's letter had failed. No results were attained until Bonham himself went to Shanghai in May and threatened to continue on to the north — the Chinese correspondence reveals why.[19]

To begin with, Hsü and Yeh at Canton had maintained their policy of disregarding barbarian complaints. In February 1850 they reported to Peking that the American and French chiefs were conferring with Bonham to send a joint communication to the English king; since trade had gradually increased in the half year since discussion regarding entrance to Canton city was stopped, it could be seen that the barbarians were not seeking a quarrel; steady profit made everyone happy, and so contentment with the trade would produce international accord; the English, being left in isolation, would have even less means of gaining their desires.[20] This was a most reassuring, if brief, summary of the situation which had provoked the British minister a few months previously to advocate hostilities. The contrast between actual British feeling and the contemporary Chinese impression of it is instructive: a few days before the court received this complacent report, Bonham had received instructions from Palmerston to explain to the Chinese authorities at the Peiho that he sought "confidential communication with the proper officers of the government . . . to remove by personal representations and explanations those causes of just complaint, which, if suffered to continue, might involve the two governments and countries in very unpleasant discussions, if not in hostile collision." [21]

This stubborn insensitivity of the Canton authorities was the more dangerous because of their sole responsibility for foreign relations. The Shanghai taotai, Lin Kuei, took the position that all matters relating to foreign affairs must be taken up with the imperial commissioner; and the Nanking governor-general, Lu Chien-ying, reported on such matters to Canton rather than to the court.[22] For this reason, when Bonham arrived at Shanghai on May 3 and told the taotai of the proposed trip of the steam sloop *Reynard* to the Peiho, Lu Chien-ying was left to meet the situation alone and save himself from it as best he could. If he went too far in accommodating the barbarians he might be censured; if he did not prevent their going to the north he would certainly be reproved. Lacking explicit authority himself to deal with barbarian affairs, he was obliged, like so many before him, to follow a twofold policy aimed at placating both the court and the barbarians. In this case he consented to receive a letter from Bonham of May 13, forwarding Palmerston's formal communication (*chao-hui*), and these two documents were subsequently sent on to the capital. In his covering memorial, Lu emphasized the fact that he had accepted these letters only as a last resort to keep Bonham from going to Tientsin: the Shanghai taotai had told the British that such letters should be presented at Canton, that Tientsin was not an open port to which they might lawfully proceed, that the Chinese local authorities on the coast would inevitably delay them; again and again they had been told what they should do, yet the British had stubbornly adhered to their intention and of course could, if they wished, pass by on the many avenues of the sea.[23] This memorial to Peking was finally sent only when it became apparent that the British could no longer be detained by dilatory tactics at Shanghai.[24]

As evidence of the court's extreme sensitivity toward any barbarian approach to the capital, a dozen edicts and some ten memorials [25] were precipitated between the end of May and the middle of July (when Bonham returned to Hongkong) by the British effort to communicate with Peking. In brief, the British appeal met with a complete rebuff. Interpreter Medhurst had no success in delivering a copy of Palmerston's letter after two weeks at the Peiho,[26] and the two letters sent through Nanking, after they reached the grand secretaries, Mu-chang-a and Ch'i-ying, received an indirect reply which summarized in its most extreme form the official view as to how Sino-foreign relations should be conducted. On June 8 the Shanghai authorities informed Bonham verbally that the Nanking governor-general "had received a private note from the ministers Muchangah and Kiying desiring him to acknowledge the receipt of the two letters, to which, however, by the laws of China, they were not allowed to give official replies." [27] They referred him to Canton. On June 13 Alcock received from the taotai a dispatch embodying a similar message. A copy of this letter from the grand secretaries to Lu Chien-ying was also the answer brought back from the Peiho.[28] This document expressed surprise that the British, having said that they would stop all discussion of the city question,[29] should again have raised it. It then outlined the Chinese system for dealing with foreign relations: the high authorities of Kwangtung, Fukien, and other provinces all have "in addition to their other charges that of transacting foreign affairs and hence the treaty contains the passage 'shall be forwarded to His Majesty by the High Chinese Officers having the charge of Foreign Affairs'— but no article exists providing for a correspondence between the High Officers at the Court and the English Plenipotentiaries or Ministers." [30]

This could not be literally denied. The clause quoted, article XXXI of the American treaty, did indeed provide in its English version that "Communications . . . to the Court of China shall be transmitted through the medium of the Imperial Commissioner" or the governors-general of the coastal provinces,[31] and the Chinese version quite as clearly provided that those officials should present the original foreign document to the emperor on the foreigner's behalf; but no one in Peking was obliged by treaty to reply! [32]

Historians have generally failed to recognize that this abortive British appeal over the head of the imperial commissioner at Canton probably touched off the court's anti-foreign measures of 1850. The young Hsien-feng Emperor, who had ascended the throne on March 9, 1850, at the Chinese age of twenty, had inherited from his father a chief minister, Mu-chang-a, whose policy of conciliating the barbarians had been increasingly denounced in terms such as are now used for "appeasement." Mu-chang-a's representative, Ch'i-ying, had left Canton under such criticism in 1848, and events since then had accumulated to discredit his barbarian policy. By impudently directing unauthorized letters to these court dignitaries who were already in a very vulnerable position, Palmerston gave them the kiss of death — not the last time that a foreign imputation of power to Chinese officials has been their undoing. A decree of December 1, 1851, degraded both these servitors[33] and dramatized the end of an era in Ch'ing foreign policy.

Palmerston's thoughts of war. To understand the effect in England of this failure to establish contact with Peking, we should note that Bonham's final report of it did not reach the Foreign Office until September 17, 1850, a year and a month after Palmerston's initial letter of protest. Until this time he had continued to base his policy on the hope that negotiations with Peking would succeed where those with Canton had not, and that he could thereby satisfy the steadily more vociferous demands of the China trade in England.[b] Meantime in early September he accepted in principle the program for new treaty ports which had been outlined by Alcock the preceding February, although he still put hope in gaining it from Peking. Alcock and Bonham, he wrote, had "clearly proved the uselessness of more seaports and that Her Majesty's Government should endeavor to exchange Ningpo and Foochowfoo for Soochowfoo, Hangchowfoo and Chinkiangfoo. But . . . any proposal to this effect should be made diplomatically, and should not be accompanied by a naval demonstration. [The latter would be improper when asking for a favour] which the Chinese government is at liberty to withhold without giving thereby to this country any just cause of war. . . . Address your application to . . . Pekin and not Canton, and you might offer to go up to Pekin to settle the matter with government there if they should wish any more detailed information. The grounds [of the proposal] would, I conceive, be that when the treaty was made it was supposed that Ningpo and Foochow would be places of considerable trade between . . . the two nations; that this expectation had been disappointed, and that therefore the intention with which the two governments concluded the treaty of Nankin has been defeated, that intention having been to increase the commercial intercourse between England and China. Her Majesty's Government therefore propose that the British Consuls at Ningpo and Foochow should be transferred to Soo-

[b] On July 5, for example, he had sent Bonham a memorial from the Manchester Chamber of Commerce and Manufactures suggesting that advantage be taken of the accession of a new emperor to improve commercial relations with China. "If . . . you should go to Pekin," wrote Palmerston, you should try to get freer access to the interior for British subjects.[34] Again on July 16 Palmerston forwarded a letter from the London East India and China Association supporting a suggestion made to them by the Canton Chamber of Commerce, that Tientsin be substituted for Ningpo as one of the five ports. If you concur, added Palmerston, try to make the exchange "when you go to Pekin." A month later, on August 16, he instructed Bonham "to represent to the Government at Pekin the great injury which is inflicted on the commercial intercourse between England and China by the . . . internal Customs Houses and other restrictions to the circulation of British manufactures in the interior of China," by which the numerous Chinese were deprived of the benefits of English trade. No doubt when this is "brought to the notice of the enlightened government of Pekin," the evil will be remedied.[35]

chow," etc.; and further that British subjects should have free access to the interior for trade or health, secured by a system of passes.[36]

Three weeks later came Bonham's final report on the failure of all diplomatic efforts to get satisfaction from Peking.[37] He reiterated his belief that the only recourse "would be to dispatch a small force to anchor off Chinkiangfoo" and blockade the Grand Canal.[38] Palmerston was thus left with a formulation of what was needed in the way of new ports in China, but without any formula of means other than coercion. Toward coercion his thoughts naturally turned. On September 29, 1850, in a memorandum concerning the cutting down of the consular establishment at Ningpo and Foochow, he added the following comment: "I clearly see that the Time is fast coming when we shall be obliged to strike another Blow in China, and that blow must be the occupation of a Position on the Yangtse Kiang to cut off communication by the Great Canal. But it would not be advisable to give the Chinese any intimation that such would be our measure. They should be left to reflect upon it when and after it was done. These half civilized Governments, such as those of China Portugal Spanish America require a Dressing every eight or Ten years to keep them in order. Their Minds are too shallow to receive an Impression that will last longer than some such Period, and warning is of little use. They care little for words and they must not only see the Stick but actually feel it on their Shoulders before they yield to that only argument which to them brings conviction, the *argumentum Baculinum*." [39]

During the winter and spring of 1851 the problem of enforcing the treaty tariff in China was thus linked in Palmerston's mind with the larger problem of using force to beat down the Chinese aversion to treaty relations and the spread of British trade. Nevertheless the Foreign Office made an honest effort to engineer from London some means of checking smuggling at Shanghai.

Mercantile proposals for customs reform. The question of consular interference for the prevention of smuggling in China first achieved public prominence in England through the *Lady Mary Wood* case of June 1850. Although it was not officially known to the Foreign Office until November, it had been foreseen as early as July by Mr. Hugh Hamilton Lindsay, the same merchant who in his youth had been under the Company at Canton and in 1832 as supercargo of the *Lord Amherst* had tested the trading possibilities of the China coast.[40] Now senior partner of Lindsay and Company, with a receiving ship at Shanghai, he was one of the most influential of the China merchants in England, and a good friend of Bonham and Palmerston. In July he expressed alarm at the increase of smuggling in the legal trade. Letters from his Shanghai partner described the flagrant smuggling of the P. and O. steamer, which forced competitors to follow suit.[41]

On September 11, a week after he had approved Alcock's program for new treaty ports but while he still sought to realize it through an appeal to Peking, Palmerston took a stand as to the smuggling problem and sought to settle it also through the same channel of negotiation.

"It cannot be doubted," he told Bonham, "that this system as described by Mr. Lindsay is extremely objectionable. It is an evasion of treaty engagements, a fraud upon and a loss to the Chinese Government, an injury to the honest trader, and a discredit to European commerce; it would be very desirable to put a stop to it. The most effectual course would be that you should address a representation to the government at Pekin, setting forth the facts which may have come to your knowledge, as proving that the Chinese local authorities are in the habit of conniving at the illicit practices of some dishonest foreign traders. . . . You might state that Her Majesty's Government are the more anxious that such abuses should be brought to the knowledge of the Government at Pekin, because the British Consuls in China are bound by treaty to see that the duties legally chargeable on British commerce are paid by British subjects, and they cannot fulfil that obligation if the local authorities of the Chinese Government, with a view to their own profit, encourage the foreign traders to evade the payment of the full amount due by those traders."[42]

The ground was thus prepared for the receipt on November 19, 1850, of Bonham's report on the *Lady Mary Wood.* As regards smuggling Bonham saw "no remedy for putting it down unless the Consul were to take upon himself the duties of an excise officer." But this would not prevent British subjects from smuggling "through the intervention of the Americans," using "American vessels for the shipment of their produce to England." Moreover the consular duties of the American merchant-consuls were "altogether subservient to their trading avocations." Hence they would not coöperate to suppress smuggling "in which . . . they themselves, as members of commercial firms, are more or less necessarily involved."[43]

The Foreign Office was now face to face with the problem, and during the next six months intermittently sought a solution. In these efforts they were helped most immediately by the China merchants in England. On November 21, for example, Lindsay asked Palmerston for an interview sometime before the 25th;[44] and on the 27th Palmerston answered Bonham's report on the *Lady Mary Wood* in a dispatch which foreshadowed the cessation of consular interference.[c]

[c] "Her Majesty's Government do not desire to depart from any obligations which they may have contracted in this matter by the treaties . . . but the obligation is reciprocal and if the Chinese Custom House officers by neglecting their duty, or betraying their trust, continue to render unavailing the measures taken by Her Majesty's consular officers to place trade upon an honest and legitimate footing, Her Majesty's Government will have to consider whether they will not be obliged to cease to take any part in regard to these matters, in so far as the agency of Her Majesty's consuls is concerned."[45]

In order to uphold the treaties as long as possible, however, the Foreign Office sought alternatives. On December 5 Lindsay suggested a remedy for smuggling: to send the consul monthly returns from the customhouses in London and Liverpool, showing exactly what each ship took to China. The consul would get them via Suez two months before the ships arrived via the Cape, and hence would know what the duties should be. From China to England, reverse the process.[46] Lindsay also noted the difficulty: "If stopped in British vessels, what is to prevent the same parties from availing themselves of other flags?" Here the Foreign Office marked in the margin "?" and "snare." Indeed there was no answer.

The Foreign Office could do better. On December 6 in a memorandum bristling with details from the trade regulations, Hammond noted that Lindsay's proposal had made no provision for the authenticity of the return to be sent from England and also would discover fraud in exports from China only when the smuggling vessel reached England. Instead Hammond suggested "a system more analogous to that established with reference to exports from Great Britain by the Acts 8 and 9 Vict., Cap. 86," whereby duplicate bills of entry should be given to the customs and a cocket received from them by the shipper; whereupon the consul could verify duty payment by inspecting the cocket and comparing one of the duplicate bills of entry received from the customs, with the bill of lading furnished by the shipper to the master of the vessel.[47]

Palmerston put little faith in cockets and duplicate bills of entry. But since the season of 1850 would be over before he could act in China, he forwarded both Lindsay's and Hammond's memoranda for Bonham to report upon.[48] The smuggling problem was left in hibernation for three months. During that time Palmerston kept it alive by directing Bonham in February 1851, since the Peiho effort had failed, to make representations to Commissioner Hsü concerning an exchange of ports, rights of residence, transit exactions, and duty evasion. The British were the more concerned over the last, which injured the honest merchant and the foreigner's reputation, "because the British Consuls in China are bound by treaty to see that the duties are regularly paid by British subjects." Hsü was to be asked to tell Peking of the corruption of the lesser Chinese officials.[49]

From its hibernation the problem was stirred in March 1851 by the unofficial report of the *John Dugdale* case of January 1851, which preceded by a full month the official dispatches on the subject. The Manchester Commercial Association sent Palmerston copies of the correspondence at Shanghai between consul and taotai. They condemned the dishonest traders as wilfully guilty, and waxed fearful of Chinese repressive measures. A week later came the suggestion of Thomas Ripley of Liverpool,[50] that weights of tea landed in England be reported to the Shanghai consul for comparison with his records.[d] The indefatigable Lindsay presented a memorial, evidently written by himself, dated March 31 and bearing the signatures of some thirty-eight firms in London, Liverpool, and Manchester. This formidable document, which might fairly claim to represent the China trade, threw the blame for the evasion of duties entirely on the Chinese. The competition among merchants at Shanghai, it asserted, prevented their profiting from the fifteen per cent saved by evading duties. Evasion was the taotai's fault, who hoped to farm the revenue for a small sum. To save the British trade from being transferred to ships of other nations, the consuls should "be authorized to declare the Chinese tariff suspended." The merchants asked Palmerston to give them an equal footing before the next season's business commenced.[52]

This proposal to suspend the Chinese tariff evidently spurred Palmerston. On April 6 he asked, "What is the treaty stipulation which mixes up our Consuls in China with the collection of Chinese Duties? and might we not declare off from that employment of them, and why was such an engagement contracted? If we were to enforce payment of Duties for goods exported in British ships w'd not the Americans get all the cargoes?" [53] In reply to this, Hammond explained the origin of consular interference — to prevent friction with the Chinese and compensate for the abolition of the Cohong — and confessed that the Americans might indeed "get all the cargoes."

This re-examination of the British obligation to enforce the treaty tariff would indicate that the foreign secretary now saw the necessity of cutting the Gordian knot, rather than picking at it further with cockets and duplicate bills. Nevertheless the Foreign Office continued for another two months to seek some alternative to the abolition of consular interference. Further memorials from Manchester and London recited the plight of honest merchants. The Foreign Office asked the Treasury for loading weights and full details of all tea and silk imported from Shanghai, thus following both Ripley's and Hammond's suggestions. A committee representing the thirty-eight signers of the recent memorial, by request, suggested specific ways of stopping smuggling: to check through the English customs; to enter all shipping details in an open book at the Chinese customhouse and have the British consul oversee the trade unofficially; to appeal directly to Peking; or to stop interfering. They agreed chiefly on the necessity of acting by the mail of April 24, 1851, since shipping began in July.[54]

On April 15 Bonham's report on the *John Dugdale* case at length arrived

[d] Alcock had already asked that copies of inward manifests received at London for goods coming from China be sent him as a help in estimating the real volume of exports from China, and this had been done.[51] Nevertheless Hammond commented that Ripley's proposal would be too roundabout, and offered a similar scheme of his own invention, which would depend for its efficiency on Chinese coöperation. "Might it not be advisable," he asked, "to have a statement exposed in the Consulate at Shanghai, in order to shame the parties into honesty?"

(written February 25, but too late to catch that month's mail). It enclosed Alcock's report of January 14, which added to the number of remedies proposed: since the Chinese customhouse had become a legal fiction, Alcock saw but two alternatives — to change the Chinese system of levying duties, or to stop interfering to prevent their evasion. To change the system, he said, induce the Chinese authorities to "collect their maritime export dues from the [Chinese] producer, at the shipping port, instead of from the foreign purchaser. The authorities here [at Shanghai] are very willing to do so. The Foreign merchants of all nations will then be on the same footing. . . . As regards imports, farm the duties for at least *one third* more than they have yet been made to yield the Imperial Revenue and thus give the Taotai a direct and personal interest in the collection of the whole. . . . Between this and a refusal to hold British subjects in any way responsible, I believe there is in effect no alternative consistent with the prosperity of our trade." [55] This would let the Chinese merchants and the Chinese customs officers bargain directly — as at Canton both before and after the war.

Last of all came the suggestions of the Liverpool East India and China Association: declare the treaty ports free by order in council until the Chinese give satisfaction; or allow no import of tea into England by anyone unless with the China consul's certificate of duties paid.[56] This completed the proposals submitted to solve the smuggling problem in China. None of them inspired Palmerston to adopt it as his own; but he forwarded the China merchants' memorial to Bonham, with authorization to have the consuls stop interfering in customs affairs, if this should become necessary to meet crises that might arise in China. As to the one constructive solution proposed from China, by Alcock, Palmerston opposed the levy of export duties on the Chinese seller instead of the British buyer, "because the Chinese might more easily raise the duties . . . and so increase the price to the English consumer." [57] Further than this the mail of April 24 carried no instructions.[e]

The decision to stop consular interference. The last mail that could pre-

[e] In the flurry of advice in which he found himself, the foreign secretary clutched at every straw that was offered. He asked the Queen's advocate about authorizing British consuls to suspend the Chinese tariff. He asked the Board of Trade about an order in council to stop all imports of tea into England not certified by the consul in China to have paid duty. This latter agency, represented by the president and secretaries rather than by its statutory composition which embraced most of the cabinet, still functioned in 1851 as an advisory body on commercial and revenue affairs to the other departments of government. Its president, Henry Labouchere, was now in his second term, and G. R. Porter, an able statistician at the end of a long career, had been joint secretary for the past decade. On behalf of the Board of Trade he replied that the new navigation laws allowed "importation under the flags of all nations and from every place." Hence it was "impossible to provide for the payment in China of the export duty upon produce coming to us thence indirectly through foreign ports" (e.g., reshipped from America). The profit gained from evading duties would pay for such indirect importation and so make any possible law unavailing. In any case, he asked, if China does not collect revenue, why should British consuls? [58]

cede the full tide of the season was to depart for China on May 24. When the Treasury complained that the customs data asked for on 250,000 packages of goods would be difficult to get from books in daily use,[59] Palmerston noted on May 20, "It might still be useful to have these returns up to the time when the Consuls shall cease to interfere." In making up his mind he had had before him the advice of the four associations of China merchants and of thirty-eight of their members jointly, as well as opinions from the Treasury and Board of Trade and the views of Bonham and Alcock.

On May 24, 1851, when no further word had come from China, Palmerston accordingly abandoned the treaty provision for consular interference. He referred to the complaints of merchants in England, the clear proof of Chinese laxity, the danger that smuggling would transfer the trade to American ships. Abondonment of the British treaty provision for consular interference had always been possible, under the most-favored-nation clause. "If the British Government has not hitherto put forward this claim, it has been from an unwillingness to break through a system calculated to obviate angry and inconvenient discussions." He therefore stood on "the twofold ground" of most-favored-nation treatment and of "the omission of the Chinese Government itself to act up to the manifest intention of the treaties." British Consuls could not do the proper work of Chinese officials. The British did not claim special privileges, but would demand equal treatment whether or not the Chinese authorities connived at duty evasion. Since Bonham's report suggesting necessary changes in the regulations had not yet reached London, he should use his own discretion in carrying out this decision in China.[60] In this way Palmerston solved the problem for the time being. His decision was not made public and became known to the merchants in England only after one of their number wrote to the Foreign Office and published its reply.[61] The decision did not reach China until the second week in July.

Meantime in China Sir George Bonham (knighted Nov. 22, 1850) had canvassed the treaty ports for a solution, but to no avail.[f] From Shanghai,

[f] He had received Lindsay's and Hammond's proposals for reform (of December 1850) in February 1851 and had sent them to Canton, Shanghai, and Amoy for comment.[62] Consul Bowring, somewhat unkindly, sent the schemes concocted in England to seven picked Canton merchants, leaving their source anonymous. Five of these merchants replied, stating plainly that the proposals sent from England must be "from someone profoundly ignorant . . . of the way business is now carried on in China." Their adoption would necessitate a "complete staff of [British] customs officers." In practice they would be "monstrous," a "national interference," and "wholly inefficient." More specifically, Lindsay's proposal that cargoes be checked on arrival in England or China by data sent ahead via Suez, was impracticable because ships in the China trade usually loaded and unloaded by degrees, getting a part of their cargoes perhaps at Shanghai and the rest at Whampoa or Hongkong, and vice versa. Moreover, it was useless, because Hongkong was a free port and any number of transfers could be made there or at Macao or Singapore, before the cargo reached Europe. Hammond's scheme for duplicate bills of entry, according to the system in England, would involve Chinese coöperation and so begged the question at issue. Bills of lading would be no help, in any case, because they usually specified merely a number of packages, "weight and contents unknown"; nor could they be compared with manifests, which carried different

Alcock replied that the one remedy in the hands of the British — to have receipts, authenticated by the consul in China, legally required at the customs in England — was prevented by the existing navigation laws. The one thing necessary to make the present system a success — having the Chinese customs verify by examination the correctness of the merchant's declaration, made by him when applying for leave to ship — was likewise unattainable. "As the first cause of the mischief was the *inefficiency of the Chinese Custom House*, so to the end this will prove an *insuperable bar*" to any prevention of irregularities.

> The error has been in taking for a basis the pre-supposed existence of habits and qualities wholly foreign to this eastern race . . . it is too much to expect a self-denying vigilance and zeal for the public interest, upon which, as a natural consequence, they must starve, after becoming an object of derision to their own people . . . The fault is with us, we have assigned to them a work which is simply impracticable, and the sooner it is amended the better.

Alcock could only reiterate his former alternatives: take care of the import duties by farming them to the taotai, and of the export duties by collecting them from the Chinese seller, instead of the British shipper; or stop interfering. He favored collecting export duties from the Chinese seller because in the larger part of the legal trade — tea and silk exporting — the foreigner would then have no contact, nor chance of collusion, with the Chinese customs.[64]

This retrogressive step in the direction of the old Canton system was advocated by the Shanghai taotai,[g] who proposed to inaugurate a new system on February 1, 1851, and appears to have done so then or a little later, after an interview with the British consul. Alcock reported in March that all Chinese goods entering Shanghai for export were registered as the property of a given individual, who was held responsible for the ultimate payment of export duty. Thus the Chinese seller could be asked to pay the duties, and from him the British exporter could obtain a duty receipt to present in lieu of duties when he shipped his goods. "The authorities here would readily adopt this system," wrote Alcock. If extortion resulted,

---

details. Finally there was no one in the Chinese Customs who could read an English document. If the Chinese Customs had any records, the consul could not get at them. Either proposal would merely handicap British trade and force it into foreign bottoms.[63]

[g] In a communication to the foreign consuls of December 15, 1850, Wu Chien-chang had already proposed a Chinese system for the prevention of smuggling in the export trade: on arrival at the military stations north and south of Shanghai, Chinese merchants bringing teas and silks would receive one copy of a manifest of their goods which had been made out in triplicate. The second copy would subsequently be given by the Chinese merchants to the tea and silk warehousemen who stored the goods pending export. The third copy would be retained by the maritime customs. Export duty on goods to be shipped could be paid at any time before shipment and a receipt obtained (on the manifest) from the government banker by either the Chinese warehousemen themselves or the foreign buyers using the warehousemen's copy of the manifest. By comparing that copy with their own the customs could then check the fact of payment.[65]

Her Majesty's Government could always revert to the former scheme, "refusing to hold British Subjects liable for any duties not ascertained to be due by examination on the part of the Custom House." But just as the consul was pursuing negotiations to introduce this system, with the concurrence of his American colleague, instructions from Palmerston forbade the arrangement as likely to give too much control to the Chinese authorities, and these negotiations at Shanghai fell to the ground leaving the same chaos as before.[66]

From Amoy Consul Sullivan reported that Lindsay's suggestions were useless since there was no direct trade with England. All the other foreign consuls (except M. de Montigny, French consul at Shanghai) were merchants, holding office mainly for commercial advantage. If asked to cooperate against smuggling, they might have to be given salaries and their home governments moved to that end. As for Hammond's duplicate bills, the Amoy consul in February 1849 had discontinued a similar system because it was so completely circumvented by collusion between the merchant's shroffs and the customs. Finally, any active interference in behalf of the Chinese revenue would certainly justify the Chinese authorities in thinking it "equally our duty to interfere and proffer them the same assistance for the suppression of the opium trade. . . . The Chinese continue to view all our proceedings with great jealousy." British concern over smuggling in the legal trade would merely suggest to them "that we have ulterior and sinister objects in view."[67]

In summarizing the problem on April 10, 1851, Bonham had outlined the two solutions suggested in China: to call on the Chinese to abolish all duties at the ports and levy them as transit duties somewhere inland; or to withhold all consular interference except when the Chinese asked for the punishment of a British subject for a charge clearly established. The first plan, if the Chinese would accept it, would be open to extortion, beyond the surveillance of the consuls, and binding only on the British traders. Hence Bonham opposed Alcock's suggestion of duties levied on the Chinese seller; and doubted also if the Chinese could be induced to farm the duties. Any such changes would involve disclosures unpalatable to the local Chinese authorities. The only expedient was to let the Chinese do their own revenue collecting. Finally, he forwarded the report of the *Canton* case, which epitomized the problem, and in fact had already forced the British officials in China toward the same solution that Palmerston was about to adopt in England.

On or about February 20, 1851, five cases of coral had been landed from the steamer *Canton* of the Hongkong and Canton Steam Packet Company, although that vessel had not first reported to the British consulate at Canton. Since a new Hoppo had arrived, Consul Bowring took the opportunity, as in the *Mayflower* case in 1849, to invite the Hoppo to a personal conference to discuss Anglo-Chinese coöperation against smuggling. The new Hoppo, however, like his predecessor, replied that "the duty of taking measures for a surveillance [against smuggling] is incumbent on each party separately."[68]

Undeterred by the Hoppo's lack of interest, Bowring proceeded to hold a consular court on March 1, which fined Captain Soames of the *Canton* $200 for his inadvertence, probably unintentional, in landing cargo without having first reported to the consul. This fine was legally due to the Chinese government. But on March 17, the Hoppo refused to accept it on the ground that, the duty having now been paid, it was customary to remit fines "if the amount of duties evaded has been inconsiderable." Thereupon the consul appealed to his superior and Bonham himself forthwith offered the fine money to the Hoppo's superior, Commissioner Hsü, who refused it in his turn. At this point the Canton manager of the packet company, W. H. Davidson, who was also Canton partner in Lindsay and Company, applied to have the fine refunded; and Bonham, believing Captain Soames to have been negligent but guiltless, favored complying.[69] Lest he seem indifferent to smuggling, however, he referred the matter to Palmerston.[h]

The exact nature of the British treaty obligation to interfere against the evasion of duties was here, as always, ill defined. Hsü Kuang-chin chose to ignore it and blandly reiterated the stand taken by the Hoppo. "Each ought in future to manage cases of smuggling according to the Treaty, and both parties adopt measures of their own to institute investigation. This will be sufficient to put a stop to this illegal practice, and not require many words for discussion." It was plain that he extended his policy of non-intercourse to the customs problem quite as completely as to every other aspect of Chinese foreign affairs. Two weeks later when Bonham obeyed Palmerston's instructions of February 1851 and made representations concerning an exchange of ports, and other British grievances including Chinese connivance at the evasion of duties, Hsü replied by ignoring entirely the customs question and asking, "Within ten years do you wish to change a treaty made for ten thousand years? Where remains then, what is called the preservation of good faith?" To Bonham's next request,

[h] Bowring, in his report on smuggling, inveighed against the consuls' "onerous and obnoxious duties as *custodes* of the revenues of China" and, citing the *Canton* case, bewailed the "thorough rottenness" of the Chinese customhouse, by which, "all my authority, all my control over British subjects and British shipping is absolutely annihilated." Even Bonham himself was irritated by Commissioner Hsü's complete indifference; on April 5 he wrote to him, on his own responsibility, "we have done all in our power towards the fulfilment of the treaty . . . and if hereafter the Hoppo should complain of any grave case of evasion of the Imperial Duties by a British Subject, I shall not consider myself bound to interfere in the matter, but shall simply direct the Consul to refer the Hoppo to the 12th article of the Supplementary treaty," which would be ample if enforced.[70] Bonham made this threat as a personal declaration, awaiting Palmerston's authorization to readdress it in the name of Her Majesty's Government.

that his representation be transmitted to the throne, the imperial commissioner retorted, "Such ordinary topics do not accord with the high dignity of the Celestial Empire." [71]

For a time, early in 1851, the exigencies of the smuggling problem at Shanghai had moved both the British merchants and the Chinese authorities in the direction of coöperation. The Shanghai British Chamber of Commerce at length even offered its coöperation against the evasion of duties. Ships of foreign flags were already being chartered for the coming season. Only five firms were reported to be paying full duties, and one firm, which was said to have evaded the payment of $80,000 in the previous season, had chartered one Dutch and three large American ships. The French and American consuls were both away temporarily, and the conscientious British consignee was terrified between the threat of interference by the British consul to maintain full payments of duties and the underbidding of American competitors who could promise shippers the opportunity to evade duties as thoroughly as anyone else.[72]

The Shanghai taotai, after much consultation with the British consul, also proposed to tighten his surveillance over the import trade by requiring foreign importers to hand more detailed manifests to their consuls for transmission to the customs. Since a system of triplicate manifests had already been adopted for all export goods, this would give the customs an equivalent check upon import cargoes. To this proposal the British consul had agreed, but the American consul felt unable fully to comply for fear of his countrymen "alleging that in my capacity of Consul I required information not necessary to the prevention of smuggling but which I availed of to my advantage as a merchant." This inability of the American consul was thereupon reported by the taotai to Commissioner Hsü at Canton, who took it up under date of May 16 with the American chargé, Dr. Peter Parker, and asked that American merchants might give manifests as detailed as the British. Although Consul Griswold had also gone to Canton on April 9, because of illness he had had no pertinent discussions with his superior. Only after an exchange of letters with Shanghai could Parker reply to Hsü, on August 28, to the effect that the provisions of the treaties were really adequate if enforced and that, as Griswold had suggested, the chief need was a competent staff of customs employees. To this Hsü replied with similar platitudes [73] and the matter was dropped. It is evident from the American records that in this case a constructive proposal emanating from the Chinese authorities had been turned down by the Americans.

The treaty port community — merchants, consuls, and merchant-consuls — by July 1851 had reached a choice of two alternatives: either somehow to secure "an efficient custom house staff to take account of goods as landed and shipped," or else to allow the Chinese authorities to collect the duties from the native merchants "as at Canton, where nine-tenths if not all the duties on Exports are collected from the Chinese." [74] The former alternative could have succeeded only on the basis of a coöperation between officials and merchants of all three nationalities which it was not possible to attain. The second alternative was marked out, as the line of least resistance, by the announcement in July of Palmerston's decision to put upon the Chinese the full onus of preventing smuggling. Bonham's announcement of this decision to Hsü under date of July 10, 1851, produced, however, no appreciable effect. At his most imperturbable, the imperial commissioner replied that no news of irregularities had come to his ears. Surely, he argued, if there is much smuggling, the duties must decrease.

> How does it then happen that the returns of late years exceed those of former times considerably? This is to me inexplicable. I shall address a letter on that subject and institute enquiries. [I cannot understand your saying that] British merchants are treated differently from all other foreign merchants. This is to me thoroughly incomprehensible. Whilst sending this reply I wish you much happiness.[75]

Meanwhile Bonham had gone up to Canton to ascertain what changes should be made in the port regulations governing British ships in order to put them on a par with the Americans. After close scrutiny of American practice, he directed Consul Bowring to tell the Hoppo that the British consulate would no longer attend to landing and shipping-off chops, but would let British merchants deal directly with the Chinese customhouse. The consul's only functions would be to report ships to the Hoppo on arrival — but send no manifest with the report — and to return the ship's papers to the merchant when he produced the Hoppo's grand chop necessary for departure.[76] Actually this changed the Canton system very little, because the British merchant was still represented in all matters by his Chinese compradore and linguist, who would continue the old practices. At Shanghai the regulations had already been revised in 1850, in order to put the British merchant in direct contact with the Chinese customhouse when exporting his tea and silk. It only remained for Alcock to notify the taotai in August 1851 that the same rule would now be applied to imports, the less important part of the trade.[i]

At Foochow and Amoy this decision which seemed so momentous to the British gained in December a tardy response which quoted the imperial commissioner as saying that he had received no communication from

[i] In brief, the consul would be concerned only when the ship reported on arrival, when the consignees produced the grand chop to get back the ship's papers on departing, and in case of dispute. Manifests of export cargo would still be filed at the consulate, but for its use only, while manifests of import cargo would be sent to the customhouse as long as merchants of other nations did the same. The British position was based on the demand for equal treatment. The taotai acquiesced and on August 16 published a list of port regulations revised accordingly.[77]

"chief Bonham" concerning smuggling.[78] This "most explicit contradiction" and denial of Bonham's correspondence with Hsü struck the British as a barefaced lie. Since the document referred to Bonham as a "chieftain" (*ch'iu*), it was returned for correction, and sent back a second time when the offensive character was only omitted and not replaced. The Tartar-general finally kept the document.[79]

Implications of Palmerston's decision. In the light of events in China the decision to stop consular interference was neither far-reaching nor constructive. In the customs procedure at Canton it modified the rules without altering the practice, since the linguist system still could cloak irregularities; while at Shanghai it found the rules already modified as regards exports, which were the vital and larger part of the trade. In denying any consular responsibility to see the duties paid, the decision was a step backward. It sacrificed the long-term principle of the British treaty system, that duties should be equal upon all according to tariff, for a temporary expedient, that duties should be equal upon all, however levied. But the consul's actual responsibility to safeguard the interests of British trade was as great as ever. All that Palmerston's decision meant for the future was that it would be, if anything, more difficult to safeguard those interests, for variations in the amounts of squeeze demanded from various shippers by individual Chinese authorities would be harder to prevent than variations from the tariff prescribed by treaty. This trouble was soon to appear as another symptom of a disease not yet cured.

Since the customs problem was but one thread in a tangled skein, Palmerston's temporary solution must be judged in the whole context of Anglo-Chinese and Anglo-American relations at the time. Coöperation between the British and American consuls was a possibility left unexplored. Anglo-American relations were, no doubt, none too friendly in 1851; the Foreign Office sought American coöperation neither through the consuls in China nor through overtures to Washington, and its exploration of alternatives was therefore incomplete. Bonham's report of his steps to stop consular interference and Hsü's indifference thereto, arrived on September 18; on September 30, Palmerston wrote the following note:

> Let me have a memo. stating our various grievances against the Chinese Government and its officers; and of the endeavours we have made by Remonstrances & Representations to obtain Redress, and let me know which is the Season of the year at which an interruption of the supplies to Peking by stopping the passage of vessels across the Yang-tsze-Kiang on their way up the Canal to Peking, would be the most effectual.[j]

[j] To this Hammond (?) replied: "With the exception of the question of the right of entry into Canton, the only grievance which can now be urged against the Chinese is the attempt to interfere with the freedom of the tea trade at Canton. . . . The Admiralty might be asked at what season an expedition should be sent up the Coast; but there is the danger in making these enquiries that a rumour

These thoughts of war merely continued the foreign secretary's train of thought begun almost a year before, as noted in November 1850. Since that time a final effort to get satisfaction through the imperial commissioner at Canton, set on foot in February 1851, had failed in April, and had been given up by Palmerston in July. In spite of the dearth of obvious grievances other than the city question and a tea tax at Canton, the British position in China had grown no better. Indeed it was weaker diplomatically in October 1851 than it had been for a decade, while the increase of British trade continued to make the treaty settlement more inadequate. Palmerston foresaw the necessity of armed coercion in the near future. His decision to stop consular interference was therefore part of a larger program.

This larger program, however, was to be long delayed. Palmerston went out of office in December 1851. His successor had no thought of war in China. In addition, the rise of the Taiping Rebellion soon created a situation in which any pressure on the imperial government in order to gain facilities for British trade would menace the peace and order on which the trade was dependent. This was pointed out by Bonham in a private letter of December 29, which forms a trenchant commentary on Palmerston's policy in 1851 in general:

"You ask me the grounds of complaint against the Chinese Government. The first is not permitting us to enter Canton. The second not receiving Lord Palmerston's letter to the address of the Ministers in a proper manner, and not making any direct reply. The third is the imposition of two mace on every picul of tea.

"On the first question, you are quite as well able to judge of the advantages as I am. On the second, I verily believe that as no minister is authorized to receive foreign communications except the Commissioner at Canton, no public officer would dare to do so, notwithstanding article XI of the Treaty. . . . Touching the tea question Seu [Hsü] has a difficult game to play. The smuggling carried on by foreigners is *truly detestable,* and I do not see that the measure complained of differs very materially from our own system of allowing tea to be landed at certain ports in England with the same object. It may be contrary to treaty I admit, but I do not see how Seu, if he be honest, can prevent the evil except by the plan he has adopted. The imposition is moreover a mere trifle: but I should be sorry to see any coercive measures resorted to at this juncture, inasmuch as such a measure *might* throw the whole of the *Two Kwangs* into a confusion, from which it might be very difficult to extract them; and it is clear that such a state of things could not be conducive to our interests."[81]

---

might get abroad of an intended attack on China, and the trade be thereby thrown into confusion." To this Palmerston replied on October 20, 1851, "Write confidentially to Sir G. Bonham to ask the latter question"; this was done next day.[80]

CHAPTER XXI

WU CHIEN-CHANG AND THE "CANTONIZATION" OF SHANGHAI 1852–53

THE CRISIS which developed at Shanghai after 1851, in the midst of civil war and local rebellion, brought into prominence a number of the new elements which we have described in earlier chapters — Cantonese adventurers who battened upon the coast trade in opium and foreign goods, including arms; a venal merchant-official, also from Canton, who as Shanghai taotai became the local "barbarian expert"; foreign merchant-consuls who used official status for private gain; and foreign officials who were reluctant either to acquiesce in the practices of the Chinese government or to take its place. Indeed, until Shanghai was actually threatened with destruction, Western policy remained relatively quiescent.

At the beginning of 1852, the center of activity in British policy-making was shifted from England to China. One of Palmerston's last acts as he left the Foreign Office had been to appoint his friend Dr. Bowring on December 23, 1851, to take Bonham's place as superintendent of trade during the latter's forthcoming leave (March 1852 to February 1853).[1] When Lord Granville, who had succeeded Palmerston, was in turn succeeded in February 1852 by Lord Malmesbury as foreign secretary in the Derby ministry, the reversal of the situation was complete: in China Bowring was by temperament an energetic diplomat where Bonham had been a cautious administrator, while in London neither Granville nor Malmesbury was sufficiently experienced in Chinese affairs or inclined by contemporary circumstances to follow Palmerston's bold course. In his eight weeks term of office, Granville had time only to forbid any measure in China likely to require the support of force, and Malmesbury in his turn sought only to improve upon these instructions. During 1852, indeed, Malmesbury was immediately occupied by the problem presented by Louis Napoleon and the necessity to "keep well with France." Neither his dispatches during his ten months in office, nor his published memoirs reveal any concern for, or in fact any knowledge of, affairs in China, least of all regarding a customs problem presumably settled eight months before by Palmerston.[2]

Dr. Bowring, on the other hand, found himself temporarily promoted over the heads of Alcock and other consuls of longer service, as he had expected, but without the continued vigorous support of Palmerston to make that promotion effective. During his term as consul at Canton since 1849 he had continued the custom, already begun by Alcock and shortly to be continued by Parkes, of bombarding the foreign office with scholarly and trenchant monographs on things Chinese. He had written privately to Palmerston bewailing the diplomatic humiliation of his position in Canton, snubbed by the Chinese and subordinated to Hongkong, and advocating prompt and active resistance to every Chinese encroachment on the rights given in the treaties.[3] Now he took up his residence at Government House as acting superintendent, "confining himself . . . strictly to his diplomatic and consular duties, while Major-General Jervois administered the Government of the Colony."[4] But this opportunity for unhampered diplomatic flights over the Chinese mainland merely increased his irritation when he found his wings clipped by the instructions of the Foreign Office, and himself ordered to stay at Hongkong and refrain from provocative discussions. During 1852, the quiescent policy of the Foreign Office was perforce maintained at Hongkong, and applied to the customs problem as to all others. Since the State Department in Washington continued as usual to ignore affairs in China, this left the British and American consuls at Shanghai free to take whatever measures they desired, so long as they would not require support from home.

The American consul at Shanghai, John N. Alsop Griswold of New York, had been at first an agent of the American firm of N. L. and G. Griswold. He had become a partner in Russell and Company on the first of January 1848, and got his commission as United States consul for Shanghai almost a year later.[5] This second event followed the first almost automatically, for the American consul's job as well as his prestige at both Canton and Shanghai derived partly from his position in the leading American firm in China. Since he corresponded directly with the secretary of state and did not depend on his consulship for a living, a merchant-consul of Russell and Company could not feel himself a subordinate, but was rather a minor colleague, of the American commissioner (or minister) to China. The latter seldom received instructions of any sort from Washington and was himself either a political appointee or a resident missionary, so that there was every opportunity for the Shanghai consul to make his own policy.

All this left the initiative more than ever to the men on the spot at Shanghai, where that fabulous character, the Cantonese taotai, Wu Chien-chang, now became a major figure. The fact that he took an interest in private commercial ventures of his own and entered into some sort of murky partnership with an American merchant-consul was typical of the period.

The emergence of "Samqua". The first taotai in charge of foreign trade at Shanghai, Kung Mu-chiu, by the latter part of 1847 had been promoted to a post as provincial judge. His "rectitude of purpose and sterling business habits" were much admired and his departure regretted by the foreign community.[6] His successor, Hsien-ling, who held the substantive office in 1848,[7] had at first been assisted by Wu Chien-chang, who appeared at Shanghai as early as March 1848 in the role of an expectant taotai sent to help smooth over the Tsingpu affair.[8] The common statement has been that this man was a former Canton hong merchant, Samqua, who had purchased his official position, and the foreign community generally gave him that name. It seems probable that he had in fact been connected with the establishment of Samqua at Canton before 1842, although it is not certain that he was the principal in it.[a] Once on the scene at Shanghai he impressed his superiors by his command of barbarian speech, which supposedly enabled him to penetrate the wiles of foreign interpreters.[13] Actually his English was none too good — "Il avait acquis ça et là un certain bagage de broken english, supérieur cependant au pidgin english que parlent les compradores et les domestiques," [14] but even so he could probably say more to the foreigners in English than he could to his own superiors in the Peking dialect. His unparalleled intimacy with foreign merchants enabled him to supply his superiors with valued insight into barbarian intentions, and the governor and governor-general were soon quoting him extensively to Peking.

Wu was the first exemplar of the treaty port type of Chinese merchant-official, who made his parasitic way upward by manipulating China's foreign relations and foreign trade. In August 1851 he became acting taotai and came to Shanghai in sole charge. The foreign community were inclined to regard his self-important comings and goings with derision (and his intentions with no little suspicion). But Samqua was undoubtedly a shrewd man gifted with persistence and relatively sophisticated in barbarian ways.[b] He was also the first Chinese official to perceive and vigor-

[a] The East India Co. records reveal that the original Samqua, who was licensed as a hong merchant in 1832, was a brother of the compradore of Magniac and Co. (which also in 1832 became Jardine, Matheson and Co.).[9] As noted in Chapter 14 above, table 7, the hong headed by Samqua (Wu Shuang-kuan) was called T'ung-shun and listed officially under Wu T'ien-yuan (a different Chinese surname from that of Howqua, Wu Ch'ung-yueh). This Wu T'ien-yuan had an elder brother named Wu T'ien-hsien who had the rank of expectant taotai, by purchase, in 1842 and who was then nominated to accompany Howqua to Kiangsu to deal with the British — a project which fell through.[10] In 1842 there was also at Canton a minor official named Wu Chien-tung,[11] who from his name might be assumed to be Wu Chien-chang's brother. The *Shanghai Gazetteer* (1871) lists Wu Chien-chang as acting taotai in 1843, but he does not appear in the documents till five years later.

In 1847 the wife of the American missionary and sinologue E. C. Bridgman was invited among others at Canton "to visit the establishments of two Chinese merchants, Samqua and Tonshing . . . These gentlemen were partners in business, and they had assembled in all about twenty children belonging to the two families" to celebrate the birthday of Tonshing's mother. By the middle of 1852 the same writer states that "Mr. Tonshing and Mr. Samqua, being rich men have both since become officers of government or 'mandarins', a rank somewhat above the Mayor of a city." Toyama Gunji is inclined to identify Wu Chien-chang with the original hong merchant.[12]

[b] In 1852 he refused to see the French minister except on terms of equality, claiming that as

ously pursue the fiscal potentialities of the Shanghai customs. He came upon the scene at the opportune moment when customs reform by Palmerston had proved impossible, when the foreign community asked only equality of opportunity in smuggling, and the Chinese government, ignorant of the Eldorado at its door, would particularly welcome all official contributions for the suppression of the Rebellion in Kwangsi. Samqua, who remembered the Cohong, saw this silver-lined opportunity more clearly than his superiors who had mastered the classics.

The new British policy of non-interference in smuggling [16] played into Wu Taotai's hands. His new port regulations eliminated the foreign consul from all but the beginning and end of customs procedure.[c] There was now no obstacle to collusion between the Chinese authorities and all merchants willing to evade the full payment of duties. Moreover, it soon became the general practice for consignees of ships to report verbally to the customs through their compradores and thereupon break bulk without waiting for a written permit, thus saving a day; while the rule that consignees of shipments in the vessel should apply for a written permit before discharging cargo fell into complete desuetude.

For the first few weeks of this "non-interference system," all went well. The consuls stood ready to assist the customs if called upon, having already warned their respective communities that Chinese measures to protect the imperial revenue, if they were just, necessary and impartially applied, would receive every support.[18] On the initiative of twenty-three merchants an American citizen, Nicholas Baylies, was made harbor-master and began to apply a set of regulations assented to by the taotai and all but the French consul, on September 24, 1851. After the non-coöperation of some captains threatened to destroy his effectiveness, it was arranged by Sir G. Bonham and Wu Taotai that the harbor-master's fees should

taotai he was a "high provincial official" within the meaning of the French treaty and that as superintendent of customs he was of equal rank with the Canton Hoppo. After the minister, who claimed he had a cold, had sent a general to call, Wu consented to return the favor and reportedly gave the Frenchman a lecture into the bargain.[15]

[c] The new routine was very simple. Consignees of a ship would report and deposit the ship's papers at the consulate and then apply to the customhouse for a written permit to break bulk, whereupon each consignee of particular shipments in the vessel applied to the customs also for a written permit to discharge cargo, giving details. On exporting, the same procedure was followed, the consignees of the ship obtaining the customs' permission to load, each shipper then getting a permit to load his part of the cargo, giving details, whereupon a detailed report of the ship's cargo was made to the customs after loading. In paying duties, exporters of tea and silk had to produce the station-house dockets of registry, procured free from the Chinese seller, whose goods had been registered on the way into Shanghai. Accounts were then made up at the customhouse, dues were paid by the merchant through his compradore to the Chinese shroff (banker) designated by the authorities, and receipts for such payment were delivered to the customhouse directly by the merchant or his compradore. Thereupon the customs made out a triplicate grand chop or port clearance, retaining one part, giving one part to the consignees of the ship, and one part to the consul. Finally, the consignees of the ship received its papers back from the consul on showing him the grand chop. Aside from his formal duties in receiving and giving up these papers, the consul was active in this revised procedure only when requested to punish irregularities or settle disputes. Reports of cargo made to him for his own records could ordinarily be checked only by reference to the grand chop.[17]

be paid to the Chinese government banker and the receipts sent to the customs prior to the granting of port clearances, so that the harbor-master could collect them periodically from the banker without troubling the captains. This coöperative arrangement, like the cordial harmony of the British and American consuls, expressed a new spirit. When Bonham came north in September he reported that "the Superintendent of Customs at Shanghai is at present exerting more than usual vigilance . . . and smuggling has in consequence diminished."[19] Partly as a result of this, customs receipts at Shanghai in 1851, even as recorded by the foreign consuls, were almost twice the receipts of 1850, from nearly the same total number of vessels.[20]

As a Cantonese and a former merchant, it was perhaps inevitable that Samqua should try to have the trade conducted in such a way that the foreign merchants and consuls would have less cognizance of its petty ramifications, while the customs collector could more easily levy indirect taxes upon it. As the American consul observed, "the present acting Taoutae has surrounded himself with numerous Canton underlings, in the Custom House and at his own office, who have commenced with a system of intimidation and would no doubt end by a system of forcing bribes from the servants and traders connected with us if not met and checked at the outset. In numerous ways it has been shown of late that the acting Taoutae is endeavouring to introduce many of the objectionable features of the old Canton system."[21] In view of the role already played by Cantonese in the expansion of foreign trade and the diplomatic style already set by Hsü and Yeh, it is not surprising that Wu, as an experienced barbarian-tamer, should have taken a few leaves from the books of the Hoppo and the imperial commissioner. The relative paucity of Chinese documents surviving from this period supports the conclusion that barbarian affairs at Shanghai for a time almost disappeared from the view of Peking, as they had from that of London. So long as Samqua could remit large and as yet unexpected sums from the customs,[22] there was less reason for his superiors to interfere.

Constant altercations nevertheless beset the Shanghai consuls and the taotai during the year 1851–52, although recorded only on the foreign side. One source of friction was the ignorance of poorly-trained customs employees and indifferent Chinese servants, who had to deal with documents insufficiently detailed and often carelessly made out. In July 1851 cargo landed for Lindsay and Company from the American clipper *Oriental* disagreed with the manifest. It was found that 30 large bales that had originally consisted of 120 smaller bales had paid duty at Canton as 30 bales, "but their clerk in the manifest made the figure 3 look like 8, and they were by mistake entered as 80 bales," while the 120 small bales were actually landed under the Canton duty receipt.[23] A fortnight later the taotai charged the American ship *Roman* with smuggling. The consul forthwith obtained from the customhouse "their book in which the goods were entered as landed day by day" and on comparison with the manifest found that sheetings had been mistaken for drills, and long ells and white shirtings for woolens and camlets, "solely from the ignorance of the Customs officers, who do not take the trouble properly to examine the goods as landed." [d]

Stoppage of duties as a diplomatic weapon. The consuls now increasingly began to use the withholding of duties as a means of coercion. This harked back to the eighteenth century practice of the East India Company at Canton, where the "stoppage of trade" had commonly been used by either side to coerce the other. Duty stoppages at Shanghai now were symptomatic of the retrogression which came with the substitution of personal deals for a rule of law.

American enterprise led the way in this new phase. On September 16, 1851, Russell and Company reported the American ship *Panama,* and received from the customs permission to discharge her cargo of lead. On the 23rd, when two Chinese cargo boats were still alongside the ship, two customs boats suddenly came down river and "with loud shouts" seized and carried off the cargo boats and boatmen, piled the lead in the customhouse yard as smuggled goods, and claimed that the boats had not gone to the customs jetty for examination. Having as head of Russell and Company formally notified himself of this as American consul, Griswold wrote to the taotai, threatening to hold the port regulations void unless the customs subordinates were punished, and demanding compensation for the lead and release of two boatmen who were held. Further correspondence

[d] "My time," wrote Mr. Griswold to the taotai, "is too valuable to be wasted in entertaining such idle complaints. . . . The officers now trump up trivial and unfounded cases against United States vessels and take no notice of smuggling . . . in vessels of other nations. . . . If vessels under the United States flag are detained on accusation of smuggling, which afterwards proves unfounded, I shall look to you and the Chinese Government for reimbursement of all reasonable charges of demurrage, loss of markets, etc., and if need be deduct the said charges from the duties justly due.

"If some measure of this sort is not adopted," explained Mr. Griswold, "malicious persons would have it in their power at any time to delay vessels, so that their own might arrive first, simply by laying information when there was no good ground." Accordingly the consul proposed to have $150 collected from American merchants for each case of proved inadvertence and $50 from the Chinese customs officers for each unfounded charge, these sums to be "paid to me for trouble in examining the case and corresponding with you [the taotai] on the subject." On July 26 Griswold actually gave public notice that $25 would be charged for every amendment of manifest, but he was reversed by his superior a month later.[24]

This style of English was typical of merchant-consuls. What form of words was presented to the taotai is of course another matter. Griswold read the taotai's dispatches "through the medium of a linguist" and seldom saw a written English translation. The Chinese translations of his own communications, when presented to Dr. Parker, the American chargé and missionary sinologue, earned the remark, "It is now a long time since seeing the foreigner 'prostrate' or 'prostrate on the face' in Chinese correspondence. This used to be the style, but . . . I am confident you are the last man knowingly to revive it." The most fiery ultimata of the American consul probably reached the taotai in a form so tepid as to be ineffectual. At all events the taotai pursued an increasingly hostile policy, and Griswold observed that "the more latitude you give them the more they attempt to take." [25]

having got nowhere, the consul on September 26 made three formal demands upon the taotai: 1) immediate release of the boatmen, 2) public punishment of the headmen of the customs boats, 3) compensation by the taotai for the lead, for damage to the cargo boats, and for unloading the rest of the cargo, which the Chinese buyers now feared to touch. If these demands were not met, Griswold would consider the American treaty in abeyance, notify his further course, and then break off all relations "until this difficulty is settled by higher powers." In reply Wu Taotai released the boatmen and proposed arbitration by a board composed of the other consuls and two Chinese officers. This board [26] on October 4 decided unanimously against the taotai, but proposed that since no disrespect had been intended, an apology would be sufficient reparation. This closed the case, and Griswold's course was heartily approved by the American chargé, Dr. Parker.[27]

Mr. Griswold's consulship was inherited by Edward Cunningham of Boston, who succeeded him as local head of Russell and Company and so became acting American vice-consul on December 10, 1851.[28] Mr. Cunningham had reached China in 1845, and after serving as clerk in J. D. Sword and Company, had entered Russell and Company in 1846 and become a partner in 1850.[29] By March 1852, three months after entering the service of his government, he was practically declaring war on China. In defense of American interests he announced the suspension of the American treaty. This action was inspired by Wu Taotai's claim that all the land north of the Yangkingpang, in the center of what was to become the International Settlement, had already been ceded to the British consul, and that therefore three deeds of land sold to an American merchant, Roundy, could not receive the taotai's official seal and so be made legal. In combatting this claim Cunningham made the strongest possible threats short of force and gave the taotai another twenty-four hours to stamp the deeds.[30] More than twenty-four hours passed. Therefore, wrote the vice-consul on March 15, "I beg formally to apprise you that I shall hold no further communication with Your Excellency, that I consider the action of the Treaty between China and the United States suspended at this port, that no import or export dues of any kind will be paid by American vessels entering here until the right in dispute is recognized; that I shall immediately write to Canton requesting the American commissioner to dispatch a man of war with all haste, meantime organizing my countrymen resident here into a force that will be competent to defend itself until her arrival since they can no longer look to the Chinese authorities for protection." [e]

[e] "I beg also to inform your Excellency that any duties unpaid in consequence of this disputed question will never be claimed by me of the parties interested, will therefore be totally and irrecoverably lost to the Imperial Government, and moreover that if in consequence of this step on my part, any measures are taken by the Chinese officers to obstruct or impede the trading of the Chinese merchants

The result of this fiery declaration was the return of the deeds duly stamped and the publication of Cunningham's notification of March 16, that American purchases of land could be confirmed with the Chinese authorities through the American consulate "without the intervention . . . of any other foreign authority" (i.e., of the British consul).[31] The taotai's position had been indefensible, since the right claimed by Cunningham had already been acknowledged by the imperial commissioner. Even so, Cunningham had taken measures which, as Parker said, were "all but tantamount to a declaration of hostilities, the prerogative ordinarily of the Supreme power of a nation." [32] He had also made the customs duties his pawn in a diplomatic game and to that extent further complicated the tariff problem.

Consul Alcock, when similarly provoked, could not so easily threaten hostilities but he was soon withholding the payment of duties. In the case of the British vessel *Katharine Sharer* he found the taotai victimizing Chinese shippers who had theretofore been unmolested when importing from Canton on American vessels. When Wu fined the Chinese firm $4,000 on an apparent technicality, Alcock held up the payment of duties on the vessel's export cargo, letting the vessel sail and retaining the British shipper's promise to pay when called upon. From April to August 1852 he held this pecuniary club over the taotai while stalling off the reversal of his position by the Foreign Office. The taotai finally gave in. This was a game of treaty port pressure-politics which neither Bowring nor Malmesbury could approve as legally justifiable. But Bowring seems to have supported it privately as the only course available.[33]

Thus in May 1852 Alcock stopped the payment of Tls. 2,278 due as duties on the *Duke of Richmond* consigned to Smith, King and Company and used the money to reimburse Mr. Smith, who had been trying with Alcock's help for six months to get payment on a promissory note for which Chinese merchants had become security. Alcock also proposed to pay another private citizen, Dr. Murray, at the rate of $100 a day, for the delay in the building of his eye hospital caused by a local secret society, Dr. Murray having claimed compensation from the Chinese authorities.[34]

Bowring temporized. He told Alcock that "H. M. Government have objected to the arrest of duties as a means of enforcing redress of grievances," but he nevertheless referred the *Katharine Sharer* case to Malmesbury, four months away, and delayed reporting on the *Duke of Richmond*, which gave Alcock time to bring the taotai to terms.[35]

This petty squabbling at Shanghai was in the Chinese tradition of

---

with the Merchants of my country, any loss the latter may suffer will be claimed of the Chinese Government and retained from the first duties which shall accrue after the question has been settled."

personal arrangement of official business. The British consul's real inclination was far otherwise. In June 1852 we find Alcock writing to Wu Taotai as though the British government had never renounced its responsibility to enforce the treaty tariff, as Palmerston had solemnly done a year before.[f] To Bowring, Alcock suggested as an active program either the prohibition of all duty payment by British subjects, which would have to be followed up by a squadron at the Grand Canal; or a declaration that the treaty was in abeyance because of Chinese action, which would doubtless precipitate the stoppage of trade and so provide a valid *casus belli.*

On his part the energetic Wu pursued his commercial bent. Many asserted that his customs administration discriminated in favor of certain foreign firms in which he had funds of his own invested. Alcock claimed that the taotai's laxity, following upon his former vigilance, had facilitated enormous shipments of low-class teas, which had easily evaded the Chinese export duties of about 20 per cent and caused a glut in the London market. This allegation that the taotai had turned trader was supported by his dealings with merchant-consuls like T. C. Beale of Dent, Beale and Company, the consul of Portugal at Shanghai.[37] As will be seen below, Wu Chien-chang's eventual impeachment in 1855 listed as one of many crimes his going into business at Shanghai with the American *Ch'i-ch'ang* firm — namely, Russell and Company. Behind these dealings Consul Alcock saw the political program of the taotai, to use commercial means to "Cantonize" foreign relations at Shanghai. Since the previous summer, Wu apparently had been trying to control all the Chinese cargo boats of the port in order to organize a cargo boat monopoly. He was also reputedly attempting to establish a Cohong of five local Chinese firms. Like many other alleged infractions of the treaties, these measures were logical Chinese ways of regularizing the paths and profits of commerce.

The British and American governments expressed little interest in this local conflict at Shanghai. Malmesbury in his ten months as foreign secretary contributed nothing new.[38] The only reaction of the Department of State was a vague blanket instruction from Daniel Webster to the newly appointed commissioner to China, Humphrey Marshall.[39]

Yet in spite of this lack of concern in Washington and in London (where uncertain relations with the United States added to the distraction caused by France),[40] it is obvious that by 1852 the British treaty system in the ports of China was in a more critical position than ever before. The consuls at Shanghai felt themselves driven to the last extremity short of armed

[f] "Your ommission to act up to the manifest intention of the treaties makes it indeed imperative upon me to withhold for the future all interference for the protection of the Chinese revenue. I come to this decision with great reluctance, the desire of my government being now as ever to keep good faith; and to the utmost of their power to coöperate with you in securing the fair levy of all duties according to tariff, but when flagrant cases . . . are passed over, nothing further remains to be done but to withdraw altogether from any participation in your acts." [36]

coercion. Alcock in particular realized that his declaration of non-interference in June 1852 was a gesture of helplessness, for it merely reiterated Palmerston's unavailing statement of a year before. Yet he felt that he could not afford to stop interfering, in order to preserve the equal incidence of the tariff upon all traders, and had therefore done so with the weapon nearest at hand, the arrest of duties. Dr. Bowring expressed the British dilemma: he told Alcock "it is safer, wiser, easier, more economical, and more pacific to resist promptly every infraction of treaties . . . than to hesitate, forbear, temporize, [or] surrender. . . . Shanghai will become a Canton if energetic measures are not adopted." At the same time he told Malmesbury that "unless for the protection of British subjects against obvious wrong, the less of interference we exercise with regard to Custom House arrangements the better."[41] This was truly facing two ways.

The impact of the rebellion. The advance of the Taiping rebels into the Yangtze valley in 1853 came as a climax to the collapse of the treaty tariff, the growing disorder in the opium trade and on the coast, and the increasing tension in Anglo-Chinese relations. Dr. Bowring sensed that "everything portends great forthcoming changes both commercial and political, the foreshadows of which become more and more visible."[42] But while Britain's proconsuls in China might hope to cut the tangled skein of Sino-foreign relations by a resort to force, the China policy of the Foreign Office in this period remained profoundly quiescent.

In December 1852 Lord John Russell became foreign secretary in the Aberdeen ministry but soon gave up that post to save his health and work for parliamentary reform, having written hardly a dispatch to China. The Earl of Clarendon succeeded him on February 22, 1852. The difficulties over the Holy Places which eventually were to lead to the Crimean war had already begun; England was, in Clarendon's own phrase, "drifting into war." Although the new foreign secretary was a good friend of Palmerston (now home secretary) and highly esteemed by him,[43] this was no time for him to think of aggression in China, even if Palmerston, contrary to his custom, had seen fit to urge on his colleague the views which he had previously held on that subject. Clarendon's instructions to the superintendent of trade at Hongkong were in the same quiet tenor as his predecessor's.[44] At the same time Sir George Bonham resumed office at Hongkong and Dr. Bowring came home on furlough (February 16, 1853).

The rebellion now distracted attention from the snarls of Anglo-Chinese relations.[45] The rebels took Nanking on March 19, 1853, and the threat of their advance to the coast, noted by Alcock as early as January, had two immediate results. First, it obliged each foreign power to define its own attitude toward the Chinese belligerents. The imperial authorities sought to enlist foreign help,[46] while Protestant missionaries began to enlarge on the virtues of the supposedly Christian rebels, whose rapid advance seemed irresistible. While awaiting Clarendon's orders, Bonham chose a middle ground. After reaching Shanghai on March 21, he decided not to interfere in any way in favor of the Chinese government, as "I feel confident that any such interference on my part could only prolong the struggle." [47] His trip to Nanking in the *Hermes* (April 27), much as it alarmed the Chinese authorities, only strengthened his decision to remain neutral.[48] After separate American and British meetings, a general convocation of the foreign community at Shanghai on April 12 concerted plans for defense and laid a basis for coöperation between the British and American communities.

The second immediate effect of the rebellion was the complete demoralization of trade at Shanghai. This also put the foreign communities under a common pressure, although not strong enough to compel their coöperation. On March 3 Alcock had reported that "at the bare supposition of Nanking being taken, trade is at a stop." Bonham found "a kind of panic amongst the Chinese merchants and traders . . . there is at present little or no business carried on and money is very scarce." [49]

There now developed at Shanghai a peculiar situation which was to last for several years. The favorable geographic position of the port and the chaotic conditions inland led to a continued increase in the import of opium and export of tea and silk. Nevertheless, the hoarding of the one coin in which the Chinese had confidence, the Carolus dollar, together with the unsaleability of foreign manufactured goods and the resulting money stringency, necessitated enormous imports of bullion. Before these imports could begin, in the latter part of 1853,[50] even the opium market was upset, and soon reduced to a barter basis. Five of the leading British firms at Shanghai, three of which maintained receiving ships at Wusung,[51] complained to their consul on March 5 that "from the refusal of the native bankers to grant the usual facilities, it has become quite impossible to obtain payment of the Export and Import duties from the Chinese dealers, or to effect the sale of goods to meet those more directly due by the Foreign Merchants; thus leading to the detention of several outward bound ships now ready for sea." [52]

Alcock's bonding system. In response to this appeal, Consul Alcock approached Wu Taotai on March 7, proposing that "upon the Consul's becoming security for the final payment of the dues in each case, a Port Clearance should be issued." Earlier British efforts in 1844 to set up a "Bonded Warehouse System" had been fruitless, as noted in Chapter 12 above. The taotai asserted that imperial regulations still required him to send the duties collected on foreign trade to Peking at the end of every two months; [53] so strongly, indeed, was cash payment a part of the Chinese fiscal system for foreign trade that bonded warehouses were not finally set up until 1880 and not used at Shanghai until 1888.[54] When the consul proposed to let British ships depart taking their export cargoes but leaving bonds in lieu of export duties — a proposal more drastic than that of landing import cargoes in a bonded warehouse and giving bonds in lieu of import duties — Wu Taotai naturally demurred. He replied that he could not let the payment of duties stand over for more than one month. To this bare possibility he annexed further conditions which Alcock regarded as "very impracticable."

This unaccommodating spirit grieved the consul, in view of the wholly exceptional circumstances, and he proceeded to establish his own bonding system. When money could not be found, payment of duty could not be hastened by detaining vessels ready for sea. Accordingly, he notified the British community on March 10, 1853, that he would give up any British ship's papers and authorize her departure on certain conditions.[g] Bonham found this system in operation when he arrived at Shanghai on March 21. It required no prolonged reflection to determine its illegality according to treaty; yet he let it continue for three weeks. The month specified by the taotai expired unnoticed on April 10. On April 14 Alcock announced the discontinuance of his regulations by April 21; all arrear duties would have to be paid up within forty days, by May 30. Subsequently on May 27 he gave notice that the taotai was willing to extend the limit, in case the mail did not arrive by May 30, to three days after its arrival. Back duties to the amount of Tls. 168,000 (some $235,000) were accordingly paid in, and Bonham did not trouble himself to report the affair to Lord Clarendon. No other foreign consul at Shanghai had joined in it.

The opium trade seems to have had an indirect bearing on Bonham's policy. The opium market revived rapidly [56] and houses importing opium thus had resources with which to barter for their teas, which they could supplement, if necessary, with bullion imported to pay the cash duties. Importers of manufactured goods, on the other hand, continued to receive shipments already ordered from England, for which there was not the slightest market, and in addition were under the necessity of paying import duties in order to land these goods and free the ships which brought them. When the export season commenced in June 1853 and the Carolus dollar began to rise toward its highest premium of 86 per cent (August 27),[57]

[g] Alcock's conditions were: 1) delivery, by the consignees of the ship, of the usual customs certificate of the amount of duties payable; 2) delivery of as much security as the consul might wish in government paper; in title deeds of houses or land; or in foreign import goods, stored and insured, with a detailed delivery order; 3) "the signature of the consignees of the ships (one of the principals)" on a formal declaration acknowledging the amount of duties due and the security given. Where a part of the duties had been paid, the duty receipts from the customs must be listed and attached to the above form. These regulations were promulgated with no time limit specified.[55]

thirteen of the twenty-five British firms at Shanghai, representing over two-thirds of the Lancashire and Yorkshire trade, petitioned Bonham on July 7 to "demand of the Chinese Government that payment of duties in cash may be deferred until trade is revived." [58] It is significant that of the five firms which had originally petitioned Alcock on March 5, the three which had receiving ships at Wusung (Jardine, Dent, and Lindsay and Company) did not sign this second petition. Of the firms that did sign, none had receiving ships. Indeed as the petition set forth, the withdrawal of nearly all the native capital from the trade made bills on England unsaleable except at exorbitant rates: "Under these circumstances we are driven to the importation of either opium or bullion; the latter of which may be impossible and the former not generally imported by those deeply interested in the Lancashire and Yorkshire trade."

In forwarding this petition, Alcock added a strong plea on his own part. Unless relief were given, two millions sterling of British capital would be locked up in goods on hand or due to arrive, and there would be detained nine ships already in harbor and twenty-three more expected. Three millions sterling of British revenue for 1854 were concerned.

Bonham replied to the merchants on July 20, castigating them for having neither foreseen the stoppage of trade nor removed their goods to safety at Hongkong. He took a very high legal tone. "A contest . . . between the Emperor of China and a small rebellious portion of his subjects," and its effect on trade, were insufficient excuse for abrogating "one of the most important of the stipulations of the treaty existing between the Sovereign in whose Kingdom such dissensions occur, and the British Government." He could not defer payment of duties without the consent of the Chinese — which Alcock was still unable to obtain.

To this lofty declaration, Sir George added several *obiter dicta*: the names of "many influential British firms at Shanghai" were not attached to the letter. Even if he could induce the Chinese Government to forego its duties, he would, "were he so to insist, injure the parties whose names do not appear in your letter, and commit an act of which those parties would have good cause of complaint." Moreover if the average duty of 5 per cent on imports could not be paid, export produce could hardly be bought. Hence why bother to get goods landed? [59] Bonham could not minimize the seriousness of the rebellion and in the next breath assert that the merchants should have stopped all orders for imports four months previously, in fear of it; and the merchants pointed this out in rebuttal on August 16, at the same time stating that the duty on staple imports was actually from 12 to 28 per cent, as Bonham should have known. In addition he must have known that the export trade was being largely conducted by barter, and that merchants might therefore well be unable to pay cash duties on imports and still be able to collect export cargoes. The fact was, as Sir George himself put it, that "the holders of opium and rich capitalists being the only parties able to purchase produce this year, few, if any, of the Manchester firms, who made consignments to China, will share in the export business." The opium companies, in short, stood to corner the tea market.[h]

Thus the first impact of the rebellion and its disruption of trade at Shanghai divided the British merchants and officials among themselves, and left the other foreign consuls indisposed to coöperate with Alcock. Meanwhile the Cantonese taotai found an increasing opportunity for his dubious talents.

Wu Chien-chang and the Shanghai rebellion. Among the vestiges of his past which had clung to Wu Chien-chang in office, in addition to his commercial propensities, was an acquaintance of long standing with another man from Hsiang-shan near Macao. This was Liu Li-ch'uan, a brigand and ex-sugar-broker at Canton, probably an opium smuggler, who for a time at least had managed Wu's accounts and was still in close touch with him.[63] Liu had arrived in Shanghai shortly after his fellow villager, in 1849, "an ordinary looking person of very dark complexion," aged 34, rather undersized, with "little of the *boanerges,* dignified appearance expected in a warrior." [64] His importance lay in the fact that he was the leader in Shanghai of the Cantonese faction of the Triad Society or San-ho-hui.

This secret society has been identified or associated with so many names, of its own, affiliated, or separate organizations — particularly the T'ien-ti-hui (Heaven and Earth Society) or Hung-men (Hung League) — that its pervasive and yet nebulous ramifications are almost impossible to trace. It is usually said to have arisen after the extinction of the Ming as a revolutionary protest against Manchu domination. It was a brotherhood possessing a complicated ritual, not unlike that of the Masonic order, a multitude of laws, passwords, and an esoteric slang, all of which are beginning to receive the attention of historians.[65] In general the society flourished along the trade routes of South China and in the overseas com-

[h] Bonham reported concerning the merchants' rebuttal of August 16, and his reply thereto of September 2, that the British houses not signing the petition included "the influential firms of Jardine Matheson & Co., Dent Beale & Co., Lindsay & Co., and Blenkin Rawson & Co., who . . . as far as I am aware, take no part in the question." [60] All of them dealt in opium. (The last named had a branch, Ker, Rawson & Co. at Singapore.) [61] Alcock's regulations in March, allowing export under bond, were in answer to the appeal of opium importing companies, and Bonham had waited three weeks before cancelling them. The Lancashire merchants' proposal of July, much less drastic in nature, he had denied categorically, without even considering a reference to the Foreign Office. Bonham evidently steered his course with one eye on the opium interests which dominated Hongkong. The foreign secretary, with the advice of the Board of Trade, approved the sound discretion of his course,[62] which was legally incontestable.

munity in Malaya. In 1853 it was active among the Cantonese and Fukienese sailors and boatmen resident at Shanghai, who had been drawn to the north in increasing numbers with the growth of foreign trade and had been causing the local authorities serious trouble. As early as 1850 there had been riots in the eastern suburb by Cantonese junkmen, whose squeezing of the local merchants and kidnapping and racketeering set a Shanghai fashion. This extra-provincial population had collected in the district northeast of the city walls, speaking languages totally strange to the local populace. In 1851 ten robbers, with Cantonese aplomb, had fought off 120 militia and a police lieutenant sent to capture them. By the summer of 1853, inspired by the example of the Taiping capture of Nanking, this insubordinate element in Shanghai was growing increasingly restive,[66] holding meetings, brandishing their arms, and making demands upon the local officials.[i] On August 10 Wu Taotai issued a proclamation against the rebellious and dangerous bands of Canton and Fukien thieves in the city. A fortnight later the district magistrate, Yuan Tsu-te, arrested the leader of the Fukien faction (head of the Hsing-hua gild),[68] but was so strongly threatened in return that he was obliged to let him go and pay him money in addition. The taotai heard of a plan to waylay his own person and compromised by giving Liu $300, so it was said, and offering to employ his followers as militia. Whether or exactly how Wu employed this ancient tactic for dealing with banditti remains obscure. Evidently his capacity to control his fellow-Cantonese was greater than his influence over the Chinchew men from Fukien. At any rate, on August 31 the district magistrate issued a proclamation stating that it had been decided to increase the local militia, the Canton, Fukien, and Ningpo gilds having applied to the taotai with that suggestion, and that $2100 would be appropriated to maintain a superintendent and a deputy superintendent, at salaries of $50 and $40 a month, with privates at $8, and in addition two boats at $350. This promise was not enough to satisfy the leading conspirators, however, and on September 7, 1853, the rising at Shanghai occurred under the name of the Hsiao-tao-hui (variously translated as Small Knife, Dagger, or Small Sword Society), an offshoot of the Triads.

September 7 was the birthday of Confucius. On that morning several foreigners entered the walled city before dawn to see the local officials conduct sacrifices at the Confucian temple. On the street they unexpectedly met bands of men, armed with spears, short swords, and a few matchlocks, wearing on their caps and jackets red cloth badges. These rebels had

[i] To the geomancers 1853 was a year of calamities in Shanghai. In later years it was recalled that there were two earthquakes and a two-day whirlwind, lightning struck the wall, the river boiled, the earth gave forth blood and sprouted hair, a certain Mrs. Hung bore male triplets colored respectively red, white, and blue, and the city fell.[67]

seized the taotai's treasury, opened the prisons, and stabbed the district magistrate and his attendant: Yuan Tsu-te, entrusting his old mother to a brother's care, had taken his official seat and calmly met his death. Criers came by beating gongs and promising that shopkeepers might open their doors without fear; during the day several foreigners, including the American commissioner to China, "walked unmolested through the city," and even "went up to the insurgents and inspected their dress and weapons without the latter taking offence." [69] With such ease was a city of some 200,000 inhabitants wrested from the imperial grasp by a band of perhaps 2000-odd organized desperadoes.

Wu Chien-chang had not gone to worship at the Confucian temple. Warned in time, he had left his yamen to the mercies of the populace and hidden himself in a private house within the city. His chief danger was from the Fukien faction of the rebels, Chinchew men who had put the contents of his treasury [70] on junks in the river, and favored killing its owner. The Cantonese faction, on the other hand, seem to have favored the re-establishment of Wu's authority with him as their leader. Liu Li-ch'uan on the day of the rising went to the American legation and consulate (Russell and Company) in the foreign settlement and said as much to the American commissioner, Humphrey Marshall. Wu appears to have shunned this honor, however, for on the next day he appealed to the American and Portuguese merchant-consuls (Cunningham of Russell and Company and Beale of Dent, Beale and Company) for protection against the Chinchew men. Since the consuls could not become officially involved, they asked Mr. J. Caldecott Smith, a young Englishman in Dent, Beale and Company, and Dr. G. R. Hall, the surgeon of the foreign community, to rescue the taotai for them. These two gentlemen found him in the city, whereupon Wu, "putting on a plain dress with some blue stockings, large goggles over his eyes, and taking an old umbrella in his hand, sallied forth from his apartment with his friends." [71] On reaching the north wall, since the rebels were guarding the gates to prevent a general exodus of the population, Mr. Smith, Wu Chien-chang, and Dr. Hall in order were lowered over the side in a sling made from a bolt of strong cloth. Later Dr. Lockhart, medical missionary of the London Missionary Society, and Mr. E. Webb of Dent, Beale and Company, brought the taotai's family out through the gates. The fugitives found shelter in the American legation, since, although American neutrality had been proclaimed, Mr. Marshall considered it the "*office of humanity* — to shelter a defenceless man and his innocent wives," especially when the man in question came "*to beg the protection of the flag of the United States.*" [72] In Russell and Company's spacious establishment, and later in a boat on the river, the taotai stayed until September 24, powerless and inactive for over two weeks, after which he left the scene entirely for a time — "gone a-Wooing," as the *North China Herald* [73] put it.[j]

[j] The following verse celebrated Wu Chien-chang's departure, without apologies to Shakespeare (but cp. *Henry VIII*, Act III, Scene 2, end of Wolsey's soliloquy, and *Othello*, Act III, Scene 3):

Samqua's Lament.

There is, between the button we aspire to,
That ample fount of dollars, and our ruin,
More pangs and fears than wars or women have;
And when he falls 'tis like a burned up squib,
Never to blaze again. O, now for ever,
Farewell the fertile squeeze, farewell sycee!
Farewell, Grand Chop, and all the lofty words
That made my station stunning, O farewell!
Farewell the chair of state and the loud gong,
The red umbrella and all mummery,
Pride, pomp, and circumstance of Taou Tai Woo!
And O ye customs' harpies! by whose means
The all potent dollar always I obtained,
Farewell! — Old Samqua's occupation's gone.
(NCH, Nov. 5, 1853).

CHAPTER XXII

RUTHERFORD ALCOCK AND THE PROVISIONAL SYSTEM 1853–54

THE REBEL COUP AT SHANGHAI and the taotai's flight precipitated an immediate problem of customs administration. At dusk on the evening of September 7 "the rabble in the foreign settlement broke into the Chinese Custom House and completely gutted it, carrying away everything portable." [a] In port were 10 British, 11 American, and 5 or 6 other foreign ships, which would soon be ready to sail. Now that the customs administration had melted away, should these vessels, and others soon to follow them, be forced to wait, or should they pay duties and go, or go free? If they should pay duties — to whom?

Rutherford Alcock met this new administrative crisis with his usual affirmative vigor by setting up the Provisional System. Without retracing accounts of this which are already available,[2] let us note certain factors which influenced its history at Shanghai. The first of these was the precedent which had been set a few months before at Amoy.

The precedent at Amoy, May 1853. The seizure of the Chinese city of Amoy in May had had many parallels with events at Shanghai in September. The coup was similarly plotted by the Small Knife Society. This offshoot of the Triads had been organized at Amoy about 1848–49 by a certain Chinese named Ch'en Ch'ing-chen ("Tan Keng-chin"), who had acquired at Singapore the status of a British subject and become a clerk, some say a compradore, in Jardine's (see Chapter 12 above). In 1851 Tan had been seized by the local taotai, together with a list of the society members, and tortured to death. Jardine's agent and the British consul were unable to rescue him, and "his body was found on the following morning, on opening Jardine, Matheson's Hong, dressed as usual and seated in a sedan chair, opposite to his master's door." [3] Tan's successor, an energetic man named Huang Wei ("Un Wee"), swore vengeance and eventually engineered the rising of May 1853.

On May 14 the Amoy authorities called on Vice-consul Backhouse, in

[a] On the next morning, it was further plundered of its "doors, windows, planks, beams, and everything movable, which was all being carried off by coolies and countrymen, no man forbidding them"; yet as many a witness testified, the customhouse "was attacked by no mob of lawless vagabonds, but by the sober and industrious people in the neighbourhood." A single foreign guard could have prevented this, by standing at the door. On September 8, after British marines had protected the French consulate from a threatened rebel sortie, "a guard was put over the building to prevent its being utterly demolished." [1]

charge of the British consulate, to say that 2000 to 3000 armed rebels were approaching Amoy from about 25 miles away. The consul warned the foreign community and in the absence of H. M. sloop *Rattler*, which was out pirate-hunting, asked the three armed receiving ships of Tait, Jardine, and Dent to enter the harbor. He then moved the consular treasure supply and the archives on board Dent's receiving ship *Lord Amherst*. On May 18 the local authorities fled, and after a day's intermittent firing some 4000 or 5000 insurgents, joined with animation by an equal number of Amoy residents, expelled the imperial troops. Excellent order was maintained; a revolution appeared to have taken place in Amoy almost without disturbance. The consulate with its guard of twelve lascars was untroubled.

Sir George Bonham hastened up from Shanghai on H. M. S. *Hermes*, and on May 24 Backhouse announced that Bonham was "pleased to disapprove" of his having asked the receiving ships to enter port; they should therefore depart. They on their side requested the continued presence of a warship to protect the "vast amount of British property now here." The consular treasure was transshipped to the *Rattler*, which had returned from hunting pirates, and a day or two later the opium ships left the harbor. Bonham told his vice-consul that "great care should be taken not to give the Chinese any pretext for saying that the British consular authorities abet and encourage the opium trade." Evidently some discussion ensued, for a week later he amplified this statement by explaining that he did not disapprove of the receiving ships anchoring in Amoy harbor, he disapproved only of their having been brought there *at the request of the consulate*. Their presence might again be useful for protection and he would not object to their returning to the harbor and remaining there as long as the Chinese authorities did not object, "should the masters of these vessels see fit to bring them there *on their own responsibility*."[4] This they soon did.

The insurgent leaders who had captured Amoy so easily now began to have their troubles. Three of the council of six leaders were from Singapore. Some of their lieutenants were Chinese of the lowest type, who had been in foreign employ and even dismissed for misconduct. Financially their regime was weak, the pay of soldiers fell from 100 to 60 cash per day, and Amoy shopkeepers were already trying to remove their property. Forced contributions from Chinese merchants met only a part of the regime's expenses of some $1000 a day. Local rice stocks were unreplenished and diminishing. In August the insurgent chieftain, Huang, published a customs tariff in an effort to raise legitimate funds, but the rate was so low, perhaps to please the Singapore element arriving from the Straits, that little revenue could be expected. The consul had considered whether in the absence of a customs administration he ought to exact promises of duty payment from British vessels leaving port, but he had thought better of it. The trade of Amoy was not large enough to create the problem faced at Shanghai three months later.

On August 28 imperial forces returned by sea to recover the port. The Amoy taotai had asked the British vice-consul in June to "get a couple of war vessels ready, with a full complement of stores, so as to coöperate" in the recapture and set commerce afoot again. To this and all other overtures the British authorities had replied with strict neutrality, and on the approach of the imperial fleet British vessels moved from the harbor between Kulangsu and the Amoy waterfront to anchor in back of Kulangsu and leave room for the battle. Only H. M. S. *Rattler* stayed in front of the foreign hongs, with steam up so as to move nimbly about if fighting came near. The insurgent fleet of thirty or more junks along the waterfront were out-numbered by the imperial flotilla, but after the first day's inconclusive cannonade it developed that the best forces of the latter were "west coast boats," that is, Cantonese pirates, hired for the occasion and not inclined to annihilate their brethren on shore. After three weeks of daily battles the British consular observers were certain that the greatly superior forces of the imperial admiral, though easily strong enough to gain the victory, were held back by their collusion with the rebels. The admiral was sincerely determined, but his fleet made more noise than destruction, except for damage to the innocent bystanders among the population. Victorious attacks on land were followed by quiet retreats at the end of the day. This continued for two months and a half, the insurgents being gradually worn down by desertion and loss of manpower and resources. Prices skyrocketed, among them that of gunpowder, in which the foreign merchants appear to have done a rousing business. Gunpowder supplies accumulated on Kulangsu to the point of endangering the community.[b] Tait and Company early in November reported $113,660 worth of property stored in various warehouses. In December after the battle was over Syme, Muir and Company promised at the consul's request to remove a large stock of powder "sufficient to destroy the whole range of buildings"; they had already negotiated for its sale to the mandarins. This foreign pecuniary interest in the local situation appears at first to have been on the side of the rebels; the *Lord Amherst* and perhaps other foreign ships in port fired several shots of grape and canister into an imperial war junk, killing one man, during the first battle on August 28. Admiral She complained, the *Rattler* confirmed the fact, and the mate of the *Lord Amherst* was brought to the consulate and "reprimanded and warned." When Admiral She on his part asked the

[b] Admiral She in a note to the consulate received on September 21 ventured to "request that when the said rebels come to the British residents to buy powder they will decidedly refuse to sell it to them. The rebels being without powder will without doubt be quickly defeated."

services of a British war-steamer in order to bring from Foochow the treasure he needed to finance his attack, which could not safely be brought overland, he was naturally refused on grounds of neutrality.

The siege ended on November 11, 1853, when the insurgent leaders quietly decamped and the imperialists scaled the walls of the citadel. The latter then, "having employed themselves all the morning in seizing such people as they could catch, began beheading them." At first the prisoners were brought to the waterfront in batches of twenty and their heads chopped off, "the bodies falling over in the mud," but as the work continued it was speeded up and "with bill-hooks, spears, and clubs they destroyed them by dozens; finally from the junks within fifty yards from the [British] men of war they began decapitating them; some were slashed with a knife and knocked overboard, others tied by one leg and hand and hove into the water to drown. The harbor was covered with struggling human beings, many of them being boys c. 12 years of age." After maintaining strict neutrality for four hours, Vice-consul Robertson at last abandoned it and told Admiral She to stop. British boats then rescued more than two hundred from drowning, many of them badly cut up, and many of them innocent coolies and farmers. Thus the Amoy rebellion which began so gently, in the end reached its white terror.[5]

Duties were not paid to the customhouse again until the Chinese authorities announced the resumption of its activities on December 15, 1853.[6] Thus the Amoy incident had several features later applicable to Shanghai: the foreign community on Kulangsu protected itself by arms and remained relatively unmolested, foreign merchants plied a profitable arms trade, the imperial customhouse was out of action and foreign ships went free.

The first steps in the Anglo-American coöperation. Another factor which influenced the history of Alcock's Provisional System was the gradual development of a common Anglo-American policy in China. First, both powers, together with France, prepared to seek treaty revision in 1854. This was a claim which demonstrated the miraculous efficacy of the most-favored-nation clause: Britain had secured her Nanking treaty in 1842. Her Supplementary treaty of 1843 contained the most-favored-nation clause. The American and French treaties of 1844 promised treaty revision in twelve years, or 1856. For Britain this meant twelve years from 1842, or 1854. Therefore it meant 1854 for the United States and France also.

Again, the approach of the Crimean war (Russian occupation of the principalities began on June 22, 1853) gave the French and English governments a common program in Europe which could easily be extended to China; and the Clayton-Bulwer Treaty of 1850 had begun a movement toward the settlement of Anglo-American differences which the efforts of the British government and of Webster and Fillmore in 1852 had advanced in spite of the checks occurring at the beginning of Pierce's administration.[7] Diplomatic coöperation was further facilitated by the presence in China of French and American ministers, M. de Bourboulon [8] and Commissioner Humphrey Marshall,[9] who were on the scene at Macao and Shanghai, respectively, in the Spring of 1853. The most immediate factor, however, was the progress of the Taiping Rebellion, which drew together all three treaty powers, and especially the two trading nations, in a common danger. Clarendon was to make the overtures for Anglo-American coöperation, but the situation at Shanghai was the vital stimulus in bringing it about.

After receiving Bonham's dispatches of March 1853, asking what course to follow toward the Rebellion, especially in the event of the fall of Shanghai, Clarendon drafted on May 7 a reply which defined a policy of strict neutrality toward both sides in China and of British coöperation with the United States and France, with an eye to treaty revision. He did not send this reply at once; and on May 17 through his ambassadors in Paris, St. Petersburg, and Washington he invited coöperation "with the view of turning to the best account the opportunity offered by the present crisis in China for opening that Empire to the commercial enterprise of foreign nations." Having received from Paris the reply that Bourboulon would be given instructions in this spirit, Clarendon on June 8 sent his draft of May 7 to Bonham. On July 8 he forwarded a similar reply from Washington, and a tepid one from St. Petersburg.[10]

The policy thus inaugurated in London was carried out immediately by Bourboulon and Bonham, who conferred at Hongkong early in August 1853 and agreed on cordial coöperation. Bonham favored perfect neutrality while Bourboulon, presumably in the interests of Catholic missions, slightly favored the imperialists as against the supposedly Protestant Taipings, and suggested sending a few warships up the Yangtze as moral support against the rebels. Bonham, however, felt that the interests of trade necessitated awaiting the outcome of a close and doubtful contest. Treaty revision also must wait — so he wrote Clarendon — since a treaty with the imperialists would involve active support of them and better terms might eventually be got from the rebels, if they were victorious. To this Clarendon replied on October 3 that treaty revision was optional, not necessary at the moment.[11] During the rest of 1853 Anglo-French coöperation on this point remained in abeyance.

Meanwhile, President Pierce and his secretary of state, W. L. Marcy, had been wary of Clarendon's overtures. Marcy's instructions to Marshall were very brief and very general. The key sentence read: "Without knowing what course the British authorities may deem it expedient to take in furtherance of the object in view; the President does not enjoin upon you co-operation but only cordial relations and free conference with them." [12]

In brief, the American commissioner, being left to his own devices, followed a policy that reflected his own personality. Marshall was a Kentuckian and after graduating from West Point had been in succession a lawyer in Louisville, a colonel of state cavalry in the Mexican War, and a representative in Congress. Now at the age of forty-one he was the third appointee and even later choice as commissioner to China of an administration about to go out of office.[13] In addition to possessing a shrewd intellect, he combined all the provincialism of a middle-Westerner, in the days when Anglo-American relations were none too cordial, with a fervid sense of the importance of his position; and had soon antagonized nearly all the other foreign officials in China, beginning with Commodore Perry and his American colleagues.[c]

When he came to deal with the British, Mr. Marshall was embittered by the comparative inadequacy of the American consular establishment. During Marshall's stay in China, the American merchant-consul at Canton went home for a year, leaving his partner as deputy. The consul at Amoy, who had been living at home in Connecticut for some time, withdrew his authority from his son, who had acted for him; and the Amoy consulate was closed. Letters arrived from the State Department for a mysterious "Dwight Webb, United States Consul at Fuchow," who had never been heard of in China. Finally, Dr. Peter Parker, the secretary of legation, claimed the right to receive sealed instructions from Washington, contents unknown to the commissioner.[15] When Marshall contrasted this haphazard establishment with Sir George Bonham's, the British power seemed ominous indeed. Sir George wrote home: "The Commissioner, Marshall, is a big, coarse, headstrong man, has never been out of Kentucky before he came here, and will I fear give us annoyance and embarrass our proceedings — he already wants to have a squabble with me but I will not afford him the opportunity if I can possibly avoid it." [16]

Meanwhile, Marshall had written to Washington: "Great Britain has exhibited in her eastern conquests neither fear of Heaven nor love of justice among men. Nevertheless I will obey your instructions to confer freely when a conference shall promise to be advantageous, and the confidence shall appear to be reciprocal between the British minister and myself — an event I am not simple enough to anticipate from my past experience and observation." [17]

It should not be inferred, however, that Marshall was an anglophobe because he was simple-minded. His chief opponent, Rutherford Alcock,

[c] The day after landing at Hongkong, for instance, he had written: "To the Commanding Officer of the United States Squadron, . . . I request that you will furnish me, at Macao, immediately, a suitable vessel-of-war . . . , to convey me to such point as it may be necessary for me to visit, in order to enter upon my official intercourse with the court of China." [14] This inaugurated strained relations with the United States Navy, which refused to grant him a private warship.

later praised him with superlatives. Although Marshall lacked a background knowledge of China, could not travel about, and had no interpreter but a Cantonese linguist, yet in Alcock's opinion "for his sound judgment and statesmanlike views, with a clear insight into what was passing around him in China (always excepting a certain monomania he brought with him from Kentucky about the British and their aims and plottings) . . . he is deserving of very high praise. We doubt whether the whole body of [British] interpreters — educated men, familiar with the people and the language — have ever produced anything to be compared with [Marshall's] dispatches." [18]

On July 4, 1853, through the intercession of Wu Chien-chang, Marshall had an interview at K'un-shan (Quinsan) near Shanghai with the Nanking governor-general, I-liang. I-liang and Wu opened Marshall's credentials, which he had sealed for the court, and found his request for an audience at Peking — a right not allowed by treaty: they observed that tributary envoys came to court at fixed times and practiced the kotow, whereas the Americans were not subservient but "proud as Yeh-langs"; they told Marshall to await a reply at Shanghai.[19] Marshall's impression of all this was that the imperial government was "impotent, ignorant, conceited, . . . superlatively corrupt. The rebels . . . struggle merely for *power*. . . . The people of China are indifferent." Nevertheless he had advocated coming to an agreement with the emperor to open the Yangtze to steam, to "tranquilize China and elevate her condition to the end that Russia and Great Britain shall not make partition of her noble domain." [20]

Owing to these views and to Marshall's own temper, Anglo-American cooperation at Shanghai in 1853 rested upon a very dubious foundation. When the draft of a joint proclamation was sent to the American legation, Mr. Marshall returned it "in pieces patched together with various cuttings out, additions, and emendations and among the rest a characteristic heading of his own, . . . 'The citizens of the United States of America and the subjects of Great Britain and France!' " [21] Equal discord was soon to curse the Provisional System born on September 9.

The Provisional Rules of September 9, 1853. When the Shanghai rising occurred on September 7, Consul Alcock's first thought was for the British trade and its treaty basis. As he put the dilemma: "if I let the ships depart without taking any measures for verifying the amount of duties and obtaining security for their final payment, British interest would be protected at the expense of Chinese, contrary to the express provisions of the Treaty. If on the other side I detained the vessels until a Custom-House should be re-established for the issue of a Grand Chop, I ran the risk of totally sacrificing British property and trade for the benefit of a Government no

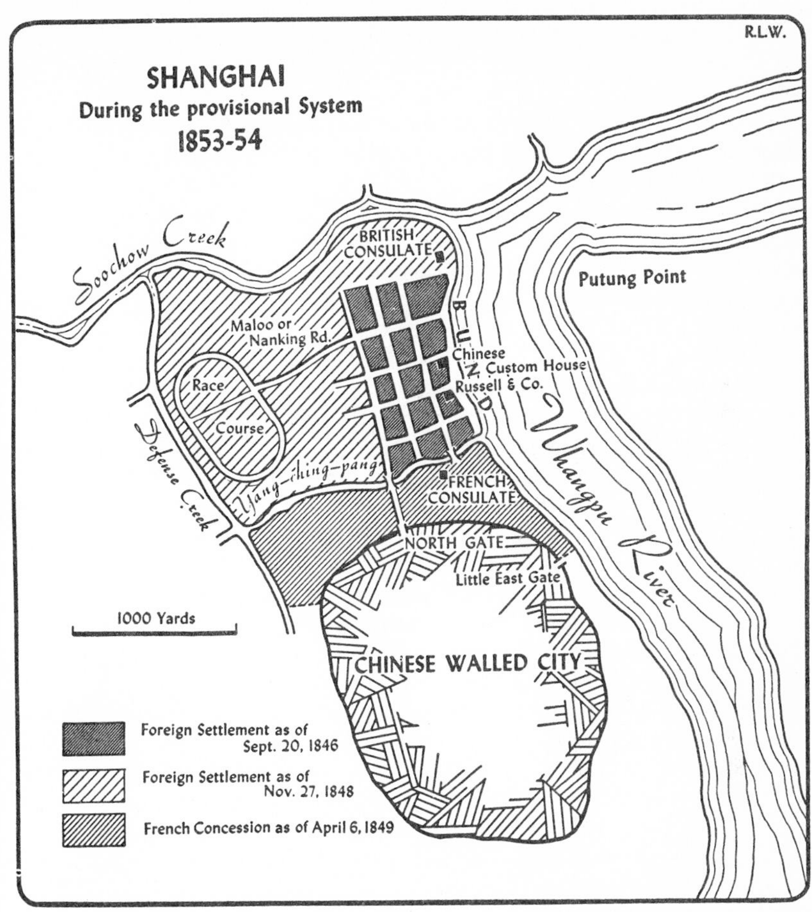

longer in a position to fulfil the conditions of that Treaty, and which might before long cease to exist. Neither alternative could be accepted." [22]

It was this sense of responsibility on the part of the British consul which chiefly brought the Provisional System into being. As Stanley Wright has emphasized,[23] Alcock was intent on preserving a legal treaty basis on which trade could continue, even in the absence of a Chinese customhouse. In order to let vessels go without the customs port clearance provided by treaty, he had to have some substitute arrangement. Money being scarce, he took promissory notes.

On September 9, after consultation between Alcock and Marshall, the British and American consuls issued notifications informing their nationals that in the absence of the Chinese authorities, promissory notes for the full amount of all customs duties due to the Chinese government would be collected by the two consulates respectively, and they each appended a set of rules governing this procedure. These rules were stated to be, and were evidently meant to be, identical in every respect.[d] But there was one important difference: British merchants could give promissory notes which would be payable "provided the sanction of H. B. M.'s Government to that effect be received," whereas this proviso was omitted in the American rules. Alcock later stated that this clause had been "introduced into the bond, after I had drafted it and was laid prostrate with sickness . . . at the earnest instance of the Merchants and for the avowed purpose of protecting them from any demand for payment until the decision of their own Government should be taken. . . ."[25] Its effect was to permit the British consul to wait for instructions from London before rescinding his system or taking any further steps with regard to bonds that might have been collected.

The American provisional rules were almost word for word the same and were stated by Cunningham to be "similar to those adopted by H. B. M.'s Consul";[26] but the omission of the proviso above quoted made their effect vastly different. The American authorities were left in a position to act as they saw fit. Some have suggested that Marshall omitted this proviso, that his home government must decide as to the validity of any bonds given for duties, because he wished to bolster the imperial cause and thwart the designs of the British. No doubt he had this attitude; but Alcock's testimony indicates that the difference was less consciously planned. British

[d] The British Notification asserted that "the capture of an isolated sea-port on the coast of a vast Empire can in no sense abrogate a solemn treaty entered into between the two Sovereigns of Great Britain and China. The obligations continue to exist on either side." Consequently, the Chinese authority being gone, and there being no legal source for the issuance of a port clearance on presentation of which the British consul would ordinarily return a ship's papers and allow it to depart, the consul, in letting ships depart under any provisional arrangement, must do so upon his own responsibility. Hence he can accept this responsibility only on his own conditions:

1. That the consignees of the ship hand in a declaration naming all consignees of import goods or shippers of outward cargo;

2. That these importers or shippers declare in writing the quantity and description of their goods, and

3. Supply further documentary evidence on the subject if demanded by the consul;

4. That the consignees of the ship "present a collective schedule of the particulars of cargo and Duties payable on goods and ship, corresponding with the several declarations of Importers and Shippers in what concerns these and with the addition of Tonnage dues."

5. "The amounts thus shown to be due from Importers, Shippers and Consignees of vessels to be paid into this office; either in Silver, as they would have had to pay if the Custom-House Bankers had to receive the duties, or by the bill of the several parties payable on demand at forty days sight in Shanghai to the Chinese Superintendent of Customs, provided the sanction of H. B. M.'s Government to that effect be received."

6. "These preliminaries arranged to the satisfaction of H. M.'s Consul, the consignees will receive on application the Ship's Papers and a Port Clearance under the Consular Seal," after which they may leave the port.[24]

officials regularly sought Foreign Office confirmation of their acts. American officials in China were on their own. Conscious of his plenary powers, Marshall felt no hesitation in sanctioning definitive measures.

The Provisional System met trouble from the first. On the day before its establishment, in fact, T. C. Beale of Dent, Beale and Company — a leading British merchant who was now Portuguese consul, Dutch vice-consul, and acting Prussian vice-consul — had allowed the Prussian vessel, *Preussischer Adler*, to leave the port with duties unpaid on receipt of an amazing written promise that it would absolve him — how is not stated — from all claims which the Chinese government might make against him for recovery of the duties.[27] This action by one of Shanghai's leading exporters set an alarming precedent. British and American merchants foresaw that, while their own vessels must promise to pay duties, vessels of other flags might go free without promising anything. Shippers by these foreign vessels could undersell in the London market; the foreign vessels themselves might get the carrying trade of the port. On September 12 four leading American firms in a letter to the American commissioner argued that the inability of the emperor's officials to protect the trade of Shanghai relieved the foreign merchants of all liability for duties and made Shanghai a free port.[e] Commissioner Marshall replied on September 14: "*The treaty is not dead* . . . The obligations of both parties survive the invasion of Shanghai." [29]

In this way three points of view began to emerge. Marshall sought to uphold the treaties and see that China got the duties due to her under them. Alcock was ready to do the same, provided the Foreign Office agreed. The merchants generally saw no reason at all why they should pay duties when China was not able to collect them, and advocated making Shanghai a free port like Trieste.[30] In the end all three were to have their way: Marshall succeeded in re-establishing the treaty tariff, Alcock waited successfully for his instructions from London, and the merchants were able to invalidate most of the promissory notes which they had given. Since the Department of State at this time seldom even sent instructions to its single full-time representative in China, it remained for the British government as usual to lead the way in dealing with the question of duties at Shanghai. As often happened, the final victory went to the British merchants in China and England. They presented their case against the Provisional System so effectively that the law officers of the crown were not aware, until too late, of the many and intricate extenuating circumstances which the Chinese

[e] In addition they objected strongly to letting their fellow merchant and chief competitor, of Russell and Co., demand in his capacity as vice-consul any of their accounts and papers that he might "see fit to require," and even receive and use their silver, if they should ever tender any in payment of duties. Alternatively they proposed to give written obligations for duties which would be payable only forty days after due notice "that the fulfillment of this obligation is demanded by the Emperor, and this demand is sanctioned by our Government." [28]

government, if it had indulged in diplomatic relations, might have brought forward to support its claim for duties.

Sir George Bonham favored applying to Shanghai the same completely negative policy which he had applied to Amoy. Yet, characteristically, since Alcock had taken the responsibility upon his shoulders, Sir George did not propose to shift it to his own by abrogating the Provisional System; he left it to the Foreign Office. Would "the sanction of H. B. M.'s Government" be received or not?

Clarendon was fully occupied at this time by affairs connected with the Crimean war. He took the complaints which arrived from the British Chamber of Commerce at Shanghai, forwarded through the East India and China Associations of London and Liverpool and their Manchester colleagues, and referred them to the Board of Trade. His decision followed verbatim the recommendation of that agency: if a Chinese government should be re-established at Shanghai, either by the rebels or by the imperial authorities, the duty payments held by Alcock in promissory notes should be paid over to it; otherwise, they should be given back to the merchants.[31] These instructions reached Bonham in the middle of January 1854 and Alcock received an answer four and a half months after his first question. Before that time arrived, the Provisional System had changed its nature.

Foreign neutrality at Shanghai (October — December 1853). While the British consul's dispatches were traveling half way around the world to be dealt with by bureaucrats who had never been in China, Shanghai had become an armed camp. From the foreign point of view there could be no thought of allowing the taotai to re-establish himself within the limits of the foreign settlement, much less collect duties on a trade he could not protect. In the military crisis Rutherford Alcock became dictator of Shanghai and under the banner of neutrality preserved both the British trade and the Provisional System which he had designed to protect it, against much opposition and in the midst of constant danger.

Among the rebels the leaders of both the Fukienese and the Cantonese factions had issued proclamations; Liu Li-ch'uan asserted it was his mission to revive the Ming dynasty and cast out the Manchu barbarians, and soon also began to claim a connection with the Taipings at Nanking. The Triads wrote to Nanking asking to become affiliated, but the overture was not accepted. Meanwhile risings occurred all around Shanghai. The nearby walled cities of Paoshan, Kiating, Tsingpu, Nanhwei, and Chuansha were seized in succession. For almost a month the imperial power was difficult to find.[32]

At the beginning of October, however, the provincial authorities returned with troops and laid siege to Shanghai by land and by water. Just before the fall of Nanking six months before, in March 1853, the governor of Kiangsu, Yang Wen-ting, had formally asked the three treaty-power consuls at Shanghai to send gunboats to help save the southern capital, a request which was repeated with some urgency later in the month.[33] Again in May the same official, now acting governor-general, had deputed officers who went with Wu Taotai to approach each of the three consuls about borrowing warships — all without avail. But Wu Chien-chang still hoped to play the role of savior to the imperial cause. In April after the U.S.S. *Susquehannah* started for Nanking with Commissioner Marshall aboard, ran aground, and came back, he boasted to his superiors that he had obtained its help from the Americans.[34] Meanwhile, realizing the value of foreign-style gunboats, he had continued his efforts to collect a fleet. In 1852 he had been able to send the schooner *Boxer* (Commodore Wang) and 12 other vessels against pirates at Ningpo. Now in April 1853 he bought two vessels, the *Agnes* and the *Antelope*, the latter a 370-ton Boston-built brig of Russell and Company's which three years previously had been making regular runs up from Hongkong with opium and back again with treasure and sundries. In June a Chinese fleet consisting of these two and another foreign-style vessel, the *Dewan*, together with 25 lorchas (foreign hull and Chinese rig), had gone up to Chinkiang. At last on September 29 an imperial fleet came down the Whangpu to Shanghai [35] and began a bloody three-day attack on the rebels.[f]

By land an imperial army advanced and besieged the walls of the city on the south, west, and northwest. By early November, the Manchu Chi-er-hang-a (contemporary romanization "Keih," also "Koerhangah") arrived upon the scene, sent from Peking to exterminate the Shanghai rebels. He proved himself an able officer and effective diplomat, became provincial treasurer in April 1854 and governor of Kiangsu a few months later.[40] The siege of the city was conducted from the first largely by militia (*yung*, "braves"), an irregular force recruited for the occasion and divided at Shanghai into a number of battalions, each having its own camp and bear-

[f] This imperial fleet was stated by the Chinese authorities to have consisted originally of thirty-two fishing smacks recruited from the Hsiang-shan district (Wu's native place) and paid for by the taotai, all under the command of local gentry.[36] By foreigners at Shanghai they were described simply as "West Coast pirate boats belonging to the notorious Apak fleet, but now locally engaged under Imperial auspices." [37] Reports of their exploits were equally at variance. The emperor was told of a naval victory off the Little East Gate on November 17 in which — after a four-hour bombardment during which the cannon sounded like thunder, the ground shook miles away, and 13,000 pounds of powder were used by the attackers — the west wind unfortunately proved too strong, the junks could not get near the shore and only managed to follow the wind and tide down to Wusung, having lost three men killed.[38] A foreign observer says of this engagement that "two junks . . . advanced close to the [rebel] battery, and running stem on, took the ground close to its guns . . . first one and then the other of the junks took fire and blew up, most of the crews being burned to death or shot down. The captains of these vessels were brave men, and did their best, but were too confident . . . [the imperial] fleet of junks was so much injured that the crews refused to engage the battery again, except at a distance." [39]

ing the name of a particular province.[g] After a siege of a year and a half, during which the population fell roughly from 200,000 to 40,000, the city of Shanghai was at last set on fire in February 1855 and the destruction of private property and public buildings completed. Among the latter were the taotai's yamen inside the Great East Gate, used as rebel headquarters, two public granaries, the yamen of the coast defense sub-prefect recently built inside the West Gate, and that of the district magistrate with the various minor offices connected with it — most of which had to be completely rebuilt.[42]

In the face of all this disorder, alarm, and popular suffering, of which the official records recount not a hundredth part, what was the attitude of the foreign community at Shanghai? The *Shanghai Almanac for 1854* lists some 270 male residents (an increase of over 100 since 1850). Of this number over 30 were temporarily absent; 40-odd had families. About a dozen were Parsee merchants. Including the opium receiving station at Wusung (but not the two or three war vessels usually on hand) Shanghai had a settled male population of less than 250 Europeans, less than one fifth of whom were married. Fully one third of the married men were among the two dozen missionaries who represented six or seven different missonary boards. Four-fifths of the male British population were between the ages of 19 and 35, and two-fifths between the ages of 25 and 30. Thus the great majority of the population were young bachelors, engaged in trade as partners or assistants in one or another of the three dozen mercantile firms, or else catering to the community.[43] In April 1853 a British volunteer corps had been organized, in which Vice-consul Thomas Francis Wade became an officer, and an American defense committee had been appointed.[44] They were custodians of unsaleable merchandise to the value of £2,000,000 which had been accumulating for six months in the dozen big warehouses and many smaller ones that lined the west bank of the Whangpu. With letters taking two months to London, the deluge of shirtings and woolens had continued unabated long after the import trade had stopped early in 1853. Thus when Shanghai fell, considerations both of self and of duty had led the foreign settlement to make itself an armed camp, from which all Chinese troops, rebel and imperialist alike, had to be excluded.

In this tense atmosphere the return of Wu Chien-chang in October raised the question of the reinstatement of his authority as superintendent of customs. A divergence now emerged between the views of Commissioner

[g] Thus after the fall of Shanghai the gentry of Kiangsu advised the enlistment of 1000 Szechwan braves, and in the report of the battle of Muddy Flat between the imperial and foreign forces in April 1854 mention is made of Szechwan, Kweichow, Kwangtung-and-Kwangsi, Hunan, Chekiang, and Ch'ao (i.e., Ch'aochoufu, Kwangtung) battalions.[41] Whether each battalion had its nominal complement of 500 men is uncertain. That it was recruited from the province of which it bore the name is doubtful. The regular Chinese provincial force (*Lü-ying* or Army of the Green Standard) was also nominally present, but according to foreign estimates only added to the confusion.

Marshall and those of Consul Alcock. The former felt himself bound to recognize the taotai's authority and tried to abolish the Provisional System at the end of October; but the British consul stuck to his guns, Marshall was defeated, and the Provisional System continued.

The United States Commissioner had a simple view of the customs problem. He regarded the resumption of duty collections in specie as an expression of faith in the treaties more than as a problem of administration. Vice-consul Wade reported that "being strongly in favour of paying the Emperor his just dues [Marshall] talks (as a matter worthy of consideration) of reinstating the Taotai as Superintendent of Customs apart from any jurisdiction as Taotai."[45] On September 20, Marshall wrote to the governor-general, I-liang, explaining the Provisional System as a device to preserve "the duties due, under the treaty, for your Emperor, when his officers are not able to collect or ascertain them."[46]

This Manchu official to whom the situation at Shanghai had thus been reported was a man of great experience and proven ability, whose long career in the service of three emperors was just drawing to its close. I-liang had been a prefect in Kwangtung as early as 1828, and in the following ten years had held high office in the provincial administrations of Kwangsi, Yunnan, Shantung, Anhwei, and Kiangsu. Transferred from the acting governorship of Kiangsu in 1838 to be governor of Kwangtung, he had remained in the thick of the Anglo-Chinese struggle that followed — Lin Tse-hsü's right hand man in fighting opium, acting superintendent of customs (Hoppo) for a time, a successful opponent of Ch'i-shan's conciliatory policy of 1840 and his successor temporarily, later an imperial commissioner and governor-general of Fukien and Chekiang. All this before 1843, when he retired because of illness. Now, having re-entered the emperor's service in 1852 and become governor-general of Kiangsu, Anhwei, and Kiangsi early in 1853,[47] I-liang was remarkable as one of the few principal actors in the tragedy of 1840–42 who had not been destroyed by his part in it. He was still an officer to whom the investigation of corruption charges and the overhauling of administrative regulations were constantly being entrusted. In 1853, however, his chief concerns were the feeding and paying of armies, to defend his provinces and the empire. Barbarian affairs at Shanghai could occupy but a small part of his attention.

I-liang replied to the American commissioner on October 8, with no little flattery, that Wu Taotai "seems disposed to maintain fidelity and honesty and is ready to try to retrieve what has been lost" and would shortly return to Shanghai and resume his duties as customs collector.[48] The taotai on October 10 officially informed both the British and American consuls[49] that, although his official seal of superintendent of customs had been lost with the city, he had, by appeal to his superiors, been deputed to use the seal of office of the director-general of grain transport of Ch'ang-chou and conduct all customs business as formerly.[h] Alcock, with Bonham's support, excluded Wu Chien-chang from the foreign settlement.[i] Undaunted, Wu Chien-chang returned to the attack from another angle, claiming the duties incurred by 10 British vessels before September 7, amounting to Tls. 45,000-odd. As to duties after September 7, either the foreign consuls on his behalf could enter them in a shipping journal and present periodic statements, to be passed on to the taotai's superiors; or he could arrange for the inland customhouses, on the main routes to Shanghai, to report entries in their books of tea and silk brought through by native merchants, from whom the taotai would proceed to collect the duties. These inland customhouses had already been ordered "to archive together every note of entry" of goods examined by them. Which of these courses would Alcock prefer? [53]

Alcock replied that the accounts of the ten British ships, which could only be closed by the customs officers, had in fact been left open when they fled on September 7. The Provisional System had taken care of them. The emperor was bound to protect British trade against unequal competition; and yet the absence of the Chinese customhouse allowed ships of other nations to go free. Efforts to collect from Chinese merchants the duties admittedly due by British merchants could only lead to "acts of reprisal" disastrous to the imperial interest.[54] The consul thus met threat with threat, and discussion ceased on October 18.

Marshall's response to the taotai's appeal on October 14 had been as clearly affirmative as Alcock's had been negative. He became alarmed at Alcock's refusal to reinstate the taotai, a position "so extraordinary and untenable." Always jealously suspicious of British designs, he saw in the posting of marines, the establishment of guardhouses, and similar measures, an approach to British political control of Shanghai, and he resolved to force the recognition of the taotai's authority. On October 24 he ordered Vice-consul Cunningham to suspend the Provisional Regulations.[55] Meanwhile he did not hesitate to notify the American merchants that the Pro-

[h] It was explained to the emperor that at the time when the rebels seized Shanghai, Wu Taotai had been hastening to Kiating to deal with the rising there but, on hearing of the trouble at Shanghai, had at once come back, and near the New Lock (Sinza) had met and fought with a rebel band, with the result that the official seal of the Su-Sung-T'ai Taotai and superintendent of maritime customs for Kiangnan, which he carried with him, had fallen into the water and been lost; and while it might be fished out sometime, it would not be very useful.[50]

[i] Bonham wrote "with reference to this individual," the taotai, that it would be imprudent to let him again take refuge in the foreign settlement, "there to concoct his schemes against the rebels." His presence would violate neutrality and might provoke a rebel attack to capture him.[51] If the taotai's own guards could not be admitted, because their presence would endanger British property, it was no less impossible to supply him with foreign support, which would violate neutrality.[52] Convinced of this even before he heard from his superior, Alcock coolly replied to the taotai, "As soon as the city of Shanghai is retaken by the Imperial troops and Your Excellency's establishment fairly reinstated in the Custom House, I shall be prepared to enter into further consideration with you of the question of Duties."

visional Regulations would cease on October 28, even though he had no assurance that a Chinese customhouse would take their place.

This public notification coerced the taotai into acting. On October 26 Wu informed the American vice-consul that he had received instructions to station one or two boats in the river off Putung Point, opposite that part of the foreign settlement farthest north from the besieged city, and transact customs business on board until the capture of Shanghai city should allow a reinstatement of the customs within the settlement as before. War vessels would soon appear for this purpose, until which time the taotai asked that the Provisional System be continued. He reiterated this request on October 27. Cunningham was immovable and asked to be notified where collections would be made.[56]

The 28th of October dawned and no word had come from Wu Chien-chang. The vice-consul appealed in haste for Marshall's instructions. But the commissioner could only add further confusion.[j] The leading American firms followed a simpler course and addressed identical letters to the representatives in Shanghai of Great Britain, France, Portugal, Holland, Prussia, and Hamburg — all the consuls there were — asking "whether, in case we desired to ship in vessels under any of (their) flags, (they) recognized any Custom House establishment; and if so, where situated?" This farce was complete when the representatives of Portugal (T. C. Beale, British merchant), of Holland (T. C. Beale, British merchant), of Hamburg (Wm. Hogg, British merchant), and of Prussia (D. O. King, partner of one of the American firms addressing the letter) all replied in chorus that they recognized no customhouse.[58]

Meanwhile, had a floating customhouse really been maintained or had it not? The evidence is fragmentary. Wu Chien-chang appears to have moored the *Antelope* and the *Agnes* off Putung Point, but he was powerless to prevent the enforcement of foreign neutrality. The *Antelope* was known to be a "crazy craft," not provided with proper magazines for her warlike stores. The two vessels moored off the Point were only twenty minutes' pull from the city and so might provoke a rebel sortie. Wu Chien-chang's not too well directed cannon, bombarding the rebels from the Putung side, had inadvertently sent a ball into the Catholic cathedral south of the city. As

[j] He replied that if anyone wanted to clear under the Provisional System, he might. Or if anyone wanted to clear according to treaty but professed "to be hindered by the absence of the Chinese Superintendent of Customs from his place of business," he might hand in a declaration of that fact and of the amount of his duties. The vice-consul should then send this to the superintendent with a formal demand of his own that the latter should "receive the duties tendered and give the port-clearance, in order that [he might] deliver the ship's register and permit her to depart." If the taotai still failed to receive duties, "protest against his violation of the treaty in attempting by such conduct to lay an embargo upon American ships in this port." Or if the Taotai consented to pay a fair demurrage "for any vessel to be delayed by his delinquency," such vessel should be detained as long as the duty on the cargo would meet the demurrage. But if the Taotai failed to do even this, the consul should take note of the vessel and let it go.[57] How many of these programs were followed does not appear.

a result the French warship *Cassini* was reported to have ordered the *Antelope* higher up the river. On the same day it was also stated that "the Taoutae placed an armed boat opposite the Custom-house which, as likely to lead to collision with the insurgents, has been ordered off by the 'Spartan' [British gunboat] and is now lying in the Soochow Creek." These actions were not aimed at preventing the existence of a floating customhouse, but they were hardly conducive to its functioning. More definite was the *Herald's* report on November 5: "We hear that a Mandarin yesterday by the ex-Taotai's orders, attempted to take possession of (and no doubt will attempt again to establish himself at) the Custom House on the Foreign ground. The guard stationed there from H. M. S. 'Spartan' of course defeated the attempt." Later it was again stated that Samqua, established on the *Antelope*, "was driven away from among the foreign shipping, as a dangerous neighbour." [59] There is little doubt that the functioning of whatever floating customhouse the taotai may have hoped to create was prevented by foreign measures of self defense. His friend the American vice-consul summed up Wu Chien-chang's difficulties: "Can it be expected that where the collector has no oversight of the great bulk of the merchantmen visiting the port, no notice of their arrivals or departures, interdicted even from sending boats to make inquiries, — for the boats must be armed for their own protection and all armed boats have been turned from the foreign anchorage by the British force, — he will be able to perform his functions with regularity? It is tying a man's hands and feet in the water and upon the result denying that he can swim." [60] Consul Alcock admitted that the situation was much as Cunningham described it.

Just at this point, to complicate the confusion, the Austrian vessel *Robert*, which had been in port since October 4 and for which there was no consul, departed on October 29 completely untaxed and leaving no bond behind. Since the American merchants had been instructed to resume cash payments of duty, they were still further alarmed: the taxing of American vessels only, while others went free, would destroy the carrying trade in American bottoms, and they protested to their vice-consul on October 31. At this juncture, also, Commissioner Marshall decided to leave for Canton. His reasons were many but not clear; he evidently hoped for an interview at last with the imperial commissioner, Yeh Ming-ch'en, and wanted to discuss with him "the strange course of the British consul at Shanghai." [61] With the American commissioner on the little coastwise steamer *Lady Mary Wood* went the British consul's dispatches for Hongkong. Their contents show Alcock in his one moment of weakness. He had just received from Bonham the opinion of the attorney general of Hongkong, who believed the Provisional System to be unnecessary, and Alcock naturally felt keenly the magnitude of his personal responsibility. Early on November 1, he now asked Bonham to order the abandonment of the Provisional System so as to have identical policies at Amoy and Shanghai "in circumstances so exactly parallel." Alcock stated his own readiness to let the taotai receive the duties "however nominal his establishment may be." But when Wu Taotai's announcement of his floating customhouse (dated October 26) reached the consul later on the same day (November 1), he replied that the decision rested with Bonham. In the end, however, Bonham ducked the responsibility of stopping the Provisional System himself.

Meanwhile, after Marshall's departure, the American consulate quietly returned to the system of promissory notes which he had ordered abandoned.[62] Vice-consul Cunningham did not relish coercing his fellow merchants.

Smith, King and Company found merchants fearful lest goods in their American ship *Jennet* be compelled to pay duties in silver and appealed to the vice-consul, who asked the taotai whether "if she loads [the Jennet] can pay her duties in notes of hand to you, as English ships continue to do through the English Consulate." The taotai replied on November 29, "I here give my consent to such a movement." [63] Having thus slid back into the train of Consul Alcock, Cunningham departed for Foochow on business,[64] leaving no deputy other than the assistant in the consulate (presumably Pedro Loureiro, Jr., one of the seven assistants in Russell and Company). Whereupon as Cunningham phrased it later, "owing to a misunderstanding upon the part of the clerk of this consulate, the latter (instead of the Taotai) received the declarations and notes of the few vessels which subsequently cleared, and without my knowledge the business was transacted in this office as under the provisional system, with the exception of that of the 'Beverley.' " [65] On December 12 the Siamese ship *Favorite* left the port scot free under the same circumstances as the *Robert*. Meanwhile American vessels gave promissory notes containing the proviso, "payable if the sanction of the United States Government is obtained." [66] Thus American vessels continued to be cleared under the Provisional System. While the System continued to be applicable to that six-sevenths of the trade of Shanghai which was carried by British and American vessels, the seventh carried by vessels of non-treaty powers continued to go free.

Having been deserted by the Americans, Wu Chien-chang's floating customhouse continued to be intimidated by the British. In preserving the neutrality of the foreign anchorage, Alcock excluded from it the boats of the floating customhouse and thus by superior force proved what he had contended — that it was incompetent. It soon disappeared.[67]

Neutrality violated (the arms trade). An anomalous situation now ensued at Shanghai. The meeting of East and West, so often romanced upon, resulted in this case in the demoralization of both; the results were more sordid than romantic. In the ensuing months of 1853–55 officials became merchants, imperialists supported the rebels, consuls neglected their trust, neutrals profited from the arms traffic, and in the midst of all this buying and selling of goods and consciences, it became less and less likely that the imperial authorities would ever be able to re-establish their authority and so resume the collection of customs duties.

Foreign neutrality was first violated in spirit when foreign adventurers entered the fray on either side. Wu Chien-chang had added to his navy by hiring fifteen hundred pirate-fishermen from the region of Macao, near his early home, who arrived at Shanghai in the beginning of November in 30-odd drag-net fishing smacks, mounting 360 guns in all.[68] Vessels of this sort, as well as "fast-crab" boats, had already been ordered from Kwangtung to clear the Yangtze of rebels, and in December the emperor commanded their use at Shanghai.[69] Wu Chien-chang's flotilla was hired for six months at $8 per man a month, but after a few successes the fishermen-pirates refused to fight their Cantonese brethren and spent their time in plundering and rapine on shore; half the boats were sent back to Kwangtung but the remainder got beyond the taotai's control and remained as an added scourge on the populace.[70] Meanwhile Wu's officers had not ignored the opportunity offered by the presence of unattached foreign seamen and vagabonds, a fly-by-night and reckless population whose members lived riotously along the Yangkingpang until lack of funds should force them to sea again. As the imperial fleet continued its operations, burning at one time 1500 houses in Lung-hua and other suburbs up the river and frequently engaging the rebel fleet, reports began to appear of the foreigners who were vigorously sailing and shooting for the taotai. By their help were captured with no little butchery the two foreign vessels *Snipe* and *Glenlyon* which the Triads had bought. But the fight was not one-sided, for foreigners in the rebel fleet, equally numerous, helped against the taotai. In a fight on November 3, what with stinkpots, gingals, and solid shot, the *Antelope* was almost ruined. By that time the taotai's fleet included, in addition to those vessels already mentioned, the 346-ton barque *Sir Herbert Compton,* the 143-ton schooner *Clown*, both ex-opium clippers, the *Eliza* and a number of Portuguese lorchas. The commanders included Chinese and Portuguese and a certain Robinson, in connection with whom other foreigners were mentioned.[71]

While western desperadoes were fighting for either side indiscriminately, the missionaries in the foreign settlement had not forgotten their calling either, and continued to enter the besieged city day by day and week by week to preach and minister to their flocks.[72] In the first month of the siege the medical missionary, Dr. Lockhart, whose new hospital had been erected by British subscriptions in 1846 just outside the North Gate of the city, had already amputated for the imperial cause "two thighs, two legs, two arms, and one foot." In the next six weeks he performed thirteen more such operations, besides innumerable minor services — dressing, bandaging, housing, feeding, removing balls from, and setting bones for, an endless flow of wounded, 60 or 70 of whom were always in his hospital. Within the city the doctor saved lives for the Triads also, although their cannon were continually sending solid shot over, around, and even into his premises outside the gate. That this and other places occupied by foreigners suffered no serious injury was most remarkable.[k]

Foreign neutrality was violated perhaps most effectively by those merchants of the Shanghai community who sold food and ammunition to the rebels. For the first year of the siege there was no impediment to non-combatants coming and going between the city and the French settlement adjoining it on the north; consequently the blockade of the city could not be made effective. I-liang and Hsü Nai-chao, governor of Kiangsu, stated the problem succinctly to the emperor in November 1853: "Barbarian establishments are spread out in the district outside the walls to the northeast. The barbarians in question fear that when the imperial troops approach the North Gate to make an attack, the rebels within the city will in return fire guns and cannon and it will be difficult for the barbarian establishments to avoid being injured; they are (therefore) hindering the imperial troops from attacking on the northeast. At present along the Yangkingpang and elsewhere there are barbarians on guard; even a few soldiers, braves, or scouts cannot advance toward those places. As to the rebels' rice and grain and gunpowder, it is highly probable that they have been secretly transported by this road to supply their needs." [74] Thus foreign neutrality impeded the attackers, as was to happen again in the 1930's.

Food supplies, to be sure, did not come entirely from foreign sources.[l] But with munitions of war it was different. Foreigners could best supply them, and did so, for a price. It was reported to Peking that "barbarian gunpowder which heretofore sold for three foreign silver dollars a keg has now risen in price to twenty-five or -six dollars. Without any doubt it is due to the rebels' buying it at all prices and to the treacherous barbarians secretly selling it for profit." [76] Before the siege was over "a deserter from

[k] One day a rebel gunner on the wall did begin to amuse himself by taking pot shots at the hospital; but Dr. Lockhart "hastened to the bastion where the gun was placed, and called out to the gunner to know what he was about . . . I insisted that he should cease his amusement . . . The man laughed, and said he did not wish to do me any harm, but as I disliked it he would not fire any more." [73]

[l] "When the day's fighting was over, the country people from the neighbouring villages would approach the walls with rice, vegetables, fish and other provisions, which . . . were hoisted over the wall. . . Hundreds of people might often be seen along the top bargaining for these articles. . . . This lasted until the Imperialists . . . caught several villagers engaged in the trade, and cut off their ears as a warning to others: this failing, they next beheaded a few and stuck the heads on poles in the road, with labels attached to them, 'Traitorous provision sellers.' " But for a long time rice remained almost as cheap inside the city as out.[75]

the marines on board an English ship of war," nicknamed the "conchologist," was said to have taught the Triads how to make brass shells, though very imperfectly.[77]

The imperial authorities were well aware of the foreign assistance which the Triads received — indeed they probably had an exaggerated opinion of its importance. Liu Li-ch'uan had at first issued proclamations stamped with the seal of a foreign trading company.[78] Several of his subordinates had had contact with the barbarians, one of the fiercest of them, Ch'en Ah-lin, having acquired a good command of English as a *ma-fu*, the sobriquet of "Skinner's horse-boy," and a pair of English shoes and stockings.[79] As time wore on and the Triad cause flourished, the provincial authorities began to report instances of foreign obstruction, partly as an excuse for their failure to recapture the city, but with feelings of real indignation. On January 13, 1854, when the expectant prefect Hsueh Huan had routed a Triad force, the latter could not be prevented by the foreign guards from escaping through the Yangkingpang region but their pursuers were stopped short. The British consul promptly apologized to Hsueh Huan, on demand, and was sharply reproved by Wu Chien-chang in addition. Again it was reported that on January 16 the rebels had been on the verge of defeat at the South Gate when suddenly a great many men wearing foreign clothes rushed out of the gate, hindered the imperial advance, and so saved the day for the Triads.[80] An active protest against foreign armament-selling was made by Chi-er-hang-a, the local imperial commander, in the middle of November 1853. Three or four hundred imperial troops, equipped with fire-pots and fire-bags, on the evening of the 14th rushed into the foreign settlement. Others landed from the river and made for the customhouse. Their object was to seize three cannon in a foreign hong, destined for the rebels. Foreign sailors and marines landed and expelled the intruders, who left six or seven dead. "A few foreigners received some slight flesh wounds."[81] Explanations ensued on all sides, Chi-er-hang-a claiming that rebels dressed as foreigners had fired on the imperialists first. Alcock issued a notification forbidding the sale of arms to the rebels but adding that the opposition of public opinion was the only thing that could really bring it to a stop.[82]

This last was a most significant statement. No British consul would relish reporting that his local community were out of hand, and none of Alcock's dispatches makes so bald a statement. Yet to Wu Chien-chang, or so Wu said,[83] Consul Alcock had spoken of the fact that "the dutiful barbarian merchants of every country hated the rebels' occupation of the city and the confusion they caused which stopped the sale of goods, but were only two tenths (of the community). Those who hoped to evade the payment of duties and supplied the rebels with gunpowder and food, fishing for profit, were actually eight tenths. Their consular officers were few. It was difficult to look after everything." [m]

What was the attitude of the Chinese authorities toward this traffic which made the recovery of Shanghai impossible? Here it is necessary to uncover the full duplicity of Wu Chien-chang. In July 1854 accusations reached Peking that Wu had all along been in league with both the rebels and the barbarians. In due course these charges were investigated and largely substantiated (April 1855) by Huang Tsung-han, the nearby governor of Chekiang (later imperial commissioner at Canton in 1858). As a result, Wu was condemned and banished (only to rise phoenix-like from his disgrace and become active at Shanghai again in 1856). The censor who impeached him recited facts we have already noted [n] and wound up with the point that Wu had set up the Ch'i-ch'ang company with the barbarians. This was the climax of the impeachment; for the food, powder, and balls of the rebels within the city were supplied by this Ch'i-ch'ang company.[85] Huang's report recited stories of how Wu had released to the company contraband of theirs which had been seized in transit; on one occasion he was said to have gone to the Ch'i-ch'ang premises in company with Liu Li-ch'uan and thence boarded a steamer in the river to hold a conference with the rebel chief. This last was not regarded by Huang as having been proved, nor had it been ascertained whether Wu, "when he and the American barbarians went into business in the Ch'i-ch'ang company, had a written agreement or not." But the taotai's guilt was overwhelming and the impeachment of July 1854 was amply sustained.[86] The evidence is concluded by the fact that Ch'i-ch'ang was the Chinese name of Russell and Company. In its "List of Foreign Hongs" at Shanghai, the *Shanghai Almanac for 1854* gives the following: "K'e-Chang, Russell & Co., Griswold, J. N. A., absent,

[m] In confirmation of this Wu had already reported a case of which he sent proof to Peking. Sometime in November his men had seized a Ningpo fishing boat in which were three barbarians, a straight double-edged sword, sixty guns, forty other swords, all foreign style, a package of foreign saltpetre and a jar of powder. One of the barbarians had a barbarian letter bearing the characters *T'ai-p'ing t'ien-kuo*, which proved to be from the treacherous English merchant *Le-na-t'u* (a foreigner's name) to the rebel chief at Chinkiang, Lo Ta-kang, and enclosed a letter from Liu Li-ch'uan. The boatman confessed that the barbarians had hired the boat to carry arms to Chinkiang for sale to the rebels, and that another boat similarly loaded had been following, but escaped. "*Wen-na-chih*" and the two other barbarians were sent to the British consul to be punished, the arms were given to the troops, and the letters seized were sent to the Grand Council at Peking.[84]

[n] The impeachment recounted how the "entire rebel party were all the said taotai's trained militia," how Wu had been warned of the rising, had fled to stay on a barbarian boat, and had left for the rebels the customs duties and subscriptions in his treasury; how the guileless Governor Hsü had believed Wu could control the barbarians and so had sheltered him and then been coerced by him; how Wu had been in foreign trade at Canton and had been relied on by the high authorities for his knowledge of English, while the barbarians made sport of him; further, how the fleet of fishing boats for which he pretended to have paid had actually got out of his control, plundered and rioted on shore, and been supported from customs funds; how customs affairs had been entirely in Wu's hands, he had concocted the barbarian chiefs' plans for them, irritated their merchants into non-payment of duties by letting Cantonese friends go duty free, shipped his peculated gains back to Kwangtung, and generally got involved with the barbarian merchants, who knew all about his crimes.

Cunningham, E., Crampton, J., Pierce, G. W., Loureiro, P. Jr.," and so on.

This makes a clear pattern. The taotai had remained at heart, as he had been at first, a merchant. What more natural than to deal as a merchant with his official peer the American vice-consul, who was also a merchant? There is some circumstantial evidence of this — Wu's purchase of Russell and Company's *Antelope*, his seeking refuge under their roof, his much touted understanding of the barbarians (among whom the British consul was not his closest friend), his various dispatches to Cunningham, asking him at one point to settle the duty question as he thought best; Wu's report to his superiors that he was secretly conspiring with the American and French chiefs in order to isolate the British.[87] All this and more besides indicates close personal relations of some sort with the American vice-consul. The evidence is not entirely limited to circumstance: a letter from an American signed "O. P. Q.," in the *Hongkong Register* of November 8, 1853, asks Cunningham point-blank: "Did you not sell your opium-clipper the *Antelope* to Samqua? Did you not furnish her sails, stores, and armament? Was she not fitted for service by a person in your employ? Did you not charter to Samqua your opium-receiving barque, the *Science*, with her armament, crew, and Captain? Did not the *Science* hoist Samqua's flag and proceed up the Yan-tze-kiang for the purpose of aiding the Imperialists?" On the other hand, we have Edward Cunningham's public denial in April 1854 that either he or his firm had ever had business connections with the taotai.[88]

Writing anonymously two years later, Alcock made this summary: "There were acts of foreigners at Shanghai — in which some at least of the parties concerned were merchants, and persons of more or less repute — *for which it is impossible to set up any valid defense in the eyes of the Chinese*, or indeed any impartial person, — some acts springing from licentiousness. . . . Others helped the people for *profit*, and thus, open sympathy, counsel, food, guns, and ammunition, passed daily from a foreign settlement, held sacred from the intrusion of imperial troops on the ground of absolute neutrality, into a blockaded city, with the professed object of prolonging the defense against the Emperor's forces!"[89] The result was that, as long as the taotai did not control the customs and the settlement boundaries sufficiently to prevent foreign goods reaching the Triads, he could not re-establish his political authority at Shanghai; but so long as he could not re-establish his authority, Alcock would not allow him to resume control of the customs. This circle was none the less vicious because the taotai helped to preserve it.

The reinstatement of the taotai. Although the rebels were not expelled from the city until February 1855, the Provisional System came to an end a year earlier. Chinese and American opposition to it became more energetic in January. Fortunately instructions from London arrived in time to afford Consul Alcock a graceful exit, and a Chinese customhouse under Wu Chien-chang's authority resumed the collection of duties in cash on February 9, 1854.

Pressure from the Chinese side to abolish the Provisional Rules came chiefly from the provincial authorities. Their superiors in Peking in the autumn of 1853, when a Taiping horde had entered Shansi and was still advancing toward the capital, could have little concern for a distant seaport. Although the fall of Shanghai was known in Peking at the end of September, an edict of October 20 still regarded the recapture of the city as merely a first step in the larger campaign against Nanking.[90] Barbarian sales of supplies to the rebels were reported to Peking in November; an edict in the usual general terms urged that means be devised to control the barbarians and prevent their collusion with the rebels; whereupon the vagabonds [91] in the city could be invested and their support cut off. This hope was reiterated by I-liang and Hsü Nai-chao in a memorial of February 21, 1854; but they added a practical program: "Wu Chien-chang thinks that it is necessary to send secret dispatches to Fukien, Chekiang, and Kiangsi to issue circular instructions to the merchants transporting Huchow silk and teas, that if there are any bringing their goods to Shanghai for sale all are to be stopped; that after the recapture of the city it will then be permitted to bring goods and sell them as before. The barbarian chiefs will lose their normal profit and necessarily desire the speedy recapture of the city. Naturally they can then make strict official inquiries and investigations; (consequently) the treacherous barbarians who help the rebels will certainly draw in their horns." Hsü Nai-chao had already written secretly to the governor of Chekiang (Huang Tsung-han) and the governor of Kiangsi to examine the matter and act accordingly.[92]

In actual fact the policy thus tardily enunciated in Chinese official correspondence had already been inaugurated. In November the American firm of Smith, King and Company, bringing out teas from Hangchow, had their teas detained by imperial troops at Sungkiang. Mr. David O. King as Prussian consul issued a pass allowing the goods to be brought on, but to no avail. Wu Chien-chang, when applied to, on November 21 admitted that he had been able previously to help the American consul (Russell and Company) secure the release of goods similarly detained, by asking Chi-erh-hang-a to give the necessary order. But recently the high provincial authorities had ordered that northern and southern stations be re-established on the trade routes leading to Shanghai, and that all dutiable goods passing those stations from Shanghai be accompanied by a document from the superintendent of customs, while native tea and silk merchants coming to Shanghai were either to report at the north or south station or at Wu Chien-chang's movable customs office.[93] In other words inland stations had been established at which if so desired the trade of Shanghai might be taxed, although the channels of trade had not yet been blocked. In December further steps were taken to make this extra-treaty-port taxation effective.[o]

Involved as Wu Chien-chang may have been in lining his own pockets at the expense of the imperial cause, it seems evident that he was actively engaged in trying to break the Provisional System. Foreign mercantile opinion was growing daily more opposed to paying up the promissory notes which had been taken by Alcock and Cunningham. If the System continued to operate, the evasions under it would steadily increase, and the validity of all the promissory notes steadily decrease. Alcock was aware of this also, and on January 14, 1854, he drew Wu's attention to evasions being practised at Wusung.[95]

Meanwhile Humphrey Marshall also sought to abolish the Provisional System.[96] Vice-consul Cunningham apparently did not disclose to him until the end of December that American vessels were clearing not through cash payments but under notes identical with the British, and so Marshall had protested to the imperturbable Yeh Ming-ch'en that American ships alone paid their duties, whereas French ships went free. Actually, there was no French shipping at Shanghai, but on the strength of such arguments Marshall decided under date of January 4 to declare Shanghai a free port for American vessels. His aim seems to have been to embarrass Great Britain more than to aid China, for he did not anticipate a return to cash collections by the Chinese and he must have foreseen that if American ships went free they would provide the best excuse [97] for not paying to China the promissory notes already given.[p]

At Shanghai, through Cunningham's tardily reported inadvertence (as Marshall failed to grasp) there had been no inequality in the conditions of payment by British and American ships. Hence the American official could hardly turn upon his British colleague with a sudden grievance. But on January 14 the long-vanished floating customhouse, which so far had cleared no ships of any sort, suddenly returned to official life. On that

[o] A proclamation dated January 12, 1854, addressed to the Chinese merchants and not made known directly to the foreign consuls, stated that Wu Chien-chang had written to Hsü Nai-chao, asking that the governors of Chekiang and Kiangsi be requested to prevent silk and tea merchants from bringing their goods into Kiangsu, and that the Hangchow customhouse ("Pihsin Kwan") be instructed to stop all goods on the way to Shanghai until peace should be restored. On December 21 the official issuing the proclamation had learned from the govenor of Kiangsu that he had already done as requested by Wu Chien-chang, and therefore it was now notified to all customs subordinates, authorized brokers, and others that goods bound for Shanghai must be stored for the time being until the rebels should be defeated.[94]

[p] Marshall wrote to Commodore Perry on December 26 ("confidential," "6 A.M.") that Yeh had not answered his protest, Shanghai would be declared a free port for American vessels, and "in the desperation to which such an order may reduce the Imperial officers at Shanghai, I cannot foretell the kind of remedy they may attempt to apply . . . but most probably *it will be one of force.*" Could the Commodore accompany him to Shanghai and Nanking in a steamer? Commodore Perry regretted that his plans for Japan must take precedence.[98]

day, the taotai received for the American ship *Beverley*, A. Heard and Company consignees, a promise to pay duties "provided the duties are collected from all Foreign ships which have loaded or discharged cargo at this port since the 7th September 1853 with the sanction of their respective Governments."[99] For this note Wu Taotai gave a port clearance, for which the *Beverley* received its papers from the United States Consulate. She did not sail until January 18. The shippers had obliged Cunningham by giving Wu Chien-chang a note which had no more validity — whether or not the taotai knew it — than the notes given under the Provisional System, but which would testify to the existence of the alternative system which Marshall had ordered in October.[100]

In order to avoid declaring Shanghai a free port, Vice-consul Cunningham acted on a clause of last resort which Marshall had inserted in his ultimatum. He asked Alcock if he would agree, in Marshall's words, to "the administration of Customs by the Chinese Superintendent on a credit system, the obligations being given at the Custom House by the shippers directly and absolutely, and without reference to the will or upon a condition over which another government has control." To this terse proposal Alcock replied as briefly, "without very clearly understanding the purport . . . whenever an Imperial Custom House is re-established here, British consignees will be required to pay their duties in the manner set forth by our treaty." Having worked out no alternative, the American vice-consul on January 20 notified his fellow citizens that he would deliver up the papers of American ships without requiring a "Chinese Custom house clearance as long as vessels under other foreign flags are allowed by the Chinese" to clear under the Provisional System. "The moment the custom house regulations are enforced upon all foreign vessels, a return to them will be required" of American vessels.[101]

Just at this moment the four and a half months cycle of correspondence with London was dramatically completed, and Consul Alcock received Clarendon's instructions of November 1853. Sir George Bonham also instructed him to meet the American claim for a free port by demanding equal treatment. Four British vessels had already gone free from Wusung and other evasions of consular authority were being planned. The Provisional System had served its purpose. The tea and silk seasons were over and a change might be made without upsetting the export trade. Alcock therefore asked Wu Chien-chang on January 30 "to state how soon you will be enabled to establish the Custom House in a fitting locality and on the footing provided by Treaty." Wu Taotai replied that his temporary customhouse was established on the north side of the Soochow creek, outside the settlement on the far side from the walled city. A joint notification of the three treaty-power Consuls, Alcock, Cunningham, and Edan, confirmed the reopening of this new customhouse on February 9, 1854.[102]

The results attained by foreign consular administration. After an interregnum of five months, nearly the whole of one season, the taotai had now been reinstated. The new location of his customhouse, outside the settlement, and the hostility of the merchants, accustomed to what they regarded as the free trade of the Provisional System, boded ill for his future collections. What had been the results of the foreign stewardship?

Between September 9, 1853 and February 9, 1854, 84 foreign vessels had departed from the port of Shanghai, not counting four or more British ships which had gone free from Wusung.[103] They amounted to some 42,000 tons of shipping under the flags of nine foreign nations; and the duties normally due upon them would have been some Tls. 887,000. No one of them had paid duties in specie. Nine of them had given no promise to pay. The rest had given declarations and promissory notes to their respective consuls, except one (*Beverley*) which had given a mocking promise to the taotai. What were the taotai's chances of collecting the duties due to China from these vessels?

Of the total of 84 ships, 45 were British and 28 were American; none at all were French. Consul Alcock held promissory notes for all 45 British ships, for duties amounting to Tls. 478,200, or well over half the total collection possible.[104] After receiving from home the opinion of the Board of Trade, he had, however, notified the taotai in accordance with that opinion that "British merchants are not to be required, unless the trade of all other nations since the capture of Shanghai be shown to have been equally taxed, to make payment of the duties ordinarily leviable." [105] This proviso, so logical in London, was a mockery in Shanghai, for vessels of non-treaty powers were outside the scope of the treaties, just as they were beyond the weak grasp of the taotai, whose hands were tied by the enforcement of foreign neutrality. Seven non-treaty vessels had departed leaving no declarations or promises of any kind.[106] Four or five others had left under flags of non-treaty powers giving declarations and promissory notes, which generally contained an impossible proviso.[107] Finally, Marshall's effort to force the hand of the British had further damaged the taotai's chances. In addition to 25 ships cleared by the American vice-consul under declarations and promissory notes similar to those for British ships, one American vessel (*Beverley*) had cleared under a bond to the taotai containing a proviso impossible of fulfilment, and two more (*Oneida* and *Science*) had gone entirely free after Cunningham's declaration of free trade on January 20. In these circumstances it was impossible to fulfill the conditions of equal duties upon all, demanded by the Board of Trade.

If the promissory notes should be held valid, the amount of duties evaded under the Provisional System ("under the best Custom House this port has ever seen," as Alcock phrased it) would be, according to his estimate, less than 10 per cent of the duties legally due on the total trade. This contrasted remarkably with the inefficiency of the Chinese customs administration. Moreover "the declarations made by the shippers . . . have been far closer to the truth than any Custom House Manifests as these are ordinarily filled in here," [108] as was only to be expected when foreign merchants dealt with their own consuls, in the same language and consciously upon their honor, and this also had insured greater equality than usual in the conditions of trade. The taotai's chances of collecting the back duties thus became a matter of interpretation for the British and American governments to decide.

In the five months during which the Provisional System had helped to keep the port open and the trade free from inland exactions, there had been shipped from Shanghai to England "not less than 18,000,000 lb. of tea and some 27,000 bales of silk, representing a trade of at least £2,200,000 sterling; and a revenue to the British Exchequer little short of the same amount." A part of this, if Shanghai had been closed, might have been diverted through other ports, but only at added cost and trouble. But Alcock confessed, "whether our national good faith may stand the better, or the large amount of duties guaranteed ever be paid, may both perhaps, but especially the latter, be less clear than could be desired, or I had once hoped. This other and unquestioned fruit of the course adopted [i.e., the exports noted above] will in any case remain and is of too much importance in reference alike to British trade and Revenue not to have been worthy of any effort it may have cost." [109] Similar feelings might have been expressed by an American administrator, if there had been one on the spot, for in the last six months of 1853 the American trade at Shanghai had reached a total value of over $5,250,000, the greater part of which was in exports of tea ($2,303,000) and silk ($1,807,000).[110]

Humphrey Marshall had sailed for home on January 27, 1854. No elaborate farewell attended his departure, although Yeh Ming-ch'en availed himself of the occasion to "trust that of late his blessings have been increasingly tranquil." [111] In the duty question at Shanghai he had set out to maintain the spirit of the American treaty by means of the Provisional System, conceiving it to be a strictly temporary measure. Finding that the British version of it was not equally temporary, and believing it to be an attempt to rob China, he had combatted it first by supporting the taotai, finally by denying the treaty. But each of these attempts to oppose the British and preserve the duties for China had in fact decreased the scope of the System and so weakened China's legal claim to the duties collected under it. Meanwhile Alcock had virtually administered the customs affairs of Shanghai, in spite of severe illness. But he had no idea at this time of keeping the Chinese customs administration under foreign control.[q] This is particularly interesting in view of the fact that it was Alcock who led the way six months later in installing foreign inspectors as consular deputies to run the Shanghai customhouse under the aegis of the taotai.

[q] In laying down his responsibility in February he wrote with evident relief, "as regards the present and future alike our course is now clear, the re-establishment of a Custom House fully recognized on the part of the three Treaty Powers relieving Foreign Consuls of all further responsibility. Nor even should the Imperialists again be driven from the Port, is it probable, after past experience, any attempt will in future be made by the former, to supply the place of the authorities, or in any way to meddle with the collection of duties."[112]

CHAPTER XXIII

SIR JOHN BOWRING AND THE FOREIGN INSPECTORATE 1854

IN THE FIVE MONTHS from March to July 1854 the customhouse re-established by Wu Chien-chang proved unable to collect duties impartially on all the foreign trade. The treaty system ceased to function and it was feared that the trade of Shanghai would be diverted elsewhere. But in this crisis the British and American officials on the spot were able to achieve a statesmanlike coöperation, and with the help of circumstances and of the promise to pay up most of the duties for which bonds had been taken from the foreign merchants, they persuaded the provincial Chinese authorities to sanction the experiment embodied in the Foreign Inspectorate.

The inauguration of this experiment in July 1854 was a constructive step of great significance. Yet it was distinctly contrary to the established policy of the British government since 1851; and through a misunderstanding on the part of the British minister, Sir John Bowring, the promise by means of which the Chinese authorities were persuaded to allow it, was broken by a decision of the British government made in England before the experiment was initiated. The introduction of foreign administrators into the Shanghai customs was also directly contrary to the deep-seated prejudice of the government in Peking and its policy of non-intercourse with the barbarians; and the provincial authorities appear to have taken the risk of allowing it (without reporting it to Peking) only because of their inability to placate the barbarians in any other way and still secure revenue to support their troops in the field against the Taiping rebels. Even so, the Foreign Inspectorate might not have been created if Wu Chien-chang had not been capable of the most unscrupulous knavery.

With the wisdom of retrospection it may appear that the foreign trade of China was bound to be regulated, by one means or another, in a manner satisfactory to the foreign powers. But within the framework of such an historical tendency, there undoubtedly were many possibilities, such as the more extensive political control of Chinese territory by foreign powers, which would have been far less desirable to China than the Maritime Customs Service by which the satisfactory regulation of foreign trade was finally achieved. Perhaps the story summarized below will prove to the reader that the establishment of the Foreign Inspectorate was an inevitable solution to the problem of customs administration. On the other hand, it may persuade him that it was an historical accident, fortuitous and fortunate.

The collapse of Wu Chien-chang's customhouse (*February-March*). At Peking the reopening of the new customhouse on the north bank of Soochow Creek went unnoticed. A memorial on February 16 (which reached Peking only on March 25) explained that from September 7, 1853, until November 20, when Wu established his temporary customhouse at the confluence of the Whangpu and Soochow Creek, no duties had been collected — as was doubtless quite true — for the reason that no merchant vessels had entered or left the port, which was decidedly not the case. From November 20 to December 30 only some Tls. 2,278 had been collected; and even this amount was reported as inland customs duties (*nei-ti shang-shui*) which it may actually have been — collected from Chinese and not foreign merchants. No official reference was made to the Provisional System nor to the reopening of the customhouse on February 9 which terminated it, and the authorities at Peking were left to expect little or no revenue from foreign trade at Shanghai until such time as the Triads could be ousted from the city.[1]

Although the reopening of the customhouse called for a return to the treaty system of collecting duties in cash at the time of landing or shipment, the necessity of defending themselves in the midst of local rebellion had enhanced the foreign merchants' natural independence of spirit, while the continued money stringency [2] and the unsaleability of imports had increased in their own minds the righteousness of their opposition to cash duties. Having, moreover, become accustomed to giving promissory notes of uncertain validity, the conscientious merchants could the more easily be led by their unconscionable brethren into the practice of open smuggling. The American claim to a free port on January 20 had induced several firms, both British and American, to ship teas and silks, duty free, down to Wusung, there to be stored on shore, "on board the opium receiving ships, and even on hired Chinese boats," [3] awaiting free shipment.

Finding on February 9 that some 4,000 tons of tea and silk had thus been sent out of port to Wusung, where the American vessel *Wild Duck* was already loading,[4] Wu Chien-chang applied to Consul Alcock for advice, preparatory to an attempt to confiscate "2,000 bales of silk and 8,000 chests of tea . . . waiting on board native and foreign craft" for free shipment from the opium station. Before he received the consul's reply, however, the taotai's officers had tried to board three of the opium receiving ships, *Folkestone, Ann Welsh,* and *Emily Jane,* reported to be holding British produce. They were promptly beaten for their temerity and one of them detained as a prisoner. The taotai's appeal to the British consul for redress and for authority to visit these ships gained only the reply that he would receive support against British subjects when he produced evidence against them. Meanwhile under the cloak of the opium trade and hence invisible to the consular eye, teas were shipped from Wusung in defiance of the Chinese authorities, who were helpless because they lacked proper legal evidence and because only foreigners could coerce foreigners.[5]

As usual, however, the taotai's plight was not so well advertised to the British government as that of the honest merchants, who demanded equal treatment.[6] The taotai, the consul, and the honest merchant were thus all three confounded by the open evasion of duties at Wusung. The taotai lacked the force and the consul the authority to prevent it, while the honest merchant felt himself unable to compete against it. The resulting tendency was for the taotai to get what revenue and profit he could by compounding with the smugglers for partial payments, while the consul alone tried to uphold the treaty system by counselling firmness to the taotai.[a] On or about February 13, the *Wild Duck* cleared from Wusung giving the taotai a promise to pay duties if the U. S. commissioner to China should "decide they are to be paid under the circumstances in which [the cargo] left port. Statement of quantity and description [of goods] hereafter to be made out in case payment is required"; but the bond was signed under protest because the ship had been loaded while Shanghai was a free port.[8] The American vessel *Helena* followed, without having entered port. On March 9 the *Sir Edward Ryan*, a British vessel, likewise left Wusung, having neither reported to the British consul nor paid duties to the taotai. By March 18, fifteen vessels had sailed. Seven had loaded at Shanghai and paid duties to the customhouse on Soochow Creek (4 British, 2 American, 1 Danish). Seven others had loaded at Wusung — of which two American ships gave bonds of a sort and the rest gave no account of cargo (3 British, 3 American, 1 Russian). The fifteenth was a Bremen ship, the *Aristides*, and the circumstances of its sailing on March 17 or 18 epitomized the situation and brought matters to a head.[9]

J. Trautmann, consignee of the outward cargo of the *Aristides*, was a member of the British firm of G. C. Schwabe and Company but, being himself a German, was amenable to no consular authority in Shanghai.[10] The *Aristides* had arrived at Shanghai on February 23 under the Bremen flag, consigned to J. Withington of Reiss and Company, who had sent an abstract of her manifest to the customhouse in Chinese. The latter contended subsequently that they thought the vessel Burmese and, as customary with Burmese vessels, gave permission for discharge of cargo without demanding that she be reported through a foreign consul. In this

[a] Alcock reported that Wu Chien-chang "several times wrote and came to me for advice, nor did I hesitate in each instance frankly to point out to him how easy and direct was the line of conduct he had to pursue if he adhered to Treaty stipulations; and how fatal to him and his Custom House would be any departure from it." [7]

way the *Aristides* was placed in the hands of J. Trautmann for the purpose of loading export cargo without having delivered up her papers. The import duties were paid in cash and promissory notes, and Trautmann began to load teas. Now the taotai had established the rule in 1850 that no foreign vessel could be reported to the customhouse except through some consul, and Palmerston in January 1851 had reversed Lord Aberdeen's decision of 1844 (that no British consul should become security for a foreign ship) by directing the British consuls to use their discretion in the matter, being careful always to take from consignees of foreign ships sufficient guarantees for the payment of all customs dues. From that time on, Alcock had copied the practice of the American consul, J. N. A. Griswold, and when a ship arrived under a flag not officially represented at Shanghai, but consigned to a British firm, he had usually satisfied the taotai's regulation by becoming security for it.[11] This would have been the customary procedure with the *Aristides*. When Trautmann, however, refused to deposit his papers with any foreign consul and likewise refused several applications to deposit them with the taotai, the latter was thus left without documentary means of coercion and without the formal help of a foreign consul. In this situation Wu apparently felt himself obliged to make the best bargain obtainable, and "despite of the volunteered and eager warnings of the British Consul [the *Aristides*] was permitted to leave the port under a compromise of duties of the most flagitious kind" [12] — namely a bond which promised to pay full duties on approximately half the cargo providing all other vessels in port paid almost full duties [b] on their entire cargoes.

The foreign community generally believed that when Wu Chien-chang went to see Trautmann personally, he had struck a bargain to his private advantage.[c] When Alcock demanded an explanation, Wu replied with ob-

[b] "I herewith promise to pay three days after demand to His Excellency, Woo, Taoutae, Superintendent of Customs, etc., etc. the sum of Six thousand two hundred and fifty Taels Sycee for duties on the Export cargo per *Aristides* provided that All the Vessels at present in Port, pay if not full duties at least (2) two taels per picul Tea, and (9) nine taels per picul Silk, duty on their entire Cargoes, the Vessels are the "Daniel Ross" "Daunebrog" "Dumfries" "Frederick 7" "John Wood" "Mandarin" "Mermaid" "Rose Standish" and "Bombay." Shanghae 17th March 1854. Signed J. Trautmann." [13]

This bond was made the less collectable by being in Trautmann's name and not in that of his firm. It provided for a full payment of duty, Tls. 6,250, on approximately one-half (2,500 piculs) of the *Aristides* cargo of tea. The treaty tariff was Tls. 2.5 per picul of tea and Tls. 10 per picul of silk.

[c] This was hotly denied by Wu's chief subordinate in the customhouse, a certain Lo Yuan-yu, in a letter to the *North China Herald*, which claimed that Wu had had to accept Trautmann's statement of the amount of his cargo, having no means of verifying it, and had been tricked by fair words. After first refusing to accept the promissory note, "at last after three days of much trouble H. E. gave the Grand Chop because he wished very much to be friendly with foreigners and thought Mr. Trautmann will not in the end do an injustice." [14] It was asserted by the officers who investigated Wu's misdeeds a few months later that in the spring of 1854 a Kwangtung merchant vessel came to Shanghai, and because it was an old acquaintance of the taotai's he remitted its duties, over forty thousand taels, with the result that the barbarian merchants became intractable.[15]

vious prevarications. J. Trautmann's complete account of the transaction was put on record and Alcock demanded that other vessels be allowed to clear on the same terms as the *Aristides*. This the taotai "refused except as a matter of favour and concession, and on the condition that I should not divulge the facts to the Consul of the United States." [16] Alcock thereupon let four British ships depart leaving in his hands conditional bonds for half duties like that left by Trautmann.[17] Since each signer of these bonds had bound himself to pay half duties providing all other signers paid more than half duties, the bonds automatically invalidated one another. They marked the birth of a bastard provisional system, which in its immediate effect obviated the need of cash payments like its legitimate predecessor; but which used, instead of bonds valid or not according to the decision of the home government, promissory notes for half duties that were absolutely worthless.

Wu Chien-chang saw his mistake, and on March 22 transmitted to Alcock, as from the imperial commissioner at Canton, a recommendation that the export duties at Shanghai should be wholly paid by the Chinese merchants, as at Canton, while the foreign merchants should continue to pay the import duties.[d] Since imports were now an almost negligible part of the legal trade, this proposal meant that the Chinese authorities would now forego tonnage dues entirely and would collect cash duties from the Chinese merchants, in lieu of having the foreign consuls collect worthless promises from the foreign merchants. The principle embodied in the treaties — that the Chinese authorities should collect from the foreign merchants — in its progressive decline had reached a seemingly final crisis. Alcock feared a complete stoppage of trade, or its diversion elsewhere.[19]

Chinese policy and the crisis at Shanghai (April). Since the maritime customs at Shanghai had yielded an official return of half a million taels in the first half of 1853,[20] why did the higher Chinese authorities not make more vigorous efforts to preserve this flow of revenue in the months after September 7? Several explanations may be offered. First, the fall of the walled city was a concrete excuse. We do not know how much revenue Wu Chien-chang was actually able to collect and pay informally; probably the Shanghai customs was still underestimated as a source of funds. In late 1853 Peking was in any case fully concentrated upon immediate survival, while the customs collector himself may have hoped to recover his revenue

[d] Three days later he informed Alcock, as from the Nanking governor-general, that since the evasion of duties forced the superintendent of customs "into discussions with the officials and merchants of different nations . . . to the great scandal of both . . . a change is therefore to be made. . . . Two stations are to be established . . . on the rivers inland. . . . As soon as these stations shall be established the responsibility of settling the duties thereat on all dutyable goods bound for Shanghai will be laid on the Chinese merchants. . . . As to the course to be pursued when peace shall have been restored, this can be considered afresh whenever the city of Shanghai shall have been recaptured." [18]

from the promissory notes due under the Provisional System — which he seems to have avoided reporting.[21] Wu's immediate superior, Hsü Nai-chao,[22] had seemingly complete confidence in him; possibly I-liang did also.[23] Behind all aspects of foreign affairs, finally, lurked the fear that the barbarians would seize the opportunity afforded by "domestic disorder" to perpetrate "foreign aggression," particularly by lending aid to the Taipings. Every incursion of a foreign vessel into the Yangtze was carefully watched and promptly reported to Peking. When the war steamer *Cassini*, for instance, reached Nanking with the French minister on December 6, 1853, the fact was known in Peking by December 20. The emperor commented [24] that if results could soon be achieved (against the rebels), the barbarians naturally would not dare continue to lie in wait for an opportunity.[e] There was a special fear that the barbarians might interfere with the transport of rice by sea to the capital [27] (as Consul Alcock had done at Shanghai at the time of the Tsingpu affair in 1848).

To this general suspicion of barbarian designs was added the plain fact that the rebels who held Shanghai continued to get extensive support from the foreign community just outside the walls to the northeast. The siege of the city had progressed with unforeseen and disconcerting slowness. Hsü Nai-chao in January 1854 was excoriated by Peking for his ineptitude in listening to rebel overtures for peace, as a result of which his delegate and the pro-imperialist supporters within the city had been killed and the defenses strengthened.[28] Edict after edict castigated him for his inability to end the siege, pointing out that Shanghai was a small and unimportant isolated city. Since it was to be foreseen that the barbarians would hinder the imperial cause, why had Hsü not devised a way to deal with them? Wu was commonly said to be thoroughly familiar with the barbarian nature; why was he now helpless and without a plan, when the barbarians secretly obstructed the imperial military strategy? [29] As the siege dragged on, the emperor sanctioned the sending of reinforcements, 1,000 men on one occasion, and the buying of foreign percussion guns, which Wu reported the rebels to have been buying from the barbarians.[30] It was typical of the contemporary aversion to foreign relations that while Peking was aware of the barbarian help that prolonged the rebels' resistance,[31] no effort seems ever to have been made from the capital to secure barbarian coöperation or compliance in putting an end to it. An edict of April 19, 1854, summed up the imperial policy: the provincial officials had reported how the bar-

[e] The provincial authorities hastened to reassure the court by reporting the explanation elicited from the French consul by Wu Chien-chang at Shanghai, that the *Cassini* had gone to Nanking only to protect the interests of a French missionary whom the rebels had coerced to follow their type of Protestantism.[25] The arrival of a Russian vessel at Shanghai at about the same time was reported with equal care, and a month later it was reiterated that neither the French nor the Russian vessel had made any demands.[26]

barians lent aid to the rebels; the court had early foreseen this and so had ordered that the rebels be attacked and routed out with all speed, to avoid complications arising.[32] There was no thought of negotiating with the barbarians in order to ameliorate the evils they caused; so the rebels continued to use the barbarians as their secret weapon,[33] while the barbarians used the rebels as a source of profit.[f]

Among others on the foreign side French missionaries, who wished to protect their converts inside the walls, tried to arrange negotiations whereby with the British and American consuls as guarantors, they might get Liu Li-ch'uan and his crew to return to their allegiance to the imperial government. Wu Chien-chang said Alcock had already made the same suggestion. But these and other proposals got nowhere.[35] The accumulating distrust and hostility came to a climax in the so-called Battle of Muddy Flat.

This historic encounter was precipitated when rowdy imperialist bands on April 3, 1854, attacked various foreigners on the edge of the settlement. The military skirmish which these attacks provoked appears to have been unpremeditated by the imperial authorities, and the Anglo-American attack on the imperial encampment west of the race-course on the following day, April 4, seems to have been equally unexpected on both sides.[36] The force of about 400 marines, bluejackets, sailors, and volunteers which formed in Kiangse Road at 3 P.M. and then marched with drums beating and colors flying down the Maloo (later Nanking Road) to the east side of the race course (Hupeh Road), half expected by their warlike attitude to secure compliance with the foreign demand for the removal of the imperial camp to the westward. When at 4 P.M. Chi-er-hang-a did not comply, "there was a marked decline in the exuberance which had characterized the march out,"[37] but the foreign force, with a British field-piece, one brass gun, and Mr. E. Cunningham's howitzer, had no alternative but to advance in the direction of the 10,000-odd Chinese troops entrenched in front of them. The British and American columns, each accompanied by their consuls,[g] did not maintain good contact and may actually have accounted for some of each other's casualties (total: four killed and eleven wounded).

[f] Dr. Lockhart wrote: "At one period the Triads would go out in small parties and kidnap any [Imperial] soldiers they found loitering astray from their camps. These were taken into the city and immediately beheaded, or cruelly tortured till they died. . . . We found that the leaders of the gangs of kidnappers were foreigners, who had deserted from English and American ships, and been tempted by the high wages given them by the Triads. They had a reward for every soldier they seized. . . ."[34]

[g] Alcock wrote on the problem of mobilizing the Shanghai community: "I said that I had kept myself as far as possible out of sight in the documents not with a view of avoiding the responsibility of my acts, but having many incoherent elements to work with — a cosmopolite community — a sensitive section of Americans, civil and military officers also, it was all important to bind them solidly together for a costly effort — and keep them so, until at least the more pressing dangers of our position were passed. In this I am happy to say, and as indeed you will see, *aided by a common danger,* I have succeeded even beyond my hopes, and such perfect accord between authorities, nations, committees and all the cosmopolite heterogeneous materials of this place a month ago would have been deemed impossible."[38]

A considerable force of rebels seized the opportunity to rush out from the city and attack the imperial south flank, and this as well as the prudence of Chi-er-hang-a must have been partly responsible for the precipitate withdrawal of the imperial forces.

The Chinese memorials reporting this affair [39] give a vivid apologia: on April 4 Chi-er-hang-a was amazed to receive an ultimatum from Alcock, whose words were many and not polite and who declined to discuss matters but soon came out leading barbarian troops. Officers were dispatched to temporize with this force — who could foresee that their speech would not be understood? The barbarians came on, the rebels rushed out of the city. A great wind rose from the northeast, barbarian fire-pots ignited the tents of the camp, guns and cannon lost their force against the wind, smoke and flame blinded the soldiers' sight, and they fled in confusion. Seeing this, the imperial troops who were then pursuing the rebels also withdrew.[40] Next day Wu Chien-chang reprimanded the foreigners, many of whom feared a counter attack. The barbarian chiefs replied very civilly, denying all intention of helping the rebels, and showing that they realized their errors. On learning of these events, the court reiterated its former policy: the barbarians were habitually crafty — since the rebel miasma had not yet been cleaned up, it was not feasible to start trouble, the only course was to put up with it. Wu Chien-chang should restrain them with righteousness, foil their plots, and quickly devise means of destroying the rebels and recapturing the city.[41] Whatever might be the possibilities of negotiation, they were left for the provincial and local authorities to explore on their own initiative and at their peril.

The revival of Anglo-American coöperation. Once again personalities determined the course of treaty-port diplomacy. The first genuine United States consul at Shanghai, Robert C. Murphy, took up his duties on March 6, 1854, and a week later the new United States commissioner to China, Robert M. McLane, reached Hongkong. McLane's father had been President Jackson's secretary of the treasury and twice minister to England; he himself had been successively a cadet at West Point, an attorney in Baltimore, and a representative from Maryland in two terms of Congress. Though not yet forty he was a capable diplomat.[42] He made friends with the U. S. Navy and received the use of a ship. As regards the duties at Shanghai, he reserved judgment.[43] He soon impressed Sir George Bonham as "well inclined to be on candid and friendly terms" with him.[44] To complete the scene, the newly appointed British minister, Sir John Bowring, reached Hongkong on April 13, and on the next day sent McLane an "informal note . . . asserting strongly his desire for hearty co-operation." [45]

Bowring brought to the customs problem a point of view less trammeled by the commercial spirit of Hongkong and more sympathetic to the Chinese side of the case. His very first dispatch asserted that "the duty question at Shanghai is by no means analogous to that of Amoy where the Imperial Government was wholly overthrown," whereas at Shanghai "it was we" who compelled the removal from the foreign settlement of the imperial force that might otherwise have enabled the taotai to collect duties. Nor could Bowring agree with Alcock that the *Aristides* case must necessarily have a "fatal retrospective action" upon the duties provisionally secured by bond under the Provisional System.[46]

The new look promised by these diplomatic officers was being taken just in time. In April foreign cargoes continued to leave Shanghai free of duty. The inland customs stations began to operate. Consul Alcock set down an analysis of why the treaty system had failed: "First the general want of energy, vigilance, and honesty in the Chinese officials; secondly, the different languages — want of any commonly acquired means of communication, either on the part of Foreigners or Natives, and even more than this, the total disparity of habits. The readiness of the Foreigner to take the law into his own hands, and resist by force the intervention of Chinese officials, and the dread and dislike of collision and violence inherent in the habits of the more peaceable Chinese of this province especially; to which is superadded a shrinking on political grounds, from any official and overt collision or act of hostility against Foreign Powers or their subjects."[47]

Thus the collapse of the customs administration at Shanghai in 1854 left the initiative in foreign hands. Moreover the slowness of correspondence with London (three months at a minimum) made it possible for the British minister to assume a power of decision which the Foreign Office considered itself still to possess. The same question regarding the payment of the promissory notes collected under the Provisional System was accordingly decided, in opposite ways, in both England and China. Arrangements made at Shanghai by Sir John Bowring (partly as a result of which the Foreign Inspectorate of Customs was established) had to be reversed shortly afterward. This contretemps deserves special note.

Bowring came back to China full of vigor and zeal, quite a different man from Bonham.[h] From his appointment as minister on the day before

[h] The quiescent policy pursued by the Foreign Office during Bowring's acting governorship at Hongkong in 1852–53 had been most irksome to him. His long reports (which justly received at the Foreign Office the heading, "from Dr. Bowring bewailing his position in China," and the comment, "his pen is prolific") had lamented "the position of a Plenipo. condemned to know nothing but what he can learn in this, his banishment from and non-intercourse with China. . . . That such a country should only be studied from a barren rock, — to which the student is stuck like a limpet, — . . . that China should be deemed only a sort of appendage to a poor, petty, profitless and expensive Colony, is a political mystery."[48] Believing as he did in the inevitable triumph of "commerce and Christianity in natural and necessary alliance to promote the progress of the pacific principle,"[49] Bowring was naturally inspired by the opportunities presented in China. At the end of his acting incumbency at Hongkong he wrote privately to Lord Granville, "I did hope that I should have been ['permitted,' crossed out] enabled during my short tenure of office to settle the several questions pending between us and the Chinese. I believe I could have arranged them satisfactorily

Christmas 1853 until his departure in the middle of February 1854, he had been constantly consulted by the Foreign Office and on the stationery of the Athenaeum Club returned voluminous opinions for Clarendon's private eye.[51] His mission was to be of great importance, to push for revision of the treaties in the interests of trade. Bowring's eminence as a scholar and experience as a diplomat also encouraged the emulation of Commodore Perry and the project of commercial treaties with Siam, Cochin-China, and Japan. During his past year's leave in England (while still nominally consul at Canton), Dr. Bowring had been no less active than usual. The Manchester associations, whose free trade ideas he embodied, had come to place high hopes in him, which they expressed to the Foreign Office, and which the Foreign Office apparently shared.[52] Knighted on February 16, 1854,[53] Sir John sailed "as a representative of the Queen, and [he later confessed] I was accredited not to Peking alone but to Japan, Siam, Cochin China and Corea, I believe to a greater number of beings . . . than any individual had been accredited before." As his critics put it, he returned "big with the fate of China and himself." [54]

Now when Bowring left in the middle of February, 1854, the reports on Shanghai came down only to December, when the Provisional System had still been functioning, and the duty question had been referred to Bonham, supposedly for his final settlement. The Foreign Office had put off the restless queries of the China trade associations with the reply that the whole matter had been referred to China.[55] Accordingly, Clarendon had neglected to give Bowring any specific instructions concerning the collection of duties at Shanghai.[i] On March 18, however, while Bowring was still traveling eastward, the Foreign Office received Bonham's decision that the question could not be satisfactorily decided in China. With his usual caution, Sir George tossed it back into the lap of the Foreign Office.[57] After six months, however, the emperor's claim to the duties as represented

and peacefully, and that my short administration might thus have been useful to my country and to mankind. But my orders to do nothing and not to quit Hong Kong have been most peremptory . . . I think there is no part of the world where so much is to be done, and I could hardly terminate my public life more honourably or more happily than by opening wider and wider the gates of access to this extensive Empire." [50]

[i] Bowring had scarcely gone when the Manchester Chamber of Commerce sent in the suggestion, on Feb. 16, that in any future treaty, British consuls should not be made to "take the initiative in matters relating to foreign Customs Duties." On their letter Clarendon noted, "I omitted to speak to Dr. J. Bowring on this subject. Has he seen the correspondence? If not write to him by next mail directing his attention to it and stating it is most desirable that the state of things at Shanghai should cease." To which the permanent undersecretary, Addington, replied that Bowring had seen the correspondence and reported on it on Jan. 21 and that Bonham had been instructed on Jan. 24, whereupon Clarendon noted: "Inst. C. of C. that Dr. Bowring is well acquainted with the whole subject and will act upon the instns. sent out last month to Sir G. B." Bowring's report of Jan. 21 had been based on Bonham's dispatches, and in general terms had agreed with Clarendon's instructions to Bonham of Nov. 24, that the decision as to payment of the duties held at Shanghai must rest on the British minister's estimate of the competence of the Imperial Government, a question which, as Bowring put it, "cannot be satisfactorily decided *here*" in London.[56]

in London had grown weaker. Clarendon already felt disposed to authorize the return of the guarantees required from the merchants "whenever Sir J. Bowring thinks the time for so doing has arrived." When Bonham reported that the Americans had declared free trade at Shanghai, Clarendon noted, "want further report before any decision is taken, but it seems to me that the Americans have taken the right course." [58]

Thus while Clarendon in London was making up his mind as to the duty question, Bowring went on his way to China, prepared to decide it there. After reaching Hongkong on April 13, 1854, he appears not to have perused in detail his predecessor's recent correspondence with the Foreign Office. For the next four months he pursued a policy based in part on the assumption that he could himself decide whether or not the back duties at Shanghai were eventually to be paid. On April 20 Bowring "conferred freely" with McLane on this question [59] and later with the French minister, Bourboulon. All three envoys concurred that as regards the customs problem "our efforts should be directed to encourage respect for treaty obligations, and that nothing but the absolute impossibility of giving effect to these obligations should induce us to recognize, patronize, or protect violations which have become almost a habit." [60] A foundation for constructive coöperation having thus been laid, McLane departed on April 21 for Shanghai. Routine duties and the menace of a Russian fleet reported in the China seas meanwhile kept Bowring at Hongkong.[61]

McLane begins negotiations. On his arrival at Shanghai McLane found that the battle of April 4 had by no means removed the foreign community's fear of collision with the imperial troops. Even the armed receiving ships from Wusung sought the protection of the six vessels of war in Shanghai harbor,[62] applying to Alcock for assurances, to which he replied that he could not protect such vessels but that under the circumstances he would not interfere against them.[63] Merchants began to complain on April 24 that export goods for which they had contracted had been charged and sometimes held for duties at the Chinese stations inland. It was felt that "unless some regularity can be established within the coming two or three most important business months . . . the trade of Shanghai will be diverted elsewhere." [64]

McLane's view of the treaty system was that the "principle of mutuality . . . providing for the presence of the authorities of the United States, is a condition precedent to the enjoyment by the Chinese Government of the duties . . . due and owing under the treaty." Hence the levy of duties inland, by violating the provisions for tonnage dues and for the presence of all the parties interested, and by changing the mode of ascertaining and levying the duties, would put "all the reciprocal obligations of the treaty at an end." He resolved "at an early date" to seek an interview with the high imperial authorities, and meanwhile established a close harmony of views with Alcock.[65] Their common determination to reassert the principles of the treaties was immediately manifest in the reply of the three treaty-power consuls (Alcock, Murphy, and Edan) on May 1, to Wu Taotai's unanswered notices of March 22 and 25 concerning inland taxation. The consuls affirmed that as the treaties "expressly provide alike for the *amount* of tariff duties, the *place*, and the *mode* of their collection; it is not in [the consuls'] province to sanction, or in any way to recognize, a departure from the specific terms of these treaties on the part of the Chinese authorities. . . ."[66]

It was at this point that Alcock first put in writing the essential idea of the foreign inspectorate:[67] "I do not relinquish all hope of success — *if the collection of duties can in any way be brought under the effective control of the Three Treaty Powers as to the executive of the Custom House Administration.* On any other basis I believe every effort to benefit the Chinese Revenue, and at the same time give that protection to the honest merchant which he can reasonably demand, must in the nature of things prove nugatory and abortive. I have stated this conviction broadly (founded, as it is, upon a lengthened experience of the Chinese Customs House Officials at this Port, and the working of the Administrative Machinery), to His Excellency the American Minister: for unless this view is taken as the point of departure for any new adjustment and practical issue out of difficulties inherent to such a question in China, I am persuaded no good can come of the best efforts all three Governments united, can make, and however straightforward and prompt they may be both in design and action."[68]

This far-reaching suggestion could come only from a maturity of experience not possessed by Commissioner McLane, yet it could be given effect only through authority such as he possessed, and only in concert with Chinese authorities of equally high rank. Fortunately the way had now been paved for more friendly relations with these authorities, for the foreign consuls had taken stricter measures to preserve foreign neutrality in fact as well as in name and so remove one chief cause of Sino-foreign friction. They had issued a joint proclamation to discourage foreign participation in the local fighting and check the sale of munitions, and had posted more guards — a measure taken by the foreigners partly for defense but reported by the Chinese officials in a better light, as a measure to check the freedom of communication between city and settlement. I-liang and Hsü Nai-chao reported to Peking at the beginning of May that, owing to the scoldings of Wu and Chi-er-hang-a, the barbarians' attitude was now respectfully submissive, the roving bandits had given up their evil courses, and the general situation at Shanghai was extremely quiet and peaceful.[69] In an interview on board the U.S.S. *Susquehannah* during the first week in May,[70] McLane told Wu Chien-chang and Chi-er-hang-a that he was deeply concerned at the disorder prevailing in China, intended at an early date to go up the Yangtze to investigate it, and would like also to obtain an interview with the governor-general, I-liang. Wu showed a strong desire to be present at such an interview, presumably so that he might "give his own directions and coloring to all matters connected with the difficulties at Shanghai." [71] When he proposed that he should make the arrangements, however, McLane "declined his civilities, really because he is himself the principal criminal in all the troubles at Shanghai." [j]

Wu Chien-chang's report of this interview with McLane deserves close scrutiny. In Governor Hsü's memorial, which was the first to reach Peking, Wu is quoted as reporting that McLane, after expressing the foreign nations' gratitude for His Majesty the Emperor's heavenly favor of trade, had confined his remarks on the customs to the following: that the rebellion at Shanghai obstructed China's customs affairs and injured the trade of all nations; and that he wished to put commercial affairs in order and make the Chinese customs show a profit. Wu himself, while impressed with the American's more than usual politeness, felt it as yet impossible to be sure whether he really wanted to put commercial affairs in order. Hsü echoed this sentiment, while the imperial edict in reply merely observed that the barbarians' nature was unfathomable,[75] and they should be ordered to go back to Canton as usual.

The memorial of I-liang, which reached Peking a week later, showed his concern to follow a course acceptable both to Peking and to the barbarians: the American envoy certainly ought not to go to Tientsin, as he threatened, but to Canton, as the emperor had ordered Marshall to do the year before; but as he now asked for an interview about May 17, Wu Chien-chang had been instructed to investigate and report.[76] Only in a supplementary memorial of the same date did I-liang cautiously bring forward another point of view: of course the imperial commands were to be followed, but McLane used Yeh Ming-ch'en's preoccupation with public business and

[j] Evidently as one result of this interview, on May 9 a joint notification of the three treaty-power consuls asked the merchants to present "in addition to the statement which they are now in the habit of making with their Invoices of Cargo, etc., *any evidence which it may be in their power to give of interior exactions, levy of duties, or other irregularities*. . . . In lieu of the specific Bond or note which they are now in the habit of giving, an obligation from the Consignee and each shipper will be taken, by which they shall undertake to hold harmless their Consuls and respective Governments from any responsibilities accruing from the departure of the ship without payment of such duties as may be due." [72] This notification expressed McLane's idea of giving the Chinese "the responsibility of disturbing the relations of friendship" so far existing. The "specific Bond or note" mentioned in it referred to the worthless bonds for half duties of the style set by the *Aristides*, under which 12 British, 6 American, 1 Danish, and 2 Hamburg vessels had left Shanghai since the 18th of March.[73] The form now substituted read as follows: "*Obligation*: We (I) hereby bind ourselves to meet any claim that may be made for duties upon our shipments by the ______ that may be adjudged by the competent authorities of the ______ to be due and owing under the Treaty of ______ with China, in the way of Import, Export, and tonnage duties." [74]

refusal to see him as a pretext. If I-liang refused him too severely, it might give him a further excuse for going to Tientsin, which would be most embarrassing at this time when there were military operations in Chihli and when grain boats were proceeding to Tientsin in continuous succession. If repeatedly refused an interview, McLane might say I-liang was afraid to see him, which would be undignified. The only course was to follow an imperial rescript of the year before, manifest broad-mindedness, and act as opportunity allowed. If, after his receiving McLane in audience, the latter should disrespectfully discuss changes in the matter of customs duties, or make other demands, I-liang could only righteously order him to go to Canton and wait on Yeh. In these impeccable terms the aged governor-general smoothly reversed himself and informed the court that he would negotiate, and an imperial rescript signified approval with orders to manage matters properly as they arose, not to stir up fresh complications, on no account to show weakness, and to restrain the barbarians from making demands [77] — in other words, to do the best he could.

Until the middle of June 1854 customs reform remained in this state of gestation. Immediately after returning from a trip to Ningpo and Foochow, McLane went up the Yangtze to Nanking on May 22 and did not return till the beginning of June. During his absence, I-liang wrote to him on May 25, fixing the period May 27 — June 5 for an interview, and again on May 28, stating that the time could be arranged after McLane's return from Nanking. While these replies studiously avoided any commitment regarding the customs and other matters raised by McLane, they expressed an encouraging readiness to confer seriously upon them.[78]

The stage was now set for diplomatic action. Rear-Admiral Sir James Stirling, in command of the East India and China station, came to Shanghai on his way to Japan and contributed vigorous views of his own to the program envisaged by Bowring and McLane. He proposed that customs duties should be paid according to treaty, "a Municipal Council should be formed, regulations established, a Police Force appointed." [79] There now ensued a series of conferences and negotiations among the Chinese, American and British officials at Shanghai which were to establish the future trade and security of the port. Between the middle of June and the middle of July 1854 the Western representatives sought to realize several objectives. They again proposed to the Chinese authorities, unsuccessfully, that foreign mediation and force if necessary should be used to secure the removal of the rebels from the city.[80] To relieve Sino-foreign friction they materially reduced, with walls and guards, the ease of access between city and settlement and by thus hindering foreign support of the rebels facilitated the imperial siege. They achieved successfully the organization of a more adequate municipal administration for the foreign settlement at

Shanghai.[81] At the same time they pushed their governments' requests for revision of the treaties, which was desired chiefly as a means of opening the Yangtze valley to trade and of establishing channels for more satisfactory diplomatic relations with Peking. In this general scheme the question of customs administration at Shanghai was only one element among several.

The customs bargain: A foreign inspectorate in exchange for back duties. With regard to customs reform, the twofold nature of the foreign program had by degrees become quite clear. It was this: if the Chinese government would in future admit a foreign element into the Shanghai customs administration, then the British and American authorities would take measures to secure the collection of the promissory notes for back duties owing to China which had remained unpaid since September 1853.

By the beginning of June 1854 there had been roughly four periods of customs administration since the capture of Shanghai in September 1853.[82] In the first period, that of the Provisional System (September 7 — February 8), promissory notes had been collected from 45 British vessels (total tonnage 18,665; total sum due the Chinese Customs, Tls. 478,300) and 25 American vessels (total tonnage 18,812; total due, Tls. 362,508). A total of 14 vessels under seven other foreign flags (but including 3 under the American flag) had during the same period given either no bonds or bonds of doubtful validity (tonnage 4,465; Tls. due 46,193). Thus out of Tls. 887,000 which had become due to the Chinese government according to the treaty tariff, Tls. 840,000 could be collected if the promissory notes held by the British and American consuls were adjudged valid by their respective governments. The taxation of foreign trade at Shanghai could thus be made over 94 per cent effective. This relatively high effectiveness of the Provisional System would make it, if the notes were collected, the most efficient customs administration that Shanghai had ever known.

In the second period, during which Wu Chien-chang's revived customhouse had functioned on Soochow Creek (February 9 — March 17), only about 14 vessels had sailed from Shanghai or Wusung (total 5501 tons). Seven of this number (including 4 British and 2 American) had paid cash duties at the customhouse. The other seven (including 3 British and 3 American) had loaded illegally outside the port of Wusung, had given either no account of cargo or a worthless bond, and had departed owing altogether about Tls. 34,313 to the Chinese government.

The sailing of the *Aristides* on March 18 had inaugurated a third period (March 18 — May 8), during which some 21 vessels (including 12 British and 6 American) had left behind them at Shanghai completely worthless promises of a kind that automatically invalidated each other (tonnage 8,316; duties due Tls. 200,620). During about the same period 5 other vessels (including 4 British) had cleared without reporting (1005 tons, Tls. 12,079).

Finally on May 9 vessels had begun to clear under the joint consular notification of that date, giving bonds which could be collected if the home governments so desired. By May 31 seven vessels (5 British and 2 American) had so departed (tonnage 1,958; duties due Tls. 26,257). To complete the picture it may here be noted that from June 1 to July 12, about a dozen more vessels cleared, half British, half American (British duties due, appproximately Tls. 22,000).

From the foregoing analysis it appears that by June 1, 1854, some 132 vessels, totaling 58,965 tons of shipping, had left Shanghai owing the Chinese government, as tonnage dues, import and export duties, a sum of Tls. 1,173,071. Of this total American merchants owed about one-third (Tls. 354,149), and British merchants nearly all the rest. No decision had as yet been announced as to the liability of the foreign merchants for these sums. The general conviction of the merchants had long been that the bonds taken under the Provisional System could not legally be collected, and in this conviction various private statements of Sir George Bonham had strengthened them.[83] Sir John Bowring, on the other hand, had already formed strong opinions on the situation at Shanghai and had a high conception of his own responsibilities: "The low vagabonds who have got the city — and the *support* of too many of the community (that part of the community who though they have charged the duties to their constituents, want to escape the paying them) have no more notions of government than a half-a-dozen Newgate birds would have. However we shall get our teas, I hope, by hook or by crook, for I never lose sight of the Chancellor of the Exchequer's mandate 'Take care of my revenues.' "[84] This last consideration made Bowring the more willing to sacrifice the past profits of the merchants if by so doing he could effect an arrangement with the Chinese that would ensure the future revenue of the British government. Once arrived on the scene, however, Bowring found on inquiry that "in almost every instance" the merchants during the Provisional System had added the amount of the prospective duties to their invoices and would thus suffer no loss if called on to pay up. As to the situations at Amoy in May and at Shanghai in September 1853, Sir John asserted that there was "in fact no analogy or resemblance between them. . . ." His argument was as follows:

At Amoy the Imperial Authority was entirely scattered — not a Mandarin, not an Imperial Soldier remained on the island, of which a mob took absolute possession. . . . The Consul himself had, for some time, to seek protection on board one of Her Majesty's ships. Trade there was none — there were neither goods to ship, nor shipping to receive them. In what respect then does the case of Amoy apply to Shanghai?

In this particular only, that a set of lawless vagabonds, all of them strangers to the locality, have seized the walled city of Shanghai, placed at a considerable distance from the foreign settlement, and from the seat of all commercial operations. It is found necessary by the foreign Consuls to require the removal of the Imperial Custom House from the settlement, in the midst of which it was situated, on the very proper ground that the foreign settlement must not be made a battle field . . . . [In the meantime, however, trade had not been interrupted but had flourished, and the merchants had prepared themselves for the payment of duties.] Ought they to pay them? The question, in my mind, admits of *no doubt*. . . . If I were to admit a position which has been sometimes put forward, that the whole charge of collecting duties is to be thrown upon the Chinese Officials, and that the coöperation of our Consular functionaries is to be withheld or denied, I should at once consent to abrogate all treaties, and *to the utter destruction of our trade with China*. Her Majesty's engagements would be made a dead letter by Her own Subjects if Her own officials are condemned to inaction. I know too well the helplessness of Chinese Authority and the corruption of Chinese Mandarins. Seven opium stations placed in the adjacency of great cities, and in which annual sales are made to the extent of between 3 and 4 millions sterling in defiance of the laws of China, are evidence of the power of the British merchants, and the feebleness of the Chinese Mandarin. These Opium Ships are armed floating depots, which no War or Customs House Junks dare approach. But our commerce with China is in the Chinese Territory, and the Chinese, though they may not be able to collect the duties without our assistance, can jeopardize and ruin the trade itself. I cannot consent to *opiumize* so valuable a commerce. If I did, I should, with open eyes and absolute foreknowledge of consequences, be a party to its annihilation.

[Consequently Bowring proposed to recover the back duties only if he could obtain from the Chinese Authorities certain conditions — among them] that satisfactory arrangements shall be made for the collection of duties on both exports and imports, arrangements by which the British Flag shall be a protection and not a disadvantage to the Queen's subjects, and by which the honourable and well disposed merchants shall be secured against the invasion of fraudulent and unscrupulous competitors.

I cannot but feel that the Imperial Authorities have just grounds to dissatisfaction. . . . For nine months they have been deprived of the resources on which, in my judgment, they had a right to calculate. The association of our interests with the cause of rebellion, is perhaps the primary reason why the local outbreak has not been subdued. The sum kept back from the Imperial revenues, and for which written obligations are held, exceeds, as I have before stated, one-third of a million of pounds sterling. . . . I am in constant intercourse with the American Commissioner, who concurs with me as regards the past, and is quite ready to enforce the payment of the duties owing to the Chinese by the citizens of the United States, and I trust we shall ere long be in a condition to submit such terms to the Viceroy as will, under Treaty conditions, restore to Shanghai its trade.[85]

Bowring had scarcely penned this dispatch when Alcock submitted to him in person a memorandum dated June 15 containing detailed "Suggestions for an improved administration of Customs and the equal levy of Duties" which elaborated his dispatch of May 1 by suggesting that a "trustworthy Foreign *Inspector of Customs* . . . as the delegate of the three Treaty Consuls . . . be nominated to his post for one year . . . by the Consuls and Taoutae conjointly and at a fixed and liberal salary." This official would have "an office *in the Custom House*" and all documents issued by it would need "*his countersignature before they can take effect.*" Alcock further specified the extent of the proposed Inspector's establishment and estimated its cost.[k]

Almost simultaneously McLane prepared for his interview with I-liang by conferring with Bowring, to whom he read extracts of his last dispatch to Washington.[86] The two ministers must have discussed Alcock's proposal, if indeed McLane did not actually see his memorandum of June 15. This discussion was the more desirable inasmuch as it was McLane who was about to see the highest provincial authority, with whom Bowring did not succeed in gaining an interview.[87] On June 16, before McLane's departure, Bowring and Stirling held an interview with Wu Chien-chang,

[k] Alcock's memorandum read in part as follows: "Of the hopelessness of any effective means being adopted to secure the impartial and efficient levy of duties by the Chinese, if left to themselves, the experience of the last ten years can leave no doubt. . . .

"The proposition now submitted for consideration consists in the association with the Chinese executive who shall be placed in charge of the Custom House Administration of a responsible and trustworthy *Foreign Inspector of Customs.* This officer as the delegate of the three Treaty Powers to be nominated to his post for one year (but subject to instant dismissal on cause shown) by the Consuls and Taoutae conjointly and at a fixed and liberal salary — sufficient to insure the services of a person of high intelligence and probity, and if possible, one possessing a knowledge of the Chinese Language. There should be placed under his orders an establishment of two first class linguists and one or more Chinese Writers and Runners; with one or more Foreigners, to serve when occasion may require, as a species of tide waiter. The total expense of the establishment may be estimated at $12,000 (as per margin) to be

Inspector, p.a.	$6000
2 Linguists at 100 p.m.	2400
Chinese Writers, Runners, etc.	600
Foreigners as supplementary Tide Waiters	3000
	$12,000

defrayed of course out of the gross revenue of duties. This Foreign Delegate or Inspector should have location for an Office *in the Custom House,* and all documents issued by the Chinese Department, port clearances — landing and shipping off chops — Duty receipts, &c., to have *his countersignature before they can take effect.* He would be required to keep *a complete set of Custom House Books,* and these together with the Chinese Records to be at all times open to the inspection of the Taoutae and the Consuls of the three Treaty Powers. The Inspector himself to be allowed *ex officio,* the freest access to the Custom House Records kept by the Chinese Officers from day to day. Or, if preferred, they might be officially examined, compared and checked at the close of every month, the three Consuls certifying the fact and noting any discrepancy.

"A machinery of this kind brought into active operation could scarcely fail to furnish a most effective check upon the venality and supineness of the Custom House Officials; and one eminently calculated to increase the Chinese Revenue to an amount far more than *ten times the cost* of the Foreign Branch Office."

RUTHERFORD ALCOCK, *Consul*

Shanghai, June 15, 1854
(FO 97/100, encl. 2 in Bowring's 77, July 7, 1854.)

at which although Bowring "avoided discussing the subject of duties," the taotai led him into the declaration, as transcribed by Interpreter H. N. Lay (later to be the first Inspector General of the Customs) that "if the Chinese officers will do their duty, Sir John will ensure the payment of duty by every merchant connected with the British Nation; while if subjects of countries not having treaties with China, be allowed to escape payment, then British subjects will be emancipated likewise."[88]

McLane was received by I-liang on June 21 at K'un-shan, which is about two-thirds of the way from Shanghai west to Soochow. He was accompanied by Wu Chien-chang and his understudy, the sub-prefect Lan Wei-wen, who later became Shanghai taotai. I-liang came from Soochow. Both arrived on the 20th and next day met in the public hall of K'un-shan. The American was polite, the Manchu frank, and their day's discussion was one of the most constructive incidents in Sino-foreign diplomacy up to that time.

After raising the questions of trade on the Yangtze and communication with Peking anent treaty revision, McLane broached the subject of the inland customhouses which were threatening to stifle the trade of Shanghai. I-liang admitted that the foreign aversion to these extra-treaty-port taxing stations was well founded. They violated the treaties. "These custom houses had been established by his express direction and persisted in after he had been advised of my instructions to the American consul to consider such a course as a practical abrogation of the treaty." After a full and very satisfactory discussion, it was agreed that the interior customhouses should be abolished and that full power should be given to the superintendent of customs at Shanghai to enter into and conclude an arrangement with the consuls of the three treaty powers for the administration of the customhouse at that port on a permanent basis.[89]

On the next day, McLane at I-liang's request submitted a memorandum of his various proposals, including the request that inland customs exactions on goods coming to Shanghai be stopped. McLane stated: "Otherwise it will be impossible to enforce the payment of duties at that port, or settle to the satisfaction of either party the difficulties that have attended the duties during the last nine months." In return for the enlargement of commercial privileges by opening the Yangtze to trade, he further promised that the American government would "at once take active and efficient means to enforce upon their citizens the prompt payment of the duties prescribed in the treaty of Wang Hia."[90]

The permission given by the Nanking governor-general for the Shanghai taotai to employ foreigners was not explicitly reported to the throne. According to I-liang's memorial, McLane had first pointed out, as an illustration of the need for revision of the old treaty system, that the Shanghai customs had been changed to Soochow Creek, a move already inconsistent with the old regulations and extremely inconvenient. McLane had full powers, and if I-liang could not negotiate, he wished him at least to memorialize the throne to send a minister with full powers. To this I-liang had replied that the Shanghai customs had been moved temporarily because of the fighting there and could be arranged as before as soon as the city was recaptured. If the barbarian merchants really had questions to raise, there was no hindrance to their discussing them equitably and properly with Wu Chien-chang, for there was no such thing as a Chinese minister with full powers.[91] I-liang further reported that McLane's memorandum of the following day concluded with the request that the new customs at Shanghai might be done away with.[92] Finally, in concluding his memorial, I-liang reiterated that the only course was to follow the imperial edict of the previous year regarding Marshall and order McLane back to Canton to await Yeh Ming-ch'en's management; meanwhile he had ordered Wu Chien-chang to take up customs affairs immediately at Shanghai, talk them over thoroughly, and manage them satisfactorily, so that the barbarians might have nothing to use as a pretext. As before, the court approved this skillfully worded memorial and ordered McLane to proceed to Canton without loitering.[93]

While it seems plain that this conference of June 21 resulted in the Shanghai taotai's being empowered to reorganize his customhouse, what was said regarding the back duties is less certain. Over these duties McLane was apparently less concerned than Bowring, whose spirit had been aroused by the antagonism of the British mercantile community toward his views. Although the American commissioner did not report to his government whether he and I-liang reached any definite agreement as to the back duties, he did write that "on my return from Kwan-shan, I apprised the British minister of the intercourse I had had with the viceroy, and we entered into cordial co-operation as to the general and local matters which had been in discussion." [94] Whereupon Bowring reported that "McLane . . . has just returned from a visit to the Viceroy and I am happy to say . . . arrangements are to be made in co-operation with, and under the sanction of the Consuls of the Three Treaty Powers, for the fair settlement of Duties according to Treaty. On this being done Mr. McLane and I have agreed that the back Duties are to be paid to the Imperial authorities — who will proceed for their recovery through the Consular Courts." [95]

Thus as early as June 27 the double nature of the customs settlement was agreed upon by McLane and Bowring. Both of them were led by their sense of justice and by their desire to conciliate the Chinese authorities to give them the opportunity of recovering back duties through the consular courts, as prescribed by treaty, at the same time that they demanded from them the opportunity to instil life into the customs in the interests of foreign trade. Bowring acknowledged this reciprocal aspect of the agreement in a second interview with Wu on June 27. Interpreter Lay reported him to have said that "with regard to the duty question (which Woo was asked whether he was fully authorized to take up, and he replied that he was) — if the arrangements for the future collection of the duties were placed upon a satisfactory basis, the Consul would be empowered to lend his best assistance towards recovering the back duties." [96] On the part of the Chinese authorities this understanding was acknowledged at the time in a communication from Hsü to Bowring on July 1,[97] in which the Kiangsu governor expressed himself much beholden "for the completeness of your arrangements," and hoped that Bowring would soon call on the merchants "to pay the duties which have accrued on exports since the 7th of September last." [l]

It is impossible to avoid the conclusion that the promise to pay up the back duties in whole or in part was used by the Anglo-American authorities as a *quid pro quo* in securing the acquiescence of the Chinese officials in the customs reform suggested by Alcock.

The inauguration of the Inspectorate. Of the two parts of this customs settlement, however, the question of future collections was the more pressing and was the first to be dealt with. On June 29 a conference between the three treaty-power consuls and Wu Chien-chang elaborated upon Consul Alcock's memorandum of June 15, to the principles of which the governor-general had already agreed.[104] "The general outline had been discussed and modifications suggested" by McLane and Bowring. The latter had, however, "been satisfied to leave the local details very much in the hands of the Consuls, who have come to a perfect unanimity of opinion and action." [105] Alcock's was naturally the dominant voice.[m] The minutes of

[l] Later, the promise that the back duties should in some manner be paid, was reiterated too plainly for mistake, in both the Chinese and foreign documents. As Mr. Wright puts it, Wu "succumbed to the tempting bait of the back duties." His superior, Hsü, reported that on his return from K'un-shan the taotai had on successive days demanded from both the American and British chiefs the duties collected by them on his behalf during the preceding nine months. They had replied that they would not dare to fall short of the full amount, but must wait till the recapture of the city.[98] Chi-er-hang-a, who succeeded Hsü as governor of Kiangsu on July 7,[99] reported that a memorandum from Bowring had asked that a minister with full powers might come to Shanghai and permit trade at other places than the five ports, whereupon he would order the merchants to pay up in toto all the unpaid duties; otherwise he would himself go to Peking.[100] In the English version of the memorandum to which Chi-er-hang-a evidently refers, sent him on July 26 in preparation for an interview the following day, Bowring said that he had full powers to arrange matters; he had already compelled British merchants to pay duty from July 12 on; he had promised to make them pay whatever was rightly owing as duties since the time the rebels took the city.[101] A similar statement had already been made by McLane, in answer to I-liang's letter of June 29 which assured him that Wu was competent to deal with customs matters and would duly report his arrangements to the imperial commissioner at Canton.[102] McLane replied on July 18 that judicious measures had been taken for the proper administration of the customs and added, "I am at the same time taking the proper measures for a settlement of the past controversies between the Imperial authorities at Shanghai and citizens of the Untied States." [103]

[m] "The Taotai met my colleagues and myself," he wrote, "at the Consulate, by appointment, for the express purpose of discussing the possibility of entering into some arrangement, by which Foreign and Chinese interests might be mutually protected and benefited. . . .

"My colleagues at once and very cordially adopted the views set forth in the Memo: of suggestions this conference marked the birth of the Foreign Inspectorate of Customs. It provided in detail for the appointment of a Board of Inspectors, for the creation of an adequate customs establishment of which they were to be the active head, and for their relations both with the taotai and with the foreign consuls and community. On July 4 the taotai formally requested the three treaty-power consuls to make their nominations for the Board of Inspectors and at the same time stated the extent of the establishment he would forthwith install and the attendant salaries. The new system would begin on July 12th and on the 6th the consuls so notified the foreign community.[107]

Before the conference of June 29 had determined upon a board of three Inspectors, the British and American consuls had suggested that M. Arthur J. Smith, interpreter in the French consulate, be appointed as the one inspector specified in Alcock's memorandum. Accordingly, when three were to be appointed, M. Smith was the first mentioned. The others were Thomas Francis Wade, British vice-consul, and Lewis Carr, of the American legation, who had shown some capacity during McLane's trip to Nanking but could not equal his colleagues in knowledge of the Chinese language. Both Mr. Carr and M. Smith retained their official positions and duties under their own governments. Under port regulations newly revised by the taotai, the new administration began on July 12, 1854. Just the day before, Wu Chien-chang had been impeached in Peking.[n]

What became of the back duties? In the ten months before July 12, 1854, British and American vessels had left Shanghai promising under certain conditions to pay customs duties totalling about Tls. 1,200,000 (say £400,000). None of the British notes was ever paid up, in spite of everything Bowring could do to reverse the view advocated so successfully in

---

and I must admit the Taoutai showed no reluctance. It is true as regarded the latter, circumstances were very favorable. He had felt his utter inability, single handed to deal with obstacles of every kind flung in the way of any collection of duties, based upon Treaty provisions, by Chinese Officials alone. The total loss of revenue with which he was menaced by this inability, made him naturally eager to profit by any suggestions that promised to re-establish his jurisdiction; to invest it with Authority, and secure the full payment of all Duties — while on the other hand it must also be confessed the magnitude of the evil threatening our Trade at the Port, and the Foreign revenue dependent upon it, was no less a matter of serious consideration." [106]

[n] Wu's later fate is instructive: in a memorial received Dec. 13, 1855, I-liang and Chi-er-hang-a condemned him after investigation, and he was banished to Ili. But on Mar. 12, 1856, by the intercession of General Hsiang Jung, Wu was left, degraded, to make amends in the imperial camp before Nanking. About Mar. 17, Hsiang Jung reported finding no proof of Wu's guilt and pointed to his laudable exertions and payments of Tls. 193,000 in procuring steamships and generally aiding the imperial cause. On Aug. 8, Yeh Ming-ch'en reported from Canton that Wu's property at Hsiang-shan had been seized but no disposition yet made of it. On Oct. 20, 1856, I-liang reported Wu's contribution of 11 large cannon, 46 smaller cannon, 224 muskets, 1900 catties of gunpowder, 2000 catties of shot, etc., for which he might well be taken back into favor.[108] He had already reappeared at Shanghai to negotiate for foreign steamers to be sent up the Yangtze, and on September 23, 1856, accompanied his successor to an interview with the American commissioner.[109] In 1858 Wu Chien-chang was still at Shanghai, now with the rank of expectant Taotai, taking an active part in the negotiations and combatting barbarian wiles as of old.[110] There is no indication that the part he played in founding the Foreign Inspectorate of Customs had been a factor of importance in causing his degradation in 1854.

England by Bonham and the merchants. Of the American duties, roughly one-third (Tls. 118,125) were finally paid to Wu Chien-chang's successor late in 1856. This was roughly one-tenth of the total promised.[111] But this perfidy seems to have disappointed the Chinese authorities more than it surprised them — they had never regarded the barbarians as particularly trustworthy. Meanwhile the new foreign collectorate at Shanghai was bringing them a greatly increased revenue.

CHAPTER XXIV

CONCLUSION: THE TREATIES SUCCEED THE TRIBUTE SYSTEM

THE FOREIGN INSPECTORATE AT SHANGHAI foreshadowed the eventual compromise between China and the West — a joint Chinese and Western administration of the modern centers of Chinese life and trade in the treaty ports. The second group of unequal treaties, negotiated after fighting in 1858 and finally ratified after further fighting in 1860, became the perfected legal basis of this Sino-Western order. Thereafter, with superior force held in reserve, the treaty powers led by Britain sought to prolong the rule of Peking in full domestic sovereignty — except for those special privileges accorded Western commercial and evangelical enterprise. For two generations after 1860 China lay open to foreign exploitation both economically and spiritually, tied by the web of treaty rights — extraterritoriality, foreign settlements and concessions, the treaty tariff which after 1858 applied to opium as well as other goods, and foreign rights of inland navigation, of proselytism and eventually even of industrial enterprise.

The Maritime Customs soon became the key institution in the use of these foreign treaty rights, no less important than the foreign consulates. Under Robert Hart as Inspector General (1863–1908) the Customs became a chief financial pillar of the Chinese government, providing both an unprecedented and reliable revenue from foreign trade and useful security for foreign loans and indemnities. Hart and his commissioners became the trusted counsellors of Chinese officialdom. They supplied at first some of the functions of a diplomatic service and supported financially the early efforts to educate and train such a corps. Lighthouses on the China coast, harbor conservancy and aids to inland navigation, hydrographic charts, pilotage and quarantine, the collection of many special dues and taxes were all by degrees added to the Customs' original functions. The great variety of Customs statistical, commercial and scientific publications partially made up for the lack of a modern Chinese government printing office. The Maritime Customs organized and until 1911 financed China's modern Postal Service. Customs commissioners of many nationalities made their contributions to scholarship as well as to diplomacy.[1] But above all the Customs set a standard of incorrupt public service and of devotion to the central administration which has been of incalculable value to the Chinese government of the twentieth century.

The lustre of this fine administrative record achieved by foreigners in the Chinese Maritime Customs is not dimmed by the fact that in the world family of nations China remained throughout the period until 1943 in the subordinate status marked by the unequal treaties. Given the Western domination of China after 1860, the Customs was useful both to Western traders and to Chinese administrators, enabling the Chinese government to meet some of its immediate problems and Western merchants to exploit their Chinese market more effectively. The Foreign Inspectorate was based on a compromise: China's limited sovereignty and the foreigners' commercial privileges were to be served jointly, by the same process of supervising and taxing foreign trade. When the foreigners' rights expanded into those of bondholders and recipients of indemnity payments, particularly after 1911, the Customs continued to serve both sides by maintaining the payments. Chinese patriots have inevitably regarded it as a device for milking the imperialists' tribute out of the Chinese economy. It is perhaps sufficient here to stop short of final moral judgment on the century of the unequal treaties, and note merely that the Chinese Maritime Customs has been the institution most thoroughly representative of the whole period.

Seen from the point of view of the Western observer, the reason for this is plain. China's century under the treaties was the era of Anglo-American commercial hegemony in a largely unindustrialized world. The aim of the Western trading powers in China was to trade but not to govern. Free trade and most-favored-nation treatment, expressive of this commercial interest, were the raison d'être of the Customs Service, whose constant purpose was to provide equal terms of competition both among individual traders and among the trading nations in China. This was the spirit of the Open Door, a British doctrine long before John Hay voiced it. It is no coincidence that in the writing of the Open Door notes of 1899, on the basis of which the United States by degrees and over the years succeeded to Britain's position of leadership in the Far East, an English commissioner of customs, Alfred E. Hippisley, "was clearly the prime mover." [2] Hippisley had worked closely under Hart and, as of 1896, had been his probable successor.[3] In the summer of 1899 he spent six weeks in Baltimore in close contact with Rockhill, who was then drafting the American notes, and the practical provisions of those documents issued in September are a clear and direct reflection of what Hart and the Customs, to say nothing of Britain, had stood for in China.[4]

Britain's diplomatic leadership among the treaty powers in late nineteenth century China no more than reflected her paramountcy in the China trade. Jardine, Matheson and Company soon added to its shipping, insurance, and miscellaneous functions as a house of agency and became an entrepreneur and investor in China's industrialization. The Hongkong and

Shanghai Banking Corporation, the Indo-China Steam Navigation Company, the Ewo Cotton Mills, the Hongkong docks, railroads, mines, engineering works, and many subsidiary enterprises came to share the vigorous attention of the firm's Scottish taipans and gave them continued influence in the City of London and in Whitehall.[5]

In the light of this growing foreign investment, Western historians have increasingly called attention to the community of interest which developed after 1860 between the treaty powers and the Manchu dynasty. Since the continuation of the Ch'ing regime would safeguard these economic rights, British officialdom, committed to the long view, soon parted company with those more eager Shanghailanders who sought constantly to take immediate advantage of Peking. This conflict between the "Old China Hands and the Foreign Office" [6] was in the cards from the moment Rutherford Alcock suggested the Foreign Inspectorate. Although Thomas Francis Wade gave place to Horatio Nelson Lay as the British inspector in 1855 and Clarendon subsequently cut the new institution adrift, declaring it to be a purely Chinese government agency,[7] it still remained headed by Englishmen who did an Anglo-Saxon job of administration. Increasingly it became the force for commercial law and order which Alcock had been seeking. It is not strange that this consul who in 1850 had voiced the aggressive designs of commercial imperialism (as noted in chapter 20) should become in the 1860's the minister at Peking most determined to hold the treaty port extremists in check and give the Ch'ing administration, with its new foreign-staffed Customs Service, a fair chance to govern China.

This brings us to a question which has seldom been asked. We know that the Customs became the lubricant that made the treaty system function smoothly for the foreigner, even to the collecting of the modest treaty tax on opium importations. It is also plain that this achievement was possible because the Customs embodied a principle of joint Sino-foreign administration — European and American commissioners serving the Chinese government on a mutually agreed basis using a mixed Chinese and Western staff. Heretofore this remarkable situation has been viewed almost entirely from the Western point of view, even by the most modern-minded (and therefore Westernized) Chinese patriots. Few have asked the question, what was the significance of this institution in Chinese terms, particularly in the context of China's long history of contact with her non-Chinese barbarian invaders?

Seen in its proper Chinese setting, I suggest that the treaty system supplanted the tribute system as a device for incorporating the foreigner into the universal state presided over by the Confucian monarchy of the Son of Heaven. This simple fact has been obscured by the attendant circumstance that tribute has signified Chinese superiority, while the treaties represented a new phase of foreign domination. The balance of power shifted spectacularly after 1842 from within to without, and this power shift has absorbed the attention of modern observers, both Chinese and Western. The underlying institutional development has been generally overlooked or misunderstood.

The key to this institutional evolution of the Chinese state in the nineteenth century lies in the fact that barbarian invaders of China had often acquired the dominant power in the Confucian state without destroying its political structure. Tribute had continued to be the mode of China's foreign relations, whether Chinese or barbarians ruled the empire, while dyarchy had served as the mode of domestic administration whenever foreign invaders were in the ascendant.[8] These political dispensations under the Confucian monarchy — tribute relations abroad and dyarchy at home — had been maintained under the Mongol and Manchu dynasties of conquest. Tribute continued, though dyarchy ceased, under the Ming. The principle of dyarchy continued, though tribute ceased, under the last Manchus. Indeed, the Westerners who turned the tribute system upside down were ipso facto admitted to the dyarchy. (Perhaps after 1860 it might better be called a Manchu-Chinese-Western "synarchy.") [a] They merely expanded their role in the Confucian state, moving from the periphery to the center. This was possible because of the peculiar nature of that state as a supranational universal order which normally included in some guise the barbarians roundabout.

Naturally, this rather sweeping proposition will be qualified as it is applied to the facts of history. Yet I suggest that it offers a starting point for the understanding of modern China in terms of Chinese tradition. A century of modern life has jarred the Chinese people loose from their past and new forces have now arisen in them; but this was not so much the case in the latter half of the nineteenth century when the Empress Dowager, Li Hung-chang and Robert Hart formed a trinity in power.

Our comprehension of both tribute and synarchy will be easier if we view them in each case as balancing mechanisms. We have noted how tribute relations were traditionally reciprocal, not unilateral — the barbarian profited from tributary trade while the emperor in receiving envoys enhanced the prestige of the dynasty. After the tables had been turned, the foreigner profited even more from his trade while seeking in self-interest to maintain the shrunken prestige of the regime. It took twenty years, from 1840 to 1860, for the balance to be shifted, but in the end the foreigner still traded

[a] I suggest that we can usefully coin here the word "synarchy," meaning joint rule or administration by two or more parties, because, first, "dyarchy" in the modern period connotes the specific arrangements made for the government of British India, with a statutory division of powers. Secondly, in China during the late Ch'ing period, Manchu, Chinese, Mongol, and Western treaty-power elements all played a part in the administration of the empire.

and the emperor still ruled. Though it was the barbarian who now called the tune, the partners were the same.

When we look at the record presented in previous chapters with this concept in mind, it is evident the Sino-Western synarchy of the treaty port era was by no means a purely Western creation. Just as the negotiators on both sides had to yield to the force of local circumstance — Ch'i-ying opening Foochow and Pottinger retaining Hongkong, both contrary to their original instructions — so the final arrangements of the treaties were actually in line with Chinese tradition. The treaty ports had their predecessors in the ports anciently assigned for tributary trade. Consular jurisdiction harked back to the custom whereby Arab headmen at medieval Zayton and Canton had taken personal responsibility for their countrymen. The most-favored-nation clause had its origin partly in the Confucian monarch's inveterate benevolence to all barbarians alike, the better to use them against one another. Even the treaty tariff, which prevented the protection of modern China's nascent industries, had its precedent in the oppressive Ch'ing taxation of production and trade. After all, licensed monopolies, export duties, and subsequently likin were all devised by a parasitic Chinese officialdom without foreign help. Finally, the use of Westerners in Chinese employ was nothing new in principle — T. F. Wade, H. N. Lay, and Robert Hart were the heirs of P'u Shou-keng, Marco Polo and Adam Schall.

Once we look for them, there are many further evidences of the dual origin of the treaty port system. That proto-capitalist, the comprador, after 1842 enlarged his functions to supplant the hong merchant as the Chinese collaborator of the foreign trader. Already, the Cantonese had served as the scouts, auxiliaries, and camp-followers of the Western commercial invaders, while the native opium dealer, though he left few records, handled the distribution of foreign drug between the receiving ship and the consumer just as eagerly as the tea and silk merchants provided export cargoes. Eventually the treaty ports grew up as a dual society of a new type, neither wholly native nor wholly foreign, with a new ricksha-culture compounded of Chinese and Western elements (a ricksha combines bicycle wheels and coolie power). Shanghailanders, for example, whatever their racial origin, found a common bond in the pursuit of profit in the Foreign Settlement. Wu Chien-chang and Edward Cunningham were Shanghailanders.

Similarly the Manchu-Chinese bureaucracy of the day put forward its new experts on the barbarians as men in whom the latter could "have confidence" — officials of the sort Ch'i-ying recruited to handle the new treaty relations, who studied the works of Wei Yuan and Hsü Chi-yü and dared to converse with consuls and missionaries. Men of this type, like Hsueh Huan at Shanghai, gained advancement through contact with foreigners.

Further analysis of the Western century in China should make it plain that the treaty system gradually became a basic component of the power structure of the Chinese state. The Westerner in this period was a partner in a Sino-Western rule over China, which by degrees came to supplant the Manchu-Chinese synarchy of the Ch'ing period. This temporary supplanting of the Manchu by the Britisher was epitomized, for example, in 1911 when the fall of the dynasty obliged the I.-G. of Customs, Sir Francis Aglen, to put China's customs revenues directly into foreign custody. The élitist tradition of Confucian government, which had made it easier than one might expect for non-Chinese warrior-administrators to seize the throne at Peking in 1644, made it similarly easy for Western traders, missionaries and travelers in the late nineteenth century to become privileged characters in the Chinese scene. They formed a foreign élite with a superior status guaranteed by their treaties and gunboats. (The fact that three generations of average Americans enjoyed contact with China on this unusual and pleasant basis no doubt contributed to the American national fondness for things Chinese.)

If the above suggests, even though sketchily, the position of the treaty system in Chinese history, it still remains an interesting question precisely how it became established. In Part I of this volume we have noted how the tradition of tribute relations handicapped and preconditioned China's response to the modern West, and in Parts II and III how the first treaties were drawn up and how the officials of Britain and China tried to make them effective. The progressive breakdown of the early treaty system, as trade expanded and diplomatic relations worsened (recounted in Part IV), has been generally lost to sight, overshadowed by the later success of the foreign powers in reaching Peking and getting the system established. Yet as indicated in Part V, it was precisely in this period of breakdown, when the local authorities at Shanghai were most hard pressed by the onrush of the Great Rebellion and local uprising, that they were constrained to accept the principle of joint administration embodied in the Foreign Inspectorate. This was the first practical step in the resuscitation of the treaty system, yet it was an on-the-spot invention made in the treaty port and soon disowned by the Foreign Office; for it ran counter to Western conceptions of inter-state relations — could foreign nationals really serve Chinese sovereignty? Nevertheless they did so, and it was possible not only because Bowring was a reformer, Alcock an administrator, and Samqua an opportunist, but also because there was in the background of the treaty ports a tradition of Sino-barbarian joint administration.

This tradition was brought into play by another background factor, the decline of the power of the Manchu dynasty, which obliged it to accept a degree of foreign partnership in order to survive its domestic and foreign crises.

Here again Chinese political institutions had their influence, for the race and nationality of the holders of power were less important in the Middle Kingdom of that day than their attitude toward the inherited social order. The agrarian-bureaucratic state could be headed by Manchus, and the latter could even be assisted by Anglo-Saxons, so long as the Chinese landlord-scholar-official class retained its customary position. Thus the suppression of pirates by British gunboats and the convoying of junks by foreign adventurers were acceptable to the waning dynasty, faute de mieux; in proportion as the Western powers made strictly limited demands, however forceful, they could be allowed to participate in the Confucian state and still not destroy it. The onset of the Taiping Rebellion was of course the immediate occasion by which the dynasty's weakness was made dramatically apparent, but it was only the climax of an accelerating process. As the Manchu power declined, the door was opened more widely to the West.

Thus if we look at the century of the unequal treaties in the context of China's institutional history, it is evident that the theory of imperialism (which was developed in Europe and is now the latest Western importation into China) is not the only avenue of approach to her modern foreign relations.

This story of a century ago indicates how the Chinese state, from its rich experience with the barbarians of Inner Asia, had no lack of institutional devices by which to accommodate foreign intruders in the domestic power structure. These devices, indeed, were all too convenient and available. They ushered the Chinese people blindly and unprepared into a new age of nationalism and industrialism. Yet even in the midst of the continuing revolution which has resulted, vestiges of the past are still discernible. Once more, a foreign element, again from the north, plays a leading part in China.

APPENDIXES

Appendix A
BRITISH PERSONNEL IN CHINA

Sec. 1: British Consular Officers at the Treaty Ports 1843-1858, listed chronologically.

Note: Since this has been compiled from a wide variety of sources, they are indicated for reference in cases of disparity. Dates are usually those of assuming duties, except when indicated as dates of appointment ("app."). The following abbreviations are used:

A	Acting	JA	Junior Assistant
AI	Assistant Interpreter	S	Supernumerary
C	Consul	SA	Senior Assistant
I	Interpreter	VC	Vice-Consul

Date of Assuming Duties	CANTON	AMOY	SHANGHAI	NINGPO	FOOCHOW
July 27, 1843[1]	C G. T. Lay				
,, ,, ,,	I R. Thom				
,, ,, ,,	SA T. T. Meadows				
,, ,, ,,	JA W. Meredith				
Nov. 2, 1843[2]		C H. Gribble			
Nov. 17, 1843[2]			C G. Balfour		
,, ,, ,,			I W. H. Medhurst		
,, ,, ,,			SA F. H. Hale		
Oct. 1, 1843 (app.)[2]				C R. Thom	
December, 1843[3]	I C. A. Sinclair				
December, 1843 (app.)[9]				SA P. Hague	
Dec. 21, 1843 (app.)[10]					
January, 1844[3]				AI C. A. Sinclair	
Feb. 7, 1844[61]		VC G. G. Sullivan			
May, 1844[4]	C F. C. Macgregor				
June, 1844[5]		I H. S. Parkes			
June, 1844[6]		SA F. Parish			
June 14, 1844[12]	I T. T. Meadows				
July 1, 1844[8]		JA C. A. Winchester			
Listed July, 1844[7]					C G. T. Lay
,, ,, ,,	VC R. B. Jackson				
,, ,, ,,	SA J. Backhouse				
,, ,, ,,	JA E. F. Giles				
,, ,, ,,				VC T. H. Layton (office abolished April, 1846)[67]	
,, ,, ,,				JA L. Hertslet	
Nov. 7, 1844[14]		C R. Alcock			
Nov. 12, 1844[15,58]		Acting I, W. R. Gingell (for Parkes)			
Nov. 20, 1844		Acting SA, L. Hertslet (for Parish)			

Date of Assuming Duties	CANTON	AMOY	SHANGHAI	NINGPO	FOOCHOW
Nov. 20, 1844		Acting JA, C. A. Winchester			
Listed January, 1845[13]					SA J. T. Walker
Listed January, 1845[13]					JA W. S. Meredith
1845-Jan. 19, 1857[64]	JA H. Oakley				
March, 1845[56]					C R. Alcock
March, 1845[57]					I H. S. Parkes
Mar. 25, 1845[16]		VC in charge, G. G. Sullivan (Alcock to Foochow)			
Mar. 25, 1845[15]		I R. Gingell			
Apr. 5, 1845[17]		C G. T. Lay			
July-Sept., 1845					Acting I, R. Gingell
Nov. 6, 1845[16]		Acting C, G. G. Sullivan (Lay dead)			
Listed January, 1846[18]					JA C. T. Watkins
,, ,, ,,			Acting JA. F. Robertson		
Apr. 15, 1846[19]		C T. H. Layton			
August, 1846 (app.)[22]					Acting I, F. Parish
August, 1846 into 1847 (app.) 5, 14			Acting I, H. S. Parkes (for Medhurst)		
August 4, 1846[20]	VC J. Backhouse (Jackson to Foochow)				
Aug. 18, 1846 (app.)[14]			C R. Alcock		
Aug. 18, 1846 (app.)[21]					C R. B. Jackson
September, 1846[3]				I C. A. Sinclair	
Sept. 12, 1846[63]				Acting C, G. G. Sullivan (Thom dead)	
Listed January, 1847[23]				JA F. Parish	
Listed January, 1847[23]	SA E. F. Giles		3rd A F. Robertson		
,, ,, ,,					JA W. S. Meredith
,, ,, ,,					I M. C. Morrison
Mar. 29-Apr. 24, 1847[33]	Acting JA, Cartwright (for Giles)				

Date of Assuming Duties	CANTON	AMOY	SHANGHAI	NINGPO	FOOCHOW
Apr. 23, 1847[26]	VC A. W. Elmslie				
Apr. 23, 1847[24]		Acting VC, J. Backhouse			
July, 1847[59]		I T. F. Wade (for Gingell)			
Listed January, 1848[26] Also January, 1846[18] + 1847[23]		I W. R. Gingell			
Mar. 25, 1848[62] - Apr. 20, 1849[27]	VC A. W. Elmslie (acting consul)				
Mar. 30, 1848[68] - August, 1849[28]		Acting VC, W. H. Medhurst (for Backhouse)			
April, 1848 (app.)			I H. S. Parkes		
Listed January, 1849[29]	SA and Acting VC, J. T. Walker				
,, - ,, ,,					SA and Acting I, F. Parish
Jan.-June, 1849[30]		Acting JA, G. S. Morrison			
Feb. 1, 1849[31]	Acting I, J. Meadows (for T. T. Meadows)				
Apr. 13, 1849[32]	C J. Bowring				
June, 1849[35]					I W. R. Gingell
June 30, 1849				SA F.Parish	
July, 1849 (app.)		I H. S. Parkes			
July 21-Aug. 21, 1849[27]	Acting C, A.W. Elmslie				
Listed January, 1850[34]			I W. H. Medhurst		
,, ,, ,,		VC J. Backhouse (dead)[60]			
,, ,, ,,		I M. C. Morrison			
,, ,, ,,			Acting SA, F. Parish (for Hale)		
January, 1850 (app.)[37]					I in charge, W. R. Gingell
Mar. 17, 1850[16]					I in charge, C. A. Sinclair (for Jackson)
June, 1850[3]					
June 15, 1850[37]					VC in charge, W. Connor

Date of Assuming Duties	CANTON	AMOY	SHANGHAI	NINGPO	FOOCHOW
July 20, 1850				Acting VC in charge, D. B. Robertson (for Sullivan)	
Aug. 15, 1850 (took over)[36]				Acting I, J. Meadows (for Sinclair)	
Aug. 20, 1850[66]			VC W. Connor		
Aug. 20, 1850[13]					I in charge, C. A. Sinclair
Jan.-Sept., 1851[3]					I in charge, C. A. Sinclair
Jan. 16, 1851[41]					
Feb. 20, 1851[10]			VC D. B. Robertson		VC in charge, W. Connor (office of Consul abolished)[21]
April, 1851[9]				VC P. Hague (office of Consul abolished) (retired Oct. 1, 1855)[9] Listed Jan., 1858[40]	
July 1, 1851[40]		JA W. H. Pedder			
3 months, 1851[40]		Acting I, W. H. Pedder			
Sept. 5, 1851					VC in charge, J. T. Walker
Nov. 21, 1851[5]	I H. S. Parkes				
In 1852[65]			VC T. F. Wade		
Listed January, 1852[42]	SA F. Parish				
,, ,, ,,			SA F. H. Hale		
Jan. 1, 1852[12]			I T. T. Meadows		
Feb.-Dec., 1852[40]		I W. H. Pedder			
Apr. 14, 1852-Feb. 14, 1853[27]	Acting C, A. W. Elmslie				
December, 1852[43]		Acting SA, G. S. Morrison			
December, 1852[3]		I C. A. Sinclair			
February, 1853 (app.)[44]	JA J. Markham				
Apr. 1, 1853[36]				Acting VC in charge, J. T. Meadows (for Hague)	
Apr. 29, 1853 (app.)[10]		C D. B. Robertson (in Canton)			
May 1, 1853 (app.)[10]	Acting C, D. B. Robertson				
June, 1853[38]			Acting SA, W. H. Fittock (for Hale)		
Oct. 14, 1853 (app.)[10]		C D. B. Robertson (took charge)			I in charge, W. R. Gingell (for Walker)
Dec. 8, 1853-Jan., 1854[27]					
Dec. 23, 1853-July 1854[27]	VC in charge, A. W. Elmslie (retired July, 1855)				

Date of Assuming Duties	CANTON	AMOY	SHANGHAI	NINGPO	FOOCHOW
Apr. 1854[44]					A J. Markham
April, 1854[45]	I M. C. Morrison				
Listed January, 1854)[46]					
Apr. 13, 1854[49]					SI P. J. Hughes
May, 1854 (app.)[48]			AVC H. N. Lay		
,, ,, ,,			I H. N. Lay		
May, 1854 (app.)[39]			C D. B. Robertson (abs. at Canton)		
July 13, 1854 (app.)[10]	Acting C, D.B. Robertson				
Aug. 10, 1854[5]		C H. S. Parkes			
Aug. 16, 1854[52]	C R. Alcock				
Aug.-Dec., 1854[27]	Acting C, A. W. Elmslie				
Sept. 8, 1854 (app.)[50]					VC F. H. Hale
Oct. 14, 1854[47]			VC T. F. Wade		
Nov. 9, 1854 (app.)[28]					C W. H. Medhurst
Dec. 14, 1854 (app.)[11]			VC F. E. B. Harvey		
Dec., 1854-Mar. 1858[8]		Acting C, C. A. Winchester			
Listed January, 1855[52]	ASA W. H. Pedder (for H. Oakley)				
Listed January, 1855[52]	AJA O. T. Lane (for G. S. Morrison				
,, ,, ,,		Acting JA, G. S. Morrison			
,, ,, ,,			S W. H. Lay		
,, ,, ,,			S J. Morgan		
January, 1855[54]		SI R. Swinhoe	SA W. H. Fittock		
January, 1855					
February, 1855[43]			Acting SA, G. S. Morrison		
March, 1855[3]			I. C. A. Sinclair		
March, 1855[8]				Acting VC, C. A. Winchester	
Mar. 9, 1855[10]			C D. B. Robertson (in charge)		

Mar. 12, 1855 (app.)[40]	I W. H. Pedder				
Mar. 29, 1855[66]					C W. H. Medhurst (took over)
June, 1855 (app.)[53]				S R. Hart	
August, 1855[45]	VC M. C. Morrison				
Dec. 6, 1855-Jan. 28, 1856[50]					VC in charge, F. H. Hale
In 1856[54]		JA R. Swinhoe			
Apr. 12, 1856 (app.)[3]				VC in charge, C. A. Sinclair	
Apr.-May, 1856[40]		Acting C, W. H. Pedder			
Apr. 14-June 11, 1856 (app.)[8]	Acting C, C. A. Winchester				
May, 1856[45]		Acting C, M. C. Morrison			
June, 1856-Sept. 1858[5]	Acting C, H. S. Parkes				
July 12, 1856[36]			Acting I, J. Meadows		
July 16, 1856[8]	VC C. A. Winchester				
Feb. 20, 1857-July, 1858[50]					VC in charge, F. H. Hale
Oct., 1857-Feb., 1858[40]		Acting C, W. H. Pedder			
Dec. 23, 1857[45]					Acting VC, M. C. Morrison
1857 and 1858[12]				VC in charge, T. Meadows	
1858 (app.)[54]		SA and Acting I, R. Swinhoe			
Feb.2-July, 1, 1858[8]	VC in charge, C. A. Winchester				
Feb. 16-Apr. 12, 1858[15]		Acting C, W. R. Gingell			
Mar. 7, 1858[50]					AC in charge, F. H. Hale
Apr. 6. 1858 (app.)[53]	JA R. Hart				
June 1, 1858 (app.)[54]			JA R. Swinhoe		
June 1, 1858[55]		JA W. H. Lay			
July 27, 1858[28]					C W. H. Medhurst (in charge)
Nov. 17, 1858[45]					VC M. C. Morrison
Nov. 26, 1858 (app.)[36]	I J. Meadows				
Dec. 21, 1858 (app.)[5]			Acting C H. S. Parkes		
Dec. 21, 1858 (app.)[10]	C D. B. Robertson (at Shanghai)				
Dec. 21, 1858 (app.)[45]					C M. C. Morrison
,, ,, ,, ,, [51]				C F. E. B. Harvey	
,, ,, ,, ,, [15]		C W. R. Gingell			
Dec. 22, 1858 (app.)[44]			VC J. Markham		

NOTES TO SEC. 1., APPENDIX A

1. CR, 1843.
2. Orders, Ordinances, Rules, and Regulations concerning the Trade in China.
3. The Foreign Office List and Diplomatic and Consular Handbook (London, January 1864), p. 145. (Cited below as FO, for the year in question.)
4. BC, 18, Macgregor's 13 to Davis, May 28, 1844.
5. FO, p. 129.
6. BA, 314, Davis' 10 to Gribble, June 20, 1844.
7. CR, July, 1844.
8. FO, p. 162.
9. Ibid., p. 93.
10. Ibid., p. 137.
11. Ibid., p. 96.
12. BC, 436.
13. CR, 1845.
14. BF, 238, Davis' 27 to Alcock, Aug. 18, 1846. BA, 35, Alcock's 75 to Davis, Nov. 12, 1844.
15. FO, p. 165.
16. BA, 67, Sullivan's 78 to Davis, Nov. 6, 1845.
17. BA, 59, Lay's 28 to Davis, Apr. 5, 1845.
18. CR, 1846.
19. BA, 73, Sullivan's 19 to Davis, Apr. 15, 1846.
20. Listed as A. V. C. in Anglo-Ch. Cal., 1847.
21. BF, 238, Davis' 44 to Alcock, Aug. 20, 1846.
22. BF, 373.
23. Anglo-Ch. Cal., 1847.
24. Orders, Ordinances, p. 50.
25. FO, p. 157.
26. Anglo-Ch. Cal., 1848.
27. FO, p. 82.
28. Ibid., p. 120.
29. Anglo-Ch. Cal., 1849.
30. FO, p. 124.
31. BC, Elmslie's 30 to Bonham, Feb. 14, 1849.
32. Ibid., 178, Bowring to Bonham (77), Apr. 13, 1849.
33. Ibid., 107, Macgregor's 23 to Davis, Mar. 29, 1847.
34. Anglo-Ch. Cal., 1850.
35. BF, Jackson's 20 to Bonham, June 4, 1849. But cp. FO, 165; Gingell became I. at Foochow in 1848.
36. FO, p. 120.
37. BF, Foochow Personnel References.
38. FO, p. 84.
39. The British Imperial Calendar for 1858 (London, 1858), p. 140.
40. FO, p. 130.
41. Ibid., p. 120.
42. Anglo-Ch. Cal., 1852.
43. FO, p. 124.
44. Ibid., p. 118.
45. Ibid., p. 124.

46. Anglo-Ch. Cal., 1854.
47. Costin, Great Britain and China, 1833-1860 (London, 1937), p. 163.
48. FO, p. 110.
49. Ibid., p. 102.
50. Ibid., p. 93.
51. Ibid., p. 96.
52. Anglo-Ch. Cal., 1855.
53. FO, p. 96.
54. Ibid., p. 152.
55. Ibid., p. 110.
56. BF, 227, Davis' 21 to Lay, Mar. 17, 1845.
57. Ibid., 228, Davis' 53 to Alcock, July 24, 1845 and 78, Sept. 29, 1845.
58. BA, 36, Alcock's 79 to Davis, Nov. 13, 1844.
59. Ibid., 339, Davis' 57 to Layton, July 9, 1847.
60. Ibid., 114, Layton's 518 to Bonham, Apr. 6, 1848.
61. Ibid., 8, Gribble's 7 to Pottinger, Dec. 11, 1843.
62. BC, 141, Elmslie's 73 to Bonham, Mar. 25, 1848.
63. BN, 77, Sullivan to Davis (17), Sept. 12, 1846. Also Davis' 37 to Sullivan, Oct. 30, 1846.
64. FO, p. 126.
65. Ibid., p. 157.
66. BF, op. cit.
67. BN, 408, Davis' 63 to Thom, Dec. 2, 1845.
68. BA, 114, Layton's 18 to Bonham, Apr. 6, 1848.

Sec. 2: Partners of Jardine, Matheson & Co., and its predecessors, to 1858.

Note: This table is drawn both from the firm's private centennial volume (Jardine, Matheson & Co.) and from Mr. Greenberg's study of the archives (British Trade), between which there are occasional discrepancies. The list of early firm names (leftmost column) is from the latter source, as well as other data in [ ].

Early firms	Name	Born-Died	Active in China	Remarks
Cox & Reid 1782	John Henry Cox	-1791	1781-1791	
	[John Reid]			
Cox & Beale 1787	Daniel Beale	1759-1842	c.1787-1797	
	David Reid			Beale, Reid & Co., 1793.
	Thomas Beale	-1842	c.1787 or 1790-1815	Partner, Beale, Reid & Co.
Hamilton & Reid & Beale 1799	Robert Hamilton		c.1793-1799	Partner, Beale, Reid & Co.
Reid & Beale 1800	Alexander Shank	-1817	c.1797-1817	Partner, Beale, Reid & Co.
Reid, Beale & Co. 1801				
Beale & Magniac 1803	Charles Magniac	1776-1824	1802-1824	Partner, Beale, Reid & Co.
Beale & Co. 1811				Formed Magniac & Co. 1817.
Shank & Magniac 1817				
Charles Magniac & Co. 1819	Hollingworth Magniac	1786-1867	1805-1827	Magniac & Co. 1817
Magniac & Co. 1824	[Daniel Magniac]			[Partner 1823-1828]
Partners of J M & Co. 1832- 1832-40	(Doctor) William Jardine	1784-1843	c.1823-1839	With Magniac & Co. [1825] c. December 1826. Formed Jardine, Matheson & Co. 1832.
1832-42	(Sir) Nicholas James Sutherland Matheson	1796-1878	1818-1842	[With Yrisarri & Co., 1821-1827]. With Magniac & Co. [1827] 1828. Jardine, Matheson & Co. 1832.
1835-41	Henry Wright		1826-1841	With Magniac & Co. 1826. Partner 1829? Partner J M & Co. 1835.
1835-36	Andrew Johnstone	1798-1857	c.1822-1836	Nephew of W. Jardine
1835-52	(Sir) Alexander Matheson	1805-1886	c.1827-1846	Nephew of J. Matheson. Head of firm 1842-1852.
1839-45	Andrew Jardine	1812-1881	1832-1843	Nephew of W. Jardine.
1842-46	William Stewart	-1846	c.1835-1846	
1843-49	Donald Matheson	-1901	-1849	Nephew of J. Matheson.
1843-56	David Jardine	1818-1856	1838-1856	Nephew of W. Jardine. Head of firm 1852.
1845-60	Joseph Jardine	1822-1861	1843-1860	Nephew of W. Jardine. Head, 1856.
1845-54	Alexander Grant Dallas	1818-1882	-1854	Junior partner 1843-1854 . Earliest representative of Co. in Shanghai.
1849-57	Alexander Campbell Maclean		c.1839-1857	

Partners of J. M. & Co.	Name	Born-Died	Active in China	Remarks
1852-82	(Sir) Robert Jardine	1825-1905	1849-1860	Nephew of W. Jardine Head, 1860.
1852-64	Alexander Perceval	1821-1866	1846-1864	Relative of J. Matheson Head in East 1860-1864.
1854-64	John Charles Bowring	1821-1893	1848-1864	Son of Sir J. Bowring
1858-61	James Macandrew	1825-1902	1847-1856	
1858-59	Malcolm Anderson Macleod		-1859	Junior partner 1858.
1858-76	James Whittall	1827-1893	c.1856-1875	Associate partner 1858. Head in East 1864-74.
c.1858-1912	William Keswick	1834-1912	1855-1886	Grand-nephew of W. Jardine. Head in East 1874-1886.
c.1858-79	Robert Alexander Houstoun	1838-1879	c.1858-1879	Related to J. Matheson.

Appendix B
DATA ON THE CH'ING CUSTOMS ADMINISTRATION AFTER THE TREATIES

Sec. 1. The rearrangement of the Hoppo's accounts in 1843.

The first five of Ch'i-ying's and the Hoppo's proposals,[1] as finally sanctioned by the emperor on August 31, 1843, indicate the "reorganization" effected in the Canton customs:

(1) The accounting system of the Canton customs included (a) regular duties (cheng-shui) levied chiefly on foreign trade, and also on merchant vessels in internal trade, (b) a fixed surplus (o-ting ying-yü), and (c) an unfixed surplus (o-wai ying-yü). The first two items had been fixed at Tls. 899,064 a year. The unfixed surplus, as reported by the customs, had varied between Tls. 100,000 and Tls. 400,000 a year. On the opening of the new ports, the total of the collections at Canton would be less than formerly (no allowance was made for an increase in the total amount of foreign trade). Therefore any insufficiency in the collection at Canton should be made up, to the fixed amount, by the transfer of funds from the new ports. This was approved.

(2) The amount of future collections at the new ports and at Canton was uncertain. Therefore no quotas of duties should be fixed for the new ports until the end of an experimental period of three years. At that time parts of the quota originally fixed for Canton could be apportioned to the customs of Fukien, Chekiang, and Kiangnan. This was approved.

(3) The category of miscellaneous duties should be abolished. This had included periodic official exactions levied in addition to the regular duties and meltage fees (hao-hsien), such as commissions, fees for entering, leaving, or remaining in port, and the like. These miscellaneous duties had been collected along with the regular duties. But now there was to be no distinction between regular duties, meltage fees, and miscellaneous duties. All were to be lumped together in the new duties. This was approved.

(4) Under this heading Ch'i-ying and his colleagues discussed, first, sums formerly remitted to make up for loss by exchange when transferring funds to the Board of Revenue. To every Tls. 100 sent to the Board, Tls. 15 had been added for this purpose. This had been increased to Tls. 25 in 1843. It was proposed and sanctioned that these payments should now be remitted to the Board out of the unfixed surplus at each customhouse.

Under the same heading, Ch'i-ying also discussed three items: (a) the annual tribute of Tls. 55,000, (b) the ginseng payments of about Tls. 100,000 a year — both of which had formerly been paid by the Cohong to the Hoppo for transmission to the imperial household — and (c) certain extra levies on the trade totalling about Tls. 40-50,000 a year which had been made by the Cohong for the support of various charities. If other countries agreed with England in demanding the abolition of the Cohong, Ch'i-ying proposed that funds for (a) and (b) should be sent to the imperial household in agreed proportions from the unfixed surpluses of the various customhouses, and funds for (c) should be derived by taking Tls. 40,000 a year from the unfixed surplus of the Canton customs. This last proposal (c) was sanctioned, but the Grand Council refused to approve the plans for (a) and (b). The ginseng money (b) was used for military and other

1. See IWSM-TK, 67.40b-45b, memorial from Ch'i-ying, Ch'i Kung, Ch'eng Yü-ts'ai and Wen-feng, Aug. 11, 1843; ibid., 68.13-20b, memorial of Mu-chang-a et al., Aug. 31, 1843; see also IWSM-TK Supp. 1615-18, mem. rec'd Nov. 7, 1843.

purposes in Peking. The Canton governor-general in 1842 had proposed that payment of it cease until at the end of four years the Cohong should have repaid its debt to the provincial government of Tls. 2,800,000. This debt had been Tls. 3,500,000 at the end of 1842. Evidently Tls. 700,000 had been paid in the first half of 1843. But the Council had proposed, and gained imperial consent, that of the Tls. 700,000 to be repaid annually by the Cohong, Tls. 100,000 should be used to keep up the payments of ginseng money. Similarly, regarding the tribute money under (a), the Council protested that it was an item of revenue much too important to be made dependent on the unfixed surplus at Canton or elsewhere. If there should be no such surplus, whence would the money come? The Hoppo should arrange the matter.

(5) Another proposal explained that the Canton customs had formerly retained a surplus of more than Tls. 100,000 every year for tribute objects and for buying things ordered by the court. It was proposed that these payments should now be met by setting aside Tls. 120,000 or 130,000 from the unfixed surplus of the Canton customs. If the Canton funds were insufficient, payments should be made from the unfixed surpluses of the other ports. The Council refused to sanction this and left the Hoppo to raise the money as he might see fit.

How far did these changes, summarized above, protect the position of the Hoppo? It is plain that under (1) he was insured against loss by being allowed to draw upon the other ports if necessary to make up his fixed payments. Also under (4), he could rely upon the other ports to avoid loss by exchange. Under (2), after three years, part of his burden of fixed payments was to be placed upon the other ports (actually, this was postponed beyond the original three-year period). He was deprived of the miscellaneous duties revenue under (3), and was made to pay Tls. 40,000 a year for charities formerly supported by the Cohong's levies (4c) and Tls. 55,000 a year for tribute money formerly paid by the Cohong (4a). On the other hand the Cohong was to continue, at least for four years, to supply the Tls. 100,000 of ginseng money (4b). The Hoppo would still be responsible for gifts to the court of Tls. 120,000 or 130,000 a year (5). Thus the burden shifted from the Cohong to him totalled nominally only Tls. 95,000.

With this may be compared the statement of the Cohong to Pottinger that their customary annual payments to the government (presumably to the Hoppo in the first instance) had included some Tls. 640,000 for building forts, Tls. 300,000 Hong duties, and Tls. 370,000 ginseng money and tribute.[2] If the Cohong had really been able in former times to pay the Hoppo this Tls. 1,310,000, of which he was now to be responsible for only Tls. 95,000, he was hardly worse off than before. Moreover, for the loss of the Cohong as a revenue collecting agency, the Hoppo was to be reimbursed from the custom-houses of the new ports. From this brief analysis, we cannot conclude that the interests of the Hoppo were damaged by the new system.

2. FO 17/66, Hong merchants' to Pottinger, Feb. 26, in Pottinger's 14 of Mar. 10, 1843.

Sec. 2: Tables of Collection Periods, 1843-1855

Note: These tables are necessary to explain the figures presented in Chapter 14, table 9, because the Ch'ing revenue reports were made for fiscal years of twelve lunar months only. Since it was necessary to add occasionally a thirteenth or intercalary month (for example, an "intercalary seventh month," jun-ch'i-yueh, after the regular lunar seventh month) to the Chinese lunar year, many solar calendar years had thirteen lunar months. This discrepant fact, however, was disregarded, with the result that the fiscal revenue year for these reports was a peculiarly retrogressive device: the thirteenth month, in any solar year which had one, was taken as the first month of a new fiscal year. We therefore find the fiscal year at Canton beginning, for example, successively in the third solar month of 1845, the second solar month of 1846 and 1847, and the first solar month of 1848. These dates have all been translated, in the table we present below, into the Western calendar. The regular customs and treaty tariff collections were for different periods, except at Canton; and the collection periods under the regular customs differed from port to port, except when Amoy and Foochow coincided. Specialists in trade statistics are welcome to pursue this subject. I am indebted to Dr. E-tu Sun for her help on it.

a. Under the Regular Customs (not including Canton)

Year	Amoy	Foochow	Ningpo	Shanghai
1843-44	8/27/43-2/13/44	3/16/43-3/3/44	10/30/43-10/18/44	11/22/43-11/9/44
1844-45	2/14/44-2/21/45	3/4/44-2/21/45	10/19/44-10/7/45	11/10/44-10/29/45
1845-46	2/22/45-2/10/46	2/22/45-2/10/46	10/8/45-9/26/46	10/30/45-10/19/46
1846-47			9/27/46-9/15/47	10/20/46-10/8/47
1847-48				10/9/47-9/26/48
1848-49	1/21/48-1/9/49	same as Amoy	9/5/48-8/24/49	
1849	1/10/49-12/28/49	" " "		
1849-50	12/29/49-12/18/50	" " "	8/25/49-8/14/50	
1850-51	12/19/50-12/7/51	" " "	8/15/50-8/3/51	9/6/50-8/26/51
1851-52	12/8/51-11/26/52	" " "	8/4/51-7/23/52	
1852-53	11/27/52-11/15/53	" " "	7/24/52-7/12/53	
1853-54			7/13/53-7/1/54	
1854-55			7/2/54-6/20/55	

b. Under the Treaty Tariff (including regular customs at Canton)

Year	Canton (treaty and regular collections combined)	Amoy (treaty tariff only)	Foochow	Ningpo	Shanghai
1843-44		11/2/43-3/13/44		12/3/43-3/13/44	11/17/43-3/13/44
1844-45	3/14/44-3/3/45	same dates as for Canton from 1844 on			
1845-46	3/4/45-2/20/46				
1846-47	2/21/46-2/10/47				
1847-48	2/11/47-1/30/48				
1848-49	1/31/48-1/19/49				
1849-50	1/20/49-1/7/50				
1850	1/8/50-12/28/51				
1850-51	12/29/50-12/17/51				
1851-52	12/18/51-12/6/52				
1852-53	12/7/52-11/25/53				
1853-54	11/26/53-11/15/54				
1854-55	11/16/54-11/4/55				

REFERENCE NOTES

Abbreviations Used In Reference Notes

AC	Archives of the United States consulate, Canton
AS	Archives of the United States consulate, Shanghai
BA	British consulate, Amoy
BC	" " Canton
BF	" " Foochow
BN	" " Ningpo
Brunnert	H. S. Brunnert, Present Day Political Organization of China, Shanghai, 1912
China	China Despatches, Department of State, National Archives, Washington, D.C., cited by volume number.
CM	China Mail, Hongkong, 1845- weekly
CR	Chinese Repository, Macao and Canton, 1832-51, monthly
CSK	Ch'ing-shih-kao (Draft History of the Ch'ing Dynasty)
CSL	Ch'ing shih-lu (Veritable Records of the Ch'ing Dynasty)
CSPSR	Chinese Social and Political Science Review, Peking, 1916- quarterly
FEQ	Far Eastern Quarterly, Far Eastern Association, 1941-
FO 17	Foreign Office Records, China correspondence, Public Record Office, London
FO 228	Legation and embassy archives, China, Public Record Office, London
HJAS	Harvard Journal of Asiatic Studies, Cambridge, 1936- quarterly
Hummel	A. W. Hummel, ed., Eminent Chinese of the Ch'ing Period (1644-1912), Washington, D.C., 2 vols., 1943-44
IWSM-HF	Ch'ou-pan i-wu shih-mo (A complete account of the management of barbarian affairs), Hsien-feng period
IWSM-TK	Ch'ou-pan i-wu shih-mo, Tao-kuang period
" " Supp.	Documents supplementary to I-wu shih-mo, selected from Grand Council archives by Dr. T. F. Tsiang (unpublished mss.)
Morse, H. B.	Conflict, vol. I, The International Relations of the Chinese Empire (Shanghai, 1910)
" " "	Submission, vol. II, ibid. (London, 1918)
" " "	Subjection, vol. III, ibid. (London 1918)
" " "	Chronicles, 5 vols., The Chronicles of the East India Company Trading to China, 1635-1834 (Oxford, 1926, 1929)
NCH	North China Herald, Shanghai, 1850- weekly
Ta-Ch'ing hui-tien	(Collected Statutes of the Ch'ing Dynasty) is cited by the reign in which an edition was published, as Chia-ch'ing hui-tien
THL	Tung-hua hsü-lu

Other abbreviations (or condensations) of titles will be found in the bibliography.

REFERENCES: CHAPTER 1.

1. John K. Fairbank, The United States and China, pp. 3-119.

2. Writings of Max Weber have provided a pervasive stimulus to sociological theory concerning China; so has the application of Marxist theory (see especially the writings of Dr. Karl August Wittfogel). See also Owen Lattimore, Inner Asian Frontiers of China.

3. This subject is treated more fully in a forthcoming source book by Ssu-yü Teng, John K. Fairbank and others, China's Response to the West, A Documentary Survey (1839-1923), to be published by the Harvard University Press.

4. Karl A. Wittfogel and Feng Chia-sheng, History of Chinese Society, Liao (907-1125), p. 24.

5. T'ung I, "I-Man-Jung-Ti yü tung-nan-hsi-pei" (The I, Man, Jung and Ti and East, South, West, North). For references to I in the classics, see e.g., The Works of Mencius (Legge trans.), bk. IV, pt. 2, ch. i, secs. 1, 2; bk. III, pt. 2, ch. v, sec. 4. See Glossary for Chinese characters in text and notes.

6. This Chinese folklore concerning barbarians was described by G. Schlegel in a series of articles, "Problèmes géographiques des peuples étrangers chez les historiens chinois," T'oung Pao, 3-6 (1892-95), passim. The subject awaits further study.

7. See Kenneth Ch'en (Ch'en Kuan-sheng), "Matteo Ricci's Contribution to and Influence on Geographical Knowledge in China," esp. p. 347 et seq.

8. See Huang-ch'ao wen-hsien t'ung-k'ao (Che-chiang shu-chü edition, 1882), ch. 298, 6-8 and 31b; Chia-ch'ing hui-tien, 31. 3-4; Chang Wei-hua, "Ming-shih Fo-lang-chi Lü-sung Ho-lan I-ta -li-ya ssu-chuan chu-shih" ("A commentary of the four chapters on Portugal, Spain, Holland and Italy in the history of the Ming dynasty"), pp. 5-6, 155-6.

9. IWSM-TK, 71.1 (March 1844); 79.17.

10. Thus Chang Hsieh, in his Tung-hsi-yang k'ao (A study of the eastern and western oceans [i.e., in Southeast Asia]), preface 1618 (Commercial Press ed., Shanghai, 1937), p. 84, notes under Hung-mao-fan that they have "deep eyes, long noses, and hair and beard all red"; he notes their similarity to traditional descriptions of the Jung in the Western Region. Likewise Ch'en Lun-ch'iung, Hai-kuo wen-chien lu (Record of things seen and heard among the maritime nations), author's preface 1730, chüan 1, Ta-hsi-yang chi, identifies Hung-mao as the generic term for Ta-hsi-yang (Europe).

11. See Chia-ch'ing hui-tien, 31.2-4; IWSM-TK, 70.1b (December 1843); 72.3 (July 1844).

12. Huang-Ch'ing chih-kung t'u (Illustrations of the regular tributaries of the imperial Ch'ing), comp. by Tung Kao et al. under imperial auspices, ordered 1751, completed 1760, Palace edition 1761, 9 chüan: ch. 1 refers to the West.

13. Ibid., 1.47.

14. Ibid., 1.40.

15. IWSM-TK, 73.3b. In a memorial received Dec. 1, 1843, Ch'i-ying had identified the Fo-lang-chi as the Portuguese at Macao, Ricci and his successors as from I-ta-li-ya, and Ta-hsi-yang as the name first used for I-ta-li-ya: ibid., 70.1. Thus he used Ta-hsi-yang for Macao, cp. ibid., 70.4.

16. C. Crow, Foreign Devils in the Flowery Kingdom, pp. 35-6. See Robert A. Hall, Jr., "Chinese Pidgin English Grammar and Texts." W. C. Hunter's Fan Kwae at Canton, among other contemporary works, gives occasional samples of pidgin. Charles G. Leland, Pidgin-English Sing-Song has a 17-page vocabulary and C. de Montigny, "Manuel du Négociant", three pages (321-3).

17. C. F. Gordon Cumming, Wanderings in China, II.54.

18. This embassy has been carefully studied by Prof. Duyvendak, "The Last Dutch Embassy."

19. For this table I am indebted to Dr. C. S. Gardner. See also the list of envoys and bibliography in Earl Pritchard's definitive article, "The Kotow in the Macartney Embassy to China in 1793," p. 200.

20. Cp. J. W. Stanton, "Russian Embassies to Peking During the Eighteenth Century;" also K. S. Latourette, The Great Century in Northern Africa and in Asia, A.D. 1800-A.D. 1914, vol. VI in A History of the Expansion of Christianity, ch. v, "The Chinese Empire." Agnes Chen, "The Eclipse of Manchuria," p. 84, notes the increased Russian incursions into Manchuria in the early nineteenth century.

21. Latourette, op.cit. The most illuminating analysis of relations between the Ch'ing and the Papacy is Father Rosso's documented study Apostolic Legations to China.

22. See the summary in Kenneth Ch'en, "Hai-lu, Fore-runner of Chinese Travel Accounts of Western Countries," pp. 210-12. For a recent survey of the growth of Western studies in the early nineteenth century, see Chang Hsi-t'ung, "The Earliest Phase of the Introduction of Western Political Science into China."

23. On these descriptions of the West, see "A Selected List of Ch'ing Works (1644-1860) on Maritime Relations" in Fairbank and Teng "Tributary System", pp. 206-219, listing 34 items, most of which await scholarly analysis. The following items may be added: Fan Tuan-ang, Yueh-chung chien-wen (Seen and heard in Kwangtung), also entitled Shuo-yueh hsin-shu (A new discussion of Kwangtung), 31 chüan in 6 ts'e 1801 (data on Macao, routes, foreign vessels); Yen Ju-i, Yang-fang chi-yao (Essentials of maritime defense), 24 chüan in 8 ts'e (data on coast defense, foreign trade and tributaries); Chou Kuang et al., Kuang-tung k'ao-ku chi-yao (Researches on Kwangtung), 46 chüan in 5 ts'e, 1893 (data on customs, shipping, Macao, etc.). See also the I-fen chi-wen (Record of the barbarian miasma) and other works by Liang T'ing-nan cited in Hummel; and Yü Ch'ang-hui, Fang-hai chi-yao (Essentials of coastal defense), chüan-shou plus 18 chüan in 10 ts'e, 1842 (see ch. xviii on maritime countries).

24. On the book of Hsieh Ch'ing-kao, see Feng Ch'eng-chün, ed., Hai-lu chu (An annotated edition of the Hai-lu). An early wood-block edition gives Yang as author; another revised edition with notes and preface by Lü T'iao-yang dated 1870 gives Hsieh (1765-1821) as author. Professor Feng's preface discusses certain problems of origin but leaves no doubt of the work's authenticity; see pp. 14-18. See also Kenneth Ch'en's useful article on the Hai-lu, loc. cit., for its data on Europe.

25. Feng, Hai-lu chu, pp. 73-74.

26. Ibid., pp. 75-76.

27. See Liang T'ing-nan, Yueh hai-kuan chih, chüan 23, Kung-po 3, Ying-chi-li, pp. 79-108.

28. See Pritchard's article, "The Kotow in the Macartney Embassy."

29. IWSM-TK, 71.27b-29.

30. Ibid., and Feng Ch'eng-chün, Hai-lu chu, pp. 73 (Ying-chi-li), 15 (Chiu-jou-fo).

31. IWSM-TK, 72.32-33b.

32. Article dated Shanghai, 1852, in Shanghai Almanac for 1854, and Miscellany.

33. Ch'en Kung-lu, Chung-kuo chin-tai shih (Modern history of China), pp. 74-75.

34. IWSM-TK, 49.28b.

35. See Fang Chao-ying in Hummel, Eminent Chinese, pp. 399-402.

REFERENCES: CHAPTER 2

1. See Hung Chün-p'ei, Ch'un-ch'iu kuo-chi kung-fa (International law of the Spring and Autumn period). This is one of several Chinese studies of "international" law among the Warring States. Others include Chang Hsin-ch'eng, Ch'un-ch'iu kuo-chi kung-fa (same title as above), a rather uncritical transposition of modern concepts back into classical times; Hsü Ch'uan-pao, Hsien Ch'in kuo-chi-fa chih i-chi (Traces of inter-state law before the Ch'in dynasty); and Ch'en Ku-yuan, Chung-kuo kuo-chi-fa su-yuan (Origins of Chinese inter-state law). One of the few analyses attempted by a Western political scientist is that of F. M. Russell, Theories of international relations, ch. ii, "Ancient China."

2. This section is chiefly based upon the data presented in J. K. Fairbank and S. Y. Teng, "On the Ch'ing Tributary System," (HJAS 1941), cited above as "Tributary System."

3. Ibid., p. 141.

4. Ibid., p. 159.

5. This point is stressed by M. Frederick Nelson, Korea and the Old Orders in Eastern Asia, p. 14, et passim.

6. Cp. regulations translated in Fairbank and Teng, "Tributary System," pp. 163-173.

7. Ibid., p. 171.

8. See J. J. L. Duyvendak, "The True Dates of the Chinese Maritime Expeditions in the Early Fifteenth Century."

9. Cp. Ta-Ming chi-li, partially translated in "Tributary System," p. 146.

10. Cp. T. F. Tsiang, "China and European Expansion," pp. 3-4.

11. See "Tributary System," p. 139.

12. Ibid., pp. 167-70.

13. These have been studied particularly by Professors Pelliot and Duyvendak in a series of monographs in T'oung Pao, esp. vols. XXX and XXXIV.

14. See Duyvendak, loc. cit. in note 8.

15. C. S. Gardner in W. L. Langer, ed., An Encyclopedia of World History, p. 134.

16. W. W. Rockhill, "Notes on the Relations and Trade of China ...," pp. 419-447. The most extensive recent work identifying these contacts is the summary volume by Professor Feng Ch'eng-chün, Chung-kuo Nan-yang chiao-t'ung shih (History of communication between China and the Southern Ocean).

17. Letter of Capt. Francis Light encl. in Cornwallis to Dundas, Jan. 7, 1789, quoted by C. E. Wurtzburg, "A Brief Account of the several countries surrounding Prince of Wales's Island", in Journal of the Malayan Branch of the R. A. S., XVI, part 1: 123-126 (July 1938).

18. See W. L. Schurz, The Manila Galleon; Chang Wei-hua, "Ming-chi Hsi-pan-ya tsai Lü-sung yü Chung-kuo chih kuan-hsi" (Sino-Spanish relations in the Philippines during the later years of the Ming dynasty), pp. 71-86.

19. See "Tributary System," pp. 174-176.

20. The most recent scholarly appraisal concludes that "China was really on the defensive from the time when the voyages ceased." See G. B. Sansom, The Western World and Japan, p. 43, also pp. 141-145. In this situation it became increasingly easy to take refuge in the great tradition of the past; for a late nineteenth century example of this, see the survey of barbarian relations on the Chinese frontier from Han through Ming compiled by Chu K'o-ching, Pien-shih hui-ch'ao (Compendium on border affairs), pub. at Changsha in 1880. Cp. Momose (Tōa) on this topic.

21. See "Tributary System," pp. 193-198, table 5.

REFERENCES: CHAPTER 3

1. Wittfogel and Feng, Liao, "General Introduction", p. 5.

2. See Franz Michael, The Origin of Manchu Rule in China, the most illuminating monograph in English on the Manchus' entrance into China.

3. See the monograph by Liu Hsuan-min, "Ch'ing-tai Tung-san-sheng i-min yü k'ai-k'en" (Colonization and opening of land to cultivation in the Three Eastern Provinces in the Ch'ing period). Also the very competent survey by Agnes Chen, "The Eclipse of Manchuria."

4. Cp. S. M. Shirokogoroff, Social organization of the Manchus.

5. On this subject W. W. Rockhill, "The Dalai Lamas of Lhasa ...", has not yet been superseded among Western studies; cp. also Lattimore, Inner Asian Frontiers.

6. See L. C. Goodrich, The Literary Inquisition of Ch'ien-lung.

7. See below, Ch. 15.

8. The master work on this early trade is that of Kuwabara Jitsuzō, "On P'u Shou-keng, a man of the Western Regions." For a general bibliography see Fairbank and Teng, "Tributary System," app. 1.

9. On Ming administration the best survey available in English is that of Chang Te-ch'ang, "Maritime Trade at Canton during the Ming Dynasty."

10. On the Japanese pirates in the Ming period, among many works, Ho Ko-en, "Ming-tai wo-k'ou ch'in-jao yen-hai ko-ti nien-piao" (Chronological table of the ravages of Japanese pirates at various places along the coast during the Ming period) gives lists and references; and Li Kuang-ming, "Chia-ching yü-wo Chiang-Che chu-k'o-chün k'ao" ("The repulse of the Wo pirates by provincial and extra-provincial armies in the provinces of Kiangsu and Chekiang during 1551-1561) uses a wealth of sources on the Chinese military defense. One very comprehensive survey is by Ch'en Mao-heng, "Ming-tai wo-k'ou k'ao-lueh" (The invasion of

China by Japanese pirates during the Ming dynasty").

11. Cp. Chang T'ien-tse, Sino-Portuguese Trade from 1514 to 1644 ... and the review by P. Pelliot in T'oung Pao, 31.58-94 (1934). On the early administration of Macao, see Boxer, Fidalgos in the Far East.

12. This analysis follows that of Chang Te-ch'ang, "Ch'ing-tai ya-p'ien chan-cheng-ch'ien chih Chung-Hsi yen-hai t'ung-shang" (Sino-Western coastal trade in the Ch'ing period before the Opium War).

13. For the ruthless early Ch'ing coast defense policy of non-intercourse, see Tanaka Katsumi, "Shinsho no Shina engai"; and Hsieh Kuo-chen, "Ch'ing-ch'u tung-nan yen-hai ch'ien-chieh k'ao".

14. Summarized from Liang T'ing-nan, Yueh hai-kuan chih (Gazetteer of the maritime customs of Kwangtung), 30 chüan, of which ch. 1-4 and 21-30 have been reprinted in the Kuo-hsueh wen-k'u series (Peiping, 1935 et seq.); latest date in the text is 1839; see ch. 7. Note the review article by Siun yuk-ching (Hsien Yü-ch'ing), "Liang T'ing-nan chu-shu lu-yao" (On Liang T'ing Nan's works). For an analysis of the evolution of Ch'ing foreign trade policy, including the conceptions underlying the Canton system, see Hirase Minokichi, Kindai Shina keizai shi, pp. 96-136.

15. Various ingenious theories have been advanced for the origin of "Hoppo." His official title was Yueh hai-kuan chien-tu; he remained actually under the Imperial Household Department rather than under the Hu-pu. For "Hoppo," The China Directory for 1864, app., gives Yueh hai-kuan pu. S. W. Williams, The Chinese Commercial Guide (Hongkong, 1863, Shortrede, 5th ed.) p. 160, declares "Hoppo" is "a corruption of hoi-po-sho, the title of a petty officer who controls the boats and police on the river. It is possible, however, that when foreign ships anchored at Canton for trade three centuries ago, their crews were placed under the supervision of the hoi-po-sho, whose title gradually came to be thus transferred to his superior." Huang P'u-sheng, "Ch'ing-tai Kuang-tung mao-i chi ch'i tsai Chung-kuo ching-chi-shih-shang chih i-i" ("The Historical Significance of Kwangtung trade under the Chin [sic] dynasty"), 175, supports Hu-pu as opposed to ho-po or hai-pu. S. Tanaka favors ho-po.

16. Juan Yuan in Kuang-tung t'ung-chih, p. 180, summarized these changes: in 1730 the Canton customs was placed under the governor-general in the eighth month, under the Canton military commandant in the ninth month; in 1735 under a vice-superintendent of customs; in 1743 under the Canton Tartar-general; in 1745 under the governor; in 1747 under the governor-general. Quoted by Liang Chia-pin, Kuang-tung shih-san-hang k'ao, p. 64.

17. See Liang T'ing-nan, Yueh hai-kuan chih, p. 7.

18. See below, ch. 14, for details of this system.

19. Morse, Conflict, p. 34.

20. The most comprehensive treatment of the Cohong is that of Liang Chia-pin, Kuang-tung shih-san-hang k'ao, from which the following account is drawn and which makes good use of Morse, Chronicles, as well as Chinese sources. The useful study by Matsumoto Tadao, "Kantō no kōshō to ikan" in Shina (China), 23.1: 52-67 (Spring 1932), and later numbers, relies mainly on Western sources; a useful survey is in Hirase Minokichi, Kindai Shina keizai shi, pp. 165-188.

21. See Liang Chia-pin, passim.

22. Cp. Liang Chia-pin, pp. 134-140, and Morse, Chronicles, passim.

23. Sansom, Western World and Japan, p. 144.

24. See Chang Te-ch'ang's article cited in note 12 above.

REFERENCES: CHAPTER 4

1. The most famous is W. C. Hunter, whose The 'Fan Kwae' at Canton before Treaty Days, 1825-44 has long been a classic. Its rosy hues have been well criticized by Ph. de Vargas in Yenching Journal of Social Studies, 1.2: 91-117 (July 1939).

2. This general view has been expressed by C. N. Parkinson, Trade in the Eastern Seas 1793-1813, but has been criticized by C. H. Philips, The East India Company 1784-1834. It appears relatively true of the Company's activities in China.

3. E. H. Pritchard, The Crucial Years of Anglo-Chinese Relations 1750-1800, p. 218.

4. Ibid., p. 265.

5. Lord Macartney's impressions are available in Helen H. Robbins, Our First Ambassador to China. See Pritchard, "The Kotow;" Chu Chieh-ch'in, "Ying-kuo ti-i-tz'u shih-ch'en lai-Hua chi" ("Account of Lord Macartney's Embassy to China"), although recent, adds little or nothing.

6. For text see Morse, Chronicles, II, 247-252.

7. Cp. "Preliminary proposals by Lt.-Col. Cathcart, Aug. 18, 1787" in Morse, Chronicles, II, 157-159: "... we require a healthy situation accessible and safe for Shipping, convenient for the Dispersion of our Manufactures and for the Collection of Teas ... Our great Depot might be placed without the Empire, in a Situation accesible to the Junks of the whole Coast ..." Cp. also Frederick Pigou's letter of 1754 quoted in Pritchard, Crucial Years, p. 126.

8. Holden Furber, John Company at Work, surveys the growth of this India-based private British trade; China was of course only one of its areas of expansion.

9. Pritchard, p. 181.

10. Ibid., p. 180.

11. Jardine, Matheson and Co., afterwards Jardine, Matheson and Co. Limited. An outline of

the history of a China House for a hundred years 1832-1932, p. 7. Cp. Morse, Chronicles, II, 142. Data in the former differs occasionally from that in the archival study by Michael Greenberg, British Trade and the Opening of China 1800-42.

12. G. J. Yorke, "The Princely House, the Story of the Early Years of Jardine Matheson and Company in China 1782-1844," ms., see p. 59. This body of quoted materials from unpublished letters deserves reworking and publication; it is used here only for concrete illustrations of conditions described in published sources. It has, however, been used very extensively with only slight acknowledgment by Maurice Collis in his Foreign Mud, a work of great readability by a facile exploiter of the historical record. The fullest detail on the ships and captains of the opium trade, evidently based in large part on records of Dent and Co., is in Basil Lubbock's compilation, The Opium Clippers.

13. Yorke and Greenberg, passim. The next paragraphs are based on Michael Greenberg's excellent monograph, drawn from the Jardine, Matheson and Co. archives at Cambridge University, which illuminates the economic role of the private traders in China before the treaties.

For a recent and independent statistical analysis based on British sources, see Etō Shinkichi, "Ahen sensō izen."

14. Yorke, p. 111.

15. The best general account is that of D. E. Owen, British Opium Policy in India and China.

16. Cp. Parliamentary Papers, House of Commons, 1855, no. 336: Returns of the Gross Revenue derived annually from the Tax on Land in India since 1792; ibid., 1857, no. 16: A Return of the Revenue derived Annually from all Sources of Taxation in India, in continuation of the above.

17. Downing, The Stranger in China, II, 157, records the estimate that 33,200,000 ounces (taels) of smoking extract were prepared in 1836 and supplied about twelve and a half million smokers. Later, in 1879, it was estimated that "average smokers" consumed daily between a fifth and a half of an ounce (2 to 5 mace) and "heavy smokers" between a half ounce and two ounces (5 to 20 mace). One-tenth of an ounce was said to fill anywhere from 3 to 20 pipes. On this basis, Robert Hart in 1881 calculated that about 200,000 chests (almost 12,000 tons) of unprepared opium were being consumed annually by two million opium smokers. This was only about two-thirds of one per cent of the population. See China, Imperial Maritime Customs, II, Special Series, no. 4, Opium (Shanghai, 1881).

The following account is based on J. G. Kerr, M.D., "Opium and the Smoking Extract," China Review, 12.1: 41-47 (July and August 1883). The author observed the preparation of opium at firsthand as supervised by the Hongkong government. The various types of opium are described by Li Kuei, Ya-p'ien shih-lueh, 2b-3.

18. Yorke, p. 107.

19. Greenberg, p. 105. Yorke, p. 91, quoting report of the Select Committee of the House of Lords, 1830.

20. Ibid., pp. 117-118; cp. Morse, Chronicles, IV, 93; Lubbock, Opium Clippers, p. 61.

21. H. H. Lindsay, Report of Proceedings on a Voyage to the Northern Ports of China in the Ship Lord Amherst. Also published in the Parliamentary Papers for 1833. Another account, lacking documentation, is in Charles Gutzlaff, Journal of three voyages (London, 1834), pp. 159-298. The Chinese originals of the correspondence translated by Gutzlaff and quoted in extenso by Lindsay were found in the Bodleian Library and published, although not identified, by Prof. Hsü Ti-shan as Ta chung chi. On the origin of the voyage see Morse, Chronicles, IV, 332-4. For a brief biography of Gutzlaff see CR, 20: 511-12 (1851).

22. Lindsay, pp. 172, 181, 194.

23. Ibid., p. 142.

24. Ibid., p. 78.

25. Ibid., p. 63.

26. Hsü Ti-shan, Ta chung chi, p. 31. This rank is normally designated First Captain of the Left (Eastern) Battalion; see Brunnert, 752 C.

27. Lindsay, pp. 92-94.

28. Ibid., pp. 131-2.

29. Ibid., pp. 111, 128, 152.

30. Liang Chia-pin, pp. 197-200.

31. Chang Te-ch'ang, "Hu-hsia-mi huo-ch'uan lai-Hua ching-kuo chi ch'i ying-hsiang" ("The significance of the voyage of Lord Amherst to the northern ports of China"). For the extensive correspondence of the Chinese authorities in 1832, see Shih-liao hsun-k'an, 13.471-75, 15.547-49, and passim; also CSL-TK, 215.7b—8b and 28; 217.8b-10 (for the latter I am indebted to Mr. C. Y. Hsü).

32. Ibid. Lindsay was long remembered on the China coast, e.g. cp. Milne's "Seven Months Residence at Ningpo," CR, XIII: 348 (1844).

33. Cp. Morse, Chronicles, IV, 332.

34. Ibid., IV, 353.

35. Yorke, p. 196, quoting "Journal kept by James Innes of the Jamesina's voyage up the East Coast of China to sell opium in November, 1832." Ms., J. M. and Co. archives.

36. Pelliot, "Un ouvrage sur les premiers temps de Macao," T'oung Pao, 31: 66, n. 2 (1934), accepts the findings of Phillips that the Chincheo of the Portuguese was Chang-chou, the important city near Amoy. For the nineteenth century there is no doubt whatever of the identity of Chinchew and Ch'üan-chou, as indicated on numerous contemporary maps. Cp. e.g. James Wyld, geographer to the Queen, Map of China (1841): "Tsiuen-tchou or Chin-chew & Harb." For How-tou-san (Tiger head hill) see S. W. Williams, Chinese Commercial Guide, app., p. 65 (1863 ed.).

37. Yorke, p. 282.

38. W. McKay to J. M. and Co., August 6, 1833; Yorke, p. 176.

39. Yorke, p. 290, citing Capt. W. McKay to W. Jardine, Dec. 1, 1835; ibid., p. 294, citing Capt. Jauncey to W. Jardine, July 8, 1836.

40. Yorke, p. 290, quoting Canton Register, April 14, 1835.

41. W. McKay to J. M. and Co., end of August, 1833; Yorke, p. 177.

42. Ibid., p. 294, Capt. J. Rees to W. Jardine, May 21, 1836.

43. Yorke, p. 292, quoting letters of 11/5/36 and 12/4/36.

44. Ibid., p. 289, Private Letter Book, March 9, 1835.

45. See FO 17/74, Public Record Office, London.

46. W. H. Medhurst, China: its State and Prospects, pp. 468-9. The Huron found the Lord Amherst well remembered all along the coast.

47. John Bowring (ed.), Observations on the Restrictive and Prohibitory Commercial System... from the Mss. of Jeremy Bentham, Esq., "preface," pp. ix-x.

REFERENCES: CHAPTER 5

1. See Li Chien-nung, Chung-kuo chin-pai-nien cheng-chih shih (Political history of China in the last hundred years), pp. 51 ff. A leading communist historian, Fan Wen-lan, stresses the vested interest of both the East India Co. and the Chinese officials in the continuance of a smuggling trade, which would tend to keep the production and the squeeze, respectively, in their hands; from this he argues that opium smuggling alone made war inevitable (Chung-kuo t'ung-shih chien-pien, I, 716-19). For a survey of the historical context, see T. F. Tsiang (Chiang T'ing-fu), "Chung-kuo yü chin-tai shih-chieh ti ta-pien-chü," esp. pp. 811 ff.

The most comprehensive Japanese account of the background of the war as visible through British sources is that of Professor T. Ueda, "Ahen sensō ron."

2. The Chinese sources are confusing because a basic account like that of Wei Yuan may appear and reappear in whole or in part under several titles with minor changes. Thus his Tao-kuang yang-sou cheng-fu chi (Record of the pacification of the foreign ships in the Tao-kuang period) has been identified textually with half a dozen other works.

Dr. S. Y. Teng, Chang Hsi, pp. 132-34, describes the relation of these to Wei Yuan's account and to E. H. Parker's translation of it (Chinese Account of the Opium War, 1888). A carefully annotated critical edition has been published by Yao Wei-yuan, Ya-p'ien chan-cheng shih-shih k'ao (A study of the historical events of the Opium War), with a preface (1933) by T. F. Tsiang and an extensive bibliography. For a comprehensive bibliography of Chinese sources on the Opium War, see the article by Chao Feng-t'ien in Yenching Journal of Social Studies, 3.1: 61-103 (October, 1940); see also Sung Mo, "Ya-p'ien chan-cheng hsin shih-liao" (New historical materials on the opium war), Kuo-wen chou-pao, 10.46,48; 11.1,3,5,8,11,13 (1933-34); and Li Kuei, Ya-p'ien shih-lueh (A brief account of the opium question), reprinted from ed. of Kuang-hsü period.

3. T'ang Hsiang-lung, "Tao-kuang shih-ch'i ti yin-kuei wen-t'i" ("Outflow of silver in the Tao-Kuang period, 1821-1839"); see also Morse, Conflict, pp. 202-204. For the earlier record, see Liang Fang-chung, "Ming-tai kuo-chi mao-i yü yin ti shu-ch'u-ju" ("The international trade and the silver movements in Ming dynasty"). For a broad survey of the flow of silver to East Asia, see Momose Hiromu's article, "Shindai ni okeru Supein doru no ryūtsū". Nozoe Shigekatsu, in his sketch of China's pre-treaty trade with the West ("Gokō kaikōzen"), follows Morse on the silver question (see 23.11: 58-62). Yano ("Shina no ahen mondai", pp. 408-9,) quotes memorials of 1704 and 1814 which associate outflow of silver with Western trade. This whole question deserves survey treatment for Western readers.

4. There were at least two instances (in Taiwan and at Chang-chou) when Chinese foreign trade dollars were minted during the Tao-kuang period; see Katō Shigeshi, "Dōkō Kampō chū Shina nite chuzoseraretaru yoshiki ginka ni tsuite" (On the foreign-style silver coins minted in China in the Tao-kuang and Hsien-feng periods), Tōhō Gakuhō, 2: 284-292 (December 1931), and addendum in ibid., 3: 351-355 (December 1932).

5. T'ang, "Tao-kuang", pp. 2-7. The arguments of the mid-thirties have been summarized by Yano Jin'ichi, "Kō Shaku-ji oyobi Rin Soku-jo".

6. Morse, Conflict, p. 204. Hirase Minokichi (Kindai Shina, pp. 70-74) draws attention to the steadily increased quotas of minted cash in the early Ch'ing period, which rose to over one billion strings in 1731; he suggests that imports of Western silver in the late eighteenth century met China's currency hunger to some extent. China's domestic currency needs in the 1830's remain to be appraised.

7. Still another (although more distant) consideration, the value of China's silver in the international market, has been studied by Wu Ch'eng-hsi, "Pai-nien-lai yin-chia pien-tung chih hui-ku" ("The price of silver, a review of its fluctuations, 1833-1931"). See also the work of Otake Fumio.

8. See Greenberg, pp. 200-203; cp. T'ang pp. 9-22; for a conventional summary, cp. Wu Yü-kan, Ya-p'ien chan-cheng shih (The Opium War). For the paper record of prohibitory regulations in the period 1830-58, see Yü En-te, Chung-kuo chin-yen fa-ling, ch.iii.

9. Some of these have been pointed out by Kuo Pin-chia, A Critical Study of the First Anglo-Chinese War. The economic factors affecting British action are pursued by Ch'ien Chia-chü, "Ya-p'ien chan-cheng-shih hsin-lun" ("The Opium War as seen from a new angle").

10. Kuo, p. 21. Cp. Costin, pp. 21-27.

11. Greenberg, p. 203.

12. See Chiang T'ing-fu, "Chung-kuo yü chin-tai," p.818; and Chung-kuo chin-tai shih, p. 22. The most recent and informative biography is that of Wei Ying-ch'i, Lin Wen-chung-kung nien-p'u. Concerning Lin's knowledge of the West, see Ch.

11 below; and Gideon Ch'en, Lin Tse-hsü, on his subsequent use of spies and translators; examples of this work are printed in the Hsiao-fang-hu chai collection.

13. The exploits of this vessel are recounted in W. D. Bernard, Narrative of the Voyages and Services of the Nemesis.

14. See Chiang T'ing-fu (T. F. Tsiang), "Ch'i-shan yü ya-p'ien chan-cheng" (Ch'i-shan and the Opium War), and the summary by Wm. R. Leete in Hummel, Eminent Chinese. By way of comment on Prof. Tsiang's article, the case against Ch'i-shan from both the military and diplomatic points of view is vigorously summarized by T'ao Yuan-chen in a review in the Ta-kung-pao t'u-shu fu-k'an (Ta-kung pao literary supplement), no. 77, May 2, 1935. The most detailed study of the documents is by Hsia Nai, "Ya-p'ien chan-cheng-chung ti T'ien-chin t'an-p'an" (The Tientsin negotiations during the Opium War).

15. Jardine, Matheson and Co., 1832-1932, p. 48; and Yorke, p. 253, Jardine's letter of May 31, 1841.

16. Yorke, p. 317, W. Jardine to J. Matheson, Feb. 6, 1840.

17. The firm's London representatives from 1834 through 1840 were Messrs. Magniac, Smith and Co.; John Abel Smith was a partner in Magniac, Jardine and Co. of London until 1848, when that firm was reorganized as Matheson and Co.; see Jardine, Matheson and Co., pp. 30, 38.

18. See R. M. Martin, China, II, 40, quoting Canton Register, Feb. 23, 1841. Martin asserts, uncritically, that this was the basis of a Foreign Office draft sent to Captain Elliot in 1841 and used by Pottinger in 1842 (p. 84). For a summary of Palmerston's draft treaty, sent to China on Feb. 20, 1840, see Costin, Great Britain and China, pp. 76-7.

19. J. Rees was captain for Lindsay in 1832, and later for J. M. and Co.

20. Yorke, p. 333, W. Jardine to J. Matheson, May 31, 1841. Collis, Foreign Mud, dramatizes Jardine's role in British policy formation, mainly on the basis of Mr. Yorke's ms. (See pp. 262 ff.) For a factual summary of the firm's influence on British officials and British politics, see Greenberg, ch. vii.

21. Yorke, p. 333, Private Letter Book, Aug. 23, 1841.

22. Palmerston to J. A. Smith, Nov. 28, 1842, in Easton, The History of a Banking House, p. 29; partially quoted in Greenberg, pp. 214-15, and in Yorke, p. 341. John Abel Smith, M. P., espoused the admission of Baron Lionel de Rothschild into Parliament in 1858.

REFERENCES: CHAPTER 6

1. This subject has been dealt with in two articles: Fairbank, "Nanking" and "Appeasement." See bibliography.

2. See summaries in Morse, Conflict; P. C. Kuo, A Critical Study of the First Anglo-Chinese war; and the article by T. F. Tsiang on "Ch'i-shan."

3. CSK, 183.5-6. Hsiao I-shan's tables in his Ch'ing-tai t'ung-shih are not entirely accurate.

4. E.g. Morse, Conflict, p. 279. On the Ch'ing use of Manchu and Chinese personnel in this period, see Fairbank, "The Manchu-Chinese Dyarchy of the 1840's and '50s."

5. See biographies of Mu-chang-a listed in Tu Lien-che and Fang Chao-ying, Index to Thirty-three Collections of Ch'ing Dynasty Biographies, Harvard-Yenching Index Series, no. 9, and particularly the biography in Hummel, Eminent Chinese. See below, Ch. 20, note 33.

6. E.g. IWSM-TK, 44.5b-7b.

7. Ibid., 51.27; 61.47b; 51.26; 58.3b, 4b, 14. A collection of forty-two manuscript documents in the Yenching University Library, dealing with the Anglo-Chinese negotiations, is described in Kuan Jui-wu, "I-wu shih-mo wai ya-p'ien chan-cheng hou Chung-Ying i-ho shih-liao shu-chien" (Some historical materials on Sino-British negotiations after the Opium War, outside the I-wu shih-mo), Shih-hsueh nien-pao, 3-4 (August 1931), 143-170, 183-194.

8. IWSM-TK, 59.17b-18b; 57.6b, 9(Aug. 3, 1842); repeated Aug. 4, ibid., 17; 59.30, 31; 58.25, 26b(Aug. 16, 1842).

9. Ibid., 57.3b, 6, 8b(all Aug. 3, 1842).

10. English observers use superlatives in describing their depredations, e.g., Ouchterlony, The Chinese War (London, 1844).

11. IWSM-TK, 57.28b-29b.

12. Ibid., 57.39-40,41; 58.10; 58.12b.

13. Ibid., 58.28-29b. An official investigation reported only 13 traitors executed and the rest of the story untrue (60.26b-30).

14. Ibid., 37-39b, see 38b lines 2-3. On this point an official investigation made no comment (60.26b-30). W. D. Bernard, Narrative of the Voyages and Services of the Nemesis, p. 412, quotes the British proclamation at Shanghai.

15. IWSM-TK, 53.10, memorial of Ch'i-ying received July 9, 1842.

16. Capt. G. G. Loch, The Closing Events of the Campaign in China, p. 159, under date Aug. 17. Loch lived with the admiral, acted as extra aide-de-camp for the general, and was given by Pottinger "the same opportunity that he himself possessed of meeting and observing the Chinese authorities."

17. IWSM-TK, 58.17-18. The reference is to hsiao-fei, "smuggler-banditti," of the Liang-huai salt-producing area.

18. Ibid., 58.19; 58.22.

19. Ibid., 58.39b-42b.

20. Ibid., 59.12-16b.

21. Ibid., 54.37-38b, mem. rec'd July 20, 1842. Ibid., edicts same date. See also ibid 57.25-26.

22. IWSM-TK, 58.39b-42b; 55.26b.

23. Cp. J. Ouchterlony, The Chinese War, pp. 224-66.

24. IWSM-TK, 44.11b; 27b-35b. On these events see also Wang Chih-ch'un, Kuo-ch'ao jou-yuan chi (Record of the ruling dynasty's graciousness to strangers), ed. 1896, 10.4-5b.

25. THL-TK, 45.8b-9; CSLC, 36.31.

26. E.g., Chin Chao-feng, Ch'ing-shih ta-kang (Outline of Ch'ing history), p. 377. Backhouse and Bland, naming no sources, elaborately state that "Wang Ting-lin (sic), Grand Secretary and Grand Councillor ... with all the strength of a masterful and sincere nature... opposed Mu Ch'ang-a's peace policy and advocated war at all costs." When the emperor refused to listen to him, Wang "indited a valedictory memorial impeaching Mu... and hanged himself." E. Backhouse and J. O. P. Bland, Annals and Memoirs of the Court of Peking, p. 397. This book would be of greater value if its Chinese sources were indicated.

27. IWSM-TK, 44.26, edict of Mar. 26, 1842; 44.22,35b; 45.10b. CSK, "Pen-chi" (basic annals), 19.3b. IWSM-TK, 44.16b; 35b. This modifies Morse's statement, Conflict, 297, n. 199, that "Kiying had been appointed Tartar General at Canton but was commissioned to negotiate the peace on his way to his post."

28. IWSM-TK, 45.16b; 10b.

29. Ibid., 47.22b; 23b, line 10-24a, line 4, received May 19, 1842. Cp. Sun-tzu, 3, "Mou-kung."

30. IWSM-TK, Supp. 1479-80, memorial sent May 13, received May 21, 1842. Cp. J. R. Morrison in CR, XII: 470 (1842).

31. Wang Chih-ch'un, 10.14, emphasizes the influence of Liu Yun-k'o on the peace policy at this time; it is not evident in the documents.

32. IWSM-TK, 47.43b-45, received May 23, 1842, quoted from p. 45. See also 48.5b, lines 7-8. Ch'i-ying mentions receiving such orders from the emperor (ibid., 45, line 1). IWSM-TK, Supp., 1496, memorial received from Ch'eng Yü-ts'ai on June 28, 1842, urges the I-li-pu negotiate (chi-mi) to delay the enemy's advance.

33. Kuang-hsü hui-tien, 23.1-7. Approximately the same figures in the Chia-ch'ing edition. The total given above is derived from adding regular duties and surplus. This was more than the Hoppo at Canton was expected to return from the foreign trade.

34. Rev. Charles Gutzlaff, The Life of Taou-Kwang, Late Emperor of China, p. 56. An undocumented account by a close student of the Peking Gazettes and purveyor of yamen gossip, one of the British interpreters in 1842. Gutzlaff is also the authority for statements that Ch'i-ying's "daughter held a most influential rank in the harem" (ibid., p. 220) and that the Tao-kuang emperor married Ch'i-ying's niece (see Sir. J. F. Davis, China During the War and Since the Peace, I, 251; an account based on "secret state papers captured during the war and translated or abstracted by Dr. Gutzlaff, interpreter to Her Majesty's Commission").

35. See successively Lieut. A. Murray, Doings in China, p. 198; "A Field Officer," The Last Year in China, p. 179; Capt. G. Loch, The Closing Events of the Campaign in China, p. 191; Murray, p. 198; Loch, p. 162.

36. See Teng, Chang Hsi, p. 21, and IWSM-TK, 47.40b.

37. Ibid., 48.1. This decision is explained by a contemporary writer, Wei Yuan, as due to the fact that "the Censor Su T'ing-k'uei had represented that the Nepaulese had attacked the English garrisons in India, and that the [British] fleet had to go to the rescue; accordingly K'iying was ordered to see if he could not seize the opportunity to retake Hongkong" (see E. H. Parker, Chinese Account of the Opium War [Shanghai, 1888], p. 62, trans. from 1878 ed. of Wei Yuan, Sheng-wu chi; also Hsiao I-shan, Ch'ing-tai t'ung-shih, p. 901). On the same day that Ch'i-ying was ordered south, a memorial from General I-ching in Chekiang reported his suspicion that the British fleet, after leaving Ningpo, had approached Chapu and Shanghai; the Chapu authorities had been warned accordingly (IWSM-TK, 48.4, received May 25, 1842).

38. Ibid., 48.5; 49.10b-11, received June 5, 1842.

39. IWSM-TK, Supp. 1479, sent May 13, received May 21. Cp. Fairbank and Teng, "Transmission

40. IWSM-TK, 48.5b-10; 48.42.

41. Ibid., 48.9, received May 26, 1842; 48.29b, received May 31, 1842; 48.40b; 51.13, received from Ch'i-ying June 25; this last memorial quotes an edict which refers to a memorial received on June 4 as the memorial "of yesterday." Cp. THL-TK under June 5. The course of these negotiations is also summarized in Yano Jinichi, Ahen sensō to Honkon, pp. 252-61.

42. IWSM-TK, 52.17, received July 3, 1842. By the British "no attention whatever was paid to these very equivocal overtures," since Sir Henry Pottinger was determined not to repeat Elliot's mistake and negotiate too soon. (See Bernard, Narrative ... of the Nemesis, p. 412).

43. IWSM-TK, 52.17b-18b.

44. Ibid., 52.12 and 15b, both received July 3; 16b; 53.7; 53.10.

45. See e.g. ibid., 53.2b, memorial from I-ching received July 9, 1842. Cf. Ouchterlony, p. 344: "So little did the government appear to have expected our attack at the valuable point chosen [i.e., Chinkiang], and so entirely preoccupied must it have been with efforts to resist an expected attempt upon the capital, that the defense of the Yang-tse-Kiang was entirely neglected until too late...."

46. IWSM-TK, 53.10, line 7, received July 9, 1842; 53.12-14.

47. IWSM-TK, Supp. 1502, memorial received from Ch'i-ying on July 20, quoting edict of July 9, 1842.

48. IWSM-TK, 53.29.

49. I am indebted on this point to Mr. John J. Nolde; see also the account by Fang in Hummel 131. See account in P. C. Kuo, pp. 161-63 and doc. no. 48, a translation of Ch'i-ying's memorial (IWSM-TK 57.31-32) received Aug. 6, 1842, summarizing his efforts of July.

50. This point has been made by Harold Hinton in his Ph.D. dissertation, The Grain Tribute System of China, 1845-1911; an Aspect of the Decline of the Ch'ing Dynasty (History Department, Harvard University, 1950).

51. Morse, Conflict, p. 15: "...delegated directly by the emperor to carry his will into effect...restricted only by the limits of his commission..."

52. IWSM-TK, 51.25b; 52.6.

53. Ibid., 55.26b, line 9-27, line 2, edict of July 26, 1842. The British demand for a ture plenipotentiary, when presented to the throne on July 9, 1842, received the comment, "How completely abominable!" (K'o-o chih chih); IWSM-TK Supp. 1500.

54. IWSM-TK, 55. 27, line 10-27b, line 5.

55. Ibid., 57.32b-33, memorial received from Ch'i-ying on August 6, 1842, in which the letters mentioned above are quoted. (Kuo merely calls these "edicts," see pp. 161, 293, 294.) Letters from the palace of the sort here referred to were a recognized form of communication, and regularly used; most edicts (shang-yü, yü-chih) at this time were transmitted to the imperial commissioner in a letter from the grand councillors (Chün-chi ta-ch'en tzu-chi). Other palace letters (t'ing-chi) were referred to on August 6 (IWSM-TK, 57.31b, line 9) and August 16 (ibid., 58.17, line 4). Chang Chung-fu points out that Lin Tse-hsü as an imperial commissioner at Canton had naturally had power "to act as circumstances might require" (pien-i hsing-shih); this later became the phrase for "plenipotentiary." See Chang Chung-fu, "Tzu ya-p'ien chan-cheng chih Ying-Fa lien-chün ch'i-chung Ch'ing-t'ing pan-li wai-chiao chih chi-kuan yü shou-hsü" (The organs and procedures of the Ch'ing court for handling foreign relations in the period from the Opium War to the Anglo-French joint expedition).

56. IWSM-TK, 57.33, line 10-33b, line 2; 58.1; 58.30, see line 7. There are one or two instances in which dispatches passed between Peking and Nanking in three days during this period. Ibid., 56.6.

57. Ibid., 58.31, line 5, received Aug. 17, 1842.

58. Loch, p. 151; Ouchterlony, p. 440. Several works state that Ch'i-ying, I-li-pu, and Niu Chien — all three — were appointed with full powers (ch'üan-ch'üan) to negotiate the treaty. See Kubota Bunzō, Shina gaikō tsūshi (A comprehensive history of Chinese foreign relations), p. 66; Huang Hung-shou, ed., Ch'ing-shih chi-shih pen-mo (A complete record of Ch'ing history), (3rd ed. Shanghai, 1925), 44.3; Chin Chao-feng, p. 392; Hsiao I-shan, p. 905; Wu Yü-kan, Ya-p'ien chan-cheng shih (The Opium War), p. 104. Saitō Yoshie, Kinsei Tōyō gaikō shi josetsu (Introduction to modern Far Eastern international relations), p. 24, omits Niu Chien from the list. There is no literal basis for such a statement in the document.

59. IWSM-TK, 58.34-35.

60. Wai-wei, see Brunnert, 752H; W. F. Mayers, The Chinese Government (3rd ed., Shanghai, 1897), no. 450. IWSM-TK, Supp. 1457, memorial received from I-ching on March 4, 1842, refers to Ch'en as from the garrison at Chen-hai below Ningpo.

61. Ouchterlony, p. 58; Davis, p. 267.

62. Loch, p. 51; Bernard, p. 412. Ouchterlony (p. 425) has "Captain White." Ibid., p. 58, explains that "his name was Showpei [Mayers, no. 446: "second captain"] Pih and he hence earned from the expedition the cognomen of 'Captain White,' pih [pai] signifying white."

63. Pai Han-chang played an important part as Ch'i-shan's emissary at the Peiho in 1840; see IWSM-TK, 12.28,29; 13.36; 14.12, 32b, 34. The documents make no reference to Ch'en Chih-kang at that time.

64. See S. Y. Teng, Chang Hsi and the Treaty of Nanking, a translation of Chang's Fu-i jih-chi. Chang is given prominent reference in the Draft History of the Ch'ing, "Pang-chiao chih", 2.6.

65. He was the same "mandarin of the name of Chang, a notorious drunkard" (Loch, p. 175), who was sent by the ailing I-li-pu to procure from the Queen off Nanking some medicine prescribed by Dr. Woosnam at the Sino-British interview of Aug. 26. The British story is that Chang got drunk, lost the instructions, and told his master to take "all the pills and liquids" at once (Loch, p. 187; Murray, p. 210). The signing of the treaty, scheduled for Aug. 27, was postponed because of the illness of I-li-pu (Pottinger's 38, Sept. 3, 1842, FO 17/57); and all accounts agree that on the twenty-ninth he was actually carried into the cabin of the Cornwallis in a much debilitated condition.

66. Teng, note 218.

67. Teng, pp. 27-34, passim.

68. Teng, pp. 44, 46.

69. As I-li-pu wrote to Chang; see Teng, p. 20.

70. Hsien-ling had formerly served as Tartar-general; Huang was a provincial treasurer. On their careers see Ch. 11.

71. IWSM-TK, 58.32b, lines 5-6, received Aug. 17, 1842. Cp. Ueda, "Shina no kaikoku," 35-37.

72. See Imperial Maritime Customs, Treaties, Conventions, etc., between China and Foreign States (Shanghai, 1887). On p. xvi it is stated that "the Treaty of Nanking, English and Chinese, has been taken from the Tsungli Yamen's original at Peking." Hsiao I-shan, 1.906, gives the preamble with the same text as the Customs' Treaties but not, like it, arranged in such a manner as to give I-li-pu the title of Ch'in-ch'ai.

73. IWSM-TK, 61.25b.

74. Loch, p. 125, under date July 26; see also Bernard, p. 440.

75. Ouchterlony, p. 424.

76. Loch, p. 134; cf. Ouchterlony, p. 438: "... Keying, a mandarin of high rank, lately arrived from Peking, to coöperate with Eleepoo." CR, XII: 515 (September, 1842), refers to Ch'i-ying as the "new commissioner" and to I-li-pu as the "old commissioner."

77. IWSM-TK, 58.32b-33, 34, edict. I-li-pu's thanks were received in Peking on Aug. 31 (ibid., 59.34).

78. Murray, p. 199. Accounts by Loch (1843), Bernard (1845), and Williams, The Middle Kingdom (1848), wrongly date this interview Aug. 19. The British and Chinese documents and other sources agree on the twentieth.

79. IWSM-TK, 58.33b; 59.31-34; trans. in Kuo, pp. 296-99.

80. On these Chinese and Manchu officials under Ch'i-ying, see below, ch. 11. Regarding Chang Hsi's button, see Teng, n . 291.

81. IWSM-TK, 55.27, lines 6-10.

82. Ibid., 58.34 (trans. in Kuo, p. 294).

83. Ibid., 59.3b, lines 7-9.

84. Ibid., 59.34b and 46b. Cp. Ueda Toshio, "Nankin jōyaku," pp. 100-102.

85. Cp. Customs, Treaties, and IWSM-TK, 59.43-46b. The Customs' text is stated to have been "taken from the Tsungli Yamen's original at Peking." The IWSM version seen by the emperor was toned down by slight changes or deletions of a character or two in nearly every clause. Needless to say, the egalitarian Chinese version known to the British became standard later in the century.

86. Davis, China During the War, I, 302.

87. As will be indicated in various instances below, the sometimes gross disparity between the literal meaning of the Chinese and English versions of the treaties of 1842 and 1843 becomes quite striking when the Chinese version is retranslated into English. Space is lacking to do this here, but cp. an imperfect attempt, "Treaty of peace, signed at Nanking between England and China, translated from the Chinese," CR, XIV: 26-30 (1845), followed by a similar translation of the American and French treaties, pp. 30-51. For the Supplementary treaty see ibid., XIII: 143-150 (1844).

REFERENCES: CHAPTER 7

1. British interest in the rule of law has been well stressed by Costin, Great Britain and China. For the Ch'ing conception of getting the barbarians under control within the established order, see the illuminating article by Banno Masataka, "Ahen sensō", esp. pp. 32-37.

2. Loch, p. 170.

3. See enc. 31 in Pottinger's 38 of Sept. 3, 1842, FO 228/18.

4. IWSM-TK, 60.14-17, mem. rec'd Sept. 29, 1842. Agreements reported to Peking in September 1842 included the following: (1) Chinese officials were to press for repayment of, but not themselves repay, merchants' debts (later embodied in general regulations of trade, art. 4); (2) malefactors were to be handed over to officials of their own country, i.e., criminal extraterritoriality (later in gen. regs. art. 13, and Supplementary treaty, 9); (3) revision of the Canton customs tariff (to implement treaty of Nanking art. 10), to which the court at first objected because an imperial tariff already existed (treaty tariff published July 22, 1843); (4) further assurances regarding rendition of Chusan and Kulangsu (treaty of Nanking art. 12, later in the Supplementary treaty, art. 11); (5) British cruisers were to be stationed at the five ports (later in gen. regs. art 14, Supp. treaty, art. 10; on this see also IWSM-TK, 6.24, 26-27); finally, British trade was to be prohibited at places other than the five ports (later in Supp. treaty, art. 4; on this see IWSM-TK, ibid., and also p. 22, mem. rec'd Oct. 17, 1842).

5. IWSM-TK, 62.18: i-wan yuan. The yuan here referred to was the "Mexican" silver dollar current in the China trade.

6. Ibid., 61.22b-23, mem. rec'd October 17, 1842; 61.18b-21, mem. rec'd Oct. 17, 1842; 23-24, same date.

7. Ibid., 61.25b, edict Oct. 17, 1842; 25b-26b, edict same date; 28b-29, edict Oct. 23, 1842.

8. Ibid., 23b, line 3; 20, lines 6-7; 22b, lines 3-4; cf. 58.34-5, mem. rec'd Aug. 17, 1842: "the demands of the barbarians are ... little more than a desire for ... trade. There are no dark schemes in them."

9. See below ch. 16, and IWSM-TK, 61-66, passim: a general reorganization of defense was ordered Oct. 26; on Nov. 1 Ch'i-ying was told to strengthen the defenses of Kiangsu; he proposed to begin his inspection of Wusung and the Yangtze shore on Nov. 24, 1842; his reports were received on Jan. 11 and Jan. 27, 1843; in the latter he recommended that water troops be trained and examined for proficiency with ships and firearms, instead of with horse and bow. During this period more correspondence by far was devoted to the defense regulations and the building of ships and batteries than to the conduct of foreign relations. See also Ch'i-ying's memorials in Shih-liao hsun-k'an, 35.287.

10. I-li-pu's subordinate position at Nanking is reflected in the documents, where in August and September 1842 some ten memorials are published as received from Ch'i-ying and I-li-pu together (in eight of these the Nanking governor-general, Niu Chien, also joined), while four were received from Ch'i-ying alone and none at all from I-li-pu alone. This alters the traditional view of I-li-pu's importance, although it does not mean that he may not have contributed decisively to Ch'i-ying's policy. Thus CSK states that on August 13 the emperor "commanded I-li-pu and his colleagues to deliberate regarding the articles of the British demands" ("pen-chi," 19.4b, line 3); but the edicts so far published for that day do not give I-li-pu this prominence (see THL same date; IWSM-TK, 58.14). Perhaps the disparity is due to I-li-pu's former prominence or to the tendency of historians

of the old school to cast aspersions upon Ch'i-ying as one who sold the country; cf. Chin Chao-feng, Ch'ing-shih ta-kang, pp. 392-3, which succeeds in mentioning Ch'i-ying only once. Ch'i-ying's patron, Mu-chang-a, has shared the same odium. As stated by the editors of Shih-liao hsun-k'an (38.394b), "Mu-chang-a perceived the emperor's frame of mind and seconded (the cause of) peace, proposing the removal of Lin Tse-hsü and the use of Ch'i-shan; when peace was concluded in 1842 with (provisions for) the indemnity and trade, because Mu-chang-a ruled the country and promoted the peace, he became the focus of the country's abuse...." Ch'i-ying succeeded Ch'i-shan as Mu-chang-a's representative in the conduct of foreign affairs; from the content of the palace letters (t'ing-chi) granting extraordinary powers which were received by Ch'i-ying on July 31 and Aug. 1, 1842, it would appear that he played the leading part at Nanking (cf. IWSM-TK, 57.32). The accounts of these negotiations in THL and CSK (foreign relations, sec. 2) are both very brief.

11. IWSM-TK, 62.36b-41, mem. rec'd Nov. 18, 1842, edict same date.

12. See summary in Morse, Conflict, p. 293; IWSM-TK, 62.15b-25b, gives the report of the Formosan authorities.

13. Ibid., 62.49b, mem. rec'd from I-li-pu Nov. 30, 1842; IWSM-TK, Supp. 1528-1538, give Chinese translations of Pottinger's dispatches to the Chinese provincial authorities.

14. IWSM-TK, 62.51b-52, 53, edicts Nov. 30, 1842; 63.33, mem. rec'd Dec. 22, 1842; THL, Dec. 21, 1842; to facilitate his going, Ch'i-ying offered to transfer to another his seal as Nanking governor-general. Cp. IWSM-TK, Supp. 1531, line 4, in mem. rec'd Dec. 27, 1842. IWSM-TK, 66.5b-8, mem. rec'd from I-liang Apr. 23, 1843; 62.50b, line 1, mem. rec'd from I-li-pu and Liu Yun-k'o, governor of Chekiang, Nov. 30, 1842. For further documents on the Pottinger-Ch'i-ying relationship in this period, see IWSM-TK, Supp. 1516-18, 1552-57, 1565-66.

15. IWSM-TK, 64.5b-7b, esp. 7, mem. rec'd Dec. 27, 1842; 64.46, edict Jan. 19, 1843.

16. BN, Thom's 33 to Davis, June 30, 1845.

17. IWSM-TK, 65.26b, mem. rec'd Mar. 6, 1843; 65.45-47, mem. rec'd Mar. 22, 1843, edict same date.

18. IWSM-TK, Supp. 1552, mem. rec'd Apr. 5, 1843; 1554-5, mem. rec'd Apr. 6, 1843.

19. IWSM-TK, 66.1-2, mem. rec'd Apr. 6, 1843; IWSM-TK, Supp. 1553, mem. rec'd same date.

20. Pottinger's 34 of Apr. 17, 1843, FO 17/67.

21. IWSM-TK, 66.2; THL, Apr. 6, 1843. This appointment seems to have been made before the arrival of all the pertinent correspondence. The Canton governor-general's suggestion that Ch'i-ying be appointed imperial commissioner, with a copy of Pottinger's dispatch requesting it, was not received at Peking until Apr. 13, 1843 (IWSM-TK, Supp. 1565-6). A memorial from Canton reporting that Pottinger had been dissuaded from his plan of going north to finish the negotiations was seen by the emperor on Apr. 7, 1843 (ibid., 1566, mem. sent by Ch'i Kung Mar. 19, 1843). It was feared that his going north again might upset popular feeling along the coast.

22. IWSM-TK, 66.23, mem. rec'd June 4, 1843. IWSM-TK, 71.18b-19, edict of Apr. 22, 1844, formally gave Ch'i-ying, as governor-general at Canton, authority over all foreign affairs at all the ports, concerning which he should memorialize with the seal of imperial commissioner — a significant centralization of authority. For trans. of edict see CR, XIII: 387 (1844).

23. Pottinger's 52 of May 14, 1843, FO 17/67.

24. Pottinger's 55 of June 8, 1843, ibid.

25. The following account is based on FO 17/68, Pottinger's 74 of July 5, 1843; and IWSM-TK, 68.3b-5b, mem. rec'd from Ch'i-ying July 30, 1843. Ch'en Kung-lu, Chung-kuo chin-tai shih (Chinese modern history), pp. 69-70, barely refers to this visit; earlier Chinese works tend to overlook it entirely.

26. A. F. Saltoun, The Frasers of Philorth, III, 202.

27. IWSM-TK, 67.5, mem. rec'd July 30, 1843; THL, same date.

28. Keying to Pottinger, encl. in Pottinger's 85 of July 19, 1843, FO 17/68. I am indebted to Mr. Chang Te-ch'ang for the information that some of the Chinese originals of these letters may be found in the British Museum, London.

29. Keying to Pottinger, rec'd Oct. 8, in Pottinger's 142 of 1843, FO 17/70.

30. Pottinger's 71 of Dec. 20, 1842, FO 17/161.

31. IWSM-TK, 73.18-20b, mem. rec'd Nov. 23, 1844; trans. by T. F. Wade in Correspondence relative to the Earl of Elgin's Special Mission to China and Japan 1857-1859 (presented to the House of Lords by command 1859), pp. 175-7. For the use made of this document in 1858, see Morse, Conflict, pp. 520-21, 524-5. Ibid., p. 521 is incorrect in dating it 1850. The present translation is from Ssu-yü Teng and John K. Fairbank, China's Response to the West, A Documentary Survey (1839-1923).

REFERENCES: CHAPTER 8

1. FO 17/190, Alcock's June 8 in Bowring's 56, June 28, 1852. Transit duties are discussed more fully in Ch. 16 below.

I regret that this Chapter was completed without the benefit of Professor Ueda's three useful articles which analyse the aspects of the treaty settlement in the context of the Chinese diplomatic documents and from the point of view of international law. Cp. Ueda Toshio, "Nankin jōyaku".

2. FO 17/57, encl. 4 in Pottinger's 36, Aug. 29; encl. 25 of Aug. 15 in Pottinger's 38; also FO 17/66, Pottinger's 6, Jan. 19, 1843. This right of free transit after a single payment is never conceded by sovereign states; cp. Ting Tso-Chao, La Douane Chinoise, p. 91.

3. FO 17/64, Aberdeen's 2, Jan. 4, 1843.

4. See Lo Yü-tung, Chung-kuo li-chin shih (History of likin in China), p. 15 et passim.

5. IWSM-TK, 61.44-46b, rec'd Oct. 29, 1842.

6. The origin of the interesting Chinese notion that Westerners would perish without a supply of China's rhubarb (tai-huang) still awaits clarification. Liang T'ing-nan (I-fen chi-wen, pp. 19-21) quotes a memorial of Lin Tse-hsü which explodes the myth: exports of rhubarb being less than 1000 piculs, how could the barbarians depend on so small a supply?

7. Cf. Dr. Morse's figure of $34,800,000 for exports of Chinese goods in the year 1836-37, calculated from foreign sources (Conflict, p. 168). Exports from China in the period 1838-43 averaged less than this (ibid., p. 366).

8. IWSM-TK, 61.46b-47, edict Oct. 29, 1842; 63.17b-19, mem. rec'd Dec. 12, 1842, edict same date.

9. FO 17/66, memorial from Hwang to Morrison, Feb. 1843, Morrison transl.; Kekung to Pottinger Mar. 9; Pottinger to Chinese authorities Feb. 20, and other enclosures in Pottinger's 24 of Mar. 25, 1843.

10. BN, Thom's 5 to Davis, Feb. 15, 1846.

11. See Customs, Treaties, "Declaration respecting Transit Duties, signed in the English and Chinese languages, at Hongkong, 26th June 1843."

12. For an authoritative technical analysis of the tariff negotiations, see S. F. Wright, China's Struggle for Tariff Autonomy 1843-1938, pp. 9-19.

13. See IWSM-TK, 65. 1-2b, mem. rec'd Feb. 6, 1843.

14. FO 17/66, Pottinger's 12 of 1843; merchants to Pottinger Feb. 8, Macao. FO 17/66, Pottinger's 6 of Jan. 19, 1843. FO 17/74, T. H. Layton to Aberdeen, Apr. 15, 1843.

15. FO 17/69, Pottinger's 118 of Sept. 11, 1843 This was Howqua III, Wu Tun-yuan; see Liang Chia-pin, Kuang-tung shih-san-hang k'ao, pp. 293-4.

16. IWSM-TK, 52.35-36b; mem. rec'd July 15, 1843, edict same date; 57.20-22, mem. rec'd Aug. 4, 1842, edict same date.

17. FO 17/66, Thom to Pottinger Mar. 10, 1843, in Pottinger's "Private" of Mar. 11.

18. IWSM-TK, 64. 40b-43; mem. rec'd Jan. 19, 1843.

19. FO 17/66, Keying to Pottinger, Feb. 26, in Pottinger's 36 of 1843, Medhurst transl.

20. FO 17/66, Keying to Pottinger, Mar. 9, encl. 20 in Pottinger's 24 of 1843.

21. Mar. 11, 1843, Pottinger to Aberdeen, Macao, "Private"; FO 17/68, memo. of June 29 in Pottinger's 85 of 1843.

22. Ibid., encl. 21 and 22.

23. FO 17/67, Pottinger's 69 of June 30, 1843.

24. Keying to Pottinger July 9 and 12 in Pottinger's 85 of 1843; IWSM-TK, 67.5b-7b, mem. rec'd July 30, 1843.

25. FO 17/68, encl. in Pottinger's 85 of July 19, 1843; FO 17/68, Keying to Pottinger July 18, encl. 4 in Pottinger's 99 of 1843. IWSM-TK, 67.39b-40b, mem. rec'd Aug. 11, 1843.

26. IWSM-TK, passim; THL, edicts Aug. 22, Sept. 6, 1842.

27. FO 17/66, encl. 22, Jan. 24, in Pottinger's 7 of 1843.

28. Ibid., encl. 24, Jan. 29.

29. FO 17/66, encl. 18 in Pottinger's 24 of Mar. 25, 1843.

30. FO 17/66, Pottinger's 6 of Jan. 19, 1843; 7 of Feb. 6; 14 of Mar. 10.

31. See below, Ch. 20. This myth that British consuls collected the Chinese duties is perpetuated in many works; see Wu Chao-hsin's survey, Chung-kuo shui-chih shih (History of the Chinese taxation system), II, 87-89; Chu Chin, Chung-kuo kuan-shui wen-t'i (The Chinese customs problem), p. 123; the currency of this error in the treaty ports is evidenced by R. S. Gundry, China, Present and Past, London, 1895, p. 186: "the Consuls seem to have found the only way ... was to undertake the collection of the duties themselves; hand ing over the amounts to the local Superintendents of Customs." Even the author of an (unofficial) Maritime Customs Gazetteer solemnly repeats the idea; see Huang Hsü-yuan, Hai-kuan t'ung-chih, I, 5: after 1842 was "the period when the foreign consuls acted on our behalf (tai-li) to levy and receive the customs duties." Again, Hsia Ching-lin, Studies in Chinese Diplomatic History, p. 200: "collecting the import duties on their own nationals and transferring the revenue thus collected to China."

32. FO 17/57, Correspondence in Pottinger's 38 of Sept. 3, 1842. This had been paraphrased in the Chinese reply: "English merchants... shall trade with whatever merchants shall best please them. And the duties they are to pay shall be paid through the English consular officers to the custom houses, so as to ensure perspicuity and simplicity." (See encl. 31) In the same vein Pottinger had rejoined at Nanking that the presence of the consuls "will be always a sufficient guarantee" that merchants pay their duties.

33. FO 17/66, encl. 19 in no. 7, Feb. 6, 1843, Pottinger to Morrison, quoting Morrison, Jan. 27, 1843; also encl. 19 in no. 24, Mar. 25, 1843, Pottinger to I-li-pu, Feb. 20. In writing to I-li-pu, Pottinger stated plainly that "the duty of the Consuls will be to see that the duties and other charges are regularly paid, that abuses do not creep in, and the smuggling be entirely prevented, ..."

34. Cp. FO 17/66, Pottinger's 24, Mar. 25, 1843: "I have observed, in reading over one or two of the enclosures to this dispatch, that they might, taken abstractedly, lead to an inference, that I mean to make Her Majesty's Consuls at the different Ports personally responsible for the realization of the

Chinese duties, and the suppression of Smuggling; but nothing is further from my intention."

35. FO 17/68, Pottinger's 88 of 1843, Pottinger to Lay, July 22, 1843. In his instructions to Consul Lay, Pottinger made it quite clear that "it is no part of the duty of the British Government or its officers to render mercantile firms or individuals any assistance in conducting their business beyond what is laid down expressly in the General Regulations ... an impression has been imbibed (or pretended to be so by some and by them inculcated in others) that government is bound by its officers and establishments to supply in some measure the loss of the agency of the abolished hong merchants." This was erroneous, he stated, as demonstrated by the fact that the new regulations applied to all the five ports, at four of which no hong merchants had ever existed.

36. IWSM-TK, 67.50-58b, mem. rec'd Aug. 16, 1843. Translated (with errors) to form encl. 1 in FO 17/71, Pottinger's 164 of Dec. 15, 1843.

37. FO 17/70, Ch'i-ying to Pottinger, Sept. 4, encl. 1 in Pottinger's 142 of 1843.

38. FO 17/69, Pottinger's 112, Sept. 1, 1843. John Robert Morrison (1814-1843) was the second son of the Rev. Dr. Robert Morrison (1782-1834), the pioneer Protestant missionary to China. In 1843 he was a member of the legislative and executive councils of Hongkong, Chinese secretary to H. M.'s mission and to the chief superintendent of trade in China, and officiating colonial secretary to the government of Hongkong.

39. BN, Thom's 33 to Davis, June 30, 1845; cp. Yorke, p. 250. For a summary of Robert Thom's rather active career in Caracas and Mexico, and in China after 1834, see CR, XVI: 242-45 (1847). He published a translation of a Chinese tale (1839), Esop's Fables ... in ... Chinese (1840), a Chinese and English Vocabulary (1843), and The Chinese Speaker, or Extracts from works written in the Mandarin language (Ningpo, 1846); see CR, XVIII: 405-407 (1849).

40. Ch'i-ying's letter was translated as follows: "Regarding Fuchow and the other Ports we must wait till the Emperor's will can be known as to when they are to be opened, but the Supplementary Treaty and Regulations not yet being settled, I really fear lest our Chinese merchants may keep looking about them and taking no active steps, so that the departure of the Foreign Merchant Ships may be much delayed. I must therefore beg, that in the midst of the pain you cannot possibly help feeling [over Morrison's death], you will yet place some moderation on your grief, and appoint some steady man to translate these Regulations into Chinese and forward them to me that the great business of reëstablishing peace and good will may be concluded, a knowledge of which cannot fail to gladden the departed spirit of Mr. Morrison in the other world." FO 17/69, Keying to Pottinger, n.d. (ca. Sept. 1, 1843), encl. 12 in Pottinger's 120 of 1843.

41. Wu T'ing-hsien was a native of Shantung and a provincial graduate. He was acting magistrate of I-ching hsien in Kiangsu and then magistrate of Shang-yuan. See Teng, Chang Hsi, note 296, citing I-cheng hsien-chih, 24.75b, and T'ung-chih Shang-Chiang liang-hsien-chih (Local history of Shang-Yuan and Kiangning of the T'ung-chih period), 1874, block-print ed., 13.38. See below, Ch. 16.

42. BN, Thom's 33 to Davis, June 30, 1845; FO 17/69, Pottinger's 102 of 1843.

43. FO 17/70, Pottinger's 154, Nov. 24, 1843. Several thousand copies were circulated and Ch'i-ying told Pottinger that one had even been placed before the emperor and the cabinet (Grand Council?) in Peking.

44. FO 17/70, Keying to Pottinger, Sept. 19, 1843, encl. 2 in Pottinger's 142.

45. IWSM-TK, 69.27-34.

46. FO 17/70, Pottinger's 142, Nov. 3, 1843; FO 17/71, Pottinger's 173, Dec. 23, 1843; FO 17/77, Aberdeen's 10, Jan. 30, 1844; FO 17/85, Aberdeen's 33 to Davis, Mar. 30, 1844.

47. The copy ratified by Queen Victoria was delivered to Huang En-t'ung by the British consul at Canton, F. C. Macgregor, on July 8, 1844. BC, Macgregor's 32, July 8, 1844.

48. See G. R. Sayer, Hong Kong, ch. iv, "Early Contacts."

49. Cp. Morse, Conflict, p. 621.

50. FO 17/62. Treasury to Canning, Jan. 29, 1842. Cp. Costin, p. 98. In January 1842 it was still the official view in London that Hongkong was held temporarily, in pawn only. The higher authorities at a distance had been similarly dubious about Albuquerque's taking Goa in 1510 and Raffles' founding Singapore in 1819. Cp. Sansom, Western World, p. 65.

51. FO 17/60, Pottinger's 8, May 20, 1842: he had made up his mind at least as early as May 1842; FO 17/57, encl. 4 in Pottinger's 36, Aug. 29, 1842; see treaty of Nanking, art. 3. Pottinger reported, "I knew that a copy of my original demands had gone to Peking, and that the change in the wording of the article could not obliterate the fact, although it spared, in some small degree the Emperor's credit in the eyes of his people." His original demands were not transmitted verbatim.

52. FO 17/64, Aberdeen's 22, Jan. 6, 1843; FO 17/63, Aberdeen's 4, Jan. 4, 1843; FO 17/75, Stanley's instructions to Pottinger as governor, no. 8, June 3, 1843, encl. in CO to FO, same date.

53. FO 17/183, W. H. Mitchell, quoting Pottinger, to Bonham, Nov. 1, 1850, encl. in Bonham's 114, encl. in Merivale to Addington, Mar. 15, 1851.

54. BN, Thom's 33 to Davis, June 30, 1845.

55. FO 17/66, encl. 18 in Pottinger's 24 of Mar. 25, 1843. Cp. Ueda, "Nankin jōyaku," pp. 157-163.

56. FO 17/66, encl. 19-24 of Mar. 25, 1843; Pottinger to Eleepoo et al., Feb. 20, 1843.

57. FO 17/68, encl. 8, n.d., in Pottinger's 85 of 1843, in reply to Pottinger's memo. of June

25; FO 17/70, encl. in Pottinger's 147 of 1843; encl. 1 in Pottinger's 85, memo. June 25, 1843.

58. BN, Thom's 33 to Davis, June 30, 1845.

59. J.K.Fairbank translation; for other versions, see CR, XIII: 147-48, 460 (1844). See Customs, Treaties, for English and Chinese texts. Robert Thom's explanation two years later was as follows: "I wrote on the occasion to Sir H. Pottinger something like the following (I am quoting from memory): 'Keying has had the Supplementary Treaty entirely recast into much better Chinese than my translation. The meaning is much about the same, there are however some alterations, and this will devolve upon me the additional trouble of retranslating their Chinese into English again.' This was accordingly done, which will explain the fact of a rough copy of said translation in my handwriting being found in the Hong Kong archives, of which enclosure No. 3 in Your Excellency's dispatch forms a portion." (BN, Thom's 33 of June 30, 1845.) The retranslation to which he referred (of the omitted passage at the end of the article) was rather rough and probably indicates his moderate competence as an interpreter. It read as follows (BN, encl. 3 in Davis' 36 to Thom, May 31, 1845): "Conclusion of the rough Translation of Article XIII of the Supplementary Treaty, omitted in copy transmitted to England... Merchants will not be permitted to request such papers or clearances for the purpose of intercourse with Hongkong at any of the other provinces of China, nor at any of the other ports or places of Quangtung, Fokien, Kiangsook or Chekiang, than the Five Ports. For instance, such passes cannot be procured at Chapoo, that Port not having the privilege of reciprocal intercourse. The Chinese officer resident at Kowlung will be instructed to consult from time to time with the English officers for the purpose of examining and making his report."

Thom's explanation (June 1845) continued: "Early in Oct. we met in Mr. Brown's house at Macao for the purpose of comparing the original English of the supplementary Treaty with my retranslation of Hwang's Chinese, previous to the documents being fair copied. There were present H. E. Sir H. Pottinger, Mr. Soliciter Burgass, Mr. Sect. Woosnam, Mr. Sec. Elmslie, myself and I think one or two others. Each article was carefully read over and compared; upon the 13th art. there was a good deal of discussion, as also upon one or two others, certain alterations in the Chinese and English were authorized and made, and at last everything being considered as understood and arranged, Mr. Sect. Elmslie was instructed to superintend the copying of the English and I was ordered to attend to the Chinese. When fairly transcribed Mr. Elmslie and I met and had the English and Chinese stitched together, but I do not remember any comparison between the English and Chinese after this.

"As Mr. Elmslie copied from Sir H.'s original English in which the clause did not exist so it did not appear in the English portion of the Treaty; whereas I copied from H. E. Hwang's Chinese and as I did not receive any orders (that I can at this moment remember) to omit the clause in question, so it was unfortunately allowed to appear in the Chinese portion. I can only surmise that H. E. Sir H. Pottinger viewed it as a parenthetical note, which the Chinese might keep for their satisfaction, if they chose, but unnecessary to us, and therefore he did not cause it to be inserted in the English portion of the Treaty."

60. FO 17/70, Pottinger's 142, Nov. 3, 1843; FO 17/96, Aberdeen's 10 of Feb. 22, 1845; BN, Thom's 33 of June 30, 1845.

61. BC, Macgregor's 57, Sept. 23, 1844; Macgregor's 57 (sic), June 26, 1845; FO 17/81, Ching to Pottinger, Mar. 30, 1844, in Pottinger's 59 of 1844. FO 17/66, Kekung to Pottinger, Mar. 9, 1843, in Pottinger's 24. FO 17/81, Pottinger to Ching, Mar. 21, 1844. Cp. Wright, Hart, p. 61.

62. FO 228/29, Canton Consulate to Gunwell (?), Aug. 21, 1843; Pottinger's 349 to Lay, Aug. 20, 1843.

63. FO 17/66, Pottinger's 24 of Mar. 25, 1843, encl. 18, 19, and 20; FO 17/68, Pottinger's 85 of late June, 1843, encl. 8 and 10. Cp. FO 17/66, memo. of Mar. 28: "The Plenipotentiary likewise intimated to the Imperial Commissioners at Nanking his perfect willingness to meet their Excellencies' suggestion that the people of Hongkong should be governed by their own laws, and Mandarins to be stationed at Kowloong for that purpose. The Plenipotentiary still accedes to that proposal (although British police jurisdiction is plainly necessary etc.) ... On this point, as well as all others reference must be had to what passed at Nanking." Cp. also FO 17/66, encl. 19 in no. 24 of Mar. 25, Pottinger to I-li-pu et al., Feb. 20, 1843: "I quite approve of Your Excellencies sending a Seunkeen [Hsun-chien] or inferior District Officer for the purpose of investigating the crimes and settling the disputes of the Chinese people residing in Hongkong and I will instruct it to be notified that all Chinese persons having complaints against Chinese may apply to him if they like ..." (continued as quoted in text above.)

64. FO 17/66, Mar. 28.

65. FO 228/38.

66. FO 17/90, Davis' 116 of Dec. 14, 1844.

67. FO 17/59, Pottinger's 70 of Dec. 10, 1842.

68. FO 17/67. Pottinger to Kekung, Apr. 13, in Pottinger's 34 of 1843; Morse, Conflict, p. 320, quoting CR, May 1843.

69. FO 17/67. encl. 2 in Pottinger's 34 of Apr. 17, 1843; Kekung to Pottinger, Thom transl., in Pottinger's 41 of 1843; FO 17/68, memo. dated June 25 in Pottinger's 85 of 1843.

70. FO 17/176, 85 to Bonham, Oct. 9, 1850. An FO minute dated Mar. 31, 1851, in response to a query by Palmerston suggests that article XII probably originated in a "desire on the part of Sir Henry Pottinger to obtain by this process an additional security against British merchants attempting to evade duties, and so giving rise to contests with the Chinese authorities....In the paper of demands first presented by Sir H. Pottinger, it was said, 'No. 10. All Hong merchants to be abolished, and British Merchants to trade with whom they like paying the just dues of the Chinese Government

through the Consular officers'. Another reason ... might have been to reconcile the Chinese Government to the abolition of the Hong Monopoly, by giving them a new species of security for obtaining payment of duties, and as said in one of the Chinese letters 'to ensure perspicuity and simplicity'." (FO 17/183).

The original British proposal or "demand", that duties should be paid through the consuls, was ordered to be discussed by an edict of July 4, 1842. Cp. Ueda, "Nankin jōyaku", p. 120, quoting IWSM-TK, 59.4.

71. FO 228/235, Pottinger's 290 to Lay, July 22, 1843, encl. in Parkes' 82 to Bowring, July 9, 1857.

72. BN, Pottinger's 8 to Balfour, Jan. 17, 1844, in Pottinger's 4 to Thom, same date.

73. IWSM-TK, 70.5-6; 8b-9.

REFERENCES: CHAPTER 9

1. The extent and persistence of the slave smuggling trade across the Atlantic down to the 1860's is described by Christopher Lloyd, The Navy and the Slave Trade.

2. See Yorke, pp. 96, 170; Gutzlaff, Journal of Three Voyages, p. 297 et seq., "Journal of a Third Voyage, 1832-33."

3. Yorke, pp. 179, 189, 260; cp. Greenberg, pp. 140-41.

4. Yorke, p. 243, quoting Private Letter Book. Cp. also pp. 234, 238, 448, 456.

5. Ibid., pp. 418, 426-7. The opium trade avoided sales on credit. In 1844 Boston merchants at Canton complained that Parsees were trusting Chinese brokers for half the purchase money; Jardine's, Russell, and Heard and Co. had lost the market, but expected some broker to fail soon and end the practice. (John Heard, Jr., to Augustine Heard, Oct. 3, 1844, vol. EM-4, Heard Papers).

6. Yorke, pp. 434, 468; it should be noted again that Basil Lubbock, The Opium Clippers, is based partly on the records of Dent and Co. and contains a great deal of information on that firm. The Report from the Select Committee on Commercial Relations with China, 1847, contains testimony from partners of both Jardine's and Dent and Co.

7. IWSM-TK, 57-60, passim.

8. FO 17/57, encl. 20a in Pottinger's 38 of Sept. 3, 1842; also printed in Papers relating to the Opium Trade in China 1842-1856, presented to the House of Commons by command, 1857. Lacking the Chinese original of this document, as of others like it, we are obliged to accept the British interpreter's translation.

9. Ibid.

10. FO 17/59, Pottinger's 70 of Dec. 10, 1842.

11. IWSM-TK, 61.22, line 10, in memorial received from Ch'i-ying Oct. 17, 1842.

12. FO 17/57, Pottinger's 38; FO 17/66, notification of Jan. 16 in Pottinger's 6 of Jan. 19, 1843.

13. FO 17/76A. This proclamation was made known to the Foochow governor-general, I-liang, at Amoy on Nov. 28 and was printed in CR, XI: 629 (1842).

14. Yorke, p. 435, Private Letter Book, Dec. 6, 1842.

15. FO 17/65, Aberdeen's 81 of Sept. 2, 1843; cp. Costin, p. 42.

16. FO 17/64, Aberdeen's 10 to Pottinger, Jan. 4, 1843.

17. Yorke, p. 438, Private Letter Book, Apr. 21, 1843.

18. I am indebted to Dr. C. C. Stelle for permission to see his ms., "American Participation in the Sino-British Opium Trade."

19. CR, XII: 168 (1843). On this whole topic see Wu Wen-tsao, The Chinese Opium Question in British Opinion. The contemporary literature on the opium question is also surveyed in Ueda Toshio, "Eikoku no ahen mitsuyu."

20. Yorke, p. 425. After the British forces withdrew, as Alexander Matheson testified in 1847, "we [J. M. and Co.] have repeatedly sent away vessels [to India] ourselves with nearly a million of dollars"; Report ... Committee on Commercial Relations, p. 341.

21. Yorke, pp. 423-5.

22. FO 17/67A under date of Nov. 24, 1843; the port clearance provided for in the harbor regulations published for Hongkong and Tinghai on Mar. 7, 1842, was not required to specify a ship's destination.

23. Ibid., Duke of Wellington to Lord Aberdeen, Nov. 24, 1843; Schoedde to Somerset, May 2, 1843.

24. FO 17/75, extract from Hope's letter of Apr. 21, 1843, in Haddington to Aberdeen, Aug. 12, 1843.

25. FO 17/67, Pottinger's 40 of Apr. 29, 1843. It is interesting to note that the collection of the Kiangnan customs reported to Peking for the year 1842 was short Tls. 33,000 (IWSM-TK, Supp. 1567-8, mem. rec'd Mar. 14, 1843).

26. FO 17/67, trans. by Harry Parkes, encl. in Pottinger's 53 of 1843.

27. FO 17/67, Pottinger's 39 of Apr. 21, 1843.

28. Ibid., Pottinger's 56 of June 9, 1843.

29. Yorke, p. 442, Private Letter Book, Sept. 10, 1843.

30. FO 17/67, Pottinger's 33 of Apr. 12, 1843, encl. Pottinger to Parker, secret and confidential, Apr. 10; Pottinger's 39 of Apr. 21, 1843.

31. Yorke, p. 437.

32. FO 17/67, Pottinger to Parker, Apr. 26, encl. in Pottinger's 40 of Apr. 29, 1843.

33. FO 17/75, Haddington to Aberdeen, Aug. 12, 1843. FO 17/65, Aberdeen's 76 of Aug. 4, 1843.

34. IWSM-TK, 63.29, mem. rec'd Dec. 15, 1842; 64.3-4b, mem. rec'd Dec. 25, 1842, edict same date; THL, same date; IWSM-TK, Supp. 1524-5.

35. IWSM-TK, 63.29b-30, edict, Dec. 15, 1842. For Kearny's request see 63.17, mem. rec'd from Kwangtung Dec. 12, 1842.

36. IWSM-TK, 65.8, mem. rec'd Feb. 11, 1842; 10b-11b, edicts same date; 41, mem. rec'd Mar. 17; 45-6, mem. rec'd Mar. 22, 1843. IWSM-TK, Supp. 1542, mem. rec'd from Liu Yun-k'o Feb. 11; 1559, mem. rec'd from Ch'i Kung, Apr. 7; 1561-4, mem. rec'd from Pao-ch'ang Apr. 8, 1843.

37. IWSM-TK, 65.27b-33, mem. rec'd Mar. 8, 1843; see esp. 30b; 65.33b, mem. rec'd Mar. 10; 66.22, mem. rec'd June 4, 1843.

38. FO 17/67, Keying to Pottinger, June 13, encl. in Pottinger's 64 of June 19, 1843.

39. IWSM-TK, 66.11-12b, mem. rec'd May 16, 1843.

40. Ibid., 13b-16, mem. rec'd May 31, 1843; edict same date.

41. Ibid., 27-28b, mem. rec'd June 18, 1843; FO 17/67, Keying to Pottinger, encl. in Pottinger's 64 of June 19, 1843.

42. FO 17/68, Pottinger to Keying, July 1, encl. in Pottinger's 75 of 1843; IWSM-TK, 67. 46b-47b, mem. rec'd from Ch'i-ying Aug. 11, 1843, quoting Pottinger's apology.

43. FO 17/67, Pottinger's 56 of June 9, 1843.

44. FO 17/64, Aberdeen's 7 to Pottinger, Jan. 4, 1843; printed in full in Morse, Conflict, app. P, excepting endorsements.

45. Yorke, p. 463, Coast Letter Book, Jan. 22, 1841.

46. Papers rel. Opium Trade (1857), Pottinger to Parker, Apr. 10, 1843.

47. FO 17/68, memo. for Keying, June 25, encl. in Pottinger's 85 of July 19, 1843.

48. FO 17/67, Pottinger's 56 of June 9, 1843.

49. IWSM-TK, 64.45, line 7, in mem. rec'd Jan. 19, 1843.

50. Ibid., 68.24b-28, mem. rec'd Sept. 23, 1843.

51. Morse, Conflict, p. 556, estimates the import into China as 28,508 chests in 1842 and 36,699 in 1843.

52. FO 17/68, Pottinger's 85 of July 19, 1843; printed in Papers rel. Opium Trade (1857); IWSM-TK, 67.1-7b, mems. rec'd July 30, 1843. Cp. Owen, p. 188.

53. FO 17/67, Pottinger's 56 of June 9, 1843.

54. FO 17/68, Pottinger's 87 of July 25, 1843; printed in Papers rel. Opium Trade (1857). Cp. IWSM-TK, 70.7-8.

55. FO 17/55, Aberdeen's 22 of July 2, 1842.

56. FO 17/67, Pottinger's 55 of June 8, 1843; cp. Morse, Conflict, p. 292. The regulation of the activities of British small craft provided for in art. XVII of the Supplementary treaty, discussed in the preceding section, concerned primarily the port of Canton; in 1843 the coast trade in small craft under foreign colors at Ningpo and northern ports had not yet begun.

57. FO 17/65, Aberdeen's 76 of Aug. 4, 1843.

58. CR, XII: 446 (August 1843).

59. Papers rel. Opium Trade (1857), encl. in Pottinger to Aberdeen, Nov. 4, 1843.

60. IWSM-TK, 67.58b-60, mem. rec'd Aug. 18, 1843; edicts same date; 68. 10-12b, mem. rec'd Aug. 31, 1843; edicts same date.

61. By the most-favored-nation clause, art.II of the French treaty of Whampoa, 1844, changed this provision to refer to cargoes only.

62. CR, XII: 558-9 (October 1843).

63. FO 17/70, Pottinger's 147, Nov. 10, 1843. See also BN, Pottinger's circular of Oct. 23, 1843.

64. IWSM-TK, 69.18b-19, in mem. rec'd Nov. 7, 1843.

65. Ibid., 19, edict Nov. 7, 1843.

66. Ibid., 70.7-8, mem. rec'd Dec. 1, 1843.

67. Ibid., 8-9, edict, Dec. 1, 1843; THL and IWSM-TK, Supp. 1628, under the same date give practically the same document; cp. Li Kuei, Ya-p'ien shih-lueh, 2.1. There are almost no works by Chinese writers referring to opium during this important period of negotiation.

68. CR, XII: 615-6 (November 1843).

69. FO 17/76A, Foreign Office to Colonial Office, Nov. 11, 1843; CO to FO, Nov. 15; Aberdeen's 87 to Pottinger, Nov. 15; FO 17/69, memo. headed "FO Nov. 6, 1843."

70. Yorke, pp. 340, 443. Consul Balfour, in testimony before the Parliamentary committee of 1847, agreed that "if profit is the question ..., the anomalous state in which [the opium trade] is even now in China is more profitable." Alexander Matheson also testified he would be "sorry to see the [opium] monopoly broken up in Bengal" because it guaranteed the quality of the product. See Report. . .Committee on Commercial Relations, pp. 334, 342.

71. A Japanese-inspired study of Britain's "economic aggression" on China, published in Peking in 1945, puts heavy stress on the role of Hongkong as the British base of operations; see Wei Hsü-chih, Ying-kuo tsai Chung-kuo ti ching-chi ch'in-lueh shih (Historical survey of England's economic agression in China), a volume in the "Greater East Asia series" (Peking, 1945), pp. 75-94.

REFERENCES: CHAPTER 10

1. Morse, Conflict, pp. 359, 362, is incorrect in stating that Amoy was opened in June 1844; and also, p. 359, in stating that Ningpo was officially opened in December 1843.

The most recent summary of the background and opening of the early ports is included in Professor Ueda's comprehensive survey of the foreign concessions in China, Shina no okeru sokai no kenkyū.

2. E. O. Reischauer, "Notes on T'ang Dynasty Sea Routes," HJAS, 5.2: 163 (June 1940).

3. Worcester, Junks and Sampans, p. 191.

4. Wu Yü-kan, "T'ang-Sung shih-tai Shang-hai tsai Chung-kuo tui-wai mao-i-shang chih ti-wei kuan"("Shanghai as an international trading port during the T'ang and Sung dynasties - a comparative study with other ports in China").

5. Worcester, p. 192.

6. E. H. Parker, China Past and Present, p. 160. For descriptions of the above topography, cp. Mayers, Dennys, and King, The Treaty Ports of China and Japan and various editions of Morrison's Chinese Commercial Guide.

7. Morrison, Chinese Commercial Guide (1844), 275-8.

8. See, e.g., book lists in Morse, Conflict, and F. C. Jones, Shanghai and Tientsin. C. A. Montalto de Jesus, Historic Shanghai, now rare, records a good deal of local color. See Balfour's testimony in 1847, Report ... Committee on Commercial Relations, p. 320, quest. 4324.

9. Mayers, Dennys, and King, The Treaty Ports, p. 353; used by Shanghai Mercury, ed., 1843-Shanghai-1893. The Model Settlement. Its Birth. Its Youth. Its Jubilee, Nov. 17, 1893, see pp. 2-5. Feetham, Report, p. 50, gives foreign population totals as 50 in 1844, 175 in 1849, and 243 in 1855. Hawks Pott, A Short History of Shanghai, p. 21, gives 90 persons for 1845. Unfortunately the Shanghai British consulate was burned with its records in 1870.

10. Mayers, Treaty Ports, pp. 396-97. Among many accounts of treaty port life see Anon., The Englishman in China, pp. 30-31; and Charles M. Dyce, Personal Reminiscences of Thirty Years' Residence in the Model Settlement, Shanghai, 1870-1900, see pp. 32-3, 56. Perhaps the most comprehensive, as well as the most sympathetic and admiring, picture of the early treaty ports is in Michie's biography of Alcock, The Englishman in China, e.g., ch. xiii, "The Traders."

11. Dyce, p. 95.

12. Sir R. Alcock, The Capital of the Tycoon, I, 38.

13. E. W. A. Tuson, The British Consul's Manual, ch. vi, devotes some 100 pages to China; the treaties of course provided only a small part of the whole legal framework.

14. FO 17/74, Pottinger to the governor of Madras, Oct. 17, 1842, in India Board to FO, May 10, 1843. G. T. Lay's Chinese name in the IWSM documents is Li-t'ai-kuo (also used for his more famous son, H. N. Lay). Ch'en Kung-lu, p. 129, makes the plausible suggestion that this was an error for Li-kuo-t'ai ("Lay, G.T."), but the error, if it is such, is consistently maintained over two decades. Lay wrote The Claims of Japan and Malyasia upon Christendom, exhibited in Notes of Voyages made in 1837 from Canton (1839), and The Chinese as they are: their moral, social, and literary character, etc, (London, 1841).

15. See Alexander Michie, The Englishman in China, passim; and R. Alcock, Notes on the Medical History of the British Legion in Spain (London, 1838), passim. Other little-known writings by Alcock include his articles in Bombay Quarterly Review (see Bibliography, below); Life's Problems. Essays: Moral, Social, and Psychological (1857); Our Policy in China (1858); The Capital of the Tycoon (1863); ed., The Journey of ... Margary (1876); Art and Industries in Japan (1878).

16. FO 17/69, Pottinger's 118 of Sept. 11, 1843.

17. FO 17/87, Davis' no. 22 of May 18, 1844; see also FO 17/88 and 86, passim.

18. FO 17/82, Pottinger's 92 of May 30, 1844.

19. BA, Gribble's 2, Nov. 10, 1843; Abeel is discussed more fully in Ch. 15. Cp. FO 228/31, Balfour's 5, Oct. 21, 1843: The American missionary E. C. Bridgman, in his capacity as president of the Morrison Educational Society at Hongkong, on the opening of Shanghai had offered the consul the services of two Chinese boys from that institution who had had three years' tuition in European and Chinese subjects with honest records. He urged that such boys, while remaining students of the school, might assist in the consulates for $8 a month, but the offer was not taken up.

20. BA, Gribble's 17, Feb. 12, 1844.

21. FO 228/29, Pottinger's 415 to Gutzlaff, Oct. 23, 1843; FO 17/64, Aberdeen's 55 of Apr. 6, 1843; FO 17/65, Aberdeen's 90 of Nov. 15, 1843.

22. BC, Hoppo to Consul, Mar. 23, and Mar. 19, 1846.

23. IWSM-TK, 73.37 and 74.5b-6b.

24. Ibid., 72.3b-4.

25. BN, Meadows to Bowring, June 14, 1852.

26. FO 17/78, Pottinger's 17 of Feb. 5, 1844. On his return to China in 1845, the Foreign Secretary recommended Wade for employment (FO 17/96, Aug. 5). Another man who followed in Wade's footsteps was W. Raymond Gingell, an assistant surgeon in the Madras forces, who came to Amoy from Chusan in November 1844 to join his corps and was drafted to take the place of Parkes as interpreter at $100 a month, during the latter's six weeks' absence on sick leave because of a return of fever. His temporary employment in China was approved by the Madras government and he became indispensable as a combined doctor and interpreter. He was sent from Amoy to Foochow in September 1845 to substitute for Parkes during the latter's absence again on sick leave, and was interpreter at Ningpo in March 1847. In 1849 he obtained Palmerston's permission to translate a history of Amoy in his leisure time for presentation to the Asiatic Societies of London and Paris. See William Raymond Gingell, trans., Hoo Pieh-seang, Chow Le Kwan Choo [Hu Pi-hsiang, Chou-li kuan-chu], "The Ceremonial Usages of the Chinese, B.C. 1121"

(London, 1852); noted in S. Y. Teng, "Chinese Influence on the Western Examination System," HJAS, 7.4: 310 (Sept. 1943).

27. Cp. S. Couling, Encyclopedia Sinica, p. 344.

28. BA, Pottinger's 283 to Gribble, Sept. 25, 1843; BC, Macgregor's 17 to Davis, June 6, 1844.

29. BN, Pottinger's circ. 6, Feb. 7, 1844.

30. Letters of G. T. Lay, mss., courtesy H. M. Lay, Barrie, Ontario. Cp. Parliamentary Papers, Return of Student Interpreters in China and Japan.

31. FO 17/75, Wise to Aberdeen, Sept. 28, 1843. By a contract of Dec. 1844, the P. and O. steamers were to be of 250 h.p. at first, and 400 h.p. after June 1846. The Ceylon-China service began Aug. 1, 1845; CR,XV: 619 (1846).

32. CM, no. 25, Aug. 7; no. 27, Aug. 21, 1845; no. 104, Feb. 11, 1847. Cp. Morse, Conflict, pp. 343-45, for data on postal services in this period.

33. FO 17/67, Pottinger's 55 of June 8, 1843; FO 17/76A, Admiralty letter of Oct. 13, 1843.

34. FO 228/29, Pottinger's 280, 332 to Parker, July, August, 1843; Pottinger's 460; FO 17/90, Davis' 111 of Dec. 5, 1844; FO 17/66, Pottinger's 40 of 1843, encl. 3.

35. BA, Gribble's 48 of July 5, 1844.

36. BN, Sullivan's 26, May 26, 1847.

37. FO 17/90, Davis' 111, Dec. 5, 1844.

38. Yorke, p. 439, Coast Letter Book, Sept. 22, 1843.

39. BN, Robertson's 49 of 1850; Winchester's 43, May 2, 1855.

40. FO 228/900, Davis to Keying, July 16, 1844; FO 228/38, Keying to Pottinger, July 24, 1844; BF, Jackson's 27, July 30, 1849; BC, Macgregor's 30, Mar. 6, 1846.

41. BN, Hague to Tung, Dec. 23; reply Dec. 31, 1851; Winchester's 30 to Hyland, June 22, 1855; Patridge to Consul, July 26, 1856.

42. BF, Jackson's 19, June 4, 1849.

43. FO 17/89, Davis' 85, Oct. 21, 1844.

44. See the articles by Alcock, "The Chinese Empire and its destinies," Bombay Quarterly Review (Bombay and London), 4 (Oct. 1855), and "The Chinese Empire in its Foreign Relations," ibid., 6 (Apr. 1856).

45. FO 228/43, Davis' 37, Oct. 21, 1844; Balfour's 54, Aug. 14, 1844.

46. Cp. Michie, The Englishman in China, pp. 129-35; Morse, Conflict, p. 392; Chinese account from Chung-Hsi chi-shih, reprinted in Hsiao I-shan, Ch'ing-tai t'ung-shih, II, 928-9.

47. BN, no. 81, Dec. 24, 1844, Thom to Ye-kwun, Yin district magistrate.

48. BF, Davis' 77, Oct. 27, 1845; Clarendon's 2, Jan. 24, 1846; both approved this course. Cp. Lane-Poole, Sir Harry Parkes, ch. iv.

REFERENCES: CHAPTER 11

1. Chih-chi chih-pi, pai-chan pai-sheng. Ch'i-ying had taken this as a motto in 1842, see Ch. 6.

2. See IWSM, passim for examples of these terms, e.g., IWSM-TK, 1.24b, line 3; 4.16, line 8; 4.19b, line 8.

3. E.g. IWSM-HF, 2.11b; 3.28, line 4; 6.10, line 2; 12.6b, line 3. This stock idea had long been current, cp. Yueh hai-kuan chih, 26.1, "The barbarians' nature is to scheme only for profit."

4. IWSM-HF, 3.30, line 6, memorial of Hsü Kuang-chin, received Dec. 31, 1850, apparently quoting Mencius, book I, ch. 1.4: "Superiors and inferiors will try to snatch this profit the one from the other, and the kingdom will be endangered." (Legge trans.)

5. IWSM-HF, 7.24.

6. On this term see above, Ch. 3.

7. See, e.g., IWSM-TK, 64.44b, line 6, memorial of Ch'i-ying received Jan. 19, 1843. Cp. ibid., 61.19, line 6, memorial of Ch'i-ying, I-li-pu, and Niu received Oct. 17, 1842.

8. Wei Yuan, Hai-kuo t'u-chih, ed. of 1844, 50 chüan. For a comparison of the different editions and discussion of authorship, see Gideon Chen, Lin Tse-hsü, pp. 23-30; Chang Hsi-t'ung, "Western Political Science in China;" and Tu Lien-che in Hummel, p. 850. The first edition, in 50 chüan, is wrongly listed by some bibliographers as 60 chüan. Ch'i Ssu-ho, "Wei Yuan", pp. 204-7, describes the 1852 edition and its Chinese and Western sources. As late as 1902 an Errata and supplements to the Hai-kuo t'u-chih was published by Sun Hao in 20 volumes; see his Hai-kuo t'u-chih cheng-shih.

9. Several items by Lin, and also by early Western missionaries, are included in the great collection (ts'ung-shu) on geography, including the barbarians, by Wang Hsi-ch'i, Hsiao-fang-hu-chai yü-ti ts'ung-ch'ao, (preface 1877, second supplement 1897, 1438 titles in 84 ts'e), see e.g., ts'e 77, chih 11, ch. 9, item 3. CR,XVI: 417-424 (1847), attributes the Hai-kuo t'u-chih entirely to Lin. On this whole subject see Chang Hsi-t'ung's article. For a biography and critique of Wei, see Ch'i Ssu-ho, "Wei Yuan." He began the Sheng-wu chi in 1828.

10. Hai-kuo t'u-chih, ch. 1. For a translation of this section see Teng and Fairbank, China's Response to the West.

11. Hai-kuo t'u-chih, 1.36-54.

12. Ibid., 1.39b-40. The current Chinese communist view is that Wei Yuan's book poineered the institutional reform movement of which K'ang Yu-wei was the climax and which represented the interests of Chinese commercial capitalism. See Hou Wai-lu, Chin-tai Chung-kuo ssu-hsiang hsueh-shuo shih, II, 604-608.

13. See Hai-kuo t'u-chih, 43.1-6.

14. Ibid.

15. See Gideon Chen, Lin Tse-hsü, ch. i.

16. Hummel, p. 606.

17. Gideon Chen, pp. 39-49.

18. Detailed manuals on coastal defense, with maps, were produced in this period, building on earlier works in a tradition coming down from the Japanese invasions of the Ming period; see Yen Ju-i, Yang-fang chi-yao, and Yü Ch'ang-hui, Fang-hai chi-yao (1842).

19. IWSM-TK, 69.1-10.

20. Ibid., 71.22-23.

21. Ibid., 72.25-30.

22. Ibid., 75.lb; 75.26b-30; 75.41-44; 76.20b-23b.

23. Ibid., 70.34-35; 70.32-34.

24. See Gideon Chen, Tseng Kuo-fan,pp. 1-9.

25. CM, no. 41, Nov. 27; no. 42, Dec. 4, 1845.

26. IWSM-TK, 74.29b-31.

27. IWSM-TK, 69.13-15.

28. IWSM-TK, 69.15-16.

29. Murray, p. 206.

30. See Teng, Chang Hsi, note 269; Loch, p. 150.

31. Th. de Ferrière le Vayer, Une Ambassade Francaise en Chine, p. 245.

32. FO 17/70, Pottinger's 142, Nov. 3, 1843. On the flimsy charge against Huang in 1846, see CR, XVI: 103, 151-52 (1847).

33. CSK, ch. 213, "Chiang-ch'en nien-piao" (Chronological table of provincial officials), 11.35b. See Teng, Chang Hsi, note. 98.

34. FO 17/57, Pottinger's 38, Sept. 3, 1842; cp. Loch, p. 149: "The Tartar General 'Chin'"; followed by S. W. Williams, The Middle Kingdom (1848), II, 565: "Tartar commandant;" 566, "Chin, the Manchu commandant"; Murray, p. 206: "The Tartar General."

35. Loch, pp. 150, 162; Murray, pp. 179-80.

36. IWSM-TK, 69.16; 70.24b.

37. IWSM-HF, 1.27b. Ch'en Kung-lu, Chung-kuo chin-tai shih, p. 93, notes that Hsien-ling got the blame for the Tsingpu affair of 1848. Cp. below, ch. 21, references 7 and 8.

38. Ibid., 70.25-28. Cp. also 68.29b-31.

39. Ibid., 70.6-7.

40. Ibid., 71.24b-25; 71.27. For Lu's later activity in Fukien in 1847, see Ch. 15 below.

41. Ibid., 73.25b-26b.

42. The Rev. W. C. Milne in his "Notes of a Seven Months Residence in the City of Ningpo, from December 7th, 1842, to July 7th, 1843" records extensive and friendly social relations with Shu Kung-shou and also with his colleagues Li Ju-lin and Lu Tse-ch'ang. He lent them books (including a copy of Wyld's map of China), discussed many topics, and got Lu cured of the itch; see CR, XIII: 16, 29, 41, 79, 90, 127, 132, 140, 142 (1844). Li Ju-lin of Shantung, reputed a chü-jen at 19, impressed Milne as "one of the most fortunate men of his day," barely 33 years of age, intelligent, unassuming, and hospitable to foreigners (ibid., p. 79).

43. Teng, notes 356, 228, 167.

44. IWSM-TK, 51.13b; Teng, notes 169 and 281. For Hsü Chi-yü's praise of Lu, see below, ch. 15, note 47.

45. Teng, note 311, corrects Ch'en Po-ling to read Ch'eng Po-ling but this is not substantiated in IWSM.

46. IWSM-TK, 72.43b; Teng, 81 ff., note 296; see above, Ch. 8. Callery, the French interpreter, reported that Wu T'ing-hsien spoke to him "with great interest" of Joan of Arc as a heroine who saved her people but later perished at their hands (Grosse-Aschhoff, p. 29).

47. IWSM-TK, 72.43b; 72.3b-4. CR, XVIII: 672 (1849), reported under date of Nov. 21, 1849, that "Chau Changling, late acting judge of Kwangtung, is reported to have been robbed of upwards of 30,000 taels by beggars when on his way to Chehkiang, with his father's coffin."

48. IWSM-TK, 72.3b-4; 72.19-20; see also Shih-liao hsun-k'an, 35.294b, a mem. of Ch'i-ying on P'an's qualifications. P'an collected and reprinted various works on foreign countries; see his Hai-shan hsien-kuan ts'ung-shu, which was printed mainly in the years 1845-49 and contains some translations on the West; cp. Grosse-Aschhoff, p. 18.

49. Ibid., 72.32b; 72.35b; 72.37; 72.43b.

50. See Hummel, p. 309.

51. IWSM-TK, 70.20-21.

52. Ibid., 71.19-22.

53. BA, Gribble's 19 of Feb. 14, 1844.

54. Davis, China during the War, p. 74.

55. Hummel, p. 309; Hsü Chi-yü, Ying-huan chih-lueh, introd.; cp. Abeel's journal in CR, XIII: 233-38 (1844).

56. See Ch. 15.

57. IWSM-TK, 70.5.

58. Ibid., 70.9-11.

59. Ibid., 70 12b-14; 70.9-11.

60. Ibid., 70.22-24.

61. FO 17/81, passim.

62. IWSM-TK, 70.11-12; 70.26b-27b; 70.30-32b.

63. FO 17/89, Davis' 85 of Oct. 21, 1844.

64. See Earl Swisher, The Management of the American Barbarians: A Study in the Relations between the United States and China from 1840 to 1860, Ph.D., dissertation, Harvard University (1941), p. 60; quoted by permission of the author.

65. Ch'i Kung sent Kearny's request for equal treatment to Peking; IWSM-TK, Supp. 1521-23, mem. rec'd Dec. 12, 1842. There is no record of an edict granting it.

66. On this whole subject see Pritchard, "The Origins of the Most-Favored-Nation and the Open Door Policies in China", and Banno Masataka, "Ahen sensō"; the latter examines the ideological bases of Ch'ing policy. See also T. F. Tsiang, "The extension of equal commercial privileges to other nations than the British after the Treaty of Nanking," CSPSR, 15.3: 422-444(October 1931); Thomas Kearny, "The Tsiang Documents ... an American viewpoint," ibid., 16.1: 75-104 (April 1932); T. F. Tsiang, "A note in reply," ibid., pp. 105-109; Thomas Kearny, "Commodore Kearny and the Open Door and Most Favored Nation Policy in China in 1842 to 1843," New Jersey Historical Society Proceedings, 50; 162-190 (1932); see also further discussion in CSPSR, XVI: 75-104 (1932); and T'ien Hsia Monthly, 3 (1936). Commodore Kearny's reports were published in 1846 in U. S. Cong. 29:1, Senate Doc. 139, pp. 1-47. Cushing's biographer (C. M. Fuess, The Life of Caleb Cushing) is uncritical on this point.

67. See Swisher, pp. 172-3; and also IWSM-TK, Supp. 1548-50, mem. of Ch'eng Yü-ts'ai, rec'd Apr. 9; ibid., 1681-82, June 8, 1844, reporting success in stopping Cushing's northern journey.

68. Macgregor to Davis, Feb. 4, 1845, in Parliamentary Papers, Returns of Trade ... July 1845, p. 6.

69. Tchang Yen-chen in his "Le Traité de Whampoa 1844," p. 57, notes how Ch'i-ying professed a great desire for intimate friendship, to Lagrené, but described him to the emperor as "rusé, sournois, soupçonneux et vicieux." This article uses IWSM, but for the most complete study, see Angelus Grosse-Aschhoff, O.F.M., Ph.D., The Negotiations between Ch'i-ying and Lagrené 1844-1846, pp. 32, 35 et passim, which gives translations of 19 documents from IWSM, makes good use of Callery's journal and other French documents and clarifies many aspects of Sino-French relations. Cp. also IWSM-TK, Supp. 1705-07, memorials from Ch'i-ying rec'd Oct. 6 and Nov. 6, 1844. The French effort at mediation in 1842 (when a French warship appeared suddenly off Shanghai on July 31, see IWSM-TK, 59.5, 18b-21) still awaits investigation. IWSM-TK, Supp. 1506-09, memorial of Niu Chien rec'd Aug. 24, 1842, indicates that Niu asked British help in getting rid of the French. Among other French materials, see J. M. Callery, Correspondence diplomatique Chinoise, Ferrière le Vayer, Th(éophile) de, Une Ambassade Francaise en Chine, and H. Cordier, "La Mission Dubois de Jancigny. ..". Shih Chao-ying, "I-pa-ssu-ssu nien Chung-Mei Chung-Fa t'iao-yueh" (The Sino-American and Sino-French treaties of 1844), uses the Chinese documents cursorily. Note the rather mystifying account of the French offers of 1842 in Wei Yuan, Hai-kuo t'u-chih, ed. 1844, 1.38b-39. The partly published Journal of the French interpreter, J.M. Callery, gives the most illuminating insight into the personalities and methods of Ch'i-ying's staff at this time.

70. IWSM-TK, 74.7b-9; 74.16.

71. Ibid., 74.16-18b. For an account of negotiations of Lannoy and others, based on the Belgian archives, see J.-M. Frochisse, S.J., La Belgique et la Chine, pp. 22-40.

REFERENCES: CHAPTER 12

1. See Morse, Conflict, ch. xiv.

2. FO 17/57, encl. 23 dated Aug. 15, in Pottinger's 38, Sept. 3, 1842.

3. Ibid.

4. Ibid., encl. 31.

5. Mayers, Dennys, and King, Treaty Ports, p. 257.

6. See Cheng Teh-k'un, "Cannons of the Opium War; a history of the campus of Amoy University."

7. BA, Pottinger's 5, Jan. 15, 1844.

8. BA, Gribble's 26, Mar. 14, 1844.

9. Cp. Yorke, p. 460.

10. IWSM-TK, 71.46-66; 71.19-23a; 72.13.

11. Ibid., 73.35-37.

12. FO 17/90, Davis' 120, Dec. 30, 1844. Aberdeen advised Davis to withhold such non-coöperative threats; FO 17/96, Aberdeen's 36, May 23, 1845.

13. IWSM-TK, 74.12-14b.

14. Ibid., 73.36-37; 74.1-2b; 12b.

15. BA, Lay's 61, Aug. 16, 1845. Consul Lay had sought self-sufficiency. "We pay a little attention to domestic economy, as we rear our poultry, ducks, geese, sheep and horses. The poultry occupy a large room near the cook-house, the ducks and geese live in a walled enclosure, the horses have a stable constructed under one wing of the verandah or corridor or gallery that runs round the second story, the sheep repose under one of the arches on which the building rests, so that we have all our stock near at hand, which is necessary as the servants are not the most honest people in the world." (Letter to H.N. Lay, Sept. 20, 1845, ms., courtesy H.M. Lay, Barrie, Ontario).

16. IWSM-TK, 74.21-22.

17. FO 228/31. Cp. Chinese Commercial Guide, ed. 1844, p. 198. Hawks Pott, A Short History of Shanghai, p. 21, states that the British consular offices were moved to their later site on July 21, 1849; the first consulate was built in 1852.

18. IWSM-TK, 70.30-32b. In February 1844 it was reported that Thom had rented a private house outside the city wall in the chiang-pei (north bank) district.

19. BA, Thom's 9, Jan. 31, 1844.

20. FO 17/89, Davis' 85, October 1844. Cp. Sir J. F. Davis, China During the War and Since the Peace, II, 72; and S. Lane-Poole, Sir Harry Parkes in China, p. 52.

21. IWSM-TK, 73.11b, line 6; 73.9b-15.

22. BF, passim, esp. Jackson's Oct. 28, 1848. After the port's awakening in 1854, Consul Medhurst paid the first three months' rent for a consulate site on Nantai on Mar. 31, 1855, and thereafter proposed to give up all but a part of the temple in the city. Cp. Chinese Commercial Guide, ed. 1844, p. 185.

23. FO 17/66, encl. 8 and 9 in Pottinger's 24 of Mar. 25, 1843.

24. On the substitution of tonnage dues for the ancient Chinese measurement fee, cp. Wright, Tariff Autonomy, pp. 48-50.

25. FO 17/81, Pottinger's 59 of 1844; FO 17/80, 43 of 1844; BA, Pottinger's 11 to Gribble, Jan. 26, 1844, et passim. The ten regulations concerned regular reports of the number of English residents, anchorage of British vessels inside the 200-gun-battery and Kulangsu, landing of goods between sunrise and sunset only, and only at the fixed landing places, control of sailors, prevention of foreigners straying into people's houses, joint control of the Cantonese and Fukienese linguists and shroffs, payment of tonnage dues in full but of duties on cargo only as landed, payment of full tonnage dues by all vessels loading or discharging cargo, exemption from tonnage dues of vessels merely calling for a few days on their passage along the coast (stay limited to 48 hours), and prevention of Chinese breaking the law by shipping in foreign vessels. These Amoy regulations were first reported to Peking in April 1844 as having been framed by Hsü on the basis of regulations drawn up for Shanghai. IWSM-TK, 71.19-22.

26. BA, Layton's 65, July 28, 1847; Layton's 38, July 19, 1848.

27. Details concerning the creation of the standard Haikuan (Customs) tael for use at all five ports and of the official assay of foreign coins made at Canton in July 1843 are given in Wright, Tariff Autonomy, pp. 25-32.

28. BC, Hoppo to Consul, no. 4, Oct. 6, 1843; FO 17/71, Pottinger's 167, Dec. 19, 1843; FO 228/31, vol. I.

29. FO 228/38, Keying to Davis, no. 37; FO 228/43, Balfour's 87.

30. BA, Gribble's 3, Nov. 13, 1843.

31. BA, Hoh and Hoh to consul, Dec. 8, 1843; Pottinger's 6, Jan. 18, 1844; Gribble's 44, June 1, 1844; FO 228/900, June 15, 1844.

32. On "touch" or "fineness", i.e., purity of silver, see Morse, Trade and Administration, ch. v.

33. BA, Alcock's 9, Feb. 8, 1845; Davis' 13, Feb. 22, 1845.

34. BA, Lay's 66, Sept. 23; Sullivan's 84, Nov. 26; Davis' 96, Dec. 4; Keying to Davis, Dec. 12, 1845; Sullivan's 13, Feb. 14, 1846.

35. On the American opium trade see Ch. 13.

36. Cushing himself claimed 16 points of excellence for his treaty—to Nelson, July 5, 1844, in CR, (December 1845), to which Morse adds another (Conflict, p. 330).

37. The French treaty signed by M. de Lagrené at Whampoa on October 24, 1844, was almost a duplicate of the American treaty, with a few minor changes. The 34 articles of the American treaty and the 36 of the French may be compared with 12 in the British treaty of Nanking, 15 in the general regulations of trade, and 17 in the Supplementary treaty.

38. BC, Bowring, July 1849, passim; BA, July 1849.

39. BC, Elmslie's 127, July 27, 1848; Bonham's 45, Mar. 24, 1849, with encl.; Elmslie's 55, Mar. 26; Bonham's 124, July 27, 1849.

40. See, for example, accounts by W. H. Medhurst of a two weeks' journey from Shanghai into Chekiang and by J. E. (Joseph Edkins) of a similar seventeen day trip of 300 miles, in Shanghae Almanac for 1855; cp. below, Ch. 16.

41. Cp. Griffin, Clippers and Consuls, p. 359.

42. FO 17/70, Pottinger's 160, Nov. 29, 1843.

43. IWSM-TK, 72.9b-10b.

44. FO 17/78, Pottinger's 11, Jan. 30, 1844; FO 17/79, no. 24, Feb. 10, 1844; FO 17/80, no. 43; BA, Thom's 9, Jan. 31, 1844.

45. FO 228/31, Balfour's 9, Dec. 2, 1843; no. 1, Jan. 27, 1844; FO 17/79, Pottinger's 20, Feb. 5, 1844.

46. FO 228/31, Balfour's 36, May 16, 1844.

47. Procl. by Chuy, June 22, 1852; Bonham's 35, Aug. 26.

48. BC, Bonham's 16, 17, 18, March 1854. Cp. House of Commons (1847-48) [930.], xlviii, 617, 699 and House of Lords (1847-48), xix, 535, Papers relating to the Murder of Six Englishmen in the Neighborhood of Canton in the Month of December 1847, etc.

49. BN, Pottinger to Balfour, Jan. 15, in Pottinger's 9 of 1844; Thom's 5, Jan. 20; Pottinger's 38 to Gribble, Apr. 17; Pottinger's circular 13, May 6, 1844; FO 17/82, Pottinger's 77, May 6, 1844.

50. IWSM-TK, 77.15b, line 2; 77.14b-16.

51. BA, passim; BC, passim. Cp. Anglo-Chinese Calendar for 1851, Shanghae Almanac for 1854, 1855, 1856.

52. BF, Medhurst's 14 to Bowring, Jan. 23, 1857. He called it Hsien-po, the usual form being Han-p'u.

53. BA, Lai to consul, Sept. 26, Oct. 9, 1851.

54. BA, passim.

55. FO 17/88, Davis' 70, Aug. 6, 1844. For a letter of Lord William Bentinck in India to the Canton authorities in 1831, touching on the protection of British subjects in foreign countries, see CR, XI: 2-4 (1842).

56. BA, Layton's 46, Sept. 9, 1846; Bonham's 20, May 1, 1849.

57. BA, Layton's 87 and 100, Nov. 10, Dec. 27, 1847; Bonham's 4, Jan. 16, 1851. BA, Chang to Sullivan, Feb. 23, 1851. A few months later the Hai-fang obligingly applied to the consul to produce

two Chinese employees of Tait and Co., who were wanted to appear in a case before him; Lai to Backhouse, July 7, 1851.

58. For this and the following paragraph, see BA, Layton's 34, July 10; 37, July 17, 1848; Chaou to Backhouse, Nov. 24; Backhouse's 60, Nov. 27; Bowring's 61, Dec. 9, 1852.

59. CM, Mar. 25, May 13, 1847.

60. Mayers, *Treaty Ports*, p. 376.

61. BN, Robertson's 4, Jan. 20, 1851.

62. BN, Hague's 4, Jan. 19, 1852; see below, Ch. 23.

63. IWSM-TK, 70.26b-27b.

64. CM, Feb. 20, 1845, Government Notification, Hongkong, Feb. 15.

65. BF, Bonham's circular 10, Apr. 11, 1850.

66. BF, Bowring's 83, Oct. 31; 85, Nov. 9, 1857.

67. BN, no. 7 to Twan taotai, Feb. 24, 1854.

68. BF, Davis' 83, Dec. 27, 1845.

69. BF, Lieut. Gov. to Alcock, Apr. 14, 1846.

70. IWSM-TK, 75.30b-34; 76.5-8b.

71. CM, no. 80, Aug. 27, 1846: Mr. Glen took passage for Suez on the *Lady Mary Wood*, Aug. 28.

72. BF, Jackson's 30, May 10, 1847; Davis' 21, May 8, 1846, *et passim*. Characters for the name of A-ping are not recorded; see Ch. 10.

73. CM, no. 8, Apr. 10, 1845.

74. CM, July 15, 1847.

75. BF, Medhurst's 114, Dec. 17, 1855; Procl., May 28, 1856.

76. BF, Bowring's 13, July 12; Walker's 33, Aug. 20, 1853.

77. BF, Medhurst's 95, Oct. 20, 1858.

REFERENCES: CHAPTER 13

1. See Charles C. Stelle, *Americans and the China Opium Trade in the Nineteenth Century*, Ph.D. dissertation, University of Chicago (1938); *ibid.*, "American Trade in Opium to China 1821-1839"; Owen, *British Opium Policy*, pp. 206-8. For a summary of the early history of Russell and Co., see State Street Trust Company, *Old Shipping Days in Boston*, pp. 16-17; also Forbes, *Personal Reminiscences*, pp. 355-360. The Heard Papers (Harvard Business School, Baker Library) give many details. Heard and Co. bought mainly through Parsee constituents in Bombay. In 1844 they chartered the schooner *Don Juan* at $1000 a month to distribute 286 chests of superior Malwa on the coast, hoping to get $820 a chest there instead of the $750 offered at Canton (John Heard, Jr., to Augustine Heard, Sept. 1, 1844, vol. EM-4).

2. Owen, p. 209.

3. An interesting study along this line has been made by Dr. Yi-faai Laai, *The Part Played by the Pirates of Kwangtung and Kwangsi Provinces in the Taiping Insurrection*, Ph.D. dissertation, University of California (1949). The Chekiang authorities in 1843 connected the growth of piracy with the growth of foreign trade in general; see *Shih-liao hsun-k'an*, 36.319b, in mem. of Liu Yun-k'o, et al.

4. BA, Misc. corresp. no. 5,6,7, Nov. 7 and 8, 1843.

5. Yorke, pp. 461-2, J. Matheson to Cap. D. Forbes, Nov. 1, 1843.

6. *Ibid.*

7. FO 17/91, Gribble to Aberdeen, Dec. 10, 1844.

8. FO 228/31, Balfour's 33, Apr. 9, 1844.

9. FO 228/31, Balfour to Taotai, Dec. 12, in *ibid.*

10. FO 228/31, Balfour's notification, Shanghai, Feb. 10, in his 8 of Feb. 12, 1844. Cp. Wright, *Hart*, p. 78.

11. *Ibid.*, Balfour's 8.

12. FO 228/235, Pottinger's 20, Mar. 2, 1844.

13. Balfour's notification, Feb. 10.

14. S. F. Wright, *Tariff Autonomy*, pp. 70-71.

15. FO 228/31, Kung to Balfour, Mar. 12, in Balfour's 19, Mar. 13, 1844.

16. FO 228/31, Balfour's 33, Apr. 9, 1844. This able statement of the problem was not forwarded to London.

17. FO 228/31, Balfour's notification, Apr. 9, in his 33, Apr. 9, 1844.

18. FO 228/31, Kung to Balfour, Apr. 14, in Balfour's 34, Apr. 15, 1844.

19. FO 228/31, Balfour's 38, May 20, 1844.

20. BF, local corresp.

21. BA, Hang to Gribble, Feb. 11, Mar. 16, 1844.

22. BA, Gribble's 16, "Report on the opium trade of Amoy," July 3, 1844.

23. BC, Lay's 6, Apr. 1, 1844.

24. BC, Macgregor's 19, Mar. 24, 1845.

25. CM, no. 10, Apr. 24; no. 12, May 8, 1845.

26. FO 228/31, Balfour's 33, Apr. 9, 1844.

27. BC, Macgregor's 30, Apr. 17, 1845, w. encl.

28. CM, no. 12, May 8, 1845.

29. BC, corresp. of consul, Hoppo *et al.*, April–June, 1845; FO 17/96, Aberdeen's 60, Aug. 8, 1845, approved the consul's course. CM, no. 14, May 22, 1845.

30. FO 17/92, encl. in Colonial Office to F.O., Feb. 17, 1844.

31. FO 17/92, Davis to Stanley, Feb. 10, 1844, in Stanley to FO, Feb. 17, 1844.

32. See House of Commons (1857), Session 2, no. XLIII, *Papers relating to the Opium Trade ... 1842-1856.*

33. See Memo. by W. H. Mitchell, Nov. 1, 1850, written at Bonham's request (in Bonham's 114 Misc. to Grey, Dec. 28, 1850, copy in Merivale to Addington, Mar. 15, 1851, FO 17/183). Mitchell had been a consular assistant at Amoy in 1844; later a merchant; on Mar. 28, 1850, already a justice of the peace at Hongkong, he was "appointed to officiate as Assistant Police Magistrate, Sheriff, Provost Marshal, Coroner, and Marshal of the Vice-admiralty Court." (Minutes of Exec. and Legis. Councils, Hongkong, 1848-53, CO 131/2). He was given twelve months leave about Mar. 22, 1853, later extended six months (CO 403/6). In June 1856 he was accused of extorting money from prisoners while in the office of Sheriff and Acting Chief Magistrate. Labouchere at the Colonial Office found the evidence conflicting and replied in August 1856 that he wished to hear nothing more of the case, whatever happened. There is no evidence that Mitchell had any animus against the opium firms. Mitchell appended the following tables:

Bengal Opium imported into China from 1845 to 1849 inclusive.

1845	18792
1846	20000
1847	21650
1848	28000
1849	36000
Chests	124442

Bombay Opium imported into China from 1845 to 1849 inclusive.

1845	20660
1846	19063
1847	20523
1848	17479
1849	18532
Chests	96275

Bengal 124,442; Bombay 96,275. Total chests 220,717.

Dr. H. B. Morse (Conflict, table p. 556) gives 212,407 chests as the total shipments from India 1845-49 and 175,407 chests as the estimated consumption in China.

34. CM, no. 12, May 8, 1845, describes an attempted robbery of J.M. and Co.'s opium godown.

35. See CM, no. 1, Feb. 20; no. 4, Mar. 13; no. 11, May 1; no. 12, May 8; no. 20, July 3, 1845; no. 125, July 8; no. 127, July 22, 1847.

36. Mitchell, loc. cit., note 33 above. Pelcovits, Old China Hands, pp. 15-17, quotes another memo. written by Mitchell in 1852, developing his ideas further, which Bonham filed but Lord Elgin sent home in 1858 (Mar. 31, FO 17/287).

37. Mitchell, loc. cit.

38. Friend of China, Mar. 1, quoted in CM, no. 159, Mar. 2, 1848.

39. Chinese Commercial Guide (1844), p. 269.

40. Mitchell, loc. cit.

41. Chinese Commercial Guide (1844), p. 68; cp. CM, no. 93, Nov. 26, also Dec. 17, 1846, et passim.

42. CM, no. 82, Sept. 10, 1846.

43. See in CM, no. 159, Mar. 2, 1848.

44. J. Tyrone Power, Recollections of Three Years in China (1853), and Robert Fortune, Three Years Wanderings (1847) give contemporary descriptions of the Namoa foreign settlement. Cp. Yorke, p. 440.

45. FO 17/80, Ching to Pottinger, Feb. 21, in Pottinger's 43 of 1844; Pottinger to Ching, Mar. 7; FO 17/81, Proclamation by Pottinger, Hongkong, Apr. 6, in his 58, Apr. 6, 1844; FO 228/38, Ching to Pottinger, Apr. 5, 1844.

46. FO 17/87-88, Davis' 23 and 35, June 18 and July 1, 1844, encl. Davis' procl. of June 28, 1844.

47. FO 17/85, Aberdeen's 4, Feb. 28, 1844; FO 17/81, Pottinger's 63, Apr. 10, 1844.

48. IWSM-TK, Supp. 1599, memorial rec'd Sept. 7, 1843; cp. ibid., 1894-6 and 1903-6, for 1846. For a more extensive account, see J. K. Fairbank, "The Legalization of the Opium Trade before the Treaties of 1858." IWSM-TK, Supp. 1443-1477, passim, give details of cases Feb. – May 1842.

49. IWSM-TK, Supp. 1443-5, 1497.

50. Ibid., 1599 as above; 1601, rec'd Sept. 7, 1843; 1642, rec'd Jan. 25, 1844; 1569, rec'd Apr. 18, 1843.

51. CM, no. 44, Dec. 18, 1845.

52. Ibid., 1780-82, mem. rec'd Aug. 27, 1845.

53. IWSM-TK, Supp. 1894, rec'd Sept. 19, 1846; 1903 as above; 2062, rec'd Aug. 31, 1848; 2065, same date; 2068, same date; 2108, rec'd Sept. 19, 1849

54. CM, no. 178, July 13; no. 161, Mar. 16, 1848.

55. IWSM-TK, Supp. 2105, rec'd Sept. 19, 1849. A translation of the proclamation of the Nanking governor-general to this effect appears in NCH, Sept. 7, 1850; see full summary of this translation in Morse, Conflict, p. 549. Peter Parker described the emperor's anti-opium edict as simply "a recapitulation of the old laws of the land regarding its use, and requiring conformity thereto." See China 6, no. 14 to Webster, Apr. 21, 1851.

56. IWSM-HF, Supp. 37, mem. rec'd Sept. 16, 1851; 38, rec'd Sept. 25, 1851; 109, rec'd June 9, 1851; 152, rec'd Apr. 3, 1854.

57. T. F. Wade, "A Note on the Condition and Government of the Chinese Empire in 1849," in NCH, Aug. 17, 1850, states it as his belief that at that time the poppy was cultivated in nine provinces, all south of the Yangtze.

58. BN, Bonham's circular 5, May 13, 1848. BC, Elmslie's 115, June 22, 1848.

59. See BC, Bowring's 41 of 1850, a comprehensive survey of the China trade.

60. BA, Layton's 15, Feb. 9; his 6 to Foochow, Feb. 10, 1847. Chimmo Bay is on the Fukien coast between Amoy and Ch'üan-chou; specifically, off Shen-hu. "Chimmo Bay will be easily recognized by the Ku-sau tah [Ku-sao, "sisters-in-law," t'a] or Chimmo pagoda, which is 760 feet above

the sea ... in latitude 24°43′ N. and longitude 118°33′ 6″ E." CR, XIV: 271 [1845], from sailing directions by Capt. Collinson

61. CM, no. 105, Feb. 18, 1847; no. 11, May 1, 1845.

62. BA, Layton's 30, Mar. 9, 1847.

63. CM, no. 132, Aug. 26; no. 141, Oct. 28, 1847; no. 171, June 1, 1848; Government notification, July 21, 1848.

64. IWSM-TK, 77.32b-35; and IWSM-TK,Supp. 1980-85 and 2000-03, memorials received Aug. 2 and Nov. 1, 1847.

65. BA, Davis' 31, Mar. 31, 1847.

66. BA, Layton's 30, Mar. 9, 1847.

67. BA, Davis' 61, July 26, 1847.

68. BA, Davis' 67, Aug. 11, 1847; Layton's 72, Sept. 1.

69. BF, Davis' 56, Oct. 16, 1846; corresp. March-July, 1847.

70. BA, Bonham's 70, Dec. 1, 1849, re opium.

71. BN, Sullivan's 5, Mar. 15; 13, May 27, 1848, et passim.

72. BN, Hague's 24 to Bonham, June 28, 1851.

REFERENCES: CHAPTER 14

1. Cp. Pottinger to Morrison, Jan. 25, 1843, in CR, XII: 94-5 (February 1843).

2. FO 17/66, I-li-pu to Pottinger, Jan. 22, in Pottinger's 7, Feb. 6, 1843.

3. IWSM-TK, 68.28-29b, mem. rec'd Sept. 23, 1843. Cp. Wright, Hart, pp. 69-70.

4. This table is based on that given in Chinese and English by S. Wells Williams in A Chinese Commercial Guide (2nd ed., revised, Macao, 1844), p. 159; romanizations have been altered to the Wade-Giles system. Liang Chia-pin, Kuang-tung shih-san-hang k'ao, traces the personnel of each hong, using Morse, Chronicles, and less voluminous Chinese sources. C. de Montigny, Manuel du Négociant Français en Chine (Paris, 1846), p. 327, copies Williams' table with one or two errors and misconceptions.

5. T. F. Tsiang, "The Government and the Co-Hong of Canton, 1839," translates a memorial of the Canton authorities in 1839 which lists hong merchants' debts to the government, accumulated since 1819, at a total of Tls. 1,464,000. Early in 1843 the hong merchants informed Pottinger (FO 17/66, letter of Feb. 26, encl. 2 in Pottinger's 14 of Mar. 10, 1843) that after deducting recent payments, they had still owed Tls. 3,500,000 to the government at the end of 1842, in addition to their debts of some $4,300,000 due to foreign merchants. Cp. IWSM-TK, 65.25, mem. rec'd from I-li-pu et al., Mar. 6, 1843.

6. IWSM-TK, Supp. 1512-13, mem. of Ch'i Kung and Wen-feng, Oct. 28, 1842.

7. Ibid., 1560, mem. of Ch'i Kung, Apr. 7, 1843; FO 17/68, Pottinger to Ch'i-ying, July 20, in Pottinger's 88, 1843.

8. FO 17/69, encl. in Pottinger's 102 of 1843; FO 17/80, Huang to Pottinger, rec'd Feb. 12, in Pottinger's 43 of 1844.

9. CM, no. 72, July 2, 1846; cp. IWSM-TK, Supp. 1756-59, hong merchants' request for postponement of payments, May 1845.

10. BC, Bowring's 140, Oct. 18, 1845, 45, Apr. 19, and 58, Apr. 22, 1850.

11. BC, Bowring's 243, Dec. 10, 1849; 7, Jan. 17; 24, Feb. 18, 1850; Bonham's 10, Feb. 7, 1850; Bowring's 74 to Robertson, Dec. 5, 1854; BC, Circulars, June 30, Dec. 15, 1855; Bowring's 170, Oct. 16, and 190, Nov. 21, 1855.

12. See Liang Chia-pin, pp. 250-255, and Momose in Hummel.

13. See China Directory, 1861, 1862, 1864. At Foochow Jardine's also used I-ho but with a different character for I. Jardine's at Hongkong and Canton used Cha-tien, but at Amoy used K'o-pei-shih. The early compradores evidently chose their own styles. In his survey of J. M. & Co., Uchida Naosaku ("Zai-Shi Eikoku", p. 224, n.1) suggests the probable explanation that they acquired Howqua's firm name because at Canton they had rented his "E-wo hong", called by foreigners the Creek Factory, and after 1842 succeeded him there. This Chinese name so inherited at Canton in time eclipsed its competitors.

14. See The Economist, Dec. 21, 1844, pp. 1538-39.

15. IWSM-TK, 67.40-43b. China's exports of cotton goods exceeded her imports until 1829 and British cotton goods' imports were unimportant until after 1843; see Yen Chung-p'ing, Chung-kuo mien-yeh chih fa-chan (The development of the Chinese cotton industry), pp. 28-29, 43. Ch'i-ying's statement of 1843 was anachronistic, doubtless through ignorance. One of the earliest official references to increased cotton goods imports was in a memorial from Liu Yun-k'o, Apr. 25, 1844; see IWSM-TK, Supp. 1660-62.

16. Wright, Tariff Autonomy, p. 14.

17. FO 17/66, Matheson et al. to Pottinger, Feb. 8, 1843, in Pottinger's 12 of 1843. They estimated the total of duty and charges as follows: in 1836, Tls. 2.5; 1839, Tls. 5; 1841, Tls. 8.5; 1843, Tls. 6.

18. BC, Macgregor's 9 of Feb. 4, 1845, and 28 of Feb. 21, 1846.

19. IWSM-TK, 67.40b-45b, Aug. 31, 1843. Several of these points were forecast in ibid., 66.40-43, mem. rec'd July 9, 1843. The British legation archives contain an unsigned summary of Mu-chang-a's recommendations with serious errors of translation, headed "Extract from Peking Gazette" (Chinese correspondence, vol. 5 for 1844, FO 228/38); the same summary, with the same errors, appears in CR, XII: 632 (December 1843).

20. The Ch'ing ginseng administration, based on Manchuria, monopolized the sales of this supposed

energy-restorer through licensed merchants. For its general regulations, marketing, and efforts to prevent smuggling, see Kuang-hsü hui-tien shih-li, ch. 232 - 233, and Ch'in-ting hu-pu tse-li, ed. 1865, ch. 33. Imports at Canton, in large part from the United States, were a late addition to the Manchurian supply.

21. IWSM-TK, 66.41b-42 in 40-43b, mem. rec'd July 9, 1843; edicts same date.

22. IWSM-TK, 67.45b; 68.20b-21.

23. IWSM-TK, 68.29, in 28-29b, mem. rec'd Sept. 23, 1843.

24. IWSM-TK, Supp. 1621-22, mem. rec'd Nov. 19, 1843; 1623-24. Sub-stations of the Canton customs were listed, inter alia, in Hu-pu tse-li, ed. 1851, 39.17-18.

25. Ibid., 1625-6, mem. sent Oct. 15, rec'd Nov. 19, 1843.

26. Ibid., 1627.

27. BC, memo. by T. T. M(eadows), re Hoppo's letter of Aug. 17, 1845.

28. T'ang Hsiang-lung, "Kuang-hsü san-shih-nien Yueh-hai-kuan ti kai-ko" ("The Reform of the Canton Customs Administration in 1904").

29. As an example see the handbook Liu-pu ch'eng-yü chu-chieh (Explanatory notes on the established terminology of the Six Boards, Kyōto, 1940), which lists and defines some 5,000 special terms to be met with in the Ch'ing administration.

30. The following section has been mainly worked out by Dr. E-tu Zen Sun, to whom I am heavily indebted.

31. This summary is based largely on data compiled from the Collected Statutes by Wang Ch'ing-yun in his Shih-ch'ü yü-chi, ch. vi; for details, see Table 8 and Appendix B.

32. See IWSM-TK, Supp. 1701, 1754-55; Hu-pu tse-li, ed. 1851, 39.11.

33. See ibid., 39.12b, 17-18; IWSM-TK, Supp., passim.

34. Ibid., 1671; 1689b and passim.

35. See IWSM-TK, Supp., passim, and Hu-pu tse-li, 39.1-7.

36. Cp. Wang Ch'ing-yun, 6.1.

37. IWSM-TK, Supp. 1859-60; IWSM-HF, Supp. 79.

38. IWSM-TK, Supp. 1621, 1634, 1684; cp. Hu-pu tse-li, 40.10, 12-13, 15.

39. See edicts in THL, Sept. 6 and Nov. 1, 1842.

40. IWSM-TK, Supp. 1899. This arrangement was extended for another three years; see Ch. 19, reference note 36.

41. Ibid., 1771-2, 1793; 2057-59, 2081b-82; IWSM-HF, Supp. 52, 244.

42. Ibid., TK, Supp. 2087; 1901-02; cp. SL-TK, 434.2.

43. IWSM-TK, Supp. 1898, 1963b; 1669, 1772, 1729, 1842-44, 1951; 1899.

44. This table is based on IWSM-TK and HF, Supp., passim.

REFERENCES: CHAPTER 15

1. FO 17/68, Pottinger's 290 to Lay in no. 88 of 1843.

2. FO 17/80, Pottinger's 41, Mar. 1, 1844; FO 17/94, F O to C O, July 6, 1844.

3. As early as 1836 Davis' compendious two volumes, The Chinese: A General Description of The Empire of China, with woodcuts, was being circulated by Harper and Bros., New York, as no. 81 of their Family Library.

4. FO 17/87 and 88, passim.

5. FO 17/85, Aberdeen's 4, Feb. 28, 1844.

6. It is worth noting that after 1819 British administrators like Raffles and Crawfurd had been at work in Singapore, which was in contact with China; see R. Coupland, Raffles, 1781-1826.

7. FO 17/84, Pottinger's 102, June 17, 1844; FO 17/87, Davis' 19, June 13, 1844.

8. FO 17/90, encl. in Davis' 121 of 1844.

9. FO 17/88, Davis' 73, Aug. 12; FO 17/90, Davis' 120, Dec. 30, 1844. In retrospect, Davis was a good deal more sympathetic with Ch'i-ying's difficulties and good intentions (Davis, China: A General Description, 1857, I,160-65).

10. CM, no. 40, Nov. 20, and no. 41, Nov. 27, 1845.

11. CM, no. 63, Apr. 30, 1846.

12. James Orange, The Chater Collection, pp. 426-27, 440; Worcester, Junks and Sampans, pp. 147-50. Both quote the Illustrated London News of Apr. 1, 1848; see also the Mariner's Mirror for October 1922.

13. See Customs, Treaties, "Convention ... 4th April 1846"; and Grosse-Aschhoff, Negotiations between Ch'i-ying and Lagrené, pp. 117-18 et passim.

14. IWSM-TK, 74.28b-29; 29b-31.

15. Ibid., 74.29b-32b. For the British agitation to keep Chusan, or exchange it for Hongkong, see CR, XIV: 546-47 (1845), referring to the Friend of China and R. M. Martin.

16. BC, Macgregor's 102, Dec. 15, 1845. American merchants did well at Canton: R. B. Forbes, enjoying one fourth of Russell and Co.'s profits, in two seasons expected to add $150,000 to his "little competency" (to A. Heard, May 15, 1850, vol. BM-8, Heard Papers).

17. BC, Bowring's 79, Apr. 9, 1851.

18. BC, Macgregor's 7, Feb. 7, 1847.

19. BC, Moller, Sec'y., to Consul, Mar. 22, 1847. For data on the Chamber, see CR, XVI: 87-92 (1847); on its predecessor, the Canton General Chamber of Commerce, see ibid. VII: 386-89 (1838-39).

20. BC, misc. corresp., 1847.

21. BC, Ponder to Consul, Nov. 23; Bowring to Imperial Commissioner, Nov. 27; Ponder to Bowring, Dec. 20, 1849.

22. AP dispatch from Canton, New York Times, Feb. 10, 1949.

23. See the summary in Costin, pp. 120-134, esp. p. 129.

24. Dr. John J. Nolde has done an illuminating Ph.d. dissertation at Cornell on this topic: The "Canton City Question," 1842-1849: A Preliminary Investigation into Chinese Anti-Foreignism and its Effect upon China's Diplomatic Relations with the West (September 1950).

25. First printed in 1874, this work was reprinted in 1937 by the Peiping Academy (Kuo-li Pei-p'ing yen-chiu yuan) and the Commercial Press, 5 chüan, 116 plus 11 pp. On the "city question," see ch. v. Cn Liang, see Momose in Hummel. For a Chinese summary of the "city question" 1843-1858, see Ch'i-hsien ho-shang tiao-sou (The old fisherman on the Ch'i-hsien river), Ying-chi-li Kuang-tung ju-ch'eng shih-mo (A complete account of the English in Kwangtung entering the city), in the Yang-shih ch'ien-ch'i-pai er-shih-chiu ho chai ts'ung-shu, Shao-hsing, Mo-jun-t'ang ed., 1927, 1st collection, 1 chüan, 17 pp. Foreign observers like J. F. Davis were aware that Cantonese xenophobia became exacerbated and organized as a result of the first war; Davis, China During the War, II,27.

26. In order to apply the motif of a "people's resistance movement," a doctrinaire revisionist like Chou Ku-ch'eng lists the whole string of incidents reported in blue blooks between 1842 and 1856; see his Chung-kuo t'ung-shih (General history of China), 1945 ed., pp. 1038-39. Dr. Nolde (note 24 above) concludes that the gentry were the real leaders of the movement; in the parlance of some recent writers this conflict at Canton naturally becomes one between "imperialist capitalism" and "reactionary feudalism" (see Wu P o [Fan Wen-lan], Chung-kuo chin-tai shih, A63).

27. See Customs, Treaties: the English text was a very free and somewhat amplified version of the Chinese.

28. On the French aspect, see Costin, p.125, and Grosse-Aschhoff as in note 13 above.

29. IWSM-TK, 77.35b et seq., 41b-42b; 78, 1-3, 19b-22.

30. The work attributed to Ch'i-ying, Yueh-t'ai yü-sung, actually contains several score poetic eulogies by officials and gentry of Canton on the occasion of his departure. On Hsü, see Fairbank and Teng in Hummel, p. 319. Ch'i-ying's policy during his last years at Canton has not been adequately studied, nor have the circumstances of his departure. Toward the end of the period (in commenting on the abilities of Hsü to handle the barbarians) Ch'i-ying describes how he himself had begun the job with spirit and vigor but had been so worn down by its travail that his hair and beard were completely white, his liver complaint was growing worse day by day, and both his vision and his strength were failing; see Shih-liao hsun-k'an, 35.298. CR, XIX: 166-67 (1850), quoting CM, Feb. 28, 1850, gives a summary of Ch'i-ying's official activity, 1848-50 ; he is stated to have had "no fewer than forty-nine audiences of his majesty." Dr. T. F. Tsiang concludes (in his article, "Chung-kuo yü chin-tai shih-chieh", p. 821) that Ch'i-ying's retirement from Canton was not due to the emperor's lack of confidence in him but to his own fear of forthcoming disaster. As to his eventual demotion by Hsien-feng, see below, Ch. 20, note 33.

31. R. K. Douglas in DNB has him governor at Singapore until 1847; the Singapore Almanack for 1856 states that Col. W. J. Butterworth, C.B., became governor in 1843. E. J. Eitel, Europe in China, has him as governor 1833 to 1842.

32. H. Morse Stephens, "The Administrative History of the British Dependencies in the Further East."

33. Eitel, Hong Kong, p. 253.

34. Ibid., p. 282.

35. See biography of Hsü in Ch'ing-shih lieh-chuan, 48.10b.

36. See Hummel, and Ch'ing-shih lieh-chuan, 40.44b.

37. See Sir J. Bowring, Autobiographical Recollections (London, 1877), passim.

38. Ibid.; see memoir by Lewin B. Bowring; also Sir J. Bowring, Matins and Vespers (London, 1895) and memoir by Lady Bowring.

39. J. H. Clapham, The Economic Development of France and Germany 1815-1914, p. 303, quotes Bowring's reports on the Prussian Commercial Union (1840).

40. J. Bowring, Autobiographical Recollections, mem. by L. B. Bowring.

41. Ibid., p. 289, pub. posthumously (Bowring died in 1872); W. A. P. Martin, A Cycle of Cathay (2nd ed., 1897), p. 27.

42. IWSM-TK, 80.10b, mem . rec'd May 7, 1849; cp. ibid., 14: "the English barbarians have now given up the discussion of entering the city [pa-i chin-ch'eng]." This is repeated in Hsü's biography in Ch'ing-shih lieh-chuan, 48.11. Bonham protested, "It is altogether impossible that the Chinese authorities could have so misconstrued my meaning" (FO 17/168, his 68 to Palmerston, July 22, 1850). Cp. Morse, Conflict, p. 397. On the emperor's delight, see IWSM-TK, 80.5, 15, 37, edict of Dec. 19, 1849. Dr. Nolde's dissertation, by an analysis of Hsü's correspondence with Peking and with Bonham, casts a new light on the high degree of initiative taken by Hsü. The contemporary historian, Hsueh Fu-ch'eng, has no hesitation in saying that Hsü secretly called upon (mi-chao) the militia to threaten Bonham; see his "Shu Han-yang Yeh-hsiang Kuang-chou chih pien," in Tso Shun-sheng, Chung-kuo chin-pai-nien shih tzu-liao, p. 51. This account by Hsueh has been translated with critical comment by Huang Yen-yü, "Viceroy Yeh Ming-ch'en". The emperor's lack of esteem for British capabilities is reflected in his interview of October 1849 with the Kwangtung financial commissioner Po-kuei, the alleged transcript of which was translated by T. T.

Meadows (The Chinese and Their Rebellions, Ch. xi).

43. See IWSM-TK, 79.25-26, edicts of Oct. 29, 1848; 27b-29b, memorial of Hsü and Yeh, rec'd Jan. 3, 1849. On the foreign side it was felt that the whole Canton community was "living on a volcano ... Canton with its million of hostile inhabitants, separated from them by a wall, can be compared to nothing else" (Berncastle, A Voyage to China, II, 172.

44. See IWSM-TK, 79.31-32, mem. rec'd Feb. 17, 1849; on the use of the term chi-mi in 1842 see Ch. 6 above. On Hsü's spies in Hongkong, cp. Shih-liao hsun-k'an, 36. 339.

45. See IWSM-TK, 80.18-19b, mem. of censor Ts'ao Lu-t'ai, rec'd May 16, 1849 (accepting the cylical date, which disagrees with the month stated), esp. 19b.

46. See IWSM-TK, Supp. 1846-49, memorial from Liu, rec'd Feb. 10, 1847, containing a great encomium of Hsü's prowess in handling the British. See Shih-liao hsun-k'an, 36.321b-23b for elequent memorials from Liu and Hsü on the British concern for Chinese official titles and seals of rank, and the need to give Lu proper status in form.

47. IWSM-TK, 79.34-35, in memorial of Liu-Yun-k'o and Hsü Chi-yü, rec'd Feb. 17, 1849.

48. See Ying-huan chih-lueh, first ed., 1850. I find that S. Wells Williams (?) in a long review in the Chinese Repository, XX: 169-94 (1851), was struck by a number of the points I have selected below. Governor Hsü's book should prove a gold mine for monographic exploitation by an enterprising student of intellectual history.

49. See K. S. Latourette, The Great Century, p. 300. Cp. "Notices of Amoy and its inhabitants,"CR, XIII: 233-38 (1844); see under Jan. 27 and Mar. 26, 1844. Abeel arrived at Kulangsu Feb. 24, 1842, and left Dec. 19, 1844; CR, XV: 355-56 (1846). Ibid., XVIII: 260-75 (1849), summarizes his life from a volume, Memoir of the Rev. David Abeel, D.P., late missionary to China, 1845, by his nephew, Rev. G. R. Williamson. Abeel wrote Residence in China and the Neighboring Countries, 1836.

50. On Ricci's influence see L. Carrington Goodrich, "China's first Knowledge of the America's;" and Kenneth Ch'en, "Matteo Ricci's Contribution to and Influence on Geographical Knowledge in China." Note Wei Yuan's discussion of previous cartographers (Ricci et al.) in Hai-kuo t'u-chih, 46. Cp. e.g. maps of Asia in Hai-kuo t'u-chih (1844), 2.4b-5, and Ying-huan chih-lueh (1850), 1.9b-10.

51. See Sung-k'an hsien-sheng ch'üan-chi (Complete collected writings of [Hsü] Sung-k'an), 4 ts'e, preface by Yen Hsi-shan (1915); wen-chi, 1.7-12b, esp. 8.

52. Ibid., tsou-su, 1.20-22, esp. 21; cp. Shih-liao hsun-k'an, 36.322b. The fact that Hsü presented sentimental verses to Bowring (see CR, XX: 433-34 [1851]) seems inconclusive as to his actual views.

53. See CR, XX: 247-50 (1851).

54. Shih-liao hsun-k'an, 36.22 ff. See IWSM-HF, 3, passim. CR, XIX: 459-62 (1850), gives a translation of an anti-British placard of the Foochow literati in 1850 — this whole incident awaits investigation.

55. The most recent appraisal of Hsü, as compared with Wei Yuan, is in Chang Hsi-t'ung's illuminating survey article, "Western Political Science in China."

REFERENCES: CHAPTER 16

1. Published by the Oxford University Press in 4 vols., 1926; vol. V (supplementary, for the years 1742-74), 1929.

2. IWSM-TK, 70.22-24, esp. 23. A foreign visitor to Shanghai in 1843 estimated that 1600 and even 1800 sea-going junks came there annually, in addition to some 5,400 vessels from the Yangtze and the interior; cp. CR, XV: 466-72 (1846). Worcester, Junks and Sampans of the Yangtze, p. 115, defines sha-ch'uan ("sand-boat") as the "generic name for the sea-going junks from Shanghai," a small form of the large sea-going "Kiangsu trader, a craft easily recognised by (its) five masts and the broad, flat stern, from which projects ... a stern gallery of 10 feet or more in length." Such junks might vary from 85 to 170 feet overall, with a mainmast of perhaps 70 feet.

On the build-up of British capital at Hongkong, there is a survey by Matsuda Tomoo, Igirisu shihon to Tōyō, but nothing has been done from company archives.

3. FO 17/69, Pottinger's 102, Aug. 24, 1843.

4. FO 17/79, Lay's 2, Jan. 31, 1844, in Pottinger's 27.

5. FO 17/79, Pottinger's 27, Feb. 12, 1844.

6. See Sargent, Anglo-Chinese Commerce and Diplomacy, pp. 126-36. Also the survey by T. R. Banister, "A History of the External Trade of China, 1834-81."

7. Sargent, pp. 126-136.

8. On this whole subject see Yen Chung-p'ing, Chung-kuo mien-yeh chih fa-chan (Development of the Chinese cotton industry), ch. xxi; esp. p. 19.

9. L. C. Goodrich, A Short History of the Chinese People, p. 197.

10. Yen, pp. 19-20.

11. Ibid., p. 29, data from Morse, Chronicles. See above, Ch. 14, note 15.

12. See Pritchard, Crucial Years, p. 160.

13. Sargent, pp. 127, 140. Marxist writers have tended to date the impact of Lancashire cotton goods a decade too early, Karl Marx having written (in a lead article in the New York Daily Tribune of June 14, 1853): "This introduction of foreign manufactures [into China] has had a similar effect on the native industry to that which it formerly

had on Asia Minor, Persia and India. In China the spinners and weavers have suffered greatly under this foreign competition, and the community has become unsettled in proportion". Marx then refers to "the destructive influence of foreign competition on native manufactures." See Dona Torr, Marx on China, p. 3. This subject awaits definitive research, but I am inclined to follow Lo Er-kang, who vigorously attacks the facile assumption that imports of foreign cotton yarn and cloth helped cause the Taiping upheaval by their competition with the established farm handicraft production. He points out that before the 1860's these foreign imports were so relatively small as to be like "one hair among nine cows;" see his T'ai-p'ing t'ien-kuo shih k'ao-cheng chi (Collected evidential studies of Taiping history), pp. 81-92.

14. R. Fortune, Three Years' Wanderings, ch. xiv. Cp. Nishijima's study of Sungkiang tea.

15. BA, Gribble's 34, Apr. 4, 1844; FO 17/91, Gribble to Aberdeen, Dec. 10, 1844. Letters in the Jardine Matheson archives as early as 1805 describe Chinchew merchants visiting Canton annually by junk to secure opium cargoes, with enough influence to get European vessels of the Macao government to convoy them home; Greenberg, p. 116.

16. Morse, Conflict, p. 366.

17. W. H. Medhurst, A Glance at the Interior of China, pp. 61-90.

18. See F. H. King, Farmers of Forty Centuries, ch. xiii; also Shanghai International Testing House, A Survey of the Silk Industry of Central China.

19. See Sargent, p. 137, and Couling, Encyclopaedia Sinica, "Silk." China, Imperial Maritime Customs, II, Special Series, No. 3, Silk (Shanghai, 1881), 163 pp., gives much detail from the various port regions for the post-Taiping period.

20. For accounts of tea production see W. Milburn, Oriental Commerce, II, 520-527; J. F. Davis, China, II, 292-294, 395-405; Couling, Encyclopaedia Sinica; Robert Fortune, Three Years' Wanderings ..., ch. ix, and A Journey to the Tea Countries. Also Hatano's valuable recent study.

21. On this region see Yü Chen-yü, Mao Chin-sheng and others, "Fu-chien Ch'ung-an Shui-chi Shao-wu ch'a-ch'ü t'u-jang" (Soil of Chungan, Shuichi and Shaowu districts, Fukien), pp. 132-3. On the activity of the numerous boat firms which carried goods on the Min River network in the early nineteenth century, see Katō Shigeshi, "Shindai Fukken Kōso no senkō ni tsuite".

22. See Ch'en Shun-nien, "Chung-Mei ch'a-yeh mao-i chien-shih" (A brief history of the Sino-American tea trade). China, Imperial Maritime Customs, II, Special Series, No. 11, Tea (Shanghai, 1889), pp. 179 English and 120 Chinese, analyzes the course and causes of the decline of the tea trade, with suggested remedies.

23. See Wang Tse-nung, "Wu-i ch'a-yen t'u-jang" ("Soil survey of the tea gardens of Wu-i hills"), Ch'a-yeh yen-chiu ("Tea Researches"), I: 106-115, 149-55 (1944); 2:44-56, 61-77.

24. Rev. G. Smith, Visit to Each of the Consular Cities of China, p. 365. This greater proximity of Foochow had long been recognized: "The comparison between the expense of conveying black teas from Fuh-keen, the province in which they are produced, to Canton, and of their conveyance to the port of Fuh-chou, in Fuh-keen, exhibits, that admission to the latter port would save the East India Company nearly 200,000 annually"; Hunt's Merchants' Magazine, 1.3: 205-6 (September 1839). C. Toogood Downing, The Stranger in China II, 151, understood that Amoy and Chinchew "adjoin the tea districts."

25. R. M. Martin, China: Political, Commercial and Social (London, 1847), II, 302-3.

26. Costin, p. 101.

27. IWSM-TK, 58.36, lines 5-6.

28. Ibid., 59.46b; this edict was received at Nanking on Sept. 7, according to Chang Hsi's diary, see Teng, p. 76. IWSM-TK, Supp. 1514-15, recorded a memorial from the fiscal expert, Lei I-hsien, dated Oct. 29, 1842. In it he argued against admitting the barbarians to Foochow, as a provincial capital of high strategic value for defense. On Lei, see above Ch. 8.

29. Liang T'ing-nan, I-fen chi-wen, p. 83, quotes a contemporary letter describing this agitation; the opening of Foochow was denounced as inimical to the national economy, the people's livelihood, and the administrative institutions (kuo-chi min-sheng cheng-t'i). See also Chung-Hsi chi-shih, 7.2-2b, and 3.14b; the court wanted to substitute Ch'üan-chou.

30. IWSM-TK, 59.39-43, [illegible] 41, line 5 et seq.; 42, line 5. Ch'i-ying later boasted to the British that in spite of the imperial refusal to allow the opening of Foochow he had "nevertheless adhered firmly to the previous agreement and begged still from the Emperor that favor." (FO 17/68, encl. 8 in Pottinger's 85 of 1843, Keying's reply to Pottinger's memo. of June 25).

31. FO 17/249, T. F. Wade to Bowring, July 21, 1856, in Bowring's 226, same date. Some British merchants denounced the non-opening of Foochow as early as 1845, attributing it to the Canton interest and to the government's need for inland transit dues; cp. CR, XIV: 548 (1845), quoting The Friend of China, Oct. 18, 1845.

32. FO 17/264, Lay to Bowring, Feb. 5, in Bowring's 65, Feb. 6, 1857. Confirmed in general in FO 17/246, Consul Robertson's 51 to Bowring, Mar. 26, in Bowring's 118, Apr. 12, 1856.

33. BF, passim. Foreign readers of the Peking Gazette noted a report from the Board of Revenue that the imperial customs duties levied on the foreign trade of Foochow in 1844 totalled Tls. 143. In the same period the collection at Amoy was reported as Tls. 40,132; CM, no. 23, July 24, 1845.

34. See (W. H. Medhurst), A glance at the interior of China obtained during a journey through the Silk and Green Tea Districts. Taken in 1845. In 1847 Consul Balfour's description of the tea routes (Report ... Committee on Commercial Relations, pp. 326-27) checked closely with Medhurst's.

35. Medhurst, p. 136.

36. Ibid., p. 169.

37. Robert Fortune, A Journey to the Tea Countries of China; Including Sung-lo and the Bohea Hills (London, 1852), passim. See also his Two Visits to the Tea Countries of China, 2 vols, 3rd ed. (London, 1853); and Stanley Wright, Kiangsi Native Trade and its Taxation, esp. ch. i, "Trade routes." Cp. Hatano Yoshihiro's article.

38. See Chang Te-ch'ang, "Ch'ing-tai ya-p'ien chan-cheng ch'ien chih Chung-Hsi yen-hai t'ung-shang" (Sino-Western coastal trade in the Ch'ing period before the opium war), pp. 122-23.

39. BC, Macgregor's 28, Feb. 21, 1846.

40. BN, Thom's 1, Jan. 10, 1846.

41. Lo Yü-tung, Chung-kuo li-chin shih, p. 11, quotes the Kuang-hsü hui-tien as listing a total of only Tls. 843,600 for the regular quota of duties to be collected in the provinces on the trade of merchants, including lo-ti shui (lit. "fall-to-the-ground duties"), shang-shui ("merchant duties"), and tsa-shui ("miscellaneous duties") — three categories under which he includes many lesser varieties. But the exact meaning of these terms is still ambiguous. Chu Ch'i, Chung-kuo ts'ai-cheng wen-t'i, explains lo-ti-shui as a tax levied on goods when imported into a market and sold in shops (at retail).

42. Professor Yang is engaged on a series of monographic studies of Ch'ing terminology.

43. See Wright, Kiangsi Native Trade, ch. iv, for a vivisection of the Kiukiang Native Customs.

44. IWSM-TK, 68.18b, line 5 gives the new duty incorrectly as Tls. 1; this must be a copyist's error.

45. Ibid., 67.40-45; 68.13-21.

46. See IWSM-TK, Supp. 1742-43, mem. of the acting governor of Kiangsu, May 17, 1845; also ibid., 2029-30.

47. BN, circular no. 5, Feb. 27, 1844.

48. FO 17/79, Balfour's 11, Dec. 6, 1843, in Pottinger's 20, Feb. 5, 1844; cp. Montalto de Jesus, Historic Shanghai, p. 31.

49. Ibid., Balfour's 12, Dec. 21, 1843, in Pottinger's 20. Balfour opined in 1847 that transit duties were "generally light" throughout China; the danger was from the illegal exactions of local officials. See Report ... Committee on Commercial Relations, p. 321.

50. IWSM-TK, 70.22-24.

51. Ibid., Pottinger's 20; FO 17/86, Aberdeen's 45 to Davis, June 4, 1844; FO 17/81, Pottinger's 63, Apr. 10, 1844.

52. BN, Balfour's 10, Jan. 27, 1846, in Balfour to Thom, Jan. 31, 1846.

53. Fortune, A Journey to the Tea Countries, pp. 268-9.

54. IWSM-TK, Supp. 1636-39, mem. sent Jan. 2, rec'd Jan. 19, 1844.

55. BN, Thom's 43, July 20, 1844; FO 228/43, Balfour's 68, Sept. 21, 1844.

56. BN, Thom's 43, July 20, 1844.

57. FO 228/43, encl. in Balfour's 68 of 1844.

58. Encl. in ibid.

59. Ibid., Balfour's 68. The orders to these two officers were said by Medhurst to have come down from the emperor via the governor-general of Fukien-Chekiang, the governor-general of the Liang-Kiang and the Kiangsu governor, and the joint-prefect of Nanchang in temporary charge of the Kuang-hsin prefecture with rank of joint-prefect in the grain transport department. "Joint-prefect" is undoubtedly a mistranslation of T'ung-chih, prefect.

60. Ibid., Balfour's 68.

61. FO 228/900, Davis' 38 to Balfour, Oct. 21, 1844; Davis to Ch'i-ying, Oct. 21, 26, and Nov. 4, 1844; FO 228/38, Ch'i-ying to Davis, Nov. 11, in Davis' 109, Nov. 26, 1844; FO 228/43, Davis' 48 to Balfour, Nov. 20, 1844.

62. CM, no. 5, Mar. 20, 1845. Copied in CR, XIV: 200 (1845).

63. BN, Chin to Thom, no. 2, Jan. 27, 1844.

64. BC, passim, and CM, no. 170, May 18, 1848.

65. Ibid. and IWSM-TK, 79.32, in mem. of Hsü, rec'd Feb. 17, 1849. Documents on the cassia trade were also published in CR, XVII: 652-55 (1848).

66. BC, passim.

67. See Hang-chou-fu chih, Hsuan-t'ung ed., 64.1 and 5-10.

68. FO 17/245, Robertson's 29, Feb. 4, in Bowring's 57, Feb. 13, 1856.

69. BN, Balfour's 86, Dec. 31, 1845, in Balfour to Thom, Jan. 20, 1846, encl. petition of Wan Suymow, et al. Robert Fortune noted the general foreign supposition that at Hangchow "they have a custom-house in which they levy duties on merchandise imported or exported by foreigners, which duties are opposed to the ... treaty of Nanking." (A Journey to the Tea Countries, p. 31).

70. BN, Thom to Balfour, Feb. 10, 1846.

71. W. H. Medhurst, A Glance at the Interior of China ... 1845, p. 160.

72. Ibid., p. 172.

73. CM, no. 168, May 4, 1848; cp. no. 148, Dec. 16, 1847.

REFERENCES, CHAPTER 17

1. Dr. T. F. Tsiang's phrase for the period between the first and second treaty settlements; see his Chung-kuo chin-tai shih (Chinese modern history), ch. i, sec. 4. This whole question of the

growth of the foreign coasting trade in China up to 1868 is dealt with in Wright, China's Struggle for Tariff Autonomy, pp. 185-197.

2. See especially BN, passim, and BC, Elmslie's 156, Oct. 8, 1852. Cp. also R. M. Martin's compilation of data in his China, II,132-37.

3. Ibid.

4. Li Tseng-chieh, Hai-wai chi-yao, in Ch'en K'un, comp. Ts'ung-cheng hsü-yü-lu,7 chüan, preface 1881, see ts'e 19-22 in Ju-pu-chi chai hui-ch'ao. Cp. also the map volumes in Yen Ju-i, Yang-fang chi-yao; Yü Ch'ang-hui, Fang-hai chi-yao; and similar works of the time.

5. BC, Elmslie's 156, 1852.

6. BN, Thom's 54, Aug. 30, 1844. BA, Alcock's 7, Feb. 3, 1845; Layton's 12, Feb. 3, 1847.

7. BN, Thom's 9, Jan. 31, 1844.

8. FO 17/79 Pottinger's 2, Jan. 16, 1844, and Pottinger's 24 of 1844; BA, Seu (Hsü) and Heng to Gribble, no. 19, Feb. 14, 1844.

9. IWSM-TK, 70.32b-34.

10. Ibid., 71.4b-6b, 19-22.

11. BN, passim.

12. FO 17/81, Pottinger's 65, Apr. 11, 1844, quoting regulations drawn up Feb. 22, 1844. Cp. Balfour's testimony that bonding had "full approval" of the Chinese authorities but "was defeated" by the re-export clause of the American treaty; Report from the Select Committee on Commercial Relations with China, p. 319, question 4319.

13. FO 228/31, Balfour's 37, May 18, 1844; FO 17/82 and 86, passim.

14. IWSM-TK, 78.8.

15. BC, passim.

16. Wright, Hart and the Chinese Customs, p. 85, citing NCH, no. 119, Nov. 6, 1852. Mr. Wright, ibid., pp. 185, 193, note 12a, explodes H. N. Lay's claim to have secured the use of drawback certificates in 1856 by citing Alcock's action of 1852. Actually, the practice seems to have gone even further back, to 1847.

17. BC, Consul to Hoppo, Aug. 8, reply Aug. 12, 1845.

18. BC, Elmslie's 79, 105, and 124, April-July, 1849.

19. Palmerston's 103, Nov. 9, 1848, in Bonham's circular 2, Jan 24, 1848.

20. BA, Davis' 38, Apr. 17; 76, Sept. 1, encl. Davis to Keying, Aug. 30; Davis' 80, Sept. 15, 1847. BN, Davis' circular 16, no. 59 to Ningpo, no. 80 to Amoy, Sept. 17, encl. Davis to Keying, Sept. 10, 1847. Davis' public notification of Sept. 17, 1847, is printed in Wright, Tariff Autonomy, pp. 697-8.

21. BA, Layton's 50, Sept. 20, 1848.

22. In this predicament the Shanghai customs affected to be uncertain whether duty had been paid at Amoy, and stalled for time by referring to the Amoy customs and the imperial commissioner. (BA, Layton's 53, Oct. 16, 1848.)

23. BF, Jackson's 45, Dec. 20, 1849; Bonham's 6, Feb. 11, 1850; Jackson's 4, Jan. 8, 1850.

24. BA, Layton's 43, July 26, 1848, with encl.

25. BA, local corresp., February-September; Parkes' 63 and notification, Sept. 21, 1854.

26. Ibid.

27. BA, Parkes to Gingell, Nov. 7, 1854.

28. BA, Parkes' 77, Nov. 20, 1854.

29. BA, Parkes' 90, Dec. 30, 1854; Bowring's 47, Dec. 4, 1854; 7, Jan. 11, 1855.

30. BN, Bowring's 11, Feb. 25, 1856.

31. BN, Winchester to Robertson, Dec. 7, 1855.

32. BN, Chin to Thom, Nov. 23, 1844.

33. BA, corresp. July – August, 1848.

34. BA, Bowring's 28, Mar. 22, 1858.

35. BC, local corresp., 1847-1849.

36. FO 17/87, Pottinger to Stanley, CO , Dec. 21, 1843, encl. in Davis' 8 of 1844; FO 17/78, minute by Pottinger, Jan. 24, in his 12 of 1844; FO 17/86, Aberdeen's 90, Nov. 16, 1844.

37. FO 17/81, Pottinger's 74, Apr. 29, 1844.

38. BC, Governor-General Ching (i.e., Ch'eng) to consul, May 24, 1844, T. T. Meadows, transl.

39. BC, memo. by Meadows, Mar. 21, 1845.

40. BC, Macgregor's 42, May 10, 1845.

41. BC, circ. to British Community, June 26, 1845; FO 17/96, Aberdeen approved these arrangements in his 94, Nov. 24, 1845.

42. BC, Macgregor's 64, Aug. 1, 1845.

43. BC, Ke to Macgregor, Dec. 11, 1845.

44. CM, no. 54, Feb. 26, 1846.

45. BC, Macgregor's 149, July 28; to Hoppo, Aug. 3, 1847.

46. BC, Bowring's 151, June 20, 1849; he was still unconfirmed by Hsü and had not asked British permission.

47. BC, Amaral to Bonham, Apr. 4, 1849.

48. BA, Layton's 82 and 83, Oct. 23, 1847.

49. BF, Jackson's 21, Apr. 17; 34, July 17, 1848. At Foochow no British sailing letters were issued, but a total of fifty-five Portuguese lorchas visited the port in the year 1850, all but two of them engaged in convoy work. BF, Sinclair's 5, Jan. 13, 1851.

50. See P. Pelliot, "Un ouvrage sur les premiers temps de Macao," p. 65; on the fort, see Montalto de Jesus, Historic Macao, p. 13; on the enigmatic Mendez Pinto, see Schurhammer in Asia Major, III: 71-103, 194-267.

REFERENCES: CHAPTER 18

1. Smith, Exploratory Visit, p. 196.

2. Cheuk-woon Taam, The Development of Chinese Libraries under the Ch'ing Dynasty, 1644-1911, p. 47 and pp. 7-10.

3. Worcester, Junks and Sampans, p. 126.

4. BN, Thom's 3, Dec. 26, 1843.

5. BN, Thom's 8, Jan. 31; 4, Jan. 20; encl. in Thom's 9, Jan. 31, 1844.

6. BN, Thom's 16, Mar. 23, 1844; Pottinger's 25, Apr. 15, 1844.

7. BN, Thom's 54, Aug. 22, 1844; Thom's 1, Jan 10, 1846; Sullivan's 19, July 31, 1848.

8. IWSM-TK, 71.24b-27; see also BN, "Extract from the Peking Gazette concerning the port of Ningpo, by the Lieut. Governor," encl. in Thom's 73, Aug. 12, 1844.

9. FO 17/87, Davis' 15, June 7, 1844; FO 17/86, Aberdeen's 75, Oct. 5, 1844; BN has a separate volume on the subject.

10. FO 17/96, Aberdeen's 59, Aug. 8, 1845. Cp. Wright, Tariff Autonomy, p. 72, and Davis to Aberdeen, May 5, 1845, in Papers Relating ... Opium Trade, pp. 22-23.

11. Smith, Exploratory Visit, ch. xii-xiv.

12. BN, Thom's 1 of 1846.

13. BN, Sullivan's 27, Oct. 18, 1846.

14. BN, Thom's 50, Aug. 6, 1844; Chinese correspondence, 1844-1846, passim; Davis' 63, Dec. 21, 1846. Continuance of this munitions trade was evidenced in 1853 when a Soochow merchant contracted for 100 bags of saltpetre from an opium captain (Hall) at Lookong (BN, Hague to Hall, June 2, July 11, 1853).

15. BN, corresp. in October 1845; Sullivan's 18, May 12, 1849.

16. BN, Notif., Nov. 3, 1847; Smith, Exploratory Visit, p. 532.

17. BN, Sullivan's 48, Aug. 26, 1847. The activity of the British navy in suppressing piracy has been very usefully summarized by Dr. Grace Fox in her British Admirals and Chinese Pirates 1832-1869.

18. BN, Sullivan's 14, June 10, 1848; Sullivan's 10, May 11, 1848.

19. Ibid. and Layton's 13, June 9, 1849; et passim 1847-49. Cp. Fox, British Admirals, pp. 101, 107.

20. BF, Jackson's 22, Apr. 29; 9, Feb. 17; 8, Feb. 2 1848.

21. See Fox, pp. 179, 190, 110-11, also 201-204, app. D.

22. BN, corresp., 1848, passim.

23. See Davis' notification May 29, in CR., XVII: 318 (June 1848); BN, Bonham's 17, June 13, 1848.

24. BN, Palmerston's 20, Apr. 14, in Bonham's circular 10, Aug. 19, 1848; Palmerston's 96, Oct. 31, 1848, in Bonham's circular 10, May 31, 1849; also in CR, XVIII: 669 (1849).

25. See documents in extenso in CM, no. 190, Oct. 5; also no. 179, July 20, and no. 181, Aug. 3, 1848; BN, Alcock's 95 to Sullivan, Aug. 22; Bonham's 30, Oct. 25, 1848.

26. Worcester, Junks and Sampans, pp. 127, 130, describes the modern Chen-hai-ch'uan (Chenhai boats), painted in "a riot of colour," usually red, green, and white on a black hull, which supply the Ningpo and Shanghai fish markets.

27. See note 25 above.

28. BN, Sullivan's 21, June 8; Bonham's 32, July 20, 1849.

29. BN, Davidson to consul, Nov. 2, 1850, misc. letters; Robertson to Davidson, Nov. 23, 1850.

30. BN, Robertson's 52, Nov. 8, 1850; Tih to Hague, July 8, 1851.

31. BN, Bonham's 3, Jan. 7, 1851.

32. BN, Robertson's 20 to Wang, Chinhai magistrate, Dec. 12, 1850.

33. NCH, Dec. 6, 1851; BN, Hague's 36, Sept. 8; Bonham's 43, Oct. 14, 1851; 10, Feb. 14, 1852.

34. BN, Hague's 18 to Guimarēs, Governor of Macao, Feb. 26, 1852. Hague's correspondence as Portuguese consul at Ningpo in 1851-52 is included in the British consular records.

35. BN, Hague's 18, Apr. 11, 1851.

36. BN, local corresp., April-September 1851.

37. See NCH, Jan. 10 and 31, 1852; and Feb. 21, quoting "Dr. Macgowan's Note Book."

38. BN, Hague's 44, Nov. 15, 1851; 7, Jan. 23, 1852.

39. BN, Juy to Hague, Jan. 28 and 29, 1852.

40. BN, Meadows' 19, Apr. 15, 1854.

41. BN, Sinclair's 111, November 1856.

42. BN, corresp., January-March 1855.

43. BN, Bowring's 103, Dec. 14, 1855; 32, Apr. 28, 1856.

44. BN, Meadows' 36, July 31, with encl. from Tuan Taotai; Bowring's 25, 26, 27, July; Guimares to Bowring, Aug. 24, in Bowring's 31, Aug. 28; BN, July-August 1854, passim.

REFERENCES: CHAPTER 19

1. BC, Lay's 6, Apr. 1, 1844. The fine of $500 was paid, more than a year later after an appeal.

2. BA, Gribble's 33, Apr. 3; Pottinger's 38, Apr. 17, 1844. FO 17/81, Pottinger's 69, Apr. 17, 1844.

3. BA, Layton's 25, Apr. 30, 1846; IWSM-TK, Supp. 1849: appointment of Ko-er-sa, a colonel (Hsieh-ling) of the Bordered Yellow Banner, was reported in a memorial received on May 15, 1846.

4. BA, passim.

5. BA, Layton's 12, Feb. 3, 1847; 9, Feb. 10, 1848.

6. BC, Bowring's 153, June 22, 1849.

7. BA, Layton's 7, Feb. 9, 1849.

8. BF, Alcock to Too, no. 39, Aug. 3, 1846.

9. BA, Layton's 17, July 11: 26, Sept. 28; Bonham's 41, Aug. 2, 1849.

10. BC, Macgregor's 26, Apr. 4, 1845.

11. BC, Hoppo to consul; Chinese correspondence, May-June 1845, T. T. M. transl.; Macgregor's 59, July 3, 1845.

12. BC, Macgregor's 9, Feb. 4, 1845; 28 of 1846, 11 of 1847, 65 of 1848, and 17 of 1849. Figures left as in originals.

13. Cp. Morse, Conflict, p. 366; also above, table 9 in Ch. 14. It will be seen that these consular figures are compatible with the Chinese fiscal reports. IWSM-TK, Supp. 1897-99, mem. from Ch'i-ying received Oct. 23, 1846, surveys the experience of the preceding three years, noting the decline of revenue.

14. BC, consul's 21, to Hoppo, Feb. 6; consul's 17 to imperial commissioner, Feb. 9, 1849.

15. BN, Davis to Keying, Sept. 10, in Davis' 59 to Sullivan (circ. 16), Sept. 17, 1847.

16. Mayers, Treaty Ports (1867), p. 126; Chinese Commercial Guide (1844), p. 87.

17. FO 17/69, Keying to Pottinger, Aug. 1; Pottinger to Keying, Aug. 10, 1843, encl. in 102; partly printed in House of Commons, XL: 9 (1847); FO 228/29, Pottinger's 347 to Lay, Aug. 19, 1843.

18. FO 17/69, Pottinger's 104, Aug. 24, 1843; CM, no. 152, Jan. 13, 1848.

19. See the list in Chinese Commercial Guide (1844), pp. 160-162.

20. CM, no. 65, May 14, 1846.

21. CM, no. 180, July 27, 1848; cp. BC, Hughesden and Co. to consul, July 5, 1847.

22. A Chinese Commercial Guide (ed. 1844), pp. 84-89, 157-173, describes the routine of trade and gives in Chinese and English the forms used in reporting vessels and cargo. Hunter, Fan Kwae, pp. 50-53, also describes the procedure. Wright, Hart and the Chinese Customs, pp. 70-71, describes the malpractices; cp. also Robert Hart's summary of them in Gundry, China, pp. 191-92.

23. The foregoing account of smuggling is based particularly on the letters of five leading Canton merchants to Bowring in March 1851, encl. in Bonham to Palmerston, Apr. 10, 1851, FO 17/176; on Parkes' "Note on the Irregularities of the Canton Custom House" of September 1854 in Bowring's 246 of 1854, FO 17/218; and on Vice-Consul Winchester's "Memorandum relative to the execution of the XII Article of the Supplementary Treaty," in Parkes' 82 of July 9, 1857, FO 228/235. Cp. also S. W. Williams, A Chinese Commercial Guide (4th ed., Canton, 1856), p. 222.

24. BC, Bowring's 177 to Bonham, Aug. 23, 1849.

25. BC, Corresp., August-November 1849, letters to superintendency; also summarized in FO 17/167; Bowring to Bonham, Mar. 23, encl. in Bonham's 53 to Palmerston.

26. FO 228/235, Bonham's 156 to Bowring, Oct. 13, 1849, et passim, September and October, encl. in Parkes' 82 of July 9, 1857.

27. FO 17/164, to Bonham, Jan. 2, 1850.

28. See T'ung-chih Shang-hai-hsien chih (T'ung-chih period, Shanghai district gazetteer), pub. at the governor's yamen, Soochow, 1871, 2.14a; a previous edition is quoted in an article, "Description of Shanghae," Chinese Miscellany, no. 4, Shanghai, 1850.

29. Cp. map in Morse, Conflict, p. 454; and Mayers, Treaty Ports, p. 378.

30. See Ta-Ch'ing chin-shen ch'üan-shu (Ch'ing dynasty official Red Book), 1852, winter ed., 1.3b, 2.32b.

31. T. T. Meadows, Desultory Notes on the Government and People of China, table, p. 100. Meadows also gives Tls. 105 and Tls. 3000 for the first two items, which accord with Red Books (lists of officials) published in 1833, 1845, 1855, 1866, 1892, and other dates.

32. See IWSM-TK, Supp. 1672-74, mem. of Sun Shan-pao, rec'd May 6, 1844. Late in 1849 the Kiangsu authorities complained that the growth of trade necessitated adding sub-stations and personnel, but allocation of Shanghai collections to Canton prevented it; IWSM-TK, Supp. 2111-14, 2119-21, memorials rec'd Nov. 19, 1849 and Feb. 22, 1850.

33. CM, no. 42, Dec. 4, 1845; gov't notif. of Nov. 29, enclosing Balfour's 65 of Nov. 7 with notifications of Jan., Mar., June, Aug. and Sept., 1845.

34. CM, no. 127, July 22, 1847; gov't notification of July 21, encl. Alcock's notif. of June 21, 1847. For the Shanghai port regulations drawn up by Alcock, see CR, XV: 566-67 (1846).

35. FO 228/43, Balfour's 85, Dec. 20, 1844.

36. IWSM-TK, Supp. 1897-99, Ch'i-ying's memorial rec'd Oct. 23, 1846; 1902, edict, same date. Cp. above, Ch. 14, note 40.

37. This three-year system had been used before; see Chinese Miscellany, no. 4: 134 (Shanghai, 1850): "The old regulation was to ascertain by comparison, the utmost amount that had been received for three years together, and then if the sum collected did not come up to this, the collector was to make it good. In 1799, this ... was discontinued." For the situation in 1850, see FO 17/167, Alcock to Bonham, Apr. 11, encl. in Bonham's 53 of 1850; FO 17/184, London East India and China Association to Palmerston, Apr. 10, 1851.

38. FO 17/176, Bonham to Palmerston, Apr. 10, 1851; FO 17/173, H. H. Lindsay to Bonham, July 22, encl. in Lindsay to Palmerston, July 27, 1850; ibid., H. H. Lindsay to Palmerston, Dec. 5, 1850.

39. FO 17/167, Bonham's 53 to Palmerston, Apr. 23, 1850, and enclosed trade reports.

40. China Instructions, vol. I, Clayton to Davis, no. 9, Oct. 18, 1849. Cp. the act of Parliament "for amending the laws in force for the encouragement of British shipping and navigation" (12 and 13 Vict. cap. 29, British and Foreign State Papers, vol. XXXVIII, 1849-50).

41. Basil Lubbock, The China Clippers, p. 106. As late as 1854, 106 days from Whampoa to London by the Cape was a quick passage; Mayers, Treaty Ports, p. 66. By 1852 American ships carried away 47 per cent of the trade of Shanghai (Morse, Conflict, p. 343); cp. Michie, The Englishman in China, I, 230.

42. FO 17/184, Directors of P. and O. to Palmerston, Apr. 29, 1851.

43. FO 17/177, Alcock's 30 to Bonham, May 1, encl. in Bonham's 47 to Palmerston, May 20, 1851; reiterated in FO 17/178, Alcock to Bonham, Aug. 9, encl. in Bonham to Palmerston, Sept. 15, 1851.

44. FO 17/169, Proceedings of a Consular Court, British Consulate, Shanghai, July 4, 1850; Jardine to Alcock, June 24, 1850, encl. in Bonham's 97 to Palmerston of Sept. 27, 1850.

45. Ibid. Cp. Wright, Hart, p. 80, and Morse, Submission, pp. 8-10.

46. Alcock to British community, Shanghai, June 23, 1850.

47. FO 17/184, P. and O. directors to Palmerston, Apr. 29, 1851; his reply, July 31; FO 17/177, Alcock to Bonham, May 1, 1851, encl. in Bonham's 47, FO 17/177. Palmerston had asked Bonham about the facts on May 20, 1851, FO 17/181.

48. FO 17/176, Bonham to Palmerston, Mar. 28, 1851; FO/174, Palmerston to Bonham, Aug. 27, 1851.

49. FO 17/181, Bonham to Addington, Dec. 29, 1851. Cp. Eitel, Hong Kong, passim.

50. FO 17/169, Bonham's 72 to Alcock, Aug. 21, 1850, encl. in his 97; FO 17/164, Palmerston's 99, Nov. 27, 1851.

51. FO 17/170, Alcock to Lin, encl. in Bonham's 144 to Palmerston, Dec. 26, 1850.

52. CR, XX: 469 (1851), Dr. Peter Parker to Commissioner Seu, Aug. 28, 1851, quoting Griswold to Parker, December 1850.

53. FO 17/173, Hogg to Lindsay, quoted in Lindsay to Palmerston, Dec. 20, 1850.

54. Lubbock, China Clippers, p. 58.

55. NCH, Jan. 11, 1851.

56. FO 17/175, Alcock's 7, Jan. 14, in Bonham's 15, 1851.

57. Ibid. On Wu see below, Ch. 21.

58. Alcock's 7 in Bonham's 15, 1851.

REFERENCES: CHAPTER 20

1. The fullest data on American consular activities in China in this period is presented in Eldon Griffin, Clippers and Consuls, ch. xiv-xviii.

2. Cp. Anglo-Chinese Calendar for the Year 1848; ibid., 1851, etc.

3. Imports of tea to Liverpool and London from Jan. 1 to July 16, 1849, were 7,193,000 lb. and 27,286,000 lb. respectively, with deliveries and stocks in about the same proportion. Gideon Nye, Jr., Tea; and the Tea Trade (New York, 3rd ed., 1850), p. 21, based on Brodribb and Coates circular, Liverpool.

4. Activities of the Manchester Chamber of Commerce are summarized in Arthur Redford, Manchester Merchants and Foreign Trade 1794-1858, ch. ix.

5. Nathan A. Pelcovits, Old China Hands and the Foreign Office (New York, American Institute of Pacific Relations, 1948) is the outstanding study of these merchant bodies in action; it is not concerned in detail with their influence before 1858.

6. Tilley and Gaselee, The Foreign Office, p. 233, quoting Hammond.

7. Ibid., p. 66.

8. Exclusive of miscellaneous letters re appointments, complaints and personal affairs filed under Domestic Various and Foreign Various, which totaled (during the five years 1852-56) 22 volumes, out of 74 of correspondence.

9. See the description of the permanent undersecretary's many-sided role in administration and diplomacy in E. Jones-Parry, "Under-Secretaries of State for Foreign Affairs, 1782-1855," pp. 315-6.

10. See F. O. List (1852), and Dictionary of National Biography (ed. 1908), art. by T. F. Henderson.

11. Tilley, The Foreign Office, pp. 91, 111, 234.

12. On the Foreign Office under Palmerston cp. C. K. Webster, "Lord Palmerston at Work, 1830-41," Politica, II: 129-144 (August 1934), and "The Foreign Minister and the Diplomatic Machine", ch. iii in The Foreign Policy of Palmerston, 1830-1841.

13. Part of this correspondence is printed in British and Foreign State Papers, XXXVIII (1849-50); see also Morse, Conflict, p. 398.

14. FO 17/166, Alcock to Bonham, Feb. 13, in Bonham's 46 of 1850.

15. FO 16/166, Bonham's 46, Apr. 15, 1850.

16. FO 17/174, Palmerston's 2, July 2, 1850.

17. Ibid., Palmerston's 17, Jan. 24, 1850.

18. FO 17/165, Bonham's 13, Jan. 30, 1850, also his 40 of Mar. 28, received May 20.

19. Costin, Great Britain and China, pp. 141-152, summarizes much of the British correspondence of this period, which is therefore omitted here. The Chinese side has been neglected.

20. IWSM-HF, 1.1, received Mar. 6, 1850.

21. FO 17/164, Palmerston's 2, Jan. 2, 1850.

22. See IWSM-HF, 1.9b, mem. of Lu received May 28, quoting dispatch received from Hsü in the second month (Mar. 3--Apr. 1, 1850).

23. Ibid.

24. FO 17/168, Bonham's 58, June 4, 1850.

25. See IWSM-HF, 1.13 to 2.5, passim, over 40 pages of text.

26. FO 17/168, Bonham's 68, July 22, 1850.

27. FO 17/168, Bonham's 62, June 11, 1850.

28. Ibid., Bonham's 68, July 22, 1850.

29. See IWSM-HF, 1.15b, line 3. Translated bv T. T. Meadows (encl. in Bonham's 63, June 16, 1850). Translations by Wade and Medhurst were also sent Palmerston (Bonham's 68, July 22, 1850). The British suggestion that the court showed weakness at Canton was rebuffed as uncultured impoliteness; in Meadows' translation: "this is by no means language such as those hold who understand political and social observances."

30. IWSM-HF, 1.16 (apparent date, May 29, 1850); see above translation by Meadows (in Bonham's 63).

31. The Chinese dispatch above noted correctly quotes the Chinese version of the Treaty of Wanghia (cp. Customs, Treaties).

32. The provision of the treaty of Nanking, article XI, that H.B.M.'s "Chief High Officer in China shall correspond with the Chinese High Officers, both at the Capital and in the Provinces, under the term 'Communication,'" was evidently based on the assumption that correspondence with the capital would take place, but in the Chinese version its sense was permissive, not mandatory that the British official and the Chinese high officers, whether in Peking or the provinces, if they corresponded, should use a certain form of dispatch.

33. I follow here the suggestion of Fang Chaoying in Hummel, p. 379; see also p. 583. Little solid evidence has thus far been adduced as to the personality of the Hsien-feng Emperor and his policies; Callery and Yvan, L'Insurrection en Chine (1855), ch. iii, paint a plausible picture by hearsay and translate a decree of Nov. 21, 1850; see also CM and CR, XX: 49-52 (1851). The causal connection between the seemingly meek departure of the Reynard from the Peiho and the fall of Ch'i-ying as an official who had exaggerated British intransigeance, is stressed in Wang Chih-ch'un, Ko-kuo t'ung-shang shih-mo chi, 13.1.

34. FO 17/164, 55 to Bonham, July 5, 1850.

35. FO 17/164.

36. FO 17/164, 73 to Bonham, Sept. 3, 1850. Partly quoted in Costin, p. 149.

37. Bonham's 63 (June 16) and 69 (July 22) were both received Sept. 23.

38. FO 17/168, Bonham's 69, July 22; cp. also Morse, Conflict, p. 399.

39. FO 17/173 (Domestic various). Memo. on "Mr. Bonham's 65, 67, 72," following an application for consular positions at Ningpo and Foochow, signed "P. 29-9-50." Partially quoted also in Costin, pp. 149-50, who, however, overlooks the change of attitude created in the foreign secretary, between Sept. 3 and 29, by the failure of his negotiations in China.

40. See above, Ch. 3; cp. Charles Gutzlaff, Journal of Three Voyages, p. 138: "Mr. Lindsay, our chief and supercargo, a man of the most humane disposition, refined manners, and enthusiastic in such an enterprise, was conversant with the Chinese language"; cp. also Morse, Chronicles IV, ch. xci; Eitel, Hongkong, p. 58. Lindsay had published pamphlets, e.g., British Relations with China, in which he defended the position of the opium trader and advocated the systematic expansion of the trade.

41. FO 17/173, Lindsay to Palmerston, July 27, 1850.

42. FO 17/164, no. 75 to Bonham, Sept. 11, 1850.

43. FO 17/169, Bonham's 97, Sept. 27, 1850. Bowring was later eloquent on the subject of foreign consuls, to Malmesbury, Jan. 10, 1853, FO 17/199.

44. FO 17/173, Lindsay to Palmerston, Nov. 21, 1850.

45. FO 17/164, Palmerston to Bonham, Nov. 27, 1850.

46. FO 17/173, Lindsay to Palmerston, Dec. 5, 1850.

47. Note on ibid.

48. FO 17/164, Palmerston to Bonham, Dec. 11.

49. FO 17/174, Palmerston's 25 to Bonham, Feb 19, 1851.

50. FO 17/183, Ripley to Palmerston, Mar. 29, 1851.

51. FO 17/170, to Bonham, Sept. 11, 1850, encl. in Bonham's 119, Oct. 26. See FO 17/173, 174: FO to Treasury, Dec. 28, 1850; Palmerston to Bonham, Feb. 6, 1851. The data supplied by the English customs proved to be insufficiently detailed; FO 17/178, Bonham to Palmerston, June 21, 1851 . When Alcock complained, the data sent proved still to be useless without the names of ships. (FO 228/147, Alcock's 53, June 3, 1852, encl. in Bowring's 62).

52. FO 17/183, China merchants to Palmerston, Mar. 31, 1850.

53. Memo. in FO 17/183 following Ripley to Palmerston, Mar. 29, 1851.

54. FO 17/184, Manchester Chamber of Commerce, and London East India and China Association, to Palmerston; FO to Treasury, Apr. 11; H. H. Lindsay, W. Magniac, Lancelot Dent, and S. G. Rathbone to Palmerston, Apr. 17, 1851.

55. FO 17/175, Alcock to Bonham, Jan. 14, enclosed in Bonham's 16, Feb. 25, 1851.

56. FO 17/184, Liverpool E. I. and China Association to Palmerston, Apr. 22, 1851.

57. FO 17/174, Palmerston to Bonham, Apr. 21, and 24, 1851.

58. FO 17/184, to Queen's advocate (enclosing China Merchants' memorial of Mar. 31), Apr. 19;

FO to Board of Trade, May 6; Porter to Addington, May 13, 1851. See Sir H. L. Smith, The Board of Trade, ch. iv, "The Board of Trade and Commerce"; British Imperial Calendar for 1851 and Dict. of Nat'l Biog., 9 (1909), art. by G. F. Russell Baker. Labouchere had been appointed Vice-Pres. 1835, Pres. 1839 (to 1841), and again 1847; and ibid. (ed. 1896), art. by W. A. S. Hewins. Porter wrote The Progress of the Nation.

59. FO 17/184, G. Cornewall Lewis to Addington, May 19, 1851.

60. FO 17/174, Palmerston's 49 to Bonham, May 24, 1851. On this whole subject see Wright, Hart, pp. 80-83.

61. FO 17/184, Sir Thomas Birch to Palmerston, June 18, and reply; published in The Times at once. Bowring's claim in 1855 (no. 186 of May 23, FO 17/309) that "Lord Palmerston's dispatch [of May 24, 1851] originated in suggestions of mine, while Consul at Canton," is of course an overstatement.

62. FO 17/175, Bonham to Palmerston, Feb. 24, 1851.

63. FO 17/176, Stephen Ponder (Dallas and Co., Chairman, Canton Chamber of Commerce); W. P. Livingston (Gibb, Livingston and Co.); Joseph Jardine (Jardine, Matheson and Co.); A. Wilkinson (Wilkinson and Sanders); and R. I. Gilman (Gilman and Co.) to Bowring, encl. in Bowring to Bonham, Mar. 24, encl. in Bonham to Palmerston, Apr. 10, 1851. John Dent (Dent and Co.) and Davidson (Lindsay and Co.) did not reply to the consul, who was not over-popular in Canton.

64. FO 17/176, Alcock to Bonham, Mar. 15, in Bonham to Palmerston, Apr. 10, 1850.

65. China, 6, Woo to Griswold, Dec. 15, 1850, in Parker's 20 to Webster, Sept. 24, 1851 (State Dept. Archives, Washington, D.C.).

66. Ibid., Seu to Parker, May 16, in Parker's 17 to Webster, June 20, 1851. FO 17/176, Alcock's Mar. 15, in Bonham's Apr. 10. See also China, 6, Griswold's of June 28, in Parker's 20, Sept. 24, 1851.

67. FO 17/176, Sullivan to Bonham, Mar. 17, in Bonham's Apr. 10, 1851.

68. FO 228/235, Bowring's 41 to Bonham, Feb. 25, 1851, and enclosures, in Parkes' 82 of 1857.

69. FO 17/176, Bonham to Palmerston and enclosures, Mar. 27.

70. Ibid., Bonham to Seu, Apr. 5, encl. in Bonham to Palmerston, Apr. 10, 1851.

71. FO 17/177, in Bonham to Palmerston, Apr. 22 and May 21, 1851.

72. FO 17/177, Alcock to Bonham, Apr. 30, in Bonham to Palmerston, May 21, 1851; FO 17/184, Sir T. Birch to Palmerston, June 18, 1851.

73. China, 6, Seu to Parker, May 16, in Parker's 17, June 20, 1851; Griswold's June 28, Parker to Seu, Aug. 28, and Seu to Parker, Sept. 12, 1851, all in Parker's 20.

74. Ibid., Griswold's June 28, 1851.

75. FO 17/178, Seu to Bonham, July 18, encl. in Bonham to Palmerston, July 22, 1851.

76. Ibid., Bonham to Bowring, July 19.

77. Ibid., Bonham to Alcock, July 21; FO 97/99, Alcock to Woo Taotai and reply, Aug. 14 and 16, encl. in Alcock's Notification to the British Mercantile Community, Aug. 19, 1851, encl. in Shanghai Chamber of Commerce to London East India and China Association, Sept. 22, 1853, encl. in same to Clarendon, Nov. 17, 1853.

78. BA, Hing to Sullivan, no. 12, Sept. 29; Sullivan's 74, Dec. 12; Bonham's 66, Dec. 20, 1851.

79. BF, Sinclair to merchants, Aug. 18; no. 56 to Ho, Aug. 19; and reply Aug. 21; Walker to Ho, Oct. 24, and reply Oct. 27; Ho to Walker, Dec. 24, 1851; see also Walker's 10, Jan. 22; and Bonham's 9, Mar. 2, 1852.

80. FO 17/178, see Note following Bonham's 80; FO 17/174, Palmerston to Bonham, Oct. 21, 1851: "As there is reason to suppose that in the event of its being at any time necessary to coerce the Chinese Government, the easiest and most effectual measure for that purpose would be to blockade the entrance of the Grand Canal," please report on the time of year most effective for a blockade and best for an expedition.

81. FO 17/181, "Extract of a letter to Sir Samuel Bonham, dated Hong Kong, Dec. 29, 1851." Bonham replied to the dispatch of Oct. 21 about coercion to this same effect: FO 17/187, to Palmerston, Jan. 26, 1852, enclosing Alcock's enthusiastic approval of the idea, to Bonham, Jan. 13, 1852. Summarized in Costin, pp. 145-46, 151-52.

REFERENCES: CHAPTER 21

1. Foreign Office List; FO 17/174, Palmerston to Bonham, Dec. 23, 1851.

2. See instructions of Granville and Malmesbury to Bowring in British and Foreign State Papers 1854-55, XLV, 918, 929, published also in Correspondence ... Relating to Entrance ... into Canton 1850-55. The French Empire was recognized on Dec. 4, 1852. Russell succeeded Malmesbury Dec. 28. Cp. Earl of Malmesbury, Memoirs of an Ex-Minister, passim; FO 17/186, Granville, Palmerston, and Malmesbury to Bonham and Bowring, January to December 1852.

3. E.g., FO 17/182, Bowring to Palmerston, private letter, Dec. 9, 1851; FO 17/187, Jan. 15, 1852.

4. From Apr. 14, 1852 to Feb. 16, 1853 (Eitel, Hong Kong, p. 254). Jervois was Lieut.-Gov. from February 1851 to April 1854 (ibid., p. 253), i.e., until Bowring's assumption of the governorship in 1854.

5. R. B. Forbes, Personal Reminiscences, app.; Morse, Conflict, p. 348.

6. CM, no. 139, Oct. 14, 1847.

7. The Anglo-Chinese Calendar for the Year 1848 (Canton, 1848), pp. 71-2, gives Hsien-ling's full title and describes him as "a steady supporter of the new and more liberal policy."

8. See IWSM-TK, 79.5b-8. CR, XVII: 373 (1848), notes that, Hsien-ling having been "displaced for imbecility ... Wu (Mr. Samqua) has taken up his residence in the old office." Ibid., p. 488: "Mr. Samqua [as of Sept. 12, 1848] had retired from that office [of taotai] but was still connected with the local government, carrying out his plans for the suppression of piracy." Cp., also, ibid., p. 544. In actual fact, the British in 1848 opposed expressing an opinion on the removal of Hsien-ling because they knew that "Sam-qua, the late Hong merchant at Canton, had been long hanging about Shanghae, open to employment, and evidently with his eye on that port as its future Taoutae, in the event of the removal of Heen-ling ...." See Correspondence respecting Insults in China, p. 156, Robertson to Alcock, Apr 7, 1848.

9. See Morse, Chronicles, IV, 327.

10. IWSM-TK, 53.36b, 57.20b-21.

11. Ibid., 58.37.

12. Mrs. Eliza Jane (Gillett) Bridgman, Daughters of China: or Sketches of Domestic Life in the Celestial Empire (New York, 1853), pp. 93,95. Toyama Gunji, Taihei tengoku, p. 40. Toyama's article on Wu, "Shanhai dōdai," summarizes the earlier part of his career.

13. IWSM-HF, 2.6b.

14. A Millac, "Les Francais à Changhai en 1853-55," Revue de l'Extrême Orient for 1883, tome 2 (Paris, 1884). Meadows (The Chinese and their Rebellions, pp. 194-95) confirms the point that Wu "had purchased all the official steps up to the Intendancy. He had not passed even the lowest of the Public Service Examinations; had little or no acquaintance with the national political literature; and could not even speak intelligibly the mandarin Chinese ... However, he could speak ... broken English ... I believe there is no other mandarin in the Imperial service ... who can converse, however, imperfectly, in an Occidental language."

15. IWSM-HF, 5.27-28.

16. Announced at Shanghai in NCH, Aug. 16, 1851; note editorial.

17. For Notification to British Community, Aug. 19, enclosing Alcock to Woo, Aug. 14, and reply, Aug. 16, see NCH, Aug. 23, 1851. Regs. also in FO 17/179, Bonham to Palmerston, Sept. 20, 1851. Summarized also in Wright, Hart, p. 83. The Customs Bank was not established until October 1852; Morse, Submission, p. 12.

18. NCH, Aug. 9, 1851, Notifications of Griswold, Aug. 1, and Alcock, Aug. 6. NCH, Dec. 20, 1851, prints Montigny to taotai, Aug. 30; also noted in Morse, Submission, pp. 11-12.

19. Ibid., and FO 17/181, Bonham to Palmerston, Dec. 4, 1851; China, 6, Parker's 24, Jan. 27, 1852, and enclosures; NCH, Sept. 27, Oct. 4, 18, Nov. 29, 1851. Alcock had proposed to appoint an American, Nathaniel Baylies, as harbor master in December 1848. (Griswold to Davis, Dec. 11, 1848, in Davis' 11, Jan. 27, 1849, China, 5.) FO 17/179, Bonham to Palmerston, Sept. 20, 1851.

20. See consular trade reports for 1851 in FO 17/187; Griswold to Parker, Oct. 4, in Parker's 22, Oct. 27, 1851, China, 6. This estimate compares with the Chinese figures; see table of customs collections in Ch. 14 above: Shanghai returns rose from Tls. 700,000 to Tls. 1,200,000.

21. China, 6, Griswold to Parker, Oct. 4, in Parker's 22, Oct. 27, 1851.

22. NCH, June 28, 1851, reported that Wu sent Tls. 140,000 from the foreign customs to Canton to be used against the rebels. Ibid., July 5, 1851, reported an edict in the Peking Gazette of May 18 to have ordered Tls. 600,000 to be sent by Wu from the Kiangnan salt and customs revenue.

23. China, 6, Griswold to Lin, July 5, to Woo, July 8, in Parker's 23, Dec. 27, 1851.

24. China, 6, Griswold to Woo, July 18, 21, 1851; Parker to Griswold, Sept. 22, 1851, in Parker's 20.

25. Ibid., Griswold to Parker, Oct. 4, in Parker's 22; Parker to Griswold, Sept. 22, 1851, in Parker's 20.

26. Alcock (British), Montigny (French), D. B. Robertson (Denmark, actually British vice-consul), T. C. Beale (Portugal and the Netherlands, actually a British citizen), Lan Wei-wen, sub-prefect of Shanghai (Hai-fang t'ung-chih), and the Shanghai district magistrate.

27. China, 6, Parker's 22 to Webster, Oct. 27, 1851, and enclosed correspondence.

28. AS, Judicial Archive no. 12 (U. S. Consulate-General, Shanghai).

29. Forbes, Personal Reminiscences, app.

30. China, 7, Cunningham to Woo, Mar. 13, in Parker's 28, Apr. 22, 1852.

31. Ibid. Notification printed in Morse, Conflict, p. 349, but as though referring particularly to land in the French Concession.

32. China, 7, see letter from Hsü, May 2, 1849, in reply to J. W. Davis' letter of Apr. 25; Parker to Cunningham, Apr. 6, in Parker's 28.

33. On this case see Alcock's 51 to Bowring, June 2, 1852, in FO 228/147; and Bowring's 63 to Malmesbury, June 30, in FO 17/190, with enclosures.

34. FO 17/192, Alcock to Bowring, May 30, encl. in Bowring's 114, Aug. 27, 1852.

35. FO 17/190, Bowring to Alcock, June 24 and 25, encl. in Bowring's 63, June 30. See also FO 17/192, Bowring's 114, Aug. 27, and Bowring's 128 to Malmesbury, Sept. 25, 1852.

36. See Bowring's 62 of 1852 and enclosures, FO 228/147, or FO 17/190, esp. encl. 3, Alcock to Woo, June 2, 1852.

37. FO 17/176, Alcock's 85 to Bonham, Oct. 9, 1850, encl. in Bonham to Palmerston, Apr. 10, 1851.

38. FO 17/186.

39. China Instructions, vol. I, Webster to Marshall, Aug. 11, 1852.

40. Cp. Malmesbury, Memoirs, p. 264, Derby to Malmesbury, Sept. 15, 1852, concerning the American fisheries, "assuredly ... I am prepared to fight for our undoubted rights rather than yield to a spirit of democratic encroachment." The Canadian reciprocity treaty was not signed until June 5, 1853.

41. FO 17/192, Bowring to Malmesbury, Aug. 26, 1852.

42. FO 17/199, Bowring to Malmesbury, Jan. 10, 1853.

43. See FO 17/198, passim; Dict. of Nat. Biog., XX, art. on Clarendon by Hon.Mr. Justice Hamilton; cp. Ashley, Life, II, 12, Palmerston to his brother William, Apr. 3, "I am very glad that Clarendon has got the Foreign Office. He will do the business well and keep up the character and dignity of the country."

44. See Br. and For. State Papers 1854-55, XLV, 935.

45. Contemporary accounts of the rise of the rebellion are mainly partisan. But cp. Callery and Yvan, History of the Insurrection in China (London, 1853); T. T. Meadows, The Chinese and their Rebellions (London, 1856); Morse, Conflict, ch. xvii; W. J. Hail, Tseng Kuo-fan and the Taiping Rebellion.

46. See appeals of the governor of Kiangsu to the Shanghai consuls cited in Bonham to Malmesbury, Mar. 11, and to Russell, Mar. 28, in FO 17/200.

47. FO 17/200, Bonham to Russell, Mar. 28, 1853 (pub. in Br. and For. State Papers 1853-54, vol. XLV, also in Corresp. re Civil War in China).

48. See IWSM-HF, 6.9-11, 12-13b; Wu Chien-chang reassured his superiors as to the British intentions.

49. FO 17/200, "Confidential" to Bonham, encl. in Bonham to Malmesbury, Mar. 11, 1853.

50. See the statement of this situation in Morse, Conflict, ch. xvii, "Shanghai in the Rebellion, 1853-1859."

51. A. G. Dallas, Lindsay and Co., Dent, Beale and Co., Gibb Livingston and Co., Mackenzie Bros. and Co.; A. G. Dallas was resident partner of Jardine, Matheson and Co. They, Dent, Beale and Co., and Lindsay and Co. had three of the nine receiving ships at Wusung listed, e.g., in the Overland China Mail, no. 87, Feb. 11, 1854. Morse, Conflict, p. 465, gives the total as ten in 1854.

52. Quoted in Alcock to British Community, Mar. 10, 1853, encl. in Bonham's 100, Sept. 4, FO 17/204; also in Morse, Submission, p. 13, quoting NCH, Mar. 12, 1853.

53. FO 17/204, Bonham's 100, enclosing W. H. Medhurst, as secretary replying for Bonham, to British merchants at Shanghai, Sept. 2. Medhurst had been interpreter to Balfour in 1844 and states in his Pamphlets issued by the Chinese Insurgents (Shanghai, 1853), p. 31, that the Chinese had just previously attempted a licensed warehouse monopoly. See also Woo to Alcock, Mar. 8 (?), cited in Alcock to Woo, Mar. 9, encl. in Alcock to British Community, Mar. 10.

54. Anon., Manual of Customs Practice at Shanghai, by "a shipping clerk of seven years standing" (Shanghai, 1894), p. 31, "Supplementary convention between Germany and China ... 31st March, 1880, Art. III, ... provides for the establishment of Bonded Warehouses in all the ports of China." Bonding was first established at Shanghai under Customs Notification of Dec. 20, 1887, in force Jan. 1, 1888, to the effect that consignees of foreign goods would have the option of either paying duty and taking immediate delivery of the same, or of deferring payment and depositing their consignments in a designated bonded warehouse. H. B. Morse was sent down from Peking in December 1887 to make the arrangements (personal statement of H. B. M.).

55. See FO 17/204, enclosures in Bonham's 100, Sept. 4, 1853.

56. In 1853 the import at Shanghai was 24,200 chests; Morse, Conflict, p. 465.

57. Morse, Conflict, chart, p. 470.

58. FO 17/203, Smith Kennedy and Co.; Hargreaves and Co.; Watson; Birley Worthington; Turner; Charles Waters P. Pro Holliday Wise; Reiss; Dirom Gray; Gibb Livingston; George Bennetts P. Pro James Macdonald; Sillar Bros.; Smith King; and Mackenzie Bros. and Co. to Bonham, July 7, encl. in Bonham's 69, July 20, 1853; quoted in part in Morse, Conflict, p. 469, from NCH, Sept. 3, 1853. For a Chinese account of these events, evidently based on Western sources, see Wang I-t'ang, Shang-hai tsu-chieh wen-t'i (The problem of the Shanghai leased territory), 3.16b.

59. FO 17/203. W. H. Medhurst for Bonham to British merchants, July 20, encl. in Bonham's 69, July 20, 1853. During the early 1850's non-opium firms like Gibb Livingston or Ripley Smith occasionally bought 5 or 10 chests of opium, perhaps for some local use (see vol. no. 223, account book for opium transactions, Heard Papers).

60. FO 17/204, Bonham's 100.

61. Established 1821; R. C. W., Singapore Almanack for 1856.

62. FO 17/209, Tennent to Addington, Oct. 1, 1853; FO 17/198, Clarendon's 71 to Bonham, Oct. 4; Addington to Board of Trade, Nov. 1; Booth to Addington, Nov. 10, 1853; Clarendon's 84 to Bonham, Nov. 12, 1853.

63. See IWSM-HF, 8.15b, 17; 10.25b.

64. NCH, Sept. 10, 1853, letter of A. B. Cabaniss, NCH, Sept. 10, 1853. Liu is also mentioned in CSK, 182, biography of Chi-er-hang-a and I-liang (chüan 401 and 377 in index).

65. Among contemporary sources, G. Schlegel, Thian Ti Hwui, The Hung-League or Heaven-Earth League (Batavia, 1866), p. 232, gives

Chinese text and translation for laws, ritual, etc.: A. Wylie, Chinese Researches (Shanghai, 1897), pt. 1, "Literary," p. 110 et seq. (same article printed in Shanghai Almanac for 1854 and Miscellany), mentions some 20 societies, and gives copy in Chinese, with English translation, of Shanghai Triads' seal; Ward and Stirling, The Hung Society (London, 1925-26, 3 vols.) interprets at length the significance of the society as found in Singapore; B. Favre, Les Sociétés Secrètes en Chine (Paris, 1933), gives a useful if unoriginal survey; see bibliography in Hsiao I-shan, "T'ien-ti-hui ch'i-yuan k'ao" (The origin of the "Heaven and Earth" Society) in Chung-shan wen-hua chiao-yü-kuan chi-k'an (Quarterly Review of the Sun Yat-sen Institute for Advancement of Culture and Education, Nanking), II.3: 777-788 (Autumn 1935). "The Triad and other Secret Societies" were ordered suppressed in Hongkong (Ord. 12 of 1845, Oct. 20, amending Ord. 1 of 1845, CM, Oct. 30, 1845). As early as 1835 W. C. Milne had described the esoteric symbols and seal, and some of the ritual of the Triads, including their separating the character Hung into a sequence of parts sounding san-pa-er-shih-i and therefore meaning "three hundred and twenty-one"; cp. CR, XIV: 59-69 (1845), a paper read to the Royal Asiatic Society in 1835. Ibid., XVIII: 281-95 (1849), presents further data.

66. NCH, Aug. 17, Oct. 5, 1850; Mar. 29, 1851. A peasant outbreak occurred at Tsingpu about June 1, 1853, under a certain Chou Li-ch'un, who then seized Kiating on Sept. 5. Toyama Gunji, Taihei tengoku, p. 33.

67. Shang-hai-hsien chih (ed. 1871). The following account is based chiefly on the accounts given in ibid., 32 et seq.; NCH, passim; A. Wylie, Chinese Researches; Wm. Lockhart, The Medical Missionary in China (London, 1861); Robt. Fortune, A Residence among the Chinese (London, 1857) - the last three being able eye-witnesses; Consul Alcock's dispatches, FO 17, passim; IWSM-HF, passim. Montalto de Jesus, Historic Shanghai (Shanghai, 1909), is picturesque and detailed, not entirely accurate; Capt. Fishbourne, Impressions of China (London, 1855), and J. Scarth, Twelve Years in China (Edinburg, 1860) both give first hand accounts. Hudson Taylor saw conditions from the inside in 1854; Dr. and Mrs. H. Taylor, Hudson Taylor in Early Years. Lanning and Couling, The History of Shanghai, p. 299 et seq., is based chiefly on NCH. Chinese accounts include Hsü Wei-nan, "Shang-hai Hsiao-tao-hui luan-shih ti shih-mo" ("Account of the Knife society insurrection at Shanghai"), in I-ching, XXVI: 28-31 (Mar. 20, 1937); Hsi Ti-ch'en, "Hsiao-tao-hui yü T'ai-p'ing t'ien-kuo shih-ch'i ti Shang-hai wai-chiao" (The Small Knife Society and foreign relations at Shanghai in the Taiping period), in Shang-hai-shih t'ung-chih-kuan ch'i-k'an (Bulletin of gazetteer office of the City of Shanghai), I: 123-146 (1933).

68. The prefecture in Fukien, not the district in Kiangsu. Hsü Wei-nan ("Shang-hai Hsiao-tao-hui") describes how the various Kwangtung and Fukien gilds joined together to form the Small Sword Society at Shanghai.

69. NCH, Sept. 10, 1853.

70. The contents of Wu's treasury were stated in the American records to be $300,000, in the Chinese records Tls. 30-40,000, in NCH, $200,000.

71. NCH, Sept. 10, 1853.

72. China, 8, Marshall's 31, Sept. 21, 1853. Wu's escape to the barbarians was notorious, and is even mentioned in CSK, 182 (biog. of Chi-er-hang-a), which states he went into hiding in a consulate.

73. "... gone a-Wooing— and our constant readers will not require us to describe the quality of the amusement ... we would say in memory of the late Intendant that, speaking after the manner of arithmeticians, the good that he did may be denoted by a 0;— the purity and loyalty of his conduct a Chemist would describe as gas ... of which Webster says 'Gases are invisible except when colored, which happens in a few instances.'" (NCH, Oct. 8, 1853).

REFERENCES: CHAPTER 22

1. NCH, Sept. 10, 1853; Fortune, A Residence, p. 120; cp. Wetmore, Recollections, p. 15.

2. I have dealt with the substance of this chapter and the next more fully in four articles in the Chinese Social and Political Science Review for 1935-36 (see in bibliography); it is also summarized in Morse, Submission, pp. 12-24, and Wright, Hart, pp. 91-110. The present discussion is condensed accordingly. For earlier accounts by Mr. Wright see his The Origin and Development of the Chinese Customs Service: 1843-1911 (Shanghai, 1939, 147 pp., for private circulation only), ch. ii; and China's Struggle for Tariff Autonomy: 1843-1938 (Shanghai, 1938), ch. ii.

3. See George Hughes, "The Small Knife Rebels (An Unpublished Chapter of Amoy History)," which is evidently based on the British consular documents. Both these sources agree in general with Liu Lien-k'o, Pang-hui san-pai-nien ko-ming shih (History of the three hundred years revolution of Chinese secret societies), p. 87. See also accounts of the Amoy rising in NCH, June 4, 1853; A. Wylie, Chinese Researches; Fishbourne, Impressions of China. Ch'ing-shih lieh-chuan, 42.12 (biography of Wang I-te) is incorrect in stating that Amoy fell in the 8th month. CR, XX: 49 (1851), states that Ch'en's corpse was sent "in a sedan to the residence of the British Consul" -- this is perhaps the degree of exaggeration to be expected in transmission of the story from Amoy to Canton. CR also says he was "born at Singapore of a Malayan mother" and could read and write English.

4. See BA, Local corresp., May-June 1853. Italics inserted.

5. BA, Local corresp., May-November 1853; Robertson's 93, Nov. 14, 1853.

6. BA, Robertson's 104, Dec. 1; Bonham's 66, Dec. 12, 1853.

7. See Cambridge History of British Foreign Policy, II, ch. vi.

8. "Ministre plenipotentiaire en Chine 20 fev. 1851, rappelé par décret du 15 avril 1852, rétabli par décret du 19 Oct. 1852"; H. Cordier, L'Expedition de Chine de 1857-58, p. 5.

9. One degree of rank below a minister. Caleb Cushing had been envoy extraordinary and minister plenipotentiary, but after him the post did not again achieve that rank until the appointment of Wm. B. Reed, Apr. 18, 1857. John W. Davis, Marshall's predecessor, had departed from China on May 24 or 25, 1850. During Daniel Webster's term as secretary of state, two men (Nelson of Tenn. and Blunt of N. Y.) were appointed and resigned. Marshall, the third, was appointed Aug. 4, 1852. Under Pierce's administration, with Marcy secretary of state, a successor (Walker of Miss.) was appointed on June 22, 1853, and resigned. Robert M. McLane of Md. was then appointed, Oct. 18, 1853, but Marshall continued actually in office until his departure from China, Jan. 27, 1854. Cp. Tyler Dennett, Americans in Eastern Asia, p. 705; FO 17/169, Bonham's 100 of Sept. 27, 1850.

10. FO 17/198, Clarendon's 29 to Bonham, May 28; 24, May 7; 37, July 8; 34, June 24, 1853.

11. FO 17/204, Bonham to Clarendon, Aug. 4, 1853; FO 17/198, no. 70 to Bonham.

12. China Instructions, 1, Marcy's 8 to Marshall, June 7, 1853; quoted in part by Dennett, Eastern Asia, p. 213.

13. See sketches of Marshall's life in R. B. Poore, The Political Register and Congressional Directory (Boston, 1878); Appleton's Cyclopaedia of American Biography (J. G. Wilson and J. Fiske, ed., New York 1888); A Biographical Congressional Directory (61st Congress, 2nd Sess., Sen. Doc. 654, Washington, 1913).

14. China, 8, Marshall to Com. Aulick, in Marshall's 4, Feb. 8, 1853. On Marshall's long squabble with the U. S. Navy in 1853, see Chester Bain's somewhat over-sympathetic article, "Commodore Matthew Perry, Humphrey Marshall, and the Taiping Rebellion."

15. Ibid., Marshall's 25, Aug. 4, 1853. Parker to Marshall, Aug. 16, 1853: "I have the honor, if such it may be considered, to be in receipt of your [letter]. You had broken the seal and opened a dispatch to my address from the Secretary of State [and told others of the contents]."

16. FO 17/200, Bonham to Hammond, private, Apr. 13, 1853.

17. China, 8, Marshall's 31, Sept. 21, 1853.

18. Unsigned art. (by Alcock) reviewing Marshall's published correspondence, in Bombay Quarterly Review, October 1855, p. 228.

19. IWSM-HF, 6.24b-26b, mem. of I-liang, rec'd July 20, 1853; and edict; cp. 27-28, mem. of Yeh Ming-ch'en, rec'd July 25, 1853.

20. China, 8, Marshall's 21, July 10, 1853.

21. Alcock in Bombay Quarterly, loc. cit. Bonham firmly avoided making this an incident (25 to Clarendon, Apr. 18, FO 17/200), and Clarendon approved his tact (48 to Bonham, Aug. 6, 1853, FO 17/198).

22. FO 97/99, Alcock's 75 to Bonham, Oct. 22, in Bonham's 128, Nov. 10; see also his 67, Sept. 7, in Bonham's 104.

23. See Wright, Hart, p. 92 ff.

24. Ibid., Notification to British Community, Shanghai, Sept. 9 (in Bonham's 109, Sept. 26, 1853). The form used was as follows: "We hereby promise to pay forty days after sight on demand the sum of Taels — at Exch.— = $ — being amount of duties due by us on Imports and Exports per British ship — as per specification handed in by us this day to H. B. M. Consul, to be paid to the Chinese Superintendent of Customs provided that the sanction of H. B. M.'s Government to that effect be obtained." (in Bonham's 15, Jan. 23, 1853, FO 97/99).

25. FO 17/310, Alcock to Bowring, Dec. 4, 1855, in Bowring's 386.

26. China, 8, notification of Sept. 9, in Marshall's 31, Sept. 21, 1853. The American rules differed from the British only in (1) omitting in rule 4 the phrase "with the addition of tonnage dues," (2) omitting all of rule 6, and (3) omitting the proviso just noted, that the sanction of the home government must be received. Cunningham stated in a letter of Apr. 27, 1854 (Forbes Papers, case 1) that the American notes also required U. S. Government approval, but this seems to have been true only later, in December 1853.

27. The guaranty read: "In consequence of our inability to obtain any statement of the amount of duties due on the 'Preussischer Adler,' we have to request your handing us the papers of that vessel so as to admit of her clearing today; and in consideration of your so doing, we guarantee to hold you harmless from all charge that, at any time, may be made against you for recovery of same, by any properly authorized officer of the Imperial Government, and to subscribe to any conditions that may be adopted as a general measure of security by the other consuls here for their protection under similar circumstances." (In Shanghai Chamber of Commerce to East India and China Association of London, in letter to Clarendon, Nov. 17, 1853, FO 97/99).

28. China, 8, American firms (Smith, King and Co., Wetmore and Co., Augustine Heard and Co., Bull, Nye and Co.) to Marshall, Sept. 12, in Marshall's 30, Sept. 15, 1853.

29. Ibid.

30. NCH, Sept. 17, 1853 (Edit.): "Never was there a better opportunity for making Shanghai a Free Port (similar to Trieste) and thus throwing on the Chinese merchants the disagreeable onus of arranging duties with their own venal Government."

31. See corresp. in FO 97/99, a special volume on the duty question; also FO 17/205, Bonham's 116 of Oct. 10; FO 17/198, Clarendon's 96 of Nov. 24, 1853.

32. See letters, editorials, and proclamations in translation, NCH, Sept. 10 and 17, Oct. 1, 1853. The Shanghai Almanac for 1855 gives a translation from the Peking Gazette of Dec. 8, 1853, which contains a specious explanation of the Shanghai

rising and later disorders. For a discussion of the complex relationship between the Triads and the Taipings, see Lo Er-kang, T'ai-p'ing t'ien-kuo shih k'ao-cheng chi, pp. 17-30.

33. NCH, Mar. 19, Apr. 2, 1853; appeals of the Kiangsu governor to the Shanghai consuls are noted in FO 17/200, Bonham to Malmesbury, Mar. 11, and to Russell, Mar. 28, 1853; also noted in Morse, Conflict, p. 454; Fortune, A Residence among the Chinese, pp. 9-10; and other works. The article by Toyama Gunji, "Taiheiran ni okeru Shinchō no gaikoku ni taisuru enjo yōsei" (The Ch'ing dynasty's requests for help from the foreign powers during the Taiping Rebellion), passes over this period and deals with 1861.

34. See IWSM-HF, 6.12, memorial of Hsiang Jung; 6.13, Yang Wen-ting; also referred to in 6.29b-30, mem. of Yeh Ming-ch'en; see also 6.10b, mem. of Yang Wen-ting.

35. See NCH, Apr. 30, 1853; Sept. 21, Sept. 28, Nov. 2, 1850; June 4, Oct. 1, 1853. B. Lubbock, The Opium Clippers, p. 349, says the Antelope was lost in the Whangpu in 1852 and sold at auction for the benefit of the underwriters. Wu's naval activities are described at length by Meadows, The Chinese and their Rebellions, p. 195 et seq., and noted by Gideon Chen, Tseng Kuo-fan, pp. 28-9, quoting THL, 20.6 and 19.

36. IWSM-HF, Supp. 147.

37. Lanning and Couling, History of Shanghai, p. 308, based on NCH.

38. IWSM-HF, Supp. 133.

39. Lockhart, Medical Missionary, p. 301.

40. See CSK, 182 for his biography; Ch'ing-shih lieh-chuan, 43.15b is more complete .

41. IWSM-HF, 7.18-19.

42. T'ung-chih Shang-hai-hsien chih, 2.2b et seq.; Lockhart, Medical Missionary, passim, gives a vivid description.

43. Shanghai Almanac for 1854, List of Foreign Residents; NCH, May 3, 1851, census of British population.

44. NCH, Apr. 9, 1853, notification by Alcock, Apr. 8.

45. FO 97/99, Wade to Bonham, private, quoted in Bonham's 109, Sept. 26, 1853.

46. China, 8, Marshall to E, Governor-general of Siang-kiang (sic), Sept. 20, in his 31, Sept. 21, 1853.

47. For biographies of I-liang, see Hummel; and Ch'ing-shih lieh-chuan, 48.45b.

48. China, 8, Eliang (also at times romanized Eleang) to Marshall, in Marshall's 34, Oct. 30, 1853.

49. IWSM-HF, Supp. 126, memorial of I-liang, rec'd Dec. 13, 1853.

50. Correspondence in Alcock's notification of Oct. 19, in Bonham's 128, Nov. 10, 1853, FO 97/99; and in Marshall's 34 as above.

51. FO 17/205, Bonham's 116 to Clarendon, Oct. 10, 1853. Clarendon approved the exclusion of "Samqua, the ex-Taotai." (no. 99 to Bonham, Nov. 30, 1853, FO 17/198).

52. Cp. Alcock to Wu, Jan. 30, 1854: "The admittance of your authority would have utterly negatived those measures of self-defense which we had been most unwillingly compelled to adopt, while the support of Your Excellency with an armed force of our own ... would have been no less inconsistent with that ... neutrality we have been strictly enjoined to observe." (In Overland Friend of China, Feb. 10, in Bonham's 29, Feb. 11, 1854, FO 97/99.)

53. FO 97/99, see Bonham's 128.

54. Ibid. Cp. Shanghai Almanac for 1855: "H. E. the Taoutae ... threatened to take steps to collect duties inland from the Native Merchants, which H. B. M.'s Consul considered to be a hasty and ill-advised expression of opinion on the part of his Excellency."

55. See China, 8, Marshall's 34, Oct. 30, and enclosures, esp. Cunningham to Marshall, Oct. 19, in Cunningham to China Mail, Oct. 22, enclosing Liu Li-ch'uan to consuls, Oct. 16, 1853.

56. Ibid., Marshall's 34.

57. Ibid.

58. Augustine Heard and Co., Smith, King and Co., Wetmore and Co., Bull, Nye and Co., to Cunningham, Oct. 30, in Marshall's 35, Nov. 21, 1853, China 8. As to the floating customs, Bull, Nye and Co., later stated: "No one was able to discover its locality"; A. Heard and Co. said the same; and Smith, King and Co. stated that "the boats were far off and often without anyone connected with the Custom House on board, not a single officer or inspector could be found on shore." (Letters of June and July 1854 in McLane's 21, China, 10). Apparently the boats were actually there, but poorly staffed.

59. NCH, Oct. 15, 29, Nov. 5, 1853; Jan. 28, 1854.

60. FO 17/99, Cunningham to Alcock, Jan. 30, in Bonham's 38, Mar. 20, 1854.

61. See Marshall's 35, China, 8.

62. Marshall's dispatches have misled historians. The American payment of cash duties at Shanghai in 1853 is wrongly reported in two standard works: Tyler Dennett, Americans in Eastern Asia, p. 217, states that "The Americans on the other hand were ordered to pay their duties at the consulate in specie. The American merchants by the decree of the American consul, who was firmly supported by the American Commissioner, were thus placed under a severe handicap with reference to their British competitors. The one paid duties in notes of doubtful value; the other paid in cash." Likewise H. F. MacNair, Far Eastern International Relations (Morse and MacNair), p. 250: "The English required the deposit of promissory notes only, while the Americans required the payment of duties at the consulate in specie. This placed the merchants of the latter at a disadvantage, but enabled Commissioner Marshall

to carry on his policy of supporting the imperial authorities." Both these statements are incorrect. Marshall did not know what was happening.

63. China, 8, enclosure A in Marshall's 37, Dec. 8, 1853.

64. FO 17/206, Bonham to FO, private, Nov. 11, 1853.

65. FO 97/99, Cunningham to Alcock, Jan. 30, in Bonham's 38, Mar. 20, 1854. "The collection of the duties was quietly resumed by the American Vice Consul, and in spite of his own notification, the papers of American ships were not given up at the Consulate until the promissory notes were received." (Smith, King and Co. to McLane, June 13, 1854, in McLane's 21, China, 10). Cunningham's account, summarized above, was reiterated later to the American Commissioner (Cunningham to McLane, May 4, 1854, in Mclane's 21, China, 10).

66. China, 10, A. Heard and Co. to McLane, May 20, 1854, in McLane's 21; China, 8, Cunningham to Marshall, Dec. 24, in Marshall's 38, Jan. 9, 1854.

67. FO 17/205, Bonham's 148, Dec. 9, 1853; China, 8, Marshall to Yeh, Dec. 11, in Marshall's 38, Jan. 9, 1854.

68. NCH, Nov. 5, 1853.

69. See THL-HF, 23.2b, Oct. 5; 24.2b, Dec. 3, 1853. Hung-tan ch'uan are also referred to in this connection, e.g., CSK, "pen-chi", 20, for Apr. 8, 1853.

70. See IWSM-HF, 10.27 and foreign accounts already cited.

71. NCH, Oct. 15, 23, 1852; Nov. 12, 1853; Lockhart, Medical Missionary, p. 300; IWSM-HF, 7.2b, states the rebels had bought 3 foreign-type vessels; ibid., 10.27 refers to 4 foreign-style sailing ships hired by Wu and stationed at Wusung. The Eliza may be the clipper reported landing opium at Singapore in 1841 (Lubbock, Opium Clippers, p. 241) or the Anna Eliza, built at Southampton in 1827, which entered the opium trade in 1846 (ibid., p. 384).

72. Detailed accounts are plentiful, e.g., letters of W. H. Medhurst, NCH, Dec. 17; Cabaniss and Roberts, NCH, Oct. 8; Lockhart, p. 323; and even in IWSM-HF, 7.4b.

73. Lockhart, p. 306.

74. IWSM-HF, 7.2-2b, 3b; see also in 23.24b for Nov. 21, 1853.

75. Lockhart, 294; letter of Rev. Jas. Johnston, May 6, 1854, quoted in Anon., China and the Missions at Amoy (Edinburg, 1854), p. 34.

76. IWSM-HF, 7.2b.

77. Lockhart, p. 322; Scarth, Twelve Years in China, p. 191.

78. See CSK, biographies, 158. The close connection between the foreigners, Wu, Liu Li-ch'uan and the Taipings is stressed in Wang Chih-ch'un's brief summary, Ko-kuo t'ung-shang shih-mo chi, 13.1b-2.

79. T'ung-chih Shang-hai-hsien chih, 11.34b; Scarth, Twelve Years in China, p. 194.

80. IWSM-HF, 7.10, mem. of I-liang and Hsü Nai-chao, rec'd Feb. 21, 1854.

81. NCH, Nov. 19, 1853; Lockhart, p. 302. This incident appears to be referred to in an edict of Dec. 11, 1853, which states that the rebels had bought cannon from the barbarians (THL-HF, 24.6b).

82. Correspondence and notification in NCH, Nov. 19, 1853.

83. IWSM-HF, 7.11b.

84. Ibid., 7.2b, mem. of I-liang and Hsü Nai-chao, rec'd Nov. 21, 1853.

85. IWSM-HF, 8.15b et seq., memorial of Ch'eng Kung-shou, rec'd July 11, 1854.

86. Ibid., 10.25 et seq., mem. of Huang Tsung-han, rec'd Apr. 4, 1855. For Wu's later fate, see note (n) at end of Ch. 23.

87. Ibid., 7.20b, mem. of Hsü Nai-chao, rec'd Apr. 3, 1854.

88. The first full-time United States consul, R. C. Murphy, reached Shanghai on Feb. 15, 1854; see NCH, Feb. 18, 1854. A recent writer in the New Statesman and Nation, London, quoted thence in the Peking & Tientsin Times (July 12, 1934), the Living Age, N.Y. (August 1934) and the Chinese Republic (Oct. 13, 1934), states that "Mr. Cunningham ... in his capacity as American Consul during the Taiping Rebellion, placed his services at the disposal of the Emperor, and at the same time, in his capacity as head of the firm of Russell and Co., sold the rebels not only arms but also a couple of warships." The writer in question ("G.H.") then tells how, during the Shanghai siege in September 1853, some of the shells sold by the Frenchmen Montigny and Remi to the Taiping rebels exploded in the garden of the French Consulate, "damaging not only the building but the French Cathedral." As sometimes happens in journalism, the idea here is no doubt correct while the details are askew; for the month was not September, Montigny had left Shanghai several months before, the rebels were not Taipings, and the French Cathedral was over a mile from the Consulate.

Cunningham's statement: "... I had no business connection with the Toutae & never had, neither has the house to which I belong, since I have been in China nor was I even on terms of friendship.... I had been constantly at war with him upon matters connected with the interests of my countrymen & had had much cause for a feeling of enmity. This feeling disappeared under the circumstances of adversity in which he was placed.... Samqua's character has been traduced by the writers from this place & the South: He was ill-disposed towards foreigners but most faithful to the trust reposed in him by his master. Shanghae has never known so just an administrator of the laws... much of the bitter odium in which he was held... was caused by his stringent measures to suppress smuggling...." (Ms. dated Apr. 27, 1854, case 1, Forbes Papers, Baker Library, Harvard Business School).

89. Alcock in Bombay Quarterly, April 1856, p. 244.

90. THL-HF, 22.24, edict of Sept. 28; 23.10, Oct. 20, 1853. Cp. also edicts of Nov. 1 and Dec. 3, 1853, in Wen-tsung hsien-huang-ti sheng-hsün, 73.3b and 74.1b.

91. IWSM-HF, 7.3b.

92. Ibid., 7.12.

93. Wu to Alcock, Nov. 21, in NCH, Dec. 3, 1853.

94. This proclamation appears in translation in NCH, Feb. 11, 1854 and in Bonham's no. 34 (FO 97/99), but in the latter version emanates from Wu, Superintendent of Silk Revenue at Hangchow (explained to be "an official sent annually from the Court ... to superintend the revenues collected for the privy purse," evidently the Chih-tsao, cp. Mayers, The Chinese Government, no. 325). In both versions the proposal is made by Wu Chien-chang. In I-liang's official biography (CSK, biographies, 158) he himself is given credit for the policy. This policy of stopping exports through Shanghai was announced to the British at Ningpo on Mar. 2, 1854; Governor Hsü had urged it on the Chekiang authorities on Jan. 5, on the ground that the banditti would plunder all teas and silks approaching Shanghai (BN, Twan Taotai, no. 5, to Meadows, Mar. 2, 1854).

95. FO 17/309, Wade to Alcock, May 1, 1854, in Alcock's 45 to Bowring, in Bowring's 182.

96. For Marshall's suspicions, see his 37, Dec. 8, 1853, China, 8.

97. Dr. Tyler Dennett's encomium of "the battle which Marshall had undertaken at Shanghai in defence of the Imperial revenues" (Americans in Eastern Asia, p. 221) seems undeserved. Marshall confessed (no. 38, Jan. 9, 1854), "I am sure I wish the British and French authorities may continue to ... refuse to acknowledge the right of the Chinese ... to collect duties; for that position submitted to by China defines my right clearly, under the second article of the treaty to treat Shanghai as a free port." Marshall imagined that Great Britain would do likewise, "and thus she will add wrong to wrong, while my course will give me all the advantage without ever exposing me to a charge of violating the treaty."

98. See in Marshall's 38, Jan. 9, 1854, China, 8. Cp. Bain, "Commodore Matthew Perry".

99. Form of bond not mentioned in Marshall's dispatches, but given in Bonham's 38, Mar. 20, 1854, FO 97/99.

100. This inference is supported by a subsequent statement of A. Heard and Co. (to McLane, July 19, 1854, in McLane's 21, China, 10), that "vessels continued to clear by depositing notes at the U. S. Consulate until the 14th January, when our notes for clearance of the 'Beverley' were refused at the Consulate and after great difficulty and some personal risk, we succeeded in finding His Excellency Woo Taoutae (in the Camp on the Soochow Creek), who received our notes and granted a grand Chop.

"Further, as regards the case of the 'Beverley," we must observe that at the time the U. S. Consul refused to accept our notes in clearance of her, and referred us to the Chinese authorities, he must have been in possession of Colonel Marshall's instructions to declare the Port Free, as he published the declaration three days afterwards, and no vessel had arrived from the South in the interim. We therefore think it but justice that the 'Beverley' should be placed upon the same footing as the 'Oneida,' which loaded at the same time, and was allowed to leave without paying any duties, or granting any obligation." (The Oneida was dispatched by Bull, Nye and Co. The above letter, perhaps discreetly, omits to mention that, at the same time as the Oneida, the Science was dispatched by Russell and Co.).

101. FO 97/99, Bonham's 38, Mar. 20, 1854 and enclosures.

102. FO 97/99, esp. enclosures in Bonham's 15 to Clarendon, Jan. 23; 29, Feb. 10; 35, Mar. 10; and 38, Mar. 20, 1854.

103. The following summary is based upon the British and American reports, which generally agree: Alcock's "Abstract Return of all Foreign Vessels which have left Shanghae with or without payment of Duties since the 7th September, 1853" (in Bowring's 55, June 12, 1854, FO 97/99); Murphy to McLane, Shanghai, July 30, 1854, and voluminous enclosures from American merchants (in McLane's 21, Nov. 25, 1854, China, 10); letters of Shanghai (British) Chamber of Commerce to Alcock, Feb. 10 and Mar. 1, 1854 (in Bonham's 35, Mar. 10, 1854, FO 97/99; also in NCH, and quoted in Morse, Submission, p. 16); Cunningham's consular report, Dec. 31, 1853 (in Parker's 2, Feb. 22, 1854, China, 9). The American settlement is reported in IWSM-HF, 13.26.

104. Tls. 478,300 would be normally about £ 160,000; but the complexities of exchange at this time at Shanghai forbid offhand calculation; cp. Morse, Conflict, p. 468 et seq. Bonham was "credibly informed" that the bonds held by Alcock amounted to £ 250,000 in January (Bonham's 15, Jan. 23, FO 97/99), and Alcock later estimated them at more than half a million dollars (Bonham's 29, Feb. 10, 1854, FO 97/99).

105. Alcock to Wu, Jan. 30, in Bonham's 29, Feb. 10, FO 97/99.

106. They were: 1 Austrian vessel (Robert, Oct. 29), 2 Spanish (San Benito, Aurora), 2 Siamese (Favorite, Siam) - for all of which there were no consuls at Shanghai; and 2 Prussian vessels (Preussischer Adler, Belliza) for which D. O. King of the American firm of Smith, King and Co. was consul.

107. They were: 3 Dutch vessels (Syren, Hydroose, Willem de Eerst) through T. C. Beale as vice-consul; 1 Hamburg (Esmeralda) through Wm. Hogg as consul; 1 Swedish, consul uncertain. The British merchant-consuls evidently followed the British consul's example.

108. Alcock's 16 to Bonham, Feb. 14, in Bonham's 35, Mar. 10, FO 97/99; reiterated in Alcock's 42 to Bowring, Apr. 3, 1855, in Bowring's 179, FO 17/309.

109. Ibid., Alcock's 16.

110. China, 9, enclosures 15 and 16, in Parker's 2.

111. China, 8, Yeh to Marshall, Jan. 23, in Marshall's 39, Jan. 25, 1854. Humphrey Marshall later was a brigadier-general in the Confederate Army, and "one of the first Confederates whose disabilities were removed by Congress," (Appleton's Cyclopaedia of American Biography, p. 226).

112. Alcock's 16 to Bonham, in Bonham's 35, FO 97/99.

REFERENCES: CHAPTER 23

1. IWSM-HF, Supp. 148, mem. of I-liang and Hsü.

2. The Carolus dollar was still at a premium of 64 per cent; cp. Morse, Conflict, p. 470.

3. FO 97/99, Bonham's 46, Mar. 23, 1854.

4. Ibid., British Chamber of Commerce to Alcock, Feb. 10, encl. in Bonham's 35; Alcock's 32, Apr. 10, encl. in Bowring's 7, Apr. 19, 1854.

5. FO 97/100, Bowring's 55, June 12, 1854.

6. FO 97/99. See Sillar Bros. to Alcock, Feb. 27, 1854; Alcock in reply, Mar. 2, encl. in Bonham's 34 of Mar. 10, 1854. Further corresp. in Bonham's 35 of Mar. 10 and 46 of Mar. 23, 1854.

7. Ibid., Alcock to Bonham, no. 32, Apr. 10, encl. in Bowring's 7 of Apr. 19, 1854.

8. Signed, Smith, King and Co., Wetmore and Co., two of the five American firms; encl. in Adamson to Alcock, Mar. 1, encl. in Bonham's 35, FO 97/99.

9. See data in Alcock's "Abstract Return," encl. in Bowring's 55 of June 12, FO 97/100.

10. The following account of the Aristides is drawn from Alcock to Bonham, Apr. 10, 1854, encl. in Bowring's 7, FO 97/99, containing synopsis of Alcock's correspondence; "papers ... brought to the FO by Mr. Hugh Fleming, Secretary of the Manchester Commercial Association, June 2/54," including Smith,Kennedy to Alcock, Mar. 25, FO 17/219; Manchester Chamber of Commerce to Clarendon, Dec. 27, 1854, FO 17/223; East India and China Association, Liverpool, to Clarendon, Dec. 21, and Sillar Bros. to Clarendon, Dec. 18, FO 97/100; NCH, Apr. 1, May 13, 1854, and passim.

11. FO 17/170, Alcock to Bonham, Oct. 5, encl. in Bonham to Palmerston, Oct. 28, 1850; FO 17/174, see Palmerston to Bonham Jan. 15, 1851, re Aberdeen's 45 of June 4, 1844.

12. NCH, May 13, 1854; cp. Alcock's 32 to Bonham, Apr. 10, encl. in Bowring's 7, FO 97/99: "In respect to the extraordinary course voluntarily adopted by the Taoutae in the case of the Aristides, I stepped very much out of the way repeatedly to warn him of the consequences."

13. "Form of Bond given by the Bremen ship Aristides," encl. in Liverpool East India and China Association to Clarendon, Dec. 21, 1854, FO 97/100. Synopsis of Smith, Kennedy to Alcock, Mar. 23, encl. in Bowring's 7, FO 97/99, states ten vessels were listed.

14. NCH, Apr. 1, 1854.

15. IWSM-HF, 10.26b, mem. of Huang Tsung-han, rec'd. Apr. 4, 1855.

16. FO 97/99, Alcock's 32, in Bowring's 7. Robert C. Murphy, first official United States consul at Shanghai, entered upon his official duties on Mar. 6 (Murphy to McLane, May 1, 1854, encl. in McLane's 21, China, 10). On the same day he demanded an apology from the taotai for the arrest of an American pilot boat and insult to the flag (cp. Morse, Conflict, p. 421, quoting NCH, Mar. 11, 1854). This he had obtained on Mar. 21, just before the correspondence quoted above.

17. Form of bond given by the British ship Dumfries, Mar. 30, which paid exactly half duties on 3678 packages tea, weight 1938 piculs 90 catties (encl. in Liverpool East India and China Assoc. to Clarendon, Dec. 21, 1854 and in Sillar Bros. to Clarendon, Dec. 18, FO 97/100).

"We hereby promise to pay three days after demand to His Excellency Woo Taoutae Superintendent of Customs &c. &c. the sum of Two thousand four hundred and twenty three Taels, 6 Mace, and 3 Candareens of Sycee for duties on our Exports per Dumfries, provided that all the following Vessels pay if not full duties at least two Taels per Picul Tea, and Nine Taels per Picul Silk, duty on their entire Cargoes.

"The Vessels are the Frederick VII Mermaid Rose Standish Bombay Onward Early Bird Jacob Bell. Signed Sillar Brothers."

18. FO 97/100, Wu to Alcock, Mar. 25, encl. in Bowring's 55, June 12; synopsis in Bowring's 7, FO 97/99; Chinese version not found.

19. Ibid., Alcock's 32, Apr. 10, encl. in Bowring's 7, Apr.18, 1854.

20. IWSM-HF, Supp. 141, a memorial from Canton, dated Dec. 19, 1853, rec'd. Feb. 17, 1854, reported a Shanghai revenue of Tls. 545,687 for the period Dec. 7, 1852, to July 1, 1853.

21. IWSM-HF makes no reference to the system nor does a review of two years customs administration at Shanghai (for 1853-55) by Chi-er-hang-a in IWSM-HF, Supp. 246.

22. Hsü was acting governor of Kiangsu from the third month of 1853 (Apr. 8 - May 7) and was made governor on Apr. 9, 1854; see Hsiao I-shan, Ch'ing-tai tu-fu piao, 174b, and THL-HF, 26.8.

23. Cp. ibid., 21. 19b: "Wu Chien-chang is well acquainted with the barbarian nature, it is not feasible for him to go far away from Shanghai."

24. IWSM-HF, 7.4; cp. NCH, Dec. 24, 1853.

25. IWSM-HF, 7.4b-5.

26. Ibid., 7.4b, 9b, rec'd at Peking Jan. 2, Jan. 24, 1854.

27. Ibid., 7.29, rec'd May 17, 1854.

28. THL-HF, 24.27b, edict of Jan. 24, 1854. A vivid account is given by Lockhart, p. 205: "a number of Canton men from the district of Kia-ying-chau [Chia-ying-chou, Kwangtung] had determined to go over to the Imperialists .... The Triads discovered the plot ... watched for the sig-

nal and ... caught two hundred of them in various parts of the city ... [nearly all of whom] were beheaded in front of the Confucian temple."

29. THL-HF, 25.9b, edict of Feb. 21, 1854. CSL-HF, 119.13, gives complete copy of same edict, which is abbreviated in THL.

30. THL-HF, 26.3b, 4b, edicts of Apr. 2, 1854; noted by Gideon Chen (Tseng Kuo-fan, p. 8), quoting Shih-ch'ao sheng-hsun, Hsien-feng period, 21.3; also THL-HF, 25.4, edict of Mar. 8, 1854.

31. Cp. IWSM-HF, 7.20b-22b, mem. from Hsü on British obstructions.

32. Ibid., 7.23, edict of Apr. 19, 1854, refers to the open clash of arms.

33. IWSM-HF, 7.20b-21, rec'd Apr. 19, 1854.

34. Lockhart, p. 312.

35. IWSM-HF, 7.11, rec'd Feb. 21, 1854. Ch. B.-Maybon and Jean Fredet, Histoire de la Concession Française de Changhai (Paris, 1929, based on French archives) gives a detailed picture of the situation at Shanghai. Consul Edan reported (Mar. 27, 1854) that the French Minister in January made efforts "pour interposer ses bons offices et amener la soumission volontaire des insurgés ..." (p. 82).

36. Cp. ibid., pp. 92-97. W. S. Wetmore, Recollections of Life in the Far East, gives the full account of an American participant; for further details see NCH and British and American corresp., passim.

37. Wetmore, Recollections ("Recollections of the Battle of Muddy Flat").

38. FO 17/219, Alcock to Hammond, personal letter, Apr. 13, 1854, marked by Clarendon "Circulate."

39. IWSM-HF, 7.18, 19, 20b (rec'd Apr. 19, 1854), 22b (edict, same date), 23b (rec'd Apr. 30), 28 (rec'd May 17).

40. IWSM-HF, 7.19, memorial of Hsü Nai-chao, rec'd Apr. 19, 1854.

41. Ibid., 7.22b, edict of Apr. 19, 1854.

42. See Ben Poore, The Political Register (Boston, 1878), p. 516. McLane held office as commissioner to China, Oct. 15, 1853 – Dec. 12, 1854. He was afterwards minister to Mexico (1859-60) and to France (1885-89). Cp. Dennett, p. 191.

43. China, 9, McLane's 1, Mar. 20, 1854.

44. FO 97/99, Bonham's 47, Mar. 23, 1854.

45. See Eitel, 297; China, 9, McLane's 3, Apr. 20, 1854.

46. FO 17/213, Bowring's 1, Apr. 15, 1854; FO 97/99, Bowring's 15 to Alcock, Apr. 18, quoting Alcock's 32 of Apr. 10, encl. in Bowring's 7 of Apr. 19, 1854.

47. Ibid., Alcock's 32 to Bonham, Apr. 10, encl. in Bowring's 7, Apr. 19, 1854.

48. FO 17/207, Granville to Russell, Jan. 18, 1853.

49. J. Bowring, The Political and Commercial Importance of Peace, A Lecture delivered in the Hall of Commerce, London (London, n.d., Peace Society), evidently published before the outbreak of the Arrow War of 1856-58.

50. FO 17/207 (Domestic various).

51. Bowring and Clarendon were old acquaintances. Cp. Lammer Moor, Bowring, Cobden and China, a Memoir (Edinburgh, 1857), p. 6; Maxwell, Life of Clarendon, p. 62, gives an account of their joint commercial mission to France in 1831, an "entirely successful" enterprise; Gladstone (War in China, speech of Mar. 3, 1857, pub. London, 1857, p. 40) stated "that [Bowring's] appointment was made ... without the knowledge or consent of the Cabinet ... it was ... allowed to pass [by Lord Aberdeen] with a declaration that the consular services of Sir J. Bowring would doubtless have given him a knowledge of China which might be useful ...." For Bowring's memoranda to Clarendon in 1853-54, see FO 17/212, e.g., Jan. 7, Jan. 20 (re Siam); Feb. 8 (re interpreters); Feb. 13 (re Amoy riot claims); Feb. 16 (re light-draught warships).

52. Cp. Manchester Chamber of Commerce and Manufactures to Clarendon, Jan. 28, 1854, FO 97/99; FO to Commercial Association of Manchester, Feb. 28, 1854, FO 12/220. For Bowring's instructions in 1854 see FO 17/210, drafts, nos. 1, 2, and 3 to Dr. Bowring, Feb. 13, 1854. No. 2 (re treaty revision) is given in Morse, Conflict, app. Q.

53. FO List, 1854, 2nd ed.

54. Bowring's Autobiography, quoted by Eitel, p. 297; ibid., p. 295; Lane-Poole, Life of Sir Harry Parkes, reflects the derogatory opinion of Bowring's egotism.

55. FO 97/99, cp. Addington to Manchester Chamber of Commerce, Jan. 30, and to East India and China Assoc., Liverpool, Feb. 6, 1854.

56. Ibid., Bagley to Addington, Feb. 16, 1854; Bowring to Addington, Jan. 21, 1854.

57. Ibid., no. 15, Jan. 23, 1854.

58. Ibid., Addington to Board of Trade, Mar. 21, 1854; Bonham's 29, Feb. 10, 1854.

59. China, 9, McLane's 1, Mar. 20; 3, Apr. 20, 1854.

60. FO 97/100, Bowring's 31; for Bowring's opinion to Alcock Apr. 18, see Bowring's 7, FO 97/99.

61. Ibid. At this time he sent to Shanghai to relieve Vice-consul Wade of the duties of interpreter, a certain H. N. Lay, who had made good progress in the Canton and Mandarin dialects. Bowring's 11, Apr. 20, FO 17/213.

62. U. S. sloop Plymouth, U. S. S. Susquehannah, British brig Grecian, steamers Encounter and Styx, French steamer Colbert; see China, 9, McLane's 4, May 8, 1854.

63. FO 17/213, Bowring's 21 to Alcock, May 16, re Alcock to Bowring of May 3, encl. in Bowring's 28, May 16, 1854. It must be noted that Alcock mentioned "the menace of a war with Russia" as partial justification for his procedure, ibid.; Clarendon approved it (98 to Bowring, Aug. 5, 1854, FO 17/210). Two American receiving ships

had already been withdrawn from Wusung; Morse, Conflict, p. 465: "There is no record to show whether the withdrawal of the American ships was due to ... [the arrival of R. C. Murphy, Feb. 15], or to the increasing risks of the commercial situation."

64. Russell and Co. to Murphy, Apr. 24, re 58 bales silk, Augustine Heard and Co. to Murphy, Apr. 26, re 136 cases silks, encl. in Murphy to McLane, Apr. 27, encl. B in no. 4, China, 9; cp. Wu to Alcock, May 22, 1854, encl. in Bowring's 55, June 12, FO 97/100.

65. China, 9, McLane's 4; cp. Alcock's 40 to Bowring, May 1, and McLane to Bowring, May 8, encl. in Bowring's 31, FO 97/100.

66. Consuls to Wu, May 1, encl. in Bowring's 55, June 12, FO 97/100 and in McLane's 4, China, 9.

67. McLane reported this was done "according to my suggestion"; ibid.

68. Alcock's 40, May 1, encl. in Bowring's 31, FO 97/100, partly quoted in Morse, Submission, p. 23; cp. also A. Michie, The Englishman in China, I,148-54.

69. IWSM-HF, 7.28b, rec'd May 17, 1854. Chi-er-hang-a had been promoted from taotai (Ch'ang-Chen-t'ung hai-tao) to Kiangsu provincial treasurer by an edict of Apr. 2 (THL-HF, 26.4b) and had received a peacock feather for efforts at Shanghai, edict of Apr. 30 (THL-HF, 26.17).

70. McLane's 5 (May 21, 1854, China, 9) is not clear as to the date of this interview, which evidently occurred after the date of his dispatch no. 4 (May 4); Hsü (IWSM-HF, 7.29b, rec'd May 17, 1854) states it was May 3, quoting Wu; I-liang (ibid., 32b, rec'd May 24) quotes Wu's report of it, which he received May 7. IWSM-HF, Supp. 166-67, a memorial from Hsü, also reports on McLane's proposed trip (rec'd May 10).

71. China, 9, McLane's 5, May 21, 1854.

72. FO 97/100, Consuls to Foreign Community, May 9, encl. in Bowring's 55. Cp. also Morse, Submission, p. 17, quoting NCH, May 20, 1854.

73. Alcock's "Abstract Return," encl. in Bowring's 55.

74. Encl. in ibid.

75. IWSM-HF, 7.30, mem. rec'd May 17, 1854; 32, edict same date.

76. Ibid., 33, rec'd May 24, 1854. On this whole period, see M. Banno's valuable study of Ch'ing diplomacy in the treaty revision negotiations of 1854 (Kokusaihō gaikō zasshi, 48.4 and 6 (October and December 1949).

77. IWSM-HF, 7.34b-35.

78. Translations in McLane's 6, June 14, 1854, China, 9.

79. FO 17/223, Stirling's 41 to Admiralty, June 19, 1854, in Admiralty to FO, Dec. 19, 1854.

80. Reported by Chi-er-hang-a, IWSM-HF, 8.30, mem. rec'd Aug. 30, 1854. IWSM-HF, Supp. 170, report of Hsü Nai-chao, July 7, 1854, indicates the very correct diplomatic language used by the Kiangsu authorities in these negotiations.

81. Among the various works on Shanghai, see Kotenev, Shanghai: its Mixed Court and Council, p. 9. These events were reported in FO 17/214.

82. Figures below are based on Alcock's "Return" in Bowring's 55, June 12, 1854, FO 97/100; Alcock's 42 in Bowring's 179, Apr. 3, 1855, FO 17/309; Murphy to McLane, July 30, 1854, and other enclosures in McLane's 21, China, 10.

83. Statement of R. I. Gilman and G. G. Nicol in letter to Bowring, July 4, FO 97/100.

84. FO 17/213, Bowring to Hammond, Private. May 18, 1854.

85. FO 97/100, Bowring's 55, June 12, 1854.

86. I. e., his no. 6, June 14, in China, 10, according to Bowring's 61, June 17, FO 17/214. This dates the interview between June 14-17.

87. Corresp. referred to in IWSM-HF, 8.26, mem. of I-liang rec'd Aug. 8, 1854.

88. FO 97/100, Bowring's 68, June 27, 1854.

89. McLane's 7, China, 10.

90. See China, 10, McLane to Eleang, encl. in his 8, July 28.

91. IWSM-HF, 8.20-20b, rec'd July 15, 1854. IWSM-HF, Supp. 173, report of I-liang, July 15, 1854, gives his very orthodox reply to McLane that all matters must be referred to Canton.

92. Ibid., 21, (hsin-kuan); the new customs referred to thus briefly may have been either that formerly established on the Bund outside the city walls or that just recently set up on Soochow Creek.

93. Ibid., 21; 22, edict of July 15, 1854. For other accounts of McLane's meeting with I-liang, see Toyama Gunji, Taihei tengoku, pp. 48-50; Yano Jin'ichi, Kindai Shina gaikō shi, p. 409.

94. McLane's, 8, July 27, China, 10.

95. Bowring's 68, June 27, FO 97/100.

96. Memo. encl. in Bowring's 74, July 6, FO 17/214. Stirling and Chi-er-hang-a were also present.

97. Heu [Hsü] to Bowring, July 1, encl. in Bowring's 74, FO 17/214.

98. See Wright, Hart, p. 103. IWSM-HF, 8.21b, rec'd July 15, 1854.

99. For edicts degrading Hsü for incapacity in recapturing Shanghai, and promoting Chi-er-hang-a, see THL-HF, 27.13, July 7, 1854; referred to also in IWSM-HF, 8.12, edict of July 7. A memorial from Hsü as Governor was received at Peking July 15, ibid., 21b.

100. Ibid., 31, rec'd Aug. 30, 1854.

101. Encl. in Bowring's 100, July 27, 1854, FO 17/215.

102. Eleang to McLane, June 29, in McLane's 8, July 27, China, 10.

103. McLane to Eleang, July 18, ibid. On Aug. 2 the three consuls wrote to Wu that they had

"reason to believe that any money payment finally determined on can hardly be under a million dollars. And to this satisfactory solution all things we hope are tending." (Consuls to Wu, in Bowring's 19, 1856, FO 17/312).

104. McLane (no. 7, July 7) enclosed the consular notification of July 6 (quoted below) as "an outline of the system agreed upon with" the governor-general (viceroy).

105. Bowring's 77, FO 97/100.

106. Alcock's 56, July 6, encl. in Bowring's 77, FO 97/100. For a summary of the "Minutes of a Conference of June 29, 1854," see Wright, Hart, pp. 104-105.

107. FO 97/100, encl. in Bowring's 77, July 7, 1854; China, 10, McLane's 8. Lanning's Memorandum on the establishment of the ... Customs in 1854 (Customs Publication, Shanghai, 1915), adds nothing to this account.

108. See "Extracts from Peking Gazettes, 1856" in Miscellany or Companion to the Shanghai Almanac for 1857; also in NCH, passim. Dates in these summaries are imprecise: cp. THL-HF, 36.1b, edict of Dec. 13, 1855; THL-HF, 37.6b, edict of Mar. 12, 1856.

109. IWSM-HF, 13.28, mem. of I-liang rec'd Oct. 11, 1856.

110. Cp. ibid., 19.10, 20, 20.2b.

111. The tortuous complexities of the back duty settlement, in which almost everyone reversed himself at least once, is summarized in my article, "The Creation of the Foreign Inspectorate" CSPSR, XX.1: 70-89 (April 1936), and in Wright, Hart, pp. 107-110.

REFERENCES: CHAPTER 24

1. See Wright, Hart and the Chinese Customs, Introduction.

2. A. Whitney Griswold, The Far Eastern Policy of the United States, p. 65: "Rockhill gratefully assured Hippisley that he was but the latter's 'mouthpiece'." Cp. Chas. S. Campbell, Special Business Interests and the Open Door Policy, p. 54. George Kennan points out that the Open Door notes "did not represent English policy of the moment" (American Diplomacy, ch. ii, see p. 36).

3. Morse, Subjection, p. 407. Cp. Wright, Hart, passim.

4. Wright, Hart, pp. 720-22, quotes Hippisley's memoranda for Rockhill.

5. See Uchida Naosaku, "Zai-Shi Eikoku", for a survey of J. M. & Co. subsidiaries.

6. This is the theme of Pelcovits' Old China Hands.

7. See J. K. Fairbank, "The Definition of the Foreign Inspectors' Status, 1854-55."

8. Cp. Fairbank, "The Manchu-Chinese Dyarchy in the 1840's", a statistical study.

BIBLIOGRAPHY

The following lists of works cited in the text avoid the useless display of simply listing all publications available, and lack of space forbids evaluation of each item. A critical bibliography should rest on far greater use than I have yet made of these intricate masses of literature; many more volumes will be based on them, particularly on the Chinese documentary collections. The present volume adumbrates only faintly the vast scope of the records awaiting study.

My primary sources have been the unpublished correspondence of the British officials and the recently published correspondence between Chinese authorities in the provinces and at Peking, supplemented from the United States, French, and Chinese archives. The British consuls, being closest to the scene of action on the China coast, left the most detailed record of events there. Complete files (either drafts or originals) of consular correspondence were kept at each port, arranged in the following three major series:

(1) *To* and *From the Superintendency of Trade* (also labelled *Hong Kong*, *Government House*, or *Legation*). The Hongkong end of this correspondence is filed under FO 228 in the Public Record Office in London.

(2) *To* and *From the Chinese Authorities* (sometimes labelled *Superintendent*, i.e., of Customs). English versions only.

(3) *To* and *From Miscellaneous* (or *General Letters*), including correspondence with British officers at other ports or on H.M. vessels, and with local British residents and local foreign consuls.

Despatches received from the Chinese authorities and, ordinarily, the Chinese drafts of those sent to them were filed in the interpreter's office, while English versions of both were filed by the consul as indicated under (2) above.[a]

In London the records of the Superintendency of Trade (filed in the Public Record Office under FO 228, *Embassy and Consular Archives, China*; volumes no. 19-177 are for 1842-54) contain the British minister's correspondence from Hongkong with the consulates and with the Foreign Office. They really form another copy, in draft or in original, of the documents kept in original or in draft by the consulates or by the Foreign Office, respectively. A suprisingly large number of the documents received at the consulates from local sources were enclosed in despatches to Hongkong and thence often to the Foreign Office, so that the foreign secretary usually had at hand copies of nearly all the documents pertinent to any question under consideration. This was possible, in spite of the lack of typewriters, because the actual volume of business was small, often under 100 despatches a year between two given offices.

The *Foreign Office Correspondence, China* (key number FO 17; volumes no. 55-223 are for 1842-54) contains for each year the drafts of despatches from the foreign secretary to the Superintendent of Trade, the form of which often shows the manner of their construction; the despatches received from China, usually bearing notations by the foreign secretary of his reaction at the time or of his instructions, and also notations by clerks as to the subsequent of-

(a) Details of the treaty port consular archives for the period to 1858, as found at the ports in 1934-35, are as follows (the archives of the British consulate at Shanghai were destroyed by fire in 1870):

BA: archives of the British consulate for *Amoy*: *ca*. 22 vols. in good condition. Not found: To Superintendency Oct.-Dec. 1851; To Chinese 1857; From Mis. 1843-52.

BC: *Canton*: *ca*. 46 vols. in rather poor condition (front and back covers gone on most volumes of bound correspondence; fragments of volumes partly eaten by ants). Not found: To Suptcy. 1854-56, From Suptcy. 1843-48, Aug.-Dec. 1849, Jan.-Aug. 1850, Aug.-Dec. 1851, 1856-57, Jan.-June 1858, To Chinese 1850, 1853, 1855-57, From Chinese 1853-Oct. 1858, To Misc. 1843-48.

ficial peregrinations of the despatch; and finally, volumes of Foreign and Consular Various and Domestic Various, the former containing amid much routine material some very enlightening personal correspondence between officials, the latter containing correspondence between the Foreign Office and other departments of government and between it and the merchants in England. Memoranda by the foreign secretary and the head of the Chinese Department, often of the greatest import, may be found in any of these volumes. For the years 1853-1854 a selection of documents was subsequently extracted and filed together chronologically under the heading of Duty Question at Shanghai (key number FO 97, vols. 99 and 100, classified by the P. R. O. under Supplement to General Correspondence). For historical purposes this selection, while convenient, is incomplete and must be carefully amalgamated with the material above-mentioned.

Correspondence received at the FO from China was often sent in original to the Board of Trade and to the Law Officers of the Crown or Queen's Advocate, but in nearly every case returned safely to the FO file, together with the opinions of those bodies. The Board of Trade Library in Great George Street has a few miscellaneous papers on China but did not preserve a file of trade returns. The India Office appears to have little which bears directly on China in this period. The Colonial Office correspondence with Hongkong in the P. R. O. is replete with personal details of the political feuds of the colony, but has little relation to events at the ports.

From the FO correspondence a considerable body of documents was published in the Parliamentary Papers (Blue Books) and has been used by many writers during the past century, notably by Dr. H. B. Morse in The International Relations of the Chinese Empire. More recently the FO files have been surveyed by W. C. Costin (Great Britain and China 1833-1860), together with some of the manuscript collections in the British Museum. In the present volume I have only partially collated documents used from the archives with their published versions in Blue Books, or in British and Foreign State Papers and other collections.

The American correspondence (seen by me in the archives of the Department of State but now in the National Archives, Washington) differs markedly from the British in consisting usually of general letters which treat several current topics under one despatch number. The American commissioner to China reported to his government less frequently than did the British, and often enclosed large masses of accumulated local correspondence. The fact that the consuls also corresponded directly with the State Department sometimes created friction and confusion, all of which reflected the still amorphous condition of the consular service. The American records on China are few compared with the British - a dozen large volumes of letters from the commissioners (cited above as China 8, 9, etc.), a few from the consuls, and a single volume of Instructions. Few notes and minutes accompany them, and it is evident that American relations with China before 1858 were given no more attention than the paucity of instructions would imply. In the United States consulates in China

BN: Ningpo (seen at Shanghai): ca. 64 vols. in good condition. Volumes not found: To Chinese 1849, 1857, 1858; From Chinese 1857, 1858; From Miscellaneous 1852, 1857.

BF: Foochow: ca. 21 vols. in good condition. Not found: To Superintendency 1844-47; To Chinese August 1857-58; From Chinese 1847-50, 1857-58; To Misc. no copies preserved but a Register found for 1844-51; From Misc. 1852-53.

Thus the Ningpo archives for the period appear to be practically complete, those at Foochow and Amoy are about one-fifth gone (chiefly unique local correspondence), and those at Canton are one-third missing (chiefly official correspondence with Hongkong, duplicated in the P. R. O. in London).

In addition to the above, each port had several volumes of Circulars, Notifications, Interpreter's Reports, Judicial Records, or similar miscellaneous material (e.g., at Canton, correspondence the situation was little better.[b] The records in most cases were those of missionary or merchant consuls, whose entries were brief and correspondence meagre.

With a few exceptions all the despatches of Marshall and McLane (see bibliography) were published almost immediately after those officials gave up their positions in China. The consular archives for Shanghai and Canton contain scattered references to subjects like the coast trade and the membership of the American community. The American commissioners' despatches, meanwhile, form a valuable running commentary on events; they were written by able individuals, who often occupied the position of neutral observers of British activity and did not hesitate to express their personal opinions. Tyler Dennett's Americans in Eastern Asia is based on this material, and Eldon Griffin's Clippers and Consuls gives a detailed survey of the consular letters in the American archives.

The French Archives du Ministère des Affaires Étrangères, Paris, contain about 25 volumes on China up to 1858, filed under Correspondance Politique. These include 4 volumes of despatches from the Consulate for Shanghai and Ningpo, beginning in 1848. Maybon and Fredet in their Histoire de la Concession Française de Changhai apparently used the Shanghai end of this correspondence. The French documents contain little reference to commercial matters. Those for the Lagrené mission have been surveyed by Grosse-Aschhoff.

Chinese documents. The administrative process which produced the copious Chinese documentation now available has been described in articles by Fairbank and Teng, which note the peculiar nature of memorials and of their dating when reproduced (by the date when the emperor saw them). The major published collections of edicts, or of edicts and memorials, have been described in various articles.[c] It must be noted, however, that all these compilations, like the published collections of memorials of leading officials, represent the higher level of government. Local correspondence among the officials within a province, which must have been voluminous, is not to be found in the Palace Museum archive materials, except in so far as it was copied into memorials. Whether provincial archives still exist for the period before the Taiping Rebellion is a question as yet unanswered; none, at least, has been accessible to students. There is therefore no Chinese counterpart at present to the British consular archives in the treaty ports. The Chinese documents now accesible are comparable in a general way to the British correspondence between London and Hongkong, not to that between Hongkong and the consulates.

The chief bodies of Ch'ing documents, those of the Grand Council and of the Grand Secretariat, after several vicissitudes during which a part was at one time sold as waste paper, were kept in the Palace Museum in Peiping. Some of the records of the Board of Revenue were in the possession of the Peking National University. Copies were taken of a large number of documents valuable for economic history by the Institute of Social Research of the Academia Sinica. Copies of documents of value relating to foreign affairs in the period 1834-1861 and not included in the I-wu shih-mo series were taken by Dr. T. F. Tsiang for

with the consular agent, Whampoa). Often these extra volumes are of great value, as in the case of Robert Hart's records of the Miscellaneous and Chinese correspondence of the Allied Commission at Canton in 1858.

Chinese despatches: At Foochow complete for 1844-58, in 9 volumes; at Amoy probably complete for 1843-58; at Ningpo and Canton, number not ascertained.

(b) At Shanghai there were preserved one record book from the old Ningpo consulate and half a dozen from the American consulate at Shanghai, most of the latter beginning in 1856 or 1857. All the archives of the Foochow consulate except the deed book were burned in 1868. All those at Amoy were burned about 1904. At Canton there were a dozen volumes beginning with entries earlier than 1858, the earliest entry being 1845. At Hongkong only 3 volumes survived from before 1858.

(c) For a selected list of such collections see Fairbank, Ch'ing Documents, An Introductory Syllabus.

deposit in the Tsing Hua University Library (copies of some of these supplementary documents are cited above as IWSM Supp.).

In general I have found the I-wu shih-mo collection to be the major source, supplemented by more general compilations such as the Tung-hua-lu and Shih-lu. The 4485 chüan of the latter actually contain fewer documents on foreign relations in the years 1836-1874 than do the 260 chüan of IWSM. Aside from the IWSM and other contemporary or modern collections especially compiled on foreign relations, the great body of Ch'ing dynasty official publications - such as the Collected Statutes and other works on administration - have unexpectedly little to say on the problems of Western contact.

So great was the value attached by the literati to an important or eloquent edict or memorial that versions of it may appear in several collections based on the imperial archives, while other versions turn up in the writings of contemporary chroniclers like Wei Yuan or Wang Chih-ch'un, and even in the translations of the Peking Gazette published by foreigners in the Chinese Repository (1832-1851) and North China Herald (1850—). Since each scribe might make his own omissions so as to condense a document, as is done in the Tung-hua-lu, one is never quite certain of having the full text. But few modern students will object when they find the editors of compilations trying to save us from the monstrous and overwhelming bulk of the bureaucratic scrivener's product.

Company archives. This volume has made slight use of the many hundred volumes of accounts and correspondence and the thousands of letters preserved in the archives of Jardine, Matheson and Company at the Cambridge University Library, and in the Heard and Forbes Papers at the Baker Library of the Harvard Business School. The Jardine archives have been surveyed by Michael Greenberg to 1842 and by Gerald Yorke to 1844.

Japanese materials. While there are no Japanese documentary sources directly relevant to this subject and period in China, important research on the published Chinese documents has been inaugurated in the last few years by Toshio Ueda, Masataka Banno, and others. Japanese studies of Ch'ing institutions, meanwhile, form a major key to our understanding of the old order in China; unfortunately they have been generally neglected in American research studies, including the present one. See the forthcoming volume by Fairbank and Banno, Japanese Studies of Modern China, a bibliographical guide to research on the 19th and 20th centuries.

WESTERN WORKS CITED

Note: This is a single list of books, articles, mss., and official publications arranged alphabetically by author or source. Journals and newspapers are included by title. For British Blue Books see under Parlimentary Papers, for Customs publications see under China. For certain persons, like Alcock and Bowring, I have listed more items than are cited above.

"A Field Officer," The Last Year in China (London: 1843), 197 pp.

Abeel, David, Residence in China and the Neighboring Countries (New York, 1836), 378 pp. See also Williamson.

"Notices of Amoy and its inhabitants: extracts from a Journal of the Rev. D. Abeel at Kulang su," CR, 13: 233-38 (1844).

Alcock, Rutherford, Notes on Medical History and Statistics of the British Legion of Spain, comprising the results of gunshot wounds, in relation to important questions in surgery (London, 1838), 100 pp.

"The Chinese Empire and its Destinies," Bombay Quarterly Review (Bombay and London), 4 (October 1855), 30 pp.

"The Chinese Empire in its Foreign Relations," Bombay Quarterly Review (Bombay and London), 6 (April 1856), 75 pp.

Life's Problems. Essays: Moral, Social and Psychological (London, 1857), 275 pp.

Our Policy in China, or a glance at the past, present, and future of China, in its foreign relations and commerce (London, 1858), 134 pp.

The Capital of the Tycoon, a narrative of a three years' residence in Japan, 2 vols. (London, 1863), 900 pp.

The Journey of Augustus Raymond Margary, ... to which is added a concluding chapter (London, 1875), 375 pp.

Art and Industries in Japan (London, 1878), 290 pp.

Anglo-Chinese Calendar (Canton, 1831 and later). Printed at the office of the Chinese Repository. (Issues of 1834, 1848, 1849, 1851 and 1855 found.)

Anon., China and the Missions at Amoy (Edinburgh, 1854). 40 pp.

Manual of Customs Practice at Shanghai, under the various treaties entered into between China and the Foreign Powers, etc. (Shanghai, 1894).

The Battle of "Muddy Flat," 1854. Being an historical sketch of that Famous Occurrence; written specially for the Jubilee Commemoration thereof at Shanghai, April 1904; with some additional particulars relating to the Shanghai Volunteer Corps. Printed and published at N.C.H. Office (Shanghai, 1904), 17 pp.

The Englishman in China (London, 1860), 272 pp. Preface dated July 1860.

Appleton's Cyclopaedia of American Biography, see Wilson and Fiske, editors.

Ashley, Hon. Evelyn, The Life of Henry John Temple, Viscount Palmerston, 1846-1865, with selections from his speeches and correspondence, 2 vols. (London, 1876), 750 pp.

Backhouse, E., and Bland, J. O. P., Annals and Memoirs of the Court of Peking (London, 1914), 531 pp.

Bain, Chester A., "Commodore Matthew Perry, Humphrey Marshall, and the Taiping Rebellion", FEQ, 10.3: 258-270 (May 1951).

Banister, T. R., "A History of the External Trade of China, 1834-81," in China, The Maritime Customs, I, Statistical Series: No. 6, Decennial Reports ... 1922-31, 2 vols. (Shanghai, 1933), vol. 1, pp. 1-193.

Bernard, W. D., Narrative of the Voyages and Services of the Nemesis from 1840 to 1843; and of the combined naval and military operations in China, 2 vols. (London, 1844), 960 pp.

Berncastle, Dr., A Voyage to China; including A Visit to the Bombay Presidency; the Mahratta Country; the Cave Temples of Western India, Singapore, the Straits of Malacca and Sunda, and the Cape of Good Hope, 2 vols. (London, 1851), 294 + 284 pp.

Boulais, le P. Guy, Manuel du Code Chinois, Variétés Sinologiques, no. 55 (Shanghai, 1924), 700 pp.

Bowring, Sir John, Observations on the Restrictive and Prohibitory System; especially with a reference to the decree of the Spanish Cortes of July 1820—from the Mss. of Jeremy Bentham, Esq. (London, 1821),43 pp. Preface (by Bowring), 9 pp.

The Political and Commercial Importance of Peace. A lecture delivered in the Hall of Commerce, London (no date), 24 pp.

Autobiographical recollections of Sir John Bowring. With a brief memoir by Lewin B. Bowring (London, 1877), 400 pp.

Matins and Vespers, with hymns and poems. With a memoir of his life by Lady Bowring (London, 1895). Memoir, 30 pp.

Boxer, C. R., Fidalgos in the Far East 1550-1770: Fact and Fancy in the History of Macao (The Hague: Martinus Nijhoff, 1948), 297 pp.

Bridgman, Mrs. Eliza Jane (Gillett), Daughters of China; or, Sketches of domestic life in the Celestial empire (New York, 1853), 234 pp.

British and Foreign State Papers ..., compiled by the librarian and keeper of the papers, Foreign Office (London, 1812-14, and later).

Brunnert, H. S., and Hagelstrom, V. V., Present Day Political Organization of China, translated from the Russian by A. Beltchenko and E. E. Moran (Shanghai: Kelly and Walsh, 1912), 572 + 81 pp.

Callery, J. M., Journal des Opérations Diplomatiques de la Legation Française en Chine (Macao, 1845), 276 pp.

Correspondence diplomatique Chinoise relative aux négociations du traité de Whampoa (1844), (Paris, 1879), 306 pp.

Callery and Yvan, History of the Insurrection in China, with notices of the Christianity, Creed and Proclamations of the Insurgents, translated from the French by John Oxenford (London, 1853), 325 pp.
Campbell, Chas. S., Special Business Interests and the Open Door Policy (New Haven: Yale University Press, 1951), 88 pp.
Chang Hsi-t'ung, "The Earliest Phase of the Introduction of Western Political Science into China," The Yenching Journal of Social Studies, 5.1: 1-29 (July 1950).
Chang Te-ch'ang, "Maritime Trade at Canton during the Ming Dynasty," CSPSR, 17: 264-282 (1933).
Chang T'ien-tse, Sino-Portuguese Trade from 1514 to 1644. A synthesis of Portuguese and Chinese Sources (Leyden: Late E. J. Brill Ltd., 1934), 157 pp.
Chao Feng-t'ien, "Chinese Works on the First Anglo-Chinese War," Yenching Journal of Social Studies, 3.1: 61-103 (October 1940).
Chen, Agnes Fang-chih, "Chinese Frontier Diplomacy: The Eclipse of Manchuria," Yenching Journal of Social Studies, 5.1: 69-141 (July 1950).
Chen, Gideon (Ch'en Ch'i-t'ien), Lin Tse-hsü (Peiping: Yenching University, 1934), 65 pp.

Tseng Kuo-fan (Peiping: Yenching University, 1935), 98 pp.
Ch'en, Kenneth (Ch'en Kuan-sheng), "Matteo Ricci's Contribution to and Influence on Geographical Knowledge in China," Journal of the American Oriental Society, 59.3: 325-359 (September 1939).

"Hai-lu, Fore-runner of Chinese Travel Accounts of Western Countries," Monumenta Serica, 7: 208-226 (1942).
Cheng Teh-k'un, "Cannons of the Opium War; a history of the campus of Amoy University," China Journal, 26: 4-10 (January 1937).
China Directory, 1861, 1862, 1864 (Hongkong: A. Shortrede and Co.).
China, Imperial Maritime Customs, I. Miscellaneous Series, Treaties, Conventions, etc., between China and Foreign States ... 1689-1886 (Shanghai, 1887), 1138 pp.

Imperial Maritime Customs, II, Special Series: No. 3, Silk (Shanghai, 1881), 163 pp.

Imperial Maritime Customs, II, Special Series: No. 4, Opium (Shanghai, 1881), 80 pp.

Imperial Maritime Customs, II, Special Series: No. 11, Tea (Shanghai, 1889), 179 English + 120 Chinese pp.

Imperial Maritime Customs, VI, Inspectorate Series: No. 5 (Confidential), George Lanning, Memorandum on the establishment of the Imperial Maritime Customs in 1854. Compiled by permission of the Minister for Great Britain and the Minister for the United States from the archives of the British and American Legations, Peking (Shanghai, 1915), 22 pp.

Maritime Customs, see Worcester and Wright.
China Mail (Hongkong, weekly, 1845—); 1845-58 seen in British Museum and Hongkong Public Library; 1845-53, in Colonial Secretary's office, Hongkong. For biweekly edition, see Overland China Mail.
Chinese Commercial Guide, see Morrison, also Williams.
Chinese Miscellany (Shanghai, 1849-50), printed at the Mission Press; later evidently merged with the North China Herald's Almanac.
Chinese Repository, (Macao or Canton, monthly, edited by E. C. Bridgman and S. Wells Williams 1832-51).
Chinese Social and Political Science Review, published by the Chinese Social and Political Science Association (Peking, quarterly, 1916—).
Clapham, J. H., The Economic Development of France and Germany 1815-1914 (Cambridge, 1928), 420 pp.
Clark, Arthur H., The Clipper Ship Era. An epitome of famous American and British Clipper Ships, their owners, builders, commanders, and crews, 1843-1869 (New York, 1911), 400 pp.
CM see China Mail
Collis, Maurice, Foreign Mud (London: Faber and Faber, Ltd., 1946), 318 pp.
Cordier, Henri, L'Expédition de Chine de 1857-58. Histoire Diplomatique. Notes et Documents (Paris, 1905), 450 pp.

"La Mission Dubois de Jancigny dans l'Extreme Orient, 1841-1846," Revue de l'Histoire des Colonies Françaises, 4: 1-132 (1916).
Costin, W. C., Great Britain and China 1833-1860 (Oxford University Press, 1937), 362 pp.
Couling, Samuel, The Encyclopaedia Sinica (Shanghai, 1917), 633 pp.
Coupland, R., Raffles, 1781-1826 (London, 1926), 134 pp.
CR, see Chinese Repository.
Crow, Carl, Foreign Devils in the Flowery Kingdom (New York: Harper & Brothers, 1940), 340 pp.
CSPSR, see Chinese Social and Political Science Review
Cumming, C. F. Gordon, Wanderings in China (Edinburgh and London, 1886), 382 + 370 pp.
(Cunningham, Edward) An American Resident in China, Our Commercial and Political Relations with China, pam. (Washington, February 1855) 8 pp. So attributed by Massachusetts Historical Society and Essex Institute, Salem.
Customs, Treaties, see China, Imperial Maritime Customs.
Davis, (Sir) John Francis, The Chinese: A General Description of The Empire of China and Its Inhabitants, 2 vols. (New York: Harper and Brothers, 1836).

Sketches of China; partly during an inland journey of four months between Peking, Nanking and Canton; with notices and observations relative to the present war, 2 vols. (London, 1841), 650 pp.

China During the War and Since the Peace, 2 vols. (London, 1852), 327 + 342 pp.

China: a general description of that Empire and its inhabitants, with the history of foreign intercourse down to the events which produced the dissolution of 1857, 2 vols. (London, 1857), 908 pp. A new edition, revised and enlarged.

Dennett, Tyler, Americans in Eastern Asia, A critical study of the policy of the United States with reference to China, Japan and Korea in the nineteenth century (New York, 1922), 725 pp.

Downing, C. Toogood, The Stranger in China; or, the Fan-Qui's Visit to The Celestial Empire in 1836-7, 2 vols. (London, 1838), 480 pp.

Duyvendak, J. J. L., "The last Dutch Embassy ...," T'oung Pao, 33: 1-137, 223-227 (1938); 35: 329-353 (1940).

"The true dates of the Chinese maritime expeditions in the early fifteenth century," T'oung Pao, 34: 341-412 (1939).

Dyce, Charles M., Personal Reminiscences of Thirty Years' Residence in the Model Settlement, Shanghai, 1870-1900 (London, 1906), 238 pp.

Easton, Harry Tucker, The History of a Banking House (Smith, Payne and Smiths) (London: Blades, East & Blades, 1903), 127 pp.

Eitel, E. J., Europe in China. The History of Hong Kong from the Beginning to the Year 1882 (London, 1895), 570 pp.

Fairbank, J. K., "The Legalization of the Opium Trade before the Treaties of 1858," CSPSR, 17.2: 215-263 (July 1933).

"The Provisional System at Shanghai in 1853-54; Foreign Consular Administration of the Chinese Customs," CSPSR, pt. 1, 18.4: 455-504 (January 1935); ibid., pt. 2, 19.1: 65-124 (April, 1935).

"The Creation of the Foreign Inspectorate of Customs at Shanghai," CSPSR, 19.4: 469-514 (January 1936); ibid., 20.1: 42-100 (April 1936).

"The Definition of the Foreign Inspectors' Status, 1854-55; A Chapter in the Early History of the Inspectorate of Customs at Shanghai," Nankai Social and Economic Quarterly, 9.1: 125-163 (April 1936).

"The Manchu Appeasement Policy of 1843," JAOS, 59.4: 469-484 (December 1939).

"Chinese Diplomacy and the Treaty of Nanking, 1842," The Journal of Modern History, 12.1: 1-30 (March 1940).

"Tributary Trade and China's Relations with the West," FEQ, 1.2: 129-149 (February 1942).

The United States and China (Cambridge: Harvard University Press, 1948), 384 pp.

"The Manchu-Chinese Dyarchy in the 1840's and '50's", FEQ, 12.3: 265-278 (May 1953).

Ch'ing Documents: An Introductory Syllabus (Cambridge: Harvard University Press, 1952), 100 pp.

Fairbank, J. K., and Teng, S. Y., "On the Transmission of Ch'ing Documents," HJAS, 4.1: 12-46 (May 1939).

"On the Types and Uses of Ch'ing Documents," HJAS, 5.1: 1-71 (January 1940).

"On the Ch'ing Tributary System," HJAS, 6.2: 135-246 (June 1941).

Fang, Chao-ying, "A New Technique for Estimating the Numerical Strength of the Early Manchu Military Forces," HJAS, 13.1-2: 192-215 (June 1950).

Favre, B., Les Sociétés Secretès en Chine; origine – rôle historique – situation actuelle (Paris, 1933), 222 pp.

Feetham, Richard, Report of the Hon. Mr. Justice Feetham, C.M.G., to the Shanghai Municipal Council, 2 vols. (Shanghai: North-China Daily News and Herald, 1931), 237 + 372 pp.

Ferrière le Vayer, Th. de, Une Ambassade Française en Chine. Journal de Voyage (Paris, 1854), 386 pp.

Fishbourne, Capt., Impressions of China and the present revolution: its progress and prospects (London, 1855), 400 pp.

Forbes, Robert Bennett, Remarks on China and the China Trade (Boston, 1844), 80 pp.

Personal Reminiscences, To which is added Rambling Recollections connected with China, 3rd ed., revised (Boston, 1892), 412 pp.

Fortune, Robert, Three Years' Wanderings in the Northern Provinces of China, including a visit to the Tea, Silk, and Cotton countries: with an account of the Agriculture and Horticulture of the Chinese, new plants, etc. (London, 1847), 406 pp.

A Journey to the Tea Countries of China; Including Sung-lo and the Bohea Hills... (London, 1852), 398 pp.

Two Visits to the Tea Countries of China, 2 vols., 3rd ed. (London, 1853).

A Residence among the Chinese: inland, on the coast and at sea. Being a narrative of scenes and adventures during a third visit to China, from 1853 to 1856 (London, 1857), 440 pp.

Friend of China (Hong Kong, weekly, 1841 and later). Monthly edition, Overland Friend of China.

Frochisse, J.-M., La Belgique et la Chine, Relations diplomatiques et économiques (1839-1909), (L'Édition Universelle, S. A., 53, Rue Royale, Bruxelles, Preface 1936), 459 pp.

Fuess, C. M., The Life of Caleb Cushing, 2 vols. (New York, 1923).

Fox, Grace, British Admirals and Chinese Pirates 1832-1869 (London; Kegan Paul, Trench, Trubner & Co., Ltd., 1940), 227 pp.

Furber, Holden, John Company at Work (Cambridge: Harvard University Press, 1948), 407 pp.

Gardner, C. S., "China," in Langer, W. L., ed., An Encyclopedia of World History, 1st ed. (Boston: Houghton Mifflin Co., 1940), 1155 pp.

Gladstone, W. E., War in China, speech of March 3, 1857, corrected report (London, 1857), 40 pp.

Goodrich, L. Carrington, The Literary Inquisition of Ch'ien-lung (Baltimore: Waverly Press, Inc., 1935), 275 pp.

"China's First Knowledge of the Americas," Geographical Review, 28.3: 400-411 (July 1938).

A Short History of the Chinese People (New York: Harper & Bros., 1943), 260 pp.

Greenberg, Michael, British Trade and the Opening of China 1800-42 (Cambridge: The University Press, 1951), 221 pp.

Griffin, Eldon, Clippers and Consuls, American Consular and Commercial Relations with Eastern Asia, 1845-1860 (Ann Arbor: University of Michigan Press, 1938), 533 pp.

Griswold, A. Whitney, The Far Eastern Policy of the United States (New York: Harcourt, Brace and Co., 1938), 530 pp.

Grosse-Aschhoff, Angelus, Negotiations between Ch'i-ying and Lagrené 1844-1846 (Franciscan Institute Publications, Missiology Series, no. 2, 1950), 195 pp. New York and Louvain.

Gundry, R. S., China Present and Past (London, 1895), 414 pp.

Gutzlaff, Charles, Journal of three voyages along the Coast of China in 1831, 1832, and 1833, with notices of Siam, Korea, and the Loo-Choo Islands (London, 1834), 347 pp.

China opened; or a Display of the topography, history, customs, manners, arts, manufactures, commerce, literature, religion, jurisprudence, etc. of the Chinese Empire, 2 vols. (London, 1838), 1060 pp.

The Life of Taou-Kwang, late emperor of China, with memoirs of the Court of Peking; including a sketch of the principal events in the history of the Chinese Empire during the last fifty years (London, 1852), 280 pp.

Hail, William James, Tseng Kuo-Fan and the Taiping Rebellion, with a short sketch of his later career (New Haven, 1927), 400 pp.

Hall, Robert A., Jr., "Chinese pidgin English grammar and texts," J. of the American Oriental Society, 64.3: 95-113 (July-Sept. 1944).

Harvard Journal of Asiatic Studies (Cambridge, quarterly, 1936–).

Hinton, Harold, The Grain Tribute System of China, 1845-1911; an Aspect of the Decline of the Ch'ing Dynasty, Ph.D. dissertation, Harvard University (1950), 223 pp.

HJAS, see Harvard Journal of Asiatic Studies.

Hongkong Almanack and Directory (1846 and later). Printed at the office of the China Mail.

Hongkong Government Gazette (Hong Kong, weekly, 1853-58 and later), file 1853-58 seen in Hong Kong Public Library.

Hongkong Register (Canton, 1827), later known as Canton Register, then as Hongkong Register, weekly; owned by Jardine, Matheson and Co., 1849-52; seen in Hong Kong Public Library.

Hsia Ching-lin, Studies in Chinese Diplomatic History (Shanghai, 1926), 225 pp.

Hsieh, Pao-chao, The Government of China (1644-1911) (Baltimore: Johns Hopkins Press, 1925), 414 pp.

Huang Yen-yu, "Vicery Yeh Ming-ch'en and the Canton Episode (1856-1861)", HJAS, 6.1: 37-127 (March 1941).

Huc, Evariste, A Journey through the Chinese Empire, 2 vols. (New York, 1855), 421 + 422 pp.

Hughes, George, "The Small Knife Rebels (An Unpublished Chapter of Amoy History)," China Review, 1: 244-248 (1873).

Hummel, Arthur W., ed., Eminent Chinese of the Ch'ing Period, 2 vols. (Washington, D.C.: Government Printing Office, 1943, 1944), 604 + 498 pp.

(Hunter, W. C.), an Old Resident, The "Fan Kwae" at Canton before Treaty Days, 1825-1844 (London, 1882, later reprints), 160 pp.

(Hunt's) The Merchant's Magazine and Commercial Review, ed. by Freeman Hunt (New York, monthly, July 1839 and later).

(Jardine), Jardine Matheson & Co., afterwards Jardine Matheson & Co., Limited. An outline of the history of a China House for a hundred years, 1832-1932 (Hong Kong: privately printed, 1934), 88 pp.

de Jesus, see Montalto de Jesus, C.A.

Jones, F. C., Shanghai and Tientsin (London: Oxford University Press, 1940), 182 pp.

Jones-Parry, E., "Under-Secretaries of State for Foreign Affairs, 1782-1844," English Historical Review, 49: 308-320 (April 1934).

Jurien de la Gravière, Voyage en Chine, pendant les années, 1847-1848-1849-1850, 2nd ed., 2 vols. (Paris, 1864), 390 pp.

Kearny, Thomas, "Commodore Kearny and the Open Door and Most Favored Nation Policy in China in 1842 to 1843," New Jersey Historical Society Proceedings, 50: 162-190 (1932).

"The Tsiang Documents ... an American Viewpoint," CSPSR, 16.1: 75-104 (April 1932).

Kennan, George F., American Diplomacy 1900-1950 (Chicago: University of Chicago Press, 1951), 154 pp.

Kerr, J. D., "Opium and the Smoking Extract," China Review, 12.1: 41-47 (July and August 1883).

King, F. H., Farmers of Forty Centuries (Madison 1911), 441 pp.

Kotenev, A. M., Shanghai: its mixed court and council: Material relating to the history of the Shanghai municipal council and the history, practice and statistics of the International Mixed Court: Chinese Modern Law and Shanghai Municipal Land Regulations and by-laws governing the life in the settlement (Shanghai, 1925), 600 pp.

Kuo, P. C., A Critical Study of the First Anglo-Chinese War with Documents (Shanghai: Commercial Press, 1935), 315 pp.

Kuwabara, Jitsuzō, "On P'u Shou-keng, A Man of the Western Regions, who was the Superintendent of the Trading Ships' Office in Ch'üan-chou towards the End of the Sung dynasty, together with a General Sketch of Trade of the Arabs in China during the T'ang and Sung Eras", Memoirs of the Tōyō Bunko, Tōkyō, No. 2: 1-79 (1928); 7: 1-104 (1935).

Laai, Yi-faai, The Part Played by the Pirates of Kwangtung and Kwangsi Provinces in the Taiping Insurrection, Ph.D. dissertation, University of California (1949).

Lane-Poole, Stanley, The Life of Sir Harry Parkes, K.C.B., G.C.M.G., sometime Her Majesty's Minister to China and Japan, vol. I, Consul in China (London, 1894), 100 pp.

Sir Harry Parkes in China (London, 1901), 386 pp.

Lanning, George, see under China, Customs.

Lanning, George, and Couling, Samuel, The History of Shanghai, 2 vols. (Shanghai, 1921).

Latourette, Kenneth Scott, A History of Christian Missions in China (London, 1929), 900 pp.

The Great Century in Northern Africa and in Asia, A.D. 1800 – A.D. 1914, vol. 6 in A History of the Expansion of Christianity (New York and London: Harper & Bros., 1944), 502 pp.

Lattimore, Owen, Inner Asian Frontiers of China (New York: American Geographical Society,

1940), 585 pp. (Second edition, 1951).

Lay, G. T., The Claims of Japan and Malaysia upon Christendom, exhibited in Notes of Voyages made in 1837 from Canton in the ship Morrison and brig Himmaleh, 2 vols. (New York, 1839), 200 + 295 pp.

The Chinese as they are: their moral, social, and literary character .... (London, 1841), 342 pp.

Leland, Charles G., Pidgin-English Sing-Song (London, 1887), 139 pp.

Light, Capt. Francis (letter of), encl. in Cornwallis to Dundas, Jan. 7, 1789, quoted by C. E. Wurtzburg, "A Brief Account of the several countries surrounding Prince of Wales's Island ...", in Journal of the Malayan Branch of the R.A.S., 16, pt. 1: 123-126 (July 1938).

Lindsay, H. H., Report of Proceedings on a Voyage to the Northern Ports of China in the Ship Lord Amherst (London, 1834), 296 pp.

British Relations with China (London, 1836).

Is the war with China a just one?, 2nd ed. (London, 1840), 40 pp.

Loch, Capt. G. G., The Closing Events of the Campaign in China (London, 1843), 227 pp.

Lockhart, William, The Medical Missionary in China: a narrative of twenty years' experience, 2nd ed. (London, 1861), 404 pp.

Lloyd, Christopher, The Navy and the Slave Trade. The Suppression of the African Slave Trade in the Nineteenth Century (London, New York, Toronto: Longmans, Green and Co., 1949), 314 pp.

Lubbock, Basil, The China Clippers, 4th ed. (Glasgow, 1919), 388 + xxxvi pp.

The Opium Clippers (Boston: Lauriat Co., 1933), 392 pp.

Malmesbury, Earl of, Memoirs of an ex-minister (London, 1885), 650 pp.

(Marshall, Humphrey), Correspondence between the State Department and the late Commissioner to China, ..., 33d Congress, 1st Session, vol. 16, H. Ex. Doc. 123 (1854), Ser. 734.

Martin, R. Montgomery, China; political, commercial, and social; in an official report to Her Majesty's Government, 2 vols. (London, 1847), 925 pp.

Martin, W. A. P., A Cycle of Cathay or China, South and North, with personal reminiscences, 2nd ed. (Edinburgh and London, 1896), 464 pp.

Maxwell, (Sir) Herbert, The Life and Letters of George William Frederick, Fourth Earl of Clarendon, 2 vols. (London, 1913), 620 pp.

Maybon, Ch. B., and Fredet, Jean, Histoire de la Concession Française de Changhai (Paris, 1929), 357 pp.

Mayers, William Frederick, The Chinese Government. A manual of Chinese titles, categorically arranged and explained with an appendix, 3rd ed. (Shanghai, 1897), 196 pp. (First published 1877).

Mayers, Wm. Fred., Dennys, N. B., and King, Chas., The Treaty Ports of China and Japan, a complete guide to the open ports of those countries, ... forming a Guide Book and Vade Mecum for travellers, merchants and residents in general, with 29 Maps and plans ... (London, 1867), 650 pp.

(McLane, R. M.),....All the official despatches and correspondence of the Hon. Robert M. McLane, and of the Hon. Peter Parker (1858), 35th Congress, 2nd Session, S. Ex. Doc. 22 (1859), 2 vols., Ser. 982-83.

....Instructions from the Department of State to Mr. McLane, when appointed Minister to China, 36th Congress, 1st Session, S. Ex. Doc. 39 (1860), Ser. 1033.

Meadows, Thomas Taylor, Desultory notes on the government and people of China and on the Chinese language; illustrated with a sketch of the province of Kuang-Tung, showing its division into departments and districts (London, 1847), 240 pp.

The Chinese and their Rebellions, viewed in connection with their National Philosophy, Ethics, legislation, and administration, to which is added an Essay on Civilization and its present state in the East and West (London, 1856), 625 pp.

(Medhurst, W. H.), A glance at the interior of China obtained during a journey through the Silk and Green Tea Districts. Taken in 1845 (Shanghai: North China Herald, n.d.), 192 pp.

China: its State and Prospects, with especial reference to The Spread of the Gospel ... (London, 1840), 592 pp.

Pamphlets Issued by the Chinese Insurgents.... (Shanghai, 1853).

"Reminiscences of the Opening of Shanghai to Foreign Trade," Chinese and Japanese Repository, 2.15: 79-88 (Oct. 12, 1864).

Michael, Franz, The Origin of Manchu Rule in China (Baltimore: The Johns Hopkins Press, 1942), 127 pp.

Michie, Alexander, The Englishman in China during the Victorian Era, as illustrated in the career of Sir Rutherford Alcock, K.C.B., D.C.L., many years consul and minister in China and Japan, 2 vols. (London, 1900), 442 + 510 pp.

Milburn, W., Oriental Commerce ..., 2 vols. (London, 1813), 413 + 581 pp.

Millac, A., "Les Francais à Changhai en 1853-55," Revue de l'Extrême-Orient, 1883, tome 2: 1-53. (Paris, 1884).

Milne, W. C., "Notes of a Seven Months Residence in the City of Ningpo, from December 7th, 1842, to July 7th, 1843," CR, 13 (1844), passim.

Life in China (London, 1857), 500 pp.

Montalto de Jesus, C. A., Historic Shanghai (Shanghai, 1909), 257 pp.

Historic Macao (Hongkong, 1902), 358 pp.

Montigny, C. de, "Manuel du Négociant Français en Chine," in Chine et Indo-Chine, Faits commerciaux, no. 10: 186-502 (Paris, 1846).

Moor, Lammer, Bowring, Cobden and China. A Memoir (Edinburgh, 1857), 32 pp.

Morrison, J. R., A Chinese Commercial Guide, Consisting of a Collection of Details and Regulations Respecting Foreign Trade with China, 2nd ed., revised (Macao: S. Wells Williams, 1844), 279 pp.; 4th ed. (Canton: Chinese Repository office, 1856); 5th ed. (Hongkong: Shortrede, 1863). See S. Wells Williams.

Morse, Hosea Ballou, The Trade and Administration of China, 3rd ed. (New York, Bombay and Calcutta: Longmans, Green & Co.,1921), 505 pp.

Conflict: The International Relations of the Chinese Empire, 3 vols.: vol. I, The Period of Conflict 1834-1860 (Shanghai, 1910), 727 pp.

Submission: ibid., vol. II, The Period of Submission, 1861-1893 (London, 1918), 480 pp.

Subjection: ibid., vol. III, The Period of Subjection, 1894-1911 (London, 1918), 530 pp.

Chronicles: The Chronicles of the East India Company Trading to China, 1635-1843, 4 vols. (Oxford, 1926), vol. 5 for 1742-74 (Oxford, 1929).

Morse, H. B., and MacNair, Harley Farnsworth, Far Eastern International Relations (Shanghai, 1928), 1080 pp. and (Boston: Houghton Mifflin, 1931), 846 pp.

Murray, Alexander, Doings in China (London, 1843), 320 pp.

NCH see North China Herald

Nelson, M. Frederick, Korea and the Old Orders in Eastern Asia (Baton Rouge: Louisiana State University Press, 1945), 326 pp.

Nolde, John J., The "Canton City Question," 1842-1849: A Preliminary Investigation into Chinese Anti-Foreignism and its Effect upon China's Diplomatic Relations with the West, Ph.D. dissertation, Cornell University (September 1950), 271 pp.

North China Herald (Shanghai, weekly, 1850 —) file 1850-58 in North China Daily News office, Shanghai, and Yale University Library; 1850-54 in library N.C.B.R.A.S., Shanghai, and Harvard University Library; not found in England; British Museum file begins 1862.

Nye, Gideon, Jr., Tea: and the Tea trade (New York, 1850), 56 pp.

Orange, James, The Chater Collection, Pictures relating to China, Hongkong, Macao, 1655-1860 ... (London, 1924), 528 pp.

Ouchterlony, John, The Chinese War: an account of all the operations of the British Forces from the commencement to the Treaty of Nanking, 2nd ed. (London, 1844), 520 pp.

Overland China Mail (biweekly edition of the China Mail), 1848-58, British Museum, London.

Owen, David Edward, British Opium Policy in India and China (New Haven: Yale University Press, 1934), 399 pp.

Parker, E. H., China Past and Present (London, 1903), 424 pp.

Chinese Account of the Opium War (Shanghai, 1888), 82 pp. Teng (Chang Hsi, p. 132) notes that this work, a translation of the last two chapters of Wei Yuan, Sheng-wu chi, actually translates the two final chapters of the 1878 edition, which are not found in other editions.

Parliamentary Papers (Blue Books), presented by command either to the House of Commons or the House of Lords, or to both houses, are numerous for this period. The following is a selection, omitting the annual returns of trade, Hongkong ordinances, and the like. These papers have been widely used, particularly in Morse, Conflict.

HL. 1843 (221), II, 703, Bill for the better Government of Her Majesty's Subjects resorting to China.

HL. 1843, VI, 143, Correspondence between Sir Henry Pottinger, Bart., G. C. B., and certain British Merchants in China, 10 pp.

HC. 1844 [556], LI, 359 and HL. 1844, XII, p. 225, Commissions under the Great Seal; Instructions under Her Majesty's Sign Manual; Commissions providing for the temporary exercise of the Duties of the Chief Superintendent of British Trade in China; Orders in Council and Ordinances passed and issued in virtue of the Powers conferred upon Her Majesty by the Act of the 6 and 7 Victoria c.80, 10 pp.

HC. 1844 (484), XXXIII, 632, Estimate of the Amount required to defray the Charge of the Establishment of the British Settlement at Hong Kong, and of the Consular Establishments at the Five Ports open to British Trade in China.

HC. 1844 [570], LI, 369 and HL. 1844, XV, 93, Statement of the Foreign Trade with China, and an Account of the Inland or Transit Duties of the Chinese Empire, 9 pp.

HC. 1847, V, Reports, Committees (1), 654 (Sess. Jan. 19 — July 23, 1847), Report from the Select Committee on Commercial Relations with China, etc., 593 pp.

HC. 1847 [795], XL, 1, Orders, Ordinances, Rules, and Regulations concerning the Trade in China, 60 pp.

HL. 1847, XVII, 627, and 1857, Sess. 1, VII, 309 and 315, Correspondence relative to the Operations in the Canton River, April 1847, 35 pp. and Further Correspondence in the year 1847.

HC. 1847-48. [947], XLVIII, 699, Rules and Regulations concerning the Trade in China, and Notifications promulgated in 1847, 47 pp.

HC. 1847-48 [930.] [in 947], XLVIII. 617.699 and HL. 1847-48, XIX, 535, Papers relating to the murder of Six Englishmen in the Neighborhood of Canton in the Month of December 1847, 79 pp.

HC. 1852-53 [1666], LXIX, 129 and HL. 1852-53, XXI, 413, British Subjects in China. Order of Her Majesty in Council for the government of Her Majesty's subjects being within the Dominions of the Emperor of China, or being within any ship or vessel at a distance of not more than one hundred miles from the Coast of China (Dated June 13, 1853), 15 pp.

HC. 1852-53 [1667], LXIX, 647 and HL. 1852-3, XXI, 431, Papers respecting the Civil War in China, 44 pp.

HL. 1854, XVIII, 677, Correspondence respecting the Attack on the Foreign Settlement at Shanghai, 18 pp.

HC. 1855 [255], Correspondence upon the subject of Emigration from China, 93 pp.

HC. 1855 [336], Returns of the Gross Revenue derived annually from the Tax on Land in India since 1792.

HC. 1857 [16], A Return of the Revenue derived Annually from all Sources of Taxation in India, from 1852-53 to 1855-56 (in continuation of Parliamentary Paper, No. 336, of Session 1855).

HC. 1857 [2175 Sess. 1], XII, 325, Correspondence respecting insults in China, 228 pp.

HC. 1857 [2189 Sess. 1], XII, 571 and HL. 1857, Sess. 1, VII, 291, Correspondence respecting Consular Interference for the Prevention of Smuggling in China, 5 pp.

HL. 1857, Sess. 2, XVI, 103, Return of the value of the British Manufactures exported to China, in each year since 1833: also, return of the Bullion exported from Great Britain to China in each year since 1849; and also, return of the value of Goods and Merchandise imported into

Great Britain from China in each year since 1849. (9)

Return specifying the Quantities of Specie or Bullion imported into British Possessions East of the Cape of Good Hope from China, in each year since 1849. (11) 105

HL. 1857, Sess. 1, VI, 241, Correspondence between Mr. Bonham and the Secretary of State respecting the Right of British Subjects to have free Access to Canton, during 1848 and 1849.

HL. 1857, Sess. 1, VII, 1, Correspondence relative to Entrance into Canton 1850-1855 between Sir John Bowring and the Secretary of State, 37 pp.

HL. 1857, Sess. 2, XVI, 107, Papers relating to the Colony of Hongkong, Chusan, etc. — Mr. R. M. Martin's Report on Hongkong; — Specific Report by Governor Davis, showing the points on which he dissents from Mr. Martin's Report; furnished pursuant to a Request from Lord Stanley. — Mr. Martin's Report on Chusan. — Minute on the British Position and prospect in China. By Mr. Martin.

HC. 1857 [2221 Sess. 2], XLIII, 83 and HL. 1857, Sess. 2, XVI, 161, Papers relating to the Opium Trade in China 1842-1856: - Copies of all correspondence between the British and Chinese Authorities on the subject of or having reference to Traffic in Opium in the Harbours, Rivers, and Coasts of China, 82 pp.

HC. 1859 [2571 Sess. 2], XXXIII, 1 and HL. 1859, Sess. 2, XIV, 1, Correspondence relative to the Earl of Elgin's Special Missions to China and Japan, 1857 to 1859, 488 pp.

HC. 1865 [3509], XXXVIII, 1. and HL. 1865, XIV. 1.: No. 1, Report relative to the Foreign Customs Establishment in China, 13 pp.

HC. 1865 (94), XL, 83: 18. Opium Trade. The Number of chests of Opium exported to China from Central India via Bombay, since 1830, the rate of duty, the cost of collection and establishment, and the receipts on account of the passes or the duty; — and, a similar return from Bengal, adding the advances made to the cultivators, the selling price in each year, etc.

Parkinson, C. N., Trade in the Eastern Seas 1793-1813 (Cambridge, England: The University Press, 1937), 434 pp.

Pelcovits, Nathan A., Old China Hands and the Foreign Office, (New York: American Institute of Pacific Relations, 1948), 349 pp.

Pelliot, P., "Un ouvrage sur les premier temps de Macao," T'oung Pao, 31: 58-94 (1934). A review of Chang T'ien-tse, Sino-Portuguese Trade... .

Philips, C. H., The East India Company 1784-1834 (Manchester University Press, 1940), 353 pp.

Playfair, G. M. H., The Cities and Towns of China, 2nd ed. (Shanghai, 1910), 582 pp.

Poore, R. B., The Political Register and Congressional Directory (Boston, 1878).

Porter, G. R., The Progress of the Nation, 3 vols. (London, 1836-43).

Pott, F. L. Hawks, A Short History of Shanghai, being an account of the growth and development of the International Settlement (Shanghai, 1928), 336 pp.

Power, William James Tyrone, Recollections of a Three Years' Residence in China (London, 1853), 380 pp.

Pritchard, E. H., The Crucial Years of Anglo-Chinese Relations 1750-1800, Research Studies of the State College of Washington, 4.3-4: 442 pp. (Sept.-Dec., 1936).

Pritchard, Earl H., 'The Origins of the Most-Favored-Nation and the Open Door Policies in China", FEQ, 1.2: 161-172 (February 1942).

"The Kotow in the Macartney Embassy to China in 1793," Far Eastern Quarterly, 2.2: 163-203 (February 1943).

Redford, Arthur, Manchester Merchants and Foreign Trade 1794-1858 (Manchester University Press, 1934), 251 pp.

Reischauer, E. O., "Notes on T'ang Dynasty Sea Routes," HJAS, 5.2: 142-164 (June 1940).

Robbins, Helen H., Our First Ambassador to China (London, 1908), 479 pp.

Rockhill, W. W., "The Dalai Lamas of Lhasa ...", T'oung Pao, 11: 1-104 (1910).

"Notes on the relations and trade of China ...", T'oung Pao, 15: 419-447 (1914).

Rosso, Antonio Sisto, O.F.M., Apostolic Legations to China of the eighteenth century (South Pasadena: P.D. and Ione Perkins, 1948), 502 pp.

Russell, F. M., Theories of International Relations (New York and London: D. Appleton-Century Co., 1936), 651 pp.

Saltoun, A. F., The Frasers of Philorth, 3 vols. (Edinburgh, 1879).

Sansom, G. B., The Western World and Japan (New York: Knopf, 1950), 504 pp.

Sargent, A. J., Anglo-Chinese Commerce and Diplomacy (Mainly in the Nineteenth Century) (Oxford, 1907), 332 pp.

Sayer, Geoffrey Robley, Hong Kong, Birth, Adolescence, and Coming of Age (London: Oxford University Press, 1937), 232 pp.

Scarth, John, Twelve Years in China. The People, the Rebels, and the Mandarins. By a British Resident (Edinburgh, 1860), 330 pp.

Schlegel, Gustave, Thian Ti Hwui, The Hung-League or Heaven-Earth League. A secret society with the Chinese in China and India (Batavia, 1866), 251 pp.

"Problèmes géographiques des peuples étrangers chez les historiens chinois," T'oung Pao, 3: 101-168, 490-510 (1892); 4: 323-362 (1893); 5: 178 ff (1894); 6: 1-64, 165-215, 246-257 (1895).

Schurhammer, Von G., "Fernao Mendez Pinto und Seine Peregrinacam," Asia Major, 3.1: 71-103 (1926); 3.2: 194-267 (1926).

Schurz, W. L., The Manila Galleon (New York: E. P. Dutton and Co., 1939), 453 pp.

Shanghai Almanac and Miscellany (Shanghai, 1851 and later), printed at the North China Herald Office.

Shanghai International Testing House, A Survey of the Silk Industry of Central China (Shanghai, 1925), 100 pp.

Shanghai Mercury, ed., 1843-Shanghai-1843. The Model Settlement. Its Birth. Its Youth. Its Jubilee (Nov. 17, 1893), 96 pp.

Shirokogoroff, S. M., Social Organization of the Manchus (Shanghai, 1924), 194 pp.

Singapore Almanack and Directory for the Year 1856 (Singapore, 1856).

Sirr, Henry Charles, China and the Chinese, 2 vols. (London, 1849), 900 pp.

Ceylon and the Cingalese, their History, Government, and Religion ... and Capabilities of the Island, 2 vols. (London, 1850).

Smith, George, A Narrative of an Exploratory Visit to Each of the Consular Cities of China and to the Islands of Hong Kong and Chusan in Behalf of the Church Missionary Society in the Years 1844, 1845, 1846 (London, 1847), 532 pp.

Smith, Hubert Llewellyn, The Board of Trade (London: Putnam's 1928), 280 pp.

Stanton, J. W., "Russian embassies to Peking during the eighteenth century," University of Michigan Historical Essays (Ann Arbor, 1937), 97-112.

State Street Trust Co., Old Shipping Days in Boston (1918), 49 pp.

Stelle, Charles C., "American Trade in Opium to China, 1821-1839," The Pacific Historical Review, 10.1: 57-74 (March 1941).

Americans and the China Opium Trade in the Nineteenth Century, Ph.D. dissertation, University of Chicago (1938).

Stephens, H. Morse, "The Administrative History of the British Dependencies in the Further East," American Historical Review, 4.1: 246-72 (January 1899).

Swisher, Earl, The Management of the American Barbarians: A Study in the Relations between the United States and China from 1840 to 1860, Ph.D. dissertation, Harvard University (1941), 427 pp.

Ta Chen, see Ch'en Ta.

Taam, Cheuk-woon (T'an Cho-yuan), The Development of Chinese Libraries under the Ch'ing Dynasty, 1644-1911 (Shanghai: Commercial Press, 1935), 107 pp.

Taylor, Dr. and Mrs. Howard, Hudson Taylor in Early Years. The Growth of a Soul (London, 1911), 503 pp.

Tchang, Yen-chen T. H., "Le Traité de Whampoa 1844," Yenching Journal of Social Studies, 5.1: 31-58 (July 1950).

Teng, S. Y., Chang Hsi and the Treaty of Nanking 1842 (Chicago: University of Chicago Press, 1944), 191 pp.

"Chinese Influence on the Western Examination System," HJAS, 7.4: 267-312 (September 1943).

Teng, Ssu-yü, Fairbank, J. K., and Sun, E-tu Zen, China's Response to the West, A Documentary Survey (1839-1923), draft (to be published by Harvard University Press, 1954)

Thom, Robert, trans., Lasting Resentment of Miss Wang Keaou-Iwan. A Chinese tale (Canton, 1839), 66 pp.

Esop's Fables rendered into Chinese, with a literal translation (Macao, 1840), 104 pp.

Chinese and English Vocabulary (Canton, 1843), 12 + 30 pp.

The Chinese Speaker, or Extracts from Works Written in the Mandarin Language (Ningpo, 1846), 102 pp.

Tilley, John Anthony Cecil and Gaselee, Stephen, The Foreign Office (London and New York: G. P. Putnam's Sons, Ltd., 1933), 335 pp.

Ting Tso-Chao, La Douane Chinoise (Paris: Jouve & Cie Editeurs, 1931), 214 pp.

Torr, Dona, ed., Marx on China 1853-1860, Articles from the New York Daily Tribune (London: Lawrence & Wishart, 1951), 98 pp.

Tsiang, T. F. (Chiang T'ing-fu), "The extension of equal commercial privileges to other nations than the British after the Treaty of Nanking," CSPSR, 15.3: 422-444 (October 1931).

"The Government and the Co-Hong of Canton, 1839," CSPSR, 15.4: 602-607 (January 1932).

"A note in reply," CSPSR, 16.1: 105-109 (April 1932).

"China and European expansion," Politica (London), 2.5: 1-18 (March 1936).

Tu Lien-che and Fang Chao-ying, Index to Thirty-three Collections of Ch'ing Dynasty Biographies, Harvard-Yenching Institute Sinological Index Series, no. 9 (Peiping, 1932), 392 pp.

Tuson, E. W. A., The British Consul's Manual: being a practical guide for Consuls, as well as for the merchant, shipowner, and master mariner in all their Consular transactions (London, 1856), 550 pp.

United States Congressional Documents, see Marshall, McLane.

Vargas, Ph. de, "William C. Hunter's Books on the Old Canton Factories," Yenching Journal of Social Studies, 1.2: 91-117 (July 1939).

Wade, T. F., "A Note on the Condition and Government of the Chinese Empire in 1849," North China Herald (Shanghai, Aug. 17, 1850); reprinted at Hongkong (1850), 90 pp.

Ward, J. S. M., and Stirling, W. G., The Hung Society or the Society of heaven and earth, 3 vols. (London, 1925-6).

Weber, Max, The Religion of China: Confucianism and Taoism, trans. by Hans H. Gerth (Glencoe, Ill.: The Free Press, 1951), 308 pp.

From Max Weber: Essays in Sociology, trans. by H. H. Gerth and C. Wright Mills (New York: Oxford University Press, 1946), 490 pp.

Webster, C. K., "Lord Palmerston at Work, 1830-41," Politica, 2: 129-144 (August 1934).

Webster, Sir Charles, K.C.M.G., Litt. D., F.B.A., The Foreign Policy of Palmerston, 1830-1841: Britain, the Liberal Movement and the Eastern Question, 2 vols. (London: G. Bell & Sons, 1951), 914 pp.

Wetmore, W. S., Recollections of Life in the Far East (Shanghai, 1894), 60 pp.

Williams, S. Wells, The Middle Kingdom; a survey of the Geography, Government, Education, Social Life, Arts, Religion, &c., of the Chinese Empire and its Inhabitants, 2 vols. (London, 1848 and 1883); 1204 pp. (1st ed.), 1611 pp. (rev. ed.).

The Chinese Commercial Guide, containing Treaties, Tariffs, Regulations, Tables, etc., Useful in the Trade to China & Eastern Asia; with an Appendix of Sailing Directions for Those Seas and Coasts, 5th ed. (Hongkong: A. Shortrede & Co., 1863), 266 pp. See Morrison.

Williamson, G. R., Memoir of the Rev. David Abeel, D.P., Late Missionary to China (New York: R. Carter, 1845), 315 pp.

Wilson, J. G., and Fiske, J., editors, Appleton's Cyclopaedia of American Biography, 7 vols. (New York, 1894-1900).

Wittfogel, Karl A., "Die Theorie der Orientalischen Gesellschaft," Zeitschrift für Sozialforschung (Paris, 1938), pp. 90-123.

Wittfogel, Karl A., and Feng Chia-sheng, History of Chinese Society, Liao (907-1125) (Philadelphia: The American Philosophical Society, 1949), 752 pp.

Worcester, G. R. G., The Junks and Sampans of the Yangtze, A Study in Chinese Nautical Research, Maritime Customs, miscellaneous series No. 53, vol. 1 (Shanghai: Inspectorate General of Customs, 1947), 245 pp.

Wright, Stanley F., Kiangsi Native Trade and its Taxation (Shanghai, 1920), 203 pp.

The Collection and Disposal of the Maritime and Native Customs Revenue since the Revolution of 1911. With an account of the Loan Services administered by the Inspector General of Customs (Shanghai, 1927), 275 pp.; 3rd edition revised and enlarged with the assistance of J. H. Cubben (Shanghai, 1935), 674 pp.

Hong Kong and the Chinese Customs, Maritime Customs, VI, Inspectorate Series, No. 7, Confidential (Shanghai, 1930).

China's Struggle for Tariff Autonomy 1843-1938 (Shanghai: Kelly and Walsh, Ltd., 1938), 775 pp.

The Origin and Development of the Chinese Customs Service 1843-1911 (Shanghai, 1939), 147 pp. "For private circulation only."

Hart and the Chinese Customs (Belfast: Wm. Mullan and Son, 1950), 949 pp.

Wu, Wen-Tsao, The Chinese Opium Question in British Opinion and Action (New York, 1928), 190 pp.

Wyld, James, Geographer to the Queen, Map of China, compiled from original Surveys and Sketches (Charing Cross East, London, 1842).

Wylie, A., Chinese Researches (Shanghai, 1897), 549 pp.

Yorke, G. J., "The Princely House, The Story of the Early Years of Jardine Matheson and Company in China 1782-1844" (MS.), 474 pp.

CHINESE AND JAPANESE WORKS CITED

Note: This is a single list of books and articles arranged alphabetically by author or compiler; but many works are also listed by title for cross reference, being better known by title. Periodicals are included by title separately when they have been cited more than once. For Chinese characters of romanized terms, see Glossary. Quotation marks are placed around titles of articles, and around English translations of book and article titles found in the original.

Banno Masataka 坂野正高, "Ahen sensōgo ni okeru saikeikoku taigū no mondai" 阿片戰爭後における最惠國待遇の問題 ("The Problem of the Most Favoured Nation Treatment after the Opium War"), Tōyō bunka kenkyū 東洋文化研究 ("The Oriental Culture Review"), 6: 19-41 (October 1947).

"Gaikō kōshō ni okeru Shimmatsu kanjin no kōdō yōshiki" 外交交渉における清末官人の行動樣式 ("Behaviours of the Mandarins as diplomats late in the Ch'ing Dynasty, with special reference to Treaty-Revision negotiations in 1854"), Kokusaihō gaikō zasshi, 國際法外交雜誌 ("The Journal of International Law and Diplomacy"), 48.4: 502-540 (October 1949); 48.6: 703-737 (December 1949).

Ch'a-yeh yen-chiu 茶葉研究 ("Tea Researches"), Tea Research Institute, Chungan, quarterly, Spring, 1944—.

Chang Chung-fu 張忠紱, "Tzu ya-p'ien chan-cheng chih Ying-Fa lien-chün ch'i-chung Ch'ing-t'ing pan-li wai-chiao chih chi-kuan yü shou-hsü" 自鴉片戰爭至英法聯軍期中清廷辦理外交之機關與手續 (The organs and procedures of the Ch'ing court for handling foreign relations in the period from the Opium War to the Anglo-French joint expedition), Wai-chiao yueh-pao, 2.5: 43-51 (May, 15, 1933).

Chang Hsieh 張燮, Tung-hsi-yang k'ao 東西洋考 (A Study of the eastern and western ocean [routes]), completed 1617 in 12 chüan (Shanghai: Commercial Press ed., 1937), 184 pp.

Chang Hsin-ch'eng 張心澂, Ch'un-ch'iu kuo-chi kung-fa 春秋國際公法 (International law of the Spring and Autumn period; Peiping, 1924), 360 pp.

Chang Te-ch'ang 張德昌, "Hu-hsia-mi huo-ch'uan lai-Hua ching-kuo chi ch'i ying-hsiang" 胡夏米貨船來華經過及其影響 ("The significance of the voyage of Lord Amherst to the northern ports of China"), Chung-kuo chin-tai ching-chi-shih yen-chiu chi-k'an, 1.1: 60-79 (November 1932).

"Ch'ing-tai ya-p'ien chan-cheng-ch'ien chih Chung-Hsi yen-hai t'ung-shang" 清代鴉片戰爭前之中西沿海通商 (Sino-Western coastal trade in the Ch'ing period before the opium war), Ch'ing-hua hsueh-pao, 10.1: 97-145 (January 1935).

Chang Wei-hua 張維華, "Ming-shih Fo-lang-chi Lü-sung Ho-lan I-tal-li-ya ssu-chuan chu-shih" 明史佛朗機呂宋荷蘭意大里亞四傳註釋 ("A commentary of the four chapters on Portugal, Spain, Holland and Italy in the history of the Ming dynasty"), Yen-ching hsueh-pao, monograph series no. 7 (1934).

"Ming-chi Hsi-pan-ya tsai Lü-sung yü Chung-kuo chih kuan-hsi" 明季西班牙在呂宋與中國之關係 (Sino-Spanish relations in the Philippines during the later years of the Ming dynasty), Yü-kung, 6. 8-9: 71-86 (Jan. 1, 1937).

Ch'en Ku-yuan 陳顧遠, Chung-kuo kuo-chi-fa su-yuan 中國國際法溯源 (Origins of Chinese inter-state law; Shanghai: Commercial Press, 1934), 333 pp.

Ch'en Kung-lu 陳恭祿, Chung-kuo chin-tai shih 中國近代史 (Modern history of China; Shanghai: Commercial Press, 1935), 860 pp.

Ch'en Lun-ch'iung 陳倫炯, Hai-kuo wen-chien lu 海國聞見錄 (Record of things seen and heard among the maritime nations), 2 chüan (incl. 1 of maps), author's preface 1730, other prefaces 1743, 1744, various editions.

Ch'en Mao-heng 陳懋恒, "Ming-tai wo-k'ou k'ao-lueh" 明代倭寇考略 ("The invasion of China by Japanese pirates during Ming dynasty"), Yen-ching hsueh-pao, monograph series no. 6 (Peiping, 1934), 168 pp.

Ch'en Shun-nien 陳舜年, "Chung-Mei ch'a-yeh mao-i chien-shih" 中美茶葉貿易簡史 (A brief history of the Sino-American tea trade), Ch'a-yeh yen-chiu, 1: 129-136 (1944).

Ch'i-hsien-ho-shang tiao-sou 七絃河上釣叟 (The old fisherman on the Ch'i-hsien river), Ying-chi-li Kuang-tung ju-ch'eng shih-mo 英吉利廣東入城始末 (A complete account of the English in Kwangtung entering the city), in the Yang-shih ch'ien-ch'i-pai er-shih-chiu ho chai ts'ung-shu 仰視千七百二十九鶴齋叢書, Mo jun-t'ang edition, 1st collection, 1 chüan (Shao-hsing, 1927), 17 pp.

Ch'i Ssu-ho 齊思和, "Wei Yuan yü wan-Ch'ing hsueh-feng" 魏源與晚清學風 (Wei Yuan and late Ch'ing scholarship), Yen-ching hsueh-pao, no. 39: 177-226 (December 1950).

Ch'i-ying 耆英, Yueh-t'ai yü-sung 越台輿頌, Fu-wen-chai edition, 2 ts'e (Canton, 1848).

Chia-ch'ing hui-tien: Ta-Ch'ing hui-tien 大清會典 (Collected statutes of the Ch'ing Dynasty), of the Chia-ch'ing period, 80 chüan in 80 ts'e (completed 1818).

Chiang T'ing-fu (T. F. Tsiang), 蔣廷黻, "Ch'i-shan yü ya-p'ien chan-cheng" 琦善與鴉片戰爭 (Ch'i-shan and the Opium War), Ch'ing-hua hsueh-pao, 6.3: 2-26 (October 1931).

Comp., Chin-tai Chung-kuo wai-chiao shih tzu-liao chi-yao 近代中國外交史資料輯要 (A source book of important documents in modern Chinese diplomatic history), 2 vols. (Shanghai: Commercial Press, 1931-34).

"Chung-kuo yü chin-tai shih-chieh ti ta-pien-chü" 中國與近代世界的大變局 (China and the great changes of the modern world), Ch'ing-hua hsueh-pao, 9.4: 783-827 (October 1934).

Chung-kuo chin-tai shih 中國近代史 (Chinese modern history; Changsha: Commercial Press, 1938), 128 pp.

Ch'ien Chia-chü 千家駒, "Ya-p'ien chan-cheng-shih hsin-lun" 鴉片戰爭史新論 ("The opium war as seen from a new angle"), Chung-shan wen-hua chiao-yü kuan chi-k'an, 2.3: 789-801 (Autumn 1935).

Chin Chao-feng 金兆豐, Ch'ing-shih ta-kang 清史大綱 (Outline of Ch'ing history; Shanghai: Kaiming Book Co., 1935), 504 pp.

Ch'in-ting hu-pu tse-li, see Hu-pu tse-li.

Ch'ing-hua hsueh-pao 清華學報 ("Tsing Hua Journal"), National Tsing Hua University, Peiping, semiannually, June 1924–.

Ch'ing-shih kao, see CSK

Ch'ing-shih lieh-chuan 清史列傳 (Biographical series of the History of the Ch'ing Dynasty), 80 chüan (Shanghai: Chung Hua Book Co., 1928).

Ch'ing shih-lu, see CSL

Ch'ing-tai ch'ou-pan i-wu shih-mo, see IWSM.

Ch'ing yen-fa chih 清鹽法志 (Gazetteer of the Ch'ing salt administration), 300 chüan in 65 ts'e (Peiping, 1920).

Chou Ku-ch'eng 周谷城, Chung-kuo t'ung-shih 中國通史 (General history of China), 2 vols. (Shanghai: Kaiming Book Co., 1939), 1239 pp.

Chou Kuang, et al., 周廣等, Kuang-tung k'ao-ku chi-yao 廣東考古輯要 (Researches on Kwangtung), 46 chüan in 5 ts'e (1893).

Ch'ou-pan i-wu shih-mo, see IWSM

Chu Ch'i 朱偰, Chung-kuo ts'ai-cheng wen-t'i 中國財政問題 ("China's Financial Problem"; Shanghai: Commercial Press, 1934), 248 pp.

Chu Chieh-ch'in 朱傑勤, "Ying-kuo ti-i-tz'u shih-ch'en lai-Hua chi" 英國第一次使臣來華記 ("Account of Lord Macartney's Embassy to China"), Hsien-tai shih-hsueh 現代史學 (Modern history), 3.1: 1-47 (May 25, 1936).

Chu Chin 朱進, Chung-kuo kuan-shui wen-t'i 中國關稅問題 (The Chinese customs problem; 1919), 153 pp.

Chu K'o-ching 朱克敬, Pien-shih hui-ch'ao 邊事彙鈔 (Compendium on border affairs), 12 chüan (Changsha, 1880).

Chung-Hsi chi-shih, see Hsia Hsieh

Chung-Kuo chin-tai ching-chi-shih yen-chiu chi-k'an 中國近代經濟史研究集刊 (Studies in Modern Economic History of China), Institute of Social Research, Academia Sinica, formerly Peiping, later Nanking, quarterly, 1932–

Chung-kuo she-hui ching-chi-shih yen-chiu chi-k'an 中國社會經濟史研究集刊 (known before 1937 as Chung-kuo chin-tai ching-chi-shih yen-chiu chi-k'an), Institute of Social Sciences, Academia Sinica, Nanking, semiannually, 1937–vol. V.

Chung-shan wen-hua chiao-yü-kuan chi-k'an 中山文化教育館季刊 ("Quarterly Review of the Sun Yat-sen Institute for Advancement of Culture and Education"; Nanking, Autumn, 1934–).

CSK: Ch'ing-shih kao 清史稿 (Draft history of the Ch'ing Dynasty), 536 chüan (editors' preface dated 1927).

CSL: Ta-Ch'ing li-ch'ao shih-lu 大清歷朝實錄 (The Veritable Records of the Successive Reigns of the Ch'ing Dynasty), photolithographic edition by the Manchoukuo Kuo Wu Yuan, (Council of State Affairs of the Government of "Manchoukuo,"), 4485 chüan, 1937.

Etō Shinkichi 衛藤瀋吉, "Ahen sensō izen ni okeru Eikoku shōnin no seikaku" 阿片戰爭以前における英國商人の性格 ("Activities of the British 'Country Traders' in China before the Opium War"), Tōyō bunka kenkyūjo kiyo 東洋文化研究所紀要 ("The Memoirs of the Institute for Oriental Culture"), 3: 5-80 (June 1952).

Fan Tuan-ang 范端昂, Yueh-chung chien-wen 粵中見聞 (Seen and heard in Kwangtung), also titled Shuo-Yueh hsin-shu 說粵新書, 31 chüan in 6 ts'e (1801).

Fan Wen-lan 范文瀾, ed. for Chung-kuo li-shih yen-chiu hui 中國歷史研究會 (Chinese history research society), Chung-kuo t'ung-shih chien-pien 中國通史簡編 (A general survey of Chinese history), vol. 1 (Shanghai: Hsin-chih Book Co., 1947), 766 pp. See also Wu Po.

Feng Ch'eng-chün 馮承鈞, Chung-kuo Nan-yang chiao-t'ung shih 中國南洋交通史 (History of communication between China and the Southern Ocean; Shanghai: Commercial Press 1937), 296 pp.

Hai-lu-chu 海錄注 (An annotated edition of the Hai-lu; Changsha: Commercial Press, 1938), 83 pp.

Hai-kuo t'u-chih, see Wei Yuan

Hai-kuo wen-chien lu, see Ch'en Lun-ch'iung

Hai-lu, see Feng Ch'eng-chün, Hsieh Ch'ing-kao.

Hang-chou-fu chih 杭州府志, Hsuan-t'ung ed., 178 chüan in 80 ts'e (printed 1922-26).

Hatano Yoshihiro 波多野善大, "Chūgoku yushutsucha no seisan kōzō, Ahen Sensō mae ni okeru" 中國輸出茶の生產構造，アヘン戰爭前における ("Manufacturing Structure of the Chinese tea for Export — before the Opium War"), Nagoya daigaku bungakubu kenkyū ronshū II, shigaku 1 名古屋大學文學部研究論集 II，史學 1 (Faculty of Literature, Nagoya University, March 1952), 333 pp.; see pp. 183-210.

Hirase Minokichi 平瀨已之吉, Kindai Shina keizai-shi 近代支那經濟史 (Modern Chinese economic history; Tōkyō: Chūō Kōronsha, 1942), 388 pp.

Ho Ko-en 何格恩, "Ming-tai wo-k'ou ch'in-jao yen-hai ko-ti nien-piao" 明代倭寇侵擾沿海各地年表 (Chronological table of the ravages of Japanese pirates at various places along the coast during the Ming period), Ling-nan hsueh-pao, 2.4: 136-232 (June 1933).

Hou Wai-lu 侯外廬, Chin-tai Chung-kuo ssu-hsiang hsueh-shuo shih 近代中國思想學說史 (Modern Chinese intellectual history), 2 vols., preface 1944 (Shanghai: Sheng-huo shu-tien ed., 1947) 1002 pp.

Hsi-ch'ao chi-cheng, see Wang Ch'ing-yün

Hsi Ti-ch'en 席滌塵, "Hsiao-tao-hui yü T'ai-p'ing t'ien-kuo shih-ch'i ti Shang-hai wai-chiao" 小刀會與太平天國時期的上海外交 (The Small Knife Society and foreign relations at Shanghai in the Taiping period), Shang-hai-shih t'ung-chih-kuan ch'i-k'an 上海市通志館期刊 (Bulletin of gazetteer office of the City of Shanghai), 1: 123-146 (1933).

Hsia Hsieh 夏燮, pseud. Chiang-shang-chien-sou 江上蹇叟 (lit., "the lame old man on the river"), Chung-hsi chi-shih 中西紀事 (A record of Sino-western affairs), 24 chüan in 8 ts'e, first preface 1851 (Tao-kuang 30th year, 12th month), second preface to revised edition 1859, last preface 1865; extra title-page bears date Oct. 1868.

Hsia Nai 夏鼐, "Ya-p'ien chan-cheng-chung ti T'ien-chin t'an-p'an" 鴉片戰爭中的天津談判 (The Tientsin negotiations during the Opium War), Wai-chiao yueh-pao, 4.4: 43-56 (April 15, 1934); 4.5: 95-123 (May 15, 1934).

Hsiao-fang-hu-chai yü-ti ts'ung-ch'ao, see Wang Hsi-ch'i.

Hsiao I-shan 蕭一山, Ch'ing-tai t'ung-shih 清代通史 (General history of the Ch'ing period), 3 vols.; vol. 2 (Shanghai, 1928), 929 pp.

Ch'ing-tai tu-fu piao 清代督撫表 (Tables of governors-general and governors of the Ch'ing period; Peiping, n.d.).

Ch'ing-tai ta-hsueh-shih chün-chi-ta-ch'en piao 清代大學士軍機大臣表 (Tables of Grand Secretaries and Grand Councillors of the Ch'ing period; Peiping, n.d.).

"T'ien-ti-hui ch'i-yuan k'ao" 天地會起源考 ("The origin of the 'Heaven and Earth' Society"), Chung-shan wen-hua chiao-yü-kuan chi-k'an 2.3: 777-88 (Autumn 1935).

Hsieh Ch'ing-kao 謝清高, Hai-lu 海錄 (A maritime record), 2 chüan, preface by Yang Ping-nan 楊炳南, ca. 1820 (?); see Feng Ch'eng-chün.

Hsieh Kuo-chen 謝國楨, "Ch'ing-ch'u tung-nan yen-hai ch'ien — chieh k'ao 清初東南沿海遷界攷 (On the removal [of population] on the border along the southeast coast in the early Ch'ing), Kuo-hsueh chi-k'an 國學季刊, 2.4: 797-826, map (Dec. 1930).

Hsien Yü-ch'ing ("Siun yuk-ching") 冼玉清, "Liang T'ing-nan chu-shu lu-yao" 梁廷枏著述錄要 ("On Liang T'ing Nan's works"), Ling-nan hsueh-pao, 4.1: 119-154 (April 15, 1935).

Hsü Chi-yü 徐繼畬, Ying-huan chih-lueh 瀛環志略 (A brief description of the oceans roundabout), 10 chüan in 6 ts'e, preface 1848 (1850).

(Hsü Chi-yü), Sung-k'an hsien-sheng ch'üan-chi 松龕先生全集, (Complete collected writings of [Hsü] Sung-k'an), 4 ts'e, preface by Yen Hsi-shan (1915).

Hsü Ch'uan-pao 徐傳保, Hsien Ch'in kuo-chi-fa chih i-chi 先秦國際法之遺跡 (Traces of inter-state law before the Ch'in dynasty; Shanghai, 1931).

Hsü Ta-ling 許大齡, Ch'ing-tai chuan-na chih-tu 清代捐納制度 ("The System of Purchasing Offices by Contributions during the Ch'ing period, 1644-1911"; Peking: Yen-ching hsueh-pao, monograph series, 22, 1950), 170 pp.

Hsü Ti-shan 許地山, Ta chung chi, ya-p'ien chan-cheng-ch'ien Chung-Ying chiao-she shih-liao 達衷集，鴉片戰爭前中英交涉史料 ("A Collection of Letter Writings, Appeals and Ordinances"; Shanghai: Commercial Press, 1931), 237 pp.

Hsü Wei-nan 徐蔚南, "Shang-hai Hsiao-tao-hui luan-shih ti shih-mo" 上海小刀會亂事的始末 ("Account of the Knife Society insurrection at Shanghai"), I-ching 逸經, 26: 28-31 (Mar. 20, 1937).

Hsueh Fu-ch'eng 薛福成, "Shu Han-yang Yeh-hsiang Kuang-chou chih pien 書漢陽葉相廣州之變 (in Tso Shun-sheng, 左舜生 Chung-kuo chin-pai-nien shih tzu-liao 中國近百年史資料 (Material for Chinese history of the last hundred years), 2 vols. (Shanghai, 1926), 649 pp.

Hu-pu tse-li 戶部則例 (Regulations and precedents of the Board of Revenue), 99 chüan in 72 ts'e (1851); 84 chüan (1865).

Huang-ch'ao wen-hsien t'ung-k'ao 皇朝文獻通考 (Encyclopaedia of the reigning dynasty), completed 1786 or 1787 (ed. 1822).

Huang-Ch'ing chih-kung t'u, see Tung Kao.

Huang Hsü-yuan 黃序鵷, Hai-kuan t'ung-chih 海關通志 (Maritime Customs gazetteer), 2 vols. (Peking, 1917), 788 + 412 pp.

Huang Hung-shou 黃鴻壽 ed., Ch'ing-shih chi-shih pen-mo 清史紀事本末 (A complete record of Ch'ing history), 80 chüan (1st ed., Shanghai, 1915; 3rd ed., Shanghai, 1925).

Huang P'u-sheng, 黃菩生, "Ch'ing-tai Kuang-tung mao-i chi ch'i tsai Chung-kuo ching-chi-shih-shang chih i-i" 清代廣東貿易及其在中國經濟史上之意義 ("The Historical significance of Kwangtung trade under the Chin [sic] dynasty''), Ling-nan hsūeh-pao, 3.4: 157-196 (June 30, 1934).

Hung Chün-p'ei 洪鈞培, Ch'un-ch'iu kuo-chi kung-fa 春秋國際公法 (International law of the Spring and Autumn period; Kunming: Chung-hua Printing Co., 1939), 280 pp.

IWSM-TK,-HF,-TC: Ch'ing-tai ch'ou-pan i-wu shih-mo 清代籌辦夷務始末 (The complete account of our management of barbarian affairs), photolithograph of the original compilation, 80 chüan for the later Tao-kuang period 1836-50, presented to the throne 1856; 80 chüan for the Hsien-feng period 1851-61, presented 1867; 100 chüan for the T'ung-chih period 1862-74, presented 1880 (Peiping: Palace Museum, 1930).

Juan Yuan 阮元, ed., Kuang-tung t'ung-chih 廣東通志 (Gazetteer of Kwangtung), 334 chüan (compiled 1818, reprinted 1864).

Katō Shigeshi 加藤繁, ''Shindai Fukken Kōso no senkō ni tsuite'' 清代福建江蘇の船行に就いて (On the boat firms of Fukien and Kiangsu in the Ch'ing period), Shirin 史林, 14.4: 53-61 (October 1929).

"Dōkō Kampō-chū Shina nite chūzōseraretaru yōshiki ginka ni tsuite" 道光咸豐中支那ニテ鑄造セラレタル洋式銀貨ニ就イテ (On the foreign-style silver coins minted in China in the Tao-kuang and Hsien-feng periods), Tōhō gakuhō 東方學報 (December 1931), 2: 284-292; 3: 351-355 (December 1932), Tōkyō.

Kuan Jui-wu 關瑞梧 ''I-wu shih-mo wai ya-p'ien chan-cheng hou Chung-Ying i-ho shih-liao shu-chien'' 夷務始末外鴉片戰後中英議和史料數件 (Some historical materials on Sino-British negotiations after the opium war, outside the I-wu shih-mo), Shih-hsueh nien-pao, 3-4: 143-170, 183-194 (August 1931).

Kuang-hsü hui-tien: Ta-Ch'ing hui-tien 大清會典 (Collected statutes of the Ch'ing Dynasty), of the Kuang-hsü period, 100 chüan in 36 ts'e (pub. 1899).

Kuang-hsü hui-tien shih-li: Ta-ch'ing hui-tien shih-li 大清會典事例 (Cases and precedents of the Collected Statutes of the Ch'ing Dynasty), 1200 chüan in 383 ts'e (ed. 1899).

Kubota Bunzō, 窪田文三, Shina gaikō tsūshi 支那外交通史 (A comprehensive history of Chinese foreign relations; Tōkyō, 1928), 506 pp.

Li Chien-nung 李劍農, Chung-kuo chin-pai-nien cheng-chih shih 中國近百年政治史 (Political history of China in the last hundred years), 2 vols. (Shanghai: Commercial Press, 1947), 690 pp.

Li Kuang-ming 黎光明, "Chia-ching yü-wo Chiang-Che chu-k'o-chün k'ao" 嘉靖禦倭江浙主客軍考 (''The repulse of the Wo pirates by provincials of Kiangsu and Chekiang during 1551-1561''), Yen-ching hsueh-pao, monograph series, no. 4 (December 1934), 172 pp.

Li Kuei 李圭, Ya-p'ien shih-lueh 鴉片事略 (A brief account of the opium question), 2 chüan reprinted from ed. of Kuang-hsü period (National Peking Library, 1931), 112 pp.

Li Tseng-chieh 李增階, Hai-wai chi-yao 海外紀要 (A record of essentials concerning the outer seas), in Ch'en K'un 陳坤, comp., Ts'ung-cheng hsü-yü-lu 從政緒餘錄, 7 chüan, preface 1881, see ts'e 19-22 in Ju-pu-chi chai hui-ch'ao 如不及齋彙鈔.

Liang Chia-pin 梁嘉彬, Kuang-tung shih-san-hang k'ao 廣東十三行考 (A study of the thirteen hongs at Canton; (Shanghai: Commercial Press, 1937), 414 pp.

Liang Fang-chung 梁方仲, ''Ming-tai kuo-chi mao-i yü yin ti shu-ch'u-ju'' 明代國際貿易與銀的輸出入 (''The international trade and the silver movements in Ming dynasty'') in Chung-kuo she-hui ching-chi-shih yen-chiu chi-k'an, 6.2: 267-324 (December 1939).

Liang T'ing-nan 梁廷枏, Yueh hai-kuan chih 粵海關志 (Gazetteer of the maritime customs of Kwangtung), post-1839, 30 chüan; ts'e 1, 7, and 8 (ch. 1-4, 21-25, and 26-30, respectively) reprinted in Kuo-hsueh wen-k'u 國學文庫, nos. 18, 21, and 33 (Peiping, 1935 et seq.)

I-fen-chi-wen 夷氛記聞 (Record of the barbarian miasma), 5 chüan, preface 1874; (Shanghai: Pei-p'ing yen-chiu yuan 北平研究院 [Peiping Academy], 1937), 116 + 13 pp.

Ling-nan hsueh-pao 嶺南學報 (''Lingnan Journal''), Ling-nan University, Canton, quarterly, 1929–

Liu Hsuan-min 劉選民, ''Ch'ing-tai Tung-san-sheng i-min yü k'ai-k'en'' 清代東三省移民與開墾 (Colonization and opening of land to cultivation in the Three Eastern Provinces in the Ch'ing period), Shih-hsueh nien-pao, 2.5: 67-120 (December 1938).

Liu Lien-k'o 劉聯珂, Pang-hui san-pai-nien ko-ming shih 幫會三百年革命史 (History of the three hundred years revolution of Chinese secret societies; Macao, 1940), 216 pp.

Liu-pu ch'eng-yü chu-chieh 六部成語註解 (Explanatory notes on the established terminology of the Six Boards; Kyōto: Naitō, 1940), 149 + 25 pp.

Lo Er-kang 羅爾綱, T'ai-p'ing t'ien-kuo shih k'ao-cheng chi 太平天國史考證集 (Collected evidential studies of Taiping history; Shanghai: Tu-li ch'u-pan she, 1948), 276 pp.

Lo Yü-tung 羅玉東, ''Li-chin chih-tu chih ch'i-yuan chi ch'i li-lun'' 釐金制度之起源及其理論 (The origin and principles of the likin system), Chung-kuo chin-tai ching-chi-shih yen-chiu chi-k'an, 1.1: 4-37 (November 1932), used in his Chung-kuo li-chin shih (History of likin in China) 中國釐金史.

Chung-kuo li-chin shih 中國釐金史 (History of likin in China), 2 vols. (Shanghai: Commercial Press, 1936), 649 pp.

Matsuda Tomoo 松田智雄, Igirisu shihon to Tōyō イギリス資本と東洋 (English capital and the Orient; Tōkyō: Nippon Hyōronsha 日本評論社, 1951), 290 pp.

Matsumoto Tadao 松本忠雄 ''Kantō no kōshō to ikan'' 廣東の行商と夷館 (The hong merchants and the foreign establishments at Canton), Shina 支那 (''The China Review''), 23.1: 52-67 (spec. no., Spring 1932); continued in 23.4 and 5 (April, May, 1932).

Momose Hiromu 百瀬弘, ''Shindai ni okeru Supein doru no ryūtsū'' 清代に於ける西班牙弗の流通 (Circulation of the Spanish dollar in the Ch'ing period), Shakai keizai shigaku 社會經濟史學 (Studies in social and economic history), 6 2: 1-25 (May 1936); 6.3: 37-60: (June 1936); 6.4: 43-65 (July 1936).

"Mindai ni okeru Shina no gaikoku bōeki" 明代に於ける支那の外國貿易 (China's foreign trade in the Ming period), Tōa 東亜, 8.7: 95-110 (July 1, 1935).

Nishijima Sadao 西嶋定生, "Shina shoki mengyō shijō no kōsatsu 支那初期棉業市場の考察 ("Inland Trade of Cotton Cloth in China at its Beginning Stage"), Tōyō gakuhō, 31.2: 122-148 (Oct. 1947).

Nozoe Shigekatsu 野副重勝, "Gokō kaikōzen ni okeru Shina gaikoku bōekishi no shitsuteki kentō 五港開港前に於ける支那外國貿易史の質的檢討 (A qualitative study of the history of China's foreign trade before the opening of the five ports), Shina 支那 ("The Shina, The China Review"), 23.2 (Feb. 1, 1932), cont'd. in 23.3, 7, 8, 11 (Nov. 1, 1932), and 24.2.

Otake Fumio 小竹文夫, Kinsei Shina keizaishi kenkyū 近世支那經濟史研究 (Researches in modern Chinese economic history; Tōkyō: Kōbundō, 1942), 293 pp.

Saitō Yoshie 齋藤良衛, Kinsei Tōyō gaikō shi josetsu 近世東洋外交史序説 (Introduction to modern Far Eastern international relations; Tōkyō, 1927), 509 pp.

Shang-Chiang liang-hsien-chih 上江兩縣志 (Local history of Shang-yuan and Kiangning, of the T'ung-chih period), 29 chüan in 12 ts'e, block-print ed. (1874).

Shang-hai-hsien chih, see T'ung-chih Shang-hai-hsien chih.

She-hui k'o-hsueh chi-k'an 社會科學季刊 (Quarterly Journal of Social Science), National Wuhan University, Wuchang, 1930—

She-hui k'o-hsueh tsa-chih 社會科學雜誌 (Quarterly Review of Social Sciences), Institute of Social Research, Academia Sinica, formerly Peiping, later Nanking, 1930—

She-hui k'o-hsueh ts'ung-k'an 社會科學叢刊 (Studies in Social Sciences), College of Law, National Central University, Nanking, semi-annually, May 1934—

Sheng-hsun, see Shih-ch'ao sheng-hsun, see Wen-tsung hsien-huang-ti sheng-hsun

Shih Chao-ying 時昭瀛, "I-pa-ssu-ssu nien Chung-Mei Chung-Fa t'iao-yueh" 一八四四年中美中法條約 (The Sino-American and Sino-French treaties of 1844), She-hui k'o-hsueh chi-k'an, 4.2: 291-308 (December 1933).

Shih-ch'ao sheng-hsun 十朝聖訓 (Sacred instructions of ten reigns [1616-1874]), 922 chüan in 286 ts'e, last preface 1880.

Shih-hsueh nien-pao 史學年報 ("Historical Annual"), The History Society of Yenching University, Peiping, 1929—

Shih-liao hsun-k'an 史料旬刊, (Historical materials published thrice-monthly), 40 vols. (Peiping: Palace Museum, 1930-31).

Sun Hao 孫灝, Hai-kuo t'u-chih cheng-shih 海國圖志徵實 (Errata and supplements to the Hai-kuo t'u-chih), 100 chüan in 20 ts'e (Shanghai, 1902).

Sung-k'an hsien-sheng ch'üan-chi, see Hsü Chi-yü.

Sung Mo 宋默, "Ya-p'ien chan-cheng hsin shih-liao" 鴉片戰爭新史料 (New historical materials on the opium war), Kuo-wen chou-pao 國聞週報, 10.46,48; 11.1,3,5,8,11,13.

Ta-Ch'ing chin-shen ch'üan-shu 大清縉紳全書 (Ch'ing dynasty official Red Book), 3 ts'e, (winter ed. 1852).

Ta-Ch'ing hui-tien, see Chia-ch'ing, Kuang-hsü for editions.

Ta-Ch'ing i-t'ung-chih 大清一統志 (Gazetteer of the Ch'ing Empire), 356 chüan, in 120 ts'e, compiled under imperial auspices, imperial preface dated 1744, slightly revised in 1764, reprinted in 1849.

Ta-Ch'ing li-ch'ao shih-lu, see CSL.

Ta-Ch'ing t'ung-li 大清通禮 (Current ceremonial usages of the Ch'ing Dynasty), 54 chüan in 12 ts'e (ed. 1756).

Ta-Ming chi-li 大明集禮 (Collected ceremonies of the Ming Dynasty), 53 chüan in 40 ts'e, (Palace edition, 1530).

Tanaka Katsumi 田中克己, "Shinsho no Shina enkai" 清初の支那沿海 ("Chinese coast in the early Ts'ing Dynasty"), Rekishi-gaku kenkyū 歴史學研究, 6.1: 73-81 (January 1936); 6.3: 83-94 (March 1936).

Tanaka Suiichirō 田中萃一郎, "Jūsankō" 十三行 (The thirteen hongs), Tanaka Suiichirō shigaku rombunshū 田中萃一郎史學論文集 (Tōkyō: Maruzen, 1932), 675 pp.; see pp. 61-74.

T'ang Hsiang-lung 湯象龍, "Tao-kuang shih-ch'i ti yin-kuei wen-t'i" 道光時期的銀貴問題 ("Outflow of silver in the Tao-Kuang period, 1821-1839"), She-hui k'o-hsueh tsa-chih, 1.3: 1-31 (September 1930).

T'ang Hsiang-lung 湯象龍, "Kuang-hsü san-shih-nien Yueh-hai-kuan ti kai-ko" 光緒三十年粵海關的改革 ("The Reform of the Canton Customs Administration in 1904"), Chung-kuo chin-tai ching-chi-shih yen-chiu chi-k'an, 3.1: 67-74 (May 1935).

T'ao Yuan-chen 陶元珍, "Tu 'Ch'i-shan yü ya-p'ien chan-cheng'" 讀"琦善與鴉片戰爭" (On reading "Ch'i-shan and the Opium War"), Ta-kung-pao t'u-shu fu-k'an 大公報圖書副刊 (Ta Kung Pao literary supplement), no. 77 (May 2, 1935).

THL, see Wang Hsien-ch'ien.

Toyama Gunji 外山軍治,

"Shanhai dōdai Go Kenshō 上海道台吳健彰 (The Shanghai taotai Wu Chien-chang), Gakkai 學海, 1.7: 45-54 (Dec. 10, 1944).

Taihei Tengoku to Shanhai 太平天國と上海 (The Taiping kingdom and Shanghai; Kyōto: Kōtō shoin 高桐書院, 1947), 169 pp.

"Taiheiran ni okeru Shinchō no gaikoku ni taisuru enjo yōsei" 太平亂に於ける清朝の外國に對する援助要請 (The Ch'ing dynasty's requests for help from the foreign powers during the Taiping Rebellion), Shirin 史林, 31.3,4: 32-45 (December 1947).

Tsiang, T. F., see Chiang T'ing-fu

Tso Shun-sheng 左舜生, comp., Chung-kuo chin-pai-nien shih tzu-liao 中國近百年史資料 (Material for Chinese history of the last hundred years), 2 vols. (Shanghai), 1926), 649 pp.

T'ung-chih Shang-hai-hsien chih 同治上海縣志 (Shanghai gazetteer of the T'ung-chih period), 32 chüan in 16 ts'e (1871).

Tung-hsi-yang k'ao, see Chang Hsieh.

Tung-hua (hsü-) lu, see Wang Hsien-ch'ien.

T'ung I 童疑, "I-Man-Jung-Ti yü tung-nan-hsi-pei" 夷蠻戎狄與東南西北 (The I, Man, Jung and Ti and East, South, West, North), Yü-kung 7.10: 11-17 (July 16, 1937).

Tung Kao 董誥, et al., comp., Huang-Ch'ing chih-kung t'u 皇清職貢圖 (Illustrations of the regular tributaries of the imperial Ch'ing), 9 chüan (Palace edition 1761).

Uchida Naosaku 內田直作, "Zai-Shi Eikoku shōsha Iwa yōkō no hatten shitekibunseki" 在支英國商社怡和洋行の發展史的分析 (An historical analysis of the development of the British trading firm of Jardine, Matheson and Co. in China), Shina kenkyū 支那研究, 51: 213-240 (June 1939); 52: 151-192 (Nov. 1939).

Ueda Toshio 植田捷雄, "Shina ni okeru ryōji saibanken no kigen" 支那に於ける領事裁判權の起源 (The origin of consular jurisdiction in China), Kokusaihō gaikō zasshi, 40.10: 877-907 (Dec. 1, 1941).

Shina ni okeru sokai no kenkyū 支那に於ける租界の研究 (A study of the concessions in China; Tōkyō: Ganshōdō 巖松堂 Shoten, 1941), 919 pp.

"Ahen sensō ron" 阿片戰爭論 (On the Opium War), Kokusaihō gaikō zasshi ("The Journal of International Law and Diplomacy"), 42.1: 22-47; 42.2: 135-158; 42.3: 237-270 (Jan., Feb., Mar., 1943)

"Shina no kaikoku to kokusaihō" 支那の開國と國際法 (The opening of China and international law), Tōyō bunka kenkyū 東洋文化研究, 1.1: 31-48 (October 1944).

"Eikoku no ahen mitsuyu to Nankin jōyaku" 英國の阿片密輸と南京條約 (Britain's opium smuggling and the Nanking treaty), Shina, 35.12: 1-8 (Dec. 1, 1944).

"Nankin jōyaku no kenkyū" 南京條約の研究 ("On the Treaty of Nanking"), Kokusaihō gaikō zasshi ("The Journal of International Law and Diplomacy"), 45.3-4: 93-123 (March 1946); 45.5-6: 154-175 (May 1946). Concluded in 46.3: 123-155 (February 1947) as "Zoku Nankin jōyaku no kenkyū" 續 .

"Ahen sensō to Shimmatsu kammin no shoshō" 阿片戰爭と清末官民の諸相 ("The actual attitude of the Chinese mandarins and common people towards the Opium war"), Kokusaihō gaikō zasshi 國際法外交雜誌, 50.3: 235-271 (July 1951).

Wai-chiao yüeh-pao 外交月報 ("Foreign Affairs Monthly"), Foreign Affairs Monthly Society, Peiping, monthly, 1932–.

Wang Chih-ch'un 王之春, Ko-kuo t'ung-shang shih-mo chi 各國通商始末記 (A complete account of the foreign trade with the various countries), 20 chüan in 6 ts'e (1895); identical with the same author's Kuo-ch'ao jou-yuan chi.

Kuo-ch'ao jou-yuan chi 國朝柔遠記 (Record of the ruling dynasty's graciousness to strangers, 20 chüan (1896, also 1891, 1895).

Wang Ch'ing-yün 王慶雲, Shih-ch'ü yü-chi 石渠餘紀 (also titled Hsi-ch'ao chi-cheng 熙朝紀政), 6 chüan (ca. 1850, various editions); see Hummel, pp. 813-14.

Wang Hsi-ch'i 王錫祺, Hsiao-fang-hu-chai yü-ti ts'ung-ch'ao 小方壺齋輿地叢鈔, 1438 titles in 84 ts'e (preface 1877, second supplement 1897).

Wang Hsien-ch'ien 王先謙, comp., Tung-hua hsü-lu 東華續錄 (Continuation of the Record of the Tung-hua [gate]), 252 ts'e (editor's preface 1884).

Wang I-t'ang 王揖唐, Shang-hai tsu-chieh wen-t'i 上海租界問題 (The problem of the Shanghai leased territory), 3 p'ien in 1 ts'e (n.d.); dates in text to 1913.

Wang Tse-nung 王澤農, "Wu-i ch'a-yen t'u-jang" 武夷茶岩土壤 ("Soil survey of the tea gardens of Wu-i hills"), Ch'a-yeh yen-chiu 1: 106-115 (1944), 149-55; 2: 44-56, 61-77.

Wei Hsü-chih 魏胥之, Ying-kuo tsai Chung-kuo ti ching-chi ch'in-lueh shih 英國在中國的經濟侵略史 (Historical survey of England's economic aggression in China; Peking: Hsin-min Publishing Co., 1945), 221 pp.

Wei Ying-ch'i 魏應麒, Lin Wen-chung-kung nien-p'u 林文忠公年譜 (A chronological biography of Lin Tse-hsü; Shanghai: Commercial Press, 1935), 200 pp.

Wei Yüan 魏源, Sheng-wu chi 聖武記 (A record of imperial military exploits), 14 chüan (preface to first edition 1842).

Hai-kuo t'u-chih 海國圖志 (An illustrated gazetteer of the maritime countries), 50 chüan (1844); later editions, 60 chüan (1847), 100 chüan (1852), reprint (1876), etc.

Tao-kuang yang-sou cheng-fu chi 道光洋艘征撫記 (Record of the pacification of the foreign ships in the Tao-kuang period), in Ko Shih-chün 葛士濬, Huang-ch'ao ching-shih wen hsü-pien 皇朝經世文續編 (Collected Essays on Administration of the Reigning Dynasty), Kuang-pai-sung-chai 廣百宋齋, 120 chüan, lithographic ed. (1891).

Wen-tsung hsien-huang-ti sheng-hsun 文宗顯皇帝聖訓 (Sacred Instructions of the Hsien-feng Emperor), 110 chüan in 10 ts'e.

Wu Chao-hsin 吳兆莘, Chung-kuo shui-chih shih 中國稅制史 (History of the Chinese taxation system), 2 vols. (Shanghai: Commercial Press, 1937).

Wu Ch'eng-hsi 吳承禧, "Pai-nien-lai yin-chia pien-tung chih hui-ku" 百年來銀價變動之回顧 ("The price of silver, a review of its fluctuations 1833-1931"), She-hui k'o-hsueh tsa-chih, 3.3: 323-63 (September 1932).

Wu Po 武波 (Fan Wen-lan 范文瀾), Chung-kuo chin-tai shih 中國近代史 (Modern Chinese history), vol. 1 (Shanghai: Tu-shu ch'u-pan-she, 1947), 418 pp.; rev. ed. attrib. to Fan as author (Peking, 1949).

Wu Yü-kan 武堉幹, "T'ang-Sung shih-tai Shang-hai tsai Chung-kuo tui-wai mao-i-shang chih ti-wei kuan" 唐宋時代上海在中國對外貿易上之地位觀 ("Shanghai as an International Trading Port during the T'ang and Sung Dynasties — A comparative Study with Other Ports in China"), She-hui k'o-hsueh ts'ung-k'an, 2.1: 145-216 (May 1935).

Ya-p'ien chan-cheng shih 鴉片戰爭史 ("The Opium War"; Shanghai: Commercial Press, 1931), 149 pp.

Yano Jinichi 矢野仁一, "Shina no ahen mondai" 支那の鴉片問題 (The Chinese opium problem), in *Kindai Shina no seiji oyobi bunka* 近代支那の政治及文化 (Modern Chinese politics and culture; Tōkyō, 1926), 420 pp., see pp. 370-420.

"Kō Shaku-ji oyobi Rin Soku-jo no ahen sōgi ni tsuite" 黄爵滋及び林則徐の鴉片奏議に就いて (On the memorials of Huang Chueh-tzu and Lin Tse-hsü discussing opium), in *Takase hakushi kanreki kinen Shinagaku ronso* 高瀨博士還暦記念支那學論叢 (Essays in Chinese studies commemorating the sixty-first birthday of Dr. Takase; Kyōto: Kōbundō 弘文堂, 1928), 853 pp., see pp. 757-771.

"Ahen sensō to Honkon" アヘン戰爭と香港 (The Opium War and Hongkong; Tōkyō: Kōbundō 弘文堂, 1939), 318 pp.

Yao Wei-yuan 姚薇元, *Ya-p'ien chan-cheng shih-shih k'ao* 鴉片戰爭史事考 (A study of the historical events of the opium war; Kweiyang, 1942), 266 pp.

Yen-ching hsueh-pao 燕京學報 ("*The Yenching Journal*"), Yenching University, Peiping, semi-annually, June 1927 —.

Yen Chung-p'ing 嚴中平, *Chung-kuo mien-yeh chih fa-chan* 中國棉業之發展 (Development of the Chinese cotton industry; Chungking: Commercial Press, 1943), 305 pp.

Yen Ju-i 嚴如熤, *Yang-fang chi-yao* 洋防輯要 (Essentials of maritime defense), 24 *chüan* in 8 *ts'e* (n.d.).

Ying-huan chih-lueh, see Hsü Chi-yü.

Yü Ch'ang-hui 俞昌會, *Fang-hai chi-yao* 防海輯要 (Essentials of coastal defense), *chüan-shou* + 18 *chüan* in 10 *ts'e* (1842).

Yü Chen-yü, Mao Chin-sheng *et al*. 俞震豫, 毛金生等 "Fu-chien Ch'ung-an Shui-chi Shao-wu ch'a-ch'ü chih t'u-jang" 福建崇安水吉邵武茶區之土壤 (Soil of Chungan, Shuichi and Shaowu districts, Fukien), *Ch'a-yeh yen-chiu*, 3.7-12: 131-152 (July-December 1945).

Yü En-te 于恩德, *Chung-kuo chin-yen fa-ling pien-ch'ien shih* 中國禁煙法令變遷史 (History of the changes in Chinese anti-opium laws; Shanghai: Chung-hua shu-chü, 1934), 332 pp.

Yü-kung pan-yueh k'an 禹貢半月刊 (The Chinese Historical Geography Semi-monthly Magazine), Yü-kung Research Society, Peiping, 1934 —

Yueh hai-kuan chih, see Liang T'ing-nan.

GLOSSARY OF CHINESE NAMES AND TERMS

This glossary is not designed for the edification of the general reader but to assist further research in this still unexplored field. It therefore contains Chinese character transliterations of some Western names of persons and countries in addition to characters for the Chinese and Western persons and for the places, terms and phrases cited in the text. Provinces, dynasties, and persons of other dynasties are omitted. Well-known Chinese places, when listed, follow the Chinese Post Office romanization, other places the Wade-Giles system. Characters for foreign persons and countries are given under the foreign name rather than under the romanized entry. Research would be greatly facilitated by the compilation of a full dictionary of the Chinese characters used for foreign persons and places in Chinese literature of the nineteenth century.

Entries are listed alphabetically without reference to hyphens, spaces or aspirates between letters.

Abeel (Ya-pi-li) 雅裨理
Achin (Ya-chi) 亞齊
Aigun 艾輝
Alantsai (Ya-lan-tsai) 亞蘭仔
Alcock (A-li-kuo) 阿利國，啊哩嘓
A-li-kuo see Alcock
A-li-shan-t'e-li-ah (Alexandria) 阿力山特釐阿

America (Mi-li-chien) 咪唎堅，(Ya-mei-li-chia) 亞美理駕；United States of (Ta ho-chung-kuo) 大合衆國
A-mi-ko see Omega
Amoy see Hsia-men
Anking 安慶
Annam 安南
Anunghoi (Ya-niang-hsieh) 亞娘鞋
Anyang 安陽
Ao-men (Macao) 澳門
Austria (Shuang-ying, lit. Double-Eagle) 雙鷹

Balfour (Pa-fu-er) 巴富爾
Belgium (Pi-li-shih) 比利時，(Pei-erh-jih-k'o) 吡嚫咀喀
Bengal (Ming-ya-la 明呀喇，
(Meng-chia-la) 孟加剌，
(Pang-ka-la) 榜葛剌，
(Meng-ka-la) [illegible]嘎啦
Bogue (Bocca Tigris) see Hu-men
Bohea see Wu-i
Bombay (Meng-mai) 孟買
Bonham (Wen-han) 呅嗡
Bowring (Pao-ling) 咆呤
Bridgman (Pi-chih-wen) 啤咍呅
Burut 布魯特

Callery (Chia-lueh-li) 咖略唎
Cambodia (Chien-pu-chai) 柬埔寨
Canton (Kuang-chou) 廣州
Caroline (Chia-no-lai) 甲訥來，(also K'o-le-ling) 客勒稜
Ch'a-chih-tang (Georgetown) 查治當
Cha-tien see Jardine
Chang-chia-k'ou (Kalgan) 張家口
Ch'ang-chiang (Yangtze) 長江
Chang-chou (Changchow) 漳州
Chang Hsi 張喜
Chang Hsi-t'ung 張錫彤
Chang P'an-lung 張攀龍
Changsha 長沙
Ch'ang-shan 常山
ch'ang-shui 常稅
Chang Te-ch'ang 張德昌
Chang T'ien-tse 張天澤

Chao Ch'ang-ling 趙長齡
Chao-ch'ing 肇慶
Chao Feng-t'ien 趙豐田
chao-hui 照會
Chao-ying Fang see Fang Chao-ying
Chapu 乍浦
Chefoo (Yen-t'ai) 烟臺
che-fu ch'i hsin 折服其心
Che-hai kuan 浙海關
Ch'en, Agnes Fang-chih 陳芳芝
Ch'en Ah-lin 陳阿林
Ch'en Ch'i-t'ien 陳其田
Chen-chiang see Chin kiang
Ch'en Chih-chi 陳之驥
Ch'en Chih-kang 陳志剛
Ch'en Ch'ing-chen (Tan Keng-chin, Tan King Chin) 陳慶真
Chen-hai (Chinhai) 鎮海
Chen-hai-ch'uan 鎮海船
Ch'en, Kenneth (Ch'en Kuan-sheng) 陳觀勝
Ch'en Po-ling 陳柏齡, (Ch'eng? Po-ling) 程
Ch'en Ta 陳達
Cheng Ah-er 鄭阿二
Cheng Ch'eng-kung (Koxinga) 鄭成功
ch'eng-hsin 誠信
ch'eng-i 城邑
Ch'eng Kung-shou 程恭壽
cheng-o 正額
cheng-shui 正稅
Cheng Te-k'un 鄭德坤
Ch'eng Yü-ts'ai 程矞采
Ch'i-ch'ang hang see Russell and Co.
Ch'i Chün-tsao 祁寯藻
Chi-er-hang-a ("Keih," also "Koerhangah") 吉爾杭阿
Ch'i-hsien 祁縣
Ch'i Kung (Kekung) 祁𡎴
Chi-li-pu see Gribble
Chi-lien see Glen
ch'i-lin 麒麟
chi-mi 羈縻
Ch'i-shan 琦善
Ch'i Shen 齊慎
Ch'i-ying 耆英
Chia-ch'ing 嘉慶
chia-jen 家人
Chialing 嘉陵
Chia-no-lai see Caroline
Chia-t'e-li (Catholic) 加特力
Chia-ying-chou 嘉應州
Chiang-chiao see India
Chiang-chün 將軍
Chiang-hai kuan 江海關
chiang-k'ou (ports) 港口

Chiang-k'ou see Siam
Chiang-ning 江寧
chiang-pei 江北
Chiang-pin 江彬
Chiang T'ing-fu (T. F. Tsiang) 蔣廷黻
Ch'ien-lung 乾隆
Chien-pu-chai see Cambodia
chien-sheng 監生
Ch'ien-t'ang 錢塘
Ch'ien Tuan-sheng 錢端升
chih-chi chih-pi, pai-chan pai-sheng 知己知彼，百戰百勝
chih-tao-liao 知道了
Chih-tsao 織造
Chimmo Bay, foreign name for bay off Shen-hu 深滬, Fukien
chin (catty, 1 1/3 lbs.) 斤
Ch'in-ch'ai pien-i hsing-shih ta-ch'en 欽差便宜行事大臣
Ch'in-ch'ai ta-ch'en 欽差大臣
Chinchew (Ch'üan-chou) 泉州
Chin-chih-er see Gingell
chin-shu 儘數
Ching-k'ou 京口
Ching-pao 京報
Ch'ing-p'u (Tsingpu) 青浦
Ching-te chen 景德鎮
Ching-yeh-chih (George) 京也治
Ch'ing-yuan (Ningpo) 慶元
Chinhai see Chen-hai
Chinkiang (Chen-chiang) 鎮江
chin-shih 進士
Chiu-chiang (Kiukiang) kuan 九江關
Chiu-jou-fo 舊柔佛
Chiu-lung (Kowloon) 九龍
chou 州
Chou Li-ch'un 周立春
Chou Tsu-p'ei 周祖培
Ch'ü-chou 衢州
chü-jen 舉人
chu-p'i 硃批
ch'üan-ch'üan 全權
Ch'üan-chou (Zayton, Chinchew) 泉州
Ch'uan-pi (lit. "bored nose") 穿鼻
Chuansha 川沙
ch'üan-yang chih hsing 犬羊之性
chueh-lo (chio-lo, gioro) 覺羅
Chuenpi see Ch'uan-pi
Chün-chi-ch'u 軍機處
Chün-chi ta-ch'en tzu-chi 軍機大臣字寄
Ch'ung-an (Tsungan) 崇安
Chung-ho hang see Mingqua
Chungking 重慶
Ch'ung-wen-men 崇文門
Chusan (Chou-shan) Island 舟山
Cochin 柯枝
Cohong (Kung-hang) 公行
Compradore (mai-pan) 買辦
Congou (kung-fu) 工夫
Cumsingmoon, Kumsing moon (Chin-hsing-men) 金星門
Cushing (Ku-sheng) [口顧]嘁，顧聖

Davis (Te-pi-shih) [口德][口庇][口時]，[口德]啤吐
Denmark (Huang-ch'i?) 黃旗
(Ta-ni) 大尼
(Lien-kuo) 嗹國
(Tan-mai) 丹麥
Dent and Co. (Pao-shun) 寶順

Eleepoo see I-li-pu
Elliot (I-lü) 義律
E-lo-ssu see Russia
England (Ying-chi-li) 暎咭唎
Ewo = I-ho

Fa-lan-hsi see France
fan-fang 番方
fan-hsun 犯順
fan-kuei (Fan Kwae) 番鬼
Fang Chao-ying 房兆楹
fang-fan 防範
Fatshan see Fo-shan
Fei Hsiao-t'ung 費孝通
fen-t'ou ch'a-na 分頭查拏
Feng-huang-ch'eng 鳳凰城
Feng-yang kuan 鳳陽關
Feng (Fung) Yu-lan 馮友蘭
Fokien = Fukien
Fo-lan-hsi see France
Fo-lang-chi see Portugal
Fo-lang-hsi see France
Fo-lang-hsi-ya see France
Foochow 福州
Footae = Fu-t'ai, see Kwanshing
Formosa see T'ai-wan
Fo-shan (Fatshan) 佛山
fou-fei 浮費
Fou-liang (Fu-liang) 浮梁
France (Fo-lan-hsi) 咈囒哂,
(Fa-lan-hsi) 法蘭西,
(Fu-lang-hsi) 弗朗西,
(Fo-lang-hsi) 佛朗西，狼
(Ho-lan-hsi) 和蘭西,
(Fo-lang-hsi-ya) 佛郎西亞, etc.
fu (prefecture) 府
Fuchow = Foochow
Fu-lang-hsi see France
Fu-shan 福山
Fu-t'ai hang see Kwanshing
fu-yü 撫馭
Gingell (Chin-chih-er) 金執爾
ginseng (jen-ts'an) 人參
gioro see chueh-lo
Glen (Chi-lien) 記連
Goqua or Gowqua (Hsieh Ao- kuan) 謝鰲官
(Tung-hsing hang 東興行
Hsieh Yu-jen 謝有仁
Gribble (Chi-li-pu) 記里布
Gutzlaff (Kuo-shih-la) 郭施拉

Hae Kwan = hai-kuan
Hai-fang 海防
Hai-fang t'ung-chih 海防同知
hai-kuan (Haikuan, etc) 海關
Hainan 海南
Hai-ning 海寧
hai-shui 海稅
Hai-yen 海鹽
Hamburg (Han-p'u) 漢堡
Han-chien 漢奸
Han-p'u see Hamburg
hang 行
Hangchow 杭州
Hankow 漢口
Hanlin (Academy) 翰林
hao-hsien 耗羨
hei-kuei-nu 黑鬼奴

Hei-shan (Hieshan, Sie Shan) 黑山
Heng-ch'ang 恆昌
Heung-shan see Hsiang-shan
Hien Fen = Hsien-feng
Ho-chung-kuo see America
Ho Ju-lin 何汝霖
Ho-k'ou 河口
Ho-lan see Holland
Ho-lan-hsi see France
Holland (Ho-lan) 嗬囒
Ho-lun-ti 呵輪的
Honam (Canton) 河南
hong (hang) 行
Hongkong (Hsiang-chiang) 香港
Hoochow = Hu-chou
Hoomunchai see Hu-men-chai
Hoomunkong (Hsia-men-chiang) 厦門港
Hoppo (Hu-pu) 户部 ; also see Yueh hai-kuan pu, Yueh hai-kuan chien-tu; also suggested: Ho-po 河泊, Hai-pu 海部.
Howqua (Hao-kuan) 浩官; head of the I-ho (Ewo) firm 怡和行:
Wu Kuo-ying (Howqua I) 伍國瑩,
Wu Ping-chien (Wu Tun-yuan, Howqua II) 伍秉鑑, 敦元
Wu Yuan-hua (Howqua III) 伍元華,
Wu Ch'ung-yueh (Howqua IV), Wu Shao-jung 伍崇曜, 紹榮
How-tou-san (Hu-t'ou-shan) 虎頭山
hsi-ch'un see Hyson
Hsi-feng-k'ou 喜峰口
Hsi-hsin kuan 西新關
Hsi-yang 西洋
Hsia-men (Amoy) 厦門
Hsia-pa see Parkes
Hsiang 湘
Hsiang Jung 向榮
hsiang-p'i 象皮
Hsiang-shan (Heung-shan) 香山
hsiao-chung see Souchong
hsiao-fei 梟匪
Hsiao-hsi-yang 小西洋
Hsiao I-shan 蕭一山
Hsiao-tao-hui (Small Knife Society, Small Sword Society) 小刀會
Hsieh Ao-kuan see Goqua (or Gowqua)
hsieh-chih 挾制
Hsieh-ling 協領
Hsieh Pao-chao (-ch'ao) 謝保樵
Hsieh Yu-jen see Goqua (or Gowqua)
hsien (district) 縣
Hsien-feng 咸豐
Hsien-ling 咸齡
Hsien-lo see Siam
Hsin-ch'i-p'o (Singapore) 新奇坡, mod. Hsin-chia-p'o 新加坡
Hsin-chou 新洲
Hsin-chou-fou 新洲埠
Hsin-chou-fu 新州府
Hsin-fou 新埠
hsin-kuan 新關
Hsing-Ch'üan-Yung 興泉永
Hsing-hua 興化
hsiu 秀
Hsiung-nu 匈奴
Hsü Chi-yü 徐繼畬
Hsü-chia-hui see Zikawei
Hsü Kuang-chin 徐廣縉
Hsü Nai-chao 許乃釗
Hsü Nai-chi 許乃濟

Hsueh Huan 薛煥
Hsun-chien ("Seunkeen") 巡檢
Hsun-fu 巡撫
Hu-chou 湖州
Hu-fu-te 嘑咈嘚
Hu-hsia-mi see Lindsay
Hu-Kwang 湖廣
Hu Lin-i 胡林翼
Hu-men (Bogue, Bocca Tigris) 虎門
Hu-men-chai 虎門寨
Hu-pu 户部; see Hoppo
hu-shih chu-kuo 互市諸國
Hu-shu kuan 滸墅關
hua-pu 花布
Hua-sheng-tun see Washington
Huai 淮
Huai-an kuan 淮安關
huai-jou yuan-jen 懷柔遠人
Huang-ch'ao ching-shih wen-pien 皇朝經世文編
Huang-ch'i see Denmark?
Huang Chou 黄舟
Huang En-t'ung 黄恩彤
Huang K'un-k'un 黄坤坤
Huang-p'u (Whampoa, below Canton) 黄埔 or 浦; (Whangpu, at Shanghai) 浦
Huang Tsung-han 黄宗漢
Huang Wei ("Un Wee") 黄渭
Hui-chiang 滙江
Hui-chou 徽州
Hui-tien 會典
Hung Hsiu-ch'üan 洪秀全
Hung-lou-meng 紅樓夢
Hung-mao-fan 紅毛番
Hung-men see Triad
Hung-tan ch'uan 紅單船
Hwaiyang 淮揚
Hyson (hsi-ch'un) 熙春

I 夷
Ichang 宜昌
I-ching 奕經
i-ch'ing kuei-chueh 夷情詭譎
i-ch'ing p'o-ts'e 夷情叵測
I-ho (Ewo) hang 怡和行; see Howqua. see also Jardine
I K'un-kuan see Kwanshing
Ili 伊犁
I-liang 怡良
I-li-pu 伊里布
I-lü see Elliot
India (T'ien-chu) 天竺, (Yin-tu) 印度, (Chiang-chiao) 港脚 (Giles 1245)
I-shan 奕山
i-shui 夷税
I-ta-li 意大理, Italy
I-ta-li-ya 意達里亞, see Portugal
i-wan yuan 一萬圓
I Yuan-ch'ang see Kwanshing

Jackson (Jo-sun) 若遜
Jardine (Matheson and Co.) (Cha-tien) 渣顛, 甸, (I-ho, Ewo) 怡和, 義, (K'o-pei-shih) 科孛士,
Java (Ka-la-pa) 噶喇吧
Jaya (Chaiya, Ch'ih-tzu) 赤仔
Jen-ho hang see Punhoyqua

Johore (Jou-fo) 柔佛
Jo-sun see Jackson
ju-fan shih 入番使
Juan Yuan 阮元
Jui (Juy) 瑞
jun-ch'i-yueh 閏七月
Jung 戎

Kalgan see Chang-chia-k'ou
Kan (River) 贛
Kan-chou 贛州
Kan kuan 贛關
Kan-p'u 澉浦
Kan-ssu-la ("Castilla," Spain) 干絲臘
K'ang-hsi 康熙
k'ao-chü 考據
Kashing (Chia-hsing, Kia-hing) 嘉興
K'e-la-sha-erh (Harashar) 喀喇沙爾
Kelantan (Chi-lan-tan) 急蘭丹
Keshen see Ch'i-shan
Keying see Ch'i-ying
Kiangnan 江南
Kiangsook = Kiangsu
Kiaochow 膠州
Kiating 嘉定
Kingqua (Liang Ching-kuan) 梁經官,
T'ien-pao hang 天寶行,
Liang Ch'eng-hsi 梁丞禧
Kintang (Silver Is., Chin-t'ang) 金塘
Kiukiang (Chiu-chiang) 九江
Kiying see Ch'i-ying
Ko-er-sa (Kah-ur-sah) 噶爾薩
Ko-lun-mi-ah 哥倫米阿
k'o-o chih chih 可惡之至
K'o-pei-shih see Jardine
k'o-shang 客商
kotow (k'o-t'ou) 磕頭
Kowloon (Kowlong, Chiu-lung) 九龍
Koxinga see Cheng Ch'eng-kung
Ku-sao t'a 姑嫂塔
Ku-sheng see Cushing
Kuwabara Jitsuzō 桑原隲藏,
ku-wu 鼓舞
Ku Yen-wu 顧炎武
kuan 官
kuan-fang 關防
kuan-shui 關稅
Kuang-hsin (River) 廣信
Kuang-li hang see Mowqua
Kuei-hua-ch'eng 歸化城
Kuei-liang 桂良
Kulangsu 鼓浪嶼
Kumsing moon see Cumsingmoon
K'un-shan (Quinsan, Kwan-shan) 崑山
kung 貢
Kung, Prince (Kung ch'in-wang I-hsin) 恭親王奕訢
Kung-fu see Congou
kung-hang (Cohong) 公行
Kung Mu-chiu 宮慕久
kung-shih 工食
Kung-sze (kung-ssu) 公司
kuo-chi min-sheng cheng-t'i 國計民生政體
kuo-hsin shih 國信使
Kuo-shih-la see Gutzlaff
Kwan-shan see K'un-shan
Kwanshing (I K'un-kuan 易昆官,
Fu-t'ai hang 孚泰行,
I Yuan-ch'ang 易元昌,
see Footae (Fu-t'ai)

Kwangsin = Kuang-hsin

Lagrené (La-ngo-ni) 喇萼呢, (La-ch'ih-ni) 吃
lai-hua 來化
Lambri 南渤利
Lan-ch'i 蘭谿
Lanchow 蘭州
Lannoy, J., (Lan-wa) 蘭瓦
Lan-wa see Lannoy
Lan Wei-wen 藍蔚雯
Lay, G. T., also H. N., (Li-t'ai-kuo) 李太郭, 泰
Layton (Lieh-tun) 列敦
Le-na-t'u 嘞吶吐
Lei Hai-tsung 雷海宗
Lei I-hsien 雷以諴
li (law) 例
li (distance, village) 里
Li Ch'ang-keng 李長庚
Li-chia-tao t'ou (Lee-kea-taow-tow) 李家衜頭
Li Hsing-yuan 李星沅
Li Hung-chang 李鴻章
Li Ju-lin 李汝霖
Li-ma-tou p'u-sa 利瑪竇菩薩
Li-t'ai-kuo see Lay
Li T'ing-yü 李廷鈺
liang 兩
Liang Ch'eng-hsi see Kingqua
Liang Ching-kuan see Kingqua
Liang-Huai 兩淮
Liang-Kiang 兩江
Liang-Kwang 兩廣
Liang Pao-ch'ang 梁寶常
Lieh-tun see Layton
lien-huan-ch'iang 連環鎗
Lien-kuo see Denmark
Ligor (Liu-k'un) 六崑
likin (li-chin) 釐金
Lin Ch'i-ch'i 林吉吉
Lin-ch'ing chuan-pan-cha 臨清甎版閘
Lin-ch'ing kuan 臨清關
Lindsay, Hugh Hamilton (Hu-hsia-mi) 胡夏米
Lin-kuei 麟桂
Lin-k'uei 麟魁
Lin Tse-hsü 林則徐
ling-shih 領事
Lintin (ling-ting) Island 伶仃
Liu-ch'iu 琉球
Liu Hsiang 劉相
Liu Li-ch'uan 劉麗川
liu-tu 流毒
Liu Yun-k'o 劉韻珂
Lo-lo 羅羅
Lo-pa see Roper
Lo Ping-chang 駱秉章
Lo-po-sun see Robertson
Lo-po-tan see Thom
Lord Napier (Lü-lao-pi) 律勞卑
Lo Ta-kang 羅大綱
lo-ti shui 落地稅
Loyang 洛陽
Lo Yuan-yu 羅元佑
lü 律
Lu Chi-kuang see Mowqua
Lu Chien-ying 陸建瀛
Lu-k'ang 祿康
Lü-lao-pi see Lord Napier
Lu Mao-kuan see Mowqua
Lü-sung 呂宋
Lu-ti-lan 魯低蘭
Lu Tse-ch'ang 鹿澤長

Lu Ya-ching 盧亞景
Lung-chiang kuan 龍江關
Lü-ying 綠營
Lung-hua 龍華
Lung-yu 龍游

Macao see Ao-men
Madras (Man-ta-la-sa) 曼達喇薩
ma-fu 馬夫
Ma Hsiu-kuan see Saoqua
Ma-hui see Murphy
Ma-li-lan (Maryland) 馬理蘭
Ma-li-sun see Morrison
Ma-sha-li see Marshall
Ma Tso-liang see Saoqua
mai-chi-shuang 賣雞爽
Mai-hua-t'o see Medhurst
Mai-lien see McLane
Mai-mai-chen 買賣鎮
mai-nei see Maine
Mai-pan see compradore
Mai-tu-ssu see Meadows
Maine (mien) 緬,
(mai-nei) 賣內
Malacca 滿剌加
Man 蠻
Man-ta-la-sa see Madras
Mao-hu 泖湖
Marshall (Ma-sha-li) 馬沙利
McLane (Mai-lien) 麥蓮
Meadows (Mai-tu-ssu) 麥都思
Medhurst, Walter (Mai-hua-t'o) 麥華陀
Meiling (Pass) 梅嶺
Meng-chia-la, Meng-ka-la, see Bengal
Meng-mai see Bombay
mi-chao 密召
Mi-li-chien see America
Mi-lun see Miln
Mi-shih-shih-pi (Mississippi) 密士失必
Miao-tzu 苗子
mien see Maine
mien-sheng shih-tuan 免生事端
Miln (Mi-lun) 米輪
Min (River) 閩
Mindanao (Mang-chün-ta-lao) 莽均達老
min-fang 民房
Mingan (Min-an) 閩安
Ming-ya-la see Bengal
Mingqua (P'an Ming-kuan) 潘明官,
Chung-ho hang 中和行,
P'an Wen-tao 潘文濤
Min-hai kuan 閩海關
Min-t'i-ni see Montigny
Montigny (Min-t'i-ni) 噉體呢
Morrison (Ma-li-sun) 嗎禮遜, 馬履遜
Mo-ta-man 嚤噠蠻
Mowqua (Lu Mao-kuan) 盧茂官,
Kuang-li hang 廣利行,
Lu Chi-kuang 盧繼光
Mu-chang-a 穆彰阿
Murphy (Ma-hui) 馬輝

Na-er-ching-o 訥爾經額
Nan-ao (Namoa) 南澳
Nan-hai hsien 南海縣
Nan-hsin kuan 南新關
Nan-hsiung 南雄
Namoa see Nan-ao
Nanchang 南昌
Nanhwei 南匯
Nanking 南京
Nantae see Nan-t'ai
Nan-t'ai (Nantai, Nantae) 南臺
Nan-yang 南洋
Nei-ko 內閣
nei-ti shang-shui 內地商稅
Nei-wu-fu 內務府
nei-ying 內應
Ning-kuo 寧國
Ningpo 寧波, (Sung: Ch'ing-yuan)
Ning-Shao-T'ai 寧紹太
Niu Chien 牛鑑

O-li 額利
Omega (A-mi-ko) 阿彌格, (also A-mi-k'o) 阿咪喀
o-nei ying-yü 額內盈餘
o-ting ying-yü 額定盈餘
o-wai ying-yü 額外盈餘

Pa-chia see Parker
Pa-fu-er see Balfour
Pahang (P'eng-heng) 彭亨
Pa-hsia-li see Parkes
pa-i chin-ch'eng 罷議進城
Pa-she see Persia
pai 白
Pai Han-chang 白含章
pai-hao see Pekoe
Pai-t'a-ssu 白塔寺
P'an Chen-ch'eng (Puankhequa, Puan Khe-qua) 潘振承, see Ponkhequa
P'an Cheng-wei see Ponkhequa (or Puankhequa)
P'an Hai-kuan see Punhoyqua
P'an Ming-kuan see Mingqua
P'an Shao-kuang see Ponkhequa (Puankhequa)
P'an Shih-ch'eng 潘仕成
P'an Shih-en 潘世恩
P'an Wen-hai see Punhoyqua
P'an Wen-tao see Mingqua
Pang-ka-la see Bengal
Pankhequa see Ponkhequa (Puankhequa)
Pao-ch'ang 保昌
Pao-ling see Bowring
Pao-shan 寶山
Pao-she see Persia
Pao-shun see Dent
Parker, Peter (Pa-chia) 吧嗎,
(Po-chia-pi-te) 啪嗎禪德
Parkes, Harry (Pa-hsia-li) 巴夏禮,
(Hsia-pa, = "H. P."?) 夏巴
Patani (Ta-ni) 大泥
Patna (P'ai-t'o-na) 派託拏,
(Pa-tan-na) 叭旦拏
Pei-er-jih-k'o see Belgium
Peiho 北河
Pei-hsin kuan 北新關
Peiping 北平
Peking 北京
Pekoe (pai-hao) 白毫
pen-chi 本紀
P'eng-heng see Pahang
P'eng Yun-chang 彭蘊章
Persia (Po-ssu) 波斯,
(Po-hsi) 白西,
(Pao-she) 包社,

Persia (Pa-she) 巴社,
(Po-er-she) 百爾設
Philippines (Lü-sung) 呂宋
Pi-ch'ang 璧昌
Pi-chih-wen see Bridgman
picul (tan) 擔
p'ien 篇
pien-i hsing-shih 便宜行事
pien-i ts'ung-shih 便宜從事
Pi-li-shih see Belgium
ping 稟
P'ing-yang 憑祥
Po-chia-pi-te see Parker
Po-er-she see Persia
Po-erh-tu-chia-li-ya see Portugal
Po-erh-tu-ka-erh see Portugal
Po-hsi see Persia
P'o-lo-men chiao 婆羅門教
P'o-lo-t'e-shih-tun 波羅特士頓
Ponkhequa or Puankhequa (P'an Cheng-wei)
潘正威, (-qua 官?),
T'ung-fu hang 同孚行,
P'an Shao-kuang 潘紹光,
see Puankhequa, P'an Chen-ch'eng
Portugal (Fo-lang-chi) 佛朗機,
(I-ta-li-ya) 意大里亞
(Po-erh-tu-ka-erh) 博爾都噶爾,
(Po-erh-tu-chia-li-ya) 博爾都嘉利亞,
(mod. P'u-t'ao-ya) 葡萄牙
Po-ssu see Persia
Po-to-mo (Potomac) 波多墨
Pottinger (P'u-ting-ch'a) 璞鼎查
Poyang (Lake) 鄱陽
Prussia (P'u-lu-she) 普魯社,
Mod. P'u-lu-shih 普魯士
Puankhequa (P'an Ch'i-kuan) 潘啟官, see
P'an Chen-Ch'eng, Ponkhequa
Pu-cheng-shih 布政使
pu chih ling-sheng chih-chieh 不致另生枝節
P'u-lu-she see Prussia
Punhoyqua (P'an Hai-kuan) 潘海官,
Jen-ho hang 仁和行,
P'an Wen-hai 潘文海
P'u-t'ao-ya see Portugal
P'u-ting-ch'a see Pottinger
P'u-t'o (Island) 普陀山
Putung 浦東
pu tung sheng-se 不動聲色
pu-wei wu-chien 不為無見
Pwan-tze-shing (also Pwan-sze-ching)
see P'an Shih-ch'eng

qua see kuan
Quangtung = Kwangtung
Quemoy (Chin-men) 金門

Robertson (Lo-po-sun) 羅伯遜
Roper (Lo-pa) 囉吧
Russell and Co., (Ch'i-ch'ang hang) 旗昌行
Russia (E-lo-ssu) 俄羅斯

Saddle Islands (Ma-an-shan lieh-tao) 馬鞍山列島
Sai-shang-a 賽尚阿
Samqua see Wu Chien-chang,
Wu Shuang-kuan
San-ho-hui see Triad
san-kuan 三關
San-kuan-t'ang 三官堂
san-pa-er-shih-i 三八廿一, forming hung 洪
san-shao ("samshu") 三燒
San-tien-hui see Triad
saoqua (Ma Hsiu-kuan) 馬秀官,
Shun-t'ai hang 順泰行,
Ma Tso-liang 馬佐良
Seu see Hsü
sha-ch'uan 沙船
Sha-hu-k'ou 殺虎口
Shameen (sha-mien) 沙面
Shanhaikuan 山海關
shan-hou chang-ch'eng 善後章程
Shanghai 上海
Shang-jao 上饒
Shang-pai-sha (Shang-pih-sha) 上白沙
shang-shui 商稅
shang-yü 上諭
Shang-yuan 上元
Shao-chou 韶州
Shao-hsing (Shaohing) 紹興
shao yu t'ou-hsü 稍有頭緒
shaw = hsiu
Sheklung (Shih-lung) 石龍
Shen-hu see Chimmo Bay
Shen Ping-yuan 沈炳垣
shen-shih 紳士
shih^4 是, shih^2 實, hsi^1 西, and su^1 蘇
shih-cheng 實徵
Shih-huo chih 食貨志
Shih-lung see Sheklung
Shih-po-ssu 市舶司
Shih-p'u 石浦
Shih-te-ko 士德葛
Shih-to-chi 士多吉
Shih-wei 侍衛
Shin Ping Yuan = Shen Ping-yuan
Showpei (shou-pei) 守備
Shu-hsing-a 舒興阿
Shu Kung-shou 舒恭受
Shuang-ying see Austria
shui-lei 水雷
shui-mo 水模
Shun-t'ai hang see Saoqua
Shun-t'ien-fu 順天府
Siam (Chiang-k'ou) 港口,
(Hsien-lo) 暹羅
Sian 西安
Siccawei see Zikawei
Singapore see Hsin-ch'i-p'o
Sinza (Hsin-cha) 新閘
So-li-wan see Sullivan
Soochow (Su-chou) 蘇州
Soochow Creek (Wu-sung chiang) 吳淞江
so-shu chia-chüan 所屬家眷
Souchong (hsiao-chung) 小種
Ssu-chou-chih (Gazetteer of the four continents)
四州志
Ssu-k'u ch'üan-shu 四庫全書
Ssu-te-ling see Stirling
Ssu-t'ung pa-ta ti 四通八達的
Stirling (Ssu-te-ling) 賜德齡
Su-ch'ien kuan 宿遷關
Su-chou-fu = Soochow
Sullivan (So-li-wan) 索利完
Sulu 蘇祿
Sungkiang (Sung-chiang) 淞江
Sungora (Sung-chü-lao) 宋腒朥
Su-Sung-T'ai 蘇松太
Su T'ing-k'uei 蘇廷魁
Su Wang 蘇旺

Sun Shan-pao 孫善寶
Swatow (Shan-t'ou) 汕頭
sycee (hsi-ssu) 細絲

Ta-Ch'ing 大清
Ta-hsi-yang 大西洋
ta-kuan 大關
Ta-ni see Patani, Denmark
Ta-Ying-kuo 大英國
Tae-shan see Tai-shan
Tai Chia-ku 戴嘉穀
Taichow 台州
tai-huang 大黄
T'ai Lake (T'ai-hu) 太湖
tai-li 代理
tai-pan 大班
Taiping see T'ai-p'ing t'ien-kuo
T'ai-p'ing-fu 太平府
T'ai-p'ing kuan 太平關
T'ai-p'ing t'ien-kuo (lit., Heavenly Kingdom of Great Peace) 太平天國
Tai-shan (Tae-shan) 岱山
Tait (Te-ti) 德滴
T'ai-ts'ang-chou 太倉州
Taiwan (Formosa) 臺灣
Taku (near Tientsin) 大沽
T'an Cho-yuan (Cheuk-woon Taam) 譚卓垣
Tan Ken-chin, Tan King Chin, (see Ch'en Ch'ing-chen)
Tan-mai see Denmark
Tan-tan 單呾
Tan-yang 丹陽
tao 道
Tao-kuang 道光
taotai (tao-t'ai) 道臺
Taoutae = taotai
Tchang, Yen-chen T. H. (Chang Ying-shen) 張雁深
te 德
Teen Paou see Kingqua
Te-pi-shih see Davis
Te-ti see Tait
Teng-chow 登州
Teng Ssu-yü 鄧嗣禹
T'eng-yueh 騰越
Thom, Robert (Lo-po-tan) 羅伯聃
Ti 狄
T'i-chü 提舉
T'i-tu 提督
T'ien-chin kuan 天津關
T'ien-i-ko 天一閣
t'ien-ming 天命
Tienpak (Tien-pai) 電白
T'ien-pao hang see Kingqua
T'ien-shan 天山
T'ien-ti-hui see Triad
Tientsin 天津
Ting Kung-ch'en 丁拱辰
ting-o 定額
t'ing-chi 廷寄
Tinghai 定海
to-kung 舵工
tou (peck) 斗
t'ou-hsü fen-fan 頭緒紛繁
Trengganu (Ting-chi-nu) 丁機奴
Triad Society (San-ho-hui) 三和會
(T'ien-ti-hui) 天地會 添弟會
(San-tien-hui) 三點會
(Hung-men-hui) 洪門會

tsa-shui 雜稅
Tsan-shun (Johnston?) 囋順
(Tsan-sun) 贊遜
Ts'ao Lü-t'ai 曹履泰
Ts'ao-yun tsung-tu 漕運總督
ts'e 冊
Tseng Kuo-fan 曾國藩
Tsinan (Chi-nan) 濟南
Tsingpu see Ch'ing-p'u
Tso-chuan 左傳
Tso-i 左翼
Tso-liang-t'ing 坐糧廳
Tso Tsung-t'ang 左宗棠
Tso-ying tu-ssu 左營都司
tsou-su 奏疏
Tsungan see Ch'ung-an
ts'ung-ch'üan pan-li 從權辦理
Tsungli-yamen 總理衙門
ts'ung-shu 叢書
Tsung-tu 總督
t'u^{3} 土, tu^{1} 都, tu^{4} 度, to^{1} 多, and t'u^{4} 突
Tuan Kuang-ch'ing 段光清
Tu Lien-che 杜連詰
T'un-ch'i chen 屯溪鎮
T'ung-an 同安
T'ung-chih 同知
Tungchow 通州
T'ung-fu hang see Ponkhequa (or Puankhequa)
Tung-hsing hang see Goqua (or Gowqua)
T'ung-lin 銅麟
tung nan yang 東南洋
T'ung-sheng (Tung Sang) 通生
t'ung-shih 通事
T'ung-shun hang see Wu Shuang-kuan, see Samqua
Tungting Lake 洞庭
Tung Yin-tu kung-ssu 東印度公司
Twankay see T'un-ch'i
Tze-ki (Tz'u-chi, Tszi-ki) 慈谿
Wade, Thomas (Wei-t'o-ma) 威妥瑪
wai ta-hsi-yang 外大西洋
Wai-wei 外委
Wan-kuo ti-li t'u (Illustrated geography of all countries) 萬國地理圖
wang 王
Wang Ch'i-ch'i 王七七
Wang Ch'ing-yun 王慶雲
Wang-hsia (Wanghia, Wang-hea) 望廈
Wang-hsing-teng see Washington
Wang Ting 王鼎
Wangtong (heng-tang) 橫檔
Washington (Hua-sheng-tun) 華盛頓,
(Wang-hsing-teng) 兀興騰,
(Tun) 頓
Wei-hai-wei 威海衛
Wei-t'o-ma see Wade
wei-wei er ch'ü 唯唯而去
wei-yuan 委員
wen-chi 文集
Wenchow 溫州
Wen-feng 文豐
Wen-han see Bonham
Wen-hsiang 文祥
Wen-na-chih 嗢哪咍
Whampoa see Huang-p'u
Whangpu see Huang-p'u
Woothinghien = Wu T'ing-hsien
Wuchang 武昌
Wu Chien-chang (Samqua) 吳健彰, see Wu Shuang-kuan
Wu Chien-tung 吳建勳

Wuchow 梧州
Wu Ch'ung - yueh see Howqua
Wu-erh-chi-ni-ah (Virginia) 勿爾吉尼阿
Wuhan 武漢
Wu Hao-kuan see Howqua
Wu-hu kuan 蕪湖關
Wu-i (Bohea) 武夷
Wu Kuo-ying see Howqua
Wu Ping-chien (Wu Tun-yüan) see Howqua
Wu Shao-jung see Howqua
Wu-shih-shan 烏石山
Wu Shuang-kuan (Samqua) 吳爽官,
T'ung-shun hang 同順行,
Wu T'ien-yuan 吳天垣
Wusih 無錫
Wusung (Woosung) 吳淞
Wu-sung-chiang see Soochow Creek
Wu T'ien-hsien 吳天顯
Wu T'ien-yuan see Wu Shuang-kuan (Samqua)
Wu T'ing-hsien 吳廷獻
Wu Tun-yuan (Wu Ping-chien) see Howqua
Wu-yuan (Woo-yuen) 婺源
Wu Yuan-hua see Howqua

ya-hang 牙行
Ya-lan-tsai see Alantsai
Yalu 鴨綠
Ya-ma-sun (Amazon) 亞馬孫
Ya-mei-li-chia see America
yamen 衙門
Ya-niang-hsieh see Anunghoi
Ya-pi-li see Abeel
Yang-chou 揚州
Yang king pang (yang-ching-peng) 洋涇浜, also Yang-ching-pin 濱
yang-lien 養廉
Yang Lien-sheng 楊聯陞
Yang Ping-nan 楊炳南
Yangtze (Yang-tzu-chiang) 揚子江
yang-wei chiang-chün 揚威將軍
Yang Wen-ting 楊文定
Yang Yung 楊泳
yao-hsieh, 要挾
Ye-kwun = Yeh K'un? 葉堃
Yeh-lang 夜郎
Yeh Ming-ch'en 葉名琛
Yen-chow 兗州
yen-fei 鹽匪
Yen Hsi-shan 閻錫山
Yen-p'ao t'u-shuo (Drawings on Gunnery) 演礮圖說
yen-tan 驗單
Yih-king see I-ching
Yih-shan see I-shan
Yin (Ningpo) 鄞
Yin-tai-ma 尹代嗎
yin-ti-mi-t'e 因地密特 from British Museum mss., courtesy Mr. Chang Te-ch'ang.
Ying-chi-li see England
Ying-i 英夷
Ying-kuo 英國
Ying-ni 英逆
ying-yü 盈餘
yü-chih 諭旨
Yu-i 右翼
Yü-men kuan 玉門關
Yü-shan (Yuh-shan) 玉山
Yu-ssu 由斯
Yü-yao 餘姚
Yuan-hua 源華
Yuan-shan (Yuenshan) 鉛山
Yuan Tsu-te 袁祖悳
Yueh-hai-kuan chien-tu 粵海關監督
Yueh-hai-kuan pu 粵海關部
yung 勇
Yung (River) 涌
Yung-ch'ang 永昌
Yung-cheng 雍正
Zayton see Ch'üan-chou
Zikawei (Siccawei, Hsü-chia-hui) 徐家滙

INDEX

INDEX

If China was getting tribute for glory only, why did she sometimes take charge of tributary's politics & frgn affairs & sometimes she did not take char

---

If powers only wanted economic, not political spheres, why
1) "shearing off of Chinese territory?
2) leased territory
3) separate concessions (why not just treaty ports - internat'l?)

Joint systems seem economic but exclusive systems political (This is supposedly what America protested - grabbing of zones - wanted to protect Open Door)

In Japan Westerners never got own municipal gov't whereas did in China

Did Japan resist West?
Did China? Why did Japan become imperial, but not Chi
Because J. had adopted